# Essentials for DESIGN

Julian Rickards

Taken from:

*Essentials for Design: Macromedia® Dreamweaver® MX 2004*, Level One
by Julian Rickards

*Essentials for Design: Macromedia® Dreamweaver® MX 2004*, Level Two
by Julian Rickards

PEARSON Custom Publishing

PEARSON Prentice Hall

Cover art courtesy of Eyewire/Getty Images, Inc.
Taken from:

*Essentials for Design; Macromedia® Dreamweaver® MX 2004*
by Julian Rickards

A Pearson Education Company
Upper Saddle River, New Jersey, 07458



This special edition published in cooperation with Pearson Custom Publishing.

Printed in the United States of America

10 9 8 7 6 5 4 3 2

ISBN 0-536-91665-9

2005200068

EM/LB

Please visit our web site at *www.pearsoncustom.com*

PEARSON
Custom Publishing

PEARSON CUSTOM PUBLISHING
75 Arlington Street, Suite 300, Boston, MA 02116
A Pearson Education Company

## ABOUT THE SERIES EDITOR

**Ellenn Behoriam** is president and founder of Against The Clock, Inc. (ATC), one of the nation's leading content providers. Ellenn and her staff have successfully produced many of the graphic arts industry's most popular and well-received books and related series. These works include the *Electronic Cookbook*, *Workflow Reengineering*, *Teams and the Graphic Arts*, *Adobe Photoshop Creative Techniques*, *Adobe Illustrator Creative Techniques*, and *QuarkXPress 6: Creating Digital Documents*, the foundation for the QuarkXPress Trainer certification programs. The Against The Clock series, published in concert with Prentice Hall/Pearson Education, includes more than 26 titles that focus on applications for the graphic and computer arts industries.

Against The Clock also worked with Pearson to develop the *Companion for the Digital Artist* series. These titles focus on specific and fundamental creative concepts, including design, Web-site development, photography, typography, color theory, and copywriting. The concise and compact works provide core concepts and skills that supplement any application-specific education, regardless of which textbooks are being used to teach program skills.

Under Ellenn's leadership and direction, ATC is currently developing more than 20 titles for the new *Essentials for Design* series. Her staff and long-established network of professional educators, printers, prepress experts, workflow engineers, and business leaders add significantly to ATC's ability to provide current, meaningful, and effective books, online tutorials, and business-to-business performance and workflow-enhancement programs.

## ABOUT THE AUTHOR

**Julian Rickards** has been involved in various computer-related fields over the last dozen or so years including computer instruction, technical illustration and web design and is always willing to assist someone who is struggling with a project or concept. He is an advocate of web standards and web accessibility and is a member of GAWDS.org. In his employment with the Ontario government, he oversees the database and archives of digital publications and is often called upon to assist with the development of the Internet and Intranet web sites. Julian hails from Canada where he resides with his wonderfully supportive wife, Nanette, and two sons, Sebastian and Graeme.

# ACKNOWLEDGMENTS

We would like to thank the professional writers, artists, editors, and educators who have worked long and hard on the *Essentials for Design* series.

And thanks to the dedicated teaching professionals: Kara Hardin; Scott Springfield; Doug Borton, Kellogg Community College; and David McGill, Azusa Pacific University. Your insightful comments and expertise have certainly contributed to the success of the *Essentials for Design* series.

Thanks to Debbie Davidson for her help in managing the workflow and for her work on the illustrations.

Thank you to Terry Sisk Graybill, copy editor and final link in the chain of production, for her help in making sure that we all said what we meant to say.

And a very special thank you to Erika Kendra, production designer, technical consultant, partner in crime, and friend.

And to Melissa Sabella, Anne Garcia, Jodi McPherson, and Vanessa Nuttry — we appreciate your patience as we begin this new venture together.

# CONTENTS AT A GLANCE

# TABLE OF CONTENTS

# HOW TO USE THIS BOOK

*Essentials* courseware from Prentice Hall is anchored in the practical and professional needs of all types of students. The *Essentials* series presents a learning-by-doing approach that encourages you to grasp application-related concepts as you expand your skills through hands-on tutorials. As such, it consists of modular lessons that are built around a series of numbered step-by-step procedures that are clear, concise, and easy to review.

*Essentials* books are divided into projects. A project covers one area (or a few closely related areas) of application functionality. Each project consists of several lessons that are related to that topic. Each lesson presents a specific task or closely related set of tasks in a manageable chunk that is easy to assimilate and retain.

Each element in the *Essentials* book is designed to maximize your learning experience. A list of the *Essentials* project elements, and a description of how each element can help you, begins on the next page. To find out more about the rationale behind each book element and how to use each to your maximum benefit, take the following walk-through.

# WALK-THROUGH

**Project Objectives.** Starting with an objective gives you short-term, attainable goals. Each project begins with a list of objectives that closely match the titles of the step-by-step tutorials. ▶

**OBJECTIVES**

*In this project, you learn how to*

- Explore the organization of a commercial site
- Use outlines and storyboards to plan a Web site
- Define a site and create its folders
- Build basic Web pages with text
- Examine Web pages in the Design and Code views
- Apply simple text formatting
- Use an existing page as a template
- Create page-to-page and email links

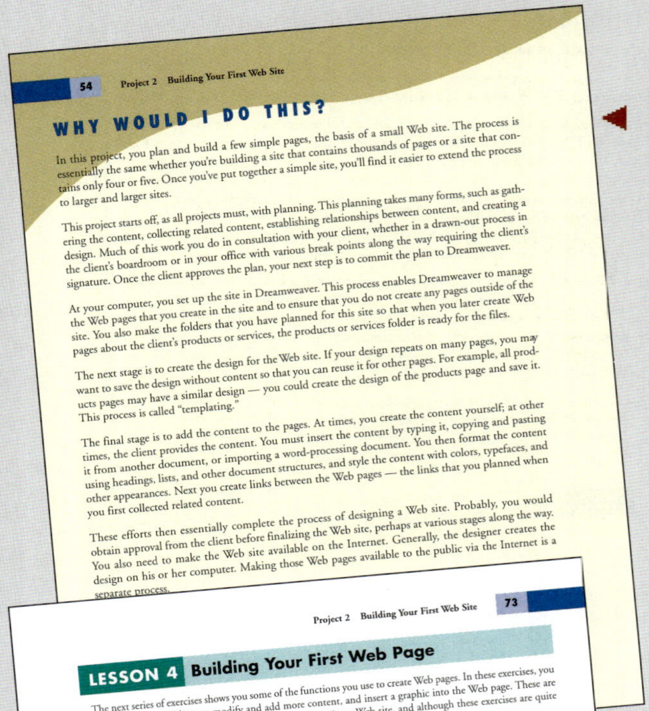

54 Project 2 Building Your First Web Site

WHY WOULD I DO THIS?

In this project, you plan and build a few simple pages, the basis of a small Web site. The process is essentially the same whether you're building a site that contains thousands of pages or a site that contains only four or five. Once you've put together a simple site, you'll find it easier to extend the process to larger and larger sites.

This project starts off, as all projects must, with planning. This planning takes many forms, such as gathering the content, collecting related content, establishing relationships between content, and creating a design. Much of this work you do in consultation with your client, whether in a drawn-out process in the client's boardroom or in your office with various break points along the way requiring the client's signature. Once the client approves the plan, your next step is to commit the plan to Dreamweaver.

At your computer, you set up the site in Dreamweaver. This process enables Dreamweaver to manage the Web pages that you create in the site and to ensure that you do not create any pages outside of the site. You also make the folders that you have planned for this site so that when you later create Web pages about the client's products or services, the products or services folder is ready for the files.

The next stage is to create the design for the Web site. If your design repeats on many pages, you may want to save the design without content so that you can reuse it for other pages. For example, all products pages may have a similar design — you could create the design of the products page and save it. This process is called "templating."

The final stage is to add the content to the pages. At times, you create the content yourself; at other times, the client provides the content. You must insert the content by typing it, copying and pasting it from another document, or importing a word-processing document. You then format the content using headings, lists, and other document structures, and style the content with colors, typefaces, and other appearances. Next you create links between the Web pages — the links that you planned when you first collected related content.

These efforts then essentially complete the process of designing a Web site. Probably, you would obtain approval from the client before finalizing the Web site, perhaps at various stages along the way. You also need to make the Web site available on the Internet. Generally, the designer creates the design on his or her computer. Making those Web pages available to the public via the Internet is a separate process.

◀ **Why Would I Do This?** Introductory material at the beginning of each project provides an overview of why these tasks and procedures are important.

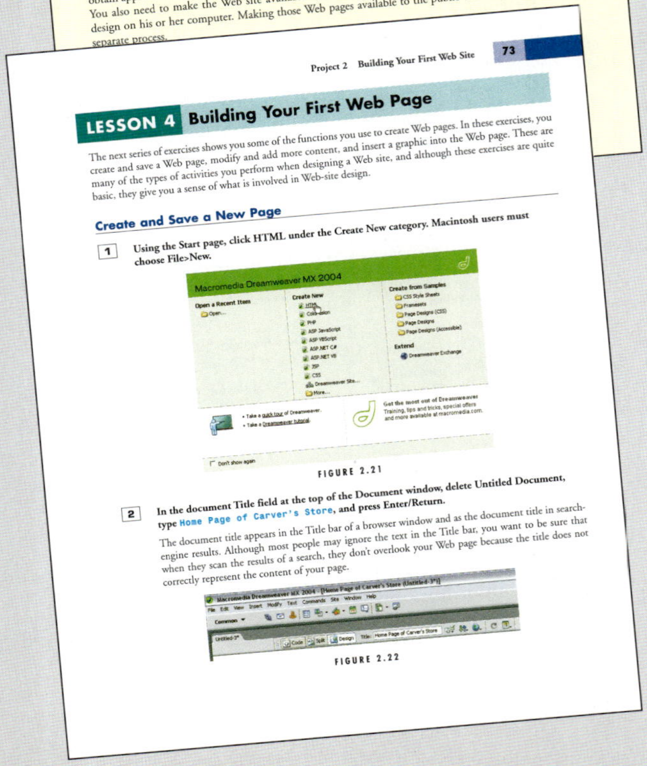

Project 2 Building Your First Web Site 73

LESSON 4 Building Your First Web Page

The next series of exercises shows you some of the functions you use to create Web pages. In these exercises, you create and save a Web page, modify and add more content, and insert a graphic into the Web page. These are many of the types of activities you perform when designing a Web site, and although these exercises are quite basic, they give you a sense of what is involved in Web-site design.

Create and Save a New Page

1 Using the Start page, click HTML under the Create New category. Macintosh users must choose File>New.

FIGURE 2.21

2 In the document Title field at the top of the Document window, delete Untitled Document, type `Home Page of Carver's Store`, and press Enter/Return.

The document title appears in the Title bar of a browser window and as the document title in search-engine results. Although most people may ignore the text in the Title bar, you want to be sure that when they scan the results of a search, they don't overlook your Web page because the title does not correctly represent the content of your page.

FIGURE 2.22

**Visual Summary.** A series of illustrations introduces the new tools, dialog boxes, and windows you will explore in each project. ▼

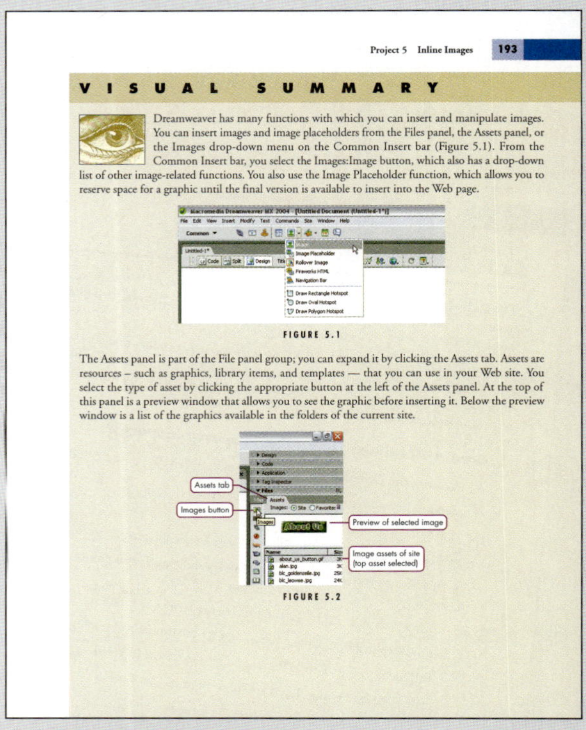

Project 5 Inline Images 193

VISUAL SUMMARY

Dreamweaver has many functions with which you can insert and manipulate images. You can insert images and image placeholders from the Files panel, the Assets panel, or the Images drop-down menu on the Common Insert bar (Figure 5.1). From the Common Insert bar, you select the Images:Image button, which also has a drop-down list of other image-related functions. You also use the Image Placeholder function, which allows you to reserve space for a graphic until the final version is available to insert into the Web page.

FIGURE 5.1

The Assets panel is part of the File panel group; you can expand it by clicking the Assets tab. Assets are resources — such as graphics, library items, and templates — that you can use in your Web site. You select the type of asset by clicking the appropriate button at the left of the Assets panel. At the top of this panel is a preview window that allows you to see the graphic before inserting it. Below the preview window is a list of the graphics available in the folders of the current site.

FIGURE 5.2

◀ **Step-by-Step Tutorials.** Hands-on tutorials let you learn by doing and include numbered, bold, step-by-step instructions.

**If You Have Problems.** These short troubleshooting notes help you anticipate or solve common problems quickly and effectively.

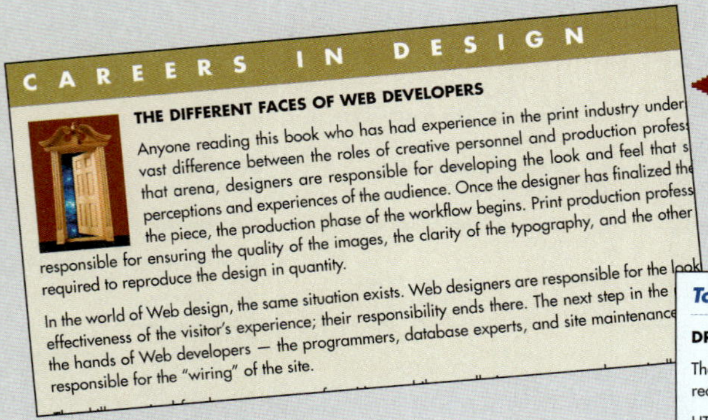

CAREERS IN DESIGN

**THE DIFFERENT FACES OF WEB DEVELOPERS**

Anyone reading this book who has had experience in the print industry under vast difference between the roles of creative personnel and production profes that arena, designers are responsible for developing the look and feel that s perceptions and experiences of the audience. Once the designer has finalized the the piece, the production phase of the workflow begins. Print production profess responsible for ensuring the quality of the images, the clarity of the typography, and the other required to reproduce the design in quantity.

In the world of Web design, the same situation exists. Web designers are responsible for the look effectiveness of the visitor's experience; their responsibility ends there. The next step in the the hands of Web developers — the programmers, database experts, and site maintenance responsible for the "wiring" of the site.

**Careers in Design.** These features offer advice, tips, and resources that will help you on your path to a successful career.

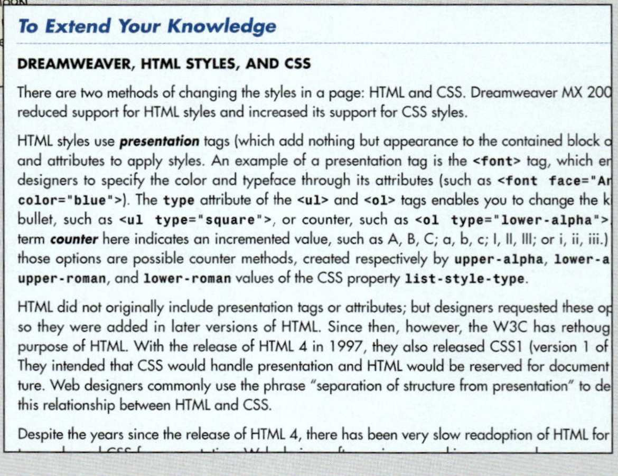

*To Extend Your Knowledge*

**DREAMWEAVER, HTML STYLES, AND CSS**

There are two methods of changing the styles in a page: HTML and CSS. Dreamweaver MX 200 reduced support for HTML styles and increased its support for CSS styles.

HTML styles use ***presentation*** tags (which add nothing but appearance to the contained block o and attributes to apply styles. An example of a presentation tag is the `<font>` tag, which en designers to specify the color and typeface through its attributes (such as `<font face="Ar color="blue">`). The `type` attribute of the `<ul>` and `<ol>` tags enables you to change the k bullet, such as `<ul type="square">`, or counter, such as `<ol type="lower-alpha">` term ***counter*** here indicates an incremented value, such as A, B, C; a, b, c; I, II, III; or i, ii, iii.) those options are possible counter methods, created respectively by `upper-alpha`, `lower-a` `upper-roman`, and `lower-roman` values of the CSS property `list-style-type`.

HTML did not originally include presentation tags or attributes; but designers requested these op so they were added in later versions of HTML. Since then, however, the W3C has rethoug purpose of HTML. With the release of HTML 4 in 1997, they also released CSS1 (version 1 of They intended that CSS would handle presentation and HTML would be reserved for document ture. Web designers commonly use the phrase "separation of structure from presentation" to de this relationship between HTML and CSS.

Despite the years since the release of HTML 4, there has been very slow readoption of HTML for

**To Extend Your Knowledge.** These features provide extra tips, alternative ways to complete a process, and special hints about using the software.

**End-of-Project Exercises.** Extensive end-of-project exercises emphasize hands-on skill development. You'll find two levels of reinforcement: Skill Drill and Challenge.

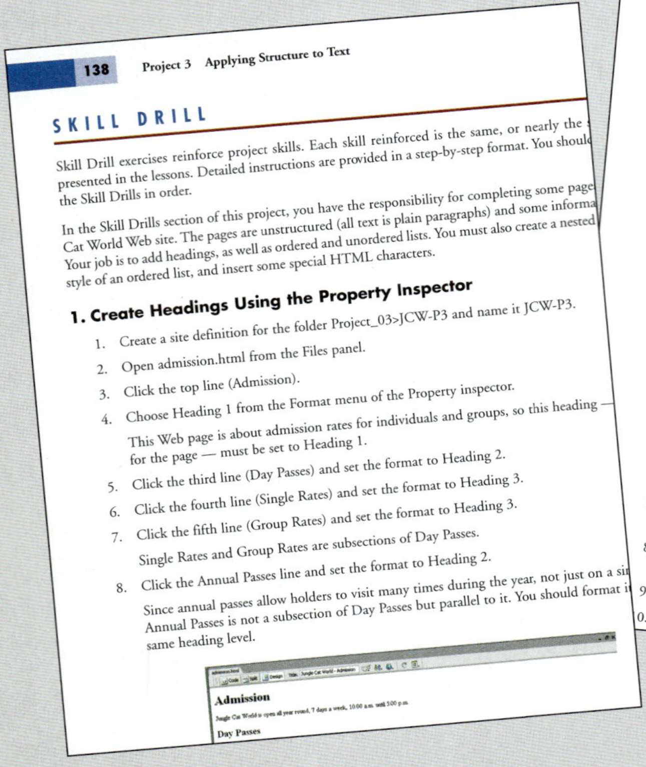

138 Project 3 Applying Structure to Text

SKILL DRILL

Skill Drill exercises reinforce project skills. Each skill reinforced is the same, or nearly the presented in the lessons. Detailed instructions are provided in a step-by-step format. You should the Skill Drills in order.

In the Skill Drills section of this project, you have the responsibility for completing some page Cat World Web site. The pages are unstructured (all text is plain paragraphs) and some informa Your job is to add headings, as well as ordered and unordered lists. You must also create a nested style of an ordered list, and insert some special HTML characters.

**1. Create Headings Using the Property Inspector**

1. Create a site definition for the folder Project_03>JCW-P3 and name it JCW-P3.
2. Open admission.html from the Files panel.
3. Click the top line (Admission).
4. Choose Heading 1 from the Format menu of the Property inspector.

   This Web page is about admission rates for individuals and groups, so this heading — for the page — must be set to Heading 1.
5. Click the third line (Day Passes) and set the format to Heading 2.
6. Click the fourth line (Single Rates) and set the format to Heading 3.
7. Click the fifth line (Group Rates) and set the format to Heading 3.

   Single Rates and Group Rates are subsections of Day Passes.
8. Click the Annual Passes line and set the format to Heading 2.

   Since annual passes allow holders to visit many times during the year, not just on a si Annual Passes is not a subsection of Day Passes but parallel to it. You should format i same heading level.

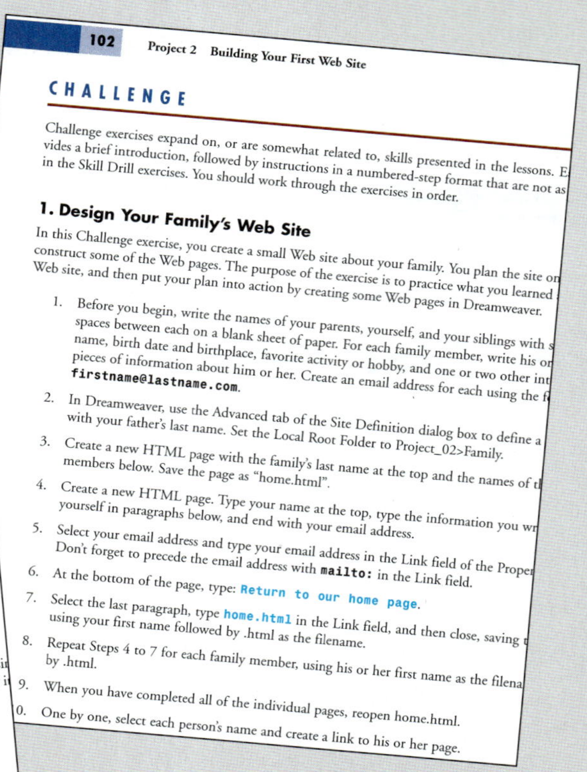

102 Project 2 Building Your First Web Site

CHALLENGE

Challenge exercises expand on, or are somewhat related to, skills presented in the lessons. E vides a brief introduction, followed by instructions in a numbered-step format that are not as in the Skill Drill exercises. You should work through the exercises in order.

**1. Design Your Family's Web Site**

In this Challenge exercise, you create a small Web site about your family. You plan the site or construct some of the Web pages. The purpose of the exercise is to practice what you learned Web site, and then put your plan into action by creating some Web pages in Dreamweaver.

1. Before you begin, write the names of your parents, yourself, and your siblings with s spaces between each on a blank sheet of paper. For each family member, write his or name, birth date and birthplace, favorite activity or hobby, and one or two other int pieces of information about him or her. Create an email address for each using the f **firstname@lastname.com**.
2. In Dreamweaver, use the Advanced tab of the Site Definition dialog box to define a with your father's last name. Set the Local Root Folder to Project_02>Family.
3. Create a new HTML page with the family's last name at the top and the names of t members below. Save the page as "home.html".
4. Create a new HTML page. Type your name at the top, type the information you wr yourself in paragraphs below, and end with your email address.
5. Select your email address and type your email address in the Link field of the Proper Don't forget to precede the email address with **mailto:** in the Link field.
6. At the bottom of the page, type: `Return to our home page`.
7. Select the last paragraph, type `home.html` in the Link field, and then close, saving t using your first name followed by .html as the filename.
8. Repeat Steps 4 to 7 for each family member, using his or her first name as the filena by .html.
9. When you have completed all of the individual pages, reopen home.html.
10. One by one, select each person's name and create a link to his or her page.

**Portfolio Builder.** At the end of every project, these exercises require creative solutions to problems that reinforce the topic of the project.

190 Project 4 Linking the Site

PORTFOLIO BUILDER

Create a Portal Site

A "Portal" site is one that provides related links and information specific to one or more subjec[ts]. There are many examples of such sites on the Web. In this assignment, you're going to create one [of] your own.

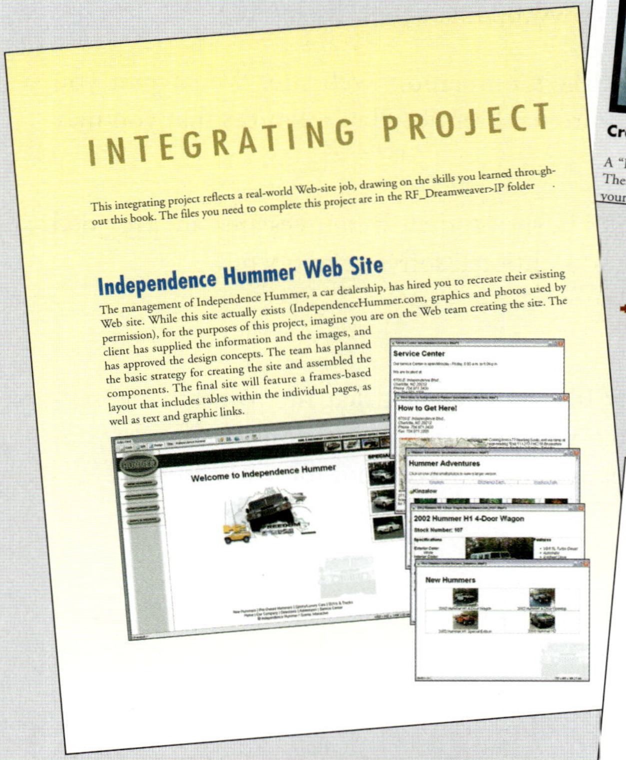

INTEGRATING PROJECT

This integrating project reflects a real-world Web-site job, drawing on the skills you learned throughout this book. The files you need to complete this project are in the RF_Dreamweaver>IP folder.

Independence Hummer Web Site

The management of Independence Hummer, a car dealership, has hired you to recreate their existing Web site. While this site actually exists (IndependenceHummer.com, graphics and photos used by permission), for the purposes of this project, imagine you are on the Web team creating the site. The client has supplied the information and the images, and has approved the design concepts. The team has planned the basic strategy for creating the site and assembled the components. The final site will feature a frames-based layout that includes tables within the individual pages, as well as text and graphic links.

**Integrating Projects.** Integrating projects are designed to reflect real-world graphic-design jobs, drawing on the skills you have learned throughout this book.

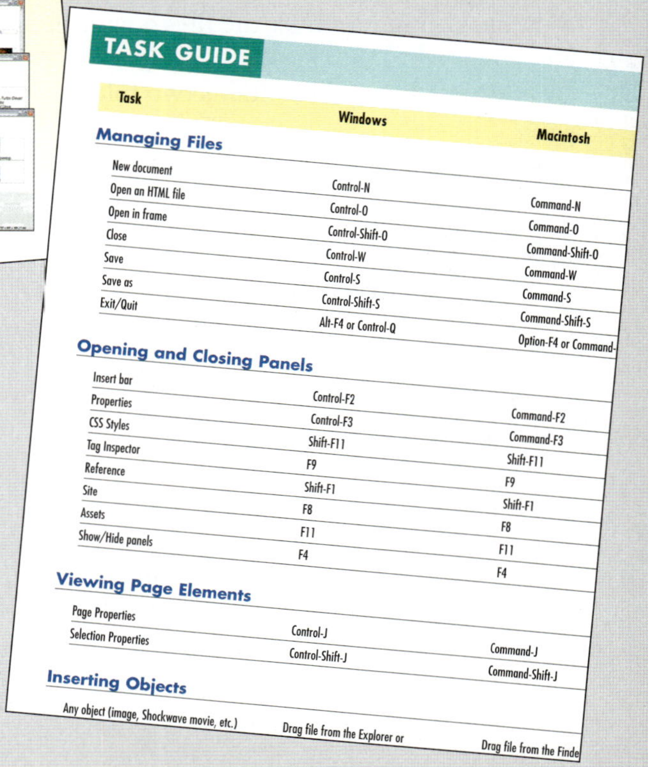

TASK GUIDE

| Task | Windows | Macintosh |
|---|---|---|
| **Managing Files** | | |
| New document | Control-N | Command-N |
| Open an HTML file | Control-O | Command-O |
| Open in frame | Control-Shift-O | Command-Shift-O |
| Close | Control-W | Command-W |
| Save | Control-S | Command-S |
| Save as | Control-Shift-S | Command-Shift-S |
| Exit/Quit | Alt-F4 or Control-Q | Option-F4 or Command- |
| **Opening and Closing Panels** | | |
| Insert bar | Control-F2 | Command-F2 |
| Properties | Control-F3 | Command-F3 |
| CSS Styles | Shift-F11 | Shift-F11 |
| Tag Inspector | F9 | F9 |
| Reference | Shift-F1 | Shift-F1 |
| Site | F8 | F8 |
| Assets | F11 | F11 |
| Show/Hide panels | F4 | F4 |
| **Viewing Page Elements** | | |
| Page Properties | Control-J | Command-J |
| Selection Properties | Control-Shift-J | Command-Shift-J |
| **Inserting Objects** | | |
| Any object (image, Shockwave movie, etc.) | Drag file from the Explorer or | Drag file from the Finde |

**Task Guides.** These charts, found at the end of each book, list alternative ways to complete common procedures and provide a handy reference tool.

## STUDENT INFORMATION AND RESOURCES

**Companion Web Site (www.prenhall.com/essentials).** This text-specific Web site provides students with additional information and exercises to reinforce their learning. Features include: additional end-of-project reinforcement material, online Study Guide, easy access to *all* resource files, and much, much more!

Before completing the projects within this text, you need to download the Resource Files from the Prentice Hall Companion Web site. Check with your instructor for the best way to gain access to these files or simply follow these instructions:

1. From an open Web browser, go to http://www.prenhall.com/essentials.
2. Select your textbook or series to access the Companion Web site. We suggest you bookmark this page, as it has links to additional Prentice Hall resources that you may use in class.
3. Click the Student Resources link. All files in the Student Resources area are provided as .exe files. These files do not require any additional software to open.
4. Click the Start Here link.
5. Once you have downloaded the proper file, double-click that file to begin the self-extraction process. You will be prompted to select a folder location specific for your book; you may extract the file to your hard drive or to a removable disk/drive.

   The Start Here file contains two folders:

   - **RF_Dreamweaver.** You can place this folder on your hard drive, or on a removable disk/drive.
   - **Work_In_Progress.** You can place this folder on your hard drive, or on a removable disk/drive.
6. Locate the project files you need from the list of available resources and click the active link to download. There is a separate file for each project in this book (e.g., Project_01, Project_02, etc.).
7. Once you have downloaded the proper file, double-click that file to begin the self-extraction process. You will be prompted to select a folder location specific to your book; you should extract the project-specific folders into the RF_Dreamweaver_L1 folder that was extracted from the Start Here file.

**Resource CD.** If you are using a Resource CD, all the fonts and files you need are provided on the CD. Resource files are organized in project-specific folders (e.g., Project_01, Project_02, etc.), which are contained in the RF_Dreamweaver folder. You can either work directly from the CD, or copy the files onto your hard drive before beginning the exercises.

Before you begin working on the projects or lessons in this book, you should copy the Work_In_Progress folder from the Resource CD onto your hard drive or a removable disk/drive.

**Resource Files.** Resource files are organized in project-specific folders, and are named to facilitate cross-platform compatibility. Words are separated by an underscore, and all file names include a lowercase three-letter extension. For example, if you are directed to open the file "graphics.eps" in Project 2, the file can be found in the RF_Dreamweaver_Project_02 folder. We repeat these directions frequently in the early projects.

**The Work In Progress Folder.** This folder contains individual folders for each project in the book (e.g., WIP_01, WIP_02, etc.). When an exercise directs you to save a file, you should save it to the appropriate folder for the project in which you are working.

The exercises in this book frequently build upon work that you have already completed. At the end of each exercise, you will be directed to save your work and either close the file or continue to the next exercise. If you are directed to continue but your time is limited, you can stop at a logical point, save the file, and later return to the point at which you stopped. In this case, you will need to open the file from the appropriate WIP folder and continue working on the same file.

**Typeface Conventions.** Computer programming code appears in a monospace font that `looks like this`. In many cases, you only need to change or enter specific pieces of code; in these instances, the code you need to type or change appears in a second color and `looks like this`.

# INSTRUCTOR'S RESOURCES

**Customize Your Book (www.prenhall.com/customphit).** The Prentice Hall Information Technology Custom PHIT Program gives professors the power to control and customize their books to suit their course needs. The best part is that it is done completely online using a simple interface.

Professors choose exactly what projects they need in the *Essentials for Design* series, and in what order they appear. The program also enables professors to add their own material anywhere in the text's presentation, and the final product will arrive at each professor's bookstore as a professionally formatted text.

To learn more about this new system for creating the perfect textbook, go to www.prenhall.com/customphit, where the online walk-through demonstrates how to create a book.

**Instructor's Resource Center.** This CD-ROM includes the entire Instructor's Manual for each application in Microsoft Word format. Student data files and completed solutions files are also on this CD-ROM. The Instructor's Manual contains a reference guide of these files for the instructor's convenience. PowerPoint slides with more information about each project are also available for classroom use.

**Companion Web site (www.prenhall.com/essentials).** Instructors will find all of the resources available on the Instructor's Resource CD-ROM available for download from the Companion Web site.

**TestGen Software.** TestGen is a test generator program that lets you view and easily edit test bank questions, transfer them to tests, and print the tests in a variety of formats suitable to your teaching situation. The program also offers many options for organizing and displaying test banks and tests. A built-in random number and text generator makes it ideal for creating multiple versions of tests. Powerful search and sort functions let you easily locate questions and arrange them in the order you prefer.

QuizMaster, also included in this package, enables students to take tests created with TestGen on a local area network. The QuizMaster utility built into TestGen lets instructors view student records and print a variety of reports. Building tests is easy with TestGen, and exams can be easily uploaded into WebCT, Blackboard, and CourseCompass.

Prentice Hall has formed close alliances with each of the leading online platform providers: WebCT, Blackboard, and our own Pearson CourseCompass.

**OneKey.** OneKey lets you in to the best teaching and learning resources all in one place. OneKey for *Essentials for Design* is all your students need for out-of-class work conveniently organized by chapter to reinforce and apply what they've learned in class and from the text. OneKey is all you need to plan and administer your course. All your instructor resources are in one place to maximize your effectiveness and minimize your time and effort. OneKey for convenience, simplicity, and success.

**WebCT and Blackboard.** Each of these custom-built distance-learning courses features exercises, sample quizzes, and tests in a course management system that provides class administration tools as well as the ability to customize this material at the instructor's discretion.

**CourseCompass.** CourseCompass is a dynamic, interactive online course management tool powered by Blackboard. It lets professors create their own courses in 15 minutes or less with preloaded quality content that can include quizzes, tests, lecture materials, and interactive exercises.

**Performance-Based Training and Assessment: Train & Assess IT.** Prentice Hall offers performance-based training and assessment in one product — Train & Assess IT.

The Training component offers computer-based instruction that a student can use to preview, learn, and review graphic design application skills. Delivered via Web or CD-ROM, Train IT offers interactive multimedia, and computer-based training to augment classroom learning. Built-in prescriptive testing suggests a study path based not only on student test results but also on the specific textbook chosen for the course.

The Assessment component offers computer-based testing that shares the same user interface as Train IT and is used to evaluate a student's knowledge about specific topics in software including Photoshop, InDesign, Illustrator, Flash, and Dreamweaver. It does this in a task-oriented, performance-based environment to demonstrate students' proficiency and comprehension of the topics. More extensive than the testing in Train IT, Assess IT offers more administrative features for the instructor and additional questions for the student. Assess IT also enables professors to test students out of a course, place students in appropriate courses, and evaluate skill sets.

# PROJECT 1

# Taking a Tour of Dreamweaver

## OBJECTIVES

***In this project, you learn how to***

- Launch Dreamweaver on your computer system
- Identify components of the Code view
- Identify components of the Design view
- Recognize features of the Property inspector
- Select HTML tags using the Tag selector
- Insert HTML tags using the Tag chooser
- Modify the Dreamweaver interface
- Obtain help with features and functions

# WHY WOULD I DO THIS?

In this project, you explore Dreamweaver and its components. You look at and try out the most important features of this program. You learn how Web pages are constructed by examining some Web pages in Dreamweaver. You explore how the Dreamweaver interface allows you to work with the components of a Web page. You see how Dreamweaver represents both the design aspect and the underlying code aspect of these pages.

Dreamweaver is a tool that grows with you. Many beginners to Web design prefer to work in a graphical environment. Dreamweaver provides a sophisticated, yet user-friendly, ***WYSIWYG*** (What You See Is What You Get) view called the "Design view." In this view, you can create styles, insert images, resize tables, and access many other functions through a click of your mouse.

The appearance of Web pages, however, is created by underlying code, ***HTML*** (HyperText Markup Language), the structural language of Web pages. When you work in the Design view, Dreamweaver creates the HTML for you. HTML is the code that identifies the graphics, fonts, colors, and more.

Dreamweaver does not include all HTML code or all options for that code in its interface. There are numerous options and features that require your manual intervention in the code. When you have enough experience and understanding of HTML, you can add these features manually. Dreamweaver provides a sophisticated interface for doing just this — the Code view. This view provides ***code hints*** (pop-up menus that offer the options for the current piece of code) and ***syntax highlighting*** (different parts of the code that are colored differently), both of which greatly assist the novice and the experienced hand-coder. (A ***hand-coder*** is a person who prefers to create directly from the code rather than through a visual interface.) Many hand-coders also greatly appreciate the sophistication of Dreamweaver's Design view — in a few seconds, they can create a complex table structure that would otherwise take them several minutes or more of hand-coding.

For these reasons, Dreamweaver is the premier Web-page authoring application for Windows and Macintosh systems. It provides you with an abundance of tools, panels, menus, and other means for creating and modifying Web pages. The interface also has many deliberate redundancies, so you have more than one way to accomplish the same task. With such a wealth of tools and other components in Dreamweaver, it is important to learn the locations, names, and functions of the components, as you do in this project, so that you can use the program efficiently. Whether you plan to create basic Web sites or manage sites of many thousands of pages, Dreamweaver is a tool that works well for you.

# VISUAL SUMMARY

At the top of the Dreamweaver Design view is the familiar Menu bar that provides access to many functions related to Web design as well as to standard document functions, such as opening, closing, and saving documents. Below it, the Insert bar gives access to many Web-design functions that are collected into groups of related functions. The Start page allows you to continue working on an unfinished recent document or create a new page from either a blank document or predesigned sample pages.

At the right, the panel groups provide access to specific functions, such as Cascading Style Sheets in the Design panel or files in the current Web site in the Files panel. Panel groups can be collapsed, like the Design panel group, or expanded, like the Files panel group. Panel groups generally consist of multiple panels, such as the Files panel group, which consists of the Files and Assets panels. Other panels, such as the Frames panel, are closed by default. At the bottom of the Dreamweaver interface, the Property inspector displays the properties of a selected item in a Web page, such as the height and width of an image.

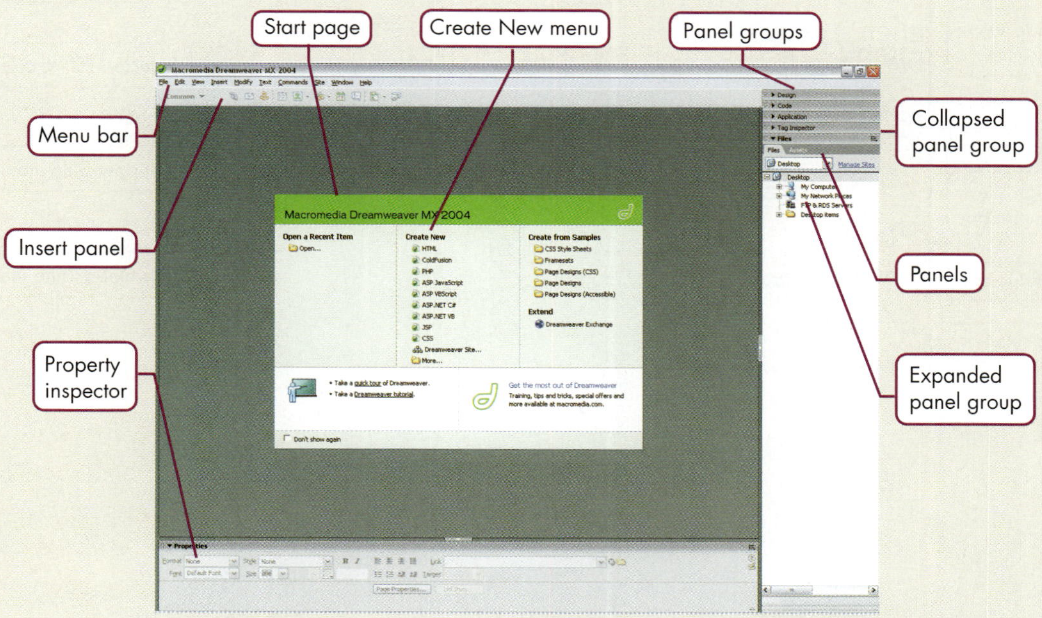


**FIGURE 1.1**

In this project, you learn about and explore the features of the Document window, the working area of the Dreamweaver interface. The following figure shows the Document window in Split view, in which you can see the Code and Design views together, but Dreamweaver can fill the Document window with either view. The Code window, the top portion of the Document window in this figure, displays the underlying HTML code that is created when you work in the Design window below it. The selected code in the Code window is the code for the figure selected in the Design window. At the top of the Document window is the Filename tab, which identifies the filename of the page you are editing; if you have multiple documents open at the same time, multiple tabs appear. The Document toolbar allows you to switch between the different views of the current Web page and also provides access to other functions related to the document as a whole. At the bottom of the Document window is the Status bar with the Tag selector on the left and the Window Size and Download Time indicators on the right.

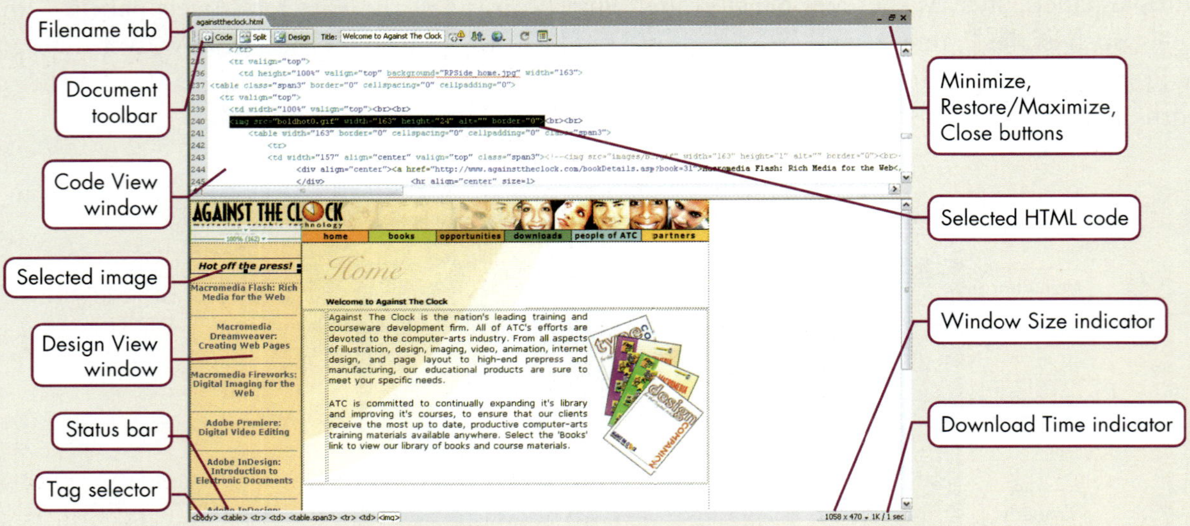


**FIGURE 1.2**

The Property inspector below the Document window changes to reflect the current and available properties of the selected item in the Document window. If you select a block of text, the Property inspector shows the format, typeface, size, color, style, alignment, and other text properties.

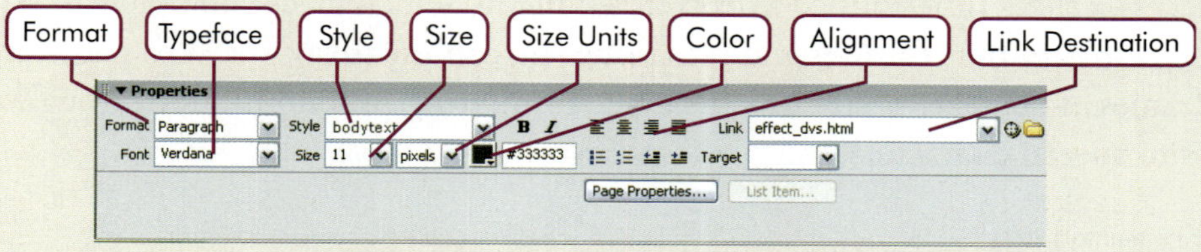


Properties of a selected paragraph

**FIGURE 1.3**

For a selected graphic, the Property inspector shows the properties of the image, such as its height, width, and location. If you have set the graphic as a link to another page, the Property inspector identifies the destination of the link. Dreamweaver provides some image-editing functions, which appear in the Property inspector when an image is selected.

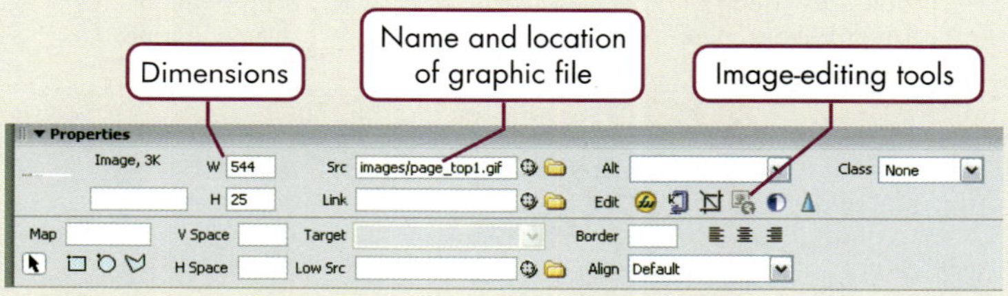


Properties of a selected image

**FIGURE 1.4**

Tables have very different properties, so when you have selected a table, the Property inspector changes to reflect the current and available properties for that table. The Property inspector is an immensely useful feature of Dreamweaver because it both displays the properties used by and available for the selected item on the Web page, and allows you to alter or add properties to the item.

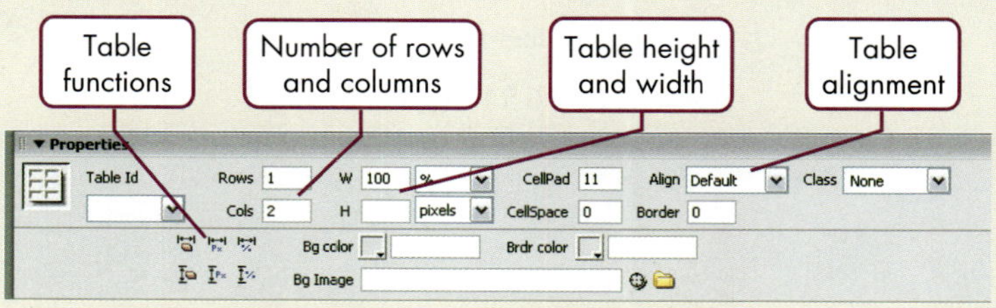


Properties of a selected table

**FIGURE 1.5**

The Insert bar provides access to many Web-page design functions. The Insert bar has a number of different forms that you can choose from the drop-down menu on the far left. The Common Insert bar contains many of the common functions that you use to create Web pages. Clicking the appropriate button accesses these functions or a drop-down menu, which gives you access to related functions. The Layout Insert bar offers features and functions you can use to lay out Web pages, including tables, layers, and frames. The Text Insert bar offers text-formatting functions and, through the drop-down menu, access to special characters.

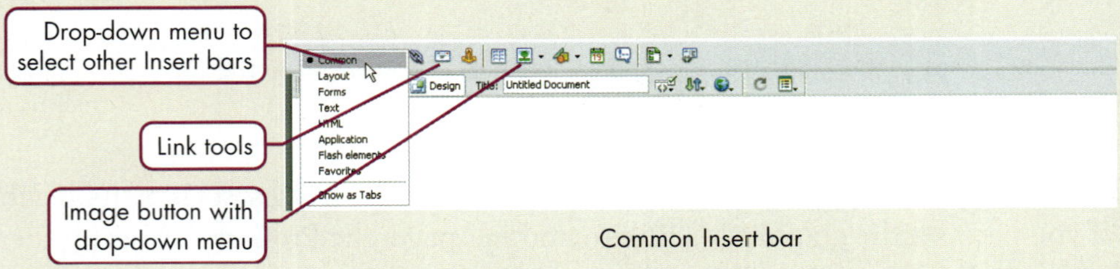


Common Insert bar

**FIGURE 1.6**

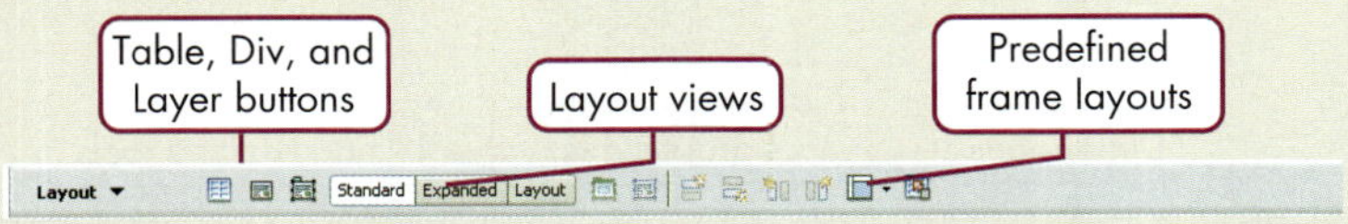


Layout Insert bar

**FIGURE 1.7**

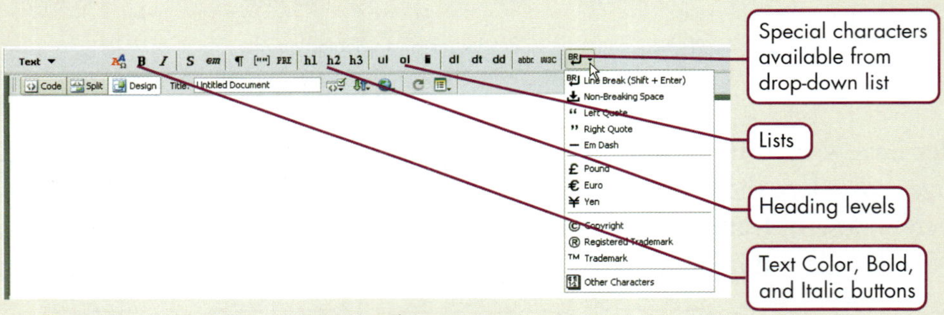


Text Insert bar

**FIGURE 1.8**

# LESSON 1 Launching Dreamweaver for the First Time

The Windows version of Dreamweaver offers a few options not available in the Macintosh version. In the Windows version, the workspace layout contains all toolbars, the Property inspector, and the panels in the Dreamweaver window. In the Macintosh version, components float in the workspace; that is, you can drag and place them separately from each other. (This layout was available for Windows users in previous versions of Dreamweaver but is no longer available in Dreamweaver MX 2004.)

In the following exercise, you launch Dreamweaver for the first time. Depending on how your system is set up, Dreamweaver may or may not display the Workspace Setup dialog box (Windows) or the Start page. In this exercise, you see these dialog boxes and discover where to enable or disable them.

Because there are some significant differences between the Windows and Macintosh workspace layouts, sometimes users on different platforms must use different methods to perform the same task. Both Windows and Macintosh users can perform all of the exercises in this book, but in this exercise, Macintosh users cannot perform one (identified) step in this exercise. Macintosh users can and should perform all other steps.

## Launch Dreamweaver for the First Time

**1** **If you are working on a Windows system, choose Start>Programs>Macromedia>Dreamweaver MX 2004. If you are working on a Macintosh computer, click the Dreamweaver icon in the Dock or the Applications folder.**

The program launches. If you are working on a Windows system and this is the first time that Dreamweaver has been started, the Workspace Setup dialog box appears, prompting you to choose the Designer or Coder workspace layout. If this is not the first time that Dreamweaver has been started or you are using a Macintosh system, skip to Step 3.

**2** **If you are working on a Windows system, choose Designer and click OK.**

Although the Coder workspace layout is available to Windows users with the simple selection of an option, it offers no additional features. This layout simply moves the Panel groups to the left and switches the Document window to Code view. Windows users can create this layout manually without using this function. Macintosh users also can create a similar layout by rearranging the panels and switching the Document window to Code view.

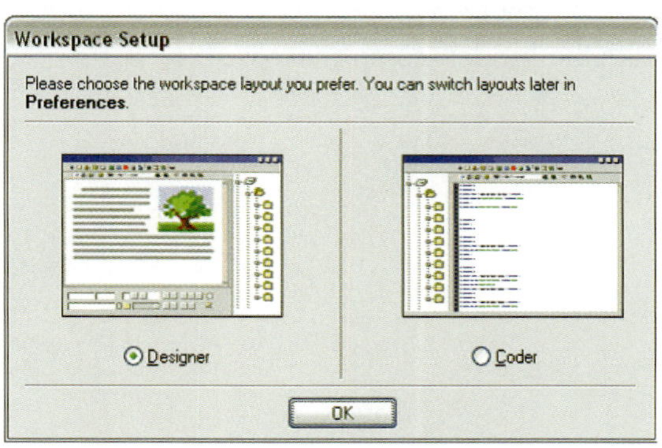


FIGURE 1.9

**3** **Choose Create New HTML document from the Dreamweaver Start Page menu.**

The Don't Show Again check box in the lower-left corner of the Start Page menu disables the Start page. Since future exercises require you to choose an option from the Start page, do not select this option at this time.

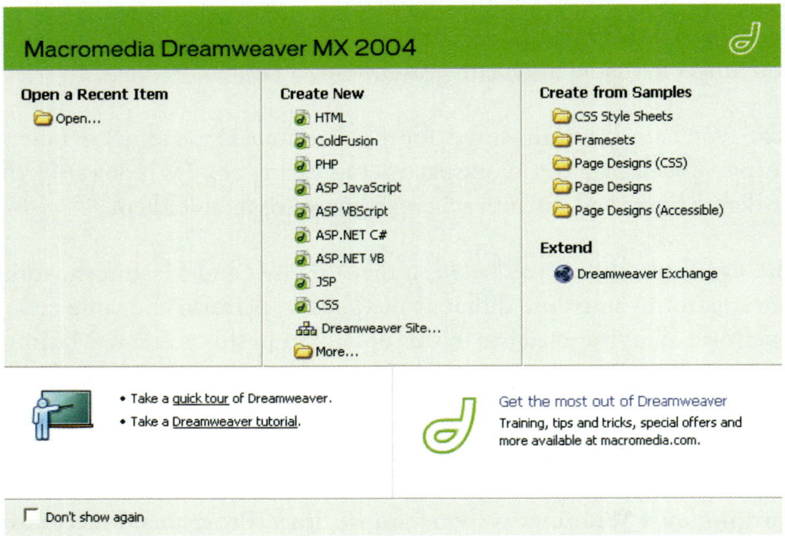


FIGURE 1.10

## To Extend Your Knowledge

### WORKSPACE LAYOUTS IN WINDOWS AND MACINTOSH

The workspace layouts are slightly different between Windows and Macintosh systems. Dreamweaver for Windows utilizes an ***MDI*** (Multiple Document Interface), in which the application encloses all open documents in the application window. Dreamweaver for Macintosh utilizes a floating workspace layout, in which the individual document windows and application components float freely in relation to each other.

The Dreamweaver setups and workspace layouts only affect the visual appearance of the application, not its functionality — all functions and features are available to all users from all layouts and setups. Some components of the interface may be visible in one setup but hidden in another. With a click of your mouse, however, you make the hidden component visible.

**4** **View the new HTML page in the Design view.**

The Design view is the WYSIWYG view, which is not unlike word-processing software. The white Document window is surrounded by the Menu and Insert bars at the top, the Panel groups on the right, and the Property inspector below. The tab at the top of the Document window indicates that the current HTML document is untitled. No HTML is visible: the only indication of HTML is the **<body>** tag in the Tag selector at the bottom-left corner of the Document window. This tag indicates that the insertion point is on the page, ready for you to type in text (body copy).

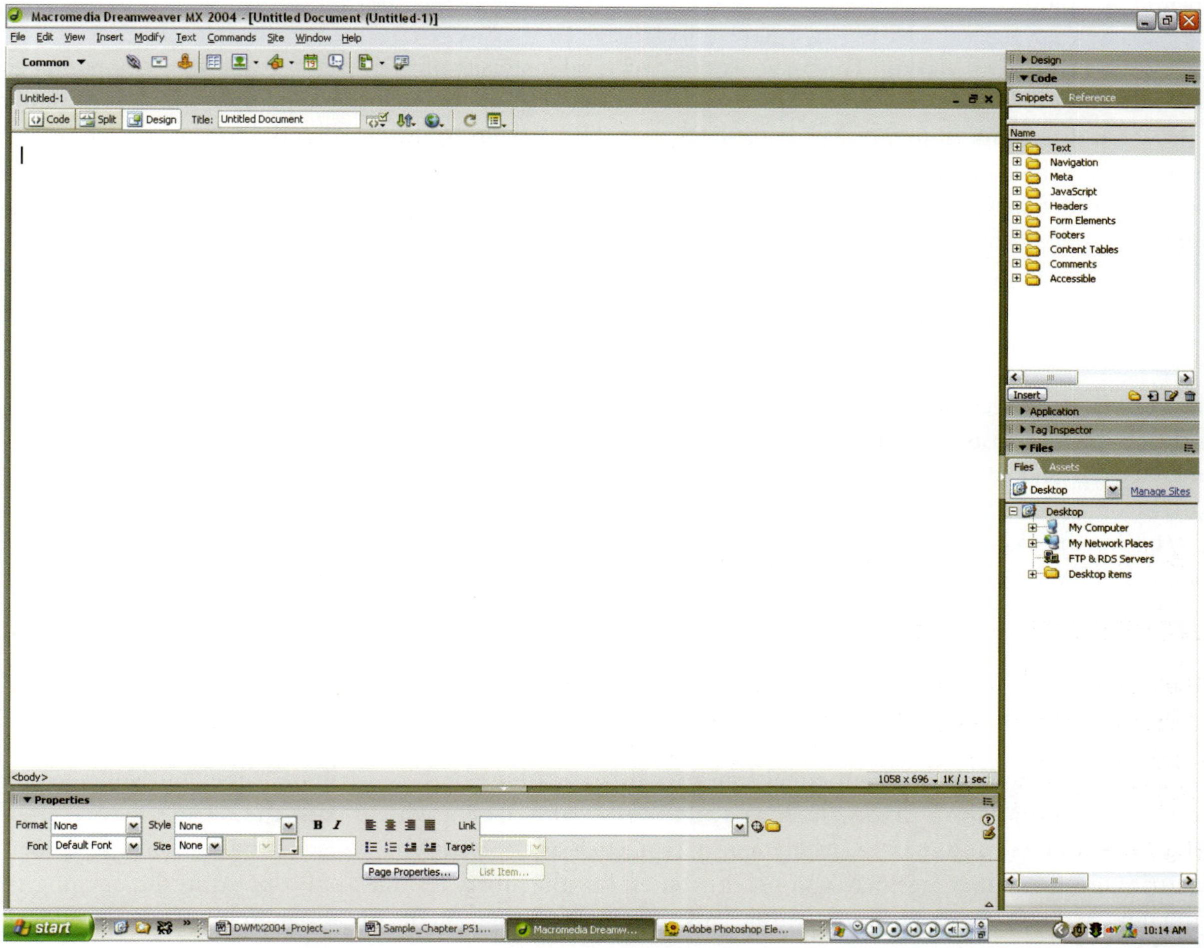


**FIGURE 1.11**

**5** **Choose File>Exit to exit Dreamweaver.**

# LESSON 2 Exploring the Code View

Dreamweaver has two basic default document views: the Design view and the Code view. The Design view, the default, is the WYSIWYG interface — the design you create in the Document window is what displays in a Web browser. The Code view displays HTML code in the Document window. A Web graphic designer might prefer the Design view while a Web programmer might prefer the Code view. At any time, however, you can switch from either setup to the other by selecting the View Select buttons at the top left of the Dreamweaver Document window.

***HTML***, or HyperText Markup Language, is the structural language of Web pages. It specifies colors, images, typefaces, and other components of a Web page. The term "Hyper" comes from hyperlink, which is the ability to provide a direct link from one Web page to another. "Text" refers to the fact that the code is written into the document as text characters. An HTML page includes not just the instructions on how to display the page but also the text that appears in the page. Code is differentiated from text content by angle brackets, < >, which surround the code. "Markup" indicates that the code is embedded amid the text in much the same way that a teacher or boss might mark up a printed page with instructions, such as "make this bold" or "add a graphic here." "Language" refers to the fact that the code must follow a standard or it won't work: to make text bold, you use `<b>`, not <bold>, because `<b>` is part of the language and <bold> is not.

The HTML language consists of HTML tags or just tags. ***Tags*** are elements surrounded by angle brackets: the bold tag, `<b>`, consists of the bold element, `b`, surround by angle brackets. HTML tags come in two forms — container tags and empty tags. ***Container tags*** surround content and have both an on and an off version of the tag. The off tag uses the same element as the on tag except that the element is preceded by a forward slash, such as `</b>` for the closing bold tag. Container tags surround content; for example, to make the word Tennessee bold, the HTML would be `<b>`Tennessee`</b>`. ***Empty tags*** do not have a closing tag, such as `<img>`, which is used to insert a graphic, or `<hr>`, which inserts a ***horizontal rule*** (a horizontal line, hence `hr`).

Tag options are known as "attributes." With rare exceptions, attributes are paired with attribute values. For example, the `<img>` (image) tag uses the `src` (source) attribute to specify the filename of the graphic. The attribute is `src` and the attribute value may be `red-rose.gif`. You format attributes and attribute values in a standard way, as well. You use an equal sign to join an attribute and its attribute value, and you surround the value with quotation marks, such as `src="red-rose.gif"`, which, with the `<img>` tag, results in `<img src="red-rose.gif">`. Many empty tags, such as the `<img>` tag, specify the content they provide by attributes. Container tags may also use attributes, but the attributes must only appear in the opening tag, never in the closing tag. For example, to specify the alignment of a paragraph, you would use `<p align="center">`paragraph text`</p>`.

## To Extend Your Knowledge

### HTML STANDARDS

Every computer language follows a particular standard. In some cases, the company that created the language maintains it, as Microsoft Corporation maintains the Active Server Pages language. In other cases, an organization maintains the language, as the ***W3C*** (World Wide Web Consortium) maintains HTML. The W3C Standards group works to continually improve HTML.

HTML is modified by two means — incorporation of new HTML code developed by browser manufacturers, or code developed by the W3C. For one dark period in the history of HTML, Netscape and Microsoft fought for control over the WWW, which they saw as an untapped market. In an attempt to improve their browsers' market share, each either created new HTML tags or "improved" upon current HTML, often to the exclusion of other browsers. This led to what is now referred to as the "browser wars." These wars created a huge headache for many corporate Web-site developers who were required to support both browsers for fear of losing a significant portion of their potential customers.

In the end, common sense prevailed; with the aid of the Web-standards advocates, W3C HTML is again the single HTML standard. During the browser wars, the mark of advanced Web developers was to show how far they could push their browser of choice, despite losing others. With the return to Web standards, the mark of advanced developers is to show how similar their Web pages look in all browsers.

Web standards are in; browser wars are out: Web developers are now measured against the W3C code standards, Web-development software is evaluated on the basis of how well it produces standards-compliant code, and browsers are evaluated by how well they display standards-compliant code. Dreamweaver produces good-quality code and, for the most part, displays it as the W3C recommends browsers should display code. Dreamweaver is not a browser, but its Design view is a very good representation of what standards-compliant browsers will display. This is one of the reasons why Dreamweaver has become the premier Web-development software.

## Explore the Code View

**1** **Launch Dreamweaver.**

**2** **Choose HTML from below the Create New heading on the Start page.**

**3** **Click the Code button at the top of the Document window and examine the HTML code in the Document window.**

Notice that the Document window contains HTML code that was not visible in the Design view. Different components of HTML are colored differently, which is helpful to a coder looking for an error. Code is blue whereas text is black, as you can see between the opening and closing `<title>` tags. Displaying different components of code in different colors is called "syntax coloring" and is only available in the better coding applications.

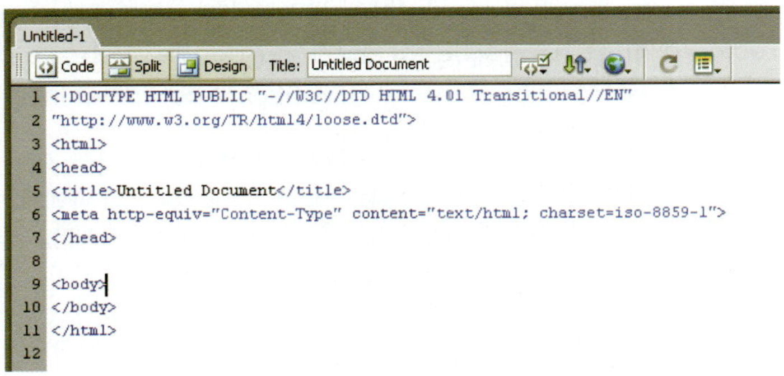


FIGURE 1.12

**4** **Click between the "y" and ">" at the end of `<body>` and press the Spacebar.**

A code prompt appears, listing all options for the `<body>` tag. (You learn more about the `<body>` tag in Lesson 5.)

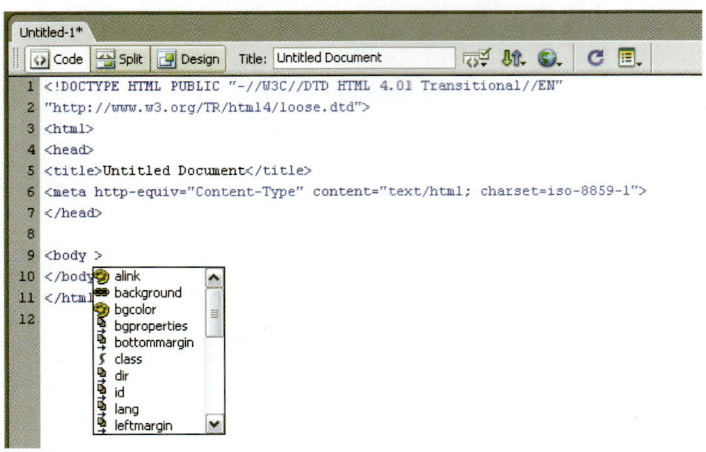


FIGURE 1.13

**5** **Move the pointer over the regions of the Document toolbar, and note the tool tips that appear.**

The filename displays Untitled until you save the file. An asterisk appears by the filename if you have modified the file since you last saved it. The No Browser Check Errors tool tip and the button graphic change when browser-check errors exist.

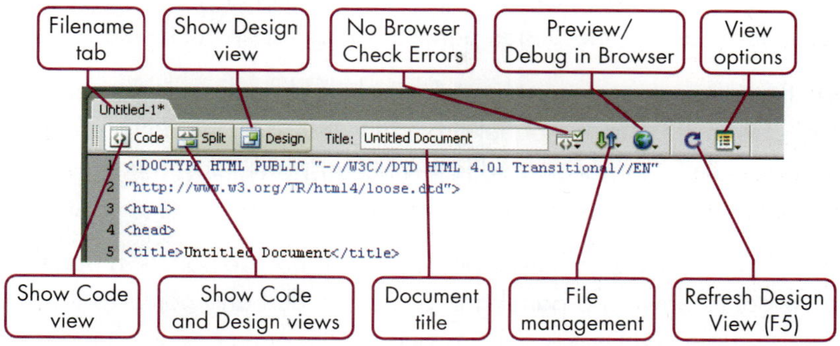


FIGURE 1.14

**6** **Move your pointer over the regions of the Common Insert bar, and note the tool tips that appear.**

The Insert bar provides access to many different functions, grouped by categories. You can select these categories through the pop-up menu at the left end of the Insert bar. By default, you select categories from a pop-up menu, but you can also change its form to a tabbed menu instead.

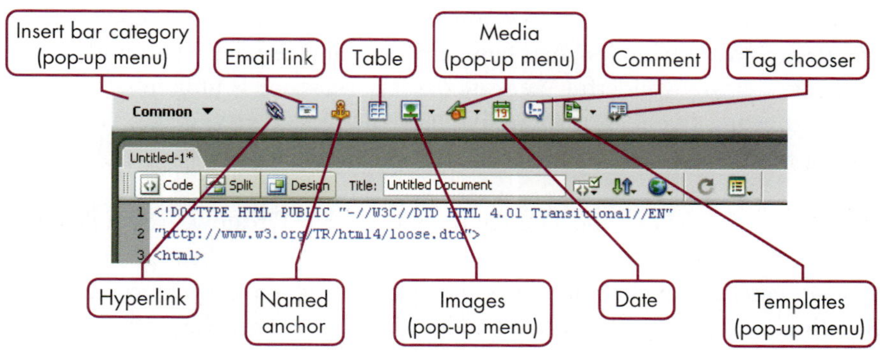


FIGURE 1.15

**7** **Click the title of the Design panel group to expand this panel group.**

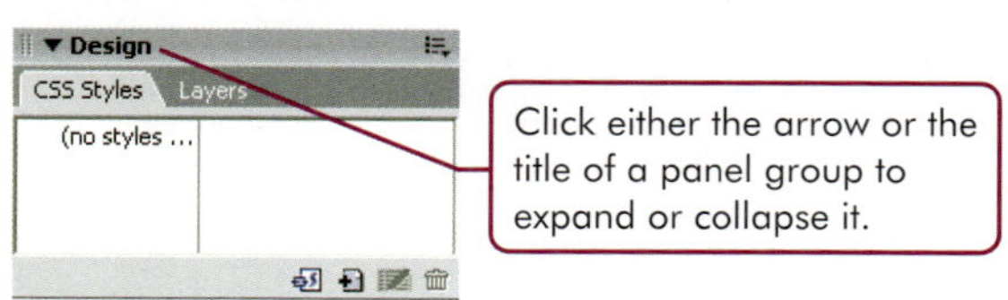


FIGURE 1.16

**8** **Click once on the Design button at the top of the Document window to switch to the Design view.**

**9** **Choose File>Exit to exit Dreamweaver. Do not save the changes to the untitled document.**

## To Extend Your Knowledge

### Expanded vs. Open, Collapsed vs. Closed

Most Dreamweaver panel groups contain panels and most, but not all, panel groups are visible on screen by default. By default, for example, the Design panel group is visible but the Results panel group is not.

Dreamweaver uses the terminology "open" and "closed" to describe whether or not the panel groups are visible and available to the user. If a panel-group title is visible, the panel group is said to be open. The Results panel-group title is not visible and is therefore closed. Closed panels may be opened from the Window menu, such as by choosing Window>Results.

The terms "expanded" and "collapsed" describe whether or not the panels in panel groups are visible. The expander arrow points down if a panel group is expanded and points to the right if collapsed. If the Styles panel tab is visible, the Details panel group is both open and expanded.

# LESSON 3 Exploring the Design View

Dreamweaver's Design view is very beneficial to beginning Web designers — it resembles word-processing software, which is familiar to most people. The common functions and features are available through a keystroke combination or a mouse click. Some people are uncomfortable working with code, so naturally prefer the Design view. Furthermore, many Web designers come from a print-design background. Their keen and experienced eyes enable them to create wonderful Web-site designs, but code is unfamiliar to them because it is not part of their print-design work. For all of these individuals, the Design view makes Web design more comfortable and natural.

The Design view permits designers to build a design on screen while Dreamweaver builds the code in the background. Although many hand-coders may argue that hand-coding gives them greater control over the code, Dreamweaver produces excellent-quality code, and the ease with which they can create tables, for example, in Dreamweaver can influence the most ardent hand-coder to give Dreamweaver a try.

As mentioned before, the Code and Design views provide access to the same functions and features of Web-page design. The primary difference between the views is how users interact with Dreamweaver to create their designs. With the Code view, the user creates the design by keying the code; with the Design view, the user commonly employs the mouse and menus to create the designs.

In the previous lesson, you saw that the Code view is just a click away. When you become more experienced with Web design, you will realize how beneficial it is to know HTML so that when you need to customize the code Dreamweaver produces, you can do so. Experienced Web designers are comfortable in both views, switching back and forth as appropriate for their needs.

## Explore the Design View

**1** **Start Dreamweaver and choose HTML from the Create New heading on the Start page.**

### If you have problems

If you don't see the Start page, choose Edit>Preferences, click the General tab, and check the Show Start Page option. Click OK to close the Preferences dialog box. The Start page does not appear immediately — you must exit Dreamweaver (File>Exit) and then relaunch it.

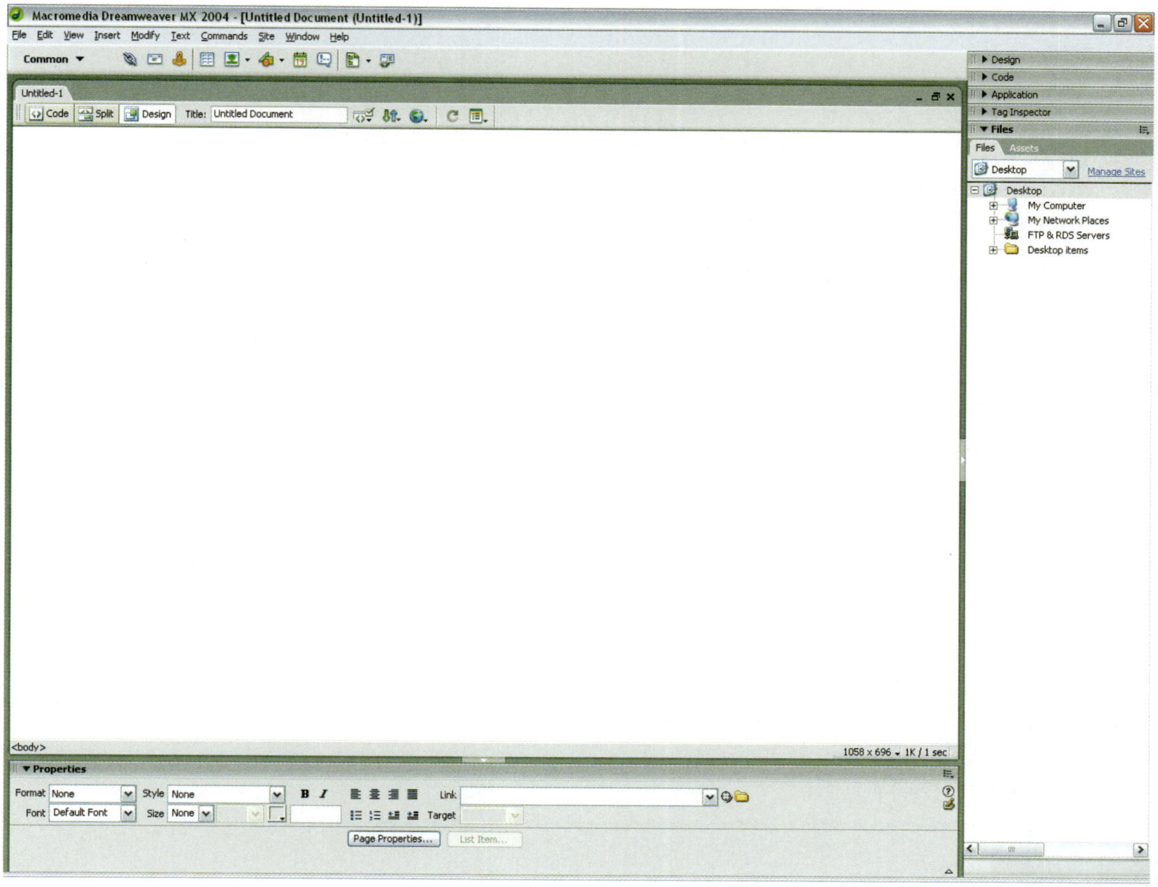


FIGURE 1.17

**2** **Click the Code button and notice that the HTML code is visible.**

**3** **Click the Split button to see the Code view in the upper portion of the Document window and the Design view in the lower portion of the Document window.**

At times it is beneficial to see both views at the same time — the Split button (the tool tip shows Show Code and Design Views) makes this possible.

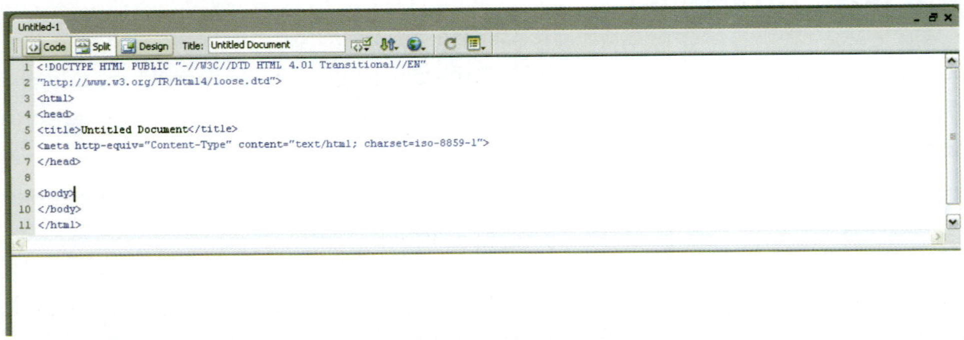


FIGURE 1.18

**4** **Move the insertion point to the end of the `<body>` tag in the Code view window, press Enter/Return once, and type your first name.**

Notice that your name does not appear in the Design view window. You must refresh the Design view in order for any code or text typed in the Code view window to be visible in the Design view window. You can also click in the Design window to refresh the Design view.

**5** **Click the Refresh Design View button in the Document toolbar.**

Notice that your name now appears in the Design view window.

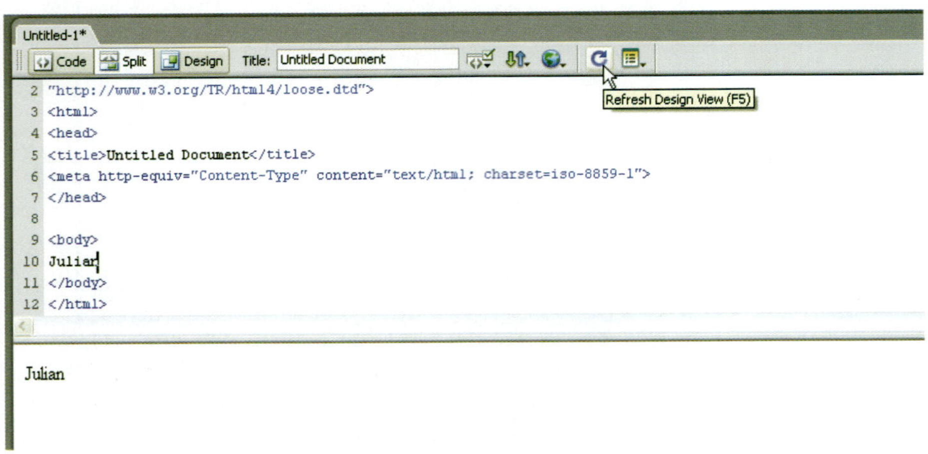


FIGURE 1.19

**6** **Close the Code view window by clicking the Design button.**

**7** **Change the Insert bar category to Layout by clicking the Insert bar category pop-up menu and choosing Layout from the list.**

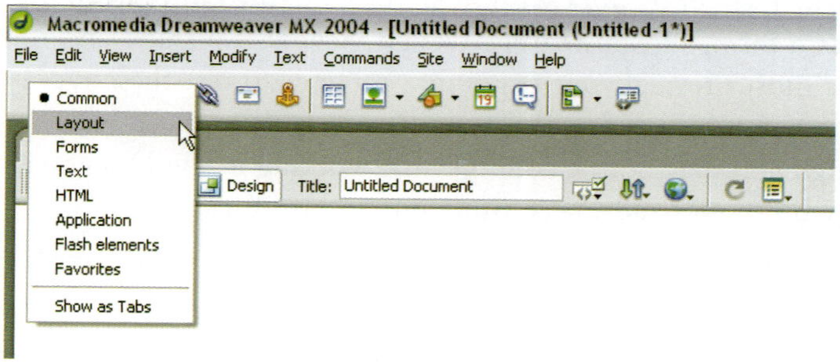


FIGURE 1.20

**8** **Close the current untitled document by choosing File>Close. When prompted, choose not to save. Leave Dreamweaver open for the next exercise.**

## LESSON 4 Exploring the Property Inspector

The Property inspector is the most important panel of the Dreamweaver interface. The Property inspector interface and options change to reflect the properties of the current selected item, such as a paragraph, table, form, or image. The Property inspector is also the means by which you can change the properties of a selected item.

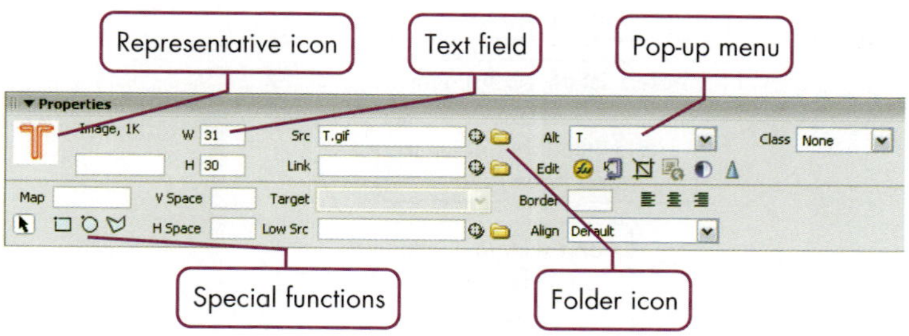


FIGURE 1.21

The Property inspector commonly uses a representative icon to indicate the type of item selected, such as a table-like icon or, in this example, a miniature of the selected image. The Property inspector provides different types of methods for changing the properties of the selected item, such as text fields in which you type, pop-up menus from which you choose, and folder icons that allow you to open a folder on your computer and select a file. For some items, the Property inspector provides access to functions that are specific to the item.

In this lesson, you use the Property inspector to explore images, headings, links, and other items without an introduction to these concepts. We assume that you have a basic understanding of basic components of a Web page, such as images, headings, and links. (We examine all of these items in much greater detail in later projects.) This lesson, however, focuses on exploring a Web page through the Property inspector. You discover how the Property inspector changes to reflect the properties of different items, how to use the Property inspector to change the item's properties, and how the Property inspector changes to reflect the changes you make to that item.

You also preview a Web page in your browser. Dreamweaver's Design view is quite like a browser, in that, for the most part, what you see in the Design view is what you get in your browser. Dreamweaver, however, emphasizes features to make it easier to work with them: black dashed lines surround each cell in a table, and a red dashed line surrounds a form. Dreamweaver's Design view is also static and unresponsive — it does not react to user actions. You must preview your pages in a browser to test these types of effects. A good rule of thumb comes from the programming community — "code a little, test a little" — which means test your design frequently. Although you may not be coding while working in the Design view, it is still good practice, especially when you move on to more advanced functions and features.

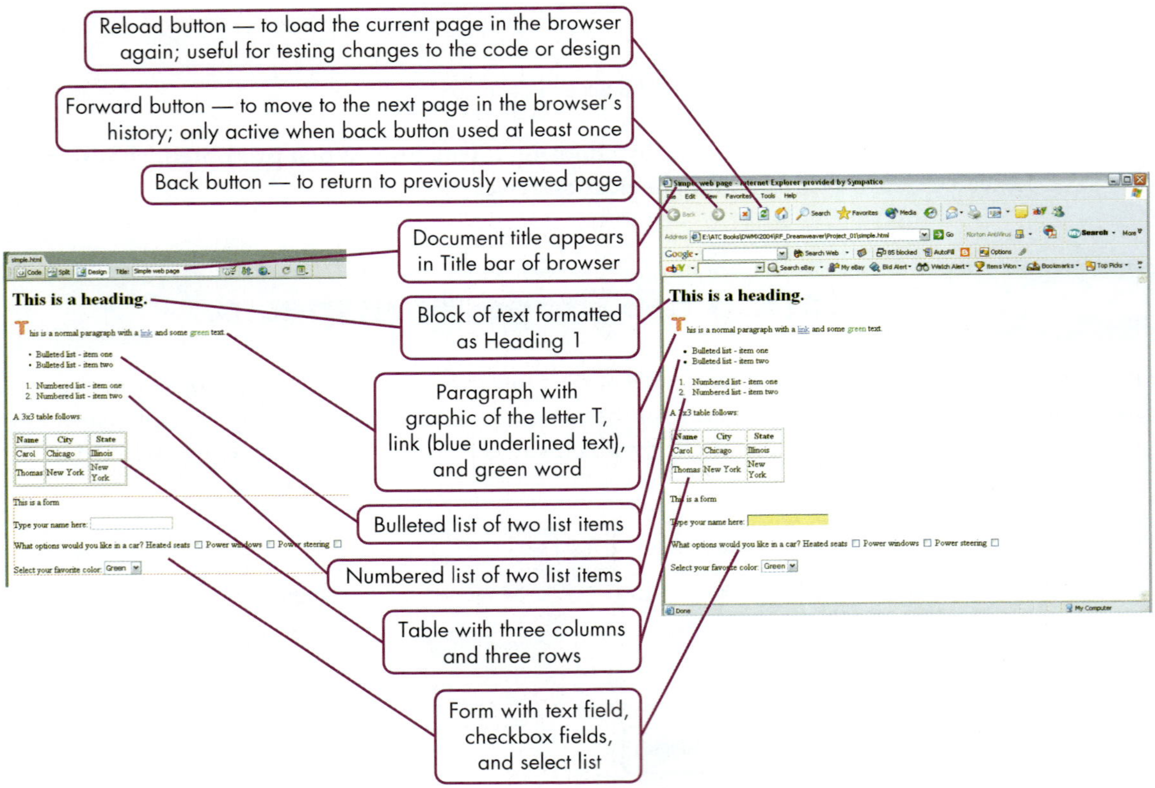


**FIGURE 1.22**

## Explore a Simple Web Page with the Property Inspector

**1** **Copy the Project_01 folder and all of its contents from the RF_Dreamweaver_L1 folder to your WIP folder.**

This step will prepare all of the files you need for Project_01.

**2** **Choose File>Open, navigate to the Project_01>Simple folder, choose the file simple.html, and click Open.**

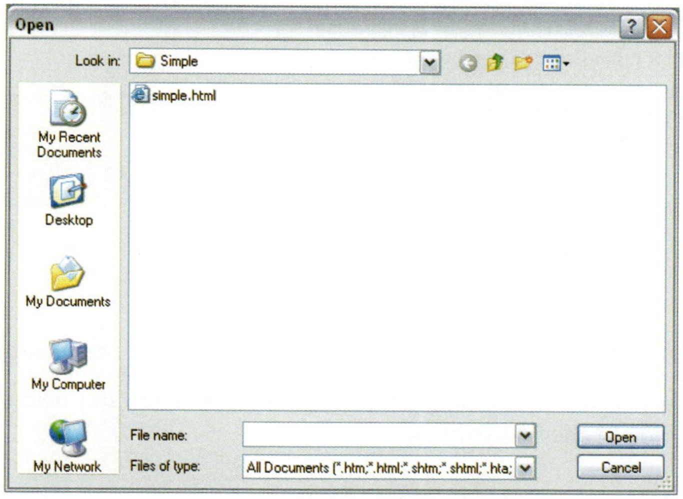


FIGURE 1.23

**3** **Click in the first sentence — this is a heading.**

Note the Property inspector indicates this sentence uses the Format Heading 1.

FIGURE 1.24

**4** **Click the graphic of the red "T."**

The Property inspector changes to display the properties of a graphic image, such as its dimensions (31 pixels wide by 30 pixels high) and its source (T.gif). Handles appear around a graphic when it is selected. The ***handles*** are the three squares that appear in the middle of the right and bottom sides and on the bottom-right corner.

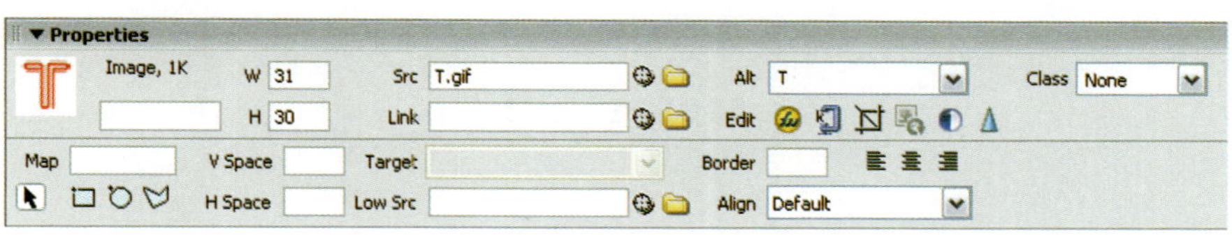


FIGURE 1.25

**5** **In the Property inspector, click to the right of the number 31, type the number 0 (making the new number 310), and press Enter/Return.**

The Property inspector both displays the properties of the selected object and allows the designer to make changes to that object's properties. In this case, you changed the graphic's width from 31 pixels to 310 pixels.

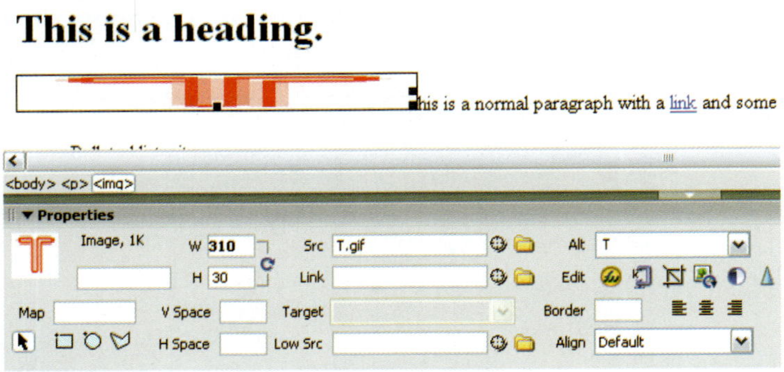


FIGURE 1.26

**6** **Click the blue underlined word link and observe the Property inspector.**

Blue underlined text is the default appearance of link text. The Link field in the Property inspector shows the destination of the selected link.

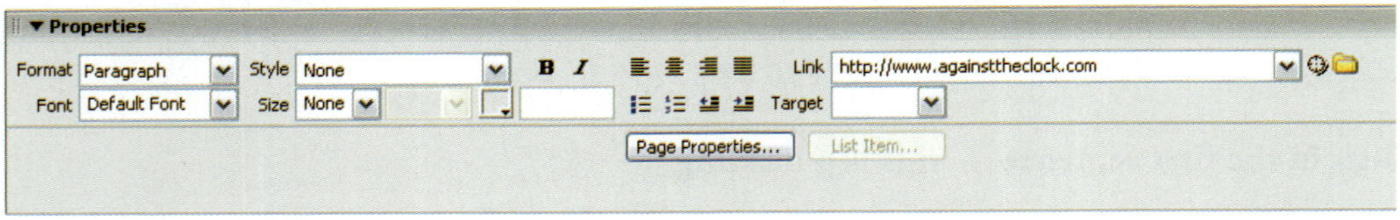


FIGURE 1.27

**7** **If necessary, scroll down so the form section is visible. Click any of the car check-box options or the color list.**

The Property inspector changes to reflect the properties of the information that those form controls collect; you cannot check any option, and the select list does not drop down to show the color options.

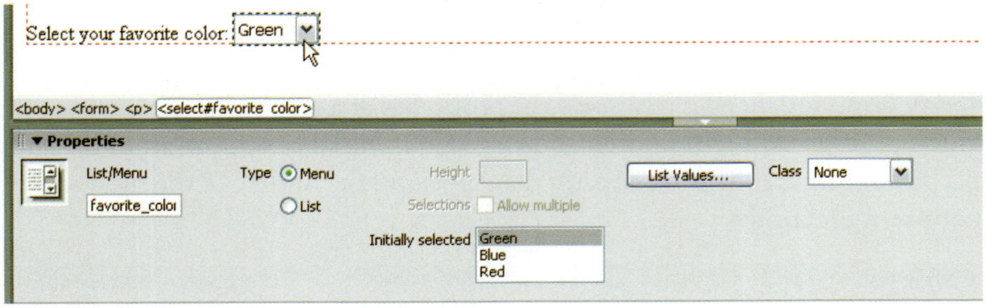


FIGURE 1.28

**8** **Preview the Web page in your browser by clicking the Preview/Debug in Browser button on the Document toolbar and choosing a browser from the list.**

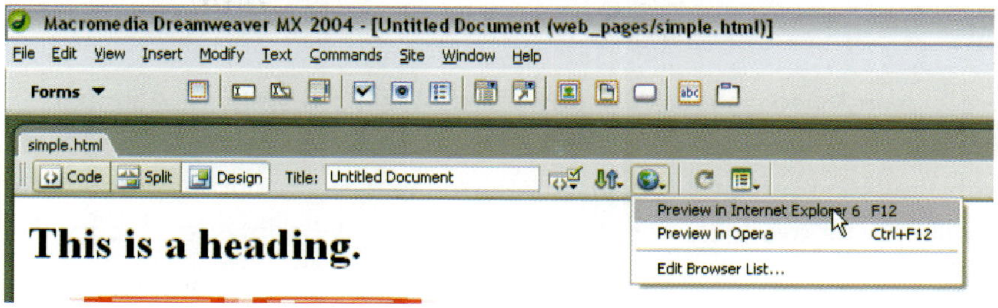


FIGURE 1.29

**9** **Click Yes to save the changes.**

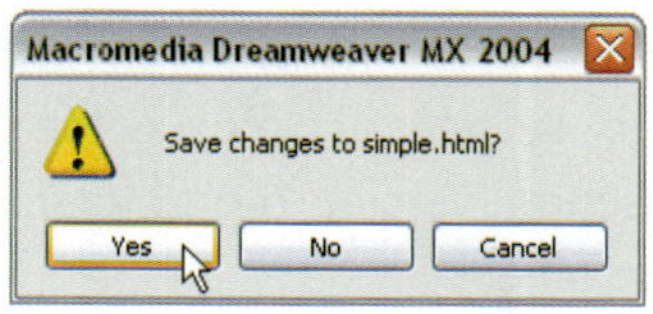


FIGURE 1.30

**10** **Click any of the car check-box options or the favorite color list, and notice that these form controls respond as you would expect them to react to user interaction.**

Although the Dreamweaver interface is WYSIWYG, it is not a browser and does not respond to user interaction in the same way a browser does. The WYSIWYG aspect of the Dreamweaver interface is for design only.

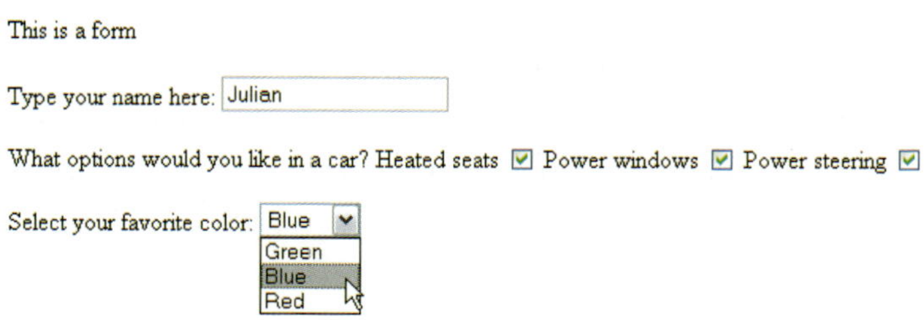


FIGURE 1.31

**11** **Close the browser and return to Dreamweaver. Leave simple.html open for the next exercise.**

## To Extend Your Knowledge

### Other Browsers

Internet Explorer (IE) is installed on most Windows and Macintosh systems. Although this browser may be the most commonly used browser, other browsers offer different experiences. IE is available at no cost. It comes with the Windows and Macintosh operating systems and upgrades are free. However, the next version will only be available with the next version of Windows, and IE for the Macintosh has been discontinued.

The Opera browser is a small, fast browser, and is available for Windows, Macintosh, and various Unix and Linux operating systems. Unlike IE, this browser comes at a cost — the free version has built-in banner advertising that you may disable for a fee of about $40.

Unlike Opera, the Netscape/Mozilla browser is entirely free to download and is available for Windows, Macintosh, and Linux/Unix systems. Firefox is the Mozilla browser for Windows, and Camino is the Macintosh version. Netscape, version 6 and later, is built from the Mozilla code — any pages that work in one will work in the other.

The Safari browser will replace IE as the default browser for the Macintosh. Apple adopted KHTML technology from a Linux windowing system called "KDE" and created the Safari browser from it. Other browsers available for Macintosh systems include iCab and OmniWeb, both for a fee.

The Lynx browser is a text or character-based browser (no graphics at all). The blind often use it in combination with a text-to-speech or text-to-Braille system to hear or read the Web site. Although it is a good browser with which to test your site for accessibility, the Opera browser (version 7 or higher) can be switched into a text-only mode for the same purposes, reducing the need to install an additional browser.

The BrowserCam.com Web site provides screenshots of your pages in up to 16 browsers. Although this service is primarily available for a fee (a limited trial is available for free), it is much cheaper than purchasing multiple computers to perform the same testing. This service can only show you how your pages look in different browsers; it cannot help you with interactive functionality, such as JavaScript.

## LESSON 5 Exploring HTML Using the Tag Selector

Most HTML tags are container tags — they have an opening and closing tag form. What you see in the Document window is content that exists within the **<body>** tag, one of the top-level HTML tags. All HTML documents start and end with the topmost **<html>** tag in its opening and closing forms. The **<html>** tag defines the beginning and end of the HTML document. The HTML document has two divisions, the head and the body, which are delimited by the **<head>** and **<body>** tags respectively. The head division contains information that is not visible to the end user with one exception — the **<title>** tag. The content of the **<title>** tag appears at the top of the browser window and also appears as the name of the document in the search-results page of a search engine. The other tags in the head include **<meta>** tags, which are commonly used to contain keywords for search engines, the **<script>** tag for JavaScript code, and the **<style>** tag for CSS code.

In this lesson, you encounter the **<h1>** tag, a heading tag. This tag is the largest and most important heading. The **<p>** paragraph tag contains standard paragraph content, which may also include the **<a>** anchor tag, the tag that creates links to other documents. The **<table>** tag, which you also encounter in this lesson, creates a table. A table consists of rows and cells in each row. Opening and closing **<tr>** table-row tags surround each row. Opening and closing **<td>** table-data tags, the tags that correspond to table cells, surround the content in each cell. Therefore, the content of a table cell is contained by **<td>** tags, which are contained by **<tr>** tags, which are contained by **<table>** tags, making the table one of the most complex structures in HTML. The **<body>** tag encloses all content that is visible in the Document window.

The Tag selector is a feature of Dreamweaver that enables the designer to view the tags used for a particular block of text, and to select a tag and its contents. The Tag selector shows the hierarchy of tags, starting with the top-left tag. It is not unlike an interactive family tree in which, when you select a particular person, the ancestry of that person is highlighted. For example, if you click in an **<a>** anchor tag (link) within a **<p>** paragraph tag within the body of the document, the Tag selector displays **<body><p><a>**. Selecting a different link in a paragraph in the body displays the same "ancestry" as the previous one. However, selecting an anchor tag in a paragraph, in a table cell, in a table row, in a table, in the body of the HTML document, displays a very different layering of tags — **<body><table><tr><td><p><a>**. When you click a tag in the Tag selector, you cause it to display the layers of tags and to select the content within the tag. Clicking the **<a>** tag selects the link text, clicking the **<p>** tag selects the paragraph including the **<a>** within it, and clicking the **<body>** tag selects everything in the body of the document.

When you want to select a few words in a sentence, Dreamweaver provides controls similar to those in word-processing software. In word-processing software, you might drag to select the words, use a particular key command to select an entire sentence, click several times to select a full paragraph, and so on. The Tag selector in Dreamweaver provides you with similar means for selecting content contained in a particular tag. Once selected, you may delete, copy, move, or style the selected content.

Although the Code view is useful for coding HTML, CSS, JavaScript, and other Web-scripting languages, Dreamweaver is primarily a WYSIWYG design tool. As mentioned before, when you draw a design in the Design view, Dreamweaver creates the HTML code in the background. Although it might seem that with Dreamweaver, you don't need to understand HTML, in fact, any understanding you can acquire of HTML benefits you, especially when you try to understand messages about the code. Dreamweaver displays code for the user in many ways, such as in the Tag selector. Without understanding HTML, you might not fully comprehend the information that the Tag selector provides. You do not need to be a hand-coder to be a Web-site designer, but if you don't understand HTML, your abilities will be compromised.

## Dreamweaver's HTML Support

Dreamweaver supports several major versions of HTML and all three subversions. By default, Dreamweaver's HTML pages are built against the HTML 4.01 transitional or frameset DTDs. A more recent version of HTML called "XHTML 1.0," however, is a better version. Most standards-aware designers build their pages against XHTML 1.0 Strict or XHTML 1.1, but Dreamweaver does not currently support XHTML 1.1. The "X" in XHTML comes from another W3C Web technology called "XML," an abbreviation for eXtensible Markup Language. ***XML*** is an extremely strict language in which, if even one component of the language is incorrect, the document does not display. The advantage of such strictness is that if the document meets the standard, it is very easy for browsers to display — guessing is not necessary. The W3C intends, with XHTML, to improve HTML and to increase the strictness of HTML, thereby making it easier for browsers to display.

## *To Extend Your Knowledge*

### CSS AND ECMASCRIPT

HTML is only one of many coding languages used in Web pages. There are numerous others, such as CSS and ECMAScript, which are both text-based coding languages that a knowledgeable user may type into an editor and view in a browser.

***CSS*** (Cascading Style Sheets) is a W3C coding language. CSS, like HTML, is not a true programming language but CSS is meant to complement HTML as a language of style. HTML was originally designed as the language defining the structure of a Web page, such as paragraphs, headings, and tables. The original intent was not to use HTML for style, such as alignment, color, or typeface options. CSS is the coding language that defines the style or look of a Web page and allows "the separation of structure and style." Despite the fact that CSS1 was released with HTML 4 in late 1996, its adoption rate has been very slow. However, Dreamweaver MX 2004, more than any previous version or competitors' products, writes most style changes using CSS rather than the outdated HTML equivalents. For this reason, many Web-standards supporters applaud Dreamweaver MX 2004's adoption of CSS.

ECMAScript, for all intents and purposes, is JavaScript, and both are client-side programming languages. ECMA is the abbreviation for the European Computer Manufacturers Association, an important standards body in Europe. The W3C has adopted their version of JavaScript as the standard for the WWW. A ***client-side*** programming language runs in the browser whereas a ***server-side*** programming language runs at the server. When you insert JavaScript code or programming instructions into a Web page, it is delivered to the browser along with the page's HTML. The browser then interprets the code and performs the required actions. JavaScript is the most popular client-side programming language, but VBScript (based on Visual Basic) and JScript (a Microsoft proprietary implementation of JavaScript), which run only in the Internet Explorer browser, are also available.

## Explore HTML Using the Tag Selector

**1** **In the open document, simple.html, click in the top paragraph — This is a heading. — and observe the Tag selector at the bottom left of the Document window.**

The Tag selector shows that the insertion point is in a paragraph that uses the **<h1>** HTML tag. This heading exists in the body of the HTML document because the **<h1>** tag follows the **<body>** tag in the Tag selector.

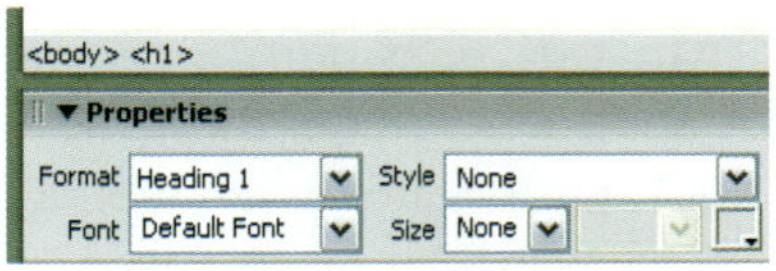


FIGURE 1.32

**2** **Click the <h1> tag in the Tag selector.**

Notice that the selected tag in the Tag selector is highlighted with a white background, and the content of the tag is selected in the Document window.

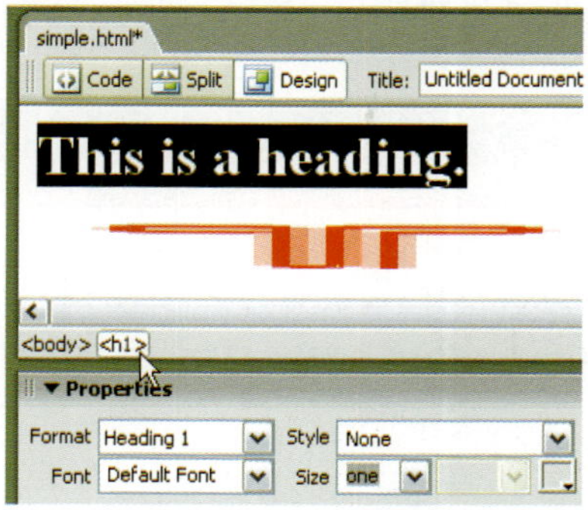


FIGURE 1.33

**3** **Click the Split button at the top of the Document window.**

When a tag is selected in the Tag selector, the text (enclosed in the tag) in the document and the code in the Code window are selected, as well. The text "This is a heading." is surrounded by **<h1>** and **</h1>** tags, indicating that the text is formatted as Heading 1.

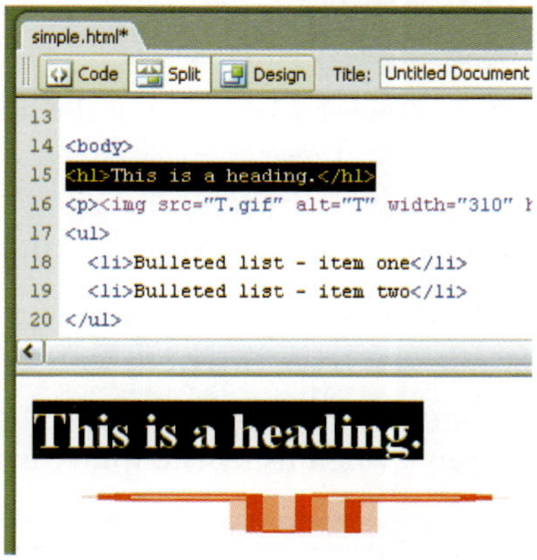


FIGURE 1.34

**4** **Click in the Carol cell of the 3 × 3 table and notice the string of HTML tags that appear in the Tag selector.**

A table is a complex HTML construct that, in its simplest form, requires a **<table>** tag to denote the beginning and ending of a table, a table-row (**<tr>**) tag for each row, and a table-data (**<td>**) tag for each data cell.

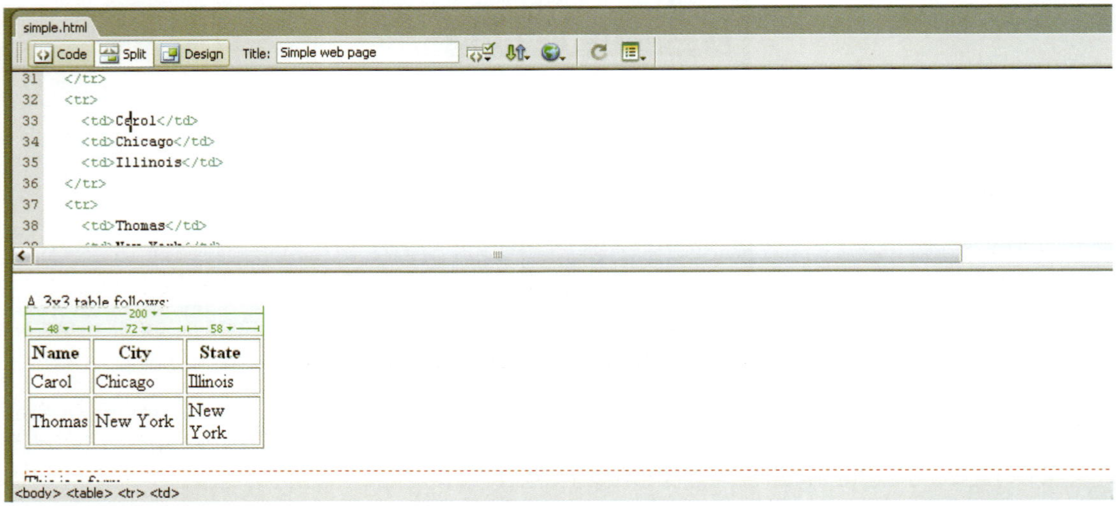

FIGURE 1.35

**5** **Click the <table> tag in the Tag selector and observe the amount of code that is selected in the Code window.**

**6** **Drag the divider between the Code and Design windows downward to increase the height of the Code window.**

The height of the Code window may not be sufficient to see a large block of code, such as you need for this small table. You can raise or lower the divider between the Code and Design windows to increase or decrease the amount of code visible when using the split-window feature.

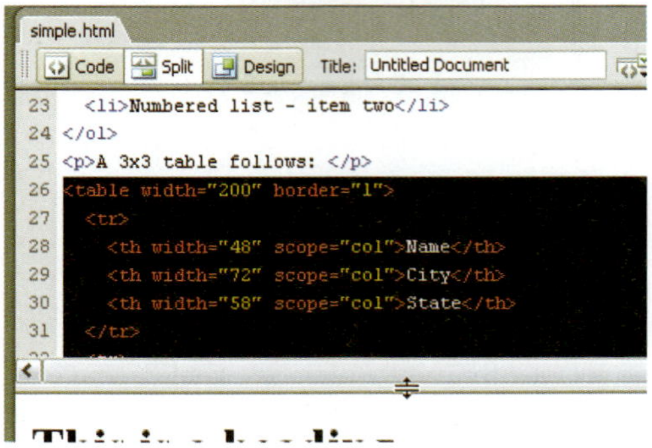

FIGURE 1.36

**7** **Note the number and variety of tags required to create a table.**

The table begins and ends with the **<table>** tag, each row begins and ends with the **<tr>** tag, and each cell begins and ends with either the **<th>** (table-header) or the **<td>** (table-data) cell. Some tags have additional properties, such as **width**, **border**, and **scope**.

**8** **Close the Code window by clicking the Design button at the top of the Document window. Leave simple.html open for the next exercise.**

## To Extend Your Knowledge

### THE DTD TAG

You probably noticed that above the opening **<html>** tag is another tag with a rather odd format: **<!DOCTYPE HTML PUBLIC "-//W3C//DTD HTML 4.01 Transitional//EN" "http://www.w3.org/TR/html4/loose.dtd">**. This is the ***DTD***, the document-type definition tag. There have been different versions of HTML, each new version introducing new tags and removing others. The DTD identifies the version of HTML used, making it easier for browsers to display the Web page. In the past, many designers and their Web-design software did not insert a DTD at the beginning of the HTML document, forcing browsers to make a best guess at what version was used and, therefore, how to display the Web pages. This was particularly difficult during the time between HTML 2.0 and HTML 4.0, the dark ages of the browser wars, when, even if you specified a DTD, the mixture of tags between the W3C HTML standard and the Netscape and Internet Explorer proprietary tags rendered the DTD essentially useless.

With the return to W3C-standard HTML, the DTD plays an important role. The DTD identifies which version of HTML the document should be measured against. When the HTML in the document meets the standard identified in the DTD, the HTML is said to be "valid" or "compliant with the standard." Dreamweaver MX 2004 has a built-in validator that you can run by selecting File>Check Page>Validate Markup.

# LESSON 6 Exploring HTML Using the Tag Chooser

Like other computer applications, Dreamweaver provides access to its most common functions through buttons and pop-up menus in the main window of the application. The most commonly used HTML tags are available from the Insert bar, the Property inspector, or both. Other tags are less prominently displayed but are available through Dreamweaver. The Tag chooser is the most visible feature that provides access to all HTML tags. Furthermore, the Tag chooser offers the Tag Info window, providing information about the tag, such as its attributes, attribute values, and use.

The Code window is the obvious place to insert HTML code by hand. However, you must have a basic sense of the name of the tag or attribute before you start: is it **q** or quote, **b** or bold, abbrev or **abbr**? The ***code hints***, which are the pop-up menus that appear when you type in the Code window, are helpful, but you may not know whether the **<q>** (quote) tag or the **<blockquote>** tag is appropriate for your needs, and this type of information is not available from the Code window.

The Tag chooser enables you to choose from all tags that are available to HTML. The tags are organized into categories, and when you click a tag, the lower portion of the Tag Chooser dialog box displays reference information about the selected tag. This reference window, Tag Info, appears in other dialog boxes, too. From the reference information, you can learn more about the tags and their uses. When you click the Insert button, you open the other component of the Tag chooser — the Tag editor. You use the Tag editor to create the tag and make changes to the attributes of the tag.

In addition to HTML, the Tag chooser provides information and assistance with other languages, such as CFML, ***ASP.Net*** (the current and more-advanced version of ASP), and ***JSP*** (Java-servlet pages, another server-side programming language). In all cases, you click the plus symbol to the left of the language to see categories of tags. You click the category to see the tags within it. In the HTML language, categories may be further subdivided to show general (current), browser-specific, deprecated, and obsolete tags. Where possible, avoid deprecated and obsolete tags. It is useful to look through the deprecated and obsolete tags to see which tags fall in these categories. Unless you select the deprecated or obsolete groups, it is not clear that they are in this category.

In this lesson, you use the Tag chooser to insert the **<address>** tag, which is not available from the other menus or functions. You use the **<address>** tag to format a block of text that is the address of a person or business. By default, text in the address tag is italicized.

## Insert the Address Tag

1. **With simple.html open, click below the red dashed line of the form.**

   Notice the empty paragraph.

2. **Click the Tag Chooser button at the right side of the Common Insert bar.**

FIGURE 1.37

3. **Click the plus symbol to the left of HTML Tags.**

4. **Click the plus symbol to the left of Formatting and Layout.**

**5** **Click General, and then click Address in the right pane.**

The **<address>** tag is described in the lower window. You may need to drag the bottom of the Tag Chooser dialog box down and drag its sides out to read the full content.

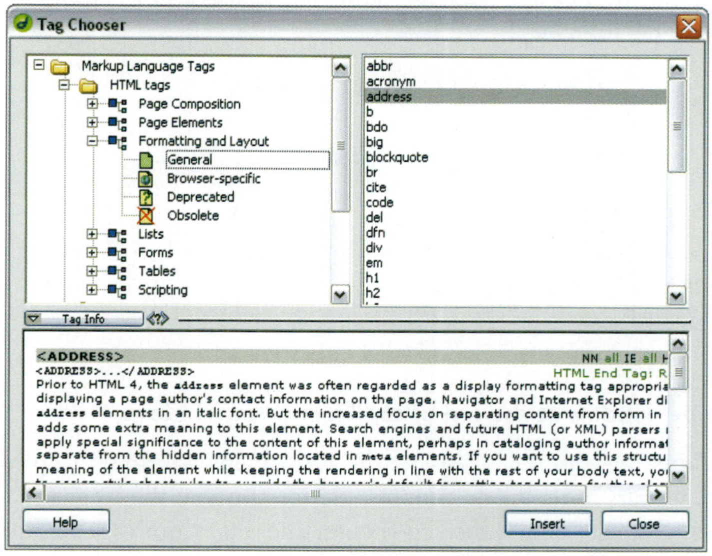


FIGURE 1.38

**6** **Click the Insert button in the lower-right corner of the Tag Chooser dialog box.**

**7** **Click the Language category of the Tag Editor – Address dialog box, and choose en English from the list of languages.**

**8** **Click the Content category; in the Address – Content field, type:**

`My address is 31 Walnut Grove, Sarasota, Florida.`

The Tag Editor dialog box provides access to the options or attributes of the selected tag, allowing you to apply any attributes available for that particular tag.

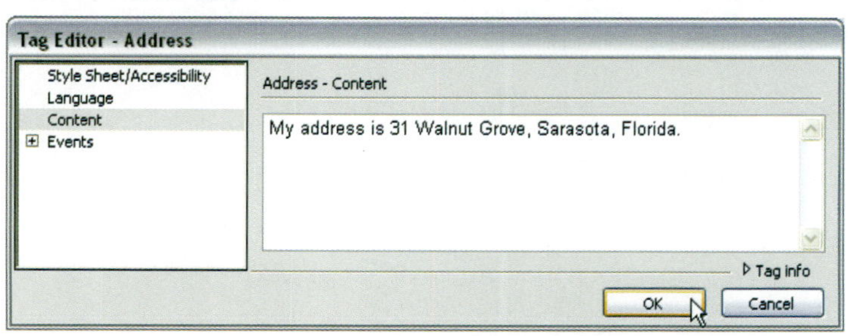


FIGURE 1.39

**9** **Click OK to insert the <address> tag.**

**10** **Click the Close button in the Tag Chooser dialog box.**

Examine the Web page and observe that the address you had typed in the Address – Content field is inserted into the page. Notice that the text is italicized. If you read the description of the **<address>** tag in the bottom portion of the Tag Chooser dialog box, you see that most browsers display content of the **<address>** tag in italics.

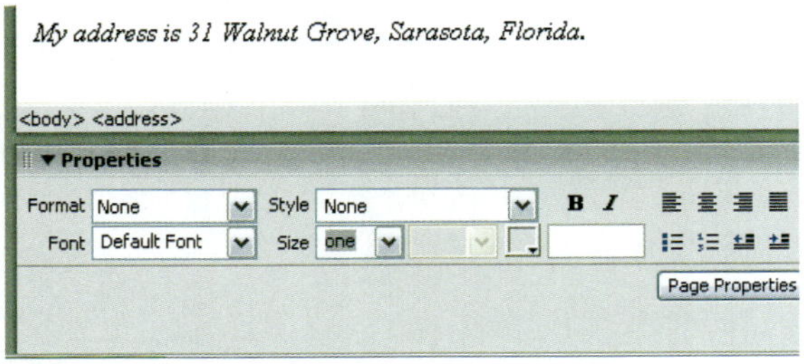

FIGURE 1.40

**11** **Look at the Code window at the top of the Document window.**

When you use the Tag chooser, it opens the Document window in Split view. You see that the **<address>** tag appears in the Code window. Notice also that the language attribute is set to English using **lang="en"**. When you use the Tag chooser and Tag editor to select and apply a tag, any attributes you make use of are applied to the code.

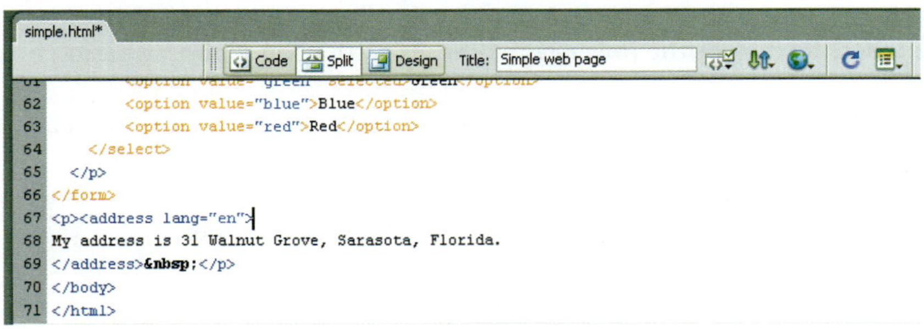

FIGURE 1.41

**12** **Click the Design button to close the Code window. Save the changes but leave simple.html open for the next lesson.**

# LESSON 7 Configuring the Document Window

No two installations of Dreamweaver or any other computer application look the same after a few hours of use — people have their own preferences for how they want to have components of the application laid out. Dreamweaver has many options for personal configuration, such as displaying the download time and resizing the Document window for different browser dimensions.

There are a number of panel groups, most of which appear on the right side of the Dreamweaver application. You can expand or contract them by clicking the name of the panel group. The Design panel group is often open so that you can work with the CSS Styles panel. Also the Files panel is almost always open so that you can work with the files in your site.

You can collapse the panel groups as a whole by clicking the Collapse button. The Collapse button allows you to hide the panels, giving you more working screen width. Having more screen width is especially beneficial if you are working in code. A Collapse button also appears between the bottom of the Document window and the Property inspector, allowing you to collapse the Property inspector and work with the additional height of the Document window.

Commonly, the Document window is set to maximized. However, there are times when you need to ensure that your designs work within specific screen resolutions, such as 1024 × 768, 800 × 600, or even 640 × 480. The document Window Size function on the bottom-right side of the Document window Status bar allows you to change the dimensions of the Document window to test different resolution. There are several preconfigured, common dimensions, but you may also create your own custom dimensions, for example for a cell phone or a PDA. You cannot set the size of the Document window larger than your current resolution, just smaller.

Dreamweaver also has a Download Time indicator next to the document Window Size indicator. This feature enables you to see the file size of your current Web page. The distinction made here between HTML document and Web page allows for the size of the images — images are files that are separate from the HTML document but part of the total download. The Download Time indicator shows both the total size of the Web page and the time it will take to download. The downloading time depends on the speed of the Internet connection. You may change this preference, too, although unless you are depending on a particular audience whose Internet connection you know, you may wish to leave the connection speed set at 56K. A general rule of thumb is to keep the download to less than 30 seconds. Careful use of appropriate image formats, image sizes, and number of images minimizes the download time.

## Configure the Document Window

**1** **Click the Restore button in the top-right corner of the Title bar of the Document window (Windows). Bypass this step if you are working on a Macintosh.**

The Restore button restores the Document window to its previous dimensions.

FIGURE 1.42

**2** **Change the Window Size to 760 × 420 (800 × 600, Maximized) by choosing from the Window Sizes list at the bottom of the Design window.**

The Window Size option allows you to change the size of the window to mimic different browser dimensions so you can appreciate how your Web-page designs appear to a person using a browser with different dimensions than yours.

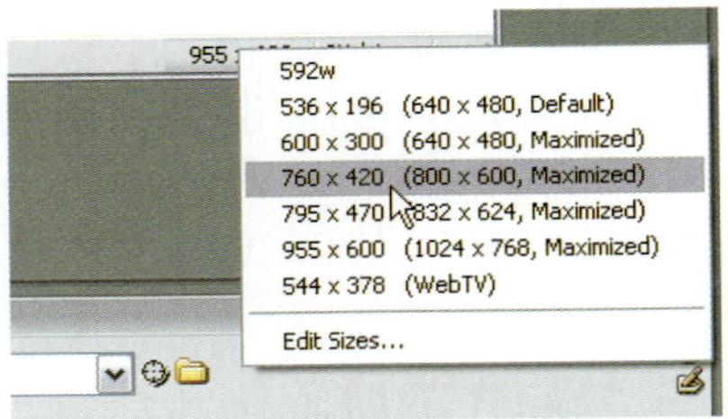


FIGURE 1.43

**3** **Choose Edit>Preferences/Dreamweaver>Preferences, then choose the Status Bar category (second from the bottom).**

This window of the Preferences dialog box allows you create new window sizes or modify existing ones. Dreamweaver uses the Connection Speed drop-down list to identify how long a person would have to wait to view the current Web page.

**4** **Change the Connection Speed to 14.4 and click OK to accept the change.**

Using a 14.4 Kb modem, a person would have to wait 2 seconds for this 3-kilobyte page to download. You can find this information through the Download Speed indicator in the bottom-right corner of the Document window.

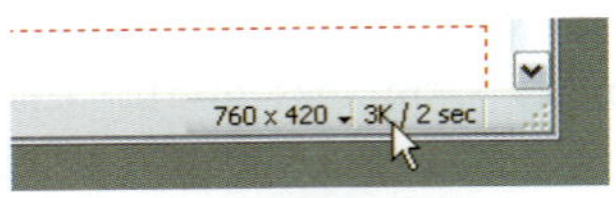


FIGURE 1.44

**5** **Reset the Connection Speed to 56 Kb by choosing Edit Sizes from the Window Sizes drop-down list, choosing 56.0 from the Connection Speed list, and clicking OK.**

Another path to the Status Bar category of the Preferences dialog box is through the Edit Sizes option at the bottom of the Window Sizes drop-down list.

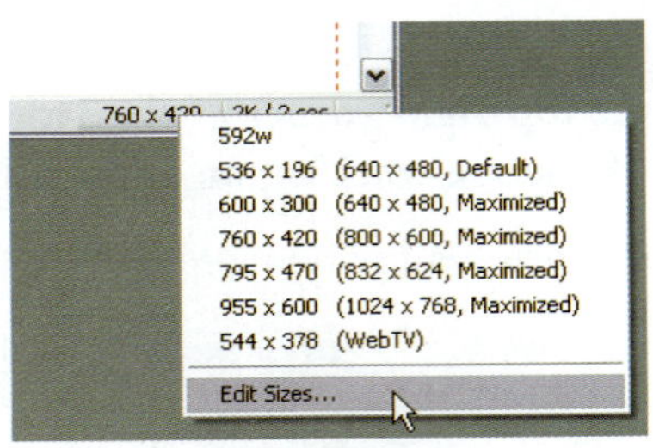


FIGURE 1.45

**6** **Reset the Document window to maximum size by clicking the Maximize button — at the top-right corner of the Document window (Windows) or the rightmost button in the top-left corner (Macintosh).**

**7** **Collapse the Property inspector by clicking the Collapse button between the Document window and the Property inspector.**

You can easily collapse and restore the Property inspector to see more of the working document.

**FIGURE 1.46**

**8** **Expand the Property inspector by clicking the Collapse button.**

**9** **Expand the width of the panel groups on the right side of the application window by dragging the Collapse button to the left.**

The panel groups on the right side of the Dreamweaver application are quite narrow and, at times, can be awkward to use in the limited space given by default. Widening the panel groups can make it easier to work with the panels.

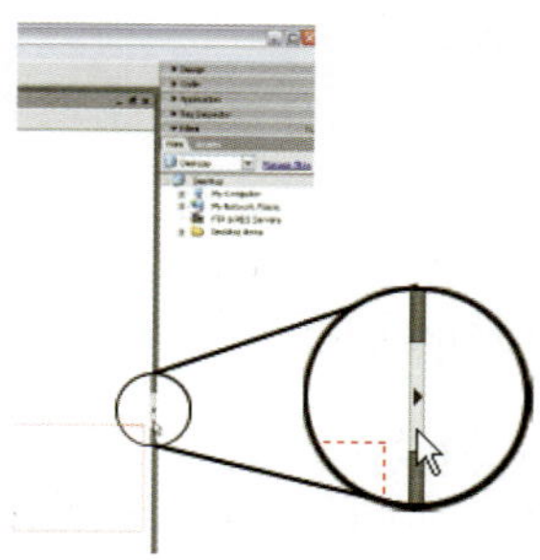

**FIGURE 1.47**

**10** **Reset the size of the panel groups by dragging the Collapse button to the right.**

You can only drag the Collapse button so far — Dreamweaver has a minimum width for the panel groups beyond which you cannot drag the Collapse button.

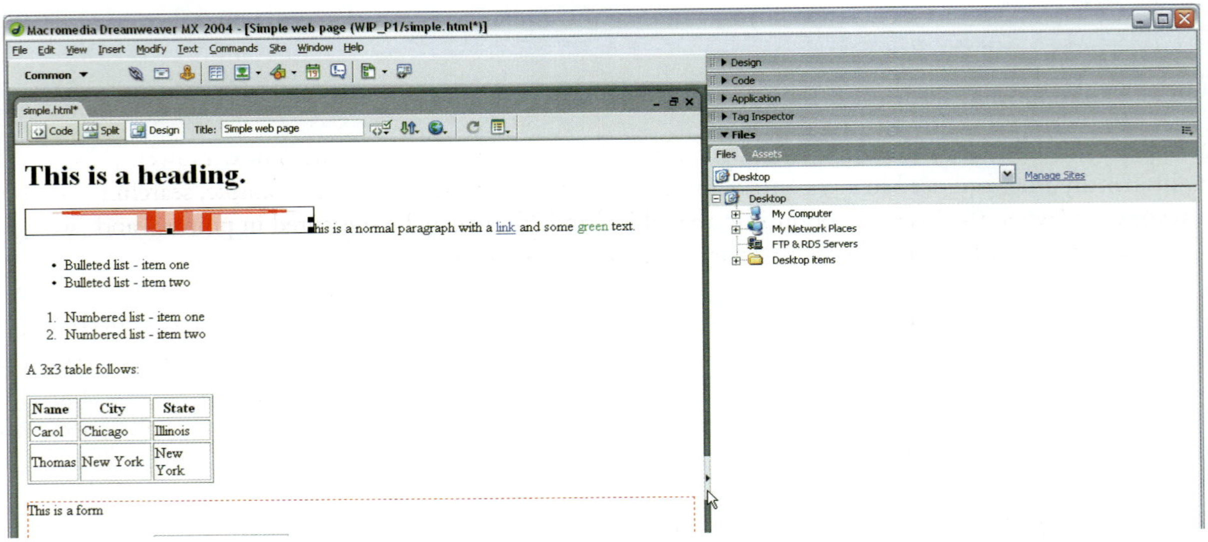


**FIGURE 1.48**

**11** **Choose File>Close to close simple.html. Keep Dreamweaver open for the next exercise.**

## LESSON 8 Exploring the Dreamweaver Help Function

The Help function of any application is very useful. The documentation for many popular computer applications is consistently extensive. It typically includes text documentation, graphics, and annotated screenshots of the application, plus numerous examples and tips on how to use the application, its functions, and its features.

The Dreamweaver Help function uses the standard help format, in which you can read the material like a book and organize it in chapters, sections, and subsections. You can find this organizational method under the Contents tab of the Help function. The Index tab provides an alphabetical listing of the important symbols, words, and phrases. You may also access the Help documentation by searching for a word or phrase using the Search tab. Dreamweaver's Help function displays in two panes. The Contents, Index, or Search results appear in the left pane and the selected page displays in the right pane.

In the Contents section, the chapters, sections, and subsections use book icons to indicate that there are multiple pages in the next level. You click a book to open it and again to close it. Pages use a different icon — when you click a page icon, the selected page appears in the right pane. The Index functionality of the Help documentation contains topics ordered alphabetically, starting with numbers, symbols, and then alphabetic characters. A large topic may have subtopics, indicated by indentation of those subtopics. As you type the name of your topic of interest in the field at the top of the left pane, you are taken to the word in the index. Typing just finds main topics, not subtopics. For example, if you type extensions, you see that installing is a subtopic of extensions, but if you type installing, you don't find extensions. You can use the Search function to search for a particular word or phrase that doesn't seem to be listed or can't be found in the index. However, the search might identify the word used in any context and also as part of a longer word. For example, searching on point turns it up in "when the insertion point is in the table," and "fonts may be measured in points," and "use your mouse pointer" — it helps to be specific when searching for some terms.

Often, the contents of a particular page may have links to terms or other related pages. These links are identified with blue, underlined text, not unlike a link in a Web page. Given that the Help pages are not created in isolation but as part of a chapter, at the bottom and top right of each page are next and previous links (blue triangles pointing to the left and right). You may use these links to read through the pages in order, according to their organization in the chapters, sections, and subsections.

In this exercise, you explore the Dreamweaver Help documentation. You open a page from the contents, locate a page from the index, and search for a page. The more familiar you are with the Help documentation, the better you will be at using Dreamweaver and resolving problems without purchasing expensive books or spending long hours on the Internet.

## Explore the Dreamweaver Help Function

1. **Choose Help>Using Dreamweaver.**

2. **In the left pane of the Dreamweaver Help documentation, click the Dreamweaver Basics book to open it.**

3. **Click Exploring the Workspace, click About the Dreamweaver Workspace, and then click The Workspace Layout.**

On Windows systems, book icons indicate that pages exist within a topic heading; on Macintosh systems, the topics appear as nested bullet items. Furthermore, on Windows systems, both the index pane (left) and the information pane (right) appear within the same dialog box; on a Macintosh system, the panes float.

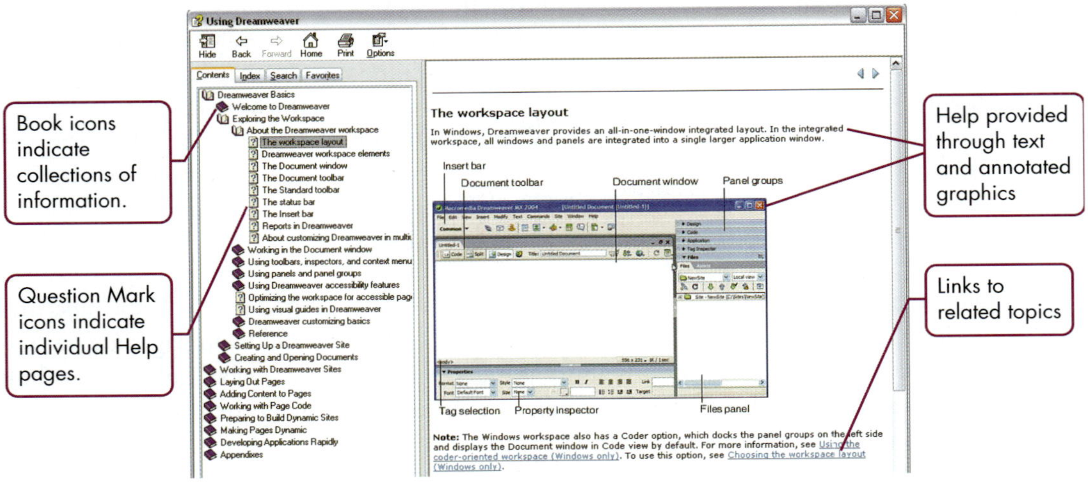


FIGURE 1.49

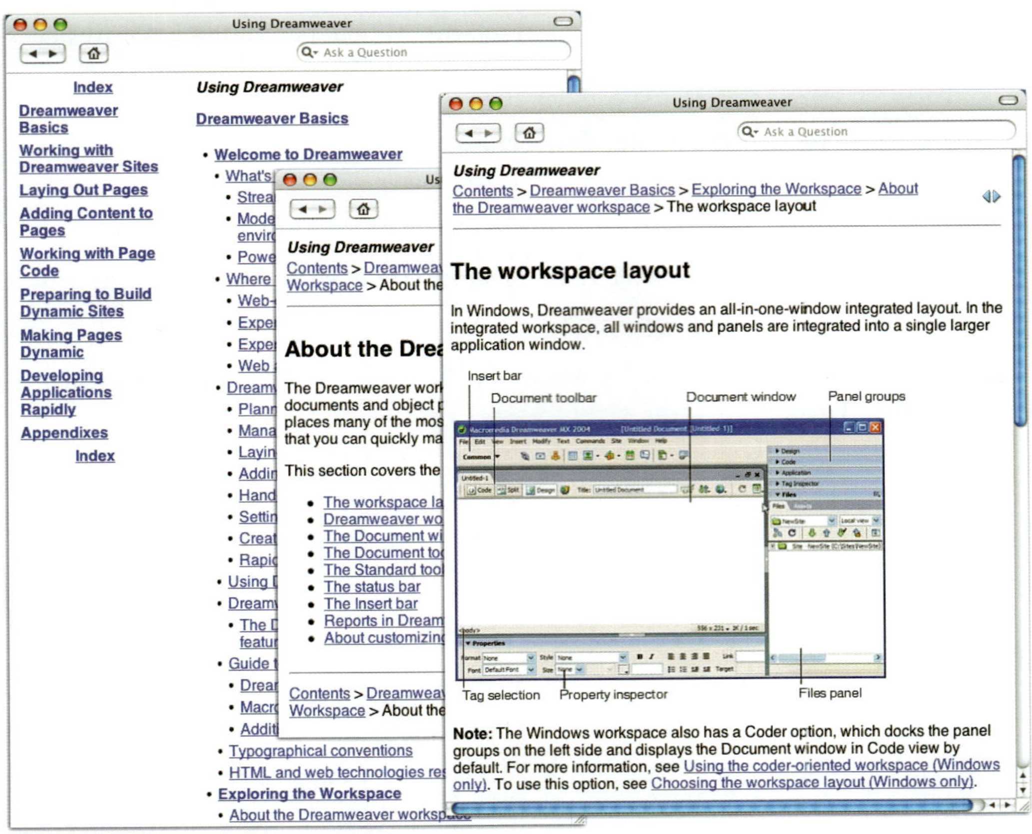


FIGURE 1.50

**4** **Click the Index tab at the top of the left pane (Windows), or Index in the first window (Macintosh).**

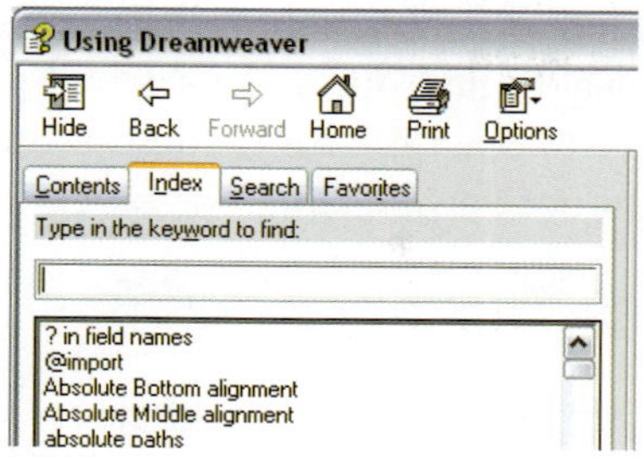


FIGURE 1.51

FIGURE 1.52

**5** **Type `downloading` in the keyword field. Choose Time from the list and click the Display button at the bottom of the left pane.**

The downloading topic in the index has four subtopics, as indicated by their indented topic headings below downloading. The Display button opens the selected page into the right pane. Alternatively, you can double-click a subtopic to open the page. You can only open subtopics, not the main topic name — you can open time but not downloading.

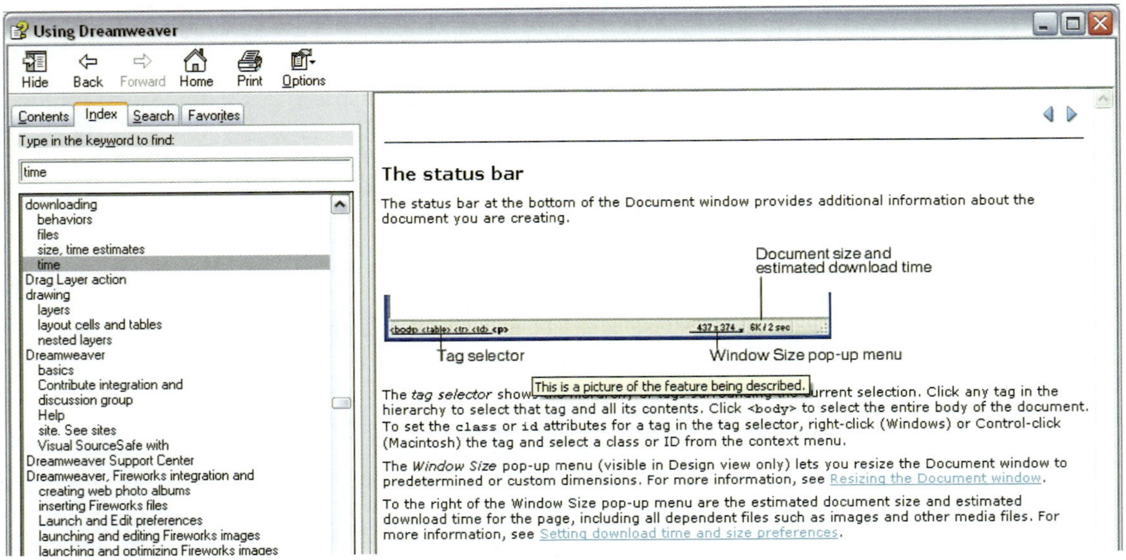


**FIGURE 1.53**

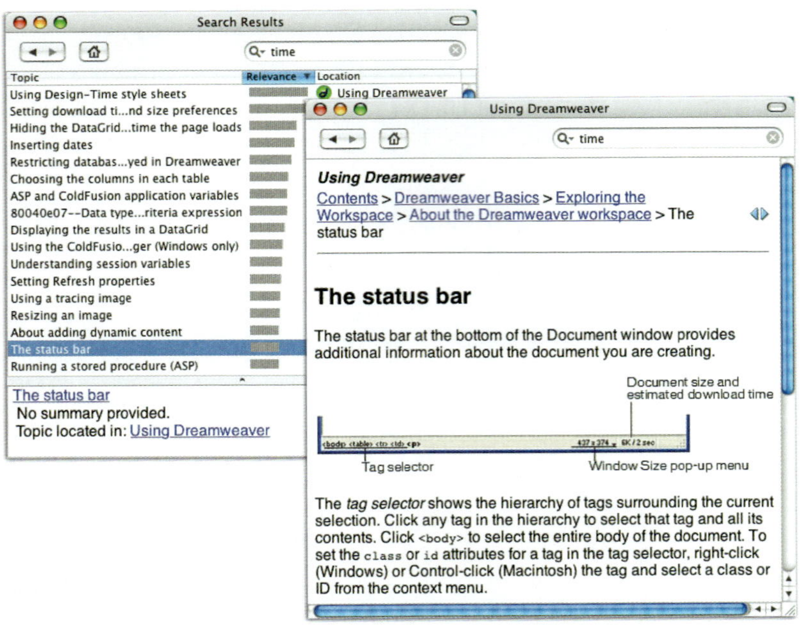


**FIGURE 1.54**

**6** **Click the Search tab. Type `acronym` in the keyword field and either click the List Topics button or press Enter/Return.**

There is only one topic with the word acronym.

**7** **Double-click the topic Setting the Acronym or Abbreviation Dialog Box Options.**

Notice that all instances of the word acronym are highlighted in the page.

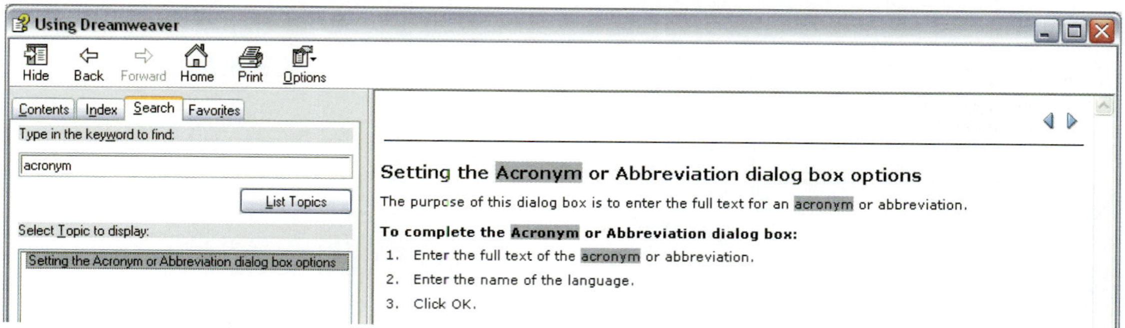


FIGURE 1.55

**8** **Click the Contents tab at the top of the Help function.**

Notice where the page on acronyms is in the Contents. Knowing where the page of interest to you is located may help you find similar pages another time or may interest you in exploring related pages in the same chapter, section, or subsection of the Contents.

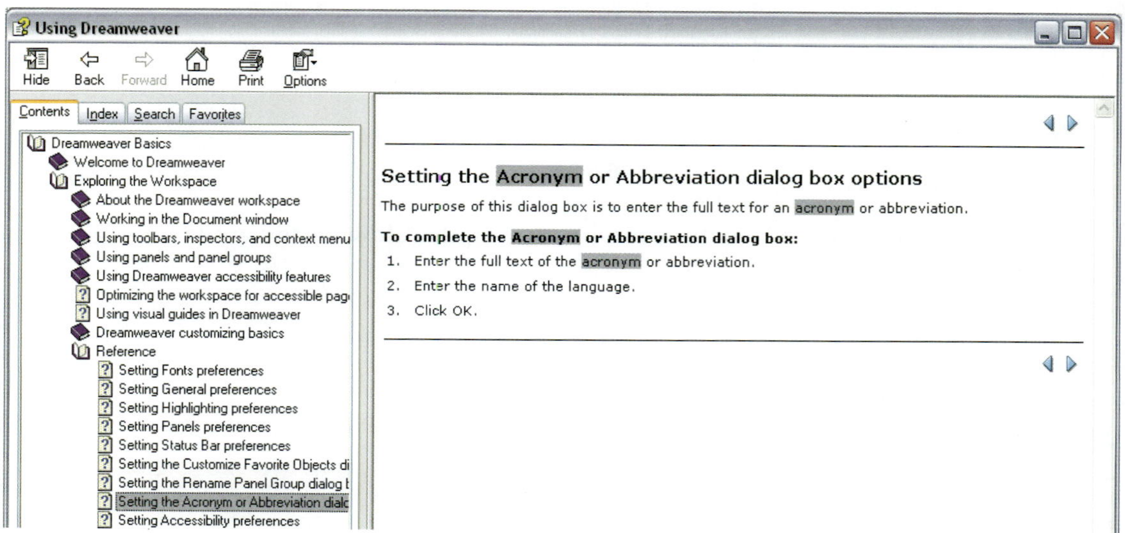


FIGURE 1.56

**9** **Return to the Search tab, and type `experienced` in the Keyword field. Double-click the Experienced Hand-Coders topic.**

The first numbered point refers to a tutorial in the Getting Started help. This is a second Help file that provides tutorial-style help on a variety of topics.

**10** **Close the Using Dreamweaver Help function by clicking the Close button at the top-right corner of the Help window.**

**11** **Select Help>Getting Started and Tutorials and, if necessary, click the Contents tab.**

The contents of this Help file provide tutorial-style help from creating simple static pages to understanding Web applications, and setting up Web servers, PHP, and MySQL. These tutorials may provide additional insight into how to use Dreamweaver and also may pique your interest in advanced topics, without forcing you to purchase additional books just to explore the topic or methodology.

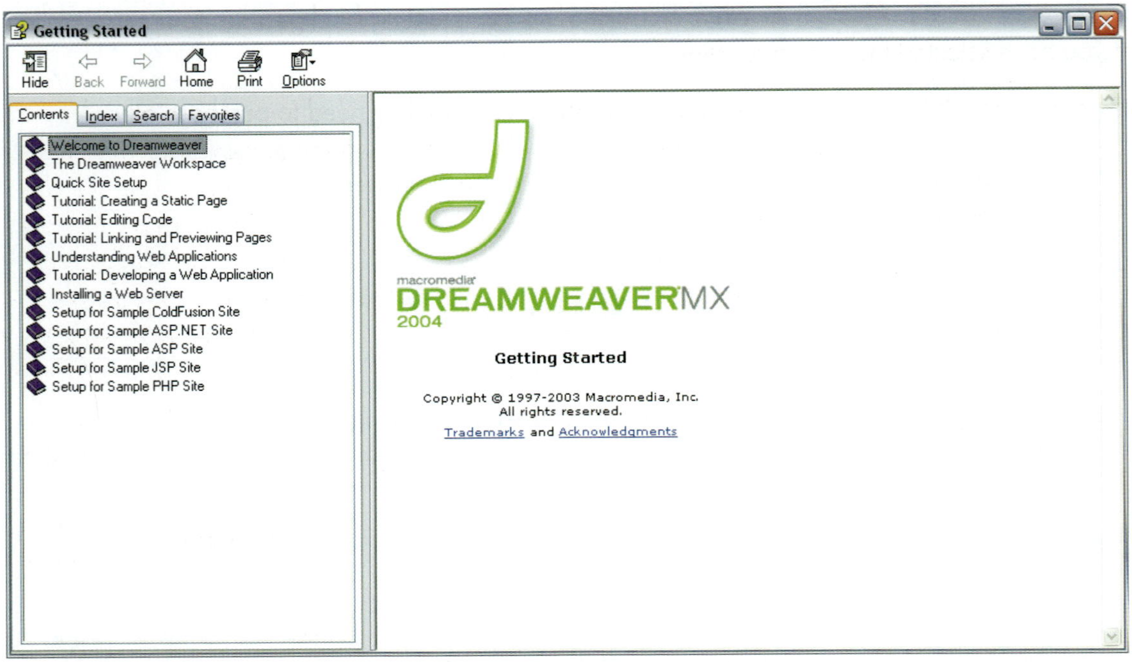


FIGURE 1.57

**12** **Close the Getting Started Help function by clicking the Close button at the top-right corner of the Help window.**

**13** **Close Dreamweaver by choosing File>Exit/Dreamweaver>Quit.**

## SUMMARY

In this project, you learned to explore Dreamweaver for the first time. You learned about the organization of the menus, toolbars, and various other features that provide access to Dreamweaver's features and functions. You discovered how to view HTML code in the Code window and saw how the Design window creates code. You learned how to select HTML using the Tag selector and how to insert an HTML tag with the Tag chooser. You saw that as you select different components of a Web page, the Property inspector changes to identify the properties of the selected component. You also learned how to obtain help on Dreamweaver's features.

## To Extend Your Knowledge

### DREAMWEAVER'S REFERENCE COLLECTION

Help functions tend to focus on aiding the user in working with the application and its functions, but not with background or reference material. For example, a word-processing application may help teach you how to make text bold or italic, but it won't teach you about proper grammar and sentence structure. The help function for a spreadsheet application may tell you what types of values you need to insert in the PV (Present Value) function, but without an accounting background, you may not realize that you have selected the wrong function.

Despite the availability of help documentation, many users find they need to purchase other books and resources for assistance. Dreamweaver supports many different coding languages, such as HTML, CSS, ColdFusion, ASP, and PHP, all of which require their own reference materials. Dreamweaver has reduced the need to purchase additional reference books somewhat by including electronic versions of reference publications within the application. The included reference material provides information for the supported languages as well as UsableNet's Accessibility Reference. In fact, the Tag Info window of the Tag chooser function draws upon these references to provide the information about the selected tag.

## KEY TERMS

Attributes
CSS
Client-side
Code hints
Container tags
Empty tags
Horizontal rule
Hand-coder
Handles
HTML
MDI
Server-side
Syntax coloring
Syntax highlighting
Tags
WYSIWYG
XML

# CHECKING CONCEPTS AND TERMS

## SCREEN ID

**Identify the indicated areas from the list below:**

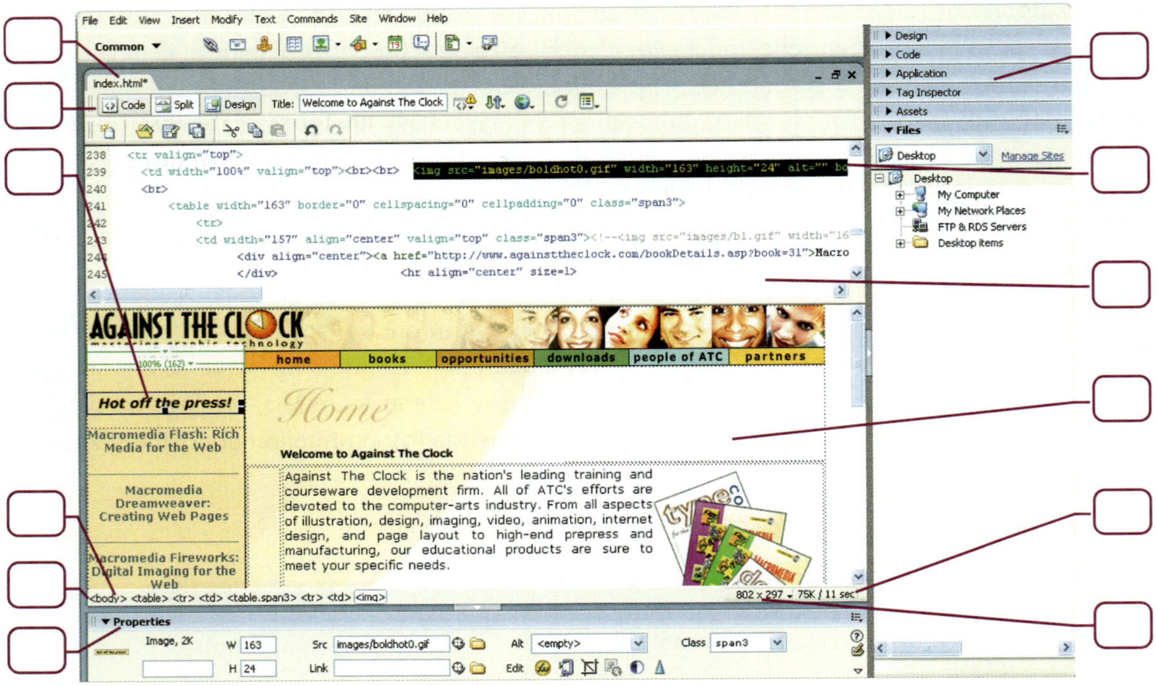


FIGURE 1.58

- **a.** Filename tab
- **b.** Document toolbar
- **c.** Selected HTML code
- **d.** Selected image
- **e.** Code View window
- **f.** Design View window
- **g.** Status bar
- **h.** Tag selector
- **i.** Window Size indicator
- **j.** Download Time indicator
- **k.** Property inspector
- **l.** Panel groups

## MULTIPLE CHOICE

**Circle the letter of the correct answer for each of the following:**

1. Dreamweaver is the premier __________.
   a. Internet browser
   b. Host server
   c. Web-page authoring and site-management application
   d. All of the above
2. What are two document views available in Dreamweaver?
   a. HTML and FTP
   b. Code and Design
   c. Digital and Analog
   d. WYSIWYG and Flash
3. In Dreamweaver, which view is always WYSIWYG?
   a. the Code view
   b. the Design view
   c. All of the above
   d. None of the above
4. HTML is __________.
   a. the structural language of Web Pages
   b. HyperText Markup Language
   c. visible in Dreamweaver's Code view
   d. All of the above
5. Using Dreamweaver, it is possible to work in both Code and Design views at the same time.
   a. True
   b. False
6. The Property inspector __________.
   a. is signified by a magnifying-glass icon
   b. changes to reflect the current and available properties of a selected item
   c. can debug HTML code
   d. None of the above
7. Which is not true of the Insert bar in Dreamweaver?
   a. It provides access to many Web-page design functions.
   b. Common, Layout, Forms, Text, and HTML are forms of the Insert bar.
   c. It is only available when using the Code view.
   d. A drop-down menu can give access to related Insert-bar functions.
8. Tags in HTML are __________.
   a. codes indicating programming errors
   b. attributes of inserted elements for graphical user interfacing
   c. only used to insert a horizontal rule
   d. elements surrounded by angle brackets
9. Which of the following is not true of the Tag chooser?
   a. It provides assistance for HTML only.
   b. It is the most visible feature that provides access to all HTML tags.
   c. It offers the Tag Info window, providing information about the tag.
   d. It provides access to the Tag editor.
10. How can you get the most up-to-date help and support available for Dreamweaver?
    a. Ask a friend who codes HTML.
    b. Choose Using Dreamweaver from the Help menu.
    c. Take an advanced course in Dreamweaver.
    d. Choose Dreamweaver Support Center from the Help menu.

## DISCUSSION QUESTIONS

1. You have explored the Code view and the Design view. Why would one view be more effective or efficient for developing a Web site? Which view would you find most practical for your work in Web-page design?

2. Even though Dreamweaver writes the HTML code for you in the background while you work in the Design view, why would it be beneficial to have a fundamental working knowledge of HTML?

## SKILL DRILL

Skill Drills reinforce project skills. Each skill reinforced is the same, or nearly the same, as a skill presented in the lessons. Detailed instructions are provided in a step-by-step format. Work through these exercises in order.

### 1. Work with Multiple Open Files

It is not uncommon to work with more than one file open at the same time. You may need to cut from one and paste to another, or just make comparisons between open files. You must be careful when working with multiple files to ensure that you do not copy from, paste to, or close the wrong file. Windows users see the filenames at the top of the Document window — the active file's tab appears light gray and all other tabs blend into the background of the top of the Document window. If you do not see the tab at the top of the Document window for the currently active file, click the Maximize button.

1. Launch Dreamweaver, if it is not already open.

2. Open index.html from the Project_01>AgainstTheClock folder. Open simple.html from the Project_01>Simple folder. Windows users: if you do not see a light-gray tab (at the top of the Document window) with simple.html on it, click the Maximize button.

3. In simple.html, move the mouse pointer over the No Browser Check Errors button.

   Note the text in the tool-tip message and the green check mark symbol in the button graphic.

4. Switch to index.html by clicking its name to the left of the simple.html tab.

5. Move the mouse pointer over the No Browser Check Errors button.

   Note that the tool-tip message has changed and the button graphic contains a yellow warning symbol.

6. Move the mouse pointer over the location of the simple.html tab and Right/Control-click.

7. Close the file simple.html by choosing Close from the pop-up menu.

8. Leave index.html open for the next Skill Drill.

## 2. Explore the Results Panel Group

When you design a Web site for the first time, redesign an existing site, or take over the management of an existing site, you may find that images, pages, and links do not work as they should. You may have an old image that is no longer in use or you may have prepared an image but not yet incorporated it into the site. In both cases, the image is known as an "orphaned file." Similarly, it is not uncommon for a large Web site to have the occasional ***dead link*** (a link that does not open the page to which it is directed). If the destination of a dead link is a page on your site, you must reestablish the link, but if the destination is another Web site that has closed, you must delete the link. When hand-coding a Web site, you perform link management in your mind, but when you properly use Dreamweaver, dead links and orphaned files can be a thing of the past for you.

Browser checking is another very practical function. Older browsers do not support the same functions, features, and versions of HTML as do current browsers. For this reason, it is useful to know which features do not work in older browsers or, sometimes, even in current browsers. Netscape 4, for example, does not support many CSS properties, and Internet Explorer 6 for Windows doesn't support the **`headers`** attribute of the table-data tag. It is helpful to know such information so that if your Web page uses a feature that depends on browser support, you are aware of the issue and may find other techniques for resolving the problem.

The Results panel group is not normally open, which means the Title bar for the Results panel group is not visible. The purpose of the Results panel group is to display the results of various queries, such as the number of dead links, orphaned images, or browser-check errors. Using this information, you can make repairs. Although the Results panel group provides a large amount of functionality, you don't need it constantly. By knowing how to open and close it, you can use it when needed and save the space it takes when you don't need the panel group.

1. Click the Target Browser Check button on the Document toolbar, and choose Show All Errors from the pop-up menu.

   Observe that the Results panel group opens at the bottom of the screen, below the Property inspector.

2. Scroll through the browser-check errors (red), warnings (yellow), and informative messages (white). Read the messages and determine which browsers have the problems.

3. Click any of the tabs in the Results panel group to explore the other features available from this panel group.

4. Collapse the Results panel group.

5. Right/Control-click the Results panel group Title bar, and choose Close Panel Group from the pop-up menu. Keep index.html open for the next exercise.

## 3. Explore a Complex Web Page

Most Web-page designs are complex in structure, employing tables to lay out the page. (***Layout*** is positioning different blocks of content on a Web page, the same meaning as in the print industry.) Tables offer numerous layout options, such as spanned cells and nested tables. Generally, Web pages use a two- or three-column layout. The three rows of a layout table may be the header at the top, the footer at the bottom, and the main content in the middle row. The middle row is commonly divided into two or three columns: the left for the navigation bar, the center for the primary content, and sometimes a right column with either advertising or additional information. ***Spanned cells*** in HTML are the equivalent of merged cells in word-processing or spreadsheet applications — two or more cells in a table or spreadsheet joined into one. Another table technique that you can use for design is ***nesting tables*** — inserting a table in a cell of an outer table. It is easier to nest a table within another than to divide the outer table. Commonly, ***forms*** that are used to gather information, such as an order form or a username/password login in, employ a table to position the input labels and input fields.

In addition to tables, you can use other features to create complex Web pages. You can use JavaScript to enhance the page, as with image rollovers. In an ***image rollover***, when the user moves the mouse pointer over an image on a Web page, the graphic swaps out with another image; when the user moves the mouse pointer off the graphic, the original image returns. Navigation bars often use this effect to indicate that the mouse pointer is over a particular link. CSS has a similar effect, typically applied to the text of a link: when the mouse pointer moves over a link, the color changes, and when the mouse pointer moves off the link, the text color returns to its original color. You create this effect using the **hover** property of CSS. You can create both of these effects — JavaScript image rollovers and CSS **hover** — in Dreamweaver, but you cannot view the effects in the application. Dreamweaver does not display dynamic effects like these; instead, you need a browser to view them.

Working with complex Web pages can be difficult, even with Dreamweaver. The greater your familiarity with the Tag selector, the easier it is for you to deduce the layout structure of a Web page. Once you understand the structure, you can then make modifications or add content to it.

1. Click the top, banner logo graphic for Against The Clock.
2. Look at the Tag selector at the bottom of the Document window, and note that numerous tags are visible; the last one, **<img>**, is selected.

   The Tag selector shows two **<table>** tags (among other tags), which means that the selected image exists within a table that is nested in another table.
3. Click the first **<table>** tag to the right of the **<body>** tag in the Tag selector.

   Observe that a thicker black line appears around the outermost table that has handles around it. You may have to scroll down to see the bottom and bottom-right handles.
4. Click the other **<table>** tag.

   Note that it, too, selects a table that surrounds the top, banner logo graphic and the series of differently colored, graphical, navigation buttons below it. Notice that this nested table is used to lay out the horizontal navigation bar at the top of the page. A similar layout has been created at the bottom (footer) of the page, again using a table.
5. Move your mouse pointer over the dotted lines that surround the main body text.

   Observe that the mouse pointer changes to a downward-pointing arrow and that a red outline surrounds the table cell.
6. Click Username in the bottom-left corner of the Web page, and look at the Tag selector.

   This form's Username and Password labels and input fields are laid out using a nested table in the form. You see the form on the Web page as the red dashed line.
7. Press "F12" to preview this Web page in your primary browser.

   Do not save changes, if you are asked. Observe that the appearance of the Web site in Dreamweaver is virtually identical to its appearance in your browser.

8. Move your mouse pointer over any of the differently colored graphic boxes (home, books, etc.) in the top navigation bar, and note that the graphics change.

   These graphics employ the JavaScript rollover effect, which Dreamweaver does not display.

9. Move the pointer over any of the text links down the left navigation bar.

   Note that the text color changes as the pointer moves over and off each link. The CSS **hover** property creates the effect on these links. Notice, again, that you cannot view this effect in Dreamweaver, even though you can create it there.

10. Close your browser and return to Dreamweaver. Leave index.html open for the next Skill Drill.

## 4. Explore Other Helpful Resources

The Dreamweaver Help system is only one resource for assistance and primarily focuses on using Dreamweaver. Web-site design requires more, however, than just using Dreamweaver, and Dreamweaver provides other resources for help.

1. Click the Code panel group to expand it, and then click the Reference tab.

   The text in the reference books is formatted wider than the default width of the panel groups. You must widen the panel groups to read the full text.

2. From the pop-up menu of books, choose O'Reilly HTML Reference, if it is not already selected.

3. From the Tag pop-up menu, choose **body**.

4. From the secondary pop-up menu to the right of the Tag pop-up menu, select **background**.

   The secondary pop-up menu does not have a label beside it, but Dreamweaver Help refers to it as the attribute pop-up menu — **background** is an attribute of the **body** tag.

5. Read through the description of the **background** attribute of the **body** tag.

   The top line of the description identifies the name of the attribute and, on the right, browser support and the HTML version in which the **background** attribute was introduced. Optional indicates that the background attribute is optional.

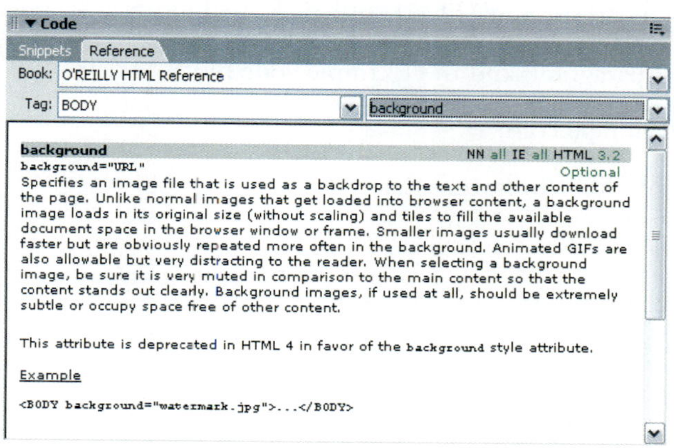


FIGURE 1.59

6. Compact the Reference panel group by choosing Window>Reference or pressing Shift-F1.
7. Expand the panel group.
8. Open Dreamweaver Help.
9. Choose the Search tab, type **css** in the Keyword field, and then click the List Topics button. Notice that the Search function finds all pages in the Help documentation that contains the phrase css.
10. Double-click Creating a New CSS Style from the list. Notice that the selected page opens in the right pane with all instances of css (in any form of capitalization) highlighted.
11. Close Dreamweaver Help. Close index.html (without saving any changes you may have inadvertently made), and then close Dreamweaver.

## CHALLENGE

Challenge exercises expand on, or are somewhat related to, skills presented in the lessons. Each exercise provides a brief narrative introduction, followed by instructions in a numbered-step format that are not as detailed as those in the Skill Drill section. You can work through one or more exercises in any order.

### 1. Explore Other HTML Reference Web Sites

In addition to the information available through the Reference panel and the Tag Info dialog box, there are many Web sites that contain excellent information on topics that you will want to learn about for Web-site design, such as HTML, JavaScript, ASP, and PHP. In this Challenge, you explore two excellent Web sites with reference material about HTML and CSS. You need access to the Internet to view these Web sites.

1. Open your browser and go to http://www.blooberry.com/indexdot/html/index.html, which is a Web site called "Index Dot HTML."
2. Click Element Index below the heading HTML Language.
3. At the bottom of the short page, click the link All.
4. Find the link to the description of HTML and click the link.
5. Read the What Is It? paragraph and the Example code block.
6. Go to http://www.htmlhelp.com.
7. Click the heading link Web Authoring Reference.
8. Click the link HTML 4.0 Reference.
9. Click the link Alphabetical List of HTML 4.0 Elements.

10. Click the link ABBR (abbreviation) and read as much of the description as you can understand. Contrast abbreviation with ACRONYM, which is described briefly in the first long paragraph.

11. Move your pointer over SQL or URL, found in the paragraph below the example block. Depending on your browser, you may not see anything happen (see the To Extend Your Knowledge sidebar that follows).

12. Close your browser.

## *To Extend Your Knowledge*

### Abbreviations, Acronyms, and Browsers

Abbreviations, when spoken aloud, are normally spelled, such as HTML and USA. Acronyms, when said aloud, are normally pronounced as a word, such as NATO (North Atlantic Treaty Organization) or MADD (Mothers Against Drunk Driving).

HTMLHelp.com points out that SQL and URL are difficult to categorize as acronyms or abbreviations. The original pronunciation of SQL was the same as the word sequel, but more recently, it is spelled out as S-Q-L (SQL means ***Structured Query Language***, a language used for interacting with databases). URL (***Uniform Resource Locator***, which means the location of a Web page, a Web graphic, or other Web file) is also pronounced similarly to the word Earl or spelled out as in U-R-L.

Still confused about whether a short form is an abbreviation or acronym? Ian Lloyd of Accessify.com created a tool called the Acrobot. Go to http://www.accessify.com/tools-and-wizards/acrobot/default.asp, type in some text with common short forms, such as "I am learning HTML in NATO", and click the Convert Acronyms button. The code returned includes the proper markup for the abbreviations and acronyms you submitted. There also is a link below the Convert button that displays all acronyms and abbreviations in the database.

When the **`title`** attribute is used to state the expanded form of an acronym or abbreviation, most browsers display the expanded form as a tool tip. Most browsers also insert a dotted underline below the abbreviation or acronym. However, Microsoft Internet Explorer for Windows does not display either the dotted underline or the tool tip. In the following figure, Mozilla 1.5 (left) and Opera 7.21 (right) both display both the dotted underline and the tool tip.

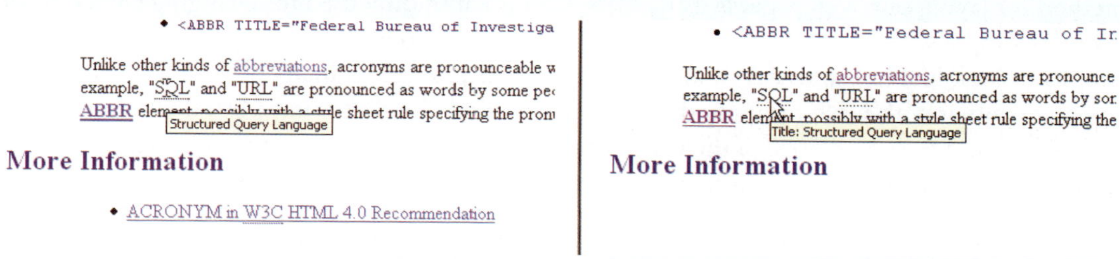


**FIGURE 1.60**

## 2. Explore a Web Page Using Tables for Layout

The Project_01>OpenCube folder contains the home page of OpenCube.com, a Web site that develops and sells JavaScript and Java technologies. This Web page uses tables for layout. Tables can become quite complex when they are embedded in others, as you see here. OpenCube.com also uses complex JavaScript effects (since the purpose of the Web site is to sell its JavaScript and Java products).

Although at first it may not be apparent, this Web page is full of graphics. Much of the text is actually a graphic of text. You learn in a later project about the limits of using fonts in your Web page — if you use a typeface in your design that others do not have, they do not to see your design exactly as you created and intended it. To counteract this, some designers create text graphics. While using text in graphics allows the visitors to see the design exactly as the designers created it, on the other hand the graphics take longer to download and therefore increase the download time.

1. Open index.html from the Project_01>OpenCube folder.
2. Observe the number of rectangles created by the dotted lines —the outlines of table cells.
3. Click the OpenCube logo in the top-left cell of the layout, and notice that the last item in the Tag selector is the **<img>** image tag. Click any of the menu items down the left side of the layout and observe the Tag selector. Note that much of the "text" on the page is, in fact, graphic text.
4. Note from the Download Time indicator in the bottom-right corner of the Document window that the page weighs in at 84 KB and will take 12 seconds to download.
5. Preview this page in your browser.
6. Observe the scrolling text in the bottom-left corner.
7. Move your pointer down over the left navigation-bar graphics (Menu, Products, Downloads, Contact, Order) and across the top menu to the right (same links) to see the drop-down menu system.
8. Close your browser and return to Dreamweaver.
9. Close index.html.

## 3. Exploring a Web Page Using a Table-Free Layout

Both OpenCube.com in the preceding Challenge exercise and index.html in Skill Drill 3 use tables for layout. Another method for laying out Web pages is using CSS. CSS is commonly used for changing colors, typefaces, and font sizes — simple style changes. However, CSS is much more powerful than that — you can use it to style paragraphs to look like lists and lists to look like paragraphs, as well as many other effects. You can position and size any content with CSS, meaning that it can direct a paragraph to start 10% down from the top of the browser window and to extend 50% of the width of the browser window. Advanced CSS can be very tricky, however, and some components have inconsistent support amongst the different browsers.

The Project_01>CssZenGarden contains a Web page from the CssZenGarden.com experimental Web site. CssZenGarden.com is entirely based on CSS for layout. Graphic artists have contributed their own interpretations of layout and design for the site, and visitors can switch between the different submissions.

CssZenGarden.com uses CSS properties without any tables at all. It also uses no JavaScript, but by using the CSS **hover** property it enables some links to change in style, thus seeming to mimic JavaScript rollover effects.

JavaScript, particularly complex JavaScript code, can be very long. Tables, especially multiple nested tables, can also add a large quantity of code to a Web page. CSS, however, is much lighter in code and therefore faster to download. Despite that, it is considered a relatively new concept, partly because many Web-design applications did not provide much support for CSS. Also, many Web designers create pages in other types of applications, such as Photoshop, Illustrator, and CorelDRAW, none of which support CSS well. Creating a Web page using CSS takes great skill, but the benefits are reduced code, faster download, and easier maintenance.

1. Open index.html from the Project_01>CssZenGarden folder.
2. Notice there are no dashed lines identifying table borders.
3. Note from the Download Time indicator that this page weighs in at 14 KB and would take only 2 seconds to download.
4. Preview the page in your browser.
5. Click one of the links under the heading Select a Design. The link moves you to CssZenGarden.com, where the same content is redisplayed using a different design, layout, and graphics. Take some time to explore some of the other designs.
6. Close your browser.
7. Return to Dreamweaver and close the application.

## To Extend Your Knowledge

### TABLE-BASED AND TABLE-FREE LAYOUTS

CssZenGarden.com is an experimental and demonstration Web site whose purpose is to show that, without using tables, CSS can be effectively employed for Web-page layout. Many graphic designers use applications that create table-based layouts. As a result, most graphic designers are not familiar with CSS-based layout options. This Web site demonstrates that with an excellent eye for design and knowledge of CSS, you can use CSS-based layout to produce equal, if not better design options than table-based designs. At the time of this writing, there are 143 designs submitted to the CssZenGarden — the content is always the same but the layout, colors, and graphics are different for each design.

Dreamweaver MX 2004 is much more CSS-aware than previous versions of the application. The projects in this book make use of CSS wherever possible so that you become comfortable with this better method of styling content through constant use.

PORTFOLIO BUILDER

## Learn to Judge Web Sites

The more you learn about designing Web sites, the easier it will become to recognize what's good and what's not — and how to incorporate the good and avoid the bad. We're not saying that you should copy the work of others; doing so is not only illegal, but it's in very poor taste. That being said, you should still consider an almost continual search for sites that are considered to be the best of the Web.

1. Launch your browser and go to http://www.webbyawards.com.
2. Spend some time looking around the site — pay particular attention to the current picks, which are available directly from the home page.
3. Make notes about why you feel the sites were chosen; consider the use of images, layout, animations, navigation, and anything else that catches your eye.
4. Be sure to check out the "Webby Judging" link, which will give you insight into how the judges select winners.
5. Check the site every once in a while to view new entries and winners.

# PROJECT 2

# Building Your First Web Site

## OBJECTIVES

*In this project, you learn how to*

- Explore the organization of a commercial site
- Use outlines and storyboards to plan a Web site
- Define a site and create its folders
- Build basic Web pages with text and graphics
- Examine Web pages in the Design and Code views
- Apply simple text formatting
- Use an existing page as a template
- Create page-to-page and email links

# WHY WOULD I DO THIS?

In this project, you plan and build a few simple pages, the basis of a small Web site. The process is essentially the same whether you're building a site that contains thousands of pages or a site that contains only four or five. Once you've put together a simple site, you'll find it easier to extend the process to larger and larger sites.

This project starts off, as all projects must, with planning. This planning takes many forms, such as gathering the content, collecting related content, establishing relationships between content, and creating a design. Much of this work you do in consultation with your client, whether in a drawn-out process in the client's boardroom or in your office with various break points along the way requiring the client's signature. Once the client approves the plan, your next step is to commit the plan to Dreamweaver.

At your computer, you set up the site in Dreamweaver. This process enables Dreamweaver to manage the Web pages that you create in the site and to ensure that you do not create any pages outside of the site. You also make the folders that you have planned for this site so that when you later create Web pages about the client's products or services, the products or services folder is ready for the files.

The next stage is to create the design for the Web site. If your design repeats on many pages, you may want to save the design without content so that you can reuse it for other pages. For example, all products pages may have a similar design — you could create the design of the products page and save it. This process is called "templating."

The final stage is to add the content to the pages. At times, you create the content yourself; at other times, the client provides the content. You must insert the content by typing it, copying and pasting it from another document, or importing a word-processing document. You then format the content using headings, lists, and other document structures, and style the content with colors, typefaces, and other appearances. Next you create links between the Web pages — the links that you planned when you first collected related content.

These efforts then essentially complete the process of designing a Web site. Probably, you would obtain approval from the client before finalizing the Web site, perhaps at various stages along the way. You also need to make the Web site available on the Internet. Generally, the designer creates the design on his or her computer. Making those Web pages available to the public via the Internet is a separate process.

In this project, you examine the folder structure of a well-organized Web site. Not all ideas are going to come from your own thoughts — you may use concepts and ideas inspired by other successful Web sites, as long as you don't copy them directly. (To learn from the techniques and organization used on another site, you Right/Control-click in your browser to examine the ***source code*** (HTML code) of the current page you are viewing.) You then work through the process of planning a Web site on paper, using storyboards and flowcharts. This process starts you thinking about the content, the relationships, and the design. In Dreamweaver, you define a folder on your system as the location in which you will design the Web site, and you create other folders at the same time. You insert content that you type, copy and paste, and import. You insert an image, create Web-page links, and email links. You also insert and modify HTML tags directly using the Tag editor and Tag selector.

This project gives you a quick overview of many features of Web pages and Dreamweaver that you can use as you design your own Web pages. You experience the entire process of creating a Web site, from initial planning to development of the Web pages. In the remaining projects in this book, you learn more about the individual components of Web pages and Dreamweaver functions in greater detail.

## VISUAL SUMMARY

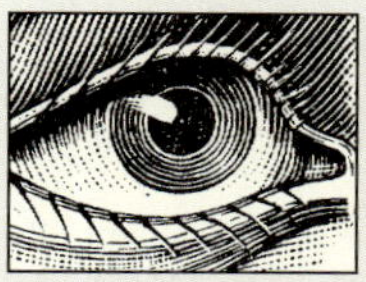

One of the first steps you take when designing a Web site is to prepare a site definition in Dreamweaver. This process allows you to state the name of the Web site. The name does not need to be the Web-site address, but can be any name that helps you remember the project, such as "Laurentian" for Laurentian University's Web site or "IBM Redesign" for the contract you were awarded to redesign IBM's Web site. You also specify the folder in which you will build the Web site, called the "local root folder." You may also record other information about the Web site, such as the HTTP address (Internet address) and what type of Web-server software you are using to create the Web site. You can use the Site Definition dialog box in either of its two forms — Basic (on the left in the following figure) and Advanced (on the right). Both forms are suitable for basic Web sites, but the Advanced form of the Site Definition dialog box has some additional options for more advanced users.

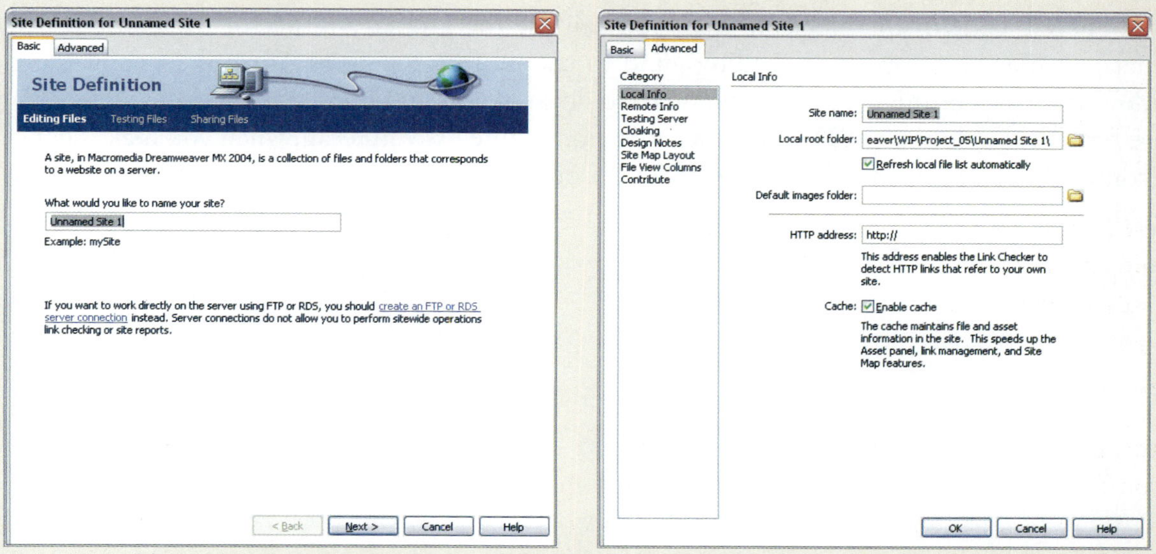


FIGURE 2.1

You create several Web pages in this project. You start by creating blank HTML documents using either the Start Page menu or the New Document dialog box. Through the New Document dialog box, you can create a variety of different types of documents. Dreamweaver groups document types into categories. To create a particular type of document, you choose the category first, and then choose the particular document type.

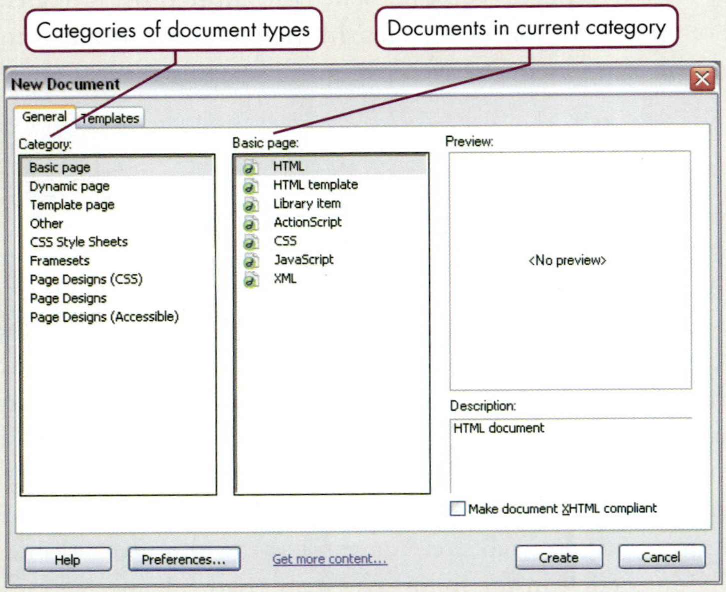


**FIGURE 2.2**

While you are adding content to pages, you may want to modify the format, the style, or even some of the HTML code of the blocks of text. You can use the Property inspector to choose text-block formats, such as paragraph and headings, and to choose font typefaces. You edit code in the Code window at the top of the Document window. To do so, you must choose the Split view to enable you to see both the Code and the Design views at the same time. As you recall, when you make changes to the content in one view, the changes appear in the other view, as well. You can also edit code using the Tag editor, an option of the Tag selector. Using the Tag selector, you can select a tag at the current position of the insertion point. The selected tag then appears with a white background. When you Right/Control-click the Tag selector, the Tag editor appears as one of the options. The Tag editor enables you to edit the selected tag. Both the Code view and the Tag editor offer you options for the current tag using the Code Hint pop-up window.

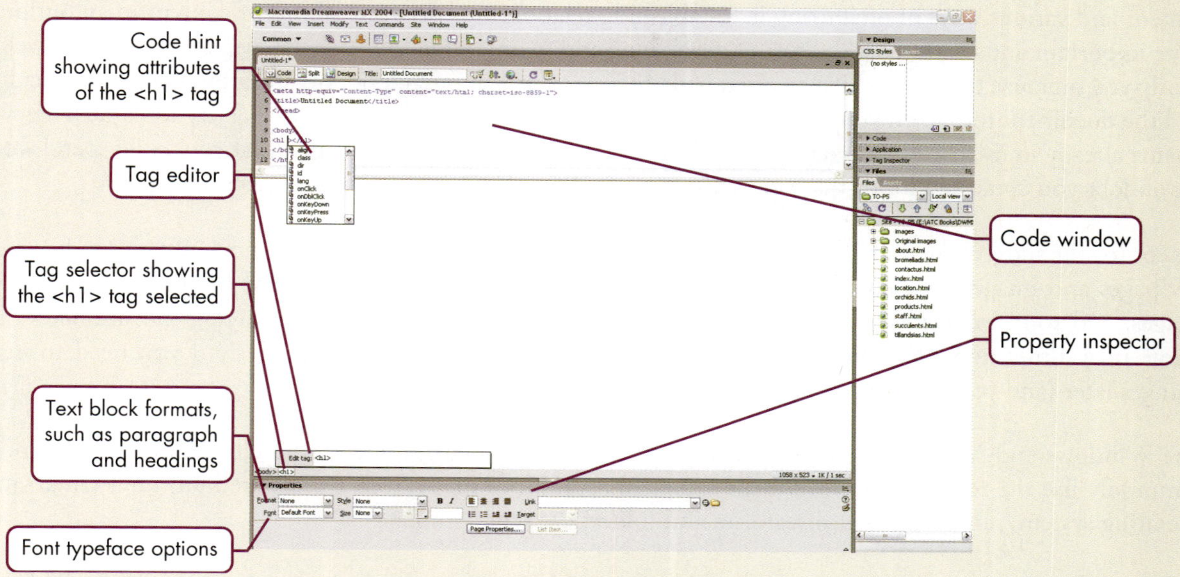


FIGURE 2.3

After creating your Web pages, you must check them by previewing them in your browser. This allows you to test the links you created. Dreamweaver cannot print the Design view of your designs — you must also preview your page in a browser to print your design.

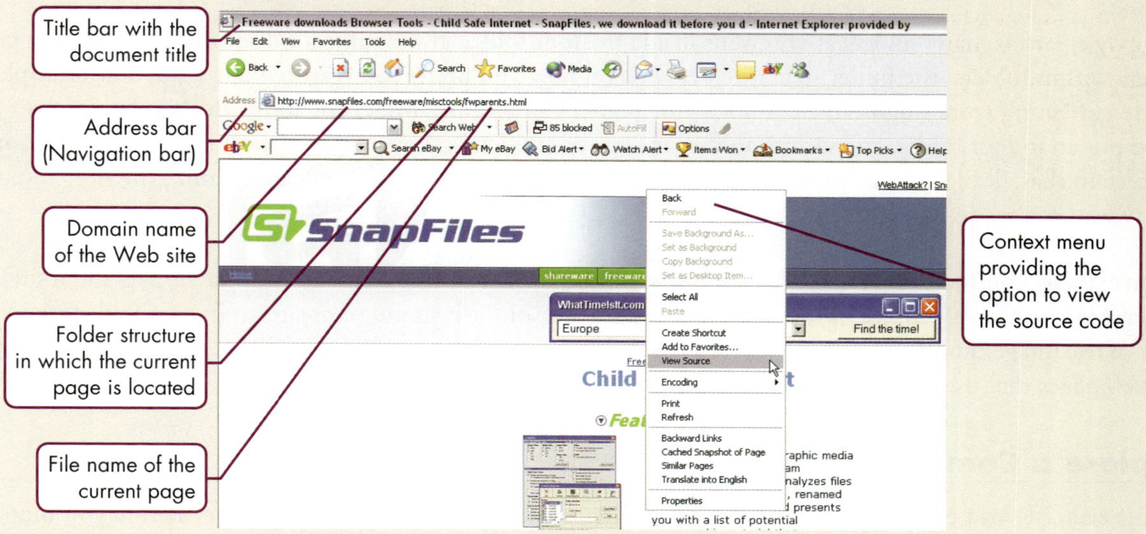


FIGURE 2.4

# LESSON 1 Exploring the Folder Structure of a Web Site

When organizing material for a Web site, you may find it very beneficial to spend some time thinking about the content and various ways of organizing it. Establishing relationships between groups of content in an outline is quite important and can impact the cost of developing and maintaining the Web site, depending on how well or poorly you organize the site. Similar to organizing files on your computer, poor organization makes it difficult to find the document for which you are searching and can create additional problems if you try to name a file with a name already in use. The better organized you are, the less time you waste — time that you could spend working on jobs you could bill for or that your employer would prefer you to use more constructively.

Except for the most elementary sites, most Web sites require some degree of organization. If your site has just a few pages and images, you could probably keep everything in one folder. Add a few hundred pages, 10,000 images, and some ***rich media*** (such as animations, sounds, and movies), and managing the site takes on a whole new dimension. Without folders to help you organize your work, particularly if you need to make changes later (and you will), managing your site is very difficult.

The Windows and Macintosh environments commonly use the term folders. The Unix/Linux environments commonly use the term directories for the same concept. Since many Web servers are built on a Unix/Linux operating system, remember that directories and folders are synonymous.

All Web sites start from a single root folder. The ***root folder*** (or the ***root***) is the starting place of the Web site. In the root folder you keep the home page of your Web site. The ***home page*** is the front door or opening page to your Web site. You can put other Web pages in the root folder, but the home page must be there. Dreamweaver and your browsers begin looking for links, graphics, objects, and pages from the root folder. Nothing contained in your site can be any ***higher*** than (outside of) the root folder. If it is, the browser won't find it. If images or media are outside the root folder, they don't appear on your Web pages.

You may create as many folders as you want inside the root folder. If the project calls for it, you can even create folders within folders; the folder structure depends on how you prefer to organize your work. For example, an online gardening store might create a folder for plants and another folder for tools. In the plants folder they could put an indoor folder, an outdoor folder, and a seeds folder. As long as you respect the root folder — making certain that all files you need for the site are in that folder or below — you can organize the site's resources in any way you want.

If you're using common objects (such as buttons, images, or logos) in a number of different pages in a site, you can end up with many copies of the same file. For this reason, it is useful to create an images folder where one copy of the image can be used by many Web pages. If the image changes, you only have to change one copy for all Web pages that use it to reflect the change.

## Explore a Commercial Site

In this exercise, you explore a few pages of SnapFiles.com, a Web site of ***shareware*** (try before you buy) and ***freeware*** (no cost) software for Windows systems. You examine the content of the pages to see what type of software they present, and you look at the Address bar to see how SnapFiles.com has organized its content. By examining a few types of software, you can determine their organizational pattern.

Web-site organization includes the filename of the Web page. The name should be logical and understandable — you wouldn't name a Web page about spreadsheet software "word-processing.html," nor would you name a Web page about word processing "spreadsheets.html." However, you could put both pages (appropriately named) in a folder called "business" for business software. You could also collect antivirus and other security software in another folder named "security." You could then put both the security folder and the business folder in a windows folder because the applications contained within it are all used on the Windows operating system. You might also create a corresponding mac folder for the same types of applications for the Macintosh operating system. Taking it a step further, given that the Macintosh computer might also require security and business software, including spreadsheets and word processing, you could repeat the names for these folder and filenames in the mac folder.

When you browse a Web site, you can look at the Address bar of your browser to see the filename of the Web page you are viewing as well as the folder structure. It is often useful to examine the folder structure of Web sites similar to yours to see how others approach organization. You might separate security from business software whereas others might combine them. Examining how others organize their sites may help you do something similar or combine several different techniques you have seen.

**1** **Open your browser and navigate to www.snapfiles.com.**

Examine the Address bar of your browser and notice that although you are viewing a Web page, no Web-page filename appears in the Address bar — the ***URL*** or address for the home page is simply shown as the ***domain name*** (the base name of a Web site — in this case, www.snapfiles.com) of the Web site.

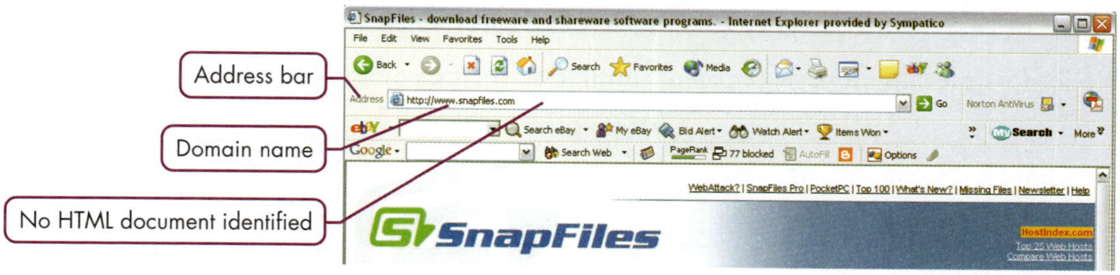


FIGURE 2.5

**2** **Near the top of the page, below the SnapFiles logo, are four green buttons. Click the Shareware button.**

Examine the Address bar of your browser, and notice that after the domain name, the Web page you are looking at is shareware.html in the shareware folder.

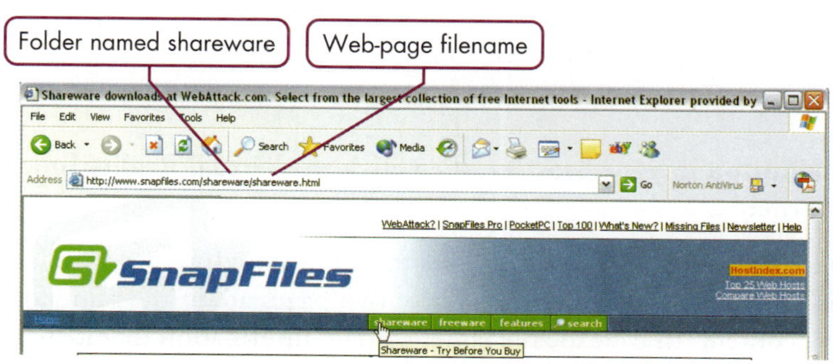


FIGURE 2.6

**3** **Click the green Freeware button below the logo.**

Notice that freeware is in a different folder than shareware. The software is separated, right from the outset, based on whether a particular application is shareware or freeware. This is the type of organization you might apply to your Web-site projects. You should review all of the content for your Web site and divide it into logical groups. Other people may have different ideas about the divisions to establish. Tucows.com, for example, is another shareware/freeware Web site; they don't separate shareware from freeware but, instead, identify the distribution format only when you read the details about the particular software.

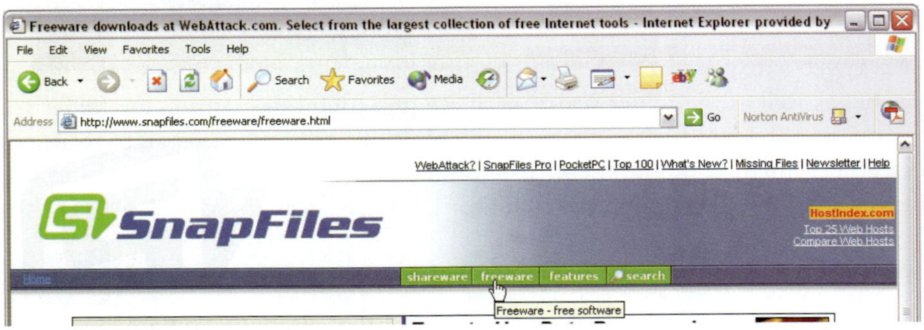


FIGURE 2.7

**4** **Click the Shareware button again.**

**5** **In the Browser Tools category (the top-left category), click Child Safe Internet.**

Notice that the current page, swparents.html, is in the misctools folder in the shareware folder.

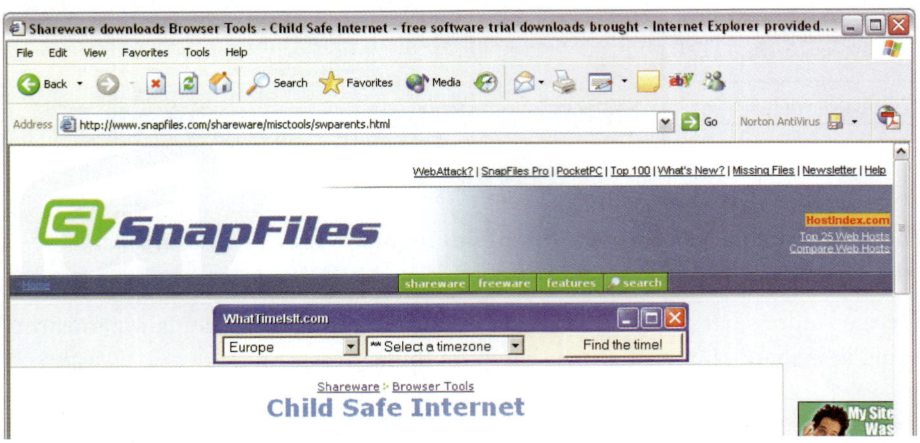


FIGURE 2.8

**6** **Click the Back button in your browser, then click the Virtual Reality link (a few links below Child Safe Internet).**

The folder structure of this page is the same as the Child Safe Internet page (shareware/misctools) but the filename is different — swvrml.html. These two pages are in the same folder but their filenames differentiate the content. In fact, the filenames contain information that identifies the type of software highlighted — swparents.html highlights Child Safe Internet shareware and swvrml.html highlights VRML shareware. The Virtual Reality category has no shareware.

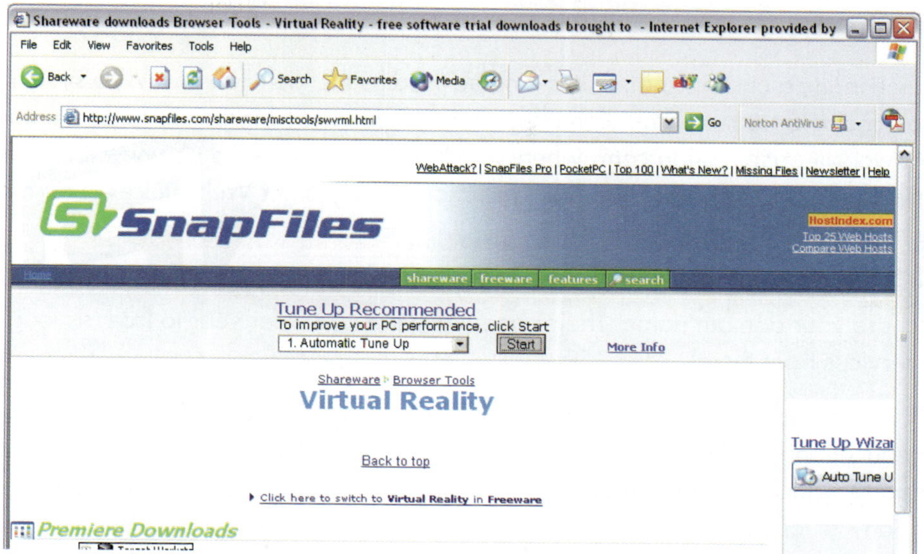


FIGURE 2.9

**7** **Below the Back to Top link is a link to Switch to Virtual Reality in Freeware. Click this link.**

The path to the Virtual Reality software in the Freeware category is identical to that of the Shareware category, except for the top-level folder. SnapFiles.com simplifies the organization of the software by keeping the folder structure identical after the shareware/freeware split. This consistent and simple organizational structure makes it much easier for the designer to manage this Web site and for users to navigate and know where they are. Another tool that is sometimes used is a ***site map***, where the folder structure is outlined, sometimes with a graphical layout and other times using text. Commonly, the graphics or text identifying folders in the site maps are links to those folders.

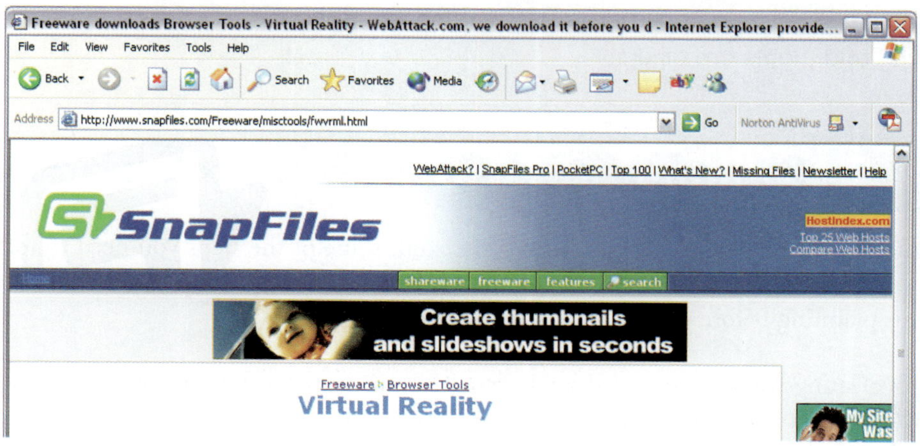


FIGURE 2.10

**8** **Close your browser.**

## To Extend Your Knowledge

### DOMAIN NAMES

A domain name is like a business name. It is a name used as the identifier of a Web site and commonly is the same as or similar to the name of the business that purchased it. Some domain names are long, such as www.websiteoptimization.com, whereas others are short, such as www.ibm.com. Although many Web sites belong to businesses and organizations, many other Web sites exist for other reasons, such as a companion Web site for a book.

Domain names must be purchased. There are many ***domain name registrars***, companies from which you can purchase your domain name. Their prices vary from $35 per year to free (as long as you purchase other services from them).

There are six top-level domains: .com (commercial), .org (organization), .mil (military), .gov (government), .edu (educational institution), and .net (originally intended for Internet providers, but often used when a company wants to create an online presence). Originally, these top-level domains suggested that the company or organization that owned the domain was from the US, but that generalization doesn't seem to apply any longer. One exception to that rule was the .int top-level domain, which was for international organizations, such as www.nato.int of the North Atlantic Treaty Organization.

In addition to the preceding domains, there are the two-letter country codes, such as .ca for Canada, .uk for the United Kingdom, and .us for the United States, which was rarely used in the past but seems to be gaining popularity. Generally, you must purchase a country-code domain name from a registrar in that country, and many countries do not allow you to purchase one unless you reside in that country. However, some countries have a very useful country code and allow nonresidents to purchase domain names using their country code. Tuvalu has a country code of .tv — you can well imagine what type of business would like to use .tv as part of their domain name. For some small countries, such as Tuvalu, their country code has provided some very beneficial revenue. New domains are developed all the time — .biz is marketed as an alternative to .com (most of the good .com domain names are gone); .info, .museum, and .name are others.

# LESSON 2 Planning and Organizing a Web Site

In this lesson and for the next few, you experience, firsthand, some of the steps you need to follow to create a Web site, such as organizing the content, outlining the site, creating a couple of pages, and adding graphics and links. You do this planning before you begin working in Dreamweaver.

Before you begin creating your pages, you should organize your content. This means working out exactly what you want to say and what you want to include on your pages. You need to determine your target audience — who they are and any other information you know about them. The more you understand your users, the better you can plan the site to suit their needs and attract their interest. Consider the purpose of the site. If you want to put up your résumé, assemble your text before you start your pages. If you're designing a business site, consider what the business is looking to achieve through its Web presence. Do you want to provide product information?

Give customers access to technical-support information and staff? Allow customers to purchase items from the site? These are just a few of the areas you should think about before you begin to design your site.

Imagine for the next few exercises that you have been asked to create a Web site for Carver's Store, a department store. Carver's Store wishes to develop an online e-commerce Web site. Your first step is to organize the products into categories. These categories will be the basis of the folder structure of the Web site.

## Sketch a Web-Site Folder Layout

Before you begin this exercise, have a sheet of paper and pencil ready. You will sketch some ideas on how to organize the Carver's Store Web site before you commit to anything. Pencil and paper are easy to work with, and even if you throw a bad idea into the recycle bin, you can still recover it.

1 **Write Carver's Store at the top of the paper and the domain name of Carver's Store's Web site, www.carvers-online.com, on the line below.**

2 **In a scratch area of the paper or on the other side, write a list of various products and/or services that might be sold or provided by the store.**

You may think of clothes for boys, girls, men, women, and babies, as well as shoes. Don't worry about the quantity of detail at this stage.

3 **Continuing on the back of the paper, group similar products and services together, making a list of three or four major categories.**

Using the example given above, clothes might be listed as a major category with boys, men, girls, women, babies, and shoes as the subcategories.

4 **On the front of the paper, write the major categories across the page below the domain name, and draw a line from the domain name to each of the category names.**

Use a single word to describe each category. For example, rather than writing "stereos, televisions, and home electronics," write "electronics" or "entertainment."

5 **List the subcategories (from Step 3) below the major categories and draw lines from the major categories down to their subcategories.**

## To Extend Your Knowledge

### KEEP IT SIMPLE

Too often, people try to use complex software to solve simple problems. In most cases, they struggle with the new-fangled software awhile and then return to something simpler and more familiar. Recently, a novice database designer made an inquiry to a discussion group looking for free software tools for database design. Someone replied: "Pen and paper is free, cross-platform, intuitive, and operating-system independent." Animated movies, such as *Finding Nemo* (by Pixar Animation Studios), start with pencil-and-paper drawings for several iterations of design before they make it into the computer. If Pixar can start their design work with pencil and paper, surely we can too.

## Create a Storyboard

Once you've outlined your plan and made some determinations about your audience, you can start developing ideas by making sketches of your layout. One effective way to sketch your layout is by creating storyboards. The term storyboard was borrowed from the film industry and is very loosely defined. Storyboards of your page can be as basic as hand-drawn sketches on scrap paper or as elaborate as complex, computerized minipages that show samples of your chosen graphics, fonts, and page colors.

Creating storyboards doesn't have to be a formal activity. You may want to make storyboards that are simple sets of notes outlining what you think you might put on each page.

When laying out your storyboard pages, use a wide or landscape orientation, since the browser window, as viewed on the typical monitor, is usually wider than it is tall. This is not to suggest that the content of a Web page must fit in the dimensions of a browser window. The reason for the landscape orientation is that studies by the print-publishing industry found that what attracts buyers is content "above the fold." On a Web page, "above the fold" is the browser window before scrolling down.

In addition to determining the content for each page, it is useful to organize the proposed pages into a flowchart so that you can sketch which pages relate to each other, which pages can be accessed from one page, and which cannot. It is not necessary that every page be accessible from all other pages on the site, but there must be a means for a visitor to get to other pages in a step or two. The flowcharting process enables you to plan the ***navigation system*** (the links that guide the visitors to other Web pages in your Web site).

1. **Gather four index cards or cut a sheet of paper into four equal pieces.**

2. **Using these cards/sheets, create a four-page storyboard for the Carver's Store Web site.**

3. **Make the first card the home page. This page introduces the store and welcomes viewers. Include a brief introduction to the store and the Web site; an attractive photograph of the interior or exterior of the store, or of a product that is currently on sale; and the location, phone number, and other information important to viewers.**

   It is essential that visitors know where they are on the Web site and what the site offers. By displaying specials or current products on the home page, you put them in front of visitors, ensuring that they immediately see these items and, hopefully, investigate further.

4. **On the second card, list the store's categories and a description of each.**

   These are the categories that you developed in the previous exercise. Although the categories may be available as links from this page for the visitor to explore, providing some information about them helps the visitor locate the products they are looking for and might entice them to look at other categories, as well: "I didn't know Carver's sells power tools."

5. **Make the third card an outline of the products found in one category. This page could be used as a template or a model for other categories.**

   Consistency is one of the keys to success. By maintaining a common look and feel throughout your site, you ensure that the customers know how to use the pages from one product to another, and from one category to another.

6 **Use the last card to represent a contact form that enables visitors to contact Carver's. This form gathers customer information, such as the customer's name and phone number, the product he or she is looking for, and the information that the customer wants to forward to the company, such as "Do you carry brand x?" or "When will my order arrive?"**

Visitors to your site need to be able to contact either you, the person in charge of the Web site, or someone from the business, such as a sales person. They might be taken to boys' underwear when they choose girls' underwear, or they might be looking for work as a salesperson with the store.

7 **On another sheet of paper, draw a rectangle at the top representing the first card.**

This rectangle represents the home page of the Web site through which most people will enter. People may be led to the Web site by radio or television advertising, by print ads, by a recommendation from a friend, or by a search engine. In most of these cases, they go to the domain name of the business, which brings them to the home page of the business.

8 **Below the top rectangle, draw a series of rectangles, which represent the major categories created in the previous exercise. In these rectangles, write the name of the categories, one per rectangle. Join each of them to the top card with a line, and join each of them to the others with a series of lines.**

From the home page, visitors choose a category to browse but may also want to look at the "home pages" of the other categories to see what is available there. The visitor may be looking for more than one item to purchase.

9 **Below each of the category rectangles, draw a series of small rectangles representing the subcategories that you developed in the previous exercise. In these rectangles, write the name of the subcategories, one per rectangle. With lines, join the subcategories to each other, adding a line from each subcategory to the main category above them and a series of short lines out from each representing links to the individual products.**

As you can see, the complexity of the linking is growing exponentially. Given the nature of this fictitious Web site, you can create a model page for each level — category level, subcategory level, and product level. Build the links into each model, and copy the model each time.

10 **Draw a circle in the center of the top rectangle, representing the area where the featured product would appear. Draw a line from the circle to one of the product lines.**

This line represents the link from the featured product on the home page to the detail page for that particular product. Unlike most of the other links you created here, this one will change often with each new special.

11 **Lastly, create a rectangle at the bottom of the page to represent the contact form you outlined in Step 6 of this exercise. Draw lines from one product line, one subcategory rectangle, one category rectangle, and the home page to this rectangle.**

In reality, you would draw these lines from every product line, subcategory, and category; there would be so many lines that the paper would be almost solid black. However, the point is that certain common pages, such as the contact form, the home page, the legal-disclaimer page, the employment page, and several other pages we haven't created or discussed, would be linked from every page on the site.

# LESSON 3 Defining the Site and Its Folders

You've organized your content into folders, outlined your basic content on cards, and obtained management's approval of your flowchart. Your next step is to set up your Web site in Dreamweaver. There are two basic steps for configuring the site: first, you specify where to store the site's files and folders on your computer; second, you create the site's folders.

To use Dreamweaver's site-management functions, you must define your Web site in the application. You do so through the Site Definition dialog box, which asks a series of questions about the Web site, such as the location of the root folder. You must create this folder before opening the Site Definition dialog box. This root folder does not need to be the root folder of your computer system, such as C:\Carvers. It could be much deeper, such as C:\Documents\Websites\Carvers\. For example, you may have the shareware folder on SnapFiles.com as www.snapfiles.com/shareware on the Web site, but you might have it as C:\Documents\Websites\Snapfiles\shareware on your computer.

The Site Definition dialog box uses terms like local, remote, and server technologies. A Web site you are designing on your computer is considered "local." When you put your Web pages on the Web server that is connected to the Internet, that computer is called the "remote" computer. We strongly recommend that you design locally and then put the files on the remote computer when finished. Although most ***Web-hosting services*** (companies that lease space on their Web servers for Web sites) have rigorous backup procedures, redundant Internet connections, backup generators, and other necessary systems, critical failures do happen. Your local copy may be the only copy that remains of your site. The term server technologies refers to special software that you could run on your local computer. Simple Web pages don't require this software, but pages that depend on a database application or server-side programming are difficult to test without it. While not difficult to install and configure, none of these technologies are necessary for this book.

The final step you take in defining a Web site in Dreamweaver is to create the folders that exist in the Web site. You can do this either in or outside of Dreamweaver. In this lesson, you use the Files panel in Dreamweaver to create the folders in the defined Web site; the Files panel acts rather like a miniature version of Windows Explorer (Windows) or the Finder (Macintosh). You might not anticipate needing certain folders during your preparation phase. Knowing how to create folders from within Dreamweaver can save you a lot of effort in switching back and forth between Explorer/Finder and Dreamweaver.

## Create a Site Definition

**1** **Copy the Project_02 folder and all of its contents from the RF_Dreamweaver_L1 folder to your WIP folder.**

Doing this prepares all of the files you need for Project_02.

**2** **Launch Dreamweaver.**

**3** **Expand the Files panel so that you can see the folders on your computer.**

You can use the Files panel as a file manager, allowing you to view the drives, folders, and files on your system, as well as add, delete, rename, copy, cut, and paste folders and files. You can also use the Files panel to create the site definition.

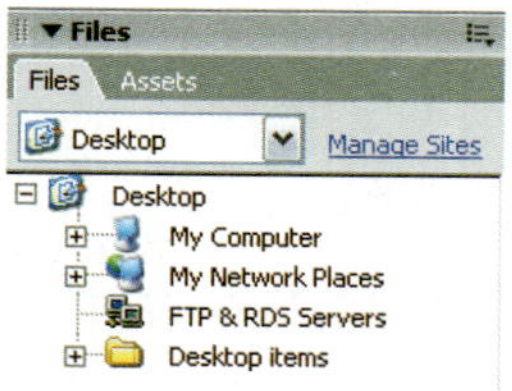


FIGURE 2.11

**4** **From the top of the Files panel, click the drop-down list and choose Manage Sites from the bottom of the list.**

The Files panel displays all drives on your computer system. You may create, delete, or rename folders and files just as if it were a miniature Explorer/Finder. You may need to do this at times when you want to create the root folder for a new Web site.

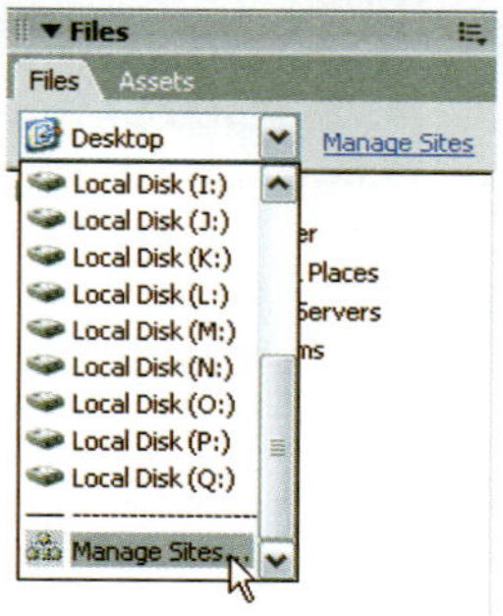


FIGURE 2.12

**5** **In the Manage Sites dialog box, click the New button and choose Site.**

***FTP*** (file transfer protocol) and ***RDS*** (remote data service) are methods of connecting to a remote Web site so that you can directly edit files on the Web server. Generally we recommend that you do neither. Some corporations, however, provide Web servers for development purposes and a different, final-production Web server that exists on the Internet. In this situation you may use either FTP or RDS as the corporation takes responsibility for maintaining the local Web server.

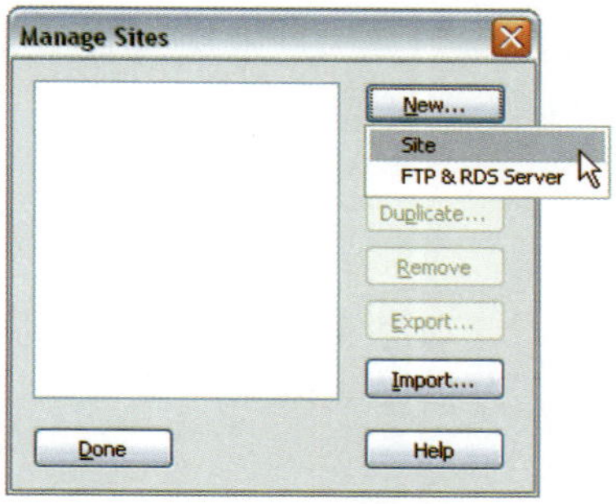


FIGURE 2.13

**6** **Type `Carver's Store` as the name of the site and click Next.**

In addition to standard ***alphanumeric characters*** (letters and numbers), Dreamweaver allows some other characters in the site name. The site name is just an internal designation that Dreamweaver uses to store the settings of your Web-site definition.

## If you have problems...

Ensure that the Basic tab is selected at the top of the Site Definition dialog box.

**7** **Click No, I Do Not Want to Use a Server Technology and click Next.**

The pages you create in this book do not require Web-server or database software, so you won't need to use any server technology.

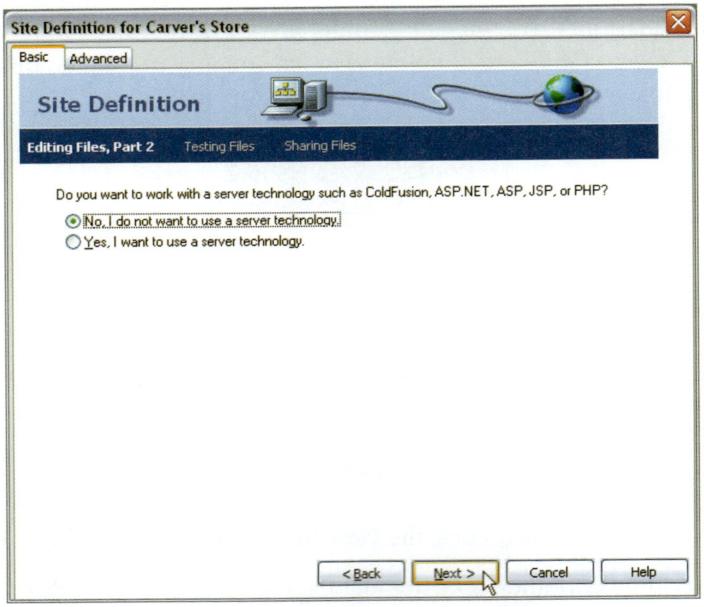


FIGURE 2.14

**8** **Click Edit Local Copies on My Machine, Then Upload to Server When Ready (Recommended), but do not click Next.**

This means that you will develop locally. To develop remotely, you have to choose FTP or RDS servers from the outset.

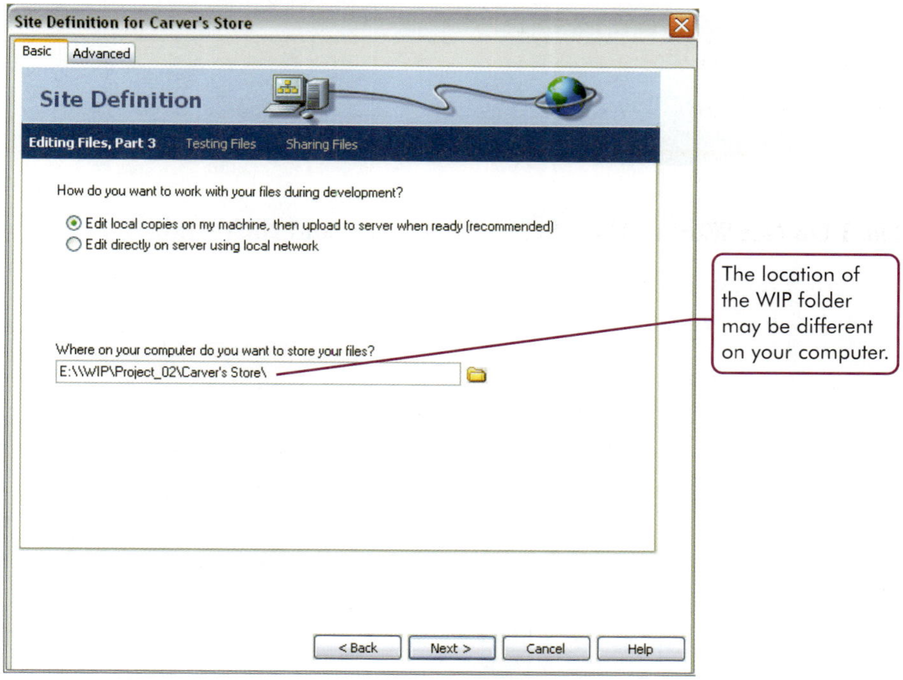


FIGURE 2.15

**9** **Click the folder icon to the right of the text field, and then navigate to and open the Project_02>Store folder. Click Select/Choose, and then click Next.**

The Store folder, which is the root folder for Carver's, has been created for you. Ordinarily you would have to create the folder before defining the Web site in Dreamweaver.

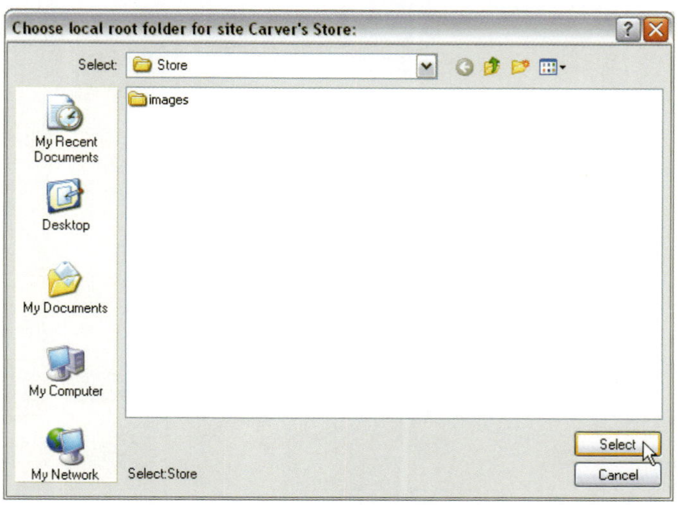


FIGURE 2.16

**10** **In response to the question about connection method to your server, choose None and click Next.**

You don't have access to an external (remote) Web server. If you did, then you could specify the settings so that after you finish the design locally, you could copy the files to the remote Web server.

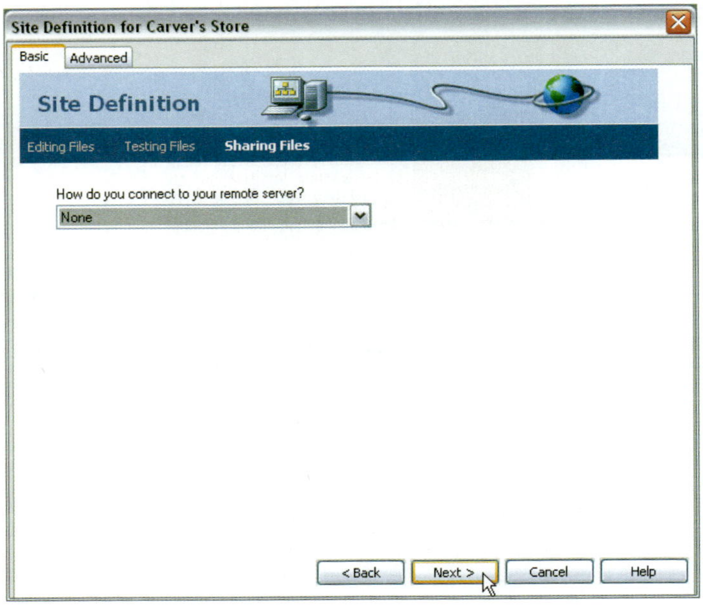


FIGURE 2.17

**11** **Click Done and then click Done again. Keep Dreamweaver open for the next lesson.**

You have set up a folder as a site in Dreamweaver. In the next exercise, you create the folders in the Web site using the structure you wrote out previously. You do this using the Files panel, which has much of the functionality of a file manager.

## Create Nested Folders

***Nested folders*** are folders within folders. Technically, you have already created a nested folder by creating the ***root*** or base folder for your Web site in your Project_02 folder, which is nested in your WIP folder. In this exercise you create folders that will exist within your Web site, not outside of it. You use the structure that you planned in the earlier exercise (Sketch a Web-Site Folder Layout).

**1** **Right/Control-click the Site folder for Carver's Store and choose New Folder from the menu.**

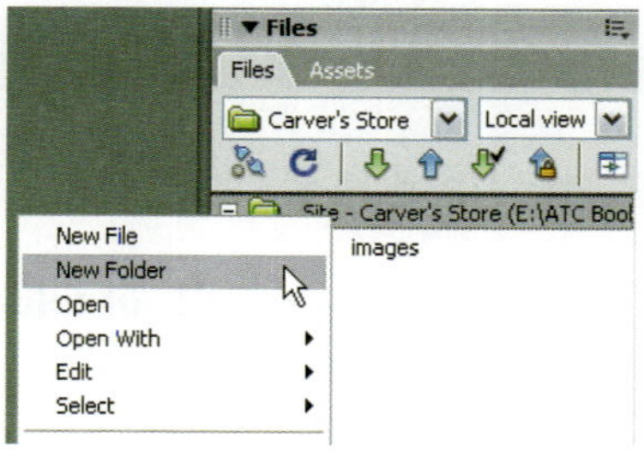


FIGURE 2.18

**2** **Type the name of your first major category, such as clothes. Use all lowercase characters.**

Although you may name filenames and folders using ***mixed-case characters*** (both upper- and lowercase characters), Windows systems ignore the character case — the folder clothes is considered the same as Clothes, CLOTHES and ClOtHeS. However, the character case of file and folder names matters on Unix and Linux systems, and because more ***Web-server software*** (software that enables an Internet-connected computer to deliver Web pages) runs on Unix or Linux operating systems than on any other operating system, you should be consistent and use lowercase. Should you have to move your Web site, even temporarily, to a case-sensitive operating system, using lowercase characters would prevent problems.

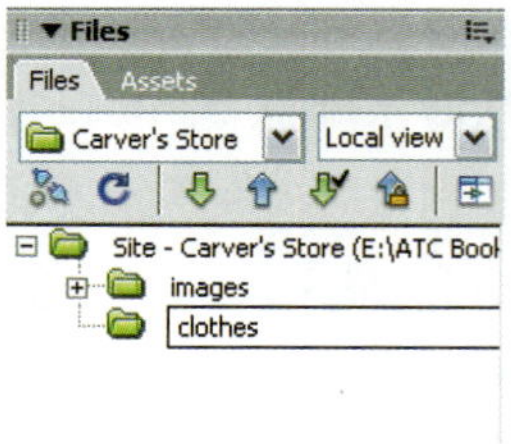


FIGURE 2.19

**3** **Create the folders for the other major categories that you wrote up in Step 3 of the Sketch a Web-Site Folder Layout exercise.**

Use the planning and site organization that you wrote up earlier as you now build your Web site in Dreamweaver.

**4** **Right/Control-click one of the category folders, create a new folder, and name it using one of the subcategory names for that folder.**

In this example, boys is a subcategory of clothes.

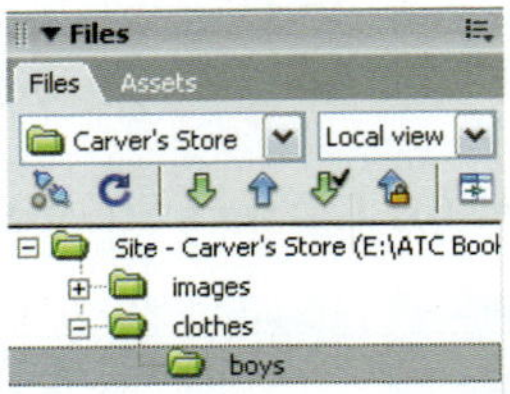


FIGURE 2.20

**5** **Repeat the process in Step 4 until you have created subfolders for all folders of your major categories.**

You have now created the folder structure for your Web site. More than this, however — you have begun the process of organizing the content in your Web site.

## To Extend Your Knowledge

### NAMING CONVENTIONS FOR FILENAMES AND FOLDERS

When naming files and folders for use on a Web server, certain characters may create problems. Avoid using spaces. Instead, use either the hyphen or the underscore character — travel-agency.html and travel_agency.html are both easier to read than travelagency.html. Don't start a filename or folder name with a numeral, but feel free to use as many numerals as you wish after the first alphabetical character. Finally, restrict the characters to alphanumeric characters (letters of the alphabet and numerals) plus hyphens and underscores. (Windows also allows the # symbol, but that character has special meaning in HTML and CSS, so it is best not to risk confusing your server by using it in a filename or folder name.)

Most current operating systems allow long filenames — up to 255 alphanumeric characters. While you can use this many characters for both filenames and folder names, it's best to keep filenames reasonably short — long enough for clarity but short enough to avoid excessive typing or errors. (Eliminating the 8-character filename and folder name limit that existed in Windows 3.1 and earlier, as well as in DOS, was a welcome enhancement to Windows 95 and later. It allowed travel-agency.html instead of trvagncy.htm. There was also a 3-character limit to filename extensions, but that was also eliminated with Windows 95. Web-page filenames may now end with .html instead of the previous .htm.)

# LESSON 4 Building Your First Web Page

The next series of exercises shows you some of the functions you use to create Web pages. In these exercises, you create and save a Web page, modify and add more content, and insert a graphic into the Web page. These are many of the types of activities you perform when designing a Web site, and although these exercises are quite basic, they give you a sense of what is involved in Web-site design.

## Create and Save a New Page

**1** **Using the Start page, click HTML under the Create New category. Macintosh users must choose File>New.**

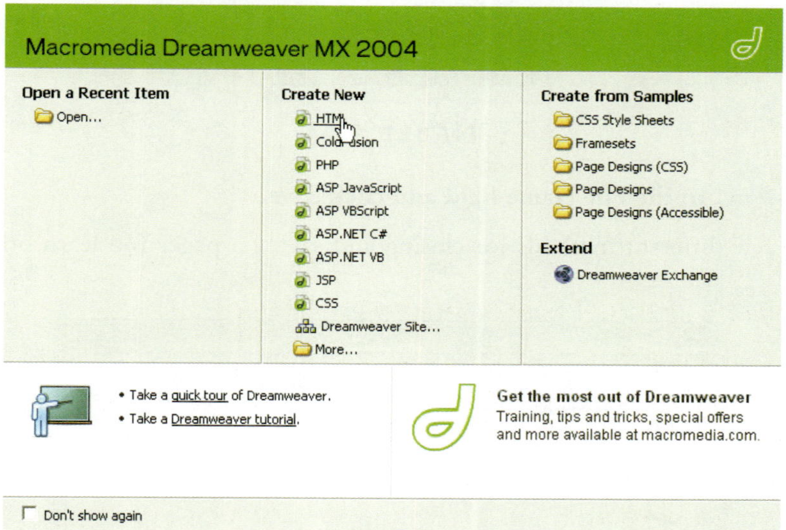


FIGURE 2.21

**2** **In the document Title field at the top of the Document window, delete Untitled Document, type `Home Page of Carver's Store`, and press Enter/Return.**

The document title appears in the Title bar of a browser window and as the document title in search-engine results. Although most people may ignore the text in the Title bar, you want to be sure that when they scan the results of a search, they don't overlook your Web page because the title does not correctly represent the content of your page.

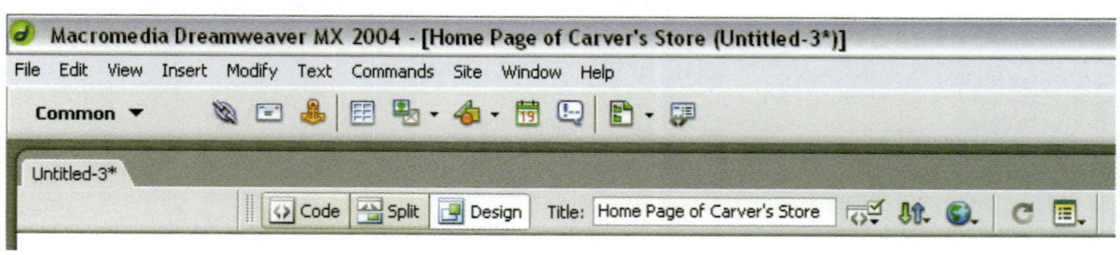


FIGURE 2.22

**3** **Choose File>Close or press Control/Command-W to close the page.**

FIGURE 2.23

**4** **Click Yes to save the changes.**

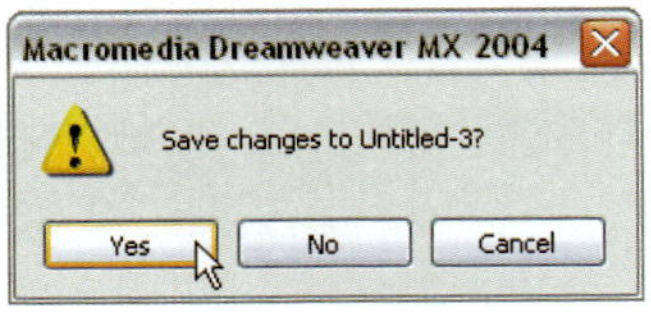


FIGURE 2.24

**5** **Type `home.html` in the File Name field and click Save.**

There are a few different methods for closing and saving a page. You learn other methods in later exercises.

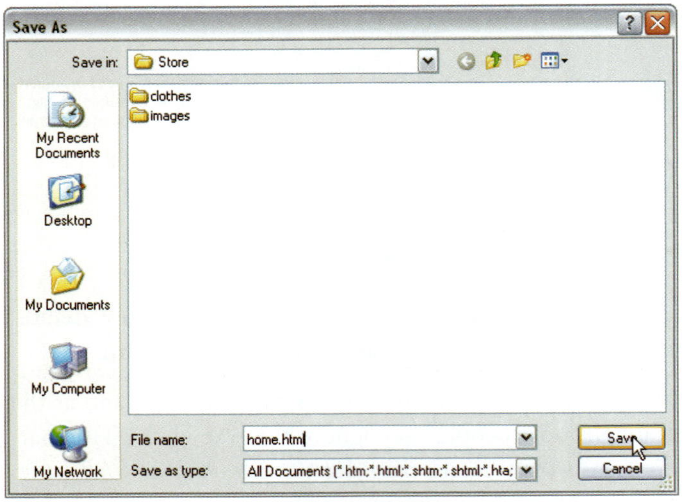


FIGURE 2.25

## Add More Text to the Page

In this exercise, you add more content to a page. The process is the same whether you add a brief greeting or more extensive content.

**1** **Open home.html by double-clicking on home.html in the Files panel.**

Double-clicking a file in the Files panel may be the easiest method of reopening an existing file; other methods include choosing File>Open or choosing File>Open Recent.

**2** **In the body area of the Document window, type `Carver's Store` and press Enter/Return.**

**3** **Type `Welcome to our store!` and press Enter/Return.**

**4** **Press Control/Command-S to save the changes made so far. Leave the file open for the next exercise.**

Control/Command-S is a keyboard shortcut for the Save procedure. You should learn some of the keyboard shortcuts because they speed up your use of those functions. Many of the keyboard shortcuts are common to all applications, making it easy to remember them. It is also a good habit to save often, so you do not lose much of your work in the event of a power failure.

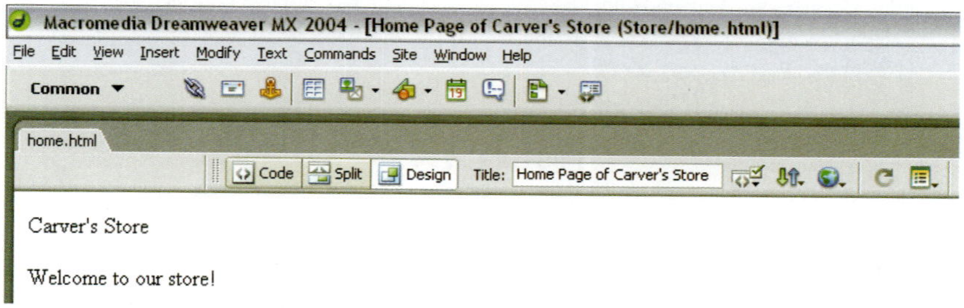


FIGURE 2.26

## Insert a Graphic

**1** **In the open file home.html, with the insertion point in the empty paragraph, choose Insert>Image.**

This is a simple method for inserting a graphic. In later projects, you learn other methods.

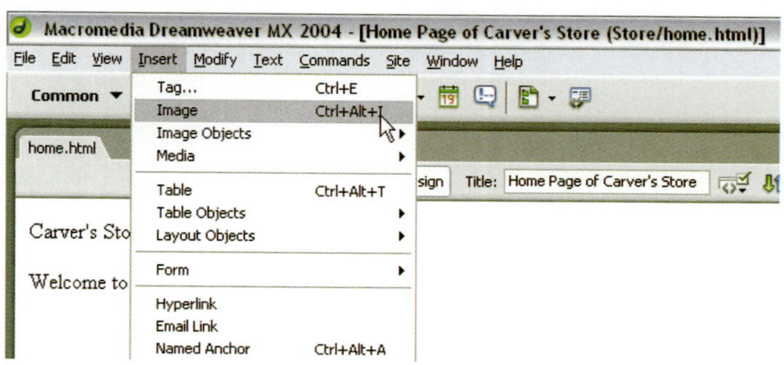


FIGURE 2.27

**2** **Double-click the images folder.**

Just as you created folders for the categories of content, you can create folders for other items, such as images and video files. Often, a Web site has many images; storing a large number of these files among the other Web-page files can be confusing.

Note that the path to the images folder on your system may be different from that shown here, depending on which drive and where on that drive you created the Project_02 folder. However, from the Project_02 folder and down, the structure of the folders is the same from system to system.

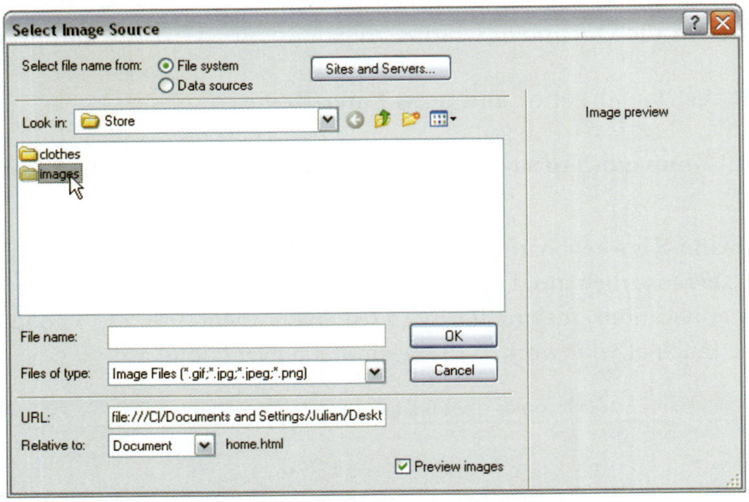


FIGURE 2.28

**3** **Click family.jpg to select the image but do not click OK.**

**4** **At the bottom of the Select Image Source dialog box, change the Relative To option to Document.**

You learn more about relative and absolute paths in Project 4. For now, consider this example. John lives at 123 Main Street and you live in the next house. A relative path from your house to John's house is: "he lives next door," whereas an absolute path to John's house is: "123 Main Street." Next door won't take someone to John's house from any house in town, only from your house. But 123 Main Street will always take someone to John's house, no matter where they start from. Relative to Document is like "next door," whereas Relative to Site is like "123 Main Street."

**5** **Click OK to insert the image.**

Notice the various properties of the image provided by the Select Image Source dialog box: an image preview, the file format, the dimensions (width, height), the size of the file, and how long (6 seconds) it will take to download.

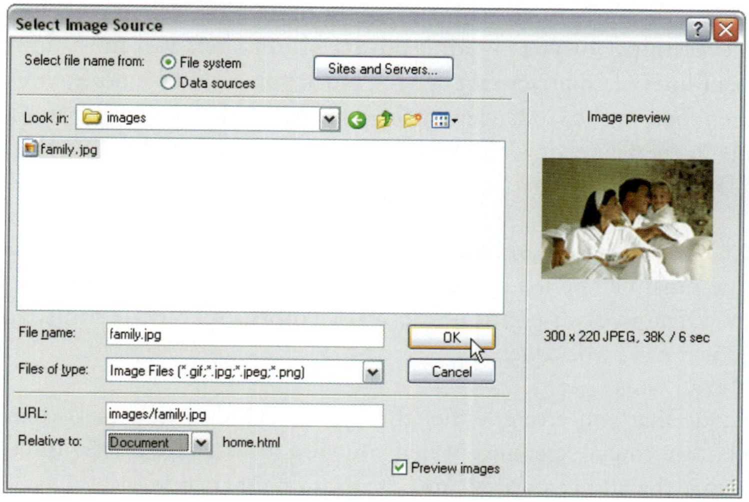


FIGURE 2.29

**6** **Choose File>Close and choose Yes to save the changes.**

## To Extend Your Knowledge

### DREAMWEAVER DOES THE HARD WORK

Inserting graphics into a Web page is very simple. So simple, in fact, that you don't realize how much other information about the image has been inserted for you. You saw in the preview window that the dimensions of this image are 300 wide and 220 high. The units are ***pixels*** — a word created from picture and elements — which are the dots on the computer monitor. In fact, Dreamweaver has specified these dimensions in the HTML code. Dreamweaver does a lot in the background when you select one of the HTML options or formats. It creates good HTML code. As you become more comfortable with the program, however, you will learn how (and be expected) to access the HTML code directly to apply options that may not be available from the Design window.

# LESSON 5 Working with Views

Most computer applications do not allow you to see or work with the code that is developed when you work with the application. The code produced when you create documents in a word-processing application, for example, is quite complex and not readable by human beings. HTML was originally developed when WYSIWYG applications were just being developed for both the Macintosh and Windows 3.0 — a WYSIWYG application for Web design was not even under consideration at the time. As a result, HTML is not very complex.

(Novices may disagree, but look at Java, C++, or another advanced programming language and you will change your mind.) For that reason, all WYSIWYG Web-design applications allow you to view and edit the code.

At times, you may need to examine the code of a particular section of the Web page. When you select a section of the design in the Design view, such as a block of text, the same block of text is selected in the Code view as well. You can then examine the code to correct it or apply something else to it. (Dreamweaver creates good code, but it cannot do everything for you — some advanced functions you must do manually.) Rather than hunt through hundreds of lines of code, looking for the block you need to modify, you can select the block in the Design view, and then look in the Code view at the selected block. The reverse is also true. You may see an unfamiliar block of code in the Code view and wonder where it fits in the Design. Selecting it also selects the related object(s) in the Design view.

When you work in the Code view, you can create code. Not all HTML options are available through the buttons and menus — some must be applied by other means, including working directly with the code. As you work in the Code view, Dreamweaver continues to assist you through code hints, a pop-up function that prompts you with options for HTML code.

Your browser uses the code that you create, either through the Design view or by hand-coding in the Code view, to display the Web page you are creating. When you view a Web page on the Internet, the code delivered to you is the same code that the author created. You can examine that code.

In this lesson, you see that the Design view and Code view are linked. You select text in the Design view and find out where it is in the Code view. You create code in the Code view and see it appear in the Design view. Finally, you examine the code that was sent to your browser to see that it is the same code you created in the Design and Code views.

## View Changes in the Code Window

**1** **Open home.html in the Files panel by double-clicking it.**

**2** **Select "Store" from the first line by double-clicking it.**

**3** **Click the Split button at the top of the Document window.**

When you select text in one window, the text is selected in the other window, as well. This feature is very useful for showing where you are both in the design and in the code.

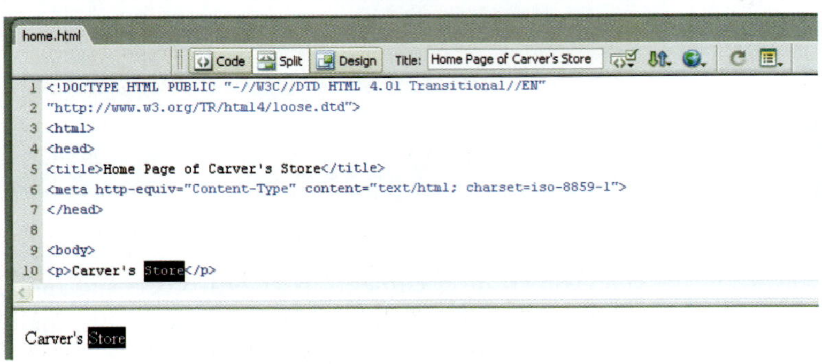


FIGURE 2.30

**4** **Press Delete and type `Online`. Leave the file open for the next exercise.**

Observe that the changes you made in the Design window are reflected in the Code window.

## View Changes in the Design Window

**1** **In the open file home.html, click to the right of the photo in the Design window.**

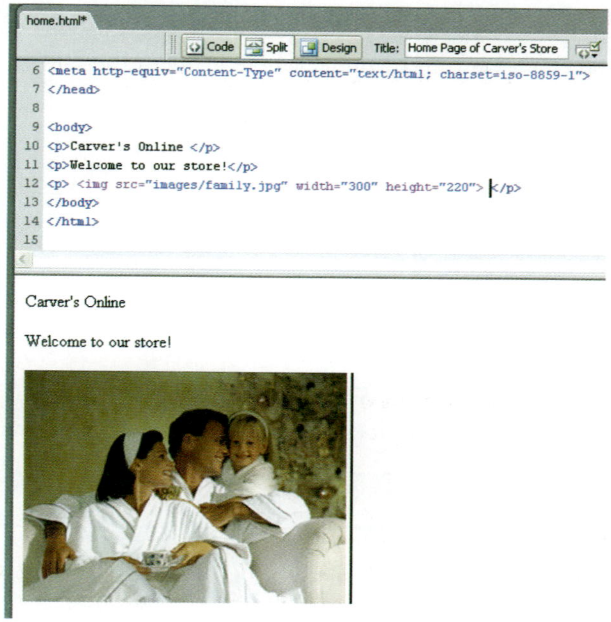


FIGURE 2.31

**2** **Click in the Code window at the end of the line (to the right of </p>, the closing paragraph tag) and press Enter/Return.**

You added another line of text and code below the graphic.

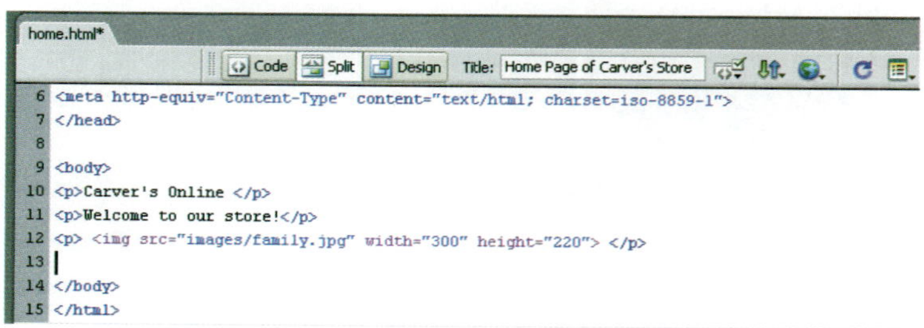


FIGURE 2.32

**3** **Type** <p>.

Notice how Dreamweaver prompts you with options for HTML tags as you type. Notice also that when you type the closing angle bracket (>), Dreamweaver adds the closing **</p>** tag for you and positions the insertion point between **<p>** and **</p>**.

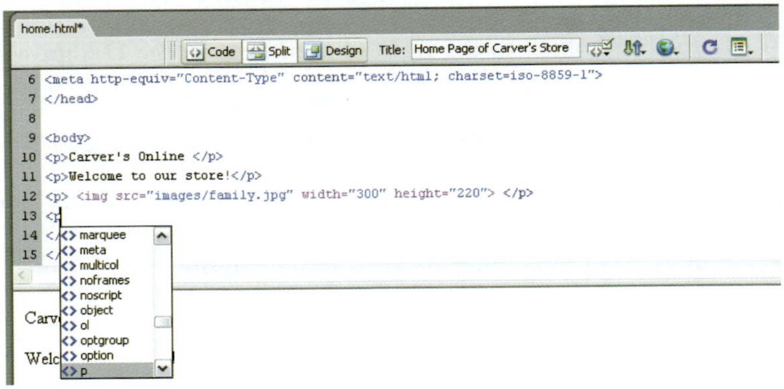


**FIGURE 2.33**

**4** **Type:** `Your favorite store for all your needs!`

Notice that the Design window below does not reflect the changes you have made (Windows).

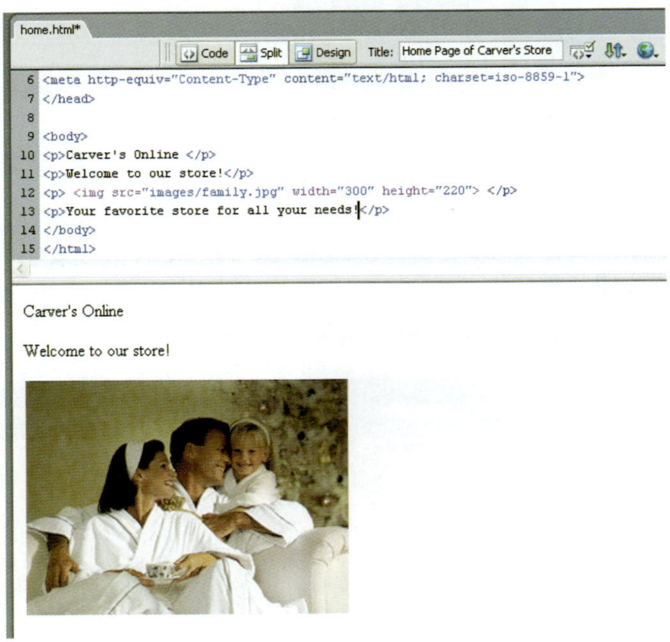


**FIGURE 2.34**

**5** **In the Property inspector, click the Refresh button.**

On a Windows system, the Design window does not dynamically change to reflect the changes in the Code window. You must use the Refresh button to make the changes appear in the Design window. On a Macintosh system, the Design window automatically reflects the changes made in the Code window.

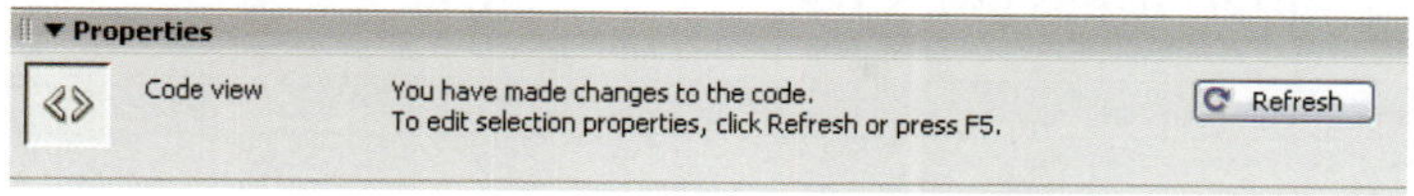


FIGURE 2.35

**6** **Click the Design button (Show Design View in the tool tip) to close the Code window.**

**7** **Press Control/Command-S to save the changes. Leave the file open for the next exercise.**

## View Source Code Sent to Your Browser

You have made changes to the Web page using both the Design view and Code view. You can examine the code in Dreamweaver, but is it the same code that is delivered to the browser? In this exercise, you examine the code that is delivered to the browser to learn that the code is exactly the same as the same code you created.

**1** **In the open file home.html, choose File>Preview in Browser and choose a browser.**

Depending on the setup of your computer, you may have only one browser or you may have many. You may choose any browser from the list to view the page you created.

**2** **Switch between Dreamweaver and your browser.**

Notice that the Web page you created in Dreamweaver looks the same in the browser window as it does in Dreamweaver's Design view.

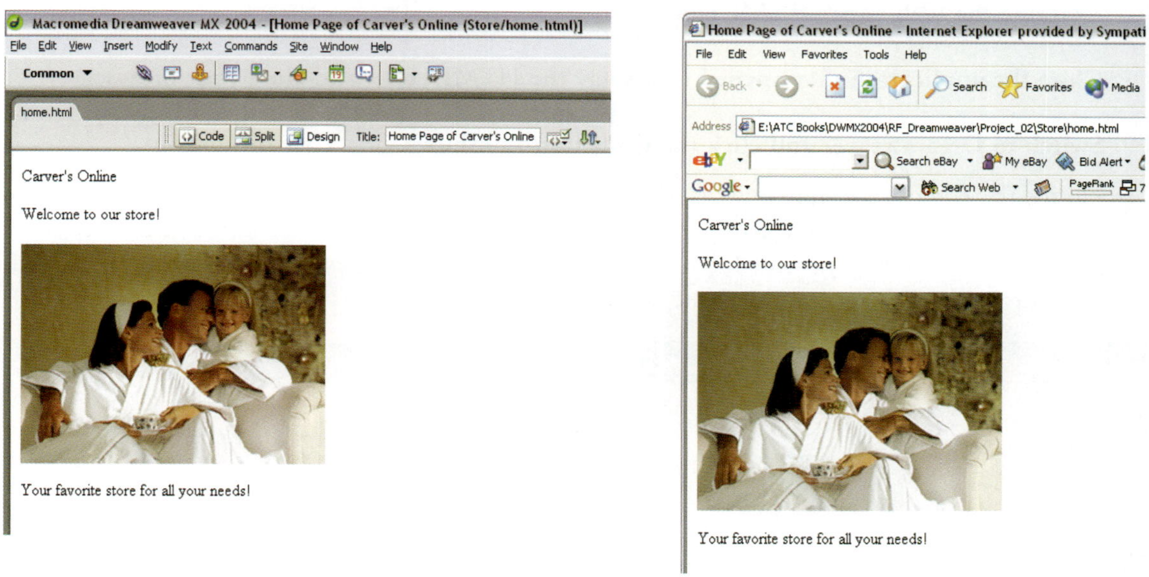


FIGURE 2.36

**3** **Right/Control-click in your browser window, and choose View Source from the pop-up menu.**

Although all browsers offer this option, different browsers may use slightly different terms for this option, such as View Page Source. Also, different browsers and computer setups display the code using different applications. For example, Internet Explorer for Windows tends to display the code in Notepad whereas Mozilla has its own Code view window.

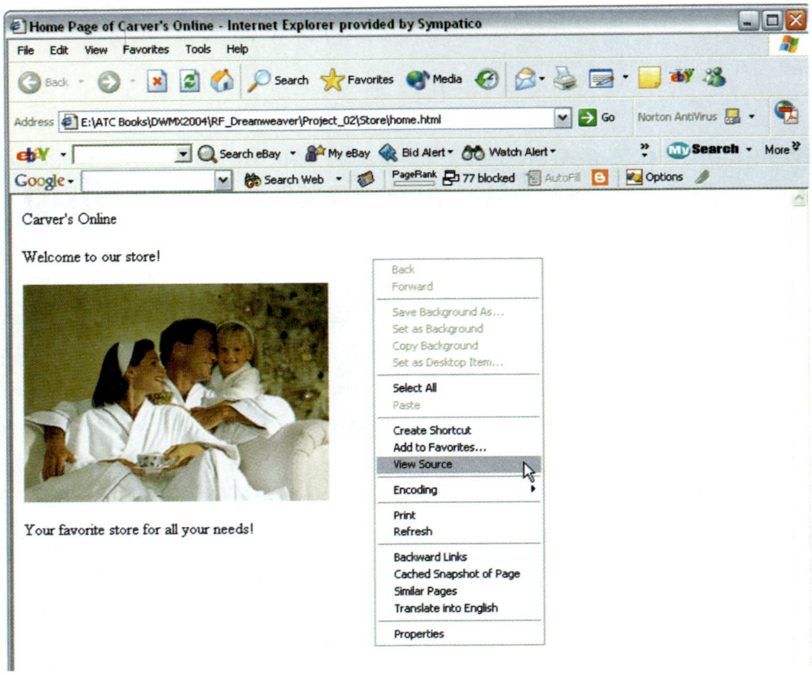


FIGURE 2.37

**4** **Examine the Web page's HTML code.**

**5** **Close the application that opened to display the HTML code, and close your browser.**

**6** **Switch to Dreamweaver and click the Code button (Show Code View in tool tip).**

Notice the code in Dreamweaver is identical to the code the browser received. Dreamweaver uses ***syntax coloring*** — different parts of the code are given different colors, such as dark blue for tags, purple for attributes, royal blue for attribute values, and black for text. Not all text or HTML editors use syntax coloring; for instance, Notepad (on the right) does not.

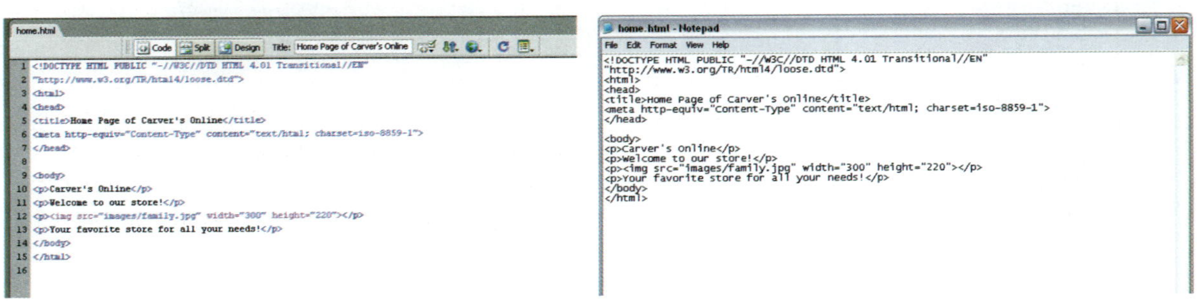


FIGURE 2.38

**7** **Click the Design button. Leave home.html open for the next exercise**

The code you created using Dreamweaver is the same code that the browser uses to display the Web page. You can use this method to examine the code of other Web pages, whose style or layout is of interest, so that you can see how they were created. The only instance when the code of the page at the Web server may differ from what the browser receives is when you use a programming language to generate the Web pages. For example, the programming code may use the current time to generate "Good Morning" or "Good Afternoon." Generally though, whatever code you create is the same code that your browser receives.

## LESSON 6 Applying Simple Text Formatting

Although Dreamweaver's focus is on creating Web pages, it also has many text functions similar to those in word-processing software. Many other types of content are available from the Internet, such as graphics, animations, videos, and music, but the primary source of content for Web pages is text. As Patrick Lynch and Sarah Horton wrote in *The Web Style Guide*, "Don't get so lost in the novelty of Web pages that basic standards of editorial and graphic design are tossed aside." HTML has all the basic text structures needed for a text-based document.

The primary structures that are most commonly used are headings, lists, and paragraphs. There are six levels of headings, starting with Heading 1, the most important, down to Heading 6. Headings are formatted with different font sizes, from the largest, Heading 1, down to the smallest, Heading 6. Heading 1 is used just once on a page and identifies the basic purpose of the page. The other headings (not all need to be used) divide and subdivide the content into chunks of easily digestible information. One common mistake that novices make is applying Heading 3 as the top heading for the page because they don't like how large Heading 1 appears. You will learn how to change the default size of text, including headings, so that you maintain the ***document structure*** (the proper use of headings and other text structures) while creating a pleasing appearance.

Other formatting options include numbered and bulleted lists, which look just like their counterparts in word-processing software. You may change the numbering style from numerals (1, 2, 3) to alphabetic (a, b, c) and other styles, and you can change the bullet characters from a circle (open circle) to a disc (filled circle) or a square bullet character. You can insert a ***horizontal rule*** (line), add an image, or format a quotation.

There are no excuses for not using proper document structure in a Web page. Your Web pages are public documents that may be viewed by thousands, hundreds of thousands, perhaps even millions of people. Using proper document structure ensures that your documents are correctly formatted for easier reading and understanding. Using proper document structure benefits the blind, as well. The blind use the Internet, too, but their experience is very different. They often use screen-reading software, such as JAWS from Freedom Scientific, or devices that convert text characters to Braille on an electronic device in front of their keyboard. Whereas sighted people can scan a page visually for large bold blocks of text representing headings, blind people cannot. They depend, instead, on proper structure of the document to let them know when they have encountered a heading or a list. It is quite possible to fake a heading by taking a standard paragraph and making the text large and bold, but the underlying code remains a paragraph, not a heading. ***Accessibility*** is the term used to describe methods and procedures for ensuring that your Web pages are just as usable by the blind as they are by sighted persons.

In this exercise, you apply simple text formatting using two different features — the Property inspector and the Tag editor. The Property inspector allows you to apply most text-formatting options by clicking the option or selecting it from a list. In the following figure, you can see that the format of the selected block of text is Heading 3. The Tag editor is somewhat like the Code view, in that you type your changes in the code. Unlike the Code view, however, only the selected HTML is visible. You first select the HTML block using the Tag selector (a function that appears in the Status bar of the Document window). The Tag selector identifies the HTML tags that are in use in the selected text, for example, Heading 3 in the following figure. When you Right/Control-click the tag in the Tag selector and choose Edit tag, a pop-up window appears, showing you the tag and its current options (no options are used in this example). You can then edit the tag in the pop-up window. Just like the Code view, code hints appear to help you select options for the tag.

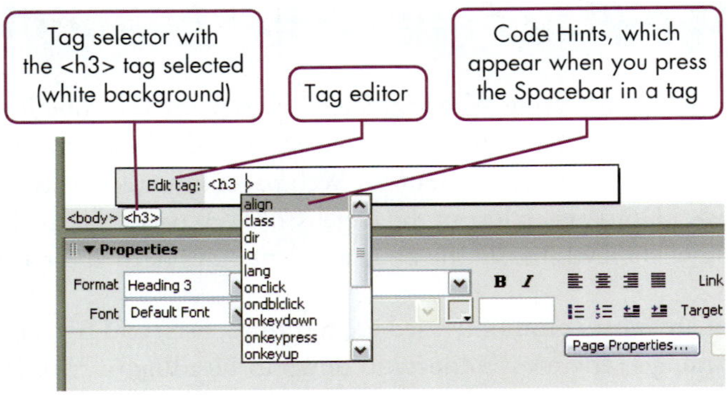


FIGURE 2.39

## Format a Heading

**1** **In the open file home.html, click in the top line of text.**

**2** **Using the Property inspector, choose Heading 1 from the Format list.**

The text becomes large and bold — this is the appearance of Heading 1 text.

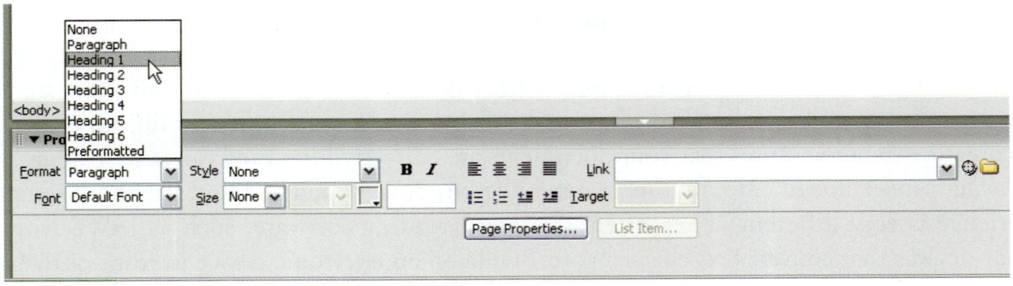


FIGURE 2.40

**3** **Drag to select the second line of text.**

**4** **Click the Bold button (B) in the Property inspector.**

You may notice that the Tag selector displays the **<strong>** tag after you apply bold. The **<strong>** tag is an accessibility feature; when screen readers encounter this tag, their computer-generated voices change to a stronger tone, indicating that the **<strong>** text is emphasized. Read aloud a sentence with bold text in it, and listen to the change in your voice. The **<b>** bold tag is being phased out in the next version of XHTML in favor of **<strong>**. Both blind and sighted users receive the same emphasis when you use the **<strong>** tag.

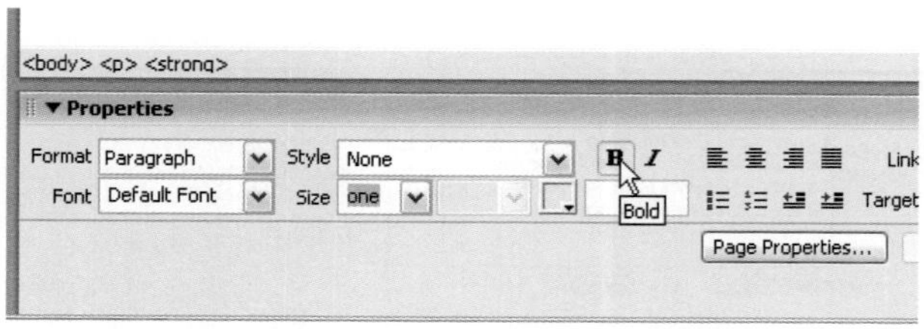


FIGURE 2.41

**5** **Click in the last line of text.**

**6** **Click the <p> in the Tag selector at the bottom of the Document window.**

When you click an HTML tag in the Tag selector, all content in that tag is selected.

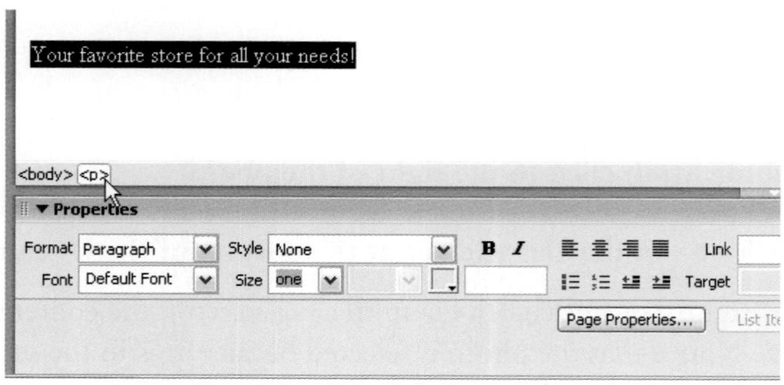


FIGURE 2.42

**7** **From the Property inspector, click the Font list and choose the second option: Arial, Helvetica, Sans-Serif.**

*Sans-serif* is French for "without serifs" (***serifs*** are the small perpendicular strokes added to parts of letters and numerals in some fonts. For example, compare **T** with **T** and notice that the first one has additional strokes perpendicular to the top crossbar and the bottom of the upright — these are serifs. Computer screens and, worse yet, television screens display text much more roughly than printers. Serif text is thus more difficult to read on a computer screen because the serifs do not display as clearly on computer screens due to their small size. Web pages tend to use sans-serif fonts because, without the serifs, the fonts appear farther apart and more distinct. Arial and Helvetica are both sans-serif fonts.

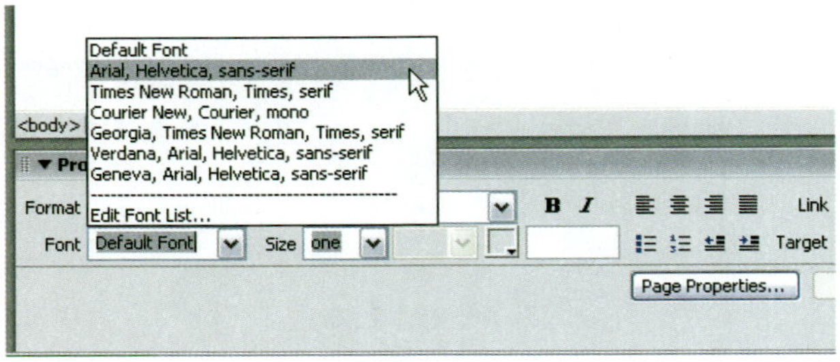


FIGURE 2.43

**8** **Close the page and save the changes. Leave the file open for the next exercise.**

## Modify Code Using the Tag Editor

The Code window is not your only means for making changes to HTML code — you can also use the Tag editor. The Tag editor, however, does not allow you to modify the content, just the code.

**1** **In the open file home.html, click to the right of the photo.**

**2** **Right/Control-click <p> in the Tag selector at the bottom of the Document window.**

When you click or Right/Control-click a tag in the Tag selector, the contents of the tag are selected in the Design window. Notice that the photo is selected because it is in the selected paragraph.

**3** **Choose Edit Tag from the pop-up menu.**

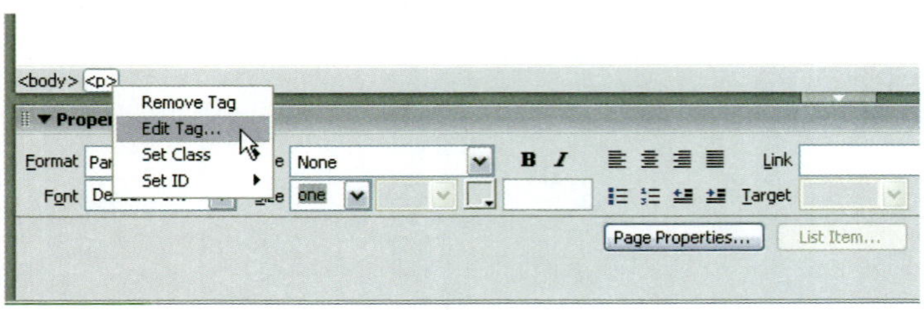


FIGURE 2.44

**4** **With the insertion point between the p and the >, press the Spacebar once and pause for a moment.**

After a moment, a pop-up menu of code hints appears. ***Code hints*** are options available for the selected HTML tag.

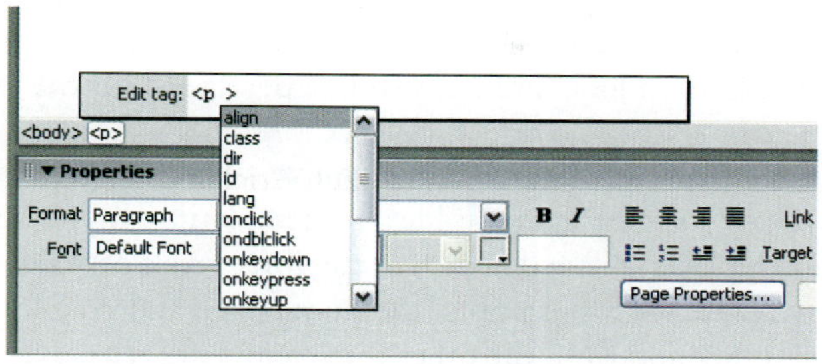


FIGURE 2.45

**5** **The first option in the list, `align`, is selected. Press Enter/Return to accept it and pause for a moment.**

That option — **`align`** — is an ***HTML attribute*** (an option) of the paragraph tag (and for numerous other tags, too). The **`align`** attribute has four ***values*** (attribute options are called "attribute values" or just "values"): **`center`**, **`justify`**, **`left`**, and **`right`**. After a moment, the four attribute values for **`align`** appear.

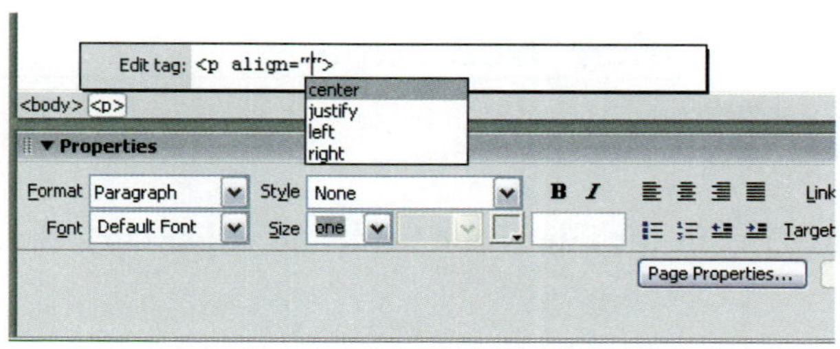


FIGURE 2.46

**6** **Note that `center`, the first attribute option for `align`, is selected. Press Enter/Return to accept it.**

When you choose **`center`**, the photo becomes centered in the Design view because the photo is in the paragraph whose property you just changed to center alignment.

**7** **Save the changes, leaving the file open for the next exercise.**

# LESSON 7 Using a Web Page as a Template

It can take a lot of time and effort, not just from you but also from others on your team, to design a Web page. If you have more than one page that uses the same basic design, differing only in content, there is no need to rebuild the page again for the second, third, or more times. Instead, build a ***template***, a document that contains the common elements you need in multiple other pages. Using the template, you efficiently build other similar pages and all retain the common look and feel you had developed for the original document.

You learned of the need for a template in Lesson 2 when you were sketching some pages at the category, subcategory, and product levels. That type of situation is ideal for templating. In the example of Carver's Store, you may only need three primary templates — one for each of the three levels of detail. Not all pages on a Web site need to tightly adhere to a template — for example, the home page and contact-form page you sketched in Lesson 2 may differ from each other and from the other three templates. However, considering that you could build most of the pages for Carver's from three such templates, you would save a lot of time and effort if you use templates.

Dreamweaver has a very strong templating function. You can create both simple and complex templates using this functionality. In this lesson, however, you don't use the Dreamweaver template functionality but something simpler — Save As. You create a document, save it, reopen it, save it as a different name, and make the changes. You then have a new document based on the template of the original document. For basic documents, there is nothing faster or easier than using the Save As menu item as a form of templating.

## Use Save as to Create Another Web Page

1. **Open home.html and choose File>Save As.**

2. **Type `home-french.html` in the File Name field, and either click the Save button or press Enter/Return.**

   You have just built your first page modeled on home.html. The next step is to make the specific content changes to this page.

3. **Select "Welcome to our store!", delete it, and in its place type:** `Bienvenue a votre magasin!`

**4** **Select "Your favorite store for all your needs!" and in its place type:** `Votre magasin favori pour tous vos besoins!`

FIGURE 2.47

**5** **Close the file, saving the changes.**

# LESSON 8 Creating Links

Hyperlinks, or links, are an integral part of Web pages. Links are what make the World Wide Web different from any other component of the Internet. They allow you to go from page to page in a news article, to jump from Web site to Web site, and, to a certain extent, to send an email. Links, whether from one Web page to another or email links, are very easy to create in Dreamweaver.

There are two basic types of Web-page links. You may link from one Web page to another page on the same site. When you create a link to another page in the same site, the domain name remains the same. All you need to do is specify the name of the page to which you wish to send the reader. If the destination page is in another folder, then you must specify the path to the page including the folder (or folders). For example, to link from the home page of Carver's Online to the OshKosh shoes page in the boys section of the shoes category, the link would be shoes/boys/oshkosh.html.

When you link from the oshkosh.html page in Carver's Online to the boys shoes page on the OshKosh B'Gosh Online Store Web site, the link would be http://www.oshkoshbgosh.com/productselection.asp?did=807. A link to a page on another site must include the domain name (www.oshkoskbgosh.com), the Web-page name (productselection.asp?did=807), the folder path (if applicable), and http:// at the beginning. ***HTTP*** is an abbreviation for HyperText Transfer Protocol, the method by which Web pages are transferred from the Web server to the browser. Browsers can display information from different types of servers — gopher, wais, http, and ftp (the first two are rare these days but http and ftp are not); to ensure that the browser and server are "speaking the same language," the protocol must be specified. ***FTP*** (File Transfer Protocol) is a protocol through which you may view files on a server, not unlike viewing the files on your computer system through Explorer/Finder. Clicking a filename on an ftp site downloads that file. If you are linking to an ftp site, you must add **`ftp://`** in front of the domain name.

In Project 4, you learn more about links and how to create them using absolute and relative paths and multiple methods in Dreamweaver. In this exercise, you create simple links. You type the link destination into the Link field, which means that you must remember to use the protocol, when needed, and must check the spelling of your link. A link to a misspelled filename takes you either to the wrong page (if the misspelling is the spelling of another page) or to no page at all (otherwise known as a "dead" or "broken" link).

## Link Pages to One Another

**1** **Open home.html from the Files panel.**

**2** **Click at the end of the last paragraph and press Enter/Return.**

When you press Enter/Return at the end of a paragraph, you create a new paragraph block with opening and closing **<p>** paragraph tags. The Tag selector shows a **<p>** at the end of the list of tags, indicating that you are working in a paragraph block.

**3** **Type: `Cette page en francais.`**

You will link this phrase, which means "This page in French", to the French page you created in the previous exercise.

**4** **In the Property inspector, click the Style list and choose None.**

The previous paragraph used style1 and the style was carried automatically to the current paragraph. Selecting None removes the style from the current paragraph.

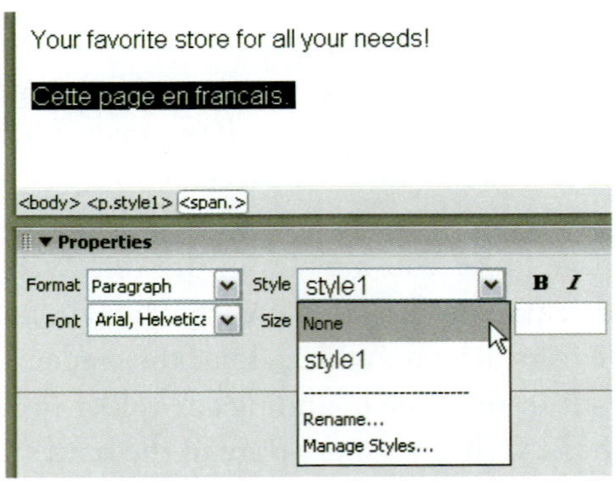


FIGURE 2.48

**5** **With the phrase selected, type `home-french.html` in the Link field of the Property inspector and press Enter/Return.**

You type the destination of the link in the Link field. There are other methods for creating a link, but even when you know the other methods, there will still be times when you need to type text into the Link field.

You must press Enter/Return after typing the link destination into the Link field. At times, Dreamweaver doesn't properly register the link destination typed into the Link field. Pressing Enter/Return forces Dreamweaver to store the value.

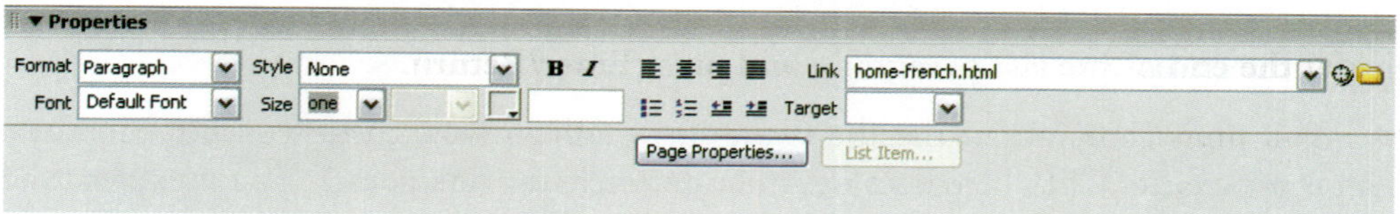


FIGURE 2.49

**6** **Close home.html, saving the changes.**

**7** **Open home-french.html.**

**8** **Click at the end of the last paragraph and press Enter/Return.**

**9** **Type: `This page in English.`**

**10** **Set Style to None.**

**11** **Select the paragraph, type `home.html` in the Link field, and press Enter/Return.**

You have now created links from home.html to home-french.html and back again.

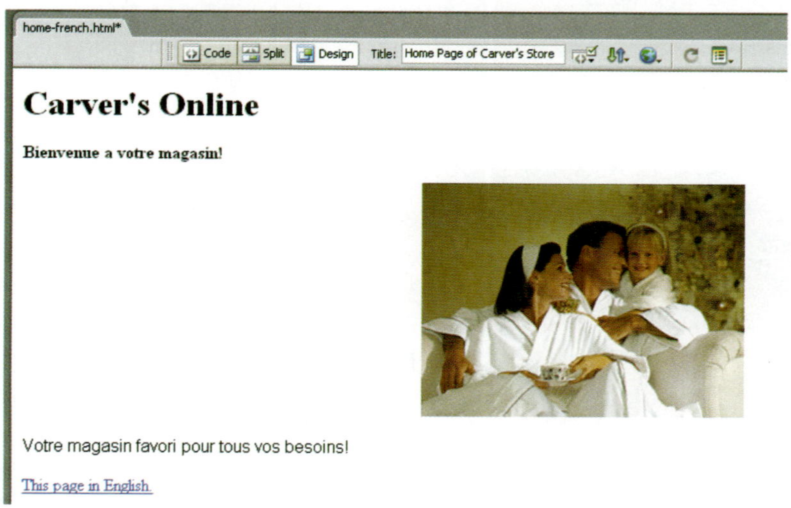


FIGURE 2.50

**12** **Close the file, saving the changes.**

## Create an Email Link

In this exercise, you create an email link. Remember that email links require **`mailto:`**, the email protocol, in front of the email address.

**1** **Open home.html.**

**2** **Click to the right of the last paragraph and press Enter/Return.**

**3** **Type:** `Please contact us if you have any questions.`

**4** **Select "contact us".**

The words "contact us" will be the link to the email address. Often, you see "click here" in a Web page, which is poor form. Click here does not indicate where the link goes — you must read the rest of the phrase or sentence to determine the purpose or destination of the link. By contrast, contact us clearly indicates the purpose of the link. Secondly, some people do not use a mouse with their computer, because they may be blind or visually impaired, or have ***motility challenges*** (such as poor hand-eye coordination, upper-body paralysis, or shakiness, such as from Parkinson's). Commonly, these people use the Tab key on their keyboard to skip from link to link. If they are using a screen reader, the screen reader reads the link text aloud. If all that these individuals hear are "click heres" on a page, they become very frustrated. You can't make sales to frustrated clients. However, if your link text is informative, your visitors understand the purpose of your links, navigate your pages with greater ease, and buy more.

**5** **In the Link field of the Property inspector, type** `mailto:info@carversonline.com` **and press Enter/Return.**

Do not insert a space between **`mailto:`** and the email address.

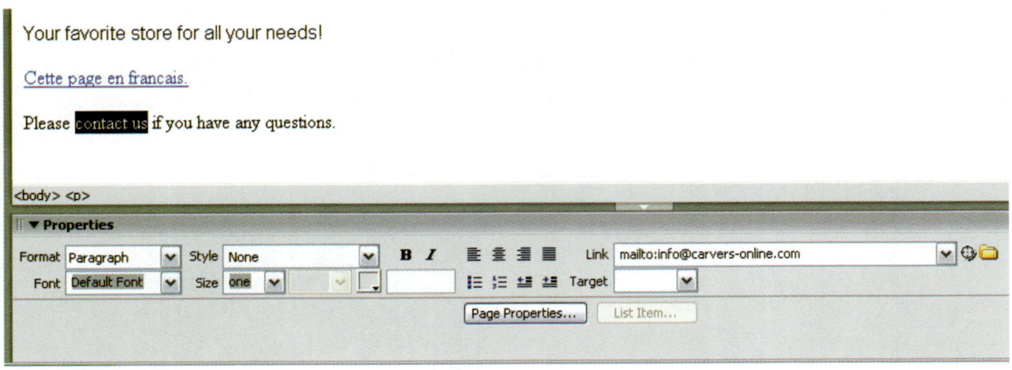


FIGURE 2.51

**6** **Save the changes, leaving the file open for the next exercise.**

## Test Your Links in a Browser

You can view many features and functions of a Web page in the Design view of Dreamweaver, but some require a browser for you to properly test your work. "Code a little, test a little" is a good principle to follow. When you create, add, or modify HTML code by hand, mistakes occasionally creep into your Web pages. Dreamweaver creates excellent-quality HTML code, but you may type an email address incorrectly or link to the wrong page. Whether you create the HTML in the Code view or work in the Design view, you should always test your links.

In this exercise, you test the links in your browser. This is a very important check since Carver's Store does not want their potential customers to be frustrated by dead links.

1. **In the open file home.html, choose File>Preview in Browser and choose a browser.**

2. **Click the link to the French page.**

3. **Click the link to the English page.**

4. **Click the email link.**

   If you do not have email software configured on your system, an alert dialog box may appear, warning you that you may need to set up email software. If so, you know that the email link is working fine.

5. **Close your browser and return to Dreamweaver.**

6. **Close home.html.**

## CAREERS IN DESIGN

### DO YOU NEED A WEB SERVER?

Experienced developers may also use a Web server to test their Web sites in a more-realistic setting. Advanced Web designers have several options for accessing and using a Web server for development purposes, such as installing Web-server software on their personal computers, setting up a separate computer that has been configured as a Web server, or purchasing Web-hosting services for development purposes only.

Access to a Web server allows you to use server-side programming to create dynamic sites. A ***dynamic site*** is one that changes regularly, such as a news site or a discussion forum. Commonly these sites use a database to store the content of the Web site. ***Server-side programming*** is a programming language that runs at the Web server; the results of this programming are returned to the visitor's browser as HTML. A ***search engine*** is a program that processes your request and returns the results in HTML, which you then see as a Web page. Search engines are dynamic in that the pages they produce are different with every request.

## SUMMARY

In this project, you learned how to plan and organize the content of a Web site and produce a flowchart from which you could create a navigation system. You learned how to define the site; create folders; and create, modify, and save basic Web pages. You also discovered how to use Save As to make one page serve as a template for another. You learned how to add text and graphics to a simple page. You learned to use the Design view to create the HTML while you work on the layout. You discovered how to use the Code view to modify the code directly, and use code hints to access a list of attributes appropriate to the selected HTML tag. You learned about HTML tags and attributes. You learned to use the Tag selector to select a block of text and the Tag editor to add an attribute to the tag. You explored creating different types of links — links to other pages on your site, and email links. You also discovered how to test your page in a browser and view the source code.

## KEY TERMS

Above the fold
Accessibility
Alphanumeric characters
Attribute values
Document structure
Domain name
Domain name registrars
Dynamic site
Freeware
FTP
Home page
HTML attribute
HTTP
Local computer
Mixed-case characters
Motility challenges
Navigation system
Nested folders
Pixels
RDS
Remote computer
Rich media
Root
Root folder
Sans-serif fonts
Search engine
Serif fonts
Server-side programming
Shareware
Site map
Source code
Templating
URL
Values
Web-hosting services
Web-server software

# CHECKING CONCEPTS AND TERMS

## SCREEN ID

**Identify the indicated areas from the list below:**

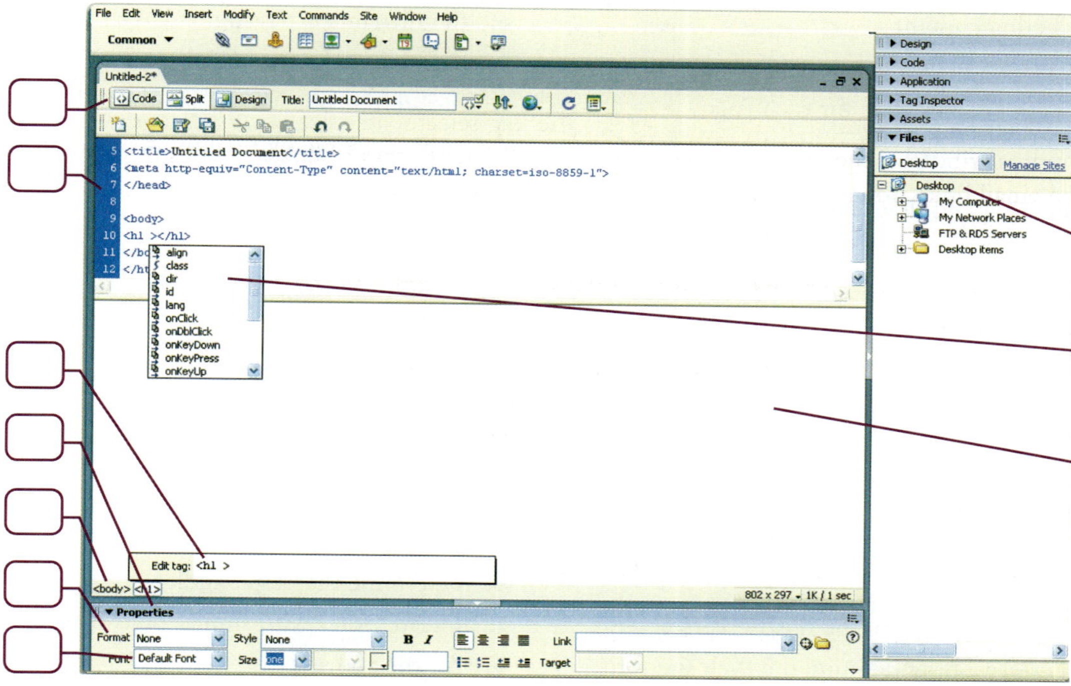

FIGURE 2.52

a. Tag editor

b. Tag selector showing the **<h1>** tag selected

c. Property inspector

d. Expanded panels group

e. Code View window

f. Design View window

g. Code hint showing attributes of the **<h1>** tag

h. Text block formats, such as paragraph and headings

i. Font typeface options

j. Layout View selection buttons

## MULTIPLE CHOICE

**Circle the letter of the correct answer for each of the following:**

1. Which of the following is not part of planning a Web project?
   a. Gathering content
   b. Collecting related content
   c. Writing HTML code for each page
   d. Creating a design concept

2. Storyboarding and flowcharting for a Web site __________.
   a. require specific HTML coding
   b. begin on paper
   c. have become obsolete in recent years
   d. are only used for Web animation

3. Site definition __________.
   a. defines thematic site design
   b. establishes the site's working title and root folder
   c. publishes the site on the host server
   d. is a creative brief defining the Web site for client approval

4. Nothing contained in your site can __________.
   a. have a file name with capital letters
   b. can have more than 256 colors
   c. be outside the root folder
   d. All the above

5. In a Web browser, you can view the source code or HTML of a Web page.
   a. True
   b. False

6. The Uniform Resource Locator or URL is __________.
   a. the filename extension of a Web page
   b. determined by the Web browser
   c. the address of a Web page
   d. only accessible by the host server

7. A domain name __________.
   a. is always capitalized
   b. must be contained in all filenames of a Web project
   c. can be registered without cost
   d. is like the name of a business

8. When designing a Web site, it is important to __________.
   a. consider the purpose of the site
   b. determine the target audience
   c. research sites with similar objectives
   d. All the above

9. FTP and RDS are both __________.
   a. image-file extensions
   b. HTML tags defining text attributes
   c. alternative programming technologies for Web development
   d. methods of connecting to a remote Web site

10. The primary source of content from Web pages is __________.
    a. video and animation
    b. music
    c. text
    d. photo images

## DISCUSSION QUESTIONS

1. You have learned that good organization and Web-site design begin with planning your content and navigation through outlining, storyboarding, and flowcharting. Why is this process more desirable than simply sitting down at the computer and beginning to design? Are there any disadvantages to working this way?

2. Organizing your content — text, images, videos, and animations — is essential for Web-site management and updating. How would you structure and organize the folders that contain the site content? How would your method of organizing result in more efficient site management and development?

3. Once you have designed the look, why are templates beneficial for Web sites that can grow to hundreds of pages? Which components of a Web page would you put into the template and why?

## SKILL DRILL

Skill Drills reinforce project skills. Each skill reinforced is the same, or nearly the same, as a skill presented in the lesson. Detailed instructions are provided in a step-by-step format. You should work through these exercises in order.

The preceding lessons and exercises provide a whirlwind tour of Dreamweaver. In the following Skill Drills, you work through similar steps to define and create Web pages, but at a slower pace, so you can learn more detail about the procedures and dialog boxes.

### 1. Define a Site with the Advanced Tab

In this Skill Drill, you define a new site using the Advanced tab of the Site Definition dialog box. The Advanced tab gives you the same options as the Basic tab , but adds many others that are needed for later projects, such as remote access and server technologies.

The site you are creating is called "Tropiflora Online" (hence the abbreviation TO). Tropiflora Online is an actual online retailer of tropical plants and supplies. (Web-site content used by permission.)

1. At the top of the Files panel, click the drop-down menu and choose Manage Sites.
2. In the Manage Sites dialog box, choose New, and then choose Site.
3. Click the Advanced tab at the top of the Site Definition dialog box.
4. Type **TO-P2** in the Site Name field.
5. Click the folder icon to the right of the Local Root Folder field.
6. Navigate to Project_02>TO-P2 and click Select/Choose.
7. Click OK.
8. Click Done.

   Working with the Advanced tab of the Site Definition dialog box seems much simpler than using the Basic tab. Unless told otherwise, use the Advanced tab of the Site Definition dialog box for all future exercises. Refer to this Skill Drill when you need to recall the process for creating a new site.

## 2. Create a New Page Using the File>New Menu

1. From the Dreamweaver Start page, click HTML from the Create New category.
2. In the Title field of the Document toolbar, type: `Home of Tropiflora Online`.
3. In the Document window, type `Tropiflora Online`, and press Return/Enter.
4. Type: `Exotic Plants For Your Home and Garden`. Press Return/Enter three times.
5. Type: `Home | Products | Location | Contact Us`.

   You type the "|" or pipe character by holding the Shift key and pressing the "\" key.

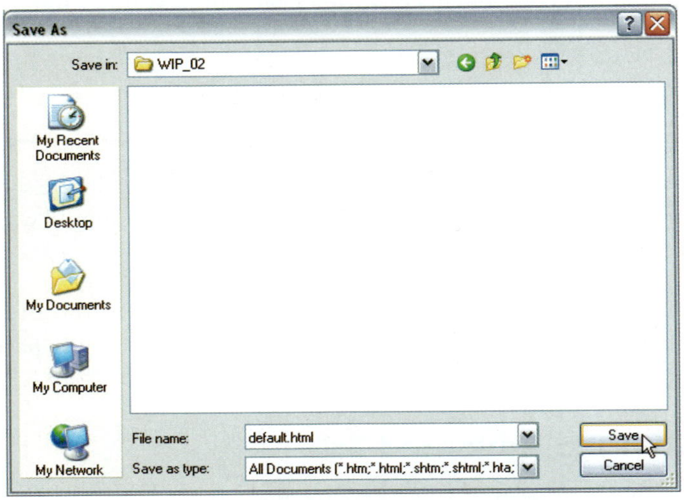


FIGURE 2.53

6. Choose File>Save and save the file as default.html in the Project_02>TO-P2 folder.
7. Click the Save button to complete the process.
8. Preview the Web page in your browser.

   Remember the proverb, "A journey of a thousand miles begins with the first step." This basic Web page is the beginning of a Web site.
9. Return to Dreamweaver.
10. Close default.html.

## To Extend Your Knowledge

### DEFAULT HOME PAGE FILENAME

Every Web site has a home page. When you go to a Web site, generally you don't type the filename of the home page but just the site's ***domain name*** (strings of letters used to name organizations, computers, and addresses on the Internet), such as http://www.ibm.com. The Web server then delivers the site's home page to your browser. With many files on a Web server, how does it know which page to deliver when the visitor does not specify the filename? The Web-hosting service configures a filename as the default, commonly either default.html or index.html.

## 3. Add Another Web Page to Tropiflora Online

Professional Web sites, small or large, consist of multiple pages that describe different aspects of a business, including products, services, and the means by which customers may contact the business. Tropiflora Online is no different, so in this exercise you add pages to the Tropiflora Online site.

1. Choose File>New.
2. From the Category list, choose Basic Page.
3. From the Basic Page category, choose HTML, and then click the Create button.
4. Delete "Untitled Document" from the Title field and replace it with **`About Tropiflora Online`**.
5. In the Document window, type the following text and then press Return/Enter the number of times indicated:

| Type this text | Press Return/Enter |
|---|---|
| **`Tropiflora Online`** | Once |
| **`About Tropiflora`** | Twice |
| **`Home | About Tropiflora | Products | Location | Contact Us`** | None |

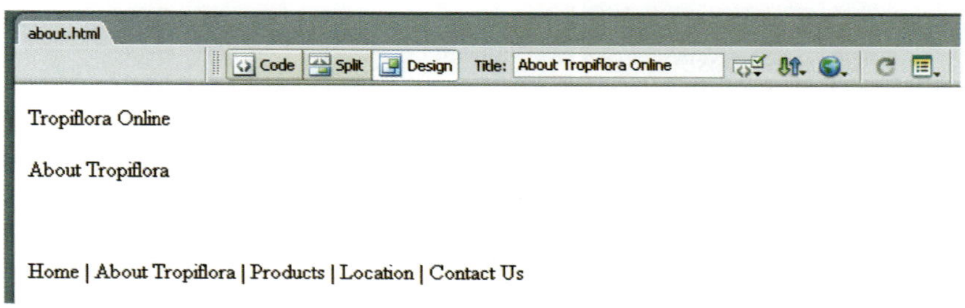


FIGURE 2.54

6. Choose File>Save, type **`about.html`** in the File Name field, and then click Save.
7. Close about.html by choosing File>Close.

## 4. Use Copy/Paste to Create New Pages

Web sites generally have a common look and feel throughout so that visitors know that they are still in the same site and understand where to find the navigation links. As you create the Tropiflora Online site with this design intent, rather than retype the common text, you use Copy and Paste.

1. Choose File>Open Recent and choose about.html from the list.
2. Choose File>New, and click Create at the bottom of the New Document dialog box.

### If you have problems

If you are unsure of the settings in the New Document dialog box for creating a new HTML page, refer to Steps 2 and 3 of the previous Skill Drill.

3. In the Title field, type: **`Products of Tropiflora Online`**.
4. In the Document window, type the following and press Return/Enter, as indicated.

| Type this text | Press Return/Enter |
|---|---|
| `Tropiflora Online` | Once |
| `Products` | Twice |
| `Top Sellers` | Twice |
| `Descriptions` | Twice |

5. Click the about.html Filename tab to bring the about.html tab in front of the Untitled page tab.
6. Drag to select the bottom line of text.
7. Press Control/Command-C to copy the selected text to the clipboard.
8. Click the filename tab to switch to the Untitled file.
9. Choose Edit>Paste (or press Control/Command-V) to paste the text at the bottom of the current page.
10. Choose File>Close, and choose Yes to save the changes.

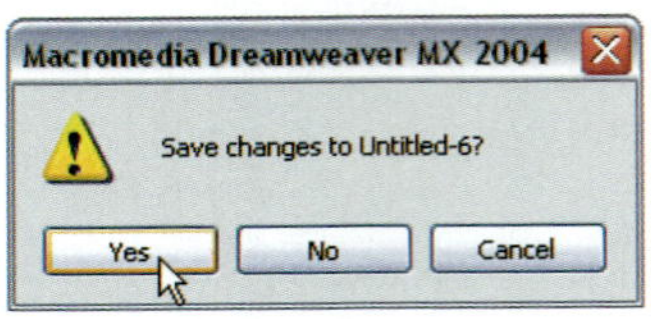


FIGURE 2.55

11. Type **`products.html`** in the File Name field, and click the Save button.

## 5. Import Content from a Microsoft Word Document

The Web designer does not have to type all content for the Web site — in many organizations, other people are responsible for supplying the content. Knowing how to import content from other files from other programs (such as word-processing documents), therefore, saves much typing time.

1. Create a new blank HTML document.

   You may either choose File>New or choose HTML from the Create New category of the Start page.

2. In the Title field, type **`Location of Tropiflora Online`**, and press Enter/Return.
3. If you are using a Windows system, choose File>Import>Word Document, select location.doc, and click Open. Continue with Step 5.
4. If you are using a Macintosh system, open location.txt, and select and copy all of the text onto the clipboard. Close locaton.txt. Paste the copied text into the current untitled page. Continue with Step 5.
5. Click the about.html tab at the top of the Document window.
6. If the navigation-bar paragraph at the bottom of the page is not selected, select it.
7. Copy the paragraph into the clipboard.
8. Switch back to the Untitled page.
9. Move the insertion point to the end of the last line and press Enter/Return.
10. Paste the copied text.

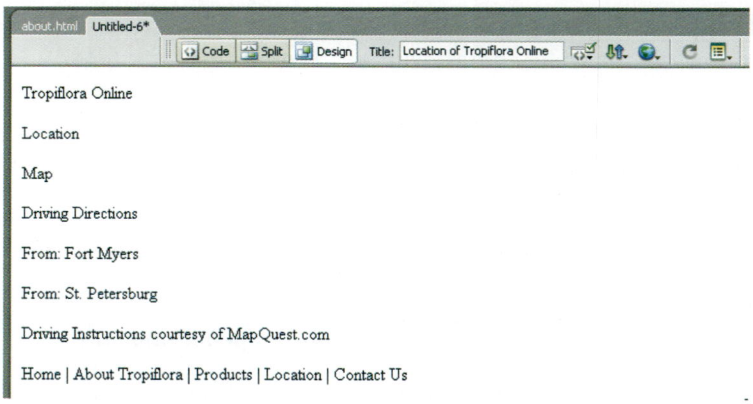


**FIGURE 2.56**

11. Close, saving the changes as "location.html".
12. Close about.html but do not save the changes if prompted — no changes should have been made.

## CHALLENGE

Challenge exercises expand on, or are somewhat related to, skills presented in the lessons. Each exercise provides a brief introduction, followed by instructions in a numbered-step format that are not as detailed as those in the Skill Drill exercises. You should work through the exercises in order.

### 1. Design Your Family's Web Site

In this Challenge exercise, you create a small Web site about your family. You plan the site on paper, and then construct some of the Web pages. The purpose of the exercise is to practice what you learned about planning a Web site, and then put your plan into action by creating some Web pages in Dreamweaver.

1. Before you begin, write the names of your parents, yourself, and your siblings with several spaces between each on a blank sheet of paper. For each family member, write his or her full name, birth date and birthplace, favorite activity or hobby, and one or two other interesting pieces of information about him or her. Create an email address for each using the format **`firstname@lastname.com`**.
2. In Dreamweaver, use the Advanced tab of the Site Definition dialog box to define a Web site named with your father's last name. Set the Local Root Folder to Project_02>Family.
3. Create a new HTML page with the family's last name at the top and the names of the family members below. Save the page as "home.html".
4. Create a new HTML page. Type your name at the top, type the information you wrote about yourself in paragraphs below, and end with your email address.
5. Select your email address and type your email address in the Link field of the Property inspector. Don't forget to precede the email address with **`mailto:`** in the Link field.
6. At the bottom of the page, type: **`Return to our home page`**.
7. Select the last paragraph, type **`home.html`** in the Link field, and then close, saving the Web page using your first name followed by .html as the filename.
8. Repeat Steps 4 to 7 for each family member, using his or her first name as the filename followed by .html.
9. When you have completed all of the individual pages, reopen home.html.
10. One by one, select each person's name and create a link to his or her page.
11. Preview the page in your browser (save when prompted) and test all of the links.
12. Close your browser and return to Dreamweaver. Close home.html.

## 2. Print a Web Page and Its Source Code

1. Open challenge1.html from the Challenges_02 site.
2. Preview the page in your browser.
3. Print the page from your browser.
4. Right/Control-click and choose View Source (or View Source Code, depending on your browser).
5. Print the source code.
6. Close the application used to view the source code (unless it happens to be Dreamweaver). Keep both Dreamweaver and your browser open for the next exercise.

## 3. Learn Techniques from the Code of Another Web Page

As you know, it is beneficial to examine the code of other sites that you admire, to see how the designer created them. You can then apply the knowledge to your own work (not just copying and pasting their code into your Web pages). In this Challenge exercise, you compare the printouts of the Web page and the code from the previous exercise to learn how the designer of these pages has constructed different text styles, such as bold, italic, and the large font size.

1. Find three occurrences each of bold and italic in the Web-page printout. Identify, in the code printout, the coding methods used to create each style.
2. Identify the code that makes the text size of the top paragraph larger than the rest.
3. In the code, identify the document title.
4. Determine where the document title appears in the browser and in the printout from the browser.
5. Close your browser.
6. Return to Dreamweaver and close challenge1.html.

# PORTFOLIO BUILDER

## Recognize How Sites are Structured

The underlying purpose of all Web sites is the presentation or delivery of information — also known as content. For information to be useful, it must be easily accessible, which requires that it be broken out into discrete categories. The method employed to categorize the information contained in a site is known as the site's structure. Your assignment is to create physical flow charts that reflect how three different Web sites are structured.

1. Select three different sites to use for the assignment.
2. Draw a rectangle at the top of a blank piece of paper and label it "home" or "index".
3. For the first site you selected, determine what major categories fall under the top box. Examples might be "About Us", "Products", "Press Releases", or similar categories.
4. Draw boxes underneath the "home" box and label them appropriately according to the categories you identified in Step 3.
5. Many of these categories offer further information broken into their own individual pages. Continue drawing boxes for each subcategory until you've charted the top three levels of the site.
6. Repeat the process for the other two sites you have chosen.
7. Keep the drawings around for reference when you're designing your own sites.

PROJECT 3

# Applying Structure to Text

## OBJECTIVES

*In this project, you learn how to*

- Structure a document with headings
- Insert line breaks in a paragraph
- Format quotations with HTML tags
- Separate content with a horizontal rule
- Use ordered and unordered lists
- Change bullet and number styles with CSS
- Create definition lists

## WHY WOULD I DO THIS?

Creating print publications has much in common with creating Web sites — both require good content and effective design. Award-winning children's books, for instance, typically have authors who write the copy, and illustrators and publishers who focus on the look and feel or design of the books. Similarly, Web sites require quality content as well as effective layout and design. That quality Web content has two dimensions — it must be meaningful and useful to your visitors, but it must also be structured correctly so that it is understandable and accessible to those same visitors. In this project you learn about the structure that underlies a Web page, why that structure is important, and how to create it.

In Project 2, you learned to plan the content of a Web site and to structure the site for easy use by visitors. You must also carefully structure the text that you put into your site, not just type it on a page and style it, as you might do for a print publication. The structure that you use is the initial basis for accessibility, a requirement for many Web sites and a key consideration for others.

Novice Web designers all too often use boldfacing and large-sized letters to indicate that particular text is a heading for the paragraphs following it. They may also use distinctive colors, fonts, and other stylistic changes. Blind users who use ***screen readers*** (computer applications that read the content aloud) to browse the Internet cannot see these stylistic changes. Instead they depend on the Web page's author to properly construct the page with headings, paragraphs, and other document structures that their screen readers can understand. Some such applications can be told (via keystrokes) to sound out just the headings, enabling listening users to skim through the headings of a document in much the same way that sighted users skip from heading to heading to see if a document or Web page may contain what they are looking for. A lack of proper headings or improper use of headings confuses users of screen readers in the same way that a book without chapter breaks can confuse sighted readers.

Lack of proper document structure negatively impacts not only users of screen-reader software, but others, as well. Some visitors use browsers that are character-based, such as the Lynx browser, which does not display styles. For their own needs, other visitors set up their browsers to use their own style settings in place of those of the Web page —paragraphs that the author made large-sized and bold text to suggest a heading would thus be reduced to mere, plain-text paragraphs. Search engines rate the quality of a page for a particular topic based, in part, on the content in headings. It is also just good form to use headings. As Patrick Lynch and Sarah Horton state in the *Web Style Guide*, "Don't get so lost in the novelty of Web pages that basic standards of editorial and graphic design are tossed aside." It is not surprising that some Web-design training organizations even offer courses in writing skills, such as "Business Writing Basics for the Web" by the HTML Writers Guild.

Many tags have ***physical appearances***, a particular look or style. In order to differentiate them from body-text paragraphs, headings tend to have the physical appearance of larger character sizes and boldfacing. Other tags may include italics or indenting, for example, as part of their physical appearance. However, structural tags, such as headings, paragraphs, lists, and block quotes, also have a ***logical significance*** — these tags play a role in the structure of the document. Headings identify the content in the following paragraphs, ordered lists are numbered lists of information, and block quotes contain material quoted from another source. Novice designers commonly use the **<blockquote>** tag solely for its physical appearance — left and right indenting — or the **<address>** tag because it italicizes the text it encloses, ignoring the intended logical significance they convey. The reverse is also true: many novice designers apply a larger font size and bold styling to a paragraph tag (**<p>**) to make it seem to be a heading. It may look like a heading but, stripped of the style applied to it, the heading is nothing more than a short paragraph, which is all a screen-reader user would "see." Clearly you need to understand the basics of good writing constructs and which HTML tags to use, after which you may apply specific style(s) to add more flair to the appearance of your Web page.

In this project, you learn about block elements and list elements, and then use them to format text. ***Block elements*** are HTML tags that structure a unit (block) of text and separate such units with white space. Included in this group are heading tags, paragraph tags, the **<blockquote>** tag, and the horizontal-rule tag. You explore the line-break tag in this chapter. You also learn to use ordered lists, unordered lists, and definition lists.

## VISUAL SUMMARY

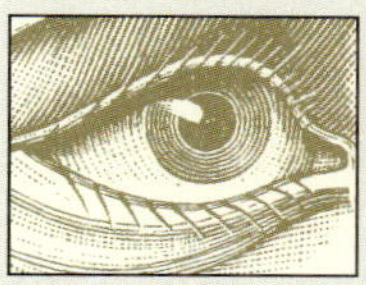

In this project, you use Dreamweaver to format headings, block quotes, and lists. There are different methods for applying functions and features. You explore some of these components while you learn about document structure and its importance to the message that you would like your Web site to convey.

The Insert bar at the top of the Document window has several different modes. Using the Insert bar pop-up menu, you may choose the mode that has the functions and features you need to perform the current task. In this project you use the HTML and Text modes of the Insert bar.

The Text Insert bar provides access to HTML tags that structure text in a Web page. You use the block-quote function to format large quotations, headings to identify the topics of content paragraphs, and list tags to format ordered (numbered) or unordered (bulleted) lists. While you probably haven't encountered definition lists outside of Web pages, in Web work you use them for associating a term with its definition or description. You use the preformatted-text tag when you want to preserve extra spaces, tabs, and carriage returns in the Web page; normally, Web browsers ignore these items.

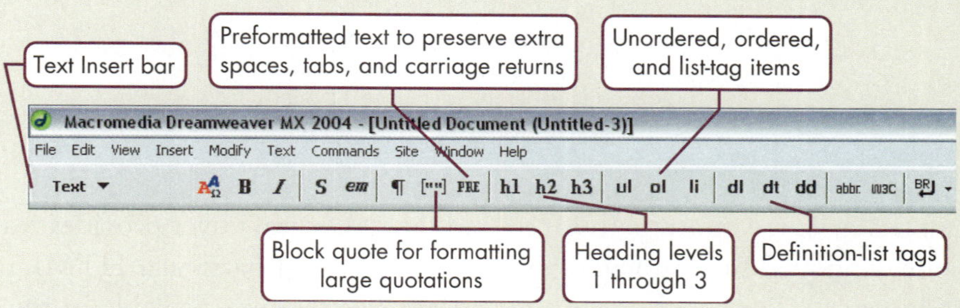


FIGURE 3.1

You use the Other Characters button at the right end of the Text Insert bar to insert characters that are helpful in text but not easily typed. As with most word-processing software, these characters are available from menus or dialog boxes. In Dreamweaver, the drop-down list provides access to the most common characters. The main button on the Text Insert bar displays an icon representing the last-used character. You can insert this character by just clicking the button — you don't need to select it from the list. At the bottom of the list is the Other Characters option, which opens the Insert Other Character dialog box, enabling you to select characters that you may need less frequently than those in the list.

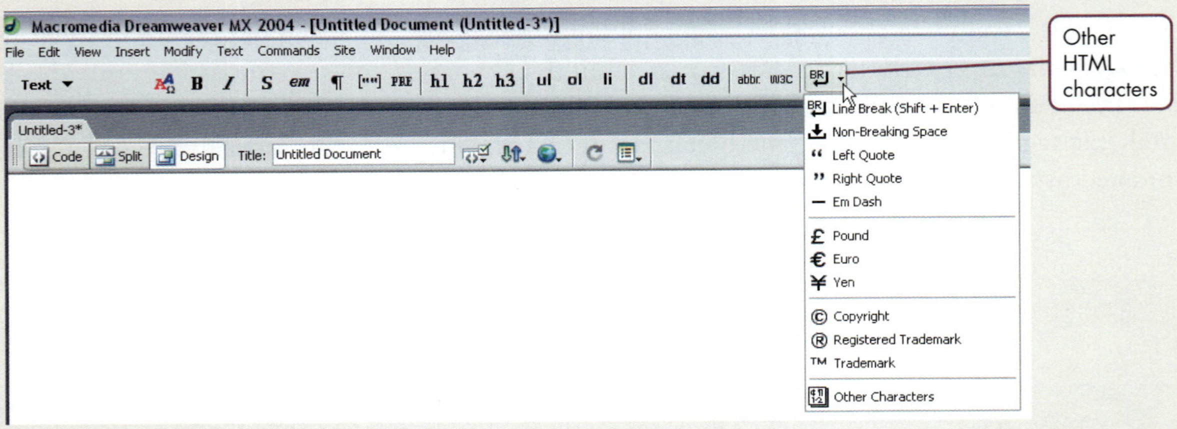


**FIGURE 3.2**

You use the Property inspector frequently in this and future projects. It may be the most commonly used component of the Dreamweaver interface as it provides access to the most commonly used functions. The Format menu allows you to format paragraphs or headings. You may create unordered and ordered lists using the appropriate buttons in the Property inspector. Text Outdent and Text Indent buttons perform two functions: you can use them to turn off and on (respectively) the **<blockquote>** tag. When combined with either ordered or unordered lists, the Text Indent button enables you to nest a list in another list.

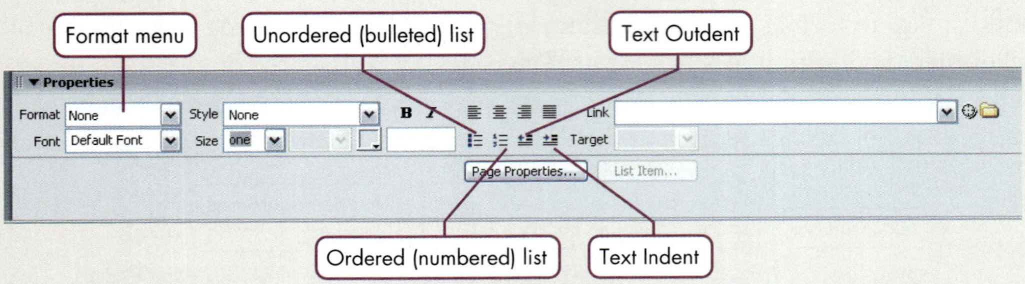


**FIGURE 3.3**

In addition to mouse-oriented controls (buttons and lists), Dreamweaver provides features for hand-coders in the Code window. This window offers many options for particular HTML tags that are not available from a button or list — all options for all HTML tags are available in the Code window.

Dreamweaver also reduces the need to memorize the various options by presenting a Code-Hint pop-up list of valid options for a particular tag. ***Valid*** means that the code adheres to the standard set by the W3C. For example, <running> is not an HTML tag as defined by the W3C and, therefore, is not valid; neither are the Canadian/British spellings of colour and centre. Although **`bgcolor`** (background color) may be an attribute of the **`<body>`** tag in HTML 4 and earlier, **`bgcolor`** is not an attribute of the **`<img>`** image tag so using it in the **`<img>`** tag is not valid. The **`bgcolor`** attribute has been removed in XHTML 1.1, and, therefore, it is not valid even for the **`<body>`** tag in that version of XHTML. The Code-Hint pop-up list only displays attributes that are valid for the specific tag and HTML version.

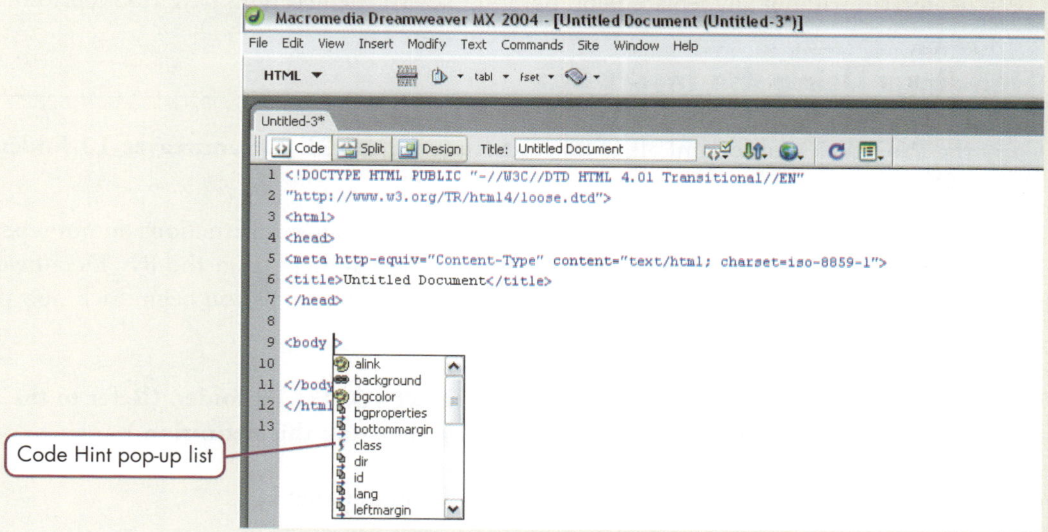


FIGURE 3.4

## LESSON 1 Inserting Headings

There are six heading levels — the largest is Heading 1 and the smallest is Heading 6. Heading 4 is the same size as normal paragraph text. Heading tags, in addition to formatting the enclosed text as a block, also boldface the text.

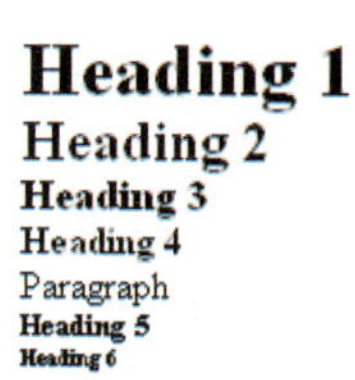


FIGURE 3.5

Every Web page should have a title, not only in the Title bar but also in the browser window. The document Title field (in the Document toolbar), which adds the document title to the **`<title>`** tag, does not produce visible text in the browser window, the area that is normally thought of as the Web page, but just to the Title bar of the browser. The document title is primarily significant to search engines, but its absence from the body of the Web page makes that page harder for viewers to understand. For this reason, you should create a title for each page and use Heading 1 for emphasis. You may use Heading 2 to create either a secondary title or sections in the document. Similarly, you may use Heading 3 and so on to further subdivide the document.

The HTML code for headings is very simple and follows a simple pattern: `<h1>...</h1>` is for Heading 1, `<h2>...</h2>` for Heading 2, and so on. Alignment (left, center, and right) is an attribute option of headings, but the alignment attribute has been deprecated in favor of CSS. ***Deprecated*** means that an item is marked for removal in a future version of HTML; the phrase ***in favor of CSS,*** used in this type of situation, suggests that the CSS property (`text-align`) can be used instead of the HTML (`align`) attribute. Some HTML tags and attributes have been deprecated without any replacement, but most stylistic deprecations have CSS replacements.

## Insert Headings Using the Insert Bar

**1** **Copy the Project_03 folder and all of its contents from the RF_Dreamweaver_L1 folder to your WIP folder.**

This step will prepare all of the files you need for Project_03. These instructions do not repeat in any later projects. You may either copy the remaining Project folders from the RF_Dreamweaver_L1 folder to your WIP folder now, or you may continue to copy them as you begin each new project in this book.

**2** **Create a site definition called TO-P3 using the Project_03>TO-P3 folder. (Refer to the instructions in Skill Drill 1 of Project 2 if you need help in creating this definition.)**

**3** **Open default.html by double-clicking the file in the Files panel.**

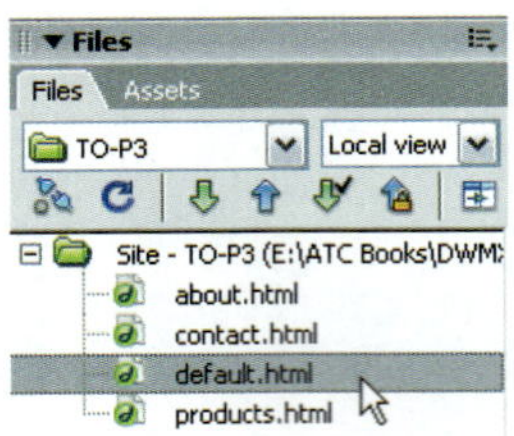


FIGURE 3.6

**4** **Click anywhere in the top line of text Tropiflora Online.**

**5** **Choose Text from the pop-up menu on the Insert bar.**

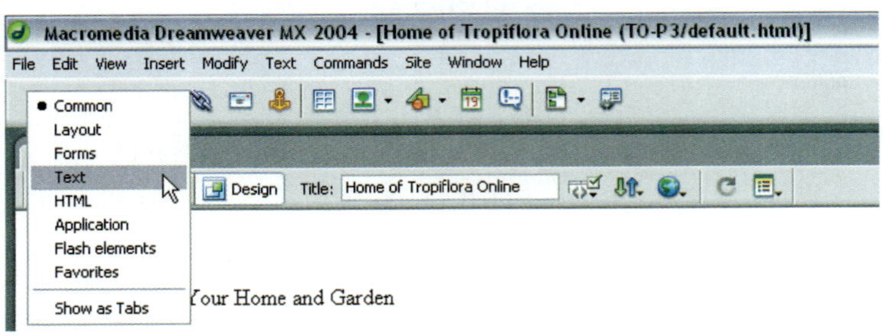


FIGURE 3.7

**6** **Click the h1 (Heading 1) button in the Insert bar.**

Observe that the block of text, Tropiflora Online, is now large and boldfaced. Heading 1 is the most important heading and produces the largest text.

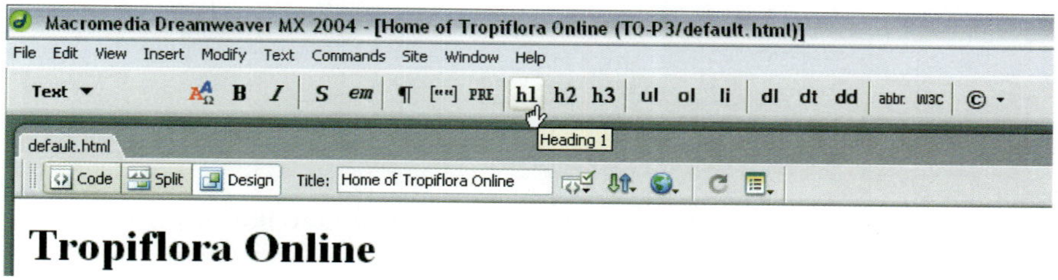


FIGURE 3.8

**7** **Click the <h1> tag in the Tag selector at the bottom of the Document window.**

Observe that the whole line is selected. This indicates that the **<h1>** tag is a block tag because Heading 1 has been applied to the entire block of text, even though you didn't select the text before applying the Heading 1. (In this figure, the Property inspector has been dragged up closer to the text so that you may easily see both.)

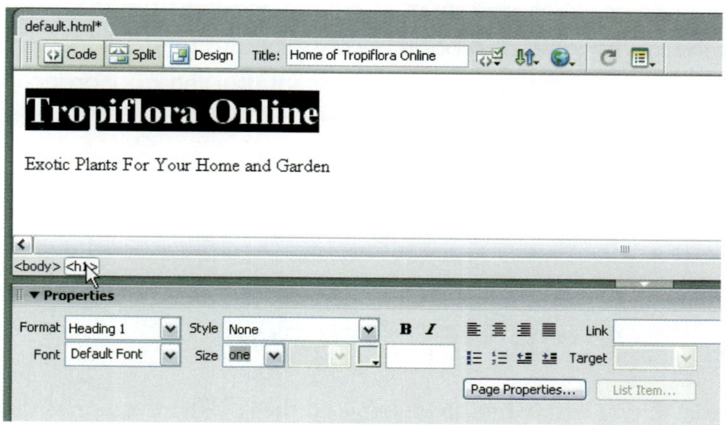


FIGURE 3.9

**8** **Observe the Format field of the Property inspector, and note that it too shows that the selected text uses the Heading 1 format.**

**9** **Click the Split button at the top of the Document window and examine the code of the selected Heading 1 text.**

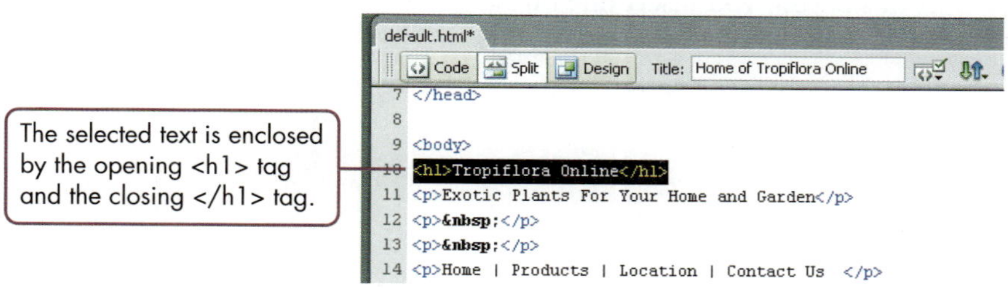


FIGURE 3.10

**10** Close the Code window by clicking the Design button at the top of the Document window.

**11** Click in the second line of the document (Exotic Plants For Your Home and Garden). Click the h2 button on the Insert bar to format the line as a Heading 2 block.

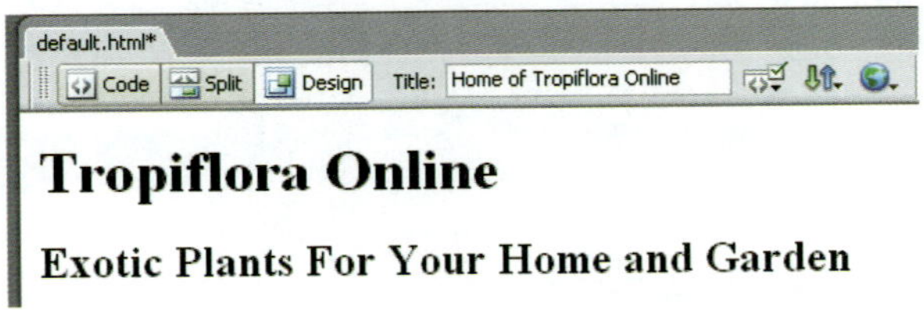


FIGURE 3.11

**12** Choose File>Close to close the document, saving the changes when prompted.

## To Extend Your Knowledge

### THE HEADINGS ARE TOO LARGE

A common complaint of novice Web designers is that the headings are too large. It is not uncommon to see Heading 3 as the top heading of a page because the designer felt Headings 1 and 2 were too large. Using headings provides structure to the document, but the appearance of the headings is a matter of style. You can easily modify the style and preserve the document structure. If it is appropriate to use Heading 2, then use it and style it smaller if it is too large for your design.

## LESSON 2 Inserting Line Breaks

Paragraphs are large blocks of text with white space between them. When you press the Enter/Return key after typing, you create a new paragraph with white space separating it from what precedes or follows. There are times, however, when you need to keep a block of text together and treat it as a single unit, but want parts of it to appear on successive lines. Consider the format of an address, for example — the entire block of text is the full address, but you usually separate the components of an address onto different lines.

Line breaks keep the content in the same paragraph block but force a new line of text to start at the left margin. The line-break code is very useful when you want to separate items but don't want the items to be in different paragraphs. In this lesson, you insert line breaks using two methods. You also examine the line-break tag, `<br>`, in the Code window.

## Insert Line Breaks in a Paragraph

**1** **Right/Control-click contact.html in the Files panel and choose Open to open the file.**

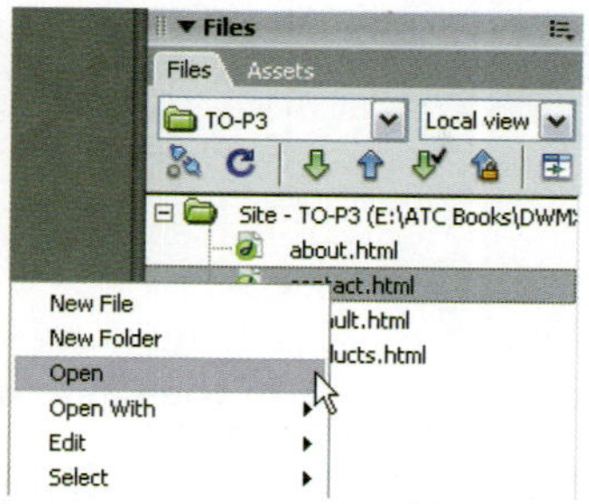


FIGURE 3.12

**2** **Click in the empty paragraph space between the Heading 3 lines (Mailing Address: and Phone Numbers:).**

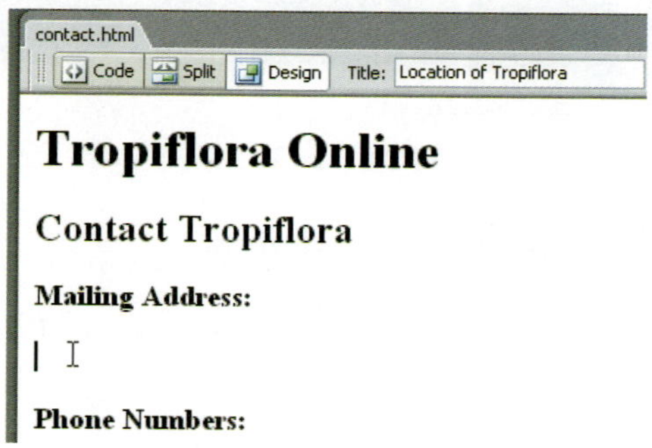


FIGURE 3.13

**3** **Type `Tropiflora`, press Shift-Enter/Return, and type `3530 Tallevast Road`.**

Observe that the space between the two lines you just typed is smaller than the space between other blocks. A line break just forces text onto another line, but the text remains in the same block.

FIGURE 3.14

**4** **Press Shift-Enter/Return, type `Sarasota, FL`, press Shift-Enter/Return, and type `34243-3890` to complete the address.**

**5** **Click the <p> paragraph tag from the Tag selector at the bottom of the Document window.**

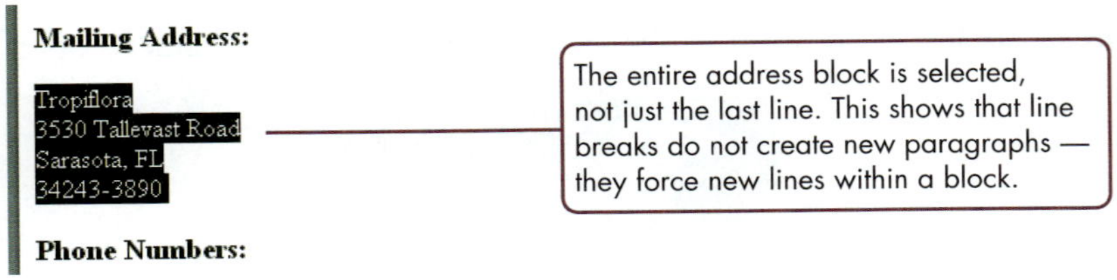


**FIGURE 3.15**

**6** **Click the Split button and observe the code in the Code window.**

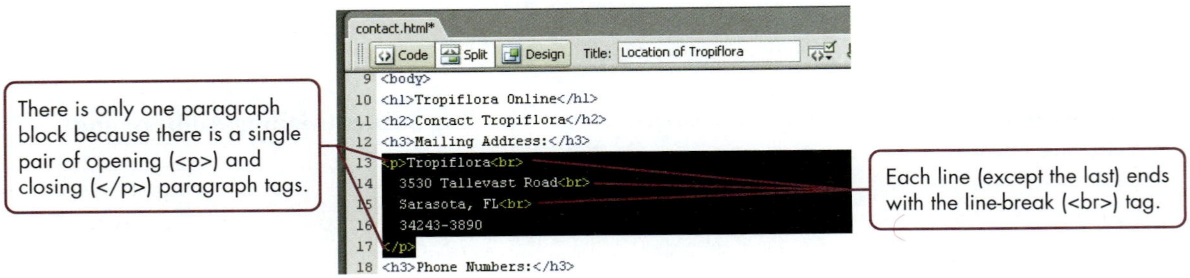


**FIGURE 3.16**

**7** **Click the Design button to close the Code window.**

**8** **Click in the blank paragraph between Phone Numbers: and Email Address:.**

**9** **Type: `Telephone: (941) 351-2267`.**

**10** **Click the drop-down list arrow to the right of the Line Break button (the last button on the Insert bar), and choose Line Break from the list.**

This is another method for inserting a line break. You can also use this method to insert other special characters.

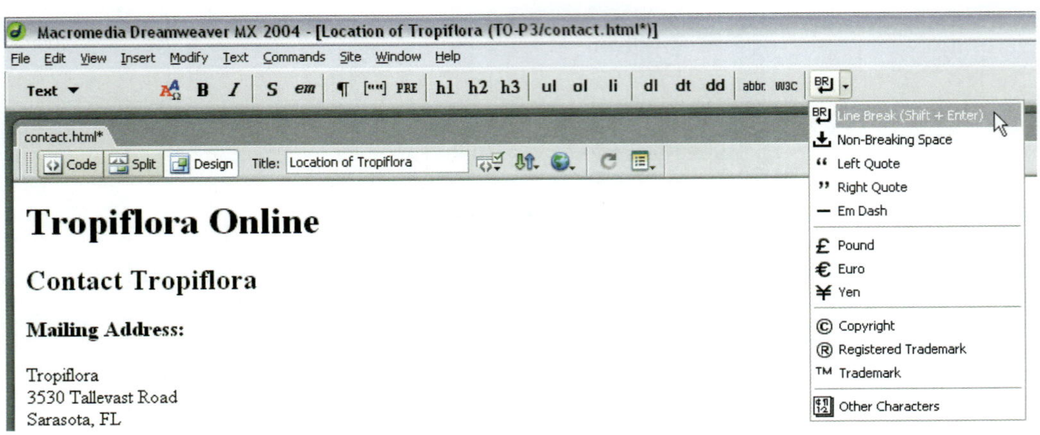


**FIGURE 3.17**

### If you have problems

If the Insert bar does not display the Text options, click the pop-up menu on the left of the Insert bar and choose Text.

11 **Type `Fax: (941) 351-6985` on the new line.**

12 **Choose File>Close to close contact.html, saving the changes when prompted.**

## To Extend Your Knowledge

### OTHER METHODS OF CREATING BREAKS

The break tag (**<br>**) is often used to break a block into separate lines without creating a new paragraph for each line. By default, paragraph tags insert extra white space between the paragraphs, whereas a **<br>** tag simply pushes the text to the next line. When formatting an address, you would commonly use the **<br>** tag to split each part of an address onto different lines. However, you can use the CSS **display** property to create the appearance of breaks in content.

Paragraphs and headings are blocks: the text in each is separated from other blocks by white space above and below. The anchor tag (**<a>**), the **<strong>** tag, and many other tags are inline tags. ***Inline tags*** do not create blocks from the enclosed content, but apply their style or functionality within the blocks. You can use the CSS **display** property to modify the layout appearance of inline content. For example, a paragraph containing only two links, such as **<p><a href="home.html">**Home**</a> <a href="about.html">**About Us**</a></p>**, appears as two links on the same line. However, if you add **style="display: block"** to each of the opening anchor tags, you change the default layout of the anchor tag from inline to block, forcing the links to display on separate lines as if they were blocks. In this way, you can create the appearance of line breaks using CSS instead of the **<br>** tag.

You may be thinking that **<br>** is much less to type each time than **style="display: block"**, but there are more efficient and advanced ways of creating and applying CSS to eliminate the duplication and make it simple to change the layout of the anchor tag to a block appearance.

# LESSON 3 Formatting a Large Quotation on a Web Page

While you or your associates will probably write most of the content on your Web sites, at times you may want to use material written by others. For instance, you might wish to use a quotation from someone else. The block quote is one of two methods you can use to format it.

The block quote, as its name suggests, is meant to format a large quotation, one large enough to warrant its own paragraph. The **<blockquote>** tag may contain one or more paragraphs, and you must surround each paragraph with the **<p>** paragraph tag. The minimum application of the **<blockquote>** tag is: **<blockquote><p>...</p></blockquote>**. Dreamweaver properly inserts paragraph tags in the **<blockquote>** tag for you: you don't have to worry about applying the paragraph format in addition to the block-quote format. Use just one pair of **<blockquote>** tags, even if a single quotation consists of multiple paragraphs — do not surround each separate paragraph with the **<blockquote>** tag.

The default appearance of the **<blockquote>** tag indents the paragraph on both the left and right. For this reason, the **<blockquote>** tag is one of the most misused HTML tags. Novice Web designers often use this tag just for its indented appearance. Many Web-design applications must also take the blame for this because they label the on/off buttons for block quotes with Text Indent and Text Outdent, as if to suggest that only style is affected; in fact, as you have just learned, the tag also has a structural purpose. Dreamweaver uses Text Indent/Outdent buttons as well as the Block Quote button to provide the block-quote structure.

The source of a quotation is known as the "citation." The **<blockquote>** tag supports this concept with the **cite** attribute. The **cite** attribute only supports a Web link as the source of the quotation, but the **<blockquote>** tag does not provide a link to the source of the quotation. Only the Mozilla browsers allow you to view the source of the citation as a property of the **<blockquote>** tag; a visitor using any other browser must view the Web page's source code to find the citation source.

In this lesson, you insert a quotation into a Web page and format the paragraphs as a block quote. You also add the citation source to the **<blockquote>** tag using the Code window.

## Insert a Block Quote

1. **Open about.html from the Files panel.**

2. **Click in the empty paragraph space below the About Tropiflora Heading 2 block.**

3. **If you are using a Windows system, choose File>Import>Word Document, select about.txt, and click Open.**

   **If you are using a Macintosh system, open about.txt, select all of the text in the file, copy it to the clipboard, and then close about.txt. Paste the text into about.html below the About Tropiflora Heading 2 block.**

4. **Click in the second inserted paragraph that begins with "Our desire was to make Tropiflora...".**

**5** **Click the Text Indent button in the Property inspector.**

Observe that the paragraph is indented from both the left and right edges of the Document window.

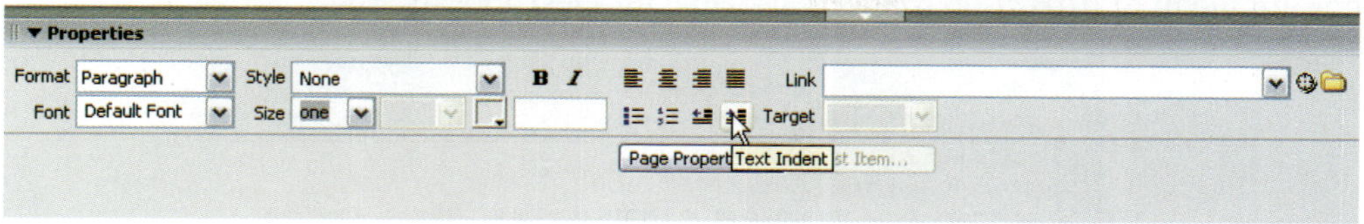


FIGURE 3.18

**6** **Click in the following paragraph that begins with "Come visit us online…". Click the Block Quote button near the middle of the Text Insert bar.**

This is another method for formatting a block as a block quote.

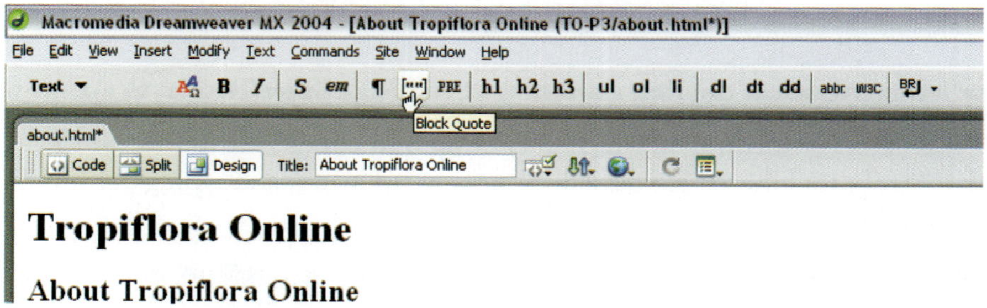


FIGURE 3.19

**7** **Click the `<blockquote>` tag from the Tag selector at the bottom of the Document window.**

Observe that both paragraphs are selected. The `<blockquote>` tag may contain multiple paragraphs.

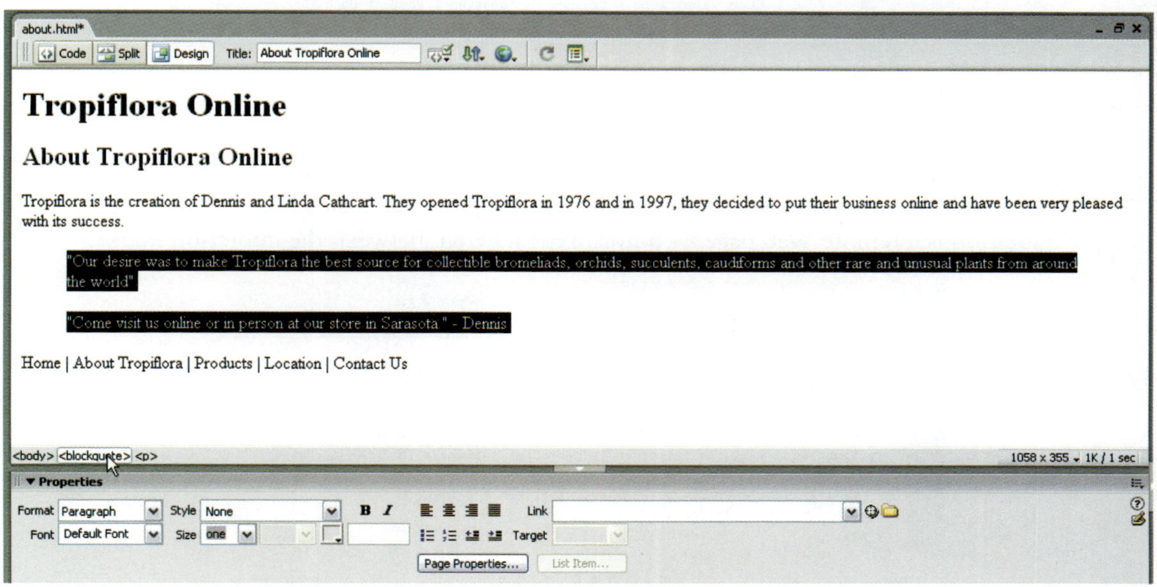


FIGURE 3.20

**8** **Click the Split button.**

**9** **Move the insertion point inside the `<blockquote>` tag just before the closing angle bracket (>), and press the Spacebar once.**

A pop-up menu of ***attributes*** (options available for tags) appears.

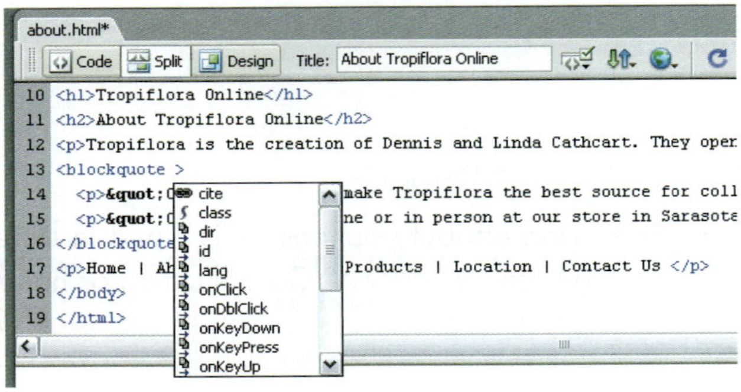


**FIGURE 3.21**

**10** **Press the letter c to select the first attribute, `cite`. Press Enter/Return to accept the selection.**

Dreamweaver's HTML editor makes it very simple to choose attributes for each tag — only the appropriate attributes for each tag display in the pop-up menu, and typing part of the attribute name selects it from the list.

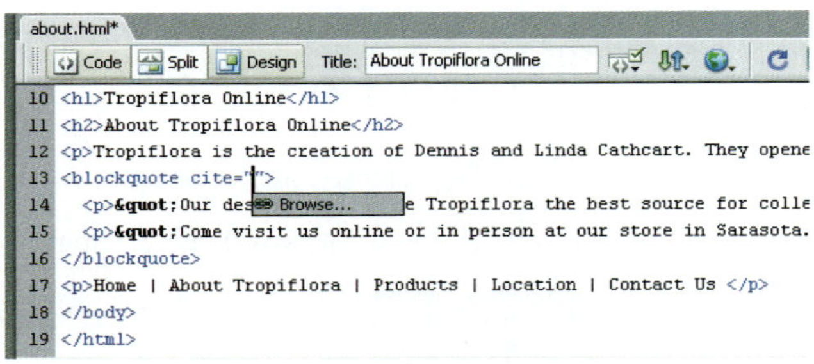


**FIGURE 3.22**

**11** **Type `http://www.tropiflora.com` between the quotation marks.**

The Browse option allows you to select a Web page using the File dialog box. However, if the source of the quotation is a remote Web page, you must type its URL between the quotation marks.

**FIGURE 3.23**

**12** **Switch back to the Design view. Press Control/Command-S to save the changes to about.html, leaving it open for the next lesson.**

## To Extend Your Knowledge

### THE CASE FOR HTML

Do you know the origin of the terms uppercase and lowercase? When printing-press operators of the nineteenth century and earlier required characters for their presses, they would retrieve the characters from their storage compartments, which were arranged in cases. Capital letters were stored in the upper case, and the smaller letters were stored in the lower case.

All HTML code — tags, attributes, and attribute options — is typed in lowercase characters. Web designers of the 1990s, whether they used a WYSIWYG application or hand-coded the HTML, commonly used uppercase characters for tags, attributes, and attribute options to distinguish them from the mixed-case characters of body text. Beginning with XHTML 1.0, however, it was recommended that all HTML, CSS, and JavaScript code be written in lowercase characters. As you recall, XHTML is an improvement on HTML that brings it closer to ***XML*** (eXtensible Markup Language). XML requires all tags, attributes, and attribute options to be in lowercase characters. This consistency ensures that an XML or XHTML browser doesn't have to convert uppercase tags to lowercase before interpreting them, thus reducing its processing time.

The only HTML tag that may use uppercase is the ***DTD*** (Document Type Definition) tag, otherwise known as the "Doctype." This tag precedes the opening **<html>** tag and, for that reason, may be written in uppercase. The Doctype that you commonly use with Dreamweaver is **<!DOCTYPE HTML PUBLIC "-//W3C//DTD HTML 4.01 Transitional//EN" "http://www.w3.org/TR/html4/loose.dtd">** which is for HTML 4.01.

## LESSON 4 Inserting a Short Quotation in a Paragraph

The **<q>** or quote tag is an ***inline*** tag — its content is contained in a block. You cannot use it by itself to create a block. You must insert an inline quotation into a paragraph or other block. This is different from the block quote, which formats its contents as a paragraph.

The physical appearance of the **<q>** quote tag surrounds the quoted text with quotation marks, although the text itself is not otherwise styled any differently than normal paragraph text. While the Opera and Mozilla browsers display the quotation marks, Internet Explorer does not. Given Internet Explorer's dominance in the browser market, it is tempting to counter this deficiency by manually inserting quotation marks in the text. However, the W3C specifically recommends against this to prevent two sets of quotation marks in compliant bowsers. Older browsers do not display the quotation marks around text that is marked up with the **<q>** tag — these browsers display the text using the default text styles of the surrounding paragraph.

You may use CSS, however, to style the text in the **<q>** tag, such as by using italics or a different color. This provides some indication that the text is a quotation. You should ensure that phraseology of adjacent text makes it clear that the specific text is a quotation, such as, "Queen Elizabeth was heard to say *Two lumps of* *sugar, please* when she placed her order for tea at Burger King." We use italics here to highlight the quotation, but even without the quotation marks, the quotation is distinct from the surrounding text. Another method you could use is JavaScript, which has functions that enable it to detect which browser the visitor is using. If the JavaScript code detects that the browser is Internet Explorer, JavaScript can surround quoted content (marked up with the **<q>** tags) with quotation marks; if any other browser is detected, JavaScript allows those browsers to insert quotation marks on their own.

In this lesson, you use the Tag chooser, an excellent utility for inserting HTML tags (and other tags) that are unavailable from the menus. The Tag chooser also enables you to apply the attributes of the tag. The **<q>** tag, for example, is not available from any of the menus and must be inserted via the Code window or the Tag chooser.

## Insert the Quote Tag

**1** **In the open file about.html, move the insertion point to the end of the block quote (to the right of "Dennis").**

**2** **Press Enter/Return once, and then click the Text Outdent button in the Property inspector.**

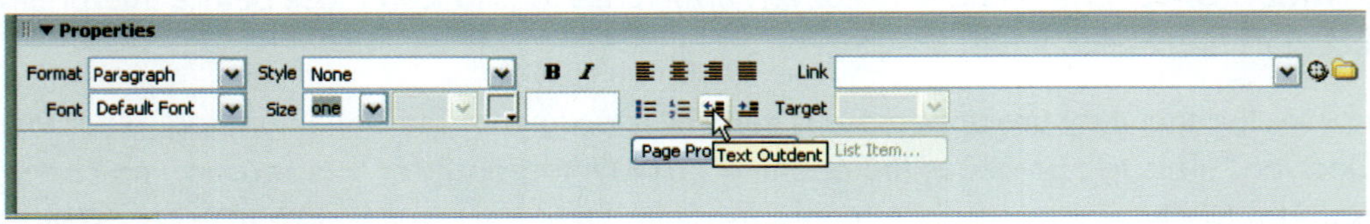


FIGURE 3.24

**3** **Type:** `Linda says These plants bring joy to our lives, let them bring joy to yours.`

**4** **Drag to select the text from "These" to "yours".**

**5** **Click the Tag chooser from the Common Insert bar.**

### ? If you have problems

If the Insert bar shows Text at the left or anything other than Common, click Text (or the other word) and choose Common from the list.

**6** **In the top-left window of the Tag Chooser dialog box, click the plus sign to the left of HTML Tags.**

**7** **Click Formatting and Layout, scroll down and click q, then click Insert.**

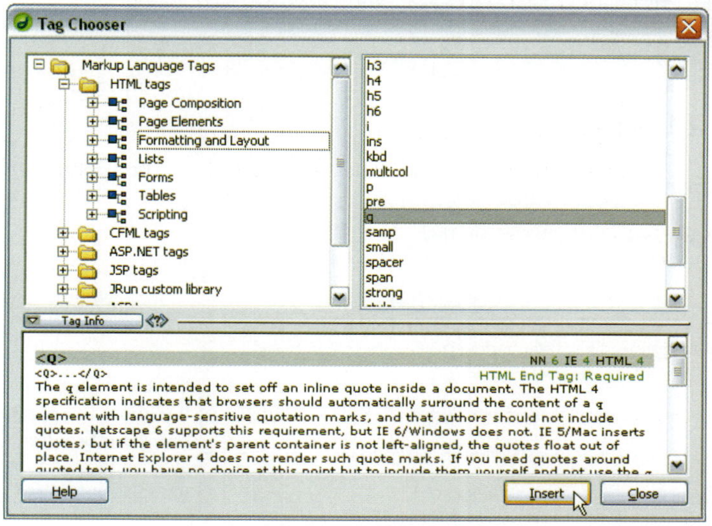

FIGURE 3.25

**8** **In the Tag Editor dialog box, type `http://www.tropiflora.com` in the Cite field, click OK, and then click Close.**

The first time you clicked Insert in the Tag Chooser dialog box after selecting **q**, the **<q>** tag was inserted into the document. The Tag Editor dialog box allows you to apply some of the attributes available for the **<q>** tag; you don't want to insert another one.

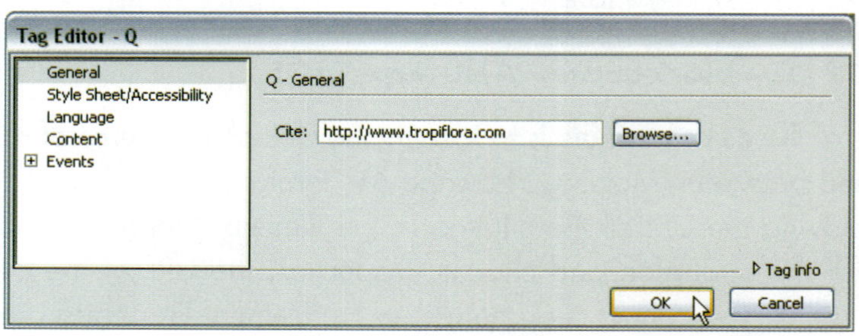


FIGURE 3.26

9 **Preview the page in your browser.**

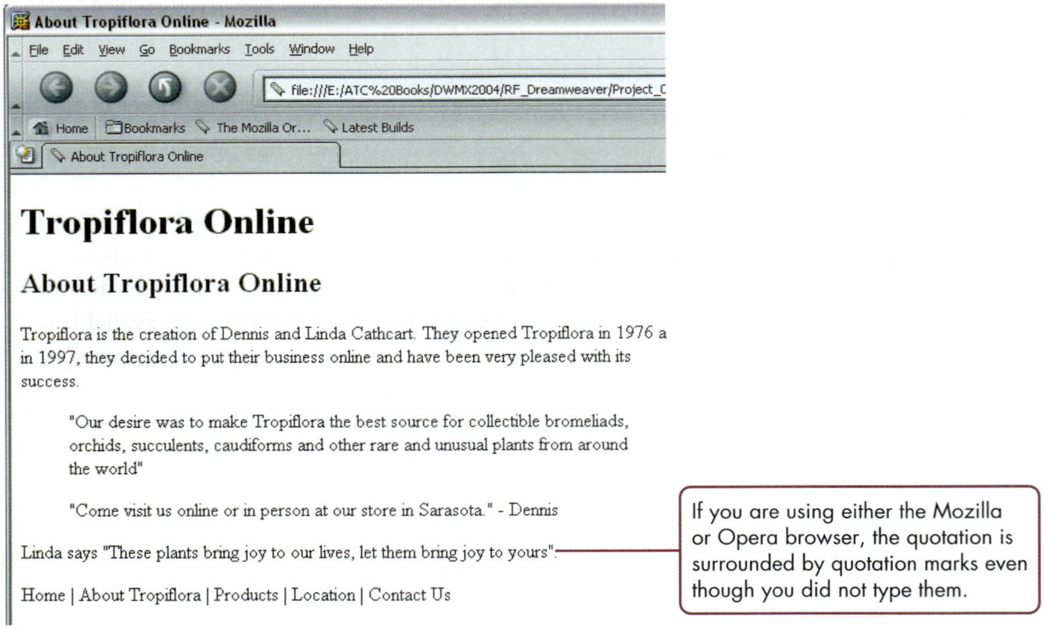


FIGURE 3.27

10 **Return to Dreamweaver.**

11 **Click the Design button and then close about.html.**

## *To Extend Your Knowledge*

### THE CITE ATTRIBUTE OF <blockquote> AND <q> TAGS

The primary purpose of the `cite` attribute is to identify the URL of the source of a quotation. However, only the Mozilla-based browsers (Mozilla, Netscape 6+, Firefox, and Camino) actually make use of this attribute by displaying the URL of the citation in the Element Properties dialog box. When you Right/Command-click the quotation and choose Properties, the URL of the citation displays. The URL, however, is not a link; you cannot click the URL in the Element Properties dialog box to go to the citation source.

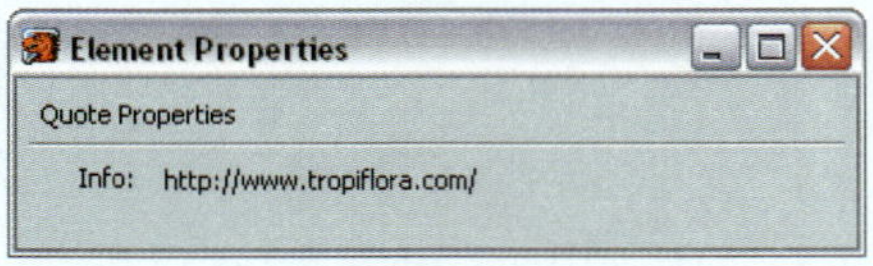


FIGURE 3.28

# LESSON 5 Separating Content Using a Horizontal Rule

The term ***horizontal rule*** comes from the print-publishing arena — it is simply a horizontal line. Although it is not used to format text, it is considered a block element because it forces apart other blocks when inserted. You cannot have a horizontal rule and a paragraph on the same line; both are blocks so they separate from one another with white space above or below.

The horizontal-rule tag, `<hr>`, has very few attributes: **`width`**, **`color`**, **`noshade`**, and **`size`**, but all have been deprecated in favor of CSS. The purpose of the **`noshade`** attribute is to eliminate the 3-D default appearance of a horizontal rule and make it just a flat colored line. Although no CSS property is yet available to replace the 3-D appearance of a horizontal rule, you can replace all other attributes of horizontal rules using CSS.

The horizontal rule is one of the few elements of HTML that does not contain content yet behaves like a block element by pushing the following paragraph below it. In this lesson, you insert horizontal rules to divide the main content of Web pages from the text that becomes navigation links in a later project.

## Insert a Horizontal Rule

1. **Open default.html.**

2. **Click in front of the "H" of Home in the bottom paragraph of the page.**

3. **Choose HTML from the pop-up menu of the Insert bar.**

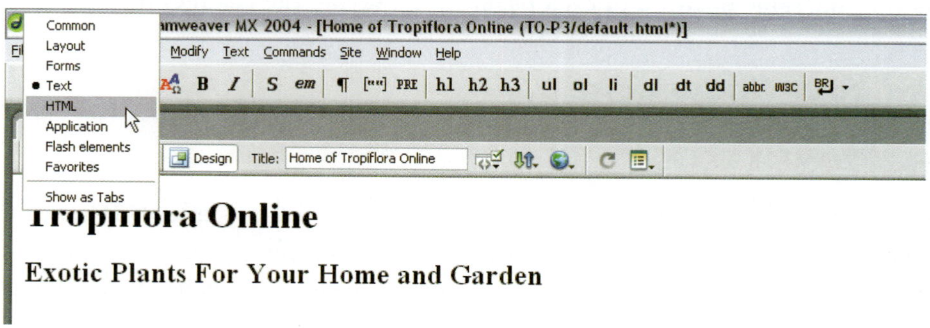


FIGURE 3.29

4. **Click the Horizontal Rule button (first button on the left) to insert a horizontal rule.**

FIGURE 3.30

**5** **Click at the end of the bottom line of text to deselect the horizontal rule.**

It is difficult to see the true appearance of the horizontal rule when it is selected.

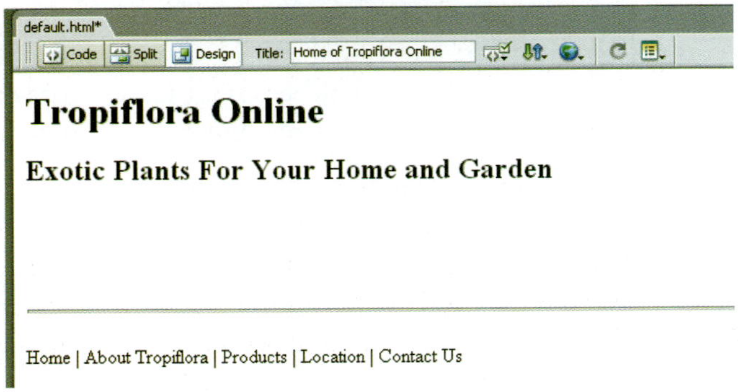


FIGURE 3.31

**6** **Close, saving the changes to default.html.**

**7** **Open about.html.**

**8** **Click in front of "Home" in the bottom paragraph.**

**9** **Choose Insert>HTML>Horizontal Rule to insert a horizontal rule from the menu.**

**10** **Close, saving the changes to about.html.**

**11** **Open contact.html and products.html one at a time and insert a horizontal rule (using either method) at the same position in each page. Close, saving the changes to each when finished.**

## To Extend Your Knowledge

### STYLING HORIZONTAL RULES

It is possible to apply CSS to horizontal rules, not only to replace the deprecated `width`, `color`, and `size` (height) attributes, but also to create a style or effect that is not possible without CSS. For example, using CSS you could create a style for a horizontal rule, such as: `style="width: 80%; height: 10px; background-image: url(flowers.gif)"`. This means that the horizontal rule would be 80% of the browser-window width, 10 pixels in height, and have a repeating background of a flowers.gif image. By using this combination of style properties for the horizontal rule, you transform the plain line into a row of flowers, but it remains a horizontal rule structurally for any browser that does not display CSS.

CSS enables us to create styles and effects that we could not achieve before CSS without adding false structure. Not only can you create many of those effects with CSS, but you also do so without adding any further structure to the Web page. For example, it was common to place content in a table to achieve a particular visual effect. If the page used CSS instead, a visitor whose browser does not render the stylistic appearances (such as a screen reader or a Braille device) would not have to wade through table structures whose only purpose was to create that particular effect. CSS allows the designer to maintain the structure prepared by the author while permitting freedom to design.

# LESSON 6 Creating Ordered and Unordered Lists

Lists might also be considered block structures, since they separate their content from other content, however, they have a special format that affects the individual items they list. Lists also have a more complicated tag structure — two or three different tags are necessary, depending on the type of list. The three types of lists you can use are ordered, unordered, and definition lists.

The two most common lists are ordered and unordered lists. They look similar except that a number precedes ordered list items and a bullet precedes unordered list items. Other computer applications, such as word-processing or other Web-design software, refer to these types of lists as "numbered" and "bulleted" lists respectively. Your decision about which list to use — ordered or unordered — depends on whether or not you wish to suggest that the first item should be done before the second, or that the first item is more important than the second. If you don't want to suggest an order of importance or procedure, use an unordered list.

## Create an Ordered List

Ordered lists have two tags — the ordered list `<ol>` tag and the list item `<li>` tag. The `<ol>` tag indicates that the list is numbered. The `<li>` tag defines the beginning and ending of a list item in the same way that a paragraph tag defines the beginning and ending of a paragraph. If an ordered list has three items, there is one pair of ordered list tags (`<ol>` ... `</ol>`) surrounding three pairs of list item tags (`<li>` ... `</li>`), each of which surrounds the list-item text.

The physical appearances of an ordered list are the number preceding each list item and the indentation of each item (and its number) from the left margin. Dreamweaver simplifies your creation of ordered and unordered lists by reducing the process to clicking a button and pressing Enter/Return.

**1** **Open products.html.**

**2** **Move the insertion point into the blank line below the Top Sellers heading.**

**3** **Click the Ordered List button in the Property inspector.**

Notice that Dreamweaver creates the first number for you.

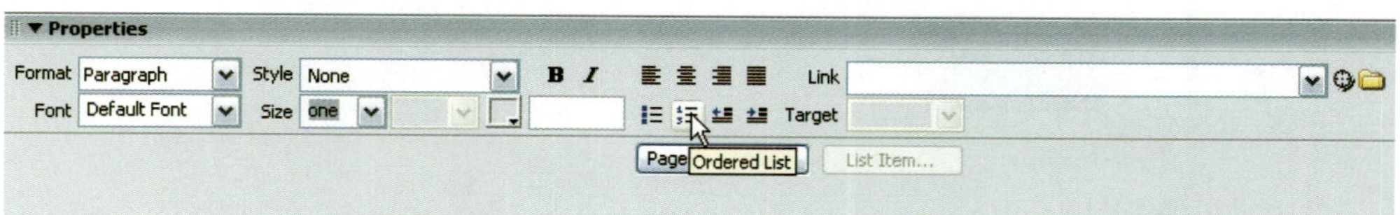


FIGURE 3.32

**4** **Type `Aechmea fulgens` and press Enter/Return.**

Dreamweaver creates the second number.

**5** **Type `Hernia zebrina`, press Enter/Return, and type `Tillandsia latifola`.**

These are the scientific or Latin names for three tropical plants.

FIGURE 3.33

**6** **Click the <li> tag in the Tag selector.**

Observe that only the last line is selected. The **<li>** tag is the list item tag, and is required for each item in the list.

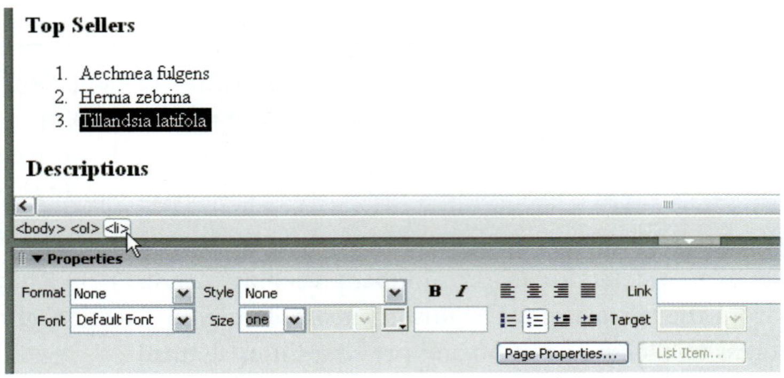


FIGURE 3.34

**7** **Click the <ol> tag in the Tag selector.**

The **<ol>** tag is the ordered list tag. The entire list is an ordered list so selecting the **<ol>** tag selects the whole list.

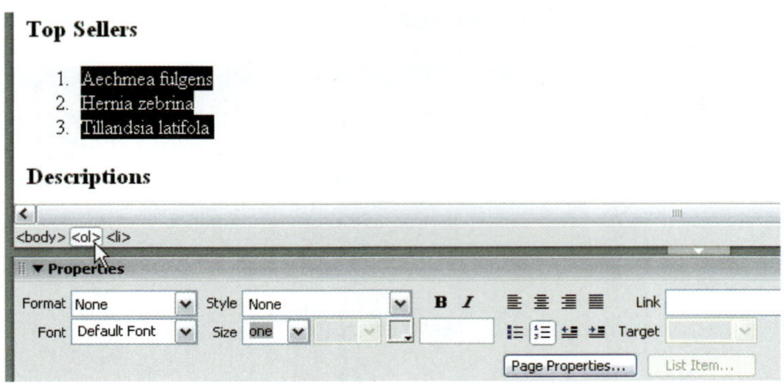


FIGURE 3.35

**8** **Switch to the Code and Design view and examine the selected code in the Code window.**

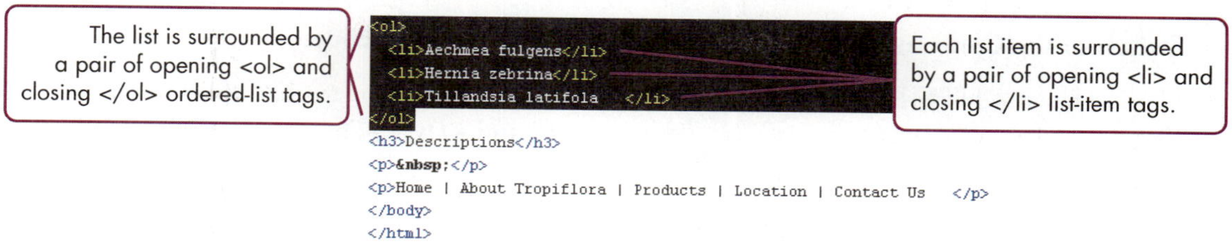


FIGURE 3.36

**9** **Switch back to the Design view, and click in the Document window outside the ordered list to deselect it.**

**10** **Choose File>Save to save the changes to the document. Leave the document open for the next exercise.**

## Create an Unordered List

As discussed earlier, you should use unordered lists if you don't want to imply an order of progression or importance. The tag format is virtually identical to that of ordered lists except that instead of a pair of ordered list tags (`<ol> ... </ol>`), you use a pair of unordered list tags (`<ul> ... </ul>`). You use list item tags (`<li> ... </li>`) in the same way — the ordered or unordered tags determine whether the list is numbered or bulleted. The physical appearances of an unordered list are the bullet preceding each list item and the indentation of each item (and its bullet) from the left margin.

**1** **In the open file products.html, click in the empty paragraph space below the Products heading.**

**2** **Click the Unordered List button in the Property inspector.**

Notice that Dreamweaver creates a bullet character in preparation for the first list item.

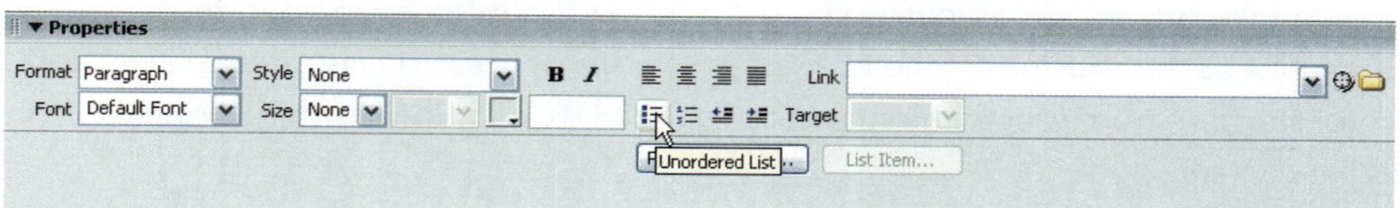


FIGURE 3.37

**3** **Type `Bromeliads` and press Enter/Return. Type `Succulents` and press Enter/Return. Type `Tillandsias`.**

FIGURE 3.38

**4** **Click the `<ul>` tag in the Tag selector.**

**5** **Switch to the Code and Design view and examine the selected code.**

Notice that the HTML coding for an unordered list is very similar to that of an ordered list, except that the `<ol>` and `</ol>` tags are replaced with `<ul>` and `</ul>`. These tags determine which type of list is created — ordered or unordered.

```
<body>
<h1>Tropiflora Online</h1>
<h2>Products</h2>
<ul>
  <li>Bromeliads</li>
  <li>Succulents</li>
  <li>Tillandsias</li>
</ul>
<h3>Top Sellers</h3>
<ol>
```

**FIGURE 3.39**

**6** **Return to Design view, and click outside the selected text to deselect it.**

**7** **Save the changes, but leave the document open for the next lesson.**

## To Extend Your Knowledge

### NAVIGATION BARS = UNORDERED LISTS

You might think that unordered lists are not used very often. However, the current teaching by accessibility and Web-standards advocates is that navigation bars are simply lists of links. You might then think that an unordered list of links would destroy any design ideas you had for the navigation bar. Not true, because you can use various properties of CSS to style the list of links. For example, **`list-style-type:none`** removes the bullets, **`list-style-image:url(yellow_ball.gif)`** adds a custom graphic as the bullet character, and **`margin-left:0px`** eliminates the left indent of the list items. You can take advantage of many other CSS properties to recreate your design while still using the unordered list as the structure of the navigation-bar list of links. This is an excellent example of the separation of structure from presentation, where you use HTML for the structure of the content and CSS for styling the content.

# LESSON 7 Styling Lists

Several different styles are available for ordered and unordered lists. The default numbering format of an ordered list is the standard Arabic numerals. With styles, however, you can also have uppercase and lowercase alphabetic characters and uppercase and lowercase Roman numerals (I, II, III, … and i, ii, iii, …).

The default style of unordered lists is a solid disc as the bullet character. The other two available styles are the open circle and a solid square. Using styles, you can also replace the bullet characters with a small graphic (even an animated graphic) but not with any other character (unless you have made that character into a graphic).

In the CSS code, you use **list-style-type:square** to change a bullet character to a square. The other options are **disc** and **circle**, but you can also remove a bullet character entirely using **list-style-type:none**. To change a numbered-list counter to uppercase alphabetic characters such as A, B, C, you would use **list-style-type:upper-alpha**. The other options are **upper-roman**, **lower-alpha**, **lower-roman**, and **decimal**. It may seem strange to list the default decimal style — why list the decimal style if all you have to do to use that style is make no change at all to the list style? There are two situations where this may be useful. If you nest lists, generally browsers display a different counter style for each level of nesting. You may want to override the default for a particular nesting level to set the counter style to decimal, or you may prefer to set all levels to decimal. Another situation might be that you set all ordered lists on your Web site to use **upper-roman**, but in one particular case, you want to override the new default and set that list to **decimal**.

You may also replace the bullet character for an unordered list with a small graphic. For example, the style definition **list-style-image: url(star.gif)** inserts a star graphic as the bullet character. However, you cannot add alt text to the graphic, so do not use a graphic that requires reading because this information will not be passed on to screen-reading software.

## Change the Bullet Style of an Unordered List

**1** **In the open file products.html, in the Property inspector, click the downward-pointing arrow to the right of the Styles list and choose Manage Styles.**

FIGURE 3.40

**2** **In the Edit Style Sheet dialog box, click New.**

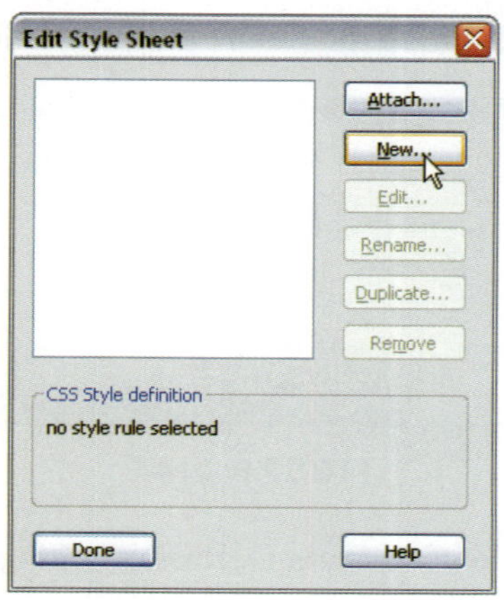


FIGURE 3.41

**3** In the New CSS Style dialog box, click Tag from the three options for Selector Type.

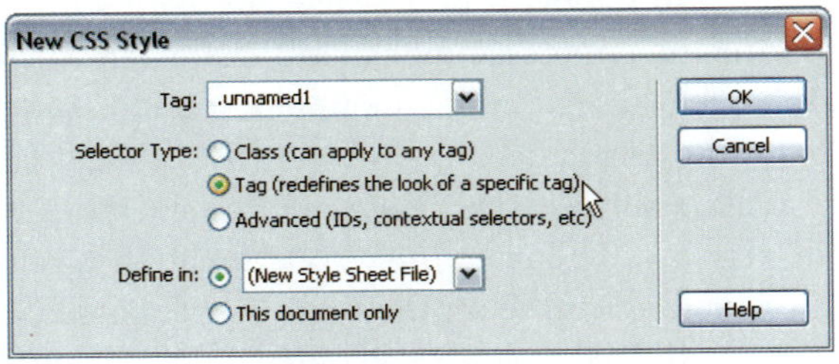


FIGURE 3.42

**4** Choose `ul` near the bottom of the Tag list.

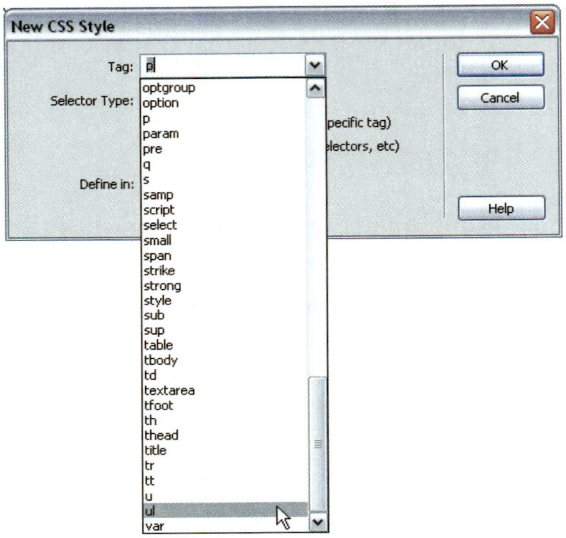


FIGURE 3.43

**5** In the Define In section, click This Document Only and click OK.

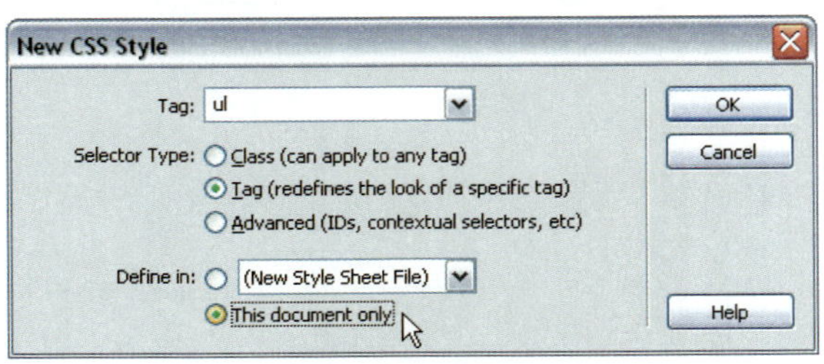


FIGURE 3.44

**6** Choose the List category in the CSS Style Definition dialog box.

7 Choose `circle` from the Type list and click OK.

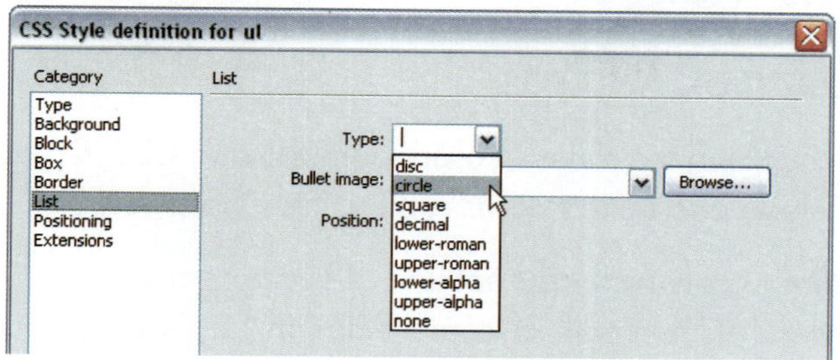


**FIGURE 3.45**

8 In the <style> dialog box, click Done.

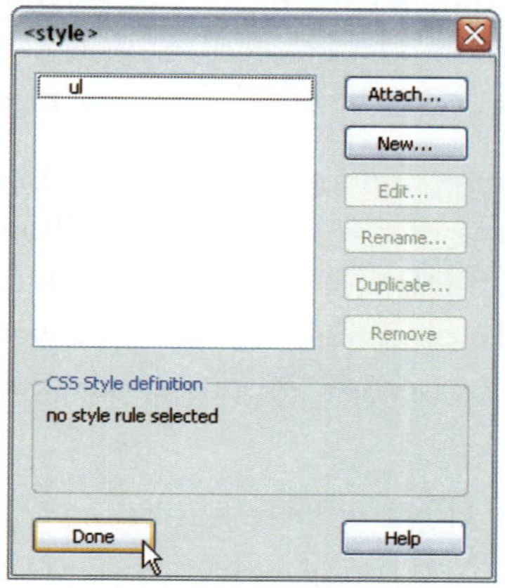


**FIGURE 3.46**

9 In the Edit Style Sheet dialog box, click Done.

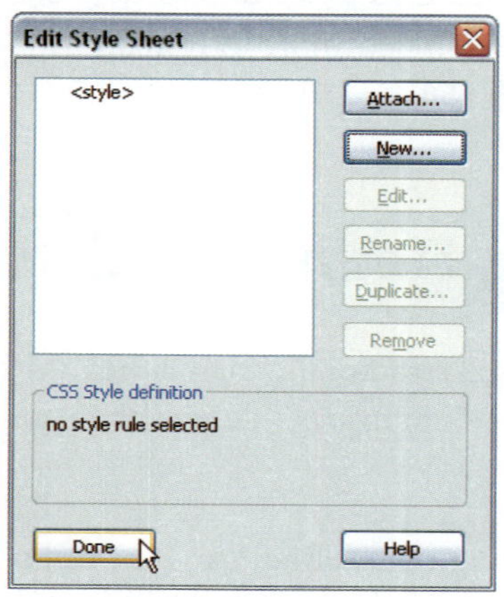


**FIGURE 3.47**

10 Notice that the bullet characters in front of all list items in both lists change to circle characters.

11 Save the changes to products.html, but leave it open for the next lesson.

## To Extend Your Knowledge

### DREAMWEAVER, HTML STYLES, AND CSS

There are two methods of changing the styles in a page: HTML and CSS. Dreamweaver MX 2004 has reduced support for HTML styles and increased its support for CSS styles.

HTML styles use ***presentation*** tags (which add nothing but appearance to the contained block of text) and attributes to apply styles. An example of a presentation tag is the **<font>** tag, which enables designers to specify the color and typeface through its attributes (such as **<font face="Arial" color="blue">**). The **type** attribute of the **<ul>** and **<ol>** tags enables you to change the kind of bullet, such as **<ul type="square">**, or counter, such as **<ol type="lower-alpha">**. (The term ***counter*** here indicates an incremented value, such as A, B, C; a, b, c; I, II, III; or i, ii, iii.) All of those options are possible counter methods, created respectively by **upper-alpha**, **lower-alpha**, **upper-roman**, and **lower-roman** values of the CSS property **list-style-type**.

HTML did not originally include presentation tags or attributes; but designers requested these options, so they were added in later versions of HTML. Since then, however, the W3C has rethought the purpose of HTML. With the release of HTML 4 in 1997, they also released CSS1 (version 1 of CSS). They intended that CSS would handle presentation and HTML would be reserved for document structure. Web designers commonly use the phrase "separation of structure from presentation" to describe this relationship between HTML and CSS.

Despite the years since the release of HTML 4, there has been very slow readoption of HTML for structure only and CSS for presentation. Web-design software is now making more and more use of CSS for presentation. Dreamweaver MX 2004, for example, primarily uses CSS for presentation — at times without even informing the user that CSS has been applied.

In this book, we deliberately emphasize CSS styles and largely omit HTML styles. There are many more CSS styles than HTML styles, they are much more powerful, and designers who use CSS are much farther ahead than those using HTML styles.

# LESSON 8 Creating Definition Lists

Definition lists are a bit more complicated structurally than either ordered or unordered lists. Whereas ordered and unordered lists consist of two tags — the tag that defines the type of list and the list item tag — the definition list uses three tags.

The definition list has a definition-list tag that defines the type of list and indicates where the definition list begins **<dl>** and ends **</dl>** (like the ordered and unordered lists that use the **<ol>** and **<ul>** tags respectively). However, the ordered and unordered lists have only one nested tag, the **<li>** tag, whereas the definition list has two. The term or phrase being defined, known as the "definition term," uses the **<dt>**...**</dt>** pair of tags; the definition or description of the term or phrase, known as the "definition description," uses the **<dd>**...**</dd>** pair of tags.

Defining words or phrases is not the only way to use definition lists. You may also use them to describe items or concepts. For that reason, it may be easier to think of definition lists as associative lists — the term and the description are associated with each other.

## Create a Definition List

**1** **In the open file products.html, move the insertion point to the blank paragraph below Descriptions.**

**2** **Click the dl (Definition List) button on the Text Insert bar.**

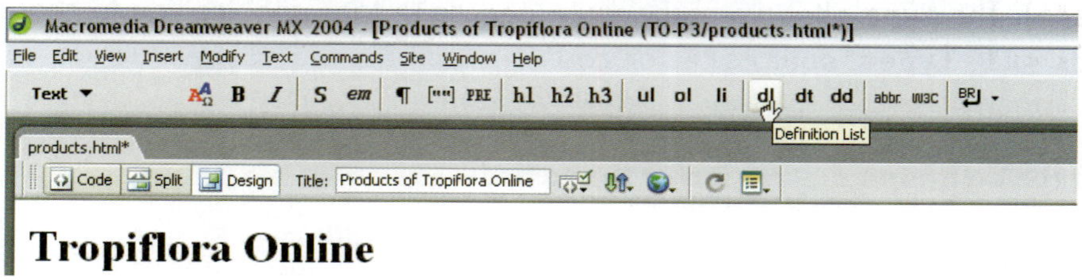


FIGURE 3.48

**3** **Type** `Bromeliads` **and press Enter/Return.**

The insertion point is indented in preparation for the description of the term Bromeliads.

FIGURE 3.49

**4** **Type:** `Bromeliads are excellent indoor plants. They have colorful, long-lasting inflorescences and some have brilliantly colored foliage as well. View our bromeliads.` **Press Enter/Return.**

The insertion point returns to the left margin in preparation for another definition term.

**5** **Type** `Succulents` **and press Enter/Return.**
**Type:** `Plants that have adjusted to the arid and semi-arid regions of the world are known as cacti and succulents. View our succulents.` **Press Enter/Return.**

**6** **Type** `Tillandsias` **and press Enter/Return.**
**Type:** `Tillandsias, or airplants, have been called the world's most unusual plants. Tillandsias are very easy to care for, exotic to look at and are a delightful addition to any home. View our tillandsias.`

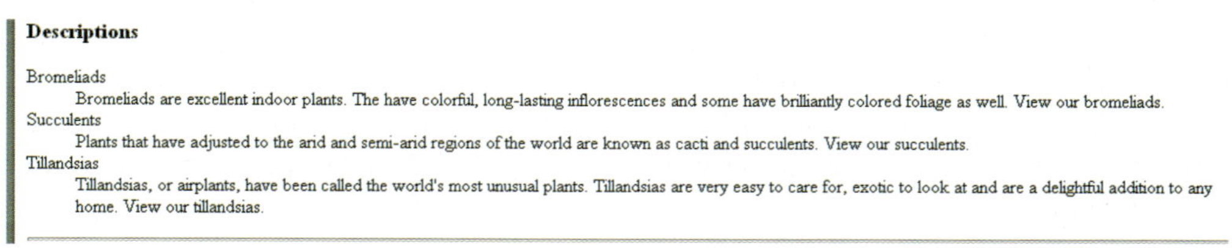


FIGURE 3.50

**7** **Click the definition term "Bromeliads" and observe the Tag selector.**

The Tag selector shows both the **<dl>** and **<dt>** tags, indicating that Bromeliads is text within the definition-term tag within a definition list.

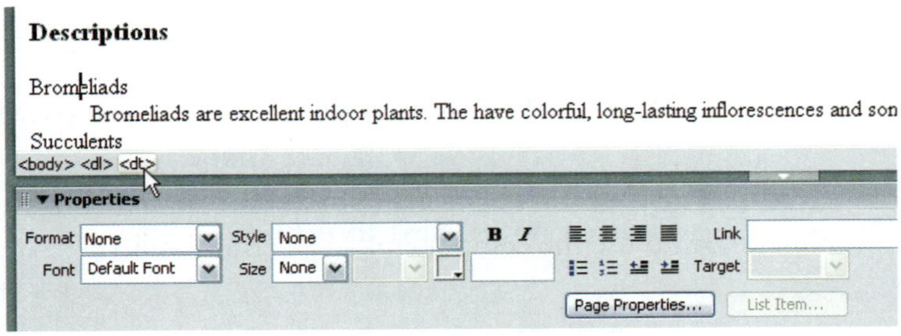


FIGURE 3.51

**8** **Click in the definition description of Bromeliads.**

Note that the Tag selector indicates the description is in a **<dd>** tag.

**9** **Click the <dl> tag in the Tag selector.**

**10** **Switch to Split view and examine the code.**

The definition list begins and ends with the **<dl>** tags. The **<dt>** tags surround the definition terms, and the **<dd>** tags surround the definition descriptions. (You may have to use the scroll bar to the right of the Code window to see all of the definition list code.)

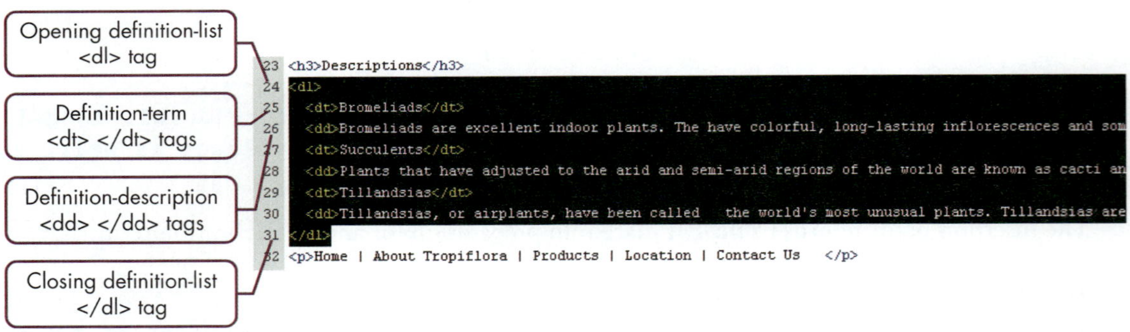


FIGURE 3.52

**11** **Return to Design view.**

**12** **Close products.html, saving your changes.**

## SUMMARY

In this project you learned about the importance of structure in text and how to create it in Dreamweaver. You discovered the different levels of headings and how to apply them with the Insert bar and the Property inspector. You became familiar with the distinctions between the different types of block elements, as well as some items that have similar roles but are not block elements. You learned how to insert line breaks and horizontal rules. You now understand the difference between text formatted as paragraphs and text formatted as block quotes. You learned how to create ordered, unordered, and definition lists, and became familiar with the distinctions between them. You learned how to use CSS to change the bullet and counter type for ordered and unordered lists. You also explored how to use the components of a definition list.

## KEY TERMS

Attributes
Block elements
Citation
Counter
Definition list
Deprecated
DTD
Heading
Horizontal rule
Inline
Inline tags
Logical significance
Ordered list
Paragraph
Physical appearances
Presentational HTML
Screen readers
Unordered list
Valid
XML

## CAREERS IN DESIGN

### THE DIFFERENT FACES OF WEB DEVELOPERS

Anyone reading this book who has had experience in the print industry understands the vast difference between the roles of creative personnel and production professionals. In that arena, designers are responsible for developing the look and feel that shapes the perceptions and experiences of the audience. Once the designer has finalized the layout of the piece, the production phase of the workflow begins. Print production professionals are responsible for ensuring the quality of the images, the clarity of the typography, and the other processes required to reproduce the design in quantity.

In the world of Web design, the same situation exists. Web designers are responsible for the look, feel, and effectiveness of the visitor's experience; their responsibility ends there. The next step in the process lies in the hands of Web developers — the programmers, database experts, and site maintenance professionals responsible for the "wiring" of the site.

The skills required for these two types of positions, while equally important, are dramatically different. This holds true in all aspects of professional communication. Creative talent ensures the quality of the user experience, while technical expertise ensures proper preparation and delivery of the content to the end user. As your career matures, it will become apparent on which side of the fence your talents lie — creative or technical.

# CHECKING CONCEPTS AND TERMS

## SCREEN ID

**Identify the indicated areas from the list below:**

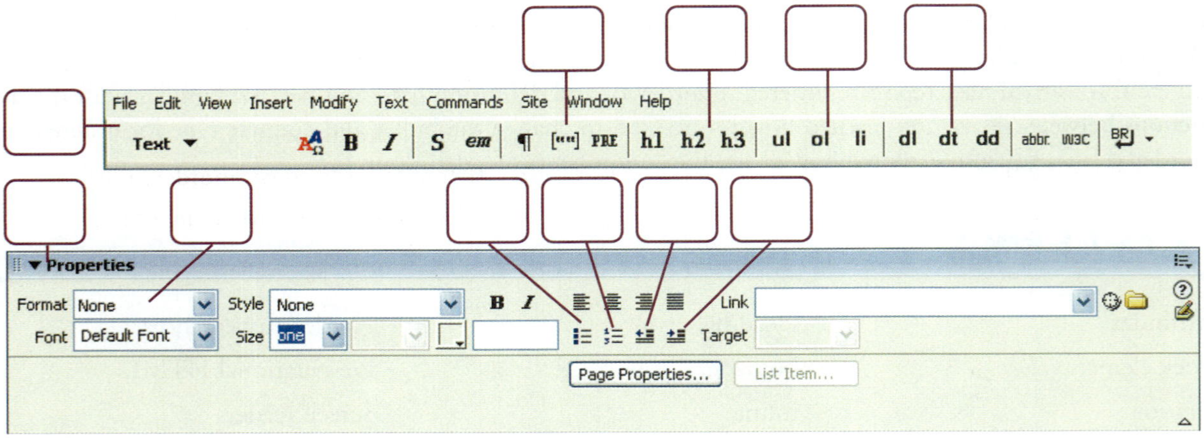


FIGURE 3.53

- **a.** Text Insert bar
- **b.** Text Indent
- **c.** Property inspector
- **d.** Headings
- **e.** Unordered list
- **f.** Definition-list tags
- **g.** Unordered- and Ordered-list tags
- **h.** Block-quote tag
- **i.** Text Outdent
- **j.** Ordered list
- **k.** Format menu

## MULTIPLE CHOICE

**Circle the letter of the correct answer for each of the following.**

**1.** Information on a Web page must be structured so that it is __________.

- **a.** meaningful and useful
- **b.** understandable and accessible
- **c.** good content with effective design
- **d.** All the above

**2.** The best way to structure text content on a Web page is by using __________.

- **a.** boldfacing and large-size letters
- **b.** distinctive colors, fonts, and stylistic changes
- **c.** headings, paragraphs, lists, and block quotes
- **d.** horizontal rules and indented paragraphs

**3.** Formatting tools similar to those used in word-processing applications can be found in the __________.

- **a.** Design panel
- **b.** Property inspector
- **c.** Layout Insert bar
- **d.** Page Properties dialog box

**4.** Headings identify __________.

- **a.** numbered lists of information
- **b.** material quoted from another source
- **c.** the content in the following paragraphs
- **d.** left and right indenting

5. Block elements are __________.
   a. HTML tags that structure a unit of text
   b. HTML tags that separate blocks of text with white space
   c. paragraph and horizontal-rule tags
   d. All of the above

6. Which text format is the largest on the computer screen?
   a. Heading 6
   b. Heading 2
   c. Paragraph
   d. Heading 1

7. Which of the following is not true of the Text Insert bar?
   a. It provides access to HTML tags that structure text.
   b. It allows text to be inserted from word-processing text files.
   c. It provides access to characters, such a copyright or trademark symbol.
   d. It allows insertion of line breaks.

8. The text in the `<title>` tag appears in the browser window.
   a. True
   b. False

9. In which of the following cases should you use a line break?
   a. Between two paragraphs
   b. After a Heading 1 or 2
   c. Before an ordered or unordered list
   d. Between the text lines of an address

10. The most commonly used component of the Dreamweaver interface is the __________.
    a. Tag chooser
    b. Help menu
    c. Property inspector
    d. Insert Other Characters dialog box

## DISCUSSION QUESTIONS

1. Explain the difference in designing and laying out Web pages considering logical significance rather than just physical appearance.

2. Pick a recipe from a local newspaper, your favorite cookbook, or any other source. Discuss how you would use at least three HTML document structures to format the recipe as a Web page. Explain why you would choose those document structures, and which others you might also consider.

3. Imagine that you have been given a list of courses offered by the Graphic Arts department of a local school to format for a Web page. Included for each course are the course code, course title, course description, and course prerequisite. Discuss which type of list (or lists) you would choose to present this information, and explain your reasoning.

## SKILL DRILL

Skill Drill exercises reinforce project skills. Each skill reinforced is the same, or nearly the same, as a skill presented in the lessons. Detailed instructions are provided in a step-by-step format. You should work through the Skill Drills in order.

In the Skill Drills section of this project, you have the responsibility for completing some pages for the Jungle Cat World Web site. The pages are unstructured (all text is plain paragraphs) and some information is missing. Your job is to add headings, as well as ordered and unordered lists. You must also create a nested list, change the style of an ordered list, and insert some special HTML characters.

### 1. Create Headings Using the Property Inspector

1. Create a site definition for the folder Project_03>JCW-P3 and name it JCW-P3.
2. Open admission.html from the Files panel.
3. Click the top line (Admission).
4. Choose Heading 1 from the Format menu of the Property inspector.

   This Web page is about admission rates for individuals and groups, so this heading — the main title for the page — must be set to Heading 1.
5. Click the third line (Day Passes) and set the format to Heading 2.
6. Click the fourth line (Single Rates) and set the format to Heading 3.
7. Click the fifth line (Group Rates) and set the format to Heading 3.

   Single Rates and Group Rates are subsections of Day Passes.
8. Click the Annual Passes line and set the format to Heading 2.

   Since annual passes allow holders to visit many times during the year, not just on a single day, Annual Passes is not a subsection of Day Passes but parallel to it. You should format it with the same heading level.

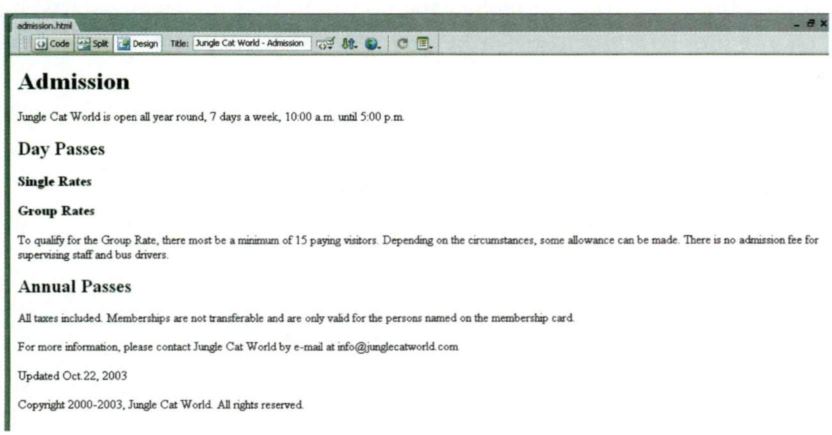


FIGURE 3.54

9. Save the changes to admission.html but keep it open for the next Skill Drill.

## 2. Create Unordered Lists

1. In the open document admission.html, click at the end of Single Rates and press Enter/Return.
2. Click the Unordered List button in the Property inspector.
3. Type the following, pressing Enter/Return as indicated:

| Text to Type | Press Enter/Return |
|---|---|
| `Adults: $12.00` | Once |
| `Teens and Seniors: $9.00` | Once |
| `Children: $6.00` | Once |
| `Children under 2: Free` | None |

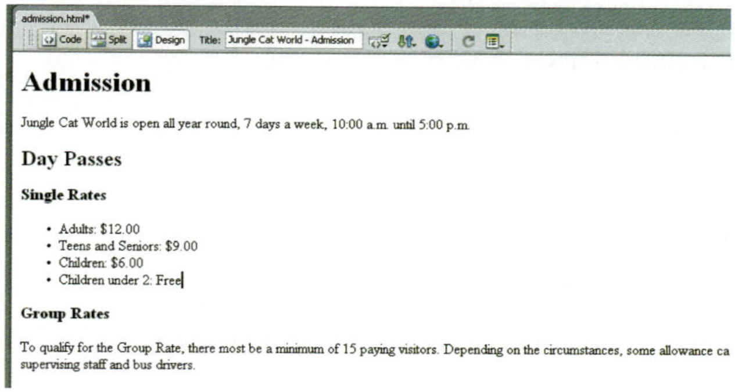


FIGURE 3.55

4. Click at the end of Group Rates and press Enter/Return.
5. Click the Unordered List button in the Property inspector.
6. Type the following, pressing Enter/Return as indicated:

| Text to Type | Press Enter/Return |
|---|---|
| `Adults: $8.00` | Once |
| `Teens and Seniors: $6.00` | Once |
| `Children: $4.00` | None |

7. Close admission.html, saving the changes.

## 3. Create and Modify the Style of an Ordered List

1. Open family_safari.html.
2. Below the Available Dates heading, drag to select the dates from June 28 to August 24, and then click the Ordered List button in the Property inspector.
3. To change the style of the ordered list, choose Manage Styles from the Style list in the Property inspector.

4. In the Edit Style Sheet dialog box, choose New. In the New CSS Style dialog box, click Tag from the Selector Type options, type **ol** in the Tag field at the top (if **ol** is already present, leave it as is), click This Document Only from the Define In options, and click OK.

5. Choose the List category in the CSS Definition dialog box, choose **upper-alpha** from the Type menu, and click OK. Click Done to close the <style> dialog box, and then click Done again to close the Edit Style Sheet dialog box.

   Observe that the numbering style changes to uppercase alphabetic.

6. Close family_safari.html, saving your changes.

## 4. Create a Nested List

1. Open admission.html.
2. Click at the end of "Annual Passes" and press Enter/Return.
3. Create an unordered list by clicking the Unordered List button in the Property inspector.
4. Type: **Family Annual Passes**. Press Enter/Return.
5. Click the Text Indent button in the Property inspector.
6. Type: **Larger Family (2 adults, up to 4 children): $80.00**. Press Enter/Return. Type: **Smaller Family (1 adult, up to 2 children): $60.00**.

   Observe the indented (nested) list. Note also that the bullets are different — they are open circles.

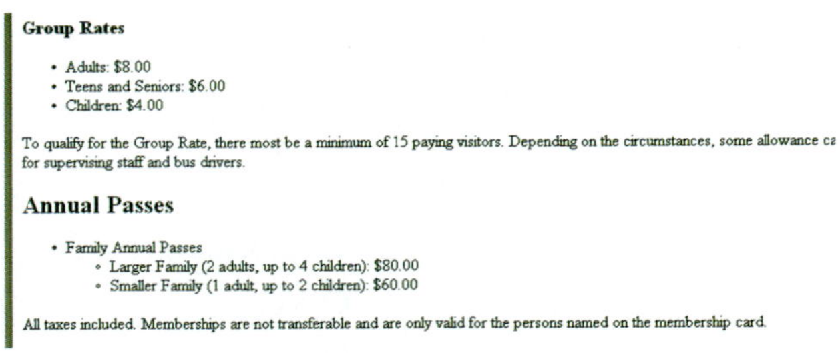


**FIGURE 3.56**

7. Observe the Tag selector at the bottom of the Document window.

   Notice that it shows **<ul>** twice. This indicates that one unordered list (the nested list) is contained in one another unordered list.

8. Press Enter/Return once more to create a new blank list item.
9. Click the Text Outdent button in the Property inspector.

   The list item shifts from the position of the nested list to the level of the initial list.

10. Type: **Individual Annual Passes: $40.00**.
11. Save admission.html, but leave it open for the next Skill Drill.

## 5. Insert Special HTML Characters

Many special characters are not easy to type. Dreamweaver provides easy access to these characters through the Text Insert bar. In this Skill Drill, you insert copyright and registered-trademark characters in the text.

1. In the open file admission.html, scroll to the bottom of the page.
2. Select the word "Copyright" and delete it.
3. At the right end of the Text Insert bar, notice a drop-down list of special characters. Click the down-pointing arrow to the right of the Characters button to view the list of common special characters.

   The Characters button changes appearance to reflect the last character you chose from this list. If you want to insert the last-selected character, you simply click the button; if you prefer to insert a different character, you click the down-pointing arrow to display the list of options.
4. Choose © Copyright from the list.
5. Click to the right of the letter "d" of World.
6. Click the drop-down list of characters, and choose Other Characters at the bottom of the list.
7. Click the Registered Trademark character ® at the top-right corner of the dialog box.

   Notice, at the top-left corner of the Insert Other Character dialog box, an Insert field with **®** in it. Special characters each have a code identifying them. When you click a code from this dialog box or from the Characters pop-up list, Dreamweaver inserts the appropriate code for you. As with all HTML, you can also type the code into the Code window.
8. Click OK to insert the registered-trademark character.
9. Click the Split button at the top of the Document window.

   Notice that the code displays as HTML code in the Code view window but as the special character in the Design view.
10. Click the Design button.
11. Close, saving admission.html.

## *To Extend Your Knowledge*

### HTML CHARACTERS

HTML and browsers support many special characters — accented characters for French, Spanish, and other Latin-based languages are available through the Insert Other Character dialog box. Different formats of code can create these special characters, such as **®** and **&0174;** which both produce the registered-trademark character (®). All formats of special HTML characters begin with the ampersand character (&) and end with a semicolon. Most named codes, such as **®** are supported by all browsers. However, the named code for the trademark (™) symbol, which is **™**, is a problem for several browsers. Dreamweaver wisely uses the numeric-code format (**&8482;**) for this special character instead of the named code. All current browsers support this numberic-code format for the trademark symbol and all other special HTML characters.

## CHALLENGE

Challenge exercises expand on or are somewhat related to skills presented in the lessons. Each exercise provides a brief narrative introduction, followed by instructions in a numbered-step format that are not as detailed as those in the Skill Drill section. These Challenge exercises should be done in order.

For these Challenge exercises, you have acquired a new client, Drummond Reid, a successful small business that sells, restores, and repairs pianos. At times, your client has lots of work for you, such as redesigning their Web site. Today, they just need you to clean up some content and structure. Some pages have no headings: you must format the heading text as proper headings. You must also modify the footers by inserting horizontal rules and converting paragraph breaks into line breaks. You need to apply these changes to all pages to provide a consistent look and feel. You must also format and style some ordered and unordered lists.

### 1. Format Headings in the Drummond Reid Web Pages

The Web pages presently just contain paragraphs. You need to format some of the paragraphs as headings.

1. From the Project_03>DR-P3 folder, create a new site definition and name it DR-P3.
2. Open index.html.
3. Format the top paragraph as Heading 1.
4. Close the file, saving the changes.
5. For each of the following files, repeat Steps 2-4, opening the file, formatting the headings as indicated, then saving and closing the file:

| File | Text | Format As |
|---|---|---|
| about.html | top paragraph Heading 1 | |
| restoration.html | top paragraph | Heading 1 |
| | Full Rebuilding | Heading 2 |
| | Restoration Costs | Heading 2 |
| | Finishes | Heading 2 |
| | One final word of advice… | Heading 2 |
| location.html | Location | Heading 1 |
| | Directions | Heading 2 |
| | Travel Time: Distance | Heading 2 |
| | four short paragraphs that begin with Coming from... | Heading 3 |
| buying_guide.html | Piano Buying Guide | Heading 1 |
| | Factors to Consider | Heading 2 |
| | Our Advice | Heading 2 |
| | Top Tips | Heading 2 |
| | Never Buy at Auction | Heading 2 |

## 2. Insert a Horizontal-Rule Divider above the Footer

1. Open index.html.
2. Click in front of the third paragraph from the bottom that begins with "Home : About".
3. Switch the Insert bar to HTML, and click the Horizontal Rule button.
4. Close, saving the changes.
5. One by one, open the four other Web pages for Drummond Reid, and insert a horizontal rule in the same position. Close the pages, saving the changes for each.

## 3. Convert a Paragraph Break to a Line Break

1. Open index.html.
2. Move the insertion point to the beginning of the second paragraph (begins with "Japanese" and is just below the horizontal rule).
3. Press the Backspace/Delete key once to merge the paragraph with the previous one, and then press Shift-Enter/Return to insert a line break separating the two lines.
4. Close, saving the changes.
5. One by one, open the four other Web pages for Drummond Reid. Merge the same two paragraphs in the footer into one, and then separate them by a line break. Close, saving the changes when finished with each Web page.

## 4. Reformat Text as Unordered and Ordered Lists

1. Open index.html.
2. Select the seven short paragraphs, from Repairing pianos to Supply of piano stools, piano parts and accessories. Format them as an unordered list.
3. Close, saving the changes.
4. Open location.html. Format as an unordered list the three short paragraphs, each starting with "From" (near the bottom of the page and below "Time Travel: Distance"). Close, saving the changes.
5. Open buying_guide.html. Format as an unordered list the four short paragraphs below the heading Factors to Consider.
6. Format as an ordered list the four paragraphs below the Top Tips heading.
7. Close, saving the changes.

## 5. Change the Numbering Style of an Ordered List

1. Open buying_guide.html.
2. Click in the ordered list of top tips.
3. Set the style of this ordered list to **`lower-roman`**.
4. Close, saving the changes.

# PORTFOLIO BUILDER

## Create an Online Résumé

Regardless of how secure you might feel in your current position, you never know when you'll find yourself seeking new employment. A résumé is a critical component in a job search. The Internet provides a perfect place for you to post your résumé so it can be accessed by potential employers.

1. If you don't already have a résumé, use a word-processing application to write one.
2. Select all the text and copy it to the clipboard.
3. Create a new Dreamweaver document and paste the information into the blank page.
4. Format the résumé so it is attractive when viewed in a browser.
5. Make sure you include an email link so interested parties have an easy way to get in touch.

# PROJECT 4

# Linking the Site

## OBJECTIVES

***In this project, you learn how to***

- Distinguish between absolute and relative paths
- Use the browse-for-file method of linking pages
- Use absolute and relative links
- Link to another Web site
- Create an email link
- Create a link from an image
- Create image maps and hotspots
- Create and link to named anchors
- Organize with default page names and subdomains

## WHY WOULD I DO THIS?

***Links*** (or hyperlinks) are the fundamental building blocks of the Internet. They enable you to direct the viewer from one page to another, from one part of a page to another, or from the current Web site to a completely different address or URL. (***URL*** is the abbreviation for Uniform Resource Locator, the location of a particular file on a Web site. A resource can be an HTML document, graphic, external style sheet, JavaScript file, or media file.)

You can create a link from a single word, a phrase, a graphic, or even a part of a graphic. When the mouse pointer is over a link, the arrow-shaped pointer normally turns into a pointing hand. You can color links differently depending on whether the visitor has visited them or not. Users find it helpful to know at a glance whether or not they have been to a particular link.

There are several types of links available for constructing your site. As noted, you can create links from one page to another, links to sections within a page, and email links. You can have any or all of these types of links in a single Web page. You can also create links that open the linked page in another browser window, or links in framed pages that change the page in another frame.

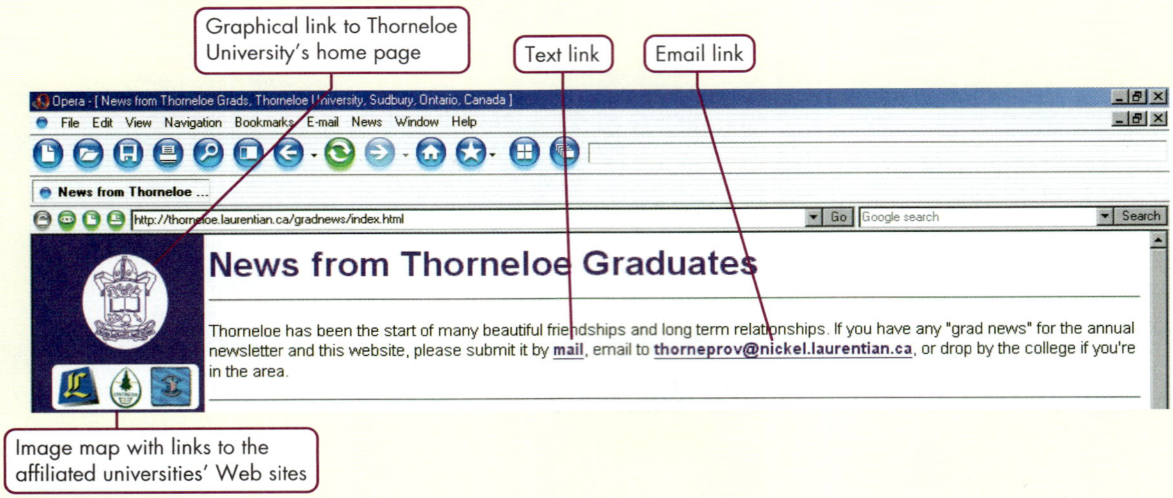


FIGURE 4.1

When you create a link from one page to another page in the same site, the URL for the link does not need to include the protocol or the domain name — in other words, it does not need http://www.domain_name.com to precede it. ***Protocol*** identifies how the browser is to handle the destination of the link: ***http*** (HyperText Transfer Protocol) means that the destination is a Web page, ***ftp*** (File Transfer Protocol) means that the destination is a file or folder on a file server, and ***mailto*** means that the destination is an email address and should be handled by an email application. When you create a link to a page on another site, however, you must use the full and complete URL, and the URL must include both the protocol and the domain name.

You can create links from text or graphics. The anchor tag **<a>** surrounds the link text or the link graphic. The anchor tag is a container tag which requires its closing **</a>** tag. Unlike many other tags, the anchor tag requires at least one attribute, the **href** attribute, which states where the link is to take the user. If the anchor tag links to products.html, the format is **<a href="products.html">**Tropiflora Products**</a>**, where the words Tropiflora Products are the link text. If you use a graphic (products.gif) as the link the image-tag information appears in place of the text Tropiflora Products, as in **<a href="products.html"><img src="products.gif"></a>**. There are other attributes of the anchor tag, but they are optional.

In addition to the **href** attribute, there is another key anchor-tag option you should know about — the **name** attribute, as in **<a name="location"></a>**. This attribute, which we discuss later in this project, creates a named anchor, sometimes referred to as a "bookmark." The **href** attribute, however, is the most commonly used attribute of the anchor tag.

In this project, you learn to create links to another page, to another Web site, to an email address, and to a particular section within a page from a block of text, a graphic, or a region of a graphic. These functions are essential to building a Web site. They enable you to provide your visitors with access to every part of your Web site. Knowing when and how to create particular types of links will serve you well as you create the numerous links you will need for your own Web sites.

## VISUAL SUMMARY

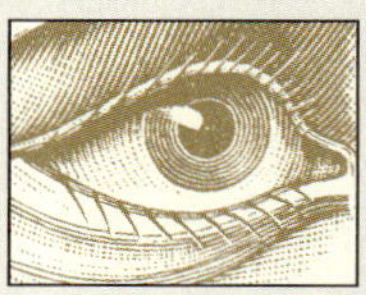

The Property inspector provides three common functions for creating links: the Point to File button, the Browse for File button (a folder icon), and the Link field. The browse-for-file function, as the folder icon suggests, opens an Explorer/Finder dialog box, allowing you to choose a file from a folder on your system. The point-to-file method uses a button that you can drag to a file in the Files panel. The Link field allows you to type the name of the file, the email address, or the URL of a Web page.

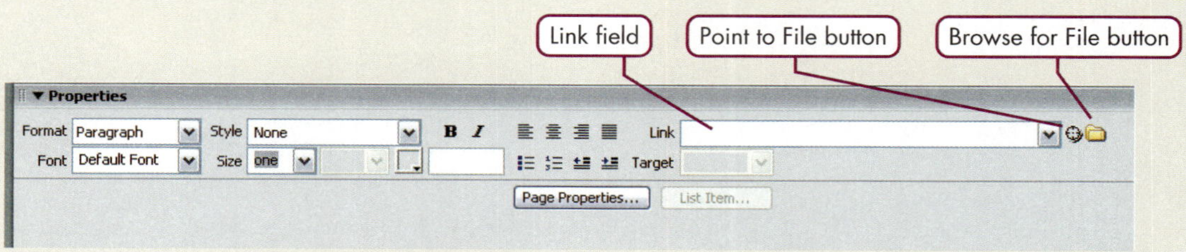


FIGURE 4.2

You can also create links from images. When you click an image in Dreamweaver, the Property inspector changes to reflect the properties of an image, and functions for creating an image map with hotspot links appear. An ***image map*** is a graphic in which different regions of the image are links. These linking regions are called "hotspots," and you use the hotspot tools to outline the hotspot region. Hotspots can be rectangles, circles (which Dreamweaver erroneously calls "ovals"), or polygons (multisided shapes, such as triangles, stars, or even the outline of a country on a map). Image maps must be named so that the code for the image map is associated with the correct image. You can use multiple image maps on a Web page, but even if you use just one image map, it can contain multiple hotspots. You must establish the association between the image-map code and the specific image.

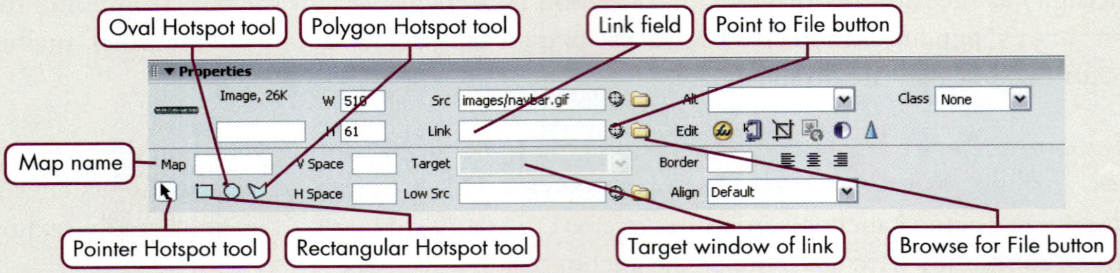


**FIGURE 4.3**

You can also create links using options available in the Common Insert bar. The Hyperlink, Email Link, and Named Anchor buttons open dialog boxes with fields that enable you to specify the particulars of these different types of links. The Images drop-down menu offers hotspot options for creating an image map. You can also Right/Control-click selected text in the Document window and choose Make Link from the context menu.

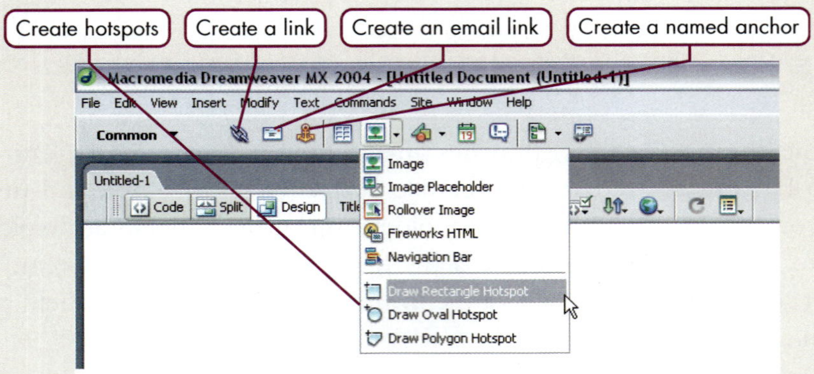


**FIGURE 4.4**

# LESSON 1 Creating Relative vs. Absolute Paths

It is important to know the difference between relative and absolute paths when creating links. Although Dreamweaver creates the link code for you when you define a link, some situations may require you to modify a link or create one by hand. If you create a link incorrectly, you will not get the results you expect.

Relative and absolute paths are two methods for describing the path from the calling page to the destination page. Relative paths use the location of the current page as the starting point. Absolute paths use the root folder of the site as the starting point.

For example, let's assume that your office is on the fourth floor of an office tower — the third office to the left of the stairs. Someone approaches your desk asking for directions to the ABC Furniture Company, which happens to be the fourth office to the left of the stairs, i.e., next door. Relative directions would be: Go back to the hallway and walk to the next office on the left. Absolute directions to the same destination would be: Go to the front door of the office tower. Take the stairs to the first floor, then to the second floor, then to the third floor, and then to the fourth floor. When you get there, turn left and walk to the fourth office. Both sets of directions would get the person to the same destination, but the absolute directions would always start from the front door of the office tower, or in Web-server terms, from the root folder of the Web site.

> Relative directions — go to: the next office to the left
>
> Absolute directions — go to: the front door/2nd floor/3rd floor/4th floor/4th office to the left

Now imagine that the person is looking for B&L Legal Services, which is located on the second floor, in the first office to the right of the stairs. Relative directions would be: Go back into the hallway. Take the stairs down to the third floor and continue down to the second floor. The office is the first on the right. Absolute directions would be: From the front door, take the stairs to the second floor. Turn to your right and the office is the first on the right.

> Relative directions — down to the 3rd floor/down to the 2nd floor/first office to the right
>
> Absolute directions — front door/2nd floor/first office to the right

## Relative Paths in URLs

There are a couple of rules to be aware of when you use relative paths. If the calling and destination pages are in the same folder, you only need to state the name of the destination page. For example, consider the folder structure of the fictitious ABC Furniture Company's Web site (Figure 4.5). Linking from bedroom.html to living_room.html in the furniture folder, the URL using a relative path would be **`<a href="living_room.html">`**.

If the destination page is in another folder, you must state the path to the folder. For example, the URL using a relative path from index.html in the root folder to index.html in the contacts folder is, **`<a href="contacts/index.html">`**, which means to go down to the contacts folder and open index.html. If you created a link in the reverse direction, the relative path of the link would be, **`<a href="../index.html">`** where **`../`** means go back or up one folder depth. You can use multiple forward or backward paths, if necessary. For example, to link from index.html in the root folder to pots_pans.html in the kitchen folder, you would create the following link path:

```
<a href= "products/kitchen/pots_pans.html">
```

The reverse would be **<a href="../../index.html">**. You can combine both forward and backward paths. Linking from bedroom.html in the furniture folder to sm_appliances.html in the kitchen folder would be **<a href="../kitchen/sm_appliances.html">**.

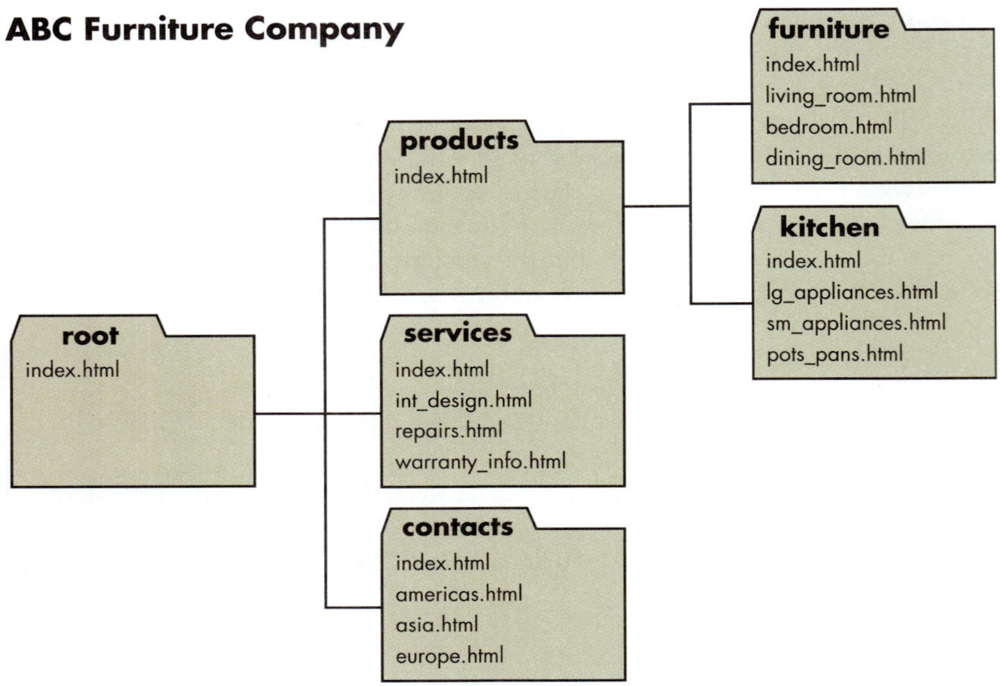


FIGURE 4.5

## Absolute Paths in URLs

When you create absolute paths, you must always create the path from the root — the path must begin with a forward slash / to indicate the root folder. It doesn't matter where the calling page is located in the site — the path always begins at the root.

To use an absolute path to link from index.html in the root folder to index.html in the services folder, the link path would be **<a href="/services/index.html">**. To link to the same page from the pots_pans.html page in the kitchen folder, the absolute path would again be **<a href="/services/index.html">**. It doesn't matter where the calling page is in relation to the destination page — the absolute path from the root folder is always the same.

## Create Relative and Absolute Paths

In this exercise, you answer questions about relative and absolute links to ensure that you understand the issues involved before you move on. Look closely at Figure 4.5 of ABC Furniture Company's Web site and answer the following questions.

1. **What is the relative path of the link from lg_applicances.html to living_room.html? What is the absolute path for the same link?**
2. **What is the relative path of the link from int_design.html to americas.html? What is the absolute path for the same link?**
3. **What is the relative path of the link from repairs.html to pots_pans.html? What is the absolute path for the same link?**
4. **What is the relative path of the link from living_room.html to sm_appliances.html? What is the absolute path for the same link?**
5. **What is the relative path of the link from asia.html to bedroom.html? What is the absolute path for the same link?**
6. **Open abc_answers.html from the Project_04 folder to view the answers to these questions.**

# LESSON 2 Linking within Your Web Site

Linking between pages within a Web site is the most common use of the anchor tag. You want to keep your visitors in your site and to allow, even promote, access to all public components of your site. Of course, this does not mean that you have to provide links *to* every page *from* every page — a large site would need hundreds or even thousands of links on every page to achieve this! Recall the flowcharting exercise in Project 2, in which you drew lines from some pages to other pages. Although you linked the major categories to one another, you did not link every product to every other, just to the category in which the product was found and to other common pages, such as the home page and the contact page.

While there is no limit to the number of links you can build on your site, you should remember that the less clicking and searching your visitors have to do to find what they're looking for, the better. Visitors are fickle and impatient — they want what they want, and they want it now. The better you organize the content and the navigation scheme, the easier it is for them to find information quickly and efficiently.

Typically, you might use the same navigation bar on every page of the site to provide links to the major sections of the site. Companies often display their logo prominently at the top of each page, frequently making it a link to the site's home page. Sometimes, a location bar or path structure highlights a path to the current Web page. For example, you can see Home/Products/Furniture, where Home, Products, and Furniture are individual links to the home page of the Web site, the home page of the furniture category, and the home page of the bedroom subcategory. This structure is commonly called "bread crumbs," reminiscent of the "Hansel and Gretel" story. You can also provide additional links to pages related to the current page, such as from bedroom furniture to living room furniture. These are all methods that you can use to help your visitors navigate around your site to learn more about the products and services of your organization.

Navigation bars, or "navbars" as they're often called, are an excellent means of creating links from every page to the major sections of your Web site. Although you can create text-link navigation bars, as we do here, you can also create graphical links. You can even incorporate JavaScript for image rollovers. Dreamweaver has a navigation-bar function for creating dynamic drop-down menus.

## Link Pages Using the Browse-for-File Method

**1** **Define the Project_04>TO-P4 folder as a site called TO-P4 using the methods outlined in Project 2.**

**2** **Open default.html from the TO-P4 site.**

You will configure the line of text along the bottom of the page as a text navigation bar. As a general rule, you wouldn't link the current page back to itself.

**3** **Select "About Tropiflora".**

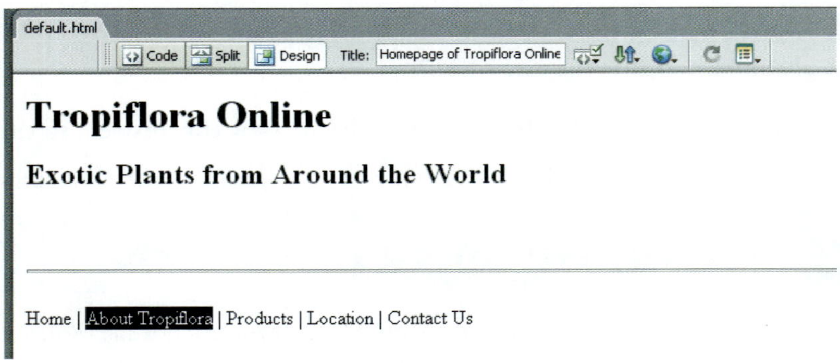


FIGURE 4.6

**4** **Click the Browse for File button (the folder icon at the right side of the Property inspector).**

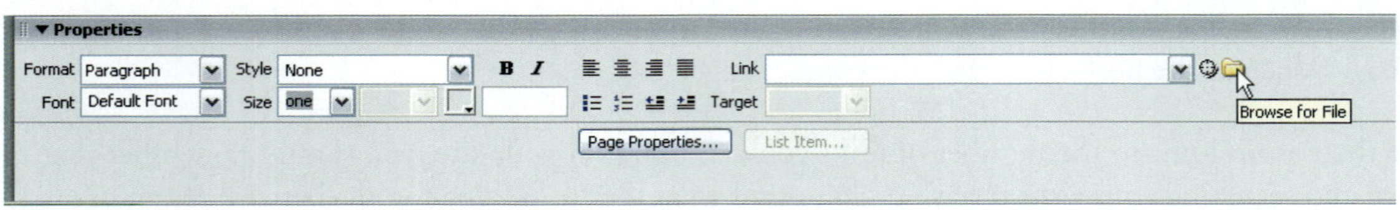


FIGURE 4.7

**5** **In the Select File dialog box, choose about.html from the list of files, choose Document in the Relative To field at the bottom of the dialog box, and click OK/Choose.**

The Relative To option creates a relative link if Document is selected, or an absolute link if Site Root/Site is selected. Unless otherwise told, you use relative links (Relative to Document) in this book.

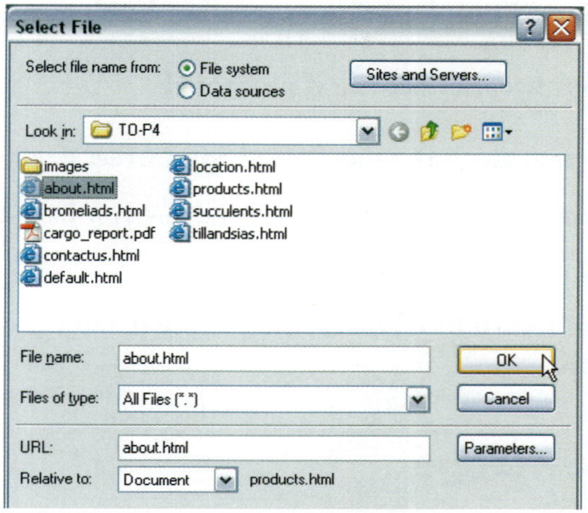


FIGURE 4.8

**6** **Preview this page in your browser, choosing Yes to save the changes to default.html when prompted.**

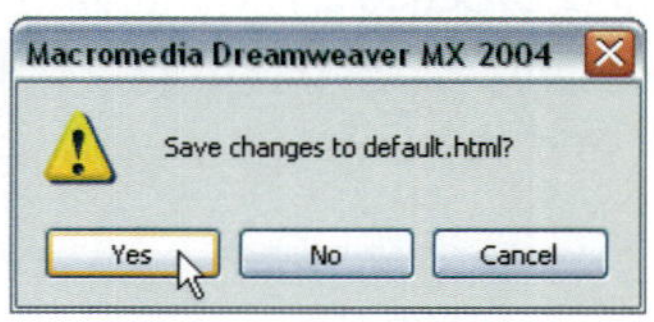


FIGURE 4.9

## If you have problems

This dialog box appears only when two conditions are met: when you have made changes to the current Web page, which has not been saved, and when you have not set Dreamweaver to display temporary files. The first condition is fairly clear: if you have saved the page, no prompt to save it appears.

The second condition may not be clear if you are new to Dreamweaver. You can set Dreamweaver to display a temporary file when you choose Preview/Debug in Browser. If you have chosen the temporary-file option, Dreamweaver creates a temporary file and sends it to your browser to display. At times, this setting may be preferable, but for this lesson it is unnecessary.

When your page displays in your browser, check the Address bar of your browser and ensure that the filename shown is the same filename you are editing. If not, choose Edit>Preferences and choose the Preview in Browser category. Uncheck the Preview Using Temporary File option and click OK. Preview the page in your browser again; this time, the filename in the browser will be correct.

**7** **Click the About Tropiflora link you created and the about.html page displays in the browser window.**

**8** **Close your browser and return to Dreamweaver.**

**9** **Link Products to products.html, Location to location.html, and Contact Us to contactus.html.**

**10** **Preview the page in your browser (saving if prompted).**

**11** **Click a link and verify that the link takes you to the correct page.**

You have not yet created the links in the other pages — you have to use the Back button in your browser to return to default.html.

**12** **Close your browser and return to Dreamweaver. Close default.html but keep Dreamweaver open for the next lesson.**

## *To Extend Your Knowledge*

### CREATE USEFUL LINK TEXT

"I wrote a review of the unauthorized biography of former President Jimmy Carter. Click here to read it." Read what — the biography or the review? Too many links use "here" as the link text, often on the same page. Instead, follow good writing practice by identifying the content of the link within the link text, such as: "I wrote a review of the unauthorized biography of former President Jimmy Carter." Now you don't need the words click here, and the link text clearly identifies to readers what they would expect to see if they click that link.

You can use the `title` attribute of the anchor tag to expand on the link-text information. The `title` attribute produces a tool-tip-like pop-up when the mouse pointer hovers over the link. You can use it to expand upon the link text. For the preceding example, the `title` attribute could be: "The Unfinished Presidency: Jimmy Carter's Journey Beyond the White House by Douglas Brinkley."

## LESSON 3 Exploring Absolute Links to a Local Web Page

Absolute links use an absolute path to the destination. Pages in the same Web site, in most circumstances, do not require absolute paths, but there are advantages to using them. For example, Web sites commonly use the company logo as a link to the home page of the Web site. Using an absolute link to /index.html works every time, no matter how many folders separate the calling page from the root folder. You may also wish to use the same code for the navigation bar. If you plan to use the navigation bar on many pages in many folders, using absolute links ensures that your links always work.

The problem with absolute paths is that they don't work correctly when you test pages located on your computer — your computer operating system interprets the root folder / as the root folder of your hard drive, not the root folder of your Web site. Dreamweaver understands where the root of the Web site is, but your browser goes to the root of your hard drive. The only way you can test links that use absolute paths is either to upload your work to a Web server or to run Web-server software on your computer.

Why should you learn absolute paths if relative links work? Some specialized Web-server applications need to know the absolute paths to certain files. When installing some discussion-forum software, for example, you must enter the absolute path to various resources, such as programming scripts or graphic folders. If you don't understand absolute paths, it would be difficult for you to install this type of software.

Although, it may not be easy to use and test absolute paths on your computer, you must use the absolute path when you link to a Web page on another Web site. Whenever you link to another Web site, you always enter the site from its root in the same way that you cannot go from your fourth-floor office directly to the fourth-floor office in the next building — you must always enter the next building from its ground-floor entrance.

In this lesson, you create an absolute link to a local Web page. You also explore the problem of testing an absolute link when developing on a local computer.

## Create an Absolute Link

**1** **Open about.html.**

**2** **Drag to select "Home" in the text navigation bar at the bottom of the page.**

**3** **Click the Browse for File button in the Property inspector.**

**4** **Choose default.html from the file list.**

**5** **From the Relative To option at the bottom of the Select File dialog box, choose Site Root/Site, and then click OK/Choose.**

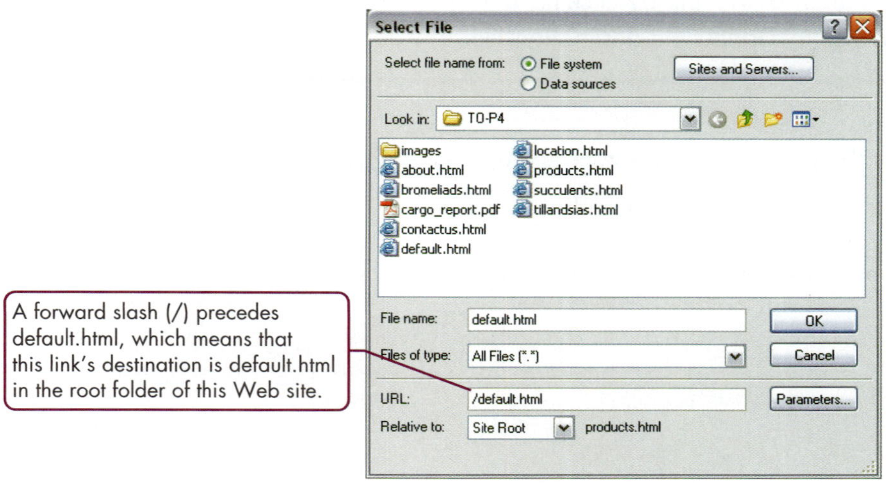


FIGURE 4.10

**6** **Preview the page in your browser (saving if prompted).**

**7** **Click the newly created link.**

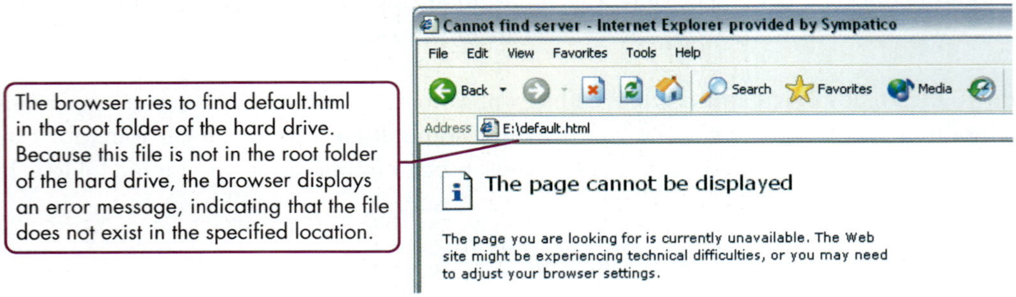


FIGURE 4.11

**8** **Close your browser and return to Dreamweaver. Keep about.html open for the next exercise.**

## Reset an Absolute Link to a Relative Link

In the previous exercise, we saw that an absolute link does not work properly on a local computer. In this exercise, we reset the absolute link to a relative link and test it in a browser.

**1** **In the open file about.html with "Home still selected", click the Browse for File button in the Property inspector.**

**2** **In the Select File dialog box, change the Relative To option from Site Root/Site to Document and click OK/Choose.**

### ? If you have problems

Even though you are just modifying the Relative To option for this link, you may still need to choose the destination of the link by clicking it. On some systems the File Name may be cleared, which requires you to reselect the destination file.

**3** **Preview the page in your browser again (saving if prompted), and retest the Home link.**

The link correctly opens the default.html page.

**4** **Close your browser, return to Dreamweaver, and close about.html.**

# LESSON 4 Linking to Other Web Sites

You must always use absolute links when linking to Web pages on another site. You can think of the domain name of a URL as the ground-floor entrance to the Web site, from which you proceed to the final destination. Links to other Web sites must be preceded by the HTTP protocol (**`http://`**).

It is not necessary to specify a Web-page name when you link to the root of a Web site — the Web server delivers the default page (the home page) when you link to the root of the Web site. Furthermore, you may not know the name of the home-page file. Is it index.htm, index.html, default.asp, index.php, or even a custom default filename? It doesn't really matter, because you can simply link to the Web site, and the Web server looks after the rest for you.

In this exercise, you create a link to MapQuest.com, a popular Web site for maps of most regions in the U.S. and many other countries. When you create a link to an external Web site, remember to add the protocol at the beginning of the URL. In addition, be sure to always test your link soon after you create it, so that if there is a problem with it, you can fix it immediately before your forget and leave a dead link.

## Create a Link to MAPQUEST

**1** **Open location.html.**

**2** **Scroll down to the bottom and select the word MapQuest at the end of the last sentence.**

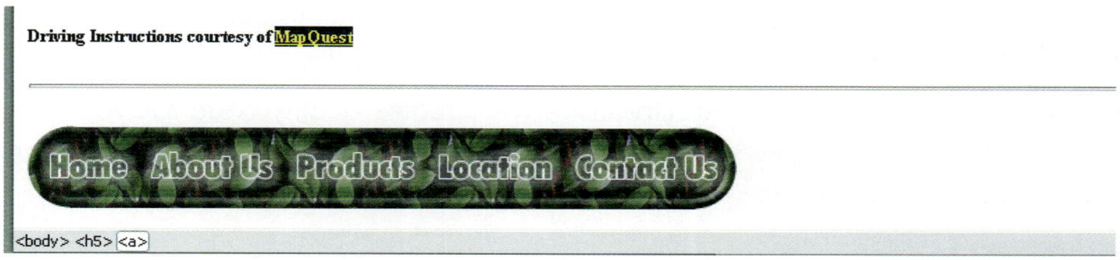


FIGURE 4.12

**3** **Type `http://www.mapquest.com` in the Link field of the Property inspector.**

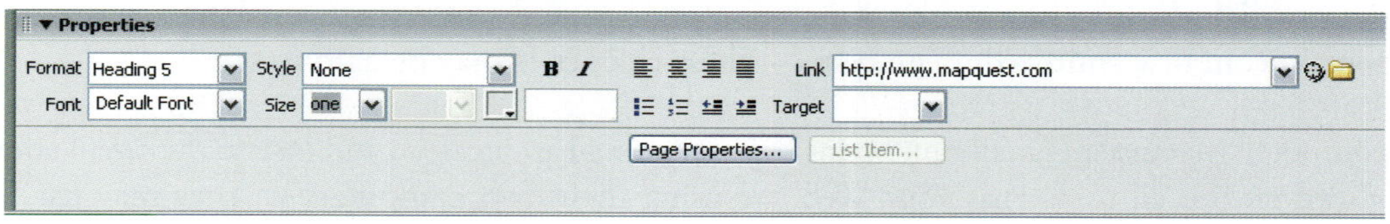


FIGURE 4.13

**4** **Preview the page in your browser (saving if prompted).**

**5** **Click the link to the MapQuest Web site.**

If you created the link correctly, MapQuest.com loads into your browser window. Correct it if necessary.

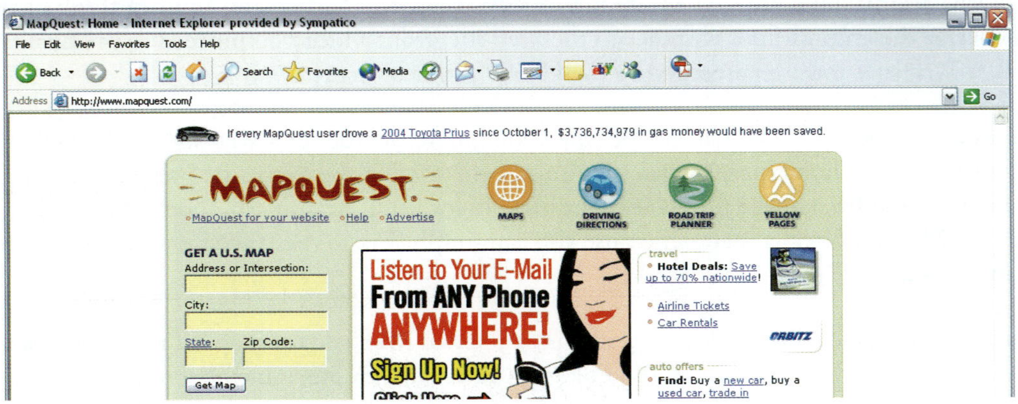


FIGURE 4.14

**6** **Close your browser, return to Dreamweaver, and close location.html.**

## *To Extend Your Knowledge*

### PREVIEW FREQUENTLY

"Code a little, test a little" is a phrase that makes a lot of sense when building Web pages. Given that Dreamweaver is a WYSIWYG design application, you don't need to check your code quite as frequently as a hand-coder would because Dreamweaver creates quality code for you. However, you should always verify links as soon as you have created them to ensure that they are correct.

# LESSON 5 Creating Email Links

Email links do not have a path but they do have a specific protocol; without `mailto:` preceding the email address, the email link does not work. Watch for periods and underscores in email addresses, such as j.smith@domain.com or j_smith@domain.com — these characters may be hard to see.

On most computer systems, an email link opens the user's email application and inserts the email address in the To field. However, not all users visit your Web site using their own computers — they may use Web-based email such as HotMail or Yahoo! Mail. By not using your email address in the email link — for example: "Send me an email" — you hide your email address from the user. However, most browsers display the link destination (in this case the email address) in the browser's Status bar at the bottom of the browser window (Internet Explorer and Mozilla) or in the form of a tool tip (Opera). Nonetheless, visitors must take the extra step of writing out the email address and then typing it in the To field of their Web-based email application. It is good etiquette (and simpler) to use the actual email address as the email link. If you use a graphic as a link, it is good etiquette to also provide the email address in text form, so the user can select the link text and copy and paste it into the To field.

In this exercise, you create an email link. The Email Link button on the Common Insert bar is simple to use. You type the link text in the Text field and the email address in the E-Mail field. You don't need to type the **mailto:** protocol — this function inserts it for you automatically. Dreamweaver also remembers the last email address you used with this function. This memory can simplify working with this function if you use the same email address repeatedly, but if you insert different email addresses, you must remember to change the email address each time. You can also create an email link by typing the email link in the Link field of the Property inspector. If you do so, however, unlike with the Email Link function, you must remember to insert the **mailto:** protocol. Although you can use the Link field for many protocols, it does not automatically insert the protocol for you.

## Create an Email Link

**1** **Open contactus.html.**

**2** **Scroll down to the email address (the last paragraph above the horizontal rule).**

**3** **Drag to select "sales@tropiflora.com".**

**4** **Click the Email Link button in the Common Insert bar.**

FIGURE 4.15

### If you have problems

The Email Link button appears in the Common Insert bar. If you do not see the envelope icon, click the Insert bar pop-up menu and choose Common from the list.

**5** **The Email Link dialog box should complete both the Text and E-Mail fields with "sales@tropiflora.com". If it doesn't, type the text into the fields. Click OK.**

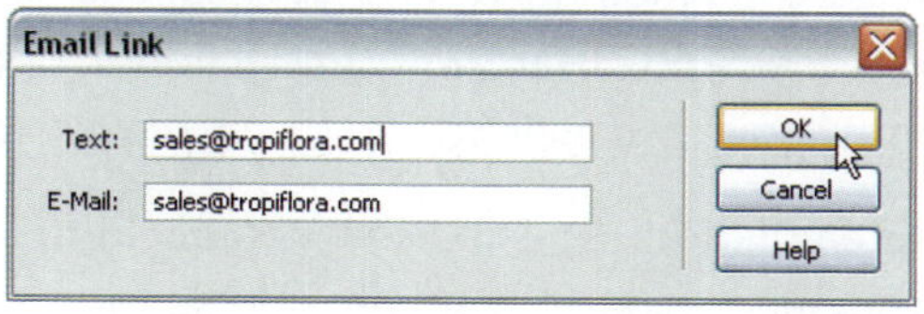


FIGURE 4.16

**6** **Preview the page in your browser (saving if prompted).**

**7** **Move the mouse pointer over the email link, and note the email address appears in the Status bar (or in the tool tip if you are using Opera).**

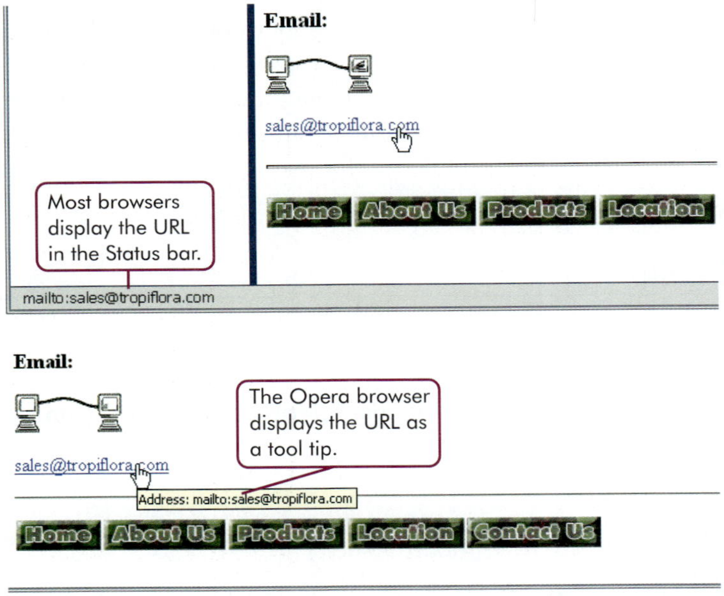


FIGURE 4.17

**8** **Close your browser and return to Dreamweaver. Leave contactus.html open for the next lesson.**

## To Extend Your Knowledge

### HIDING AN EMAIL ADDRESS FROM SPAMMERS

***Spam*** or ***U.C.E.*** (unsolicited commercial email) is a problem for everyone. Many different methods have been attempted to prevent ***spammers*** (people who send spam) from harvesting your email address from a Web site. The general assumption is that harvesting is done using a computer application that looks for the `mailto:` link and grabs the email address from the link. In response to this, many people have used JavaScript scripts to obscure the email address. However, a browser can run the JavaScript code and legibly display the email address for you. The problem with JavaScript obfuscation is that if a browser can run the JavaScript, so can email-harvesting applications. Others add obvious nonsense to the email address, assuming the end user will understand and remove it (for example, my.name@nospam.domain.com). Again, this method can be circumvented because it is commonly used.

The best method for hiding your email address is to use a contact form that sends you the message via a server-side script. The programming code of a server-side script cannot be accessed, so an email address stored in it cannot be harvested.

# LESSON 6 Using Images as Links

So far, you have only created text links; but, as you know, you can also use graphics as links. At this point, we don't discuss how to insert graphics, but instead focus on how to set existing graphics as links.

The process of creating a link from an image is very similar to creating a link from text. You select the graphic and use either the browse-for-file or point-to-file method to link to the file. There is one attribute that, although a graphics attribute, plays an important role when you use graphics as links. Visitors using nonvisual browsers can't see the graphics or know their purpose unless you use the Alt-text attribute. ***Alt-text*** is a shortened form of ***alternate text***, a text description of the graphic that is provided as an alternative to the graphic.

The vision-impaired population may not be the only ones who access your site with nongraphical browsers — other individuals may access the Internet from countries in which computer and telecommunications technology limit browser options to Lynx or other text-based browsers. Furthermore, some users with good vision and good-quality technologies still prefer to browse with graphics turned off for faster download times. The Alt-text attribute helps make your Web site accessible to all.

In this exercise, you create links from graphical buttons in the bottom navigation bar of a Web page and link them to different pages. You also create an email link from a graphic. Graphics are often used in navigation bars to dress up the links and to produce rollover JavaScript effects. You learn more about graphics in Project 5, and about JavaScript in *Essentials for Design: Dreamweaver MX 2004 Level 2*.

## Create a Link from a Graphic

**1** **In the open file contactus.html, scroll to the bottom of the page to the graphical navigation bar.**

**2** **Click the Home graphic.**

Notice that the Property inspector changes significantly to reflect the numerous different properties available for images.

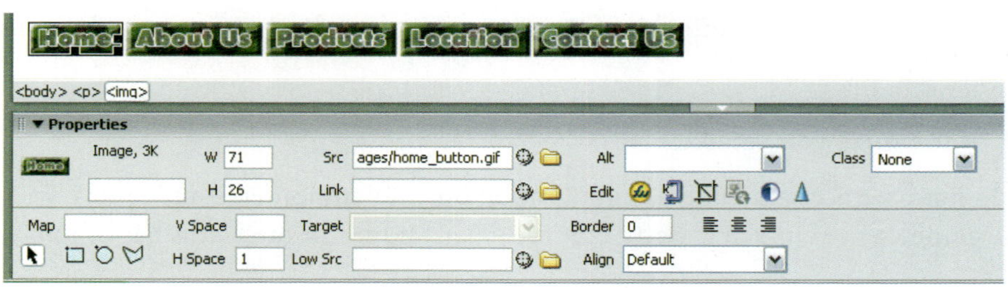


FIGURE 4.18

**3** **In the Property inspector, click the Browse for File button to the right of the Link field.**

**4** **Choose default.html and click OK/Choose.**

**5** **Type `Home` in the Alt field.**

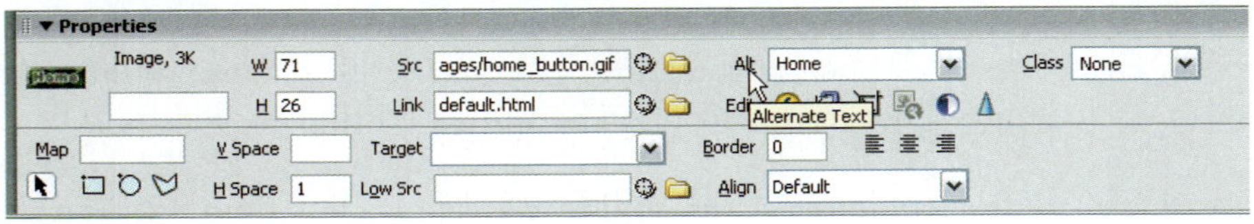


FIGURE 4.19

**6** **Continue with the rest of the graphic links, as follows.**

Contact is not linked, as there is no need to link this page to itself.

| Button | Link Destination | Alternate Text |
|---|---|---|
| About Us | about.html | About Us |
| Products | products.html | Products |
| Location | location.html | Location |

**7** **Click the email graphic above the text "sales@tropiflora.com".**

**8** **In the Link field, type: `mailto:sales@tropiflora.com`.**

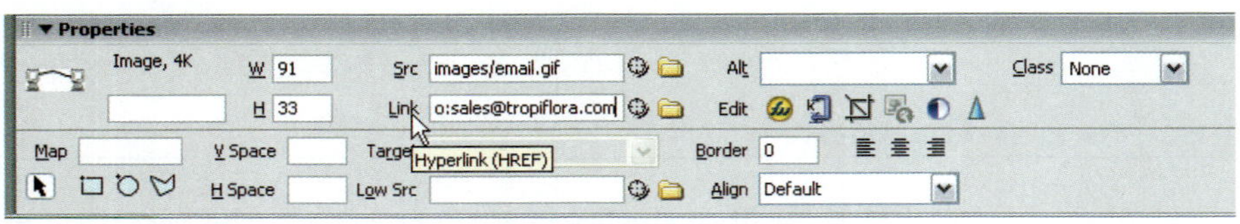


FIGURE 4.20

**9** **In the Alt field, type: `Please send us your comments.`**

**10** **Preview the page in your browser (saving if prompted).**

From this point forward, assume that if the Save Changes dialog box appears when previewing a page, you should choose Yes to save.

**11** **Test all of the links you created.**

If you do not have access to an email application on your computer, simply move your mouse pointer over the graphic email link and verify that the email address in the Status bar or tool tip is correct.

**12** **Close your browser and return to Dreamweaver. Close contactus.html.**

## To Extend Your Knowledge

### APPROPRIATE ALT TEXT FOR GRAPHICAL LINKS

It is tempting to use "Link to Home page of Tropiflora Online" as the alternate text for the Home graphic link. This elaboration is unnecessary. Those who have never used a browser through a text-to-speech system such as JAWS would not know what users of these types of software need to be able to browse our Web sites with equal facility as the fully sighted. However, JAWS and other similar software do indicate to the users that they have encountered a link — it is unnecessary to put "Link to" in the alternate-text description. Furthermore, if the graphic of the word Home is sufficient for sighted users to understand that it is a link to the home page of the current Web site, then "Home" is sufficient alternate text for those who use screen readers.

# LESSON 7 Creating Image Maps

In the Contact Us page in the previous lesson, you saw that each of the graphics in the navigation bar is a separate graphic. You could also use a single graphic, in which different regions of the graphic are links to different pages. In some cases, the graphic is no more sophisticated than a combination of several simple graphics. In other cases, it is difficult to separate one region from another. For example, consider a map of the world — the continents are irregular in shape so would be very difficult to divide from each other. As you recall, a single graphic containing different link regions or hotspots is known as an "image map." As your mouse pointer moves over the different hotspots of an image map, the coordinates of the mouse pointer determine which link is activated.

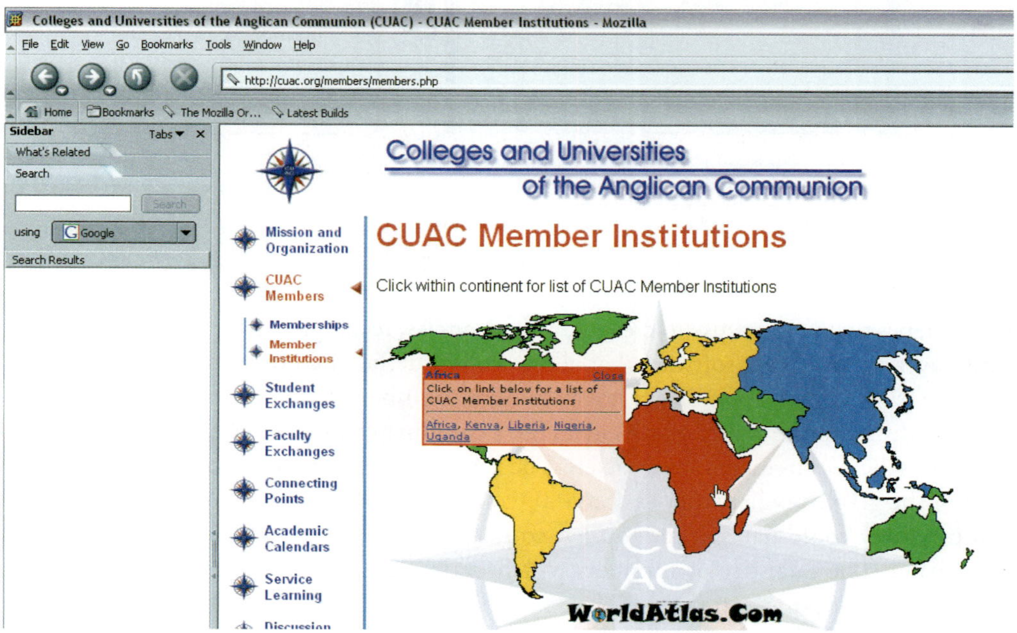


FIGURE 4.21

Furthermore, it is possible to have image-map hotspots tied to ***DHTML*** or Dynamic HTML (an advanced form of JavaScript that may be used to dynamically create and modify HTML). On the CUAC Web site (see Figure 4.21), each region of the world map is a hotspot tied to a pop-up DHTML function that provides links to member countries in each region.

There are two types of image maps: client-side and server-side. The difference between them is whether the Web server (***server-side***) or the browser (***client-side***) processes the mouse-pointer coordinates and delivers the appropriate destination in response. In most cases, client-side image maps are sufficient, but in some specialized cases, where any point in the graphic may be significant, server-side image maps are used. Server-side image maps require specialized software on the server to process the mouse-pointer coordinate. Unless you are running a Web server, you cannot test the results of a server-side image map on your computer.

MapQuest.com, for example, employs server-side image maps that use the exact position of your mouse click either to zoom into that point or to center the map on that point. Dreamweaver has the tools to create client-side image-map hotspots, but not server-side image maps. To create server-side image maps, you must write the appropriate HTML code and server-side programming code yourself, without any help from Dreamweaver.

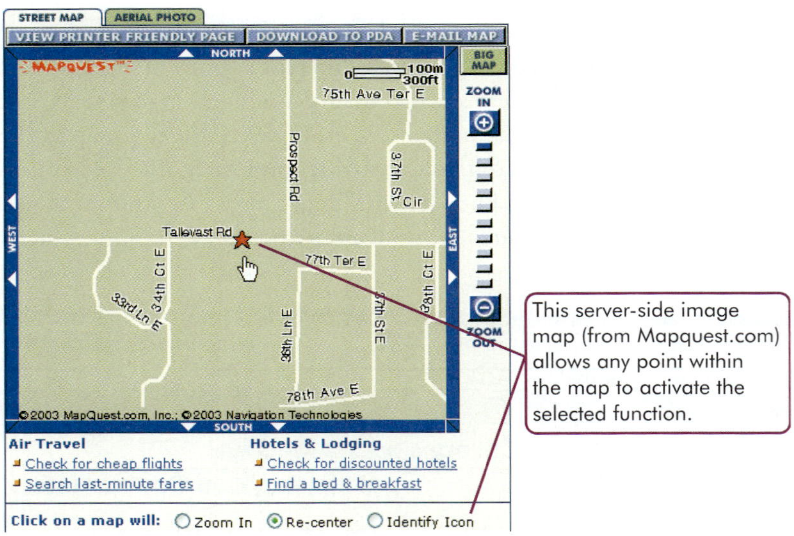


**FIGURE 4.22**

There are three shapes that you can use to create hotspots: circles, rectangles, and polygons (multisided figures). Using Dreamweaver, or any other software that allows you to define the hotspots of an image map, you must identify the shape, size, and position of the hotspot. Three numbers define the position and size of a circular hotspot: the x coordinate of the center of the circle, the y coordinate of that center, and the measurement of the radius of the circle. All measurements are in pixels. The x and y coordinates of a position are measured from the top-left corner of the graphic, where they start at 0,0. Four numbers define the position and size of a rectangular hotspot: the x and y coordinates of the top-left corner of the rectangle, and the x and y coordinates of the bottom-right corner. The quantity of numbers which define the position and size of a polygonal hotspot depend on the number of points on the polygon: each point has both an x and y coordinate, and all of these coordinates are needed to define the polygonal hotspot. A triangle, for example, has three points and therefore needs six numbers to define its size and position.

## Create Simple Hotspot Shapes

In this exercise, you create image maps in rectangular and circular shapes. You also link the hotspots to movie pages on the Internet Movie Database Web site.

**1** **Open image_map.html from the Project_04 folder.**

**2** **Click the yellow graphic with the three colored shapes.**

**3** **Type `MovieLinks` in the Map field on the left side of the Property inspector.**

Every image map requires a name. This allows the image-map coordinates to be associated with the correct graphic, which is especially important if there are multiple image maps on the same page.

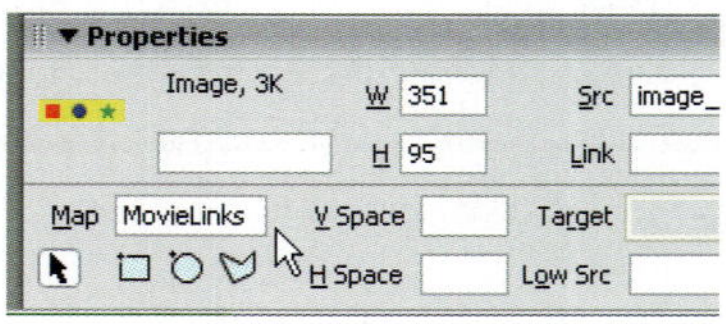


FIGURE 4.23

**4** **Click the Rectangular Hotspot Tool button at the bottom left of the Property inspector.**

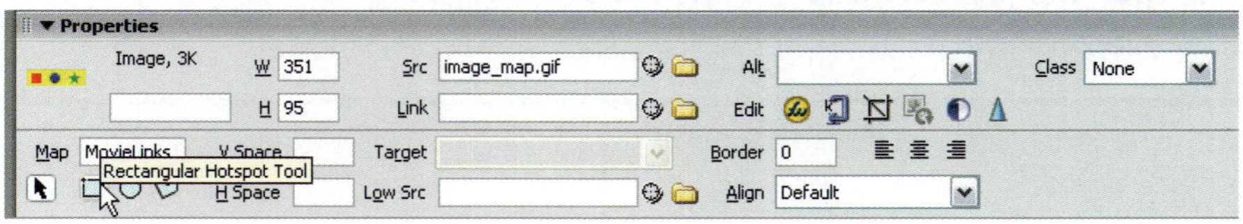


FIGURE 4.24

**5** **Drag from one corner of the red square to the diagonally opposite corner.**

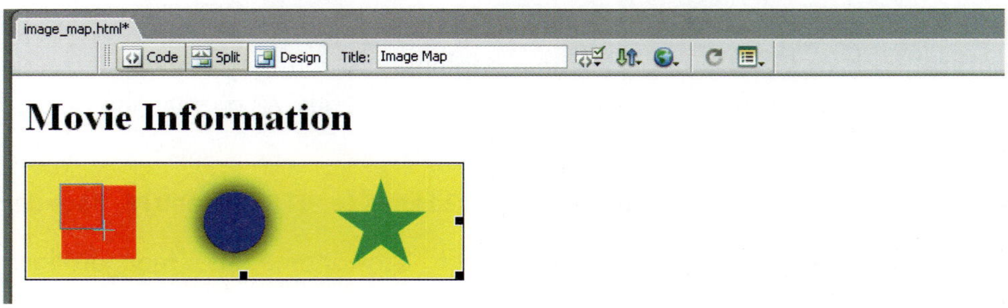


FIGURE 4.25

**6** **In the Link field of the Property inspector, delete the pound symbol (#) and type `http://us.imdb.com/Title?0099062`. Type `Arthur and the Square Knights of the Round Table` in the Alt field. Choose `_blank` from the Target list.**

**7** **Click the Oval Hotspot tool in the Property inspector.**

**8** **Drag horizontally across the blue circle until you have created a hotspot circle that is approximately the same size as the blue circle.**

You create a circle by dragging along a diagonal — drag on a 45° angle from the top-left edge of the circle (the position of the hour hand on a clock at 10:30) to the bottom-right edge of the circle (4:30).

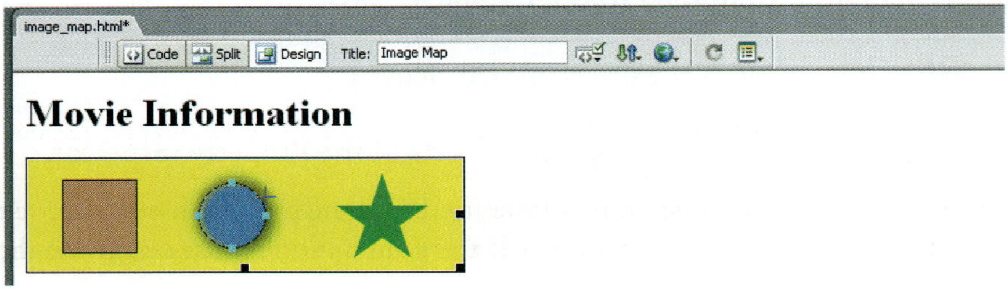


FIGURE 4.26

## If you have problems

The Oval Hotspot tool can be difficult to master. If the circle is not the right size, it is actually easier to redraw it than resize it. While it is still selected, press the Delete key to delete it. Click the Oval Hotspot tool in the Property inspector and redraw the circle. If it is simply out of position, click the Pointer Hotspot tool (the arrow tool to the left of the Rectangular Hotspot tool) and drag the circular hotspot into position.

## To Extend Your Knowledge

### DEEP LINKS

***Deep links*** point to specific content in a site, allowing readers to bypass the site's front page. Many large Web sites, such as CNN.com and search engines, are run by database technology — the content is stored in databases and may be retrieved through queries. As a result, the URLs can be quite long, such as this query for a deep link using Google.com:

```
http://www.google.com/search?sourceid=navclient&ie=UTF-8&oe=UTF-8&q=deep+link
```

As another example, this link to the story about Arnold Schwarzenegger's inauguration speech on CNN.com at:

```
http://www.cnn.com/2003/ALLPOLITICS/11/17/arnold.speech/index.html
```

You should copy and paste long URLs like these into the Link field of the Property inspector, rather than typing them, to prevent errors.

Some Web sites do not allow deep linking because advertising on the home page generates more revenue than advertising on other pages. Skipping the home page and going directly to a deep link reduces the advertising revenue of the Web site.

**9** In the Link field, delete the pound symbol and type `http://us.imdb.com/Title?0286106`. Type `Signs, a movie about crop circles` in the Alt field. Choose `_blank` from the Target list.

**10** Save the changes, but leave image_map.html open for the next exercise.

## Create a Polygonal Hotspot Shape

You have practiced creating some simple-shaped hotspots. In this exercise, you create hotspots from a polygon, a multisided shape which requires that you mark each point of the shape. Points to remember include: name the image map; create alt text for each hotspot; it is easier to delete and redo than resize a circular hotspot; and if a polygonal hotspot is missing a point, you cannot add the point — you must redraw the hotspot.

**1** In the open file, image_map.html, click the Polygon Hotspot Tool button.

**2** Going around the star, click each outer and inner point until you have created all 10 points.

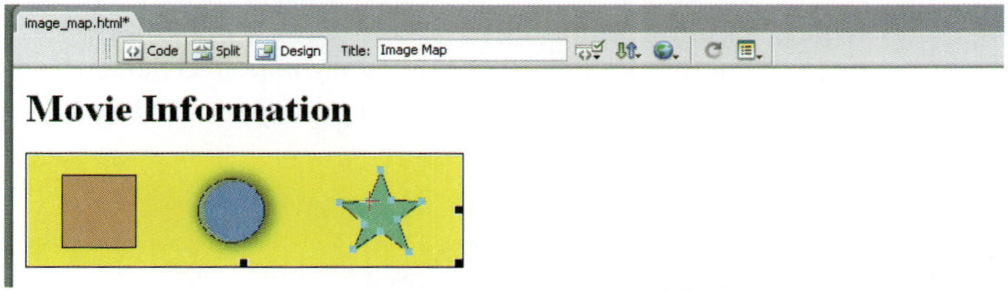


FIGURE 4.27

### If you have problems

If you have missed a point, you must delete the hotspot and redraw it. If one or more of the points are not positioned to your satisfaction, switch to the Pointer Hotspot Tool (arrow), click the point that is out of position, and drag it into position.

**3** In the Link field of the Property inspector, type: `http://us.imdb.com/Title?0121766`. Type `Star Wars, Episode III` in the Alt field. Choose `_blank` from the Target list.

**4** Preview the page in your browser. Click any of the shapes to go to the selected movie in another browser window.

The `_blank` target opens the link destination in a new browser window.

**5** Close your browser, return to Dreamweaver, and close image_map.html.

## To Extend Your Knowledge

### LINK TARGETS

Most links open the destination page in the same browser window as the originating page. However, it is possible to open a link in a new browser window — you use the `target` attribute of the anchor tag to do so. There are four predefined targets — `_blank`, `_parent`, `_top`, and `_self` — which, as you can see, all begin with the underscore character. The `_blank` target opens the link in a new browser window and is sometimes used by one Web site to open a link to another Web site in another browser window.

Framed layouts make use of the three other predefined target attributes. You can also assign names to targets; this is also a feature of framed layouts, enabling a link to open a page in the named frame. The designer decides the names of the frames, such as bottomFrame, mainFrame, and topFrame.

There are accessibility issues with using targets. The `_blank` target "breaks the Back button," which is a phrase describing the fact that you cannot use the Back button on a browser to return to the originating page because the originating page is in another window. A sighted user can see that a new browser window has opened, but it is more difficult for a visually impaired person to recognize this. It is recommended that you add an alert (with the Code window) using the `title` attribute to inform the user that "This link opens in a new browser window."

# LESSON 8 Linking within Pages

You can also set links to take the user to a section within a page, not just to a new page. The links discussed previously just take the user to the top of the linked page, not to a particular position on that page. When Web pages must be long, it is useful to create ***named anchors*** or bookmarks in the pages so that you can link directly to those specific positions on the Web page. ***FAQs*** (Frequently Asked Questions) are great examples of Web pages that use this technique. Often FAQs are set up so that the questions, listed at the top of the page, are linked to the answers below. This approach makes it easier for the user to quickly find a particular question at the top of the page and jump down directly to the answer.

Thorneloe University uses named anchors on the pages that list the courses offered by each department. Each course description has a named anchor, enabling the Webmaster to create a link from the course schedules, the degree requirements, or the faculty pages directly to the courses' descriptions.

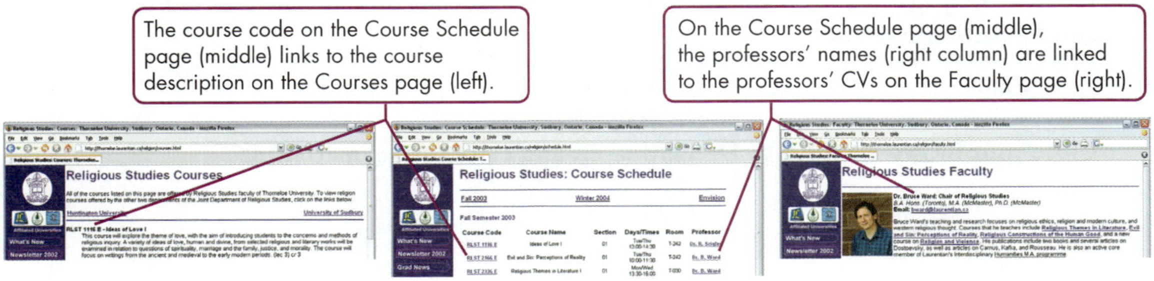


FIGURE 4.28

Links, whether page links or named anchors, require both a starting and an ending point. The starting point is the anchor tag that uses the **`href`** attribute such as **`<a href="index.html">`**. The ending point or destination in this example is a Web page. If the Web page doesn't exist, you have created a dead or broken link. If you are creating links to pages in your site, you must remember to create the destination Web pages. The same principle applies to named anchors — in order to link to a particular position in a Web page, you must create that named anchor.

Named anchors do not produce anything visible on the Web page. There are other HTML elements that also do not produce anything visible on the Web page, such as comments, divisions, and JavaScript. To aid the developer, Dreamweaver displays a shield-like symbol wherever you create an invisible element. An ***invisible element*** is HTML code that doesn't have a visible representation in a browser. Each invisible element has its own version of the shield symbol. To see the invisible elements, choose Edit>Preferences and choose the Invisible Elements category. The shield symbol for each invisible element is shown; if the element has a check mark, the shield symbol is visible in the Dreamweaver Design view.

In this exercise, you create named anchors and link to them from within the same page. Named anchors are an excellent means of directing the visitor to a particular section in a page. The page may not be long enough to justify breaking the content into different pages — named anchors provide a means of jumping directly to specific content.

## Create and Link to Named Anchors

**1** **Open products.html from the TO-P4 site.**

You will link the unordered list of products near the top of the page to the product descriptions below.

**2** **Click in front of "Bromeliads", below the "Description" heading.**

**3** **Click the Named Anchor button in the Common Insert bar.**

FIGURE 4.29

**4** **In the Anchor name field, type `bromeliads` and click OK.**

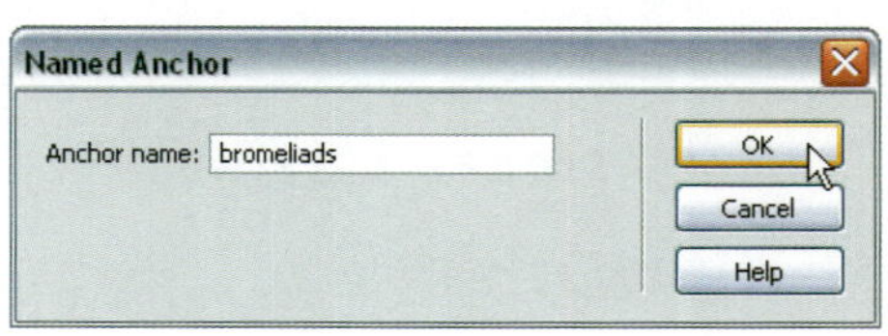


FIGURE 4.30

**5** **Click to the right of the "Bromeliads" text, and notice the yellow-shield symbol where the named anchor has been inserted.**

All invisible elements (the Dreamweaver term for elements or tags with no visible component) have a yellow symbol, indicating their location in the code; the shape of the symbol indicates the type of component.

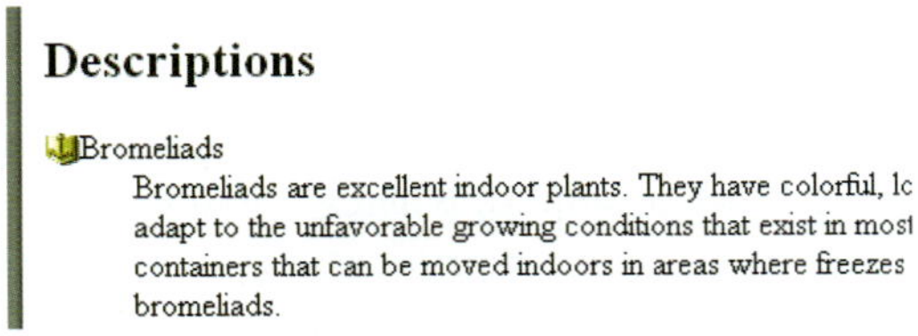


FIGURE 4.31

## If you have problems

On Windows systems, the named-anchor invisible-element indicator is visible by default, but it may have been made invisible. In the Macintosh environment, the shield symbols (including the anchor symbol) are not visible by default.

To make the invisible-element indicators visible, you first need to choose View>Visual Aids and choose Invisible Elements (to place a check mark next to that option). Next, choose Edit> Preferences, choose the Invisible Elements category, and make certain there is a check mark beside Named Anchors. If there is no check mark, click to insert one. Click OK.

**6** **Move to the top of the document and select the "Bromeliads" text just below "Products".**

**7** **Click the Hyperlink button on the Common Insert bar.**

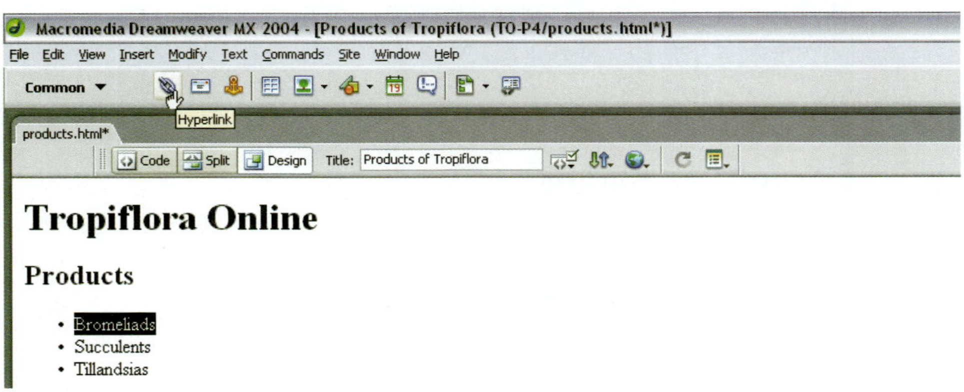


FIGURE 4.32

**8** **From the Link list in the Hyperlink dialog box, choose #bromeliads and click OK.**

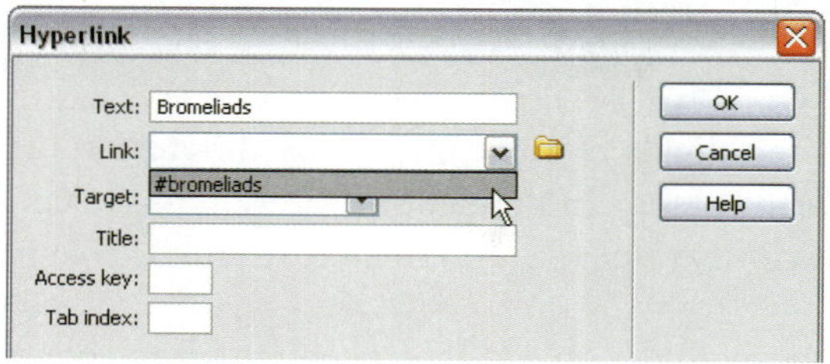


FIGURE 4.33

**9** **Preview the page in your browser and test the links.**

## If you have problems

When you click a link to a named anchor, the page should shift to bring the named anchor as close to the top of the browser window as possible. However, if the page fills the browser window, it cannot shift. To enable a demonstration of the named anchors, drag the side of the browser window inwards, so that the width is quite narrow, and test the links to named anchors. The test should be more effective.

**10** **Close the browser, return to Dreamweaver, and close products.html.**

## To Extend Your Knowledge

### NAME VS. ID

When HTML 4 was released, the W3C stated that the `name` attribute will be replaced by the `id` attribute, which means that `<a name="bookmark">` should now be `<a id="bookmark">`.

In fact, this recommendation has a much larger effect. The `name` attribute is used in only a few tags, such as the `<map>` tag and the `<a>` tag. However, the `id` attribute is a core attribute that may be used in any tag. As a result, the destination `<a href="#bookmark">` could be `<ul id="bookmark">`, `<map id="bookmark">`, or `<p id="bookmark">`. The destination does not need to be an anchor tag, just a tag with the correct `id`. Many Web developers create a bookmark as a functionless, empty tag, such as `<a name="bookmark"></a>`. By switching to the `id` attribute instead of the `name` attribute, the developer is freed from the burden of creating an empty anchor tag. Instead, the designer may simply assign the `id` to a tag that is the appropriate destination for the link.

The `id` attribute has other uses as well. It is used in JavaScript when the code is to affect a particular element, such as changing an image during a rollover. The `id` attribute also has uses in CSS and allows a developer to assign a particular style to the tag with that `id`. Now, it can also be used as a bookmark.

Unfortunately, Dreamweaver MX 2004 continues to support the named anchor and provides little support, except in the Code window, for the `id` attribute.

# LESSON 9 Using Default Pages and Subdomains to Organize a Web Site

As you recall, large Web sites often divide content into many different folders, to keep related information together in one folder. You explored content and folder organization in Project 2 with the Carver's Online store and Web site. Other methods of content organization include default filenames and subdomains.

Generally, whenever you create a new folder on a Web site, you use it to collect related pages. Creating a home page in each folder allows you to collect and disseminate general information about that particular subject and direct the visitor to more specific information. The home page for each folder should use the default home-page filename according to the Web-server configuration. Generally index.html and index.htm are the default filenames for HTML pages.

There are two benefits to using default home-page filenames. Using these default names may force you to organize general information about the contents of the folder and provide visitors with better information. Also, using these default names allows you to shorten the URL, both for linking and for providing a link in an email message to a visitor. For example, if you used the default filename for the home page of the Contacts section of your Web site, rather than linking to /contact/index.html, you need only /contact/, which then prompts the Web server to deliver the default home page of the folder (which is index.html). If you chose to ignore this advice and used contact.html as the home page, the folder URL (/contact/) would not deliver contact.html to the visitor, but would instead display an embarrassing error page. You can and should prevent this by naming the home page of the folder with the default filename.

Very large Web sites also tend to use subdomains to organize content. Laurentian University (www.laurentian.ca) has two affiliated universities that use subdomains as their domains: Thorneloe University's home page is thorneloe.laurentian.ca and Huntington University's home page is huntington.laurentian.ca. Often, subdomain URLs are more memorable than folder URLs — compare thorneloe.laurentian.ca with www.laurentian.ca/affiliate/thorneloe.

In this exercise, you explore the structure of the IBM Web site. You look at how this large company has employed default filenames and subdomains to manage its large volume of content.

## Explore the Organization of IBM.COM

**1** **Open your browser and go to http://www.ibm.com.**

Despite the fact that you did not specify a filename such as index.html, a Web page — the default for this (the root) folder — was delivered to you.

**2** **Using the Select a Country list (at the top of the navigation bar), choose Canada and, if necessary, click the Go button to the right of the list.**

Notice that even though no Web page is specified in the Address bar, the default page of the /ca/en folder is delivered to the Web browser by the Web server.

FIGURE 4.34

**3** **Click Products & Services in the top navigation bar to the right of Home.**

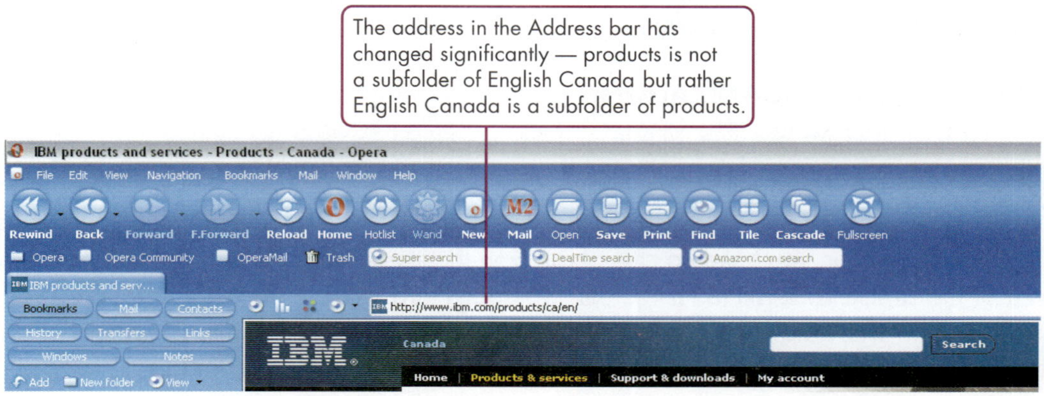


FIGURE 4.35

**4** **Near the top of the Web page in the main content area, click the Personal Computing link.**

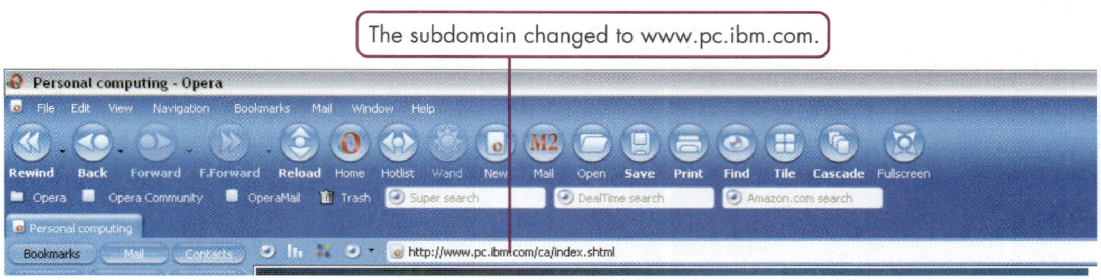


FIGURE 4.36

**5** **Click the Desktops link to explore IBM desktop computers.**

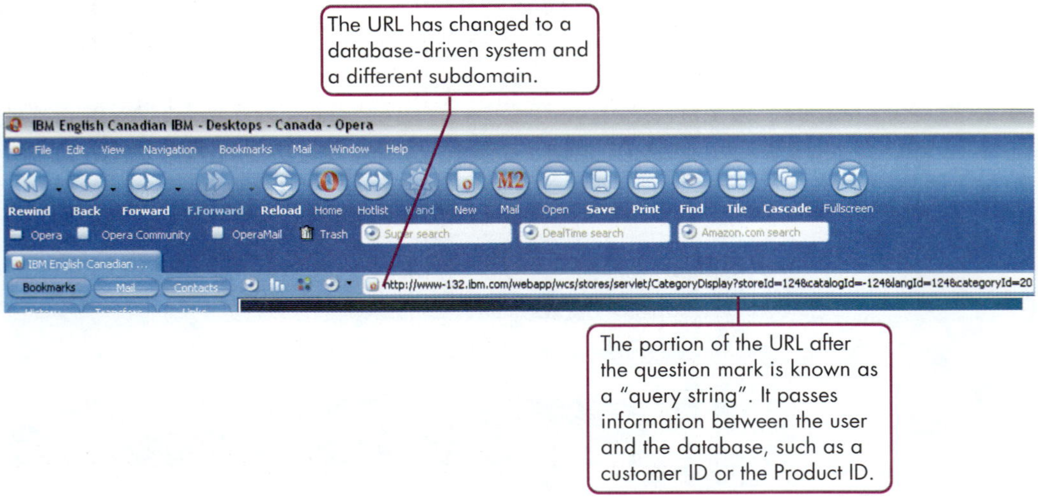


**FIGURE 4.37**

**6** **Close your browser.**

## *To Extend Your knowledge*

### DATABASE CONTENT ORGANIZATION

Some Web sites store their content in databases. Using databases to store and organize content often provides very few clues from the URL as to how the content is organized. For instance, in the URL `http://www.pcmag.com/article2/0,1759,1615757,00.asp`, notice that while you can see that there is an article2 folder, you have no clue about how the stories are grouped or categorized, or that the name of the article is "DiskPie Pro: Clean Up Your Hard Drive." However, they are organizing the articles within the database just as you would with folders — Home>Downloads>Utilities>OS Utilities>DiskPie Pro — but they're using a database structure instead of folders.

## SUMMARY

In this project, you learned about and created different types of links. You learned how to use links to let the viewer move from page to page within a site, to named anchors within a page, and to different sites. You also learned how to create and test email links. You explored the differences between relative and absolute paths, and learned how to create them. You applied links to text and graphics, and created image maps with hotspots of different shapes. You learned how you can link to a folder if a page uses the default filename, and how to use subdomains to organize content.

## KEY TERMS

Alt
Alternate text
Bookmark
Client-side image map
Deep links
DHTML
FAQs
FTP
Hotspots
HTTP
Image Map
Invisible element
Links
Mailto
Named anchors
Navigation bars
Protocol
Server-side image map
Spam/U.C.E.
URL

## CHECKING CONCEPTS AND TERMS

### SCREEN ID

**Identify the indicated areas from the list below:**

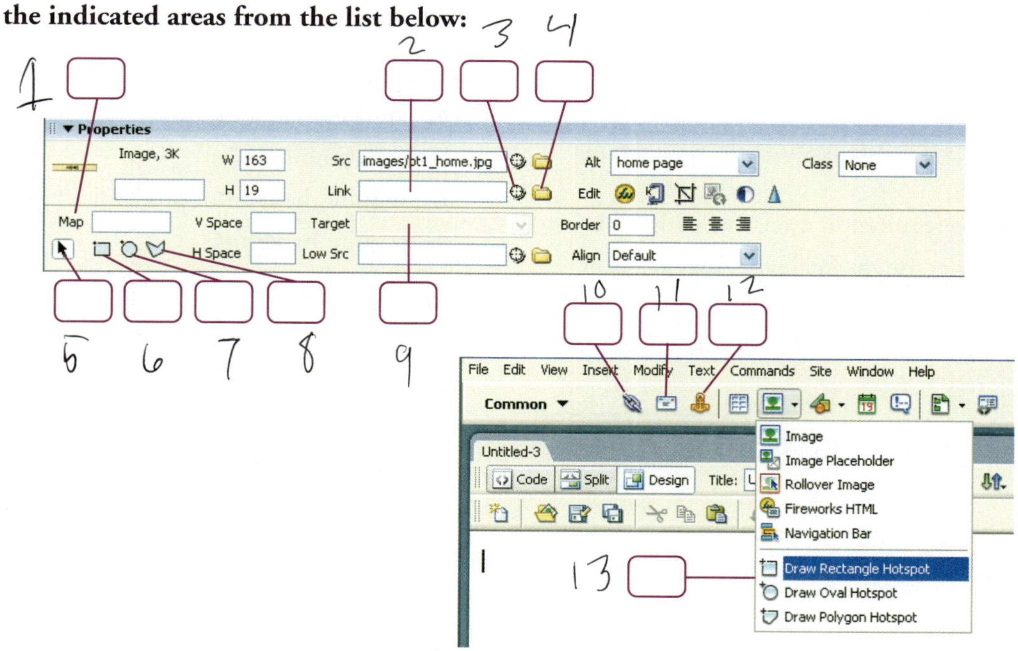


FIGURE 4.38

a. Target of link
b. Browse for File button
c. Oval Hotspot tool
d. Create a link
e. Image map name
f. Images drop-down list
g. Rectangle Hotspot tool
h. Point to File button
i. Pointer Hotspot tool
j. Create an email link
k. Polygon Hotspot tool
l. Create a named anchor
m. Link field

## MULTIPLE CHOICE

**Circle the letter of the correct answer for each of the following:**

1. Links are __________.
   - a. the fundamental building blocks of the World Wide Web
   - b. really called hyperlinks
   - c. for directing the viewer from one page to another location or resource on the Web
   - d. All of the above

2. The term protocol __________.
   - a. refers to the specific terms required for cross-platform communications
   - b. is a resource on the Internet
   - c. identifies how a browser is to handle the destination of a link
   - d. is a domain name

3. Which is not true of http?
   - a. It means that the destination is an email address.
   - b. It is not required in a relative path.
   - c. It is the acronym for HyperText Transfer Protocol.
   - d. It means that the destination is a Web page.

4. An image map in Dreamweaver __________.
   - a. must have fewer than 64 colors
   - b. must be a GIF image
   - c. has hotspot links
   - d. All of the above

5. The __________ in the Property inspector can be used to create all types of links.
   - a. Link field
   - b. Point to File button
   - c. Browse for File button
   - d. All of the above

6. Relative paths __________.
   - a. are the same as absolute paths
   - b. use the location of the current page as a starting point
   - c. are hotspots
   - d. use the root folder of the site as a starting point

7. Absolute links are necessary when linking __________.
   - a. a page to a named anchor
   - b. to a target window
   - c. to a page in another Web site
   - d. alternate text

8. Email links __________.
   - a. are Internet addresses
   - b. are absolute links
   - c. require the mailto: protocol
   - d. require hyperlinks

9. Different link regions within a single graphic __________.
   - a. are called hotspots
   - b. are an image map
   - c. do not require alternative text
   - d. All of the above

10. Links that identify sections within a page are called __________.
    - a. FAQs
    - b. target windows
    - c. named anchors
    - d. image maps

## DISCUSSION QUESTIONS

1. Some Web sites use text links and others use image maps. Describe two situations in which using image maps would be more effective than text links and explain why.
2. If you create a link to an interior page (not their home page) of another Web site, this can cause potential problems for both your visitors using the link and the Web-site owner. What might these problems be? Give an example.
3. The World Wide Web has changed the lives of everyone and every business. What role does hyperlinking play in this change?

# SKILL DRILL

Skill Drill exercises reinforce project skills. Each skill reinforced is the same, or nearly the same, as a skill presented in the project. Detailed instructions are provided in a step-by-step format. You should do the Skill Drill exercises in order.

### 1. Explore Other Methods for Creating Links

The browse-for-file method is only one method for establishing a link to a page. There are other methods that you can use to establish links to pages or named anchors. For these methods to work, the Files panel must be expanded so that the filenames are visible.

1. Open about.html from the TO-P4 site.
2. Select Home in the bottom paragraph.

3. Drag the Point to File icon from the Property inspector to default.html in the Files panel, and click default.html to set it as the destination.

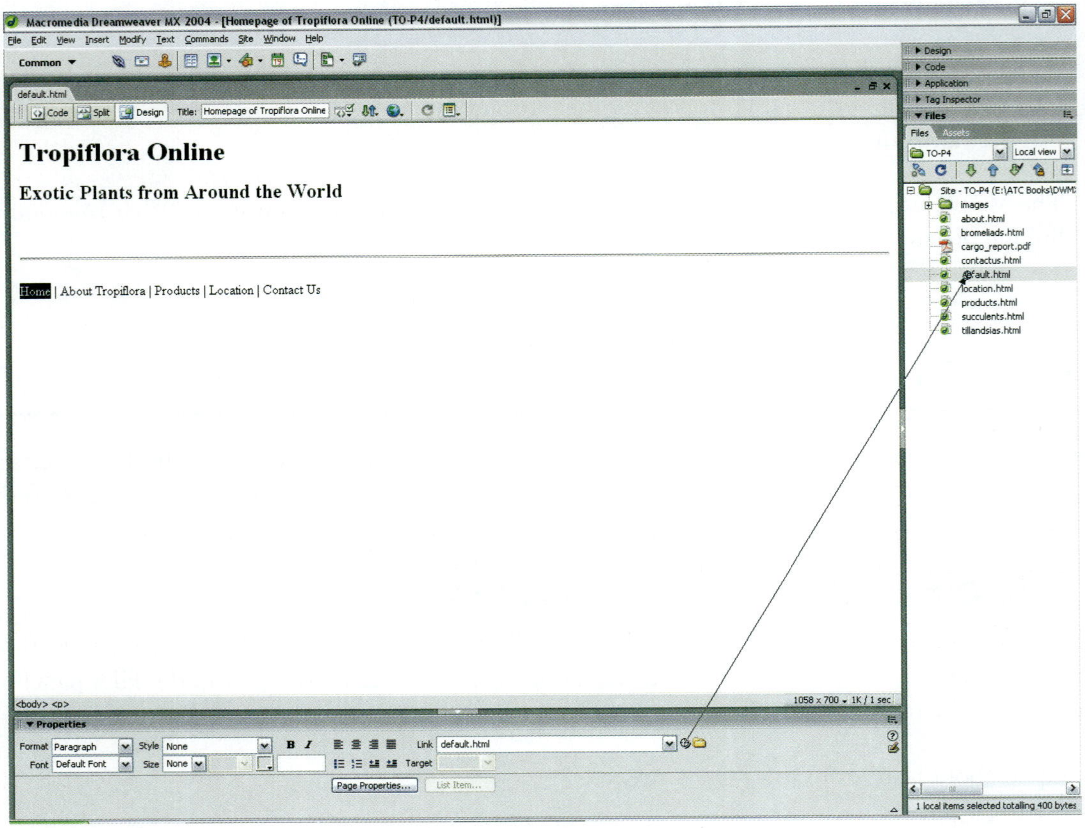

FIGURE 4.39

4. Repeat the procedure to link Products to products.html, Location to location.html, and Contact Us to contactus.html.
5. Preview the page in your browser and test the links.
6. Return to Dreamweaver and close about.html.
7. Open bromeliads.html.
8. Select "Home" at the bottom of the page.

## If you have problems

The link method outlined in Step 9 only works on Windows systems. The link methods outlined in Steps 3 and 10 work on both Windows and Macintosh systems.

9. Holding the Shift key, drag from the selected text to default.html in the Files panel.

   A line appears between Home and the mouse pointer.

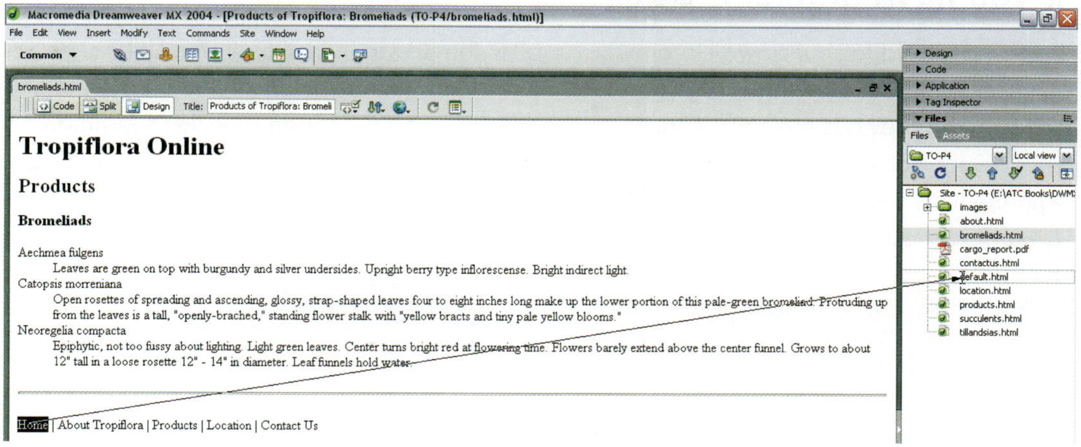

FIGURE 4.40

## If you have problems

You must hold the Shift key first before using the mouse to drag the selected text to the filename.

10. Select the "About Tropiflora" text. Right/Control-click in the selected text, choose Make Link from the context menu, choose about.html, and click OK/Choose.

    This method works in both Macintosh and Windows systems.

11. Using any of the above methods, link Products to products.html, Location to location.html, and Contact Us to contactus.html.

12. Close bromeliads.html, saving the changes.

## 2. Link Pages Using the Link List

Dreamweaver remembers the links created during a particular session and temporarily stores the links in the Link list. As it is only temporary, the Link list is emptied when you exit Dreamweaver. However, even when Dreamweaver is running, the Link list only contains links that were created during the current session. If a link to default.html was not been created during this session, it does not appear in the list.

1. Open succulents.html.

2. Select "Home" from the bottom navigation-bar paragraph.

3. Click the drop-down arrow to the right of the Link list, and choose default.html from the list.

## If you have problems

If you have had to shut down Dreamweaver after the previous Skill Drill, the Link list has emptied. To repopulate the Link list, close succulents.html, open tillandsias.html, and create the links using either of the previous methods. Close, saving tillandsias.html, reopen succulents.html, and continue with Step 2 above. By creating links using tillandsias.html, you ensure that the Link list is populated with the links needed for succulents.html.

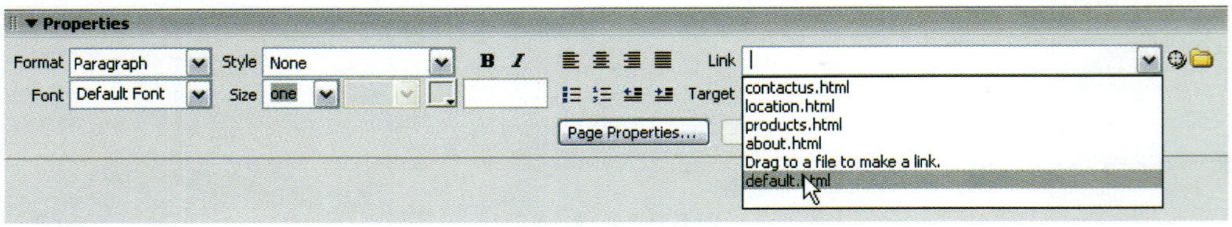


FIGURE 4.41

4. Repeat the procedure for the other items in the navigation-bar paragraph.
5. Close, saving succulents.html.
6. Open tillandsias.html. Using any method, link the items in the navigation-bar paragraph to the appropriate files. Close, saving the changes when finished.

### 3. Link to Named Anchors in Other Pages

In this Skill Drill, you create links to named anchors in pages other than the originating page. You must first create the named anchors, and then create the links.

1. Open bromeliads.html. Move the insertion point to the left of the "Aechmea fulgens" text, click the Named Anchor button in the Insert bar, type **af** as the name, and click OK. Close, saving the changes to bromeliads.html.
2. Open succulents.html. Create a named anchor called **hz** to the left of the "Hernia zebrina" text. Close, saving the changes.
3. Open tillandsias.html. Create a named anchor called **tl** to the left of the "Tillandsia latifola" text. Close, saving the changes.

4. Open both bromeliads.html and products.html. On Windows systems, choose Window>Tile Vertical to arrange the two pages side by side. On Macintosh systems, manually move and resize the two windows so they are side-by-side.

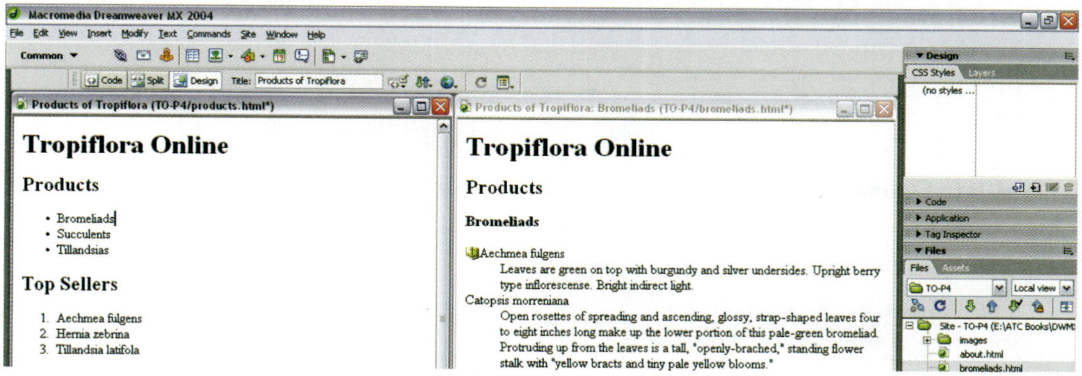

FIGURE 4.42

5. In products.html, select the "Aechmea fulgens" text below the "Products" heading.

6. Using the Point to File button in the Property inspector, drag the pointer to the **af** anchor in the bromeliads.html file.

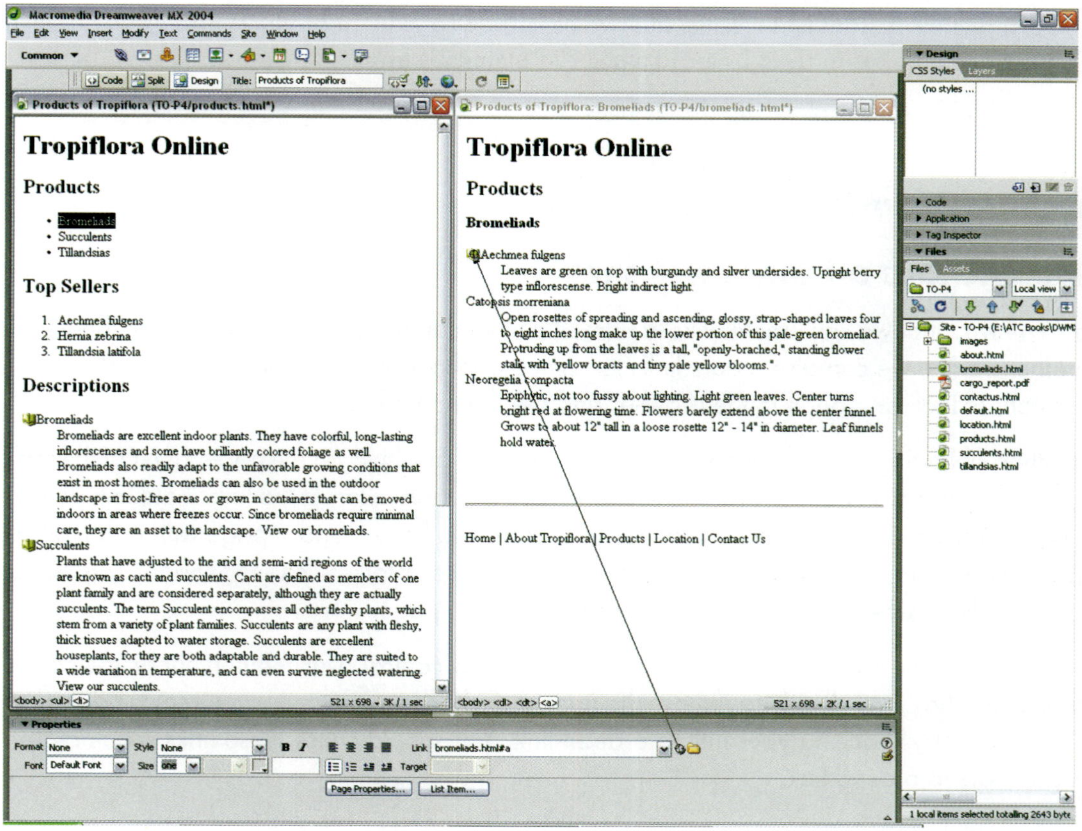

FIGURE 4.43

7. Close, saving the changes to bromeliads.html, but leave products.html open.
8. Open succulents.html and arrange the two pages side-by-side.
9. From products.html, select "Hernia zebrina" and link it to the **`hz`** named anchor in succulents.html.

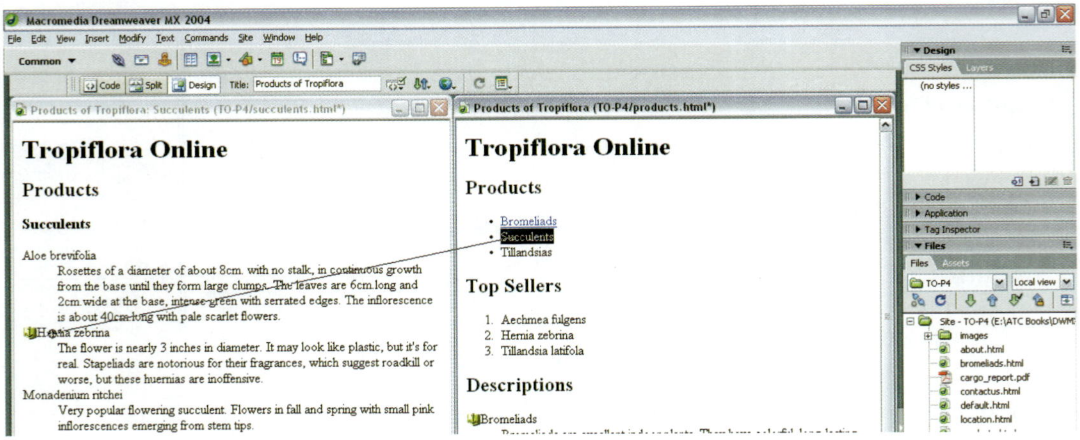


FIGURE 4.44

10. Close, saving the changes to succulents.html, but leave products.html open.
11. Open tillandsias.html and arrange the two pages side-by-side. In products.html, select "Tillandsia latifola" and link it to the **`tl`** named anchor in tillandsias.html.
12. Close both documents, saving the changes.

## To Extend Your Knowledge

### NAMED ANCHORS ON OTHER WEB SITES

In the same way that we can create links to named anchors on our own site, whether on the same page or on other pages, we can also create links to named anchors on pages of other sites. The problem is that we cannot look at a page in the browser and see the named anchors.

One method of finding named anchors on a page is to find any links on the page, often at the top of the page, move your mouse pointer over the link, and note the destination of the link. If the link points to the same page and has a # followed by text, you know that you have found a page with a named anchor. Another method is to view the actual code of the page and look for `<a name="something">`. You can then create a link to the page and the named anchor on the page.

Be aware that unlike the pages on your site, you have no control over the content or the structure of others' pages. They may decide to remove the named anchor, rename it, or even remove or rename the page itself, thereby reducing your link to a dead link. You should check these links regularly to avoid sending visitors to a dead link.

## 4. Create an Image-Map Navigation Bar

The single graphic at the bottom of the Location page was created to use as an image-map navigation bar. In this exercise, you create an image map using this graphic and link the different regions to their appropriate Web pages.

1. Open location.html.
2. Scroll to the bottom of the page and click the large graphic.

   Unlike the individual graphics in the Contact Us page that were separately linked to the appropriate pages, this single graphic will serve as a navigation bar using hotspots that link to the appropriate pages.
3. In the Map field of the Property inspector, type `navbar`.
4. Using the Rectangular Hotspot tool, outline a rectangle around the Home area of the graphic, create a link to default.html, and assign Home as the alternative text.
5. Create the remaining hotspots using the name of the area as the Alt text.
6. Preview the page in your browser.
7. Return to Dreamweaver and close location.html.

## 5. Link to a PDF Document

Most links are to other Web pages, but you may need to link to a ***PDF*** document (Portable Document Format, a Web-ready format used when the author wishes to preserve the document's original fonts and layout) or to other types of resources. For the most part, the process is the same, but because a PDF document is not a Web page, an additional attribute is recommended by the W3C. You must edit the link in the Code window to add this attribute.

1. Open products.html.
2. Click after the "Tillandsias" text in the "Products" list.
3. Press Enter/Return once and type `Grower's Supplies`.
4. Select "Grower's Supplies" and link the text to cargo_report.pdf using any method learned in this project.
5. Click the Split button at the top of the Document window.

6. At the end of the opening anchor tag **<a href="cargo_report.pdf">**, move the insertion point to the left of the closing angle bracket and type **type="application/pdf"**.

   Dreamweaver's code hints do not include the **type** attribute, although it is a valid attribute for the anchor tag since HTML 4.

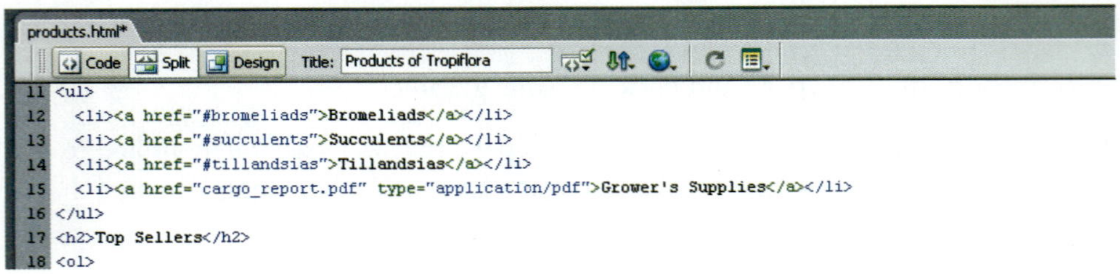


**FIGURE 4.45**

7. Close the Code window by clicking the Design button at the top of the Document window.
8. Preview the page in your browser and click the new link.

   If you have Acrobat Reader or any other PDF viewer installed on your system, the PDF document opens in the viewer or reader.

9. Return to Dreamweaver and close products.html.

## *To Extend Your Knowledge*

### MIME TYPES

***MIME*** (Multipurpose Internet Mail Extensions) was originally devised for email attachments, so that if you attached a particular type of file to a message, the recipients' email application would know how to handle the attachment, such as by playing the music, showing the video, or opening the PDF document in Acrobat Reader. MIME types also play a role in Web-page links, enabling the visitors' browsers to open the file with the appropriate application. It is not always necessary to add the MIME type to the link, especially for common types of files like PDFs. However, uncommon types of files or filename extensions, such as .pdfx, benefit from the use of the MIME type in the link; without the MIME type, users are asked by their browser which application should be used to open the file.

The MIME type is divided into the major and minor types. Major types include **application**, **audio**, and **video**, among others. In each major type, there are few to many minor types, depending on the major type. For example, the major type **application** has more than thirty minor types whereas **audio** has only a few. The MIME type format identifies the major type, followed by a forward slash, then the minor type: **application/pdf**, for example. You can find a brief description of MIME types and a breakdown of the major and minor types at http://www.ltsw.se/knbase/internet/mime.htp. The Webopedia is also a good resource for many computer-related terms: MIME types are described at http://www.webopedia.com/TERM/M/MIME.html.

## 6. Use Link Management in Dreamweaver

Without question, one of Dreamweaver's strongest features is its ability to update and fix links that, for one reason or another, get broken. The first step in managing links is to identify the current state of your links. The Check Links Sitewide function causes Dreamweaver to check every link on the site. When you issue the command, the program produces a report that categorizes all links on the site, letting you know which need attention. You can choose to look at broken links, external links, or ***orphaned files*** — files that exist in the site but aren't linked to any of the site's active pages.

If you rename a file in the site folder, Dreamweaver recognizes that other files link to this file and that their links need to change to reflect the filename change. It asks you if you want to update dependent files with the new link directions.

All of these functions are possible if you define a site in Dreamweaver. If the Project_04 folder were not set up as a site, it would still be possible to do all of the exercises in this project; if you changed a filename, you would have to manually change the links in all files that link to it. This is why defining a site is so important.

1. Right/Control-click default.html in the Files panel.
2. Choose Check Links>Entire Current Site from the menu.
3. Observe that the Results panel opens below the Property inspector.

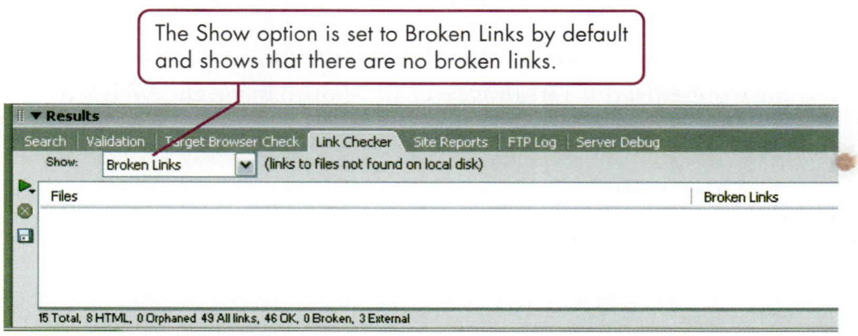


FIGURE 4.46

4. Click the down arrow to choose External Links from the Show list.

   Email links and links to external Web pages are both considered external links.

5. Choose Orphaned Files from the Show list.

   There are no pages or files in the TO-P4 folder to which there are no links.

6. Close the Results panel by clicking the panel menu at the far right of the panel, and choosing Close Panel Group.

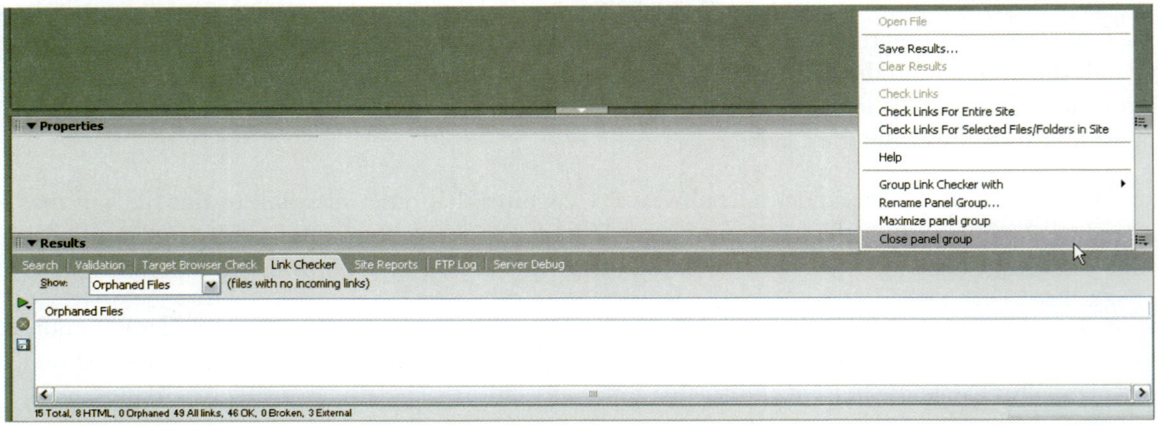


FIGURE 4.47

7. In the Files panel, Right/Control-click default.html and choose Edit>Rename.
8. Type **`index.html`** and press Enter/Return.
9. Click the Update button to update the links in the displayed files.

   All pages in this Web site are linked to default.html, the Home page. When you renamed the file, the links could have gone dead if Dreamweaver did not manage the Web site.

## CHALLENGE

Challenge exercises expand on or are somewhat related to skills presented in the lessons. Each exercise provides a brief narrative introduction, followed by instructions in a numbered-step format that are not as detailed as those in the Skill Drill section. You should do these Challenge exercises in order.

### 1. Set Links in a Page to the Others in the Site

In this Challenge, you create the links from the FAQ page to the other pages in the site. You can use any method taught previously in the Lessons or Skill Drills — this is a good opportunity to experiment with all of the methods to get comfortable with them.

The pages in this site contain graphics, JavaScript, and CSS. When you create the links in this page, the text changes color. This is a function of the styles applied to the link text.

1. Set the Project_04>DF-P4 folder as a defined site in Dreamweaver. Name it DF-P4 and ensure Access (in both the Remote Info and Testing Server categories) and Server Model are set to None.
2. Open faqs.htm.

   The two major groups of links are those down the left side of the page and along the bottom in the footer area. For the most part they are identical, except for the link to the design agency that created this Web site. This link is only in the footer area.
3. Using any method taught previously, link Home to index.htm, About to about.htm, Formal Wear to formalwear.htm, and so on in both the left navbar and the footer navbar.
4. In the footer of the page, link redrhino to http://www.redrhino.co.uk.
5. In the last paragraph above the footer, link contact us to contact.htm.
6. In the top-right corner of the page is a Contact Us graphic — link it to contact.htm.
7. Preview the page in your browser and test the links.
8. Return to Dreamweaver and leave the file open for the next Challenge.

### 2. Create Named Anchors and Links

At the top of the FAQs page are the frequently asked questions. You will link them to the appropriate paragraphs below where the questions are repeated and the answers are given. First you create the named anchors and then the links.

1. In the open file faqs.htm, click in front of the first paragraph that has the answer to the first question. You can place the named anchor in front of the sentence beginning with "How much notice" or in front of the answer immediately below it beginning with "With wedding suits."
2. Create a named anchor simply called a1 (numeral one).
3. Repeat the same procedure for the remaining eleven questions — create a named anchor either in front of the question or at the beginning of the answer.

4. Scroll to the top.
5. Select the first question in the list.
6. Using the Point to File button in the Property inspector, point to the first named anchor.
7. Select the second question in the list.
8. In the Link field of the Property inspector, type **#a2** (the named anchor for the second answer).
9. Continue to link the questions at the top with the named anchors beside the answers below.

### If you have problems

The page is too long to see the last few questions and their answers below in the same screen. To link the questions at the top and the answers at the bottom, there are two possible methods:

(1) Select the question and then type the anchor name in the Link field of the Property inspector.

(2) Select the question, scroll down until the named anchor is visible, and then drag the Point to File icon to the named anchor. The selected text does not need to be visible to create a link from it to the named anchor.

10. In the bottom-right corner is a graphic of the text Top. Click the Top graphic and link it to #top either by typing **#top** in the Link field or scrolling up and using the Point to File button to point to the named anchor in the top-left corner of the page. The purpose of this link is to return the reader quickly to the top of the page.
11. Preview the page in your browser and test the links.
12. Return to Dreamweaver and close faqs.htm.

## 3. Create Links from Appropriately Descriptive Text

You learned earlier that "click here" is not appropriate link text. In this exercise, the home page of Debonair Formalwear has been changed to include many click here phrases. Your task is to remove them and create links from appropriate words or phrases in the remaining text.

1. Open index.htm.
2. Under the section entitled Formal Wear — The last word in Black Tie, click the link text "here" and make note of the destination page for the link.
3. From that paragraph, delete the last sentence that includes the "here" text link.
4. Select an appropriate word or phrase in the remaining sentence, and create a link to the same destination to which "here" was previously linked.
5. Continue to refine the links in the main content of this page (leaving the left and bottom navigation bars alone).
6. Preview this page in your browser to ensure that the links are working correctly.
7. Return to Dreamweaver and close index.htm.

## 4. Create a List of Links to Competitive Businesses

Debonair Formalwear competes with other businesses to provide clients in the UK with formalwear. Your task is to search the Internet for five other businesses in the UK that offer formalwear for rent or purchase, and to list them as other competitive businesses.

1. Open competition.htm.

   The first business has been created for you as the first list item. You must find five others and record them using the same formatting.

2. Using your browser and your favorite search-engine Web site, search for another business in the UK that may compete with Debonair Formalwear.

   (When you perform your search, use the search term "hire" instead of "rent".) Make note of the URL to the business's Web site, a brief description (a single sentence is fine) indicating the products and/or services of the business, and the phone number of the business.

3. Type the name of the business in the next bullet.

4. Select the name of the business and link it to the URL of the business's Web site. Set the link to open in a new browser window, and add a **`title`** attribute to the opening anchor tag that reads: "Link opens in new window." Press Shift-Enter/Return and type (or copy and paste) a descriptive paragraph about the services or products of the business. Press Shift-Enter/Return and type (or copy and paste) the phone number of the business. Press Enter/Return to create a new bullet.

5. Continue to insert four more businesses in the same manner.

6. Open faqs.htm and create a link from an appropriate word or phrase in the document to competition.htm.

7. Close and save the changes to faqs.htm.

8. Preview competition.htm in your browser.

9. Return to Dreamweaver and close competition.htm.

## PORTFOLIO BUILDER

### Create a Portal Site

A "portal" site is one that provides related links and information specific to one or more subjects. There are many examples of such sites on the Web. In this assignment, you're going to create one of your own.

1. Pick a subject about which you have a personal interest. It could be anything you like to do — carpentry, fishing, hiking, skating, skiing, or some other recreational pursuit.
2. Create a Home page to act as a container for links to related sites.
3. Use Google or another search engine to locate at least twelve sites that provide information that is relevant to the subject.
4. Create links to each of the sites, including space for a small amount of descriptive text.
5. Check the links to make sure they all work as you expected them to.
6. Include an email link so visitors can submit new sites to include in the list.

# PROJECT 5

# Inline Images

## OBJECTIVES

***In this project, you learn how to***

- Choose the correct graphic format
- Insert graphics into a Web page
- Align images within a paragraph
- Set image borders and spacing
- Crop oversized images
- Resize, resample, sharpen, and adjust images
- Work with image placeholders

# WHY WOULD I DO THIS?

It wasn't so long ago that colors, images, and computing didn't coexist gracefully. Prior to the mid-1980s, most computer systems were character-based and would not display graphics, let alone multiple colors. Early computer monitors displayed text in either green or amber, and few would call those displays "color monitors." Putting images onto computer screens is a relatively recent advance.

Although the Internet was first created in the late 1960s, it wasn't until the early 1990s that images began to appear on Web pages. The appeal of graphics in Web pages was significant to the Internet, becoming part of almost everyone's life. If pictures were worth a thousand words, as the saying goes, how many words would Flash animation, videos, or downloadable music be worth? Without the media-rich content we've grown accustomed to, the Web would be a much less popular place.

Although, you can build entire Web sites using images alone, it is not recommended. Certainly some sites require an extensive number of graphics — catalog sites and artists' portfolio sites are just a few such examples. Some individuals, however, make graphics out of the text to preserve its formatting. When graphic designers create elaborate printed works, they don't have to worry about whether the text is in a standard or highly modified font. The amount of file space that the resulting brochure may take on the designer's computer does not affect the reader of the printed product. However, if you primarily use images to build your sites, you have to take into account that images weigh more, that is, they take longer to download than does type. For this reason, it is generally recommended that you use HTML and CSS to style your text instead of creating a graphic from the text.

Spotted in an email: "A picture may be worth a thousand words but a thousand words take less time to download." Selective use of images, appropriate choice of formats, and application of available image options ensures the fastest possible access speed for your visitors. Graphic designers with extensive print experience are accustomed to having many color choices and layout options available for print design; they often feel frustrated by the apparent limitation of design options available for Web work. Yet you can achieve great Web design with the right tools and knowledge.

In this project, you learn about the different types of graphic formats so you can make choices about which format is appropriate in each situation. You learn how to insert graphics on a page; align them to the left or right; place borders around them; and use Dreamweaver's image-editing tools to crop, resize, resample, and sharpen graphics. Not all Web sites need lots of graphics, but virtually all Web sites have some. This project enables you to work with graphics, few or many, in your Web pages.

# VISUAL SUMMARY

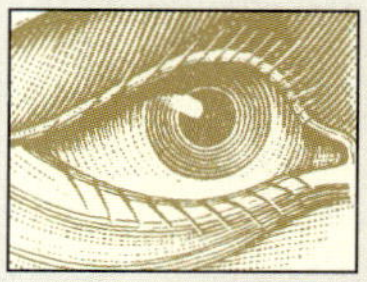

Dreamweaver has many functions with which you can insert and manipulate images. You can insert images and image placeholders from the Files panel, the Assets panel, or the Images drop-down menu on the Common Insert bar (Figure 5.1). From the Common Insert bar, you select the Images:Image button, which also has a drop-down list of other image-related functions. You also use the Image Placeholder function, which allows you to reserve space for a graphic until the final version is available to insert into the Web page.

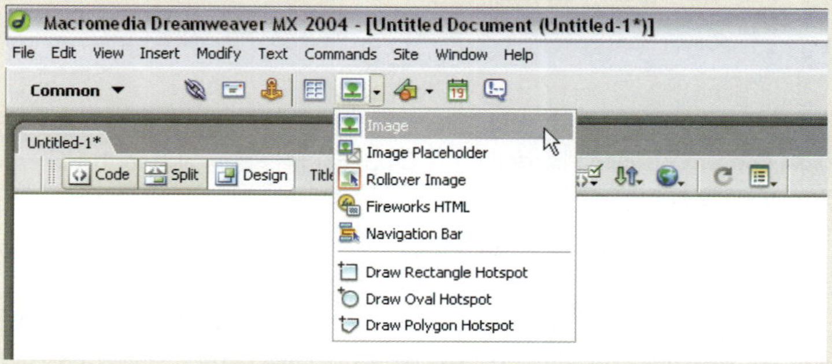


FIGURE 5.1

The Assets panel is part of the File panel group; you can expand it by clicking the Assets tab. Assets are resources – such as graphics, library items, and templates — that you can use in your Web site. You select the type of asset by clicking the appropriate button at the left of the Assets panel. At the top of this panel is a preview window that allows you to see the graphic before inserting it. Below the preview window is a list of the graphics available in the folders of the current site.

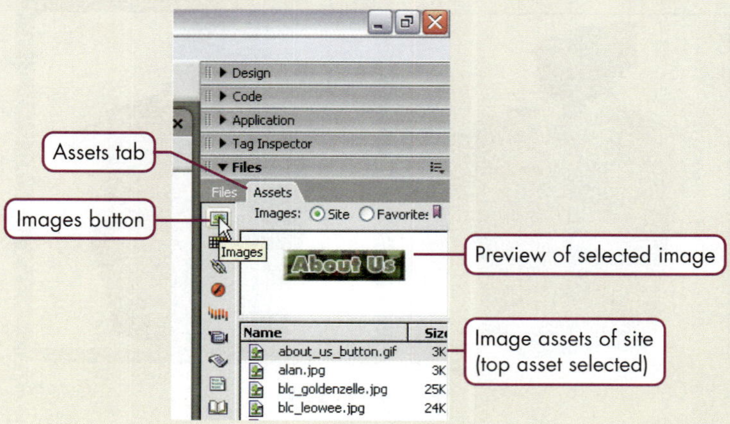


FIGURE 5.2

When you select an image, many properties of the image appear in the Property inspector, such as file size (measured in kilobytes), width, and height. The Property inspector displays other attributes of the image, such as alternate text, alignment, border, and horizontal and vertical spacing. You can view or modify any of these properties using the Property inspector.

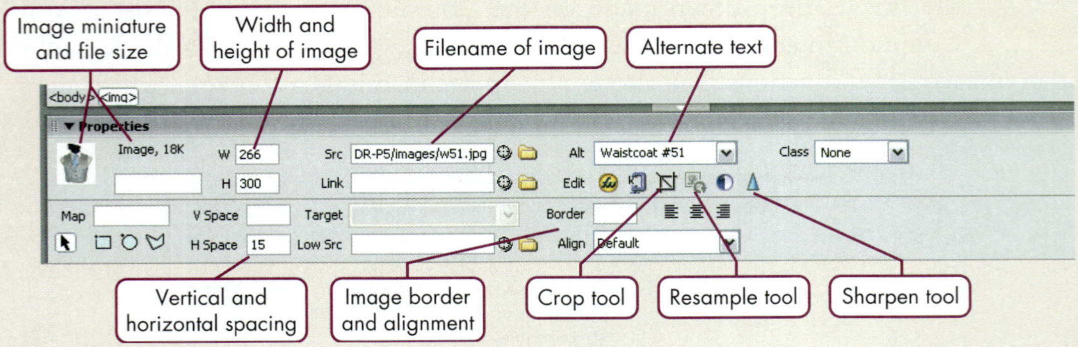


**FIGURE 5.3**

You can identify a selected image in the Document window because it has three handles. You drag these handles to enlarge or reduce the size of the image. Dreamweaver also offers some basic image-editing tools, such as the Crop, Resample, and Sharpen tools. In the following figure, the image on the right in the Dreamweaver window is ready for cropping — the crop area is outlined with a dashed line. You can resize the crop area using any of the eight handles that appear around it.

**FIGURE 5.4**

# LESSON 1 Exploring Graphic Formats

In this lesson, you learn why different types of graphics are better suited for particular situations by comparing different types of images — photographic images and text graphics. You cannot create graphics in Dreamweaver, but as a Web designer, you can work with a graphic designer who prepares the images. Knowing which formats are best suited for Web pages for different purposes will help you either guide the graphic designer or select among the graphic options. We restrict our comparisons to JPEG, GIF, and PNG graphics because visitors can view them all using most modern browsers.

There are dozens of graphic-file formats, but only a few are Web-compatible. Virtually all popular illustration and imaging programs — Macromedia Fireworks, Adobe Illustrator, Macromedia Freehand, Adobe Photoshop, and others — can convert graphics to these formats. You need to understand the differences between the different formats and the options available for each, so that you can choose the appropriate format for the situation.

Image formats for the Web fall into two broad categories. ***Bitmap images*** are comprised of individual pixels, each containing a specific color or tone value. This group includes GIF (.gif), JPEG (.jpeg or .jpg), and PNG (.png) graphic formats.

The GIF format is the most common image format used for Web graphics. ***GIF*** is an acronym for Graphic Interchange Format. It's best to use this GIF format for relatively simple graphics with large areas of solid (also called "flat") color, such as button elements, because the GIF format can only contain 256 colors (also referred to as "8-bit color" because $2 \times 2 \times 2 \times 2 \times 2 \times 2 \times 2 \times 2 = 2^8 = 256$). This format has several features and options. You can specify that it contain transparent regions by choosing one color, generally the background, to be transparent. ***Animated GIFs*** are multiple-layered GIFs in which layers display sequentially, simulating movement. You can also set GIFs to ***interlace***, that is, load in a series of steps. Each stage makes the graphic appear sharper until the image reaches its final quality. Interlacing is useful for displaying a large graphic — impatient visitors who see the progressive display of the graphic are less likely to move from your Web site before the graphic has finished loading. GIF graphics use ***lossless compression***, which means that the file size is smaller without losing any graphic information.

The ***JPEG*** graphic format (developed by the Joint Photographic Experts Group) is best for ***high-color images***, or images containing many subtle colors, such as photographs or gradients. The JPEG graphic format supports up to 16.7 million colors (or 24-bit color). In contrast to GIFs, JPEGs use ***lossy compression*** — the higher the compression, the smaller the file size and the more information is lost. Most digital cameras store their photos in JPEG format with a low compression ratio, allowing some shrinkage of the file size with limited loss of photographic information. Like GIFs, JPEGs have a progressive-loading option.

The ***PNG*** (Portable Network Graphics) graphic format is the least-common graphics format. It is a relative newcomer to the Web graphics scene, so some of its features are not supported by all browsers. It has many features similar to GIFs (which it was designed to replace) such as transparency, lossless compression, and progressive loading, but in all cases the features are much better implemented. The PNG format does not support animation, although a related format, MNG (Multiple-image Network Graphics), is being developed for that purpose. You can save PNGs in either 8-bit (256 colors) or 24-bit (16.7 million colors) format. While it may seem that the 24-bit color mode is suitable to replace JPEGs, the lossy compression routine in JPEGs produces smaller file sizes than 24-bit PNGs.

***Vector graphics*** are comprised of mathematically described lines and shapes. The use of vector graphics on the Web is relatively new, and includes Flash animation and SVG. CorelDraw, Adobe Illustrator, and Macromedia Freehand and Fireworks all primarily create vector graphics, but often users convert their illustrations to GIF, PNG, or JPEG format for use in a Web page.

Flash objects can be static or animated, and can even change in response to user actions, such as responding to the position of the mouse pointer or to keystrokes. The Flash format is compressed, enabling quick downloads. Dreamweaver cannot create complex Flash objects or animations, but it can create static Flash text and some simple Flash-animated buttons. For more information about Flash and to learn how to create elements that you can use in your Dreamweaver sites, refer to *Essentials for Design: Macromedia Flash MX 2004 Level 1.*

The ***Scalable Vector Graphics*** (SVG) format is a new vector format that can incorporate vector graphics, bitmap images, and text. It can be both dynamic and interactive. Although some graphic-illustration software (such as CorelDraw and Adobe Illustrator) can save to the SVG format, browsers cannot display these images without a plug-in. There is much hope that this format will be widely adopted but, given the seven years since the PNG format was recommended by the W3C without yet achieving complete acceptance by the general population and all browsers, the SVG format may be a few years away from widespread adoption. SVG is a text-based format, like HTML, in which code describes the shapes, positions, and colors, as in Figure 5.5, in which the sixth line in the code describes the red circle shown to the left.

```
<?xml version="1.0" encoding="ISO-8859-1" standalone="no"?>
<!DOCTYPE svg PUBLIC "-//W3C//DTD SVG 20010904//EN"
    "http://www.w3.org/TR/2001/REC-SVG-20010904/DTD/svg10.dtd">
<svg xmlns="http://www.w3.org/2000/svg"
     xmlns:xlink="http://www.w3.org/1999/xlink">
     <circle cx="25" cy="25" r="20" fill="red"/>
</svg>
```

FIGURE 5.5

Until you compare images using these formats, you cannot truly appreciate the differences between them and how one can be better than another in different circumstances. To what degree does JPEG's lossy compression have an effect on the quality of the image? Does the 256-color depth of GIF images limit its use? How do the compression routines of GIF and PNG images compare in terms of final file size? Should you choose index or alpha transparency? Although you cannot create graphics in Dreamweaver, knowing about the different graphic formats will enable you to work with a graphic designer to make the best choices and give good advice.

## Explore Different Image Formats for Photographs

In this exercise, you learn that the JPEG format is best for photographs, even when there are few enough colors in the photos for the GIF format. File size rather than image quality becomes the determining factor in the choice of graphic formats.

1. **Define the Project_05>Graphics folder as a site called Graphics using the methods outlined in previous projects. Do not click Done — leave the Site Definition dialog box open for the next step.**

**2** **Click the first site in the list and click the Remove button. When asked to confirm the removal, click Yes. Repeat until you have removed all sites from the list (except the Graphics site you defined in Step 1). Click Done when finished.**

As you create more and more Web sites and site definitions, your list of sites in the Files panel and Site Definition dialog box can become long and cumbersome. By removing the site definitions, it is easier to work with your current Web-site projects. Removing a site definition from the site listing does not delete the site from your computer — the folders and files remain as they were, but they are just not listed in the sites list. You can recreate the site definition for removed sites at any time to work on them again.

## ? If you have problems

Complex sites may have remote access, testing server, and other advanced settings that require more effort to recreate the site definition. For these more-complex site definitions, record all settings before removing the site definition. The site definitions in this book are very simple and require very little effort to recreate if you wish to do so.

**3** **Open photos.html in Dreamweaver and preview it in your browser.**

**4** **Compare the photos in cells 1a and 1b.**

Both are high-quality images, but the lossy compression routine in the JPEG format makes possible a smaller file size.

FIGURE 5.6

**5** **Compare the photos in cells 2a, 2b, and 2c.**

The JPEG format is better for photographs because it supports a wider range of colors and tones — the 8-bit GIF and PNG formats do not smoothly render the blending of greens in the background. If the JPEG compression setting is too high (2a), the quality of the image is sacrificed.

FIGURE 5.7

**6** **Compare the photos in cells 3a, 3b, and 3c.**

A black-and-white photograph (as a digital file) can contain up to 256 shades of gray. The GIF and 8-bit PNG formats support up to 256 colors, allowing the formats to display all of the shades of gray. However, accurate rendering of a black-and-white photograph in these GIF and PNG images comes at a cost in file size — more than double that of the JPEG image.

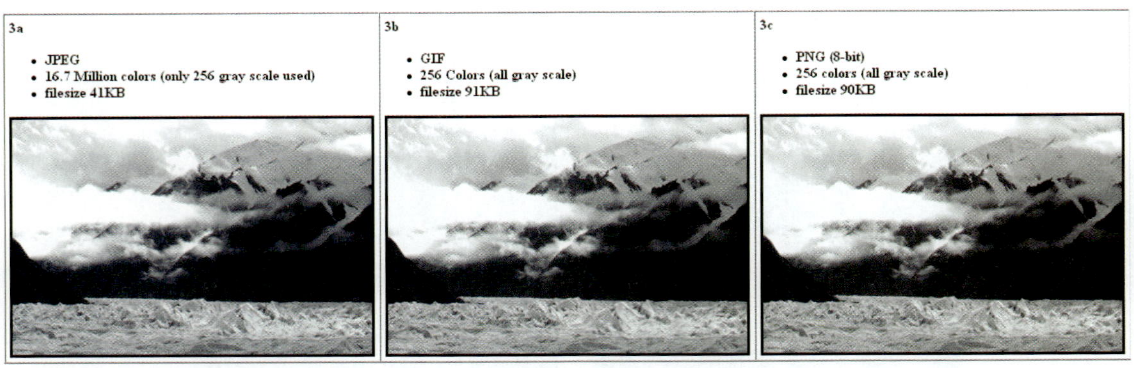


FIGURE 5.8

**7** **Return to Dreamweaver and close photos.html.**

## *To Extend Your Knowledge*

### FAVICON IMAGES

***Favicon*** is a word created from favorite and icon. It refers to the icon that appears at the left end of the Address bar or at the left end of a bookmark entry in your Favorites list (hence favorite). Commonly the icon is similar to the logo of the company or the Web site. A favicon is a 16 × 16 pixel image saved in a special icon format. Not all graphics applications can create this type of image, but you can go to favicon.co.uk to create one for free online. (They email the resulting image to you.)

To use the icon so that people visiting your Web site sees it in their browsers' address bar, you must save the icon as favicon.ico in the root folder of your Web site, not in the graphics folder or any other folder. You must also add the following code in the **<head>** section of your Web pages: **<link rel="shortcut icon" href="/favicon.ico" type="image/x-icon">** . You must code this manually, as Dreamweaver does not have any menu functions to assist you.

## Explore Different Image Formats for Simple Graphics

In this next exercise, you discover that GIF and PNG formats are best suited to simple graphics. You also observe that splitting a graphic into complex and simple components reduces the total download time by optimizing the different parts of the graphics for the appropriate file type.

**1** **Open buttons.html in your browser.**

**2** **Compare the images in cells 1a and 1b.**

The file-size difference is obvious although, in reality, using the JPEG image only adds 11KB to the total download. However, if every simple image were saved in JPEG format instead of the GIF format, the ***weight*** of the Web page (the number of bytes used by the Web page between images, HTML, and other resources) would climb unnecessarily.

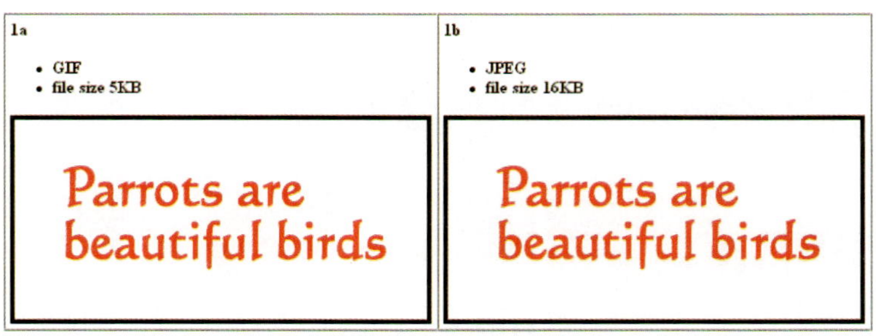


FIGURE 5.9

**3** **Compare the images in cells 2a and 2b.**

GIF animation can add some interest to a page, but can also be distracting. These animations have much larger file sizes than static images, even with optimization.

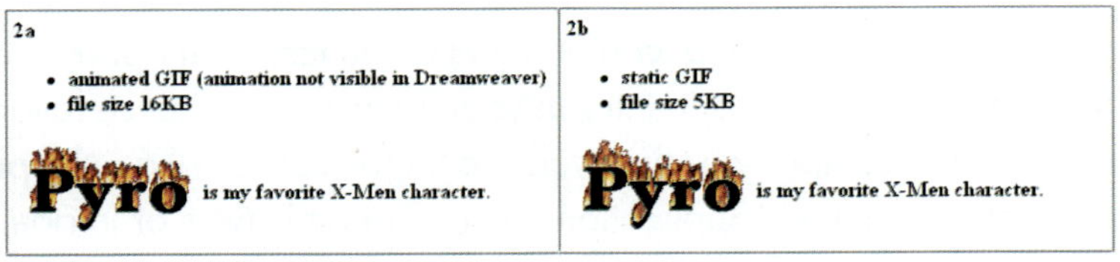


FIGURE 5.10

**4** **Compare the images in cells 3a and 3b.**

Setting a color to be transparent in a GIF image does not take any additional file space.

FIGURE 5.11

**5** **Compare the images in cells 4a, 4b, 4c, and 4d.**

These four cells compare the transparency options of PNG and GIF graphic formats. Cell 4a contains a PNG with ***alpha-transparency***, a form of transparency that supports a range of transparency from opaque to transparent. No version of IE displays a PNG with alpha-transparency — cell 4c displays a screenshot image of how cell 4a should appear in a supporting browser. Only PNG images can use alpha-transparency. Both GIF (cell 4b) and PNG (4d) can use ***index transparency***, a form of transparency in which you can set one color, generally the background color, to 100% transparent. Again, the PNG graphic is smaller than the identical graphic in GIF format.

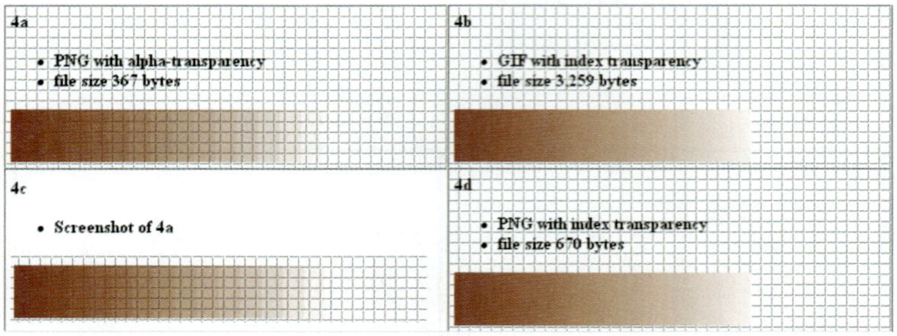


FIGURE 5.12

**6** **Switch to Dreamweaver without closing your browser.**

Notice that Dreamweaver displays the PNG image in cell 4a with its alpha-transparency, but all PNGs have an incorrect color. Until this is corrected, do not depend on the color of PNG graphics in Dreamweaver for color matching. Use a graphics application, such as Macromedia Fireworks, to identify the colors in PNG graphics.

**7** **Return to your browser and compare the images in cells 5a and 5b.**

The banner in 5a is a single, large JPEG image. You learned that JPEG is a good format for photos, but wastes file space where the graphic information is simple. The banner in 5b was split into two parts — the left photo of the birds and the right black box with red text.

FIGURE 5.13

**8** **Return to Dreamweaver and close buttons.html.**

## To Extend Your Knowledge

### INDEX VS. ALPHA TRANSPARENCY

As you saw, both GIF graphics and PNG graphics can employ transparency. Both formats support index transparency — one specific color, generally the background color, is set to 100% transparency.

Alpha transparency is not limited to a single color, or to 100% transparency. Each pixel in a graphic has an ***RGB*** (red, green, blue) code that specifies how much of each color should be used to create the color of the pixel. Images that support alpha transparency use a color palette that is sometimes referred to as "RGBa," where the "a" represents the alpha channel. The alpha channel, just like the R, G, and B channels (or colors) in an image, has a range of values from 0 to 255, but instead of a color, the alpha channel specifies the transparency of the pixel — 0 is opaque and 255 is transparent. This means that adjacent pixels of different colors may have different levels of transparency.

# LESSON 2 Inserting Images into a Web Page

An ***inline image*** is a graphic that you insert into the foreground of the Web page among the other content. (We discuss background images in Project 6.) You can use inline images in interesting and novel ways in a Web site. For a client company, you might use the corporate logo as a link to the home page. You could use images in navigation bars to dress up parts of a Web page, as you saw in Project 4. You could use photos to accompany news stories. In a Web-based photo album, you might link ***thumbnails*** (miniature photos) to larger versions of the photos for better viewing.

While you can use images effectively and creatively, remember that graphic images cost more in download time than text. The term cost may seem odd, given that most ***ISPs*** (***Internet Service Providers*** — businesses that provide access to the Internet) offer unlimited access to the Internet for a fixed fee. If your ISP doesn't charge based on usage, how could a large image cost more than a small image? ISPs may not charge based on ***bandwidth*** (the quantity of megabytes being transferred to and from their Web servers), but Web-hosting providers and high-volume Internet connections do. If your image-dense designs cost your clients large bandwidth fees, they will not be happy. Before you use a graphic, evaluate its value, size, format, and quality — controlling all of these will enable you to balance design needs, download speed, and bandwidth costs.

An image uses the **`<img>`** tag, an empty tag. This tag has two required attributes — the **`src`** (source) attribute and the **`alt`** (alternate text) attribute. An **`<img>`** tag without an image source does not produce an image, so this attribute is never omitted. However, many people do not realize that the **`alt`** attribute is also required. An **`<img>`** tag without alternate text hinders people who use screen-reader software, character-based browsers, or browsers with graphics disabled from being able to use your Web site efficiently.

Once you've determined which images you want to use, you need to know how to place them on pages and how Dreamweaver handles images as components of a defined site. On the Common Insert bar is an Images button that opens the Image dialog box, allowing you to select an image. You can also drag an image from the Files panel into the page. Do not, however, double-click an image in the Files panel — that action tries to open the image in an image-editing application, such as Fireworks.

## Insert Images from the Insert Bar

There are several different methods for inserting inline images into your Web page. Inserting images from the Common Insert bar is just one of them. Through this project, you learn other methods as well.

1. **Define the Project_05>TO-P5 folder as a site called TO-P5 using the methods outlined in previous projects.**

2. **Open index.html and delete the top Tropiflora Online heading.**

**3** **From the Common Insert bar, click the Images:Image button.**

The button is called Images:Image because it is a drop-down button providing access to several image options. The current function is the Image function for inserting images into the page. The button's tool-tip text and icon change to reflect the last image function used, such as Images:Image Placeholder or Images:Rollover Image.

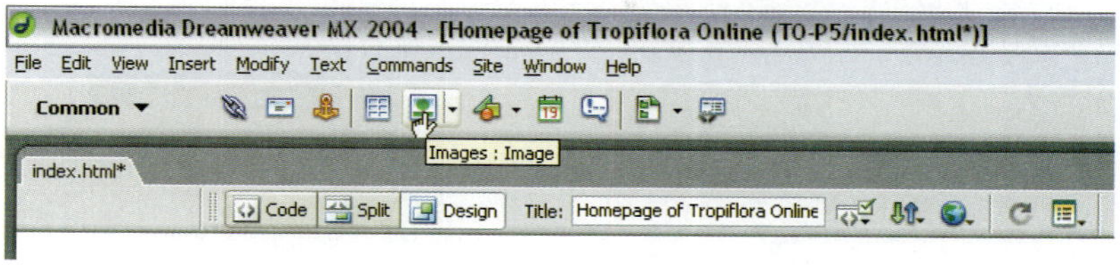


FIGURE 5.14

## If you have problems

If the Common Insert bar is not visible, use the pop-up menu at the left of the Insert bar and choose Common. If the fifth button from the left does not look like the Images button, click the drop-down list arrow to the right of the fifth button and choose Images from the top of the list. The Images:Image button changes its icon to represent the last image function selected from this list.

**4** **In the Select Image Source dialog box, double-click the images folder.**

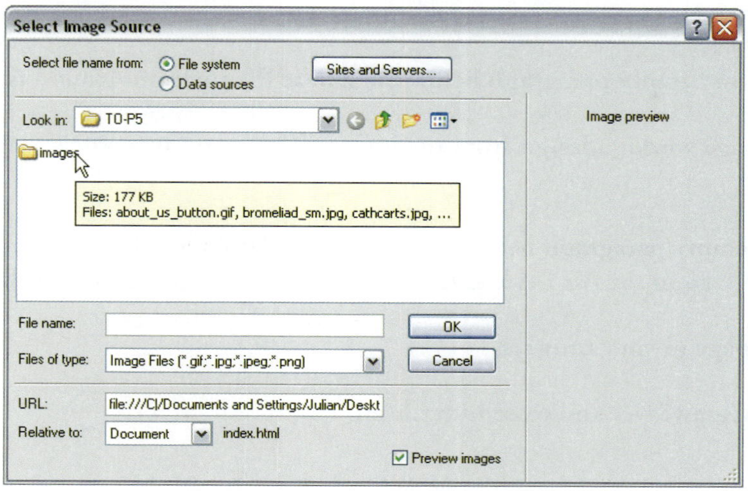


FIGURE 5.15

**5** Choose tropiflora_online.jpg and click OK/Choose.

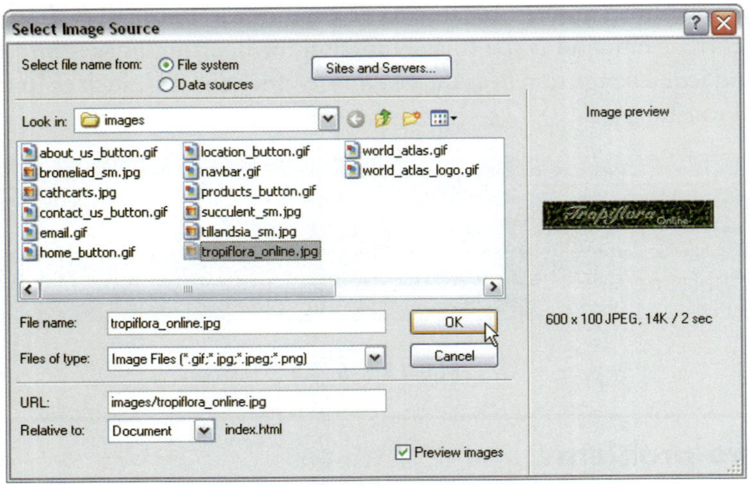


FIGURE 5.16

**6** In the Alt (alternate text) field of the Property inspector, type `Tropiflora Online`.

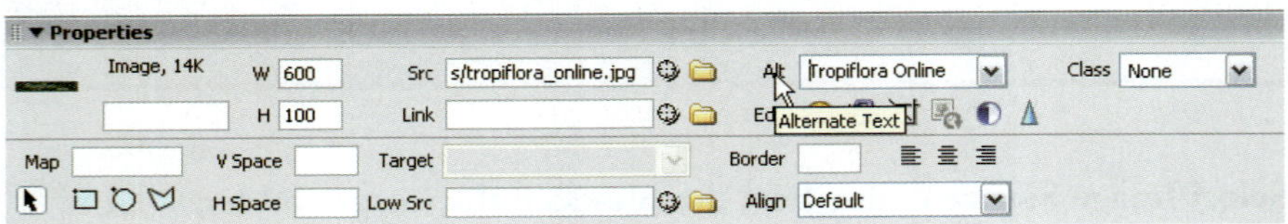


FIGURE 5.17

**7** Click in the first empty paragraph below the Exotic Plants from Around the World heading.

**8** Insert the image world_atlas.gif from the images folder, and type `World Atlas` in the Alt field.

**9** Click in the empty paragraph below, insert world_atlas_logo.gif, type `Logo of WorldAtlas.Com` in the Alt field, and link the image to http://www.worldatlas.com.

**10** Preview the page in your browser.

**11** Return to Dreamweaver and close index.html.

## To Extend Your Knowledge

### APPROPRIATE ALTERNATE TEXT FOR IMAGES

All images should have alternate text so users not viewing the graphics receive the appropriate information about images they encounter. You first categorize the image as decorative, simple, or complex. This categorization helps you determine what amount or type of alternate text is appropriate.

Decorative images provide no content to the Web page. The appropriate alternate text is **`alt=""`**, which is known as an "empty alt." In Dreamweaver, the **`<empty>`** option in the Alt field inserts an empty alt.

Simple images include button graphics or company logos. When these graphics are simply graphical text, make the alternate text the text in the image. Otherwise, keep this text very brief: "Home" for a home page, and the company name for a corporate logo, such as "IBM Corporation".

Complex images include maps or charts from spreadsheet applications. Since these images convey a large amount of information, explain them, but briefly. Although there is no limit to how much text you can put in the alternate-text attribute, when a screen reader encounters alternate text, it reads it all to the user who is forced to listen to it all before moving on. The general rule of thumb is to limit alternate text to a few words at most.

# LESSON 3 Aligning Images

You can align images in your Web designs, but with somewhat more limited options than you would have in print design. The most common alignment options used for Web graphics are left and right. However, when you select left or right alignment for an image, the alignment works a bit differently than text alignment. Of course, the image shifts to the left or right, as selected, but the text of the paragraph flows around the image on the opposite site — text flows (wraps) around a left-aligned image on its right side and vice versa. If the image is taller than the height of the paragraph in which it is inserted, the following paragraph also wraps around it until, reaching the bottom of the image, the text flows below it. The other result of choosing left or right alignment is that the top of the image aligns with the top of the characters. Without any alignment chosen, by default, the bottom of the graphic aligns with the bottom of the characters.

There is no center option for alignment of graphics — you must apply center alignment to the entire paragraph (or other block element) in which the graphic resides. In addition, any text in the same centered paragraph does not flow around it on either or both sides. Generally, you center an image if it is the only content in a paragraph.

## Align Images

**1** **Open products.html.**

**2** **In the Descriptions section of the page, click to the left of the named anchor on the left of the Bromeliads text.**

**3** **Using the Images:Image button in the Insert bar, insert bromeliad_sm.jpg from the images folder.**

When you insert an image, by default, it displays with the bottom of the image aligned with the bottom of the surrounding text.

**4** **Align the image to the right by choosing Right from the Align list in the Property inspector, and give the image an `<empty>` alternate-text attribute.**

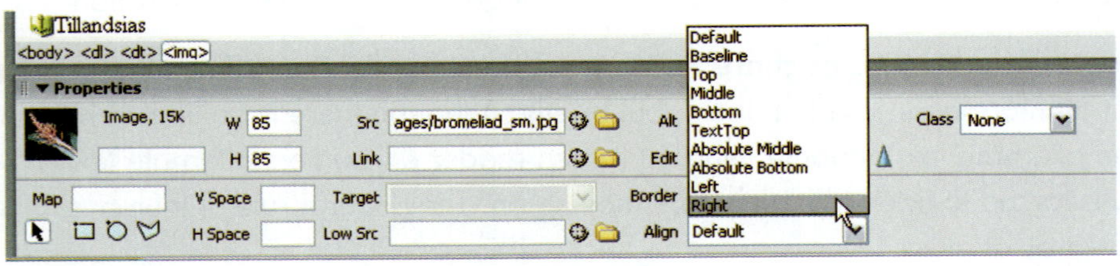


**FIGURE 5.18**

**5** **Click in front of the Succulents text in the next section.**

**6** **Insert succulents_sm.jpg, align it to the right, and give it an empty alternate-text attribute.**

**7** **Insert tillandsia_sm.jpg in front of the Tillandsia text, align it to the right, and give it an empty alternate-text attribute.**

**8** **Close, saving the changes to products.html.**

## *To Extend Your Knowledge*

### IMAGE ALIGN VS. PARAGRAPH ALIGN

Just above the Align list are three icons representing left, center, and right alignment. You may wonder why we did not use these options instead of the alignment list. These options apply to the paragraph as a whole, not just to the selected image, so all text shifts to the left, center, or right. The alignment-options list applies to the image only and floats the image within the paragraph. Choosing right alignment of the paragraph pushes all text and images to the right, but the image does not float to the right of the paragraph text.

# LESSON 4 Specifying Image Height and Width

Attributes of the **<img>** tag include **height** and **width**. These attributes specify the size of the image in ***pixels***, the individual dots on your computer screen. (Pixels is a shortening of picture elements.) You can modify the width and height of an image using **height** and **width**, but doing so can reduce the quality of the image. Enlarging a 100 × 100 image to 300 × 300 reduces its quality even though the proportions are the same. Compressing a 300 × 300 to 100 × 100 does not affect image quality as much as enlarging it, but if you want the image to display at 100 × 100 pixels, you should properly reduce the image itself so that its true or natural size is 100 × 100. A 300 × 300 image has a much larger file size than a 100 × 100 version of the same image, and a longer download time.

You should always specify the height and width of an image. Browsers take more time to ***render*** (display) a Web page if you haven't specified the image dimensions, because until the image finishes downloading, the browser does not know its size. The content around it shifts back and forth as the image loads, because the browser must keep making room for it. If you specify the dimensions, however, the browser reserves that space for it and the text content remains fixed. Users can start to read the text content during the image download, which gives the impression of a faster download time. To make this easy for you, Dreamweaver always automatically inserts the image dimensions.

Dreamweaver enables you to resize images by changing their height and width attributes after you've inserted them into the Web page. Using the height and width attributes, however, isn't the appropriate way to resize an image. Resizing a graphic using the image attributes does not change its file size, just the amount of space in which it displays on the Web page. If the image is not the correct size, use image-editing software to resize it or create the image at the correct size.

To select an image in a Web page in Dreamweaver, click it. Selected images display three handles — one each at the right side, the bottom-right corner, and the bottom side.

## Explore Image Height and Width

**1** **Open index.html.**

**2** **Click the Tropiflora Online graphic at the top of the page to select it.**

Note that the Property inspector indicates that this graphic has a width of 600 and a height of 100. Note also that the Property inspector identifies the image as 11K (11 kilobytes) in size.

FIGURE 5.19

**3** **Drag the right handle of the graphic to the left until the Property inspector shows that the width is 300 pixels.**

Observe that the 300 in the Width field displays in bold characters, indicating that the current dimension is not the natural size of the graphic.

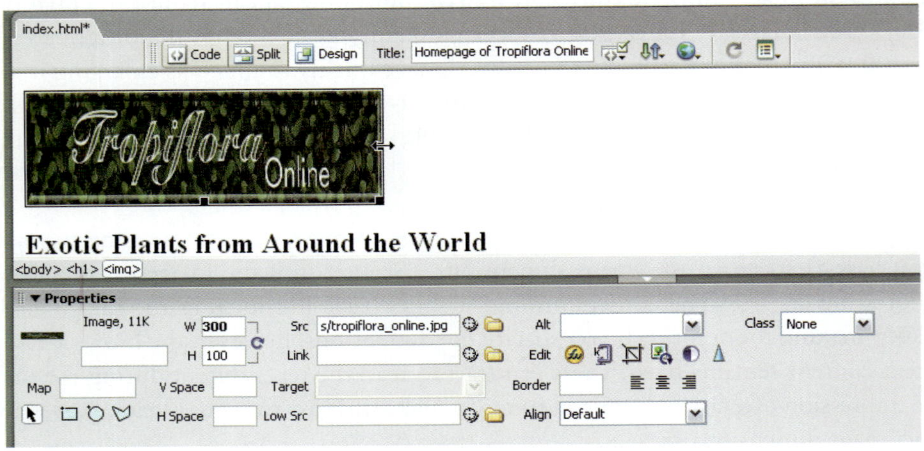


FIGURE 5.20

**4** **In the Property inspector, delete 100 from the H (Height) field, type 50, and press Enter/Return.**

The image is proportionately smaller than its original size.

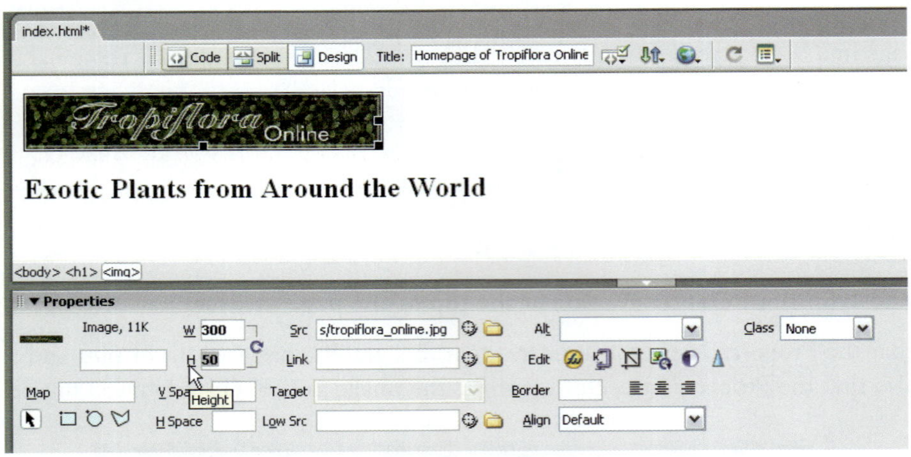


FIGURE 5.21

**5** **Note that the image size remains 11K despite the resizing of the image.**

Resizing an image, as we have done, changes the amount of space it takes on a Web page, not its file size.

**6** **Click the Reset Size/Reset Image to Original Size button to the right of the Width or Height fields in the Property inspector.**

The Reset Size/Reset Image to Original Size button does not have a tool tip to identify it. This button appears only when the size of an image (width and height) has been changed from its original size.

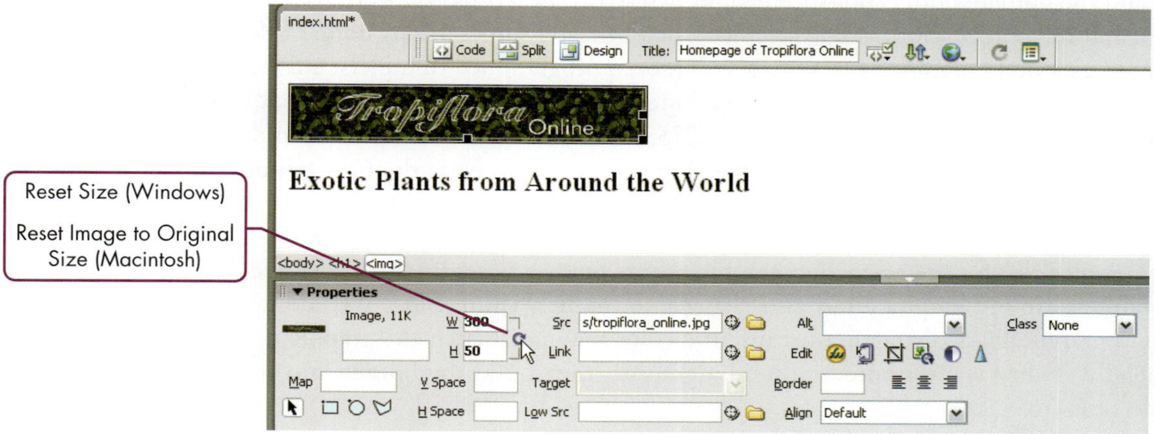


FIGURE 5.22

**7** **Close index.html. You may choose to save or not to save — the changes you made were returned to the original settings.**

## To Extend Your Knowledge

### SIZE IMAGES FIRST

When you use Dreamweaver to insert images into a Web page, the program adds the dimensions of the image to the **<img>** tag. If you find that the image is too large or too small, you can use the image's handles to resize it, but doing so distorts the image. Furthermore, as you saw, when you resize an image, it does not change the file size of the image, just the amount of space the image occupies on the Web page. Dreamweaver offers limited graphics-editing tools with which you can modify a graphic, but many professionals prefer to use graphic-editing software.

# LESSON 5 Setting Image Borders and Spacing

Browsers apply a border around a graphic at the size specified in the code. However, if you do not specify the border width, browsers treat the borders of linking and nonlinking graphics differently. If the graphic is not a link and the border width is not specified, browsers assume a 0-px (zero-pixel) border. If the graphic is used as a link and the border width is not specified, the browser assumes a 2-px border. Most developers don't like to use borders around graphics. Dreamweaver has been programmed to understand this, so if a graphic is used as a link, Dreamweaver automatically sets the border to 0 (zero). Like the alignment attribute, borders are best handled through the **`border`** property of CSS. One difference between CSS and HTML attributes is that HTML borders affect all four sides of the graphic equally, whereas the CSS **`border`** property allows you to specify different measurements, colors, thickness, and styles for each side.

The default color for links, whether graphic or text links, is blue. If you change the default color, the color of the borders around graphic links also changes to the new color. Most Web designers find the border color around graphic links distracting because the color may not match the graphic or the surrounding content. Generally, if they want a border around a graphic, they build the border into the graphic and set HTML borders to zero.

You can also put space around images, using **`hspace`** (horizontal space) and **`vspace`** (vertical space) attributes. If you set **`hspace`** to 5, a 5-pixel space appears on both the left and right sides of the image; **`vspace`** applies to both top and bottom at the same time. The **`hspace`** and **`vspace`** attributes are measured in pixels, but you don't have to specify pixels as the unit of measurement because pixels are the only unit allowed. These attributes are useful for keeping some white space around an image so that text does not butt up against them.

## Create Image Borders

1. **Open products.html.**

2. **Click the photograph of the bromeliad.**

3. **In the Property inspector, type 3 in the Border field and press Enter/Return.**

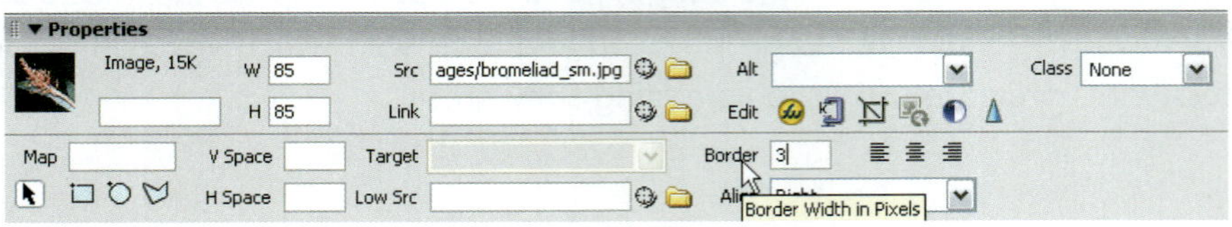


FIGURE 5.23

### ? If you have problems

It is difficult to see the border around a graphic when it is selected. Click away from the graphic to deselect it so the changes are more apparent.

**4** **Close, saving the changes to products.html.**

**5** **Open contactus.html.**

**6** **Click the email.gif graphic of the two computers.**

The Border width field is set to 0 pixels.

FIGURE 5.24

**7** **Apply a 3-pixel border to the graphic and click away from it.**

The border created around this graphic is blue because the graphic is a link.

FIGURE 5.25

**8** **Reset the Border width to 0.**

**9** **Save the changes, but leave the document open for the next exercise.**

## Set Image Spacing

**1** **In the open document contactus.html, click the Home graphic at the bottom of the Web page.**

Note that the graphics are pushed up against each other without any space between them.

**2** **Set the H Space (Horizontal Spacing in the tool tip) to 3 and press Enter/Return.**

Observe that the Home graphic now has a space between it and the About Us graphic.

FIGURE 5.26

**3** **One by one, click the remaining graphics in the navigation bar and apply 3-pixel horizontal spacing to each.**

**4** **Preview the page in your browser.**

FIGURE 5.27

**5** **Close your browser, return to Dreamweaver, and close contactus.html.**

## LESSON 6 Cropping an Image

Dreamweaver has a few basic functions for editing images, as well as the ability to use the Edit and Optimize functions in Fireworks, a Macromedia application used for image creation and editing. You can perform basic image functions in Dreamweaver, but would need a more sophisticated application for more complex image creation and editing.

The crop function allows you to specify an area of a graphic to keep. You select an image in the Document window and click the Crop button — a rectangle outlined with a dashed line appears. This outline shows the area that will be kept when cropping occurs. You can reposition the crop area by dragging the outline — the mouse-pointer cursor changes to a move cursor (four arrows) to indicate that you can move the crop area. Eight handles around the crop area allow you to select the section of the image you want to keep. In the crop area, the image displays in its full color and brightness; outside the crop area, the image is darkened. The eight handles may not be clearly visible if the surrounding area of the image is dark. If this is the case, move the mouse pointer to the approximate position of the handles — the mouse-pointer cursor changes when it is over the handle. Even with a dark image, the dashed boundary of the crop area is visible because the boundary is alternating black and white dashes.

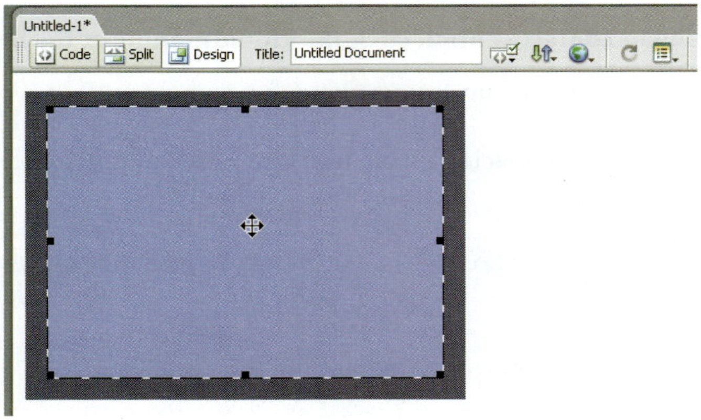


FIGURE 5.28

When you modify an image using the Crop button, you permanently change the image. For this reason, it is very important that you keep a duplicate copy of the original image elsewhere in another folder. If you make a mistake when cropping, make another copy of the original image and place it into the working image folder for your site.

## Crop an Image

In this lesson, you reduce the size of some images that are oversized. You use the crop function to crop the unnecessary surrounding image material.

**1** **Open staff.html.**

**2** **Click the photo of Jeff.**

**3** **Click the Crop button in the Property inspector.**

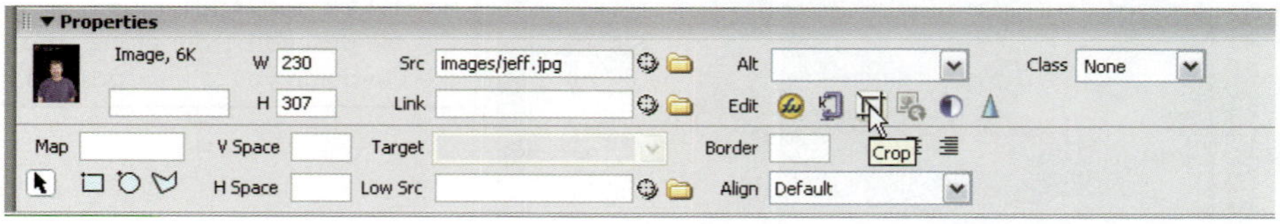

FIGURE 5.29

**4** **Read the warning and click OK. Leave the Don't Show Me This Message Again option unchecked.**

FIGURE 5.30

**5** **Click in the crop area and drag the crop area down to the base of the figure. Ensure that both of Jeff's arms are in the crop area.**

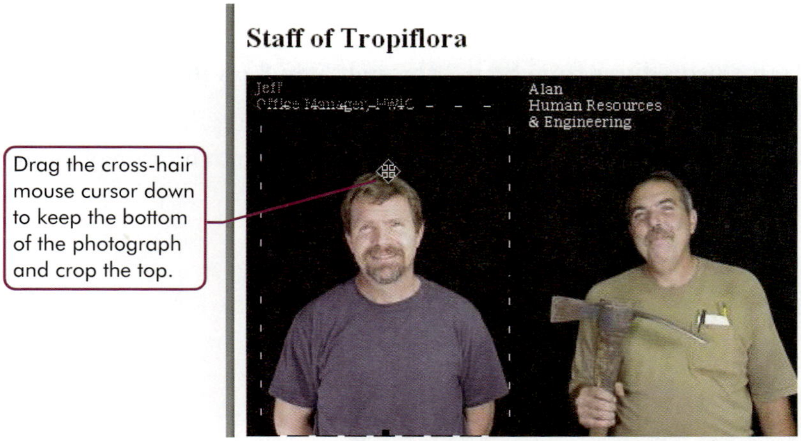


FIGURE 5.31

6 **Drag the top handle in the middle of the top dashed line down to just above Jeff's head.**

If the sides are too narrow or too wide, you can use the handles in the middle of the left and right sides to resize the width of the crop area. Drag the handle to enlarge or reduce the crop area.

FIGURE 5.32

7 **Double-click in the crop area to activate the crop function.**

## If you have problems

If you have cropped an image and the image simply resized to the dimensions of the crop area, you must relaunch of Dreamweaver to restore its functionality. Close the page without saving, shut down Dreamweaver, and then restart it. Recopy the image file from the folder in which the original is located to your site's working folder, and repeat the cropping procedure.

8 **Save the changes.**

9 **Repeat the same procedures from Step 2 through Step 8 on the photo of Alan.**

If you run into the cropping issue described in the preceding If You Have Problems sidebar while working on this photo, follow the instructions in that sidebar, but just replace the alan.jpg image.

FIGURE 5.33

### If you have problems

Dreamweaver's cropping tool is quite basic. It is difficult to crop two or more images to exactly the same size as each other — the images may slightly differ in height by a pixel or two. In the next lesson, you learn to properly resize and resample an image. If you crop these two images to different heights, proceed with the next lesson, then return to this one, and resize and resample the images so they are the same height.

10 **Preview the page in your browser.**

11 **Return to Dreamweaver and close staff.html.**

## LESSON 7 Resizing, Resampling, and Sharpening Images

When an image is not the right size, you can resize it using the height and width options in the Property inspector or by dragging the graphic's handles; but this does not alter the image's file size, just the display area. Dreamweaver offers two image-editing tools that are useful when you resize an image: Resample and Sharpen.

***Resampling*** is a two-step process that changes the number of pixels in an image: you resize the image and then resample it to add or discard pixels. After resampling, the original image is modified to the size for the width and height you set.

A side effect of resampling is that the image becomes soft. The outlines are not distinct because Dreamweaver uses ***antialiasing*** (a technique of blending bitmap-based images to reduce the stair-stepping or jagged appearance) to smooth the gradient between adjacent colors. You sharpen to increase the gradations between differing colors. ***Sharpening*** is a method of exaggerating edges in an image to give enhanced definition. Dreamweaver's sharpen function does not offer the same degree of fine control that equivalent tools in other graphic-arts software provide, but it is certainly convenient and, with care, can produce good results. Cropping does not create any softness because a portion of the image is just cut out, not resized. For this reason, the resampling option is unavailable (grayed out) when you just crop.

Like the Crop button, both Sharpen and Resample irreversibly modify the image. If you are unsatisfied with the results, you must replace the file with the original copy and retry. For this reason, you should always keep copies of the original image files elsewhere on your computer.

When you resize an image, you can resize it proportionately or disproportionately. ***Proportionate resizing*** is modifying the size of an image while keeping the ratio of width to height constant. For example, resizing a 300 × 300 image to 100 × 100 is proportionate resizing, but resizing it to 100 × 120 is disproportionate resizing. In this example, it is very easy for you to proportionately resize the image simply by typing 100 in both the width and height fields. On the other hand, as you might imagine, it would be much more difficult to proportionately resize an 843 × 539 image by calculating the ratio in your head. In Dreamweaver however, if you hold down the Shift key while dragging a corner handle, the height and width remain proportionate as you resize the image.

## Resize and Resample an Image

**1** **Open orchids.html.**

**2** **Click the first image.**

Note the file size shows as 25K in the Property inspector.

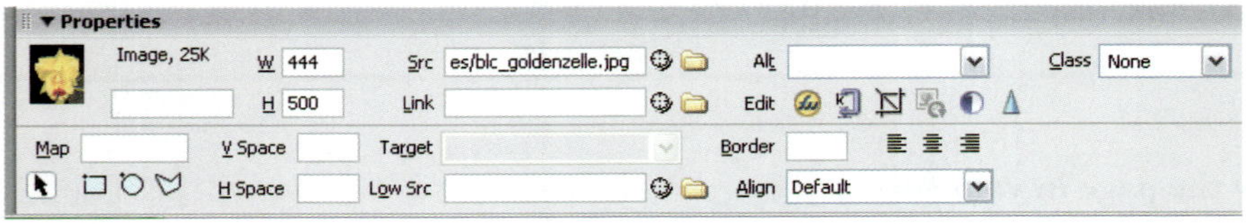


FIGURE 5.34

**3** **Holding down the Shift key, drag the bottom-right handle up toward the top-left corner of the image until the height (H) in the Property inspector reads 150; release the mouse button before the Shift key.**

FIGURE 5.35

**4** **Click the Resample button in the Property inspector.**

FIGURE 5.36

**5** **Click OK to accept the warning.**

**6** **Observe that the Property inspector shows the image's file size is now 5K and its natural dimensions are 134 pixels wide and 150 high.**

You know these are the natural dimensions of the image because the Resize Image button is not visible to the right of the Width/Height fields.

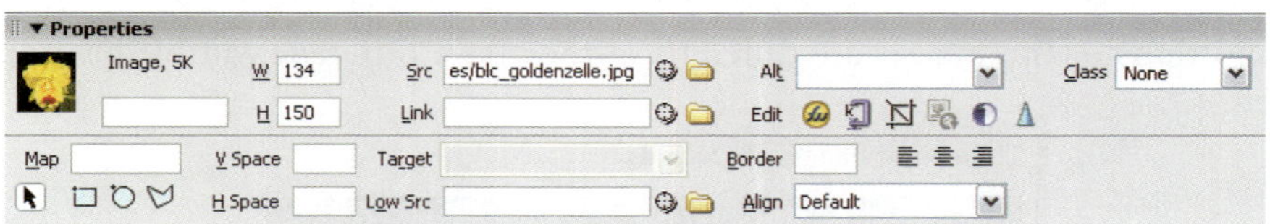


FIGURE 5.37

**7** **Save the changes to orchids.html, but leave it open for the next exercise.**

## Sharpen an Image

Resampling softens an image. In this exercise, you sharpen the image to reverse the softening effect of resampling.

**1** **In the open orchids.html file, click the resized graphic.**

**2** **In the Property inspector, click the Sharpen button and then click OK to accept the warning.**

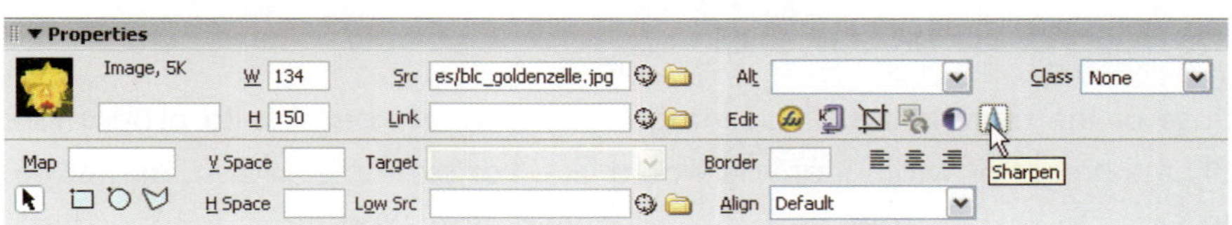


FIGURE 5.38

**3** **Move the slider to the first notch until the Sharpen setting reads 1, and click OK.**

You can experiment with other settings to find a setting you like. With the Preview option checked, the image in the Design window shows how the image will appear at each setting.

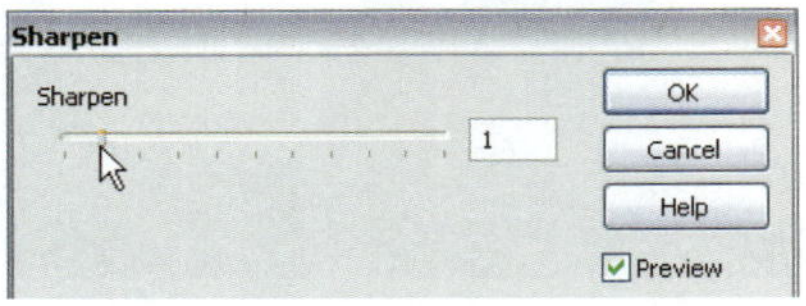


FIGURE 5.39

**4** **With the image still selected, set the H Space (horizontal spacing) field in the Property inspector to 2.**

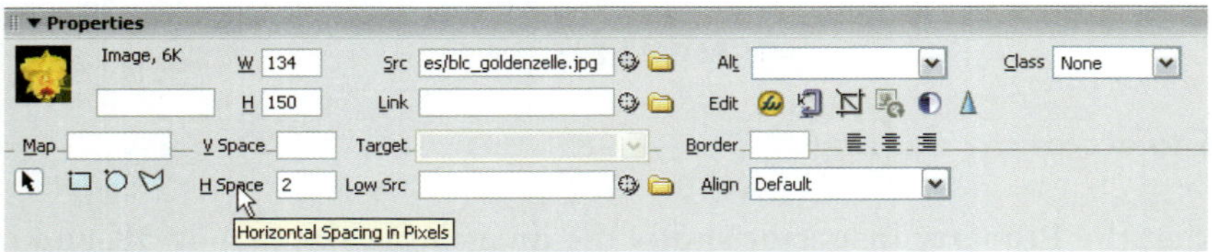


FIGURE 5.40

**5** **Apply the procedures from this and the preceding exercise to the remaining four images until you have reduced them all to 150 pixels high with 2-pixel horizontal spacing.**

The proportions of the images are different so they have different widths, but the same height of 150 pixels.

FIGURE 5.41

**6** **Preview the page in your browser.**

**7** **Return to Dreamweaver and close orchids.html.**

## To Extend Your Knowledge

### MINOR ADJUSTMENTS TO IMAGE SIZE

At times, because of the dimensions of an image, you may not be able to proportionally resize the image to exactly the height or width that you would like. For example, picture an image of 843 × 539 pixels that you want to resize from 843 to 450 pixels high. You may discover that the closest to 450 that you can achieve is 451 or 449. Given that it is only different by one pizel, resize the image to 451 or 449 and then manually type 450 in the height field before resampling. You will not be able to detect the slight distortion that this disproportionate adjustment may create.

# LESSON 8 Working with Image Placeholders

As you develop Web pages, some images may not yet be ready to place. Rather than leave the space empty, you can insert an image placeholder that reserves the space for the image and can later be replaced with the final image. Designers often work visually, creating their designs by arranging the elements in relation to one another — size, proportion, alignment, white space, and more. Using image placeholders enables them to create the page design, finalize the text in relation to the images, complete most of the technical work, and leave only minor adjustments for when they replace the placeholders with the final images. A placeholder is also a good reminder that an image is missing. Although simple to use, you may find that reminder invaluable.

## Insert and Replace an Image Placeholder

In this exercise, you are waiting for a photograph of David, the Shipping/Receiving clerk, to place on the staff page. You create the image placeholder to remind you of the missing image. A short while later, when the photograph is taken and sent to you, you replace the image placeholder with the photograph.

1. **Open staff.html.**

2. **Click to the right of Alan's photo.**

3. **From the Common Insert bar, choose Image Placeholder from the Images drop-down menu.**

4. **In the Image Placeholder dialog box, type `photo_of_david` in the Name field, `208` in the Width field, `232` in the Height field, and `Photo of David` in the Alternate Text field. Click OK.**

   The dimensions — 208 pixels wide by 232 pixels high — are based on the dimensions of the cropped images of Jeff and Alan. You may substitute other numbers if your cropped images have different dimensions.

### If you have problems

The Image Placeholder name does not allow spaces or other upper ASCII characters. If you use one or more, a warning dialog box appears and your text is removed from the Name field. To fake a space, you can use the underscore character (_) but not a hyphen (-).

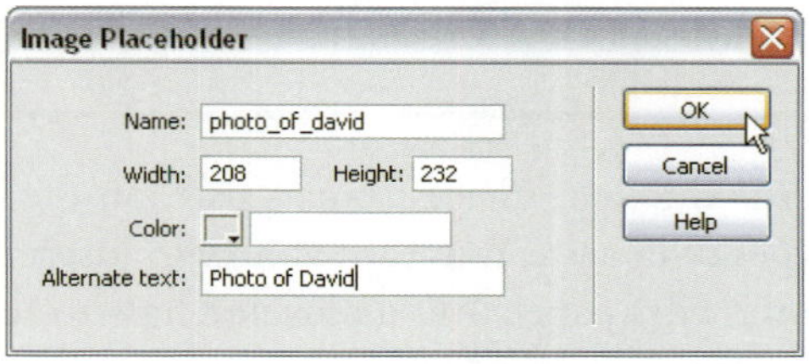


FIGURE 5.42

**5** **Preview the page in your browser.**

The placeholder displays as a missing image but the alternate text identifies the content of the image.

FIGURE 5.43

**6** **Return to Dreamweaver.**

**7** **Double-click the image placeholder and choose david.jpg from the images folder.**

When your graphic designer delivers the final image, you can use it to replace the image placeholder.

**8** **Crop the image to dimensions similar to the other two.**

**9** **Preview the page in your browser.**

FIGURE 5.44

**10** **Return to Dreamweaver and close staff.html.**

## SUMMARY

In this project, you learned about the different image formats used on the Web and how one format may be better than another for different types of images. You learned how to insert images from the Images button on the Common Insert bar and from the Files panel. You discovered how to set alignments and add borders and space around images using the Property inspector. You cropped images to remove unwanted information and resized images to different sizes. You also learned how to improve images with resampling and sharpening. You learned to create a placeholder for an image that has not arrived and then to replace the placeholder with the finished image.

## CAREERS IN DESIGN

### EXPLORING PROFESSIONAL PORTFOLIO SITES

In the early days of digital publishing technology, imaging and layout software was accepted more by graphic artists and designers than it was by "niche" professionals — people like photographers, illustrators, painters, and (little wonder) typographers. Although the widespread acceptance of what was then known as "desktop" publishing applications did in fact spell the end of certain specializations (like typesetters), other fields like photography were hardly affected at all.

Why is this important to you as a Web site designer? Because photographers in particular weathered the storm of desktop technology and emerged on the other end, evolved but in many ways exactly the same as they were before. Their ability to see the world through a lens comes through in their Web sites.

Spend time researching how professional photographers display their wares on the Web. They provide some of the best examples of portfolio sites you can imagine. Use Google or Yahoo to look for photographers in your particular region of the country who show their work on the Web. Call a few of them — particularly those whose sites you find compelling — and interview them about how they view their Web presence. What things are important to them from a design standpoint? Who designed their sites, and what software was used? You might be surprised to find that most of them were done using Dreamweaver.

## KEY TERMS

8-bit color
Alpha transparency
Animated GIFs
Antialiasing
Bandwidth
Bitmap images
Empty alt
Favicon
Flat
GIF
High-color images
Index transparency
Inline image
Interlace
Internet Service Providers (ISPs)
JPEG
Lossless compression
Lossy compression
Pixels
PNG
Proportionate resizing
Render
Resampling
RGB
Scalable Vector Graphics (SVG)
Sharpening
Thumbnails
Vector graphics

# CHECKING CONCEPTS AND TERMS

## SCREEN ID

**Identify the indicated areas from the list below:**

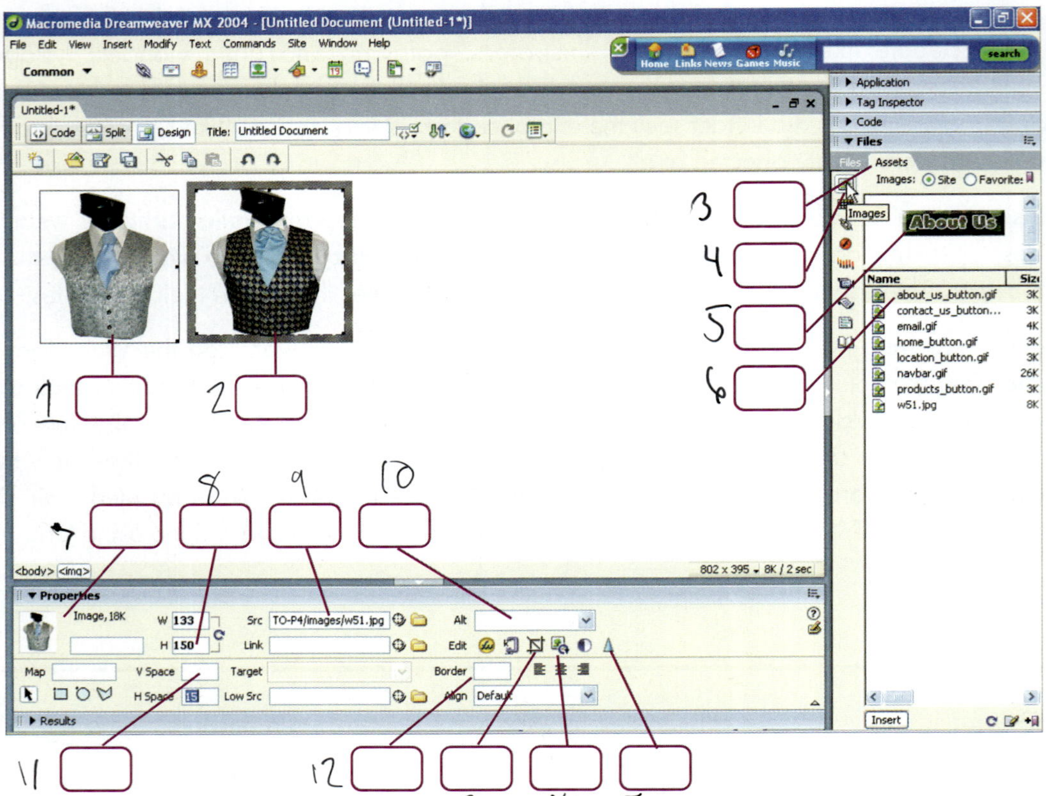


FIGURE 5.45

a. Assets tab
b. Thumbnail and file size of image
c. Alternate text
d. Selected image
e. Images button of the Assets panel
f. Sharpen tool
g. Filename of an image
h. Preview of selected image
i. Crop tool
j. Horizontal/Vertical spacing
k. Image assets of site
l. Resample tool
m. Image in crop mode
n. Width/Height of image
o. Image Border/Alignment

## MULTIPLE CHOICE

**Circle the letter of the correct answer for each of the following:**

1. Images __________.
   a. can be inserted using the Property inspector
   b. use the `<image>` tag with the **source** and **alt** attributes
   c. when selected, display eight handles
   d. All of the above

2. GIF and JPEG image formats __________.
   a. are the storage format of digital cameras
   b. are limited to 256 colors
   c. are bitmapped graphics
   d. can be animated

3. JPEGs are better than GIFs for __________.
   a. graphic text buttons
   b. background images
   c. color-photograph images
   d. None of the above

4. The PNG image format __________.
   a. is a relatively new file format
   b. can display animation
   c. is fully supported by all Web browsers
   d. uses the same compression method as a JPEG

5. Dreamweaver has the following image-editing tools:
   a. Sharpen, Crop, and Luminance
   b. Resize, Resample, and Revert
   c. Resample, Sharpen, and Crop
   d. Crop, Contrast, and Image Map

6. One Web-ready vector format is __________.
   a. 24-bit PNG
   b. CorelDRAW (CDR)
   c. SVG
   d. Fireworks

7. In Dreamweaver, image files are also referred to as __________.
   a. GIS files
   b. Assets
   c. Placeholders
   d. Paragraph attributes

8. A Web-page graphic can be aligned __________.
   a. with the paragraph-alignment tool
   b. using its handles
   c. to the left or right
   d. All of the above

9. Which of the following pairs have something in common?
   a. RGBa, animation
   b. 16.7 million colors, JPG
   c. alpha-transparency, GIF
   d. lossy compression, PNG

10. The __________ attribute does not contribute to the weight of an image file.
    a. width
    b. image format
    c. border thickness
    d. transparency color

## DISCUSSION QUESTIONS

1. Without Dreamweaver's image-editing tools, every time you want to alter an image you would have to return to a graphic-illustration program to make your changes. Which types of changes can you make to your images through Dreamweaver, and which would you have to return to the original program to do? Give an example. What limitations do Dreamweaver's image-editing tools have?

2. You have been hired by the Communications Services Branch as the organization's new Webmaster. The graphic artist who, to date, has only created printed work, has been assigned to help you. What type of guidance might you provide this graphic artist when you need graphics for the Web site?

3. Given the fact that images weigh more than text, what types of considerations would you use to evaluate which images should or should not appear on a Web site or Web page?

## SKILL DRILL

Skill Drill exercises reinforce project skills. Each skill reinforced is the same, or nearly the same, as a skill presented in the project. Detailed instructions are provided in a step-by-step format. You should work through the exercises in order.

### 1. Insert Images from the Files and Assets Panels

Dragging an image into a Web page is probably the easiest method of inserting an image. You can drag an image from the Files panel or from the Assets panel. The Files panel shows the files and folders of your Web site. The Assets panel collects and displays assets of a Web site by types, such as images. This can make finding an image much simpler rather than opening a series of folders to locate the image.

1. Open succulents.html from the TO_P5 Site.
2. Click the Assets tab in the Files panel group to expand the Assets panel.
3. Click the Images button at the top of the Assets panel to display the image assets.
4. Drag succulent_sm.jpg to the left of the Succulents text near the top of the page.

   The insertion point (black vertical bar) moves with the dragged image to indicate where the image will be inserted. Ensure that the insertion point is to the left of Succulents.

5. Click the image and choose Right from the Align menu in the Property inspector.

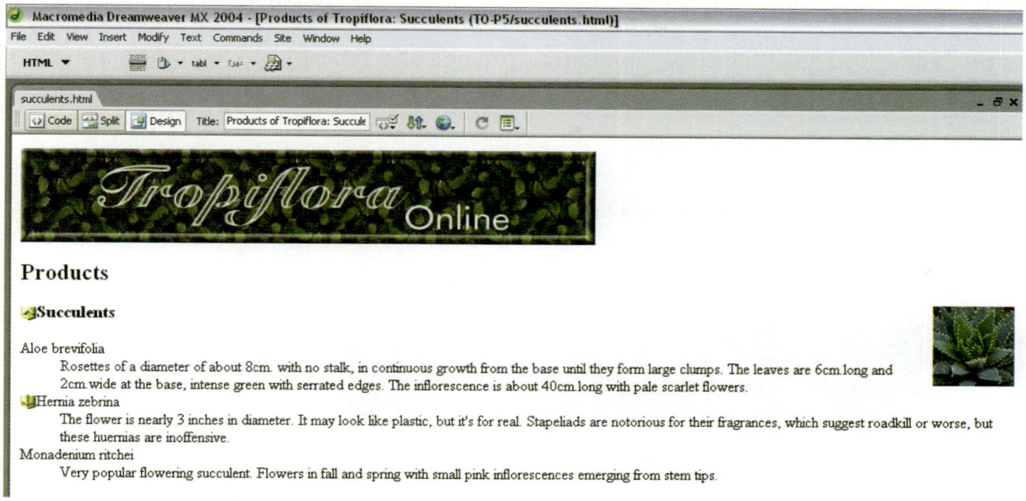


**FIGURE 5.46**

6. Close, saving succulents.html.
7. Open bromeliads.html. From the Assets panel, drag bromeliad_sm.jpg to the left of the Bromeliads text near the top of the page, and align the image to the right. Close, saving the changes.
8. Insert tillandsia_sm.jpg to the left of Tillandsias in tillandsias.html, and align the image to the right.
9. Close, saving the changes.

## 2. Adjust Image Brightness and Contrast

You may receive an image that is too bright or dark or in which the contrast is too high or too low. Dreamweaver offers a tool to correct these types of errors. As with the Crop button, this function irreversibly changes the original image. You would be wise to keep a copy of the original image in another folder if you want to be able to retry adjusting the contrast or brightness again.

1. Open about.html.
2. Click to the left of the About Tropiflora heading.
3. Insert the image cathcarts.jpg and set the alignment to left.
4. Click the image.
5. In the Property inspector, click the Brightness and Contrast button (two buttons to the right of the Crop button).
6. Click OK to acknowledge the warning.
7. Set the Brightness slider to 40 and the Contrast slider to 10.

   The slider can be difficult to position at a particular setting; you may prefer to type the values in the fields to the right of each slider.

8. Compare the image before and after the settings by unchecking and checking the Preview check box.
9. Click OK to accept the settings.
10. Set the border to 2 pixels and the horizontal spacing to 5. Type **Photo of Dennis and Linda Cathcart with their dog Bucky** in the Alternate Text field.
11. Preview the page in your browser.

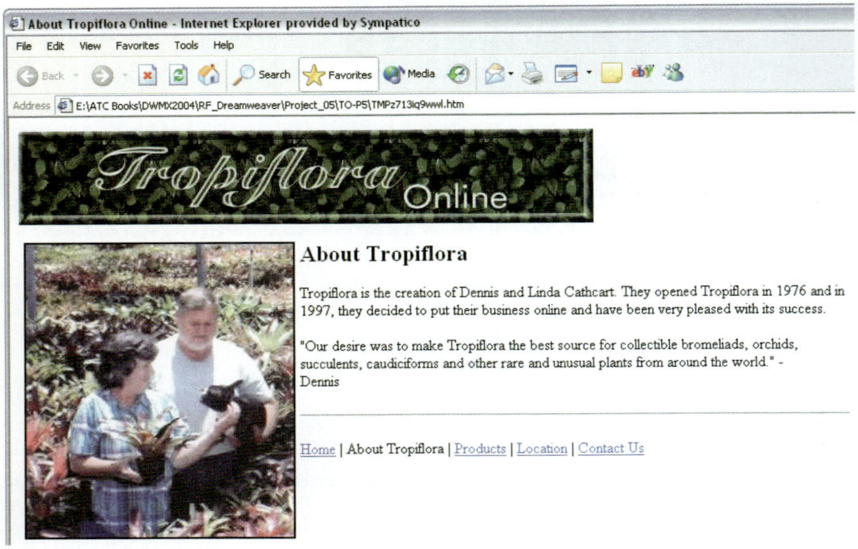


FIGURE 5.47

12. Return to Dreamweaver and close about.html.

## 3. Choose the Best Image

In this exercise, you replace each image placeholder with the best image. Three or four images are available for each placeholder. Your task is to examine all options for each placeholder and evaluate each image based on quality and file size.

1. Define a site named JCW-P5 from the Project_05>JCW-P5 folder using the standard settings.
2. Open wildlife_safari.html. (Skipping the logo_and_animal_banner placeholder), double-click the tiger_cub placeholder.
3. Choose tiger_cub1.jpg from the images folder. Examine the image for quality and make note of its file size.
4. Press Control/Command-Z to Undo the last action (or choose Edit>Undo).
5. Double-click the tiger_cub placeholder, replace it with tiger_cub2.jpg, and examine the image for quality and file size.
6. Repeat Steps 4 and 5 with tiger_cub3.jpg.
7. Evaluate the three choices and insert the best one. Set the alignment to left and the horizontal spacing to 3.

8. Repeat the process for the burmese_python placeholder, but do not set the alignment or horizontal spacing.

9. Choose the best image for the monitor placeholder, align the image to the left, and set the horizontal spacing to 3.

   Leave the placeholder for the turkey_vulture untouched for now — you deal with that image in the next exercise.

10. Scroll to the top to replace the logo_and_animal_banner placeholder.

    You must insert both a logo and an animal banner, but you may choose either two separate images or a single combined image.

11. Leave the alignment of the image (or images) that replaces the logo_and_animal_banner placeholder set to Default, but set the horizontal spacing to zero (0).

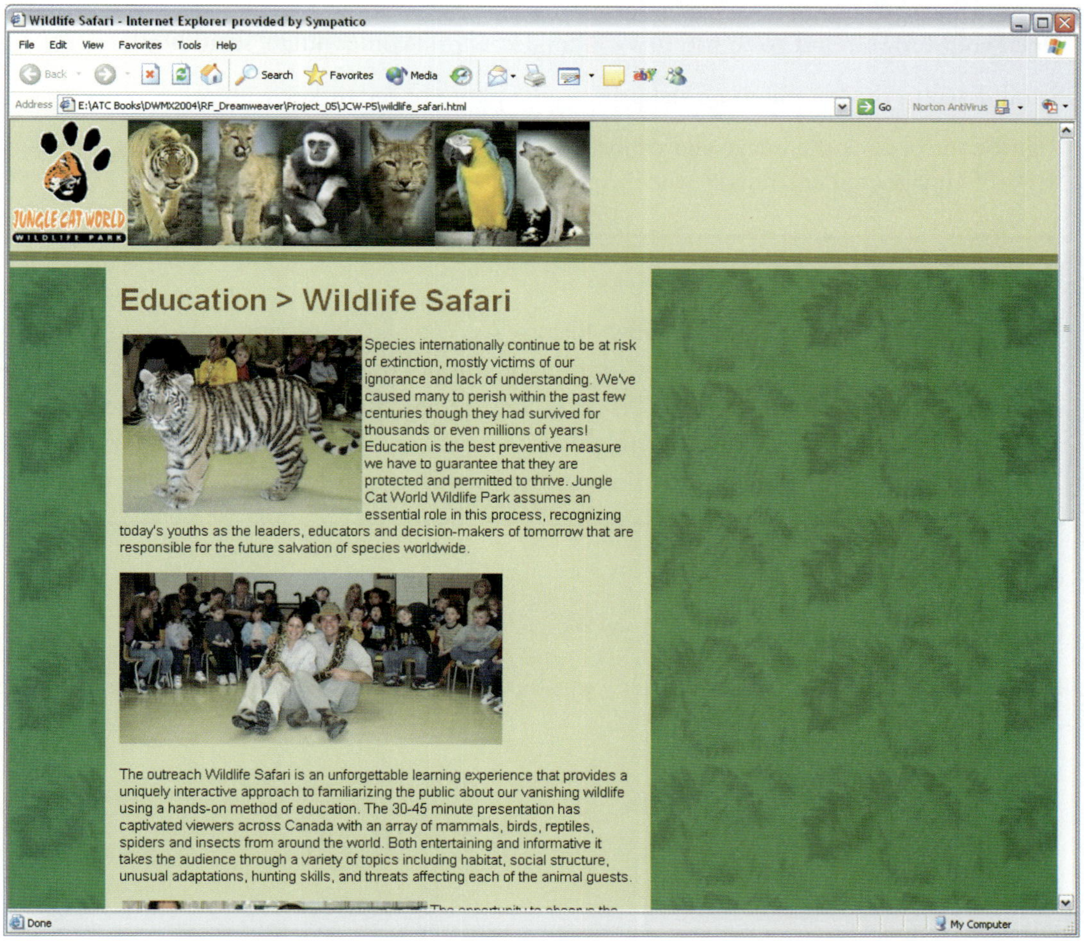


**FIGURE 5.48**

12. Close, saving your changes when finished.

## 4 Save Images from the Internet

Before you start this exercise, you need to be aware that many images on Web pages are copyrighted so you should not use these images for your own purposes, whether or not you earn any income from their use. However, it is perfectly fine to use an image as inspiration, as long as you do not copy the image directly or incorporate it into another image. You may also use an image if the author/owner of the image gives you permission to do so. Permission may come with a price tag.

There are Web sites that offer images at no cost and with no royalties attached. You may download and use these images at your leisure for personal or professional use. However, in many cases, these images are relatively low quality and may not be suitable for professional Web-site design.

In this exercise, you learn how to download and save an image for later use. (Web-site content used by permission.)

1. Define a site named JCW-P5 from the Project_05>JCW-P5 folder using the standard settings.
2. Open your browser and go to http://www.junglecatworld.com/wildlife_safari.html.
3. Scroll down to the last photo on the page — the photo of the turkey vulture.
4. Right/Control-click the image and choose Save Picture As. Navigate to your Project_05>JCW-P5>images folder, and save the image using its given filename.

### If you have problems

Internet Explorer uses the phrase Save Picture As, Mozilla/Netscape uses Save Image As, and Opera uses Save Image for the same function. If you are using the Safari browser on a Macintosh system, choose Download Image to Disk and Safari saves the image to your desktop. You can then move the image wherever you wish. In this exercise, you move it to the WIP>Project_05>JCW-P5>images folder. If you are using another browser, look for a similar command.

5. Close your browser.
6. Open wildlife_safari.html from the JCW-P5 site in Dreamweaver.
7. Replace the turkey_vulture placeholder with the downloaded image, align the image to the right, and set the horizontal spacing to 3.
8. Close, saving the changes.

## CHALLENGE

Challenge exercises expand on or are somewhat related to skills presented in the lessons. Each exercise provides a brief narrative introduction, followed by instructions in a numbered-step format that are not as detailed as those in the Skill Drills. You should do the Challenge exercises in the order given.

### 1. Link Thumbnails to Detail Pages

1. Define a site named DR-P5 from the Project_05>DR-P5 folder using the standard settings.
2. Open bechstein-details.html and expand the Assets panel.
3. Drag bechstein.jpg into the large open cell below the Comments cell.
4. Make the alternate text **Photo of a Bechstein piano**. Close, saving bechstein-details.html.
5. Open piano-stock.html.

   The Thumbnail column is reserved for thumbnail images of the various pianos available for sale. The filenames of the thumbnail images end with _thm.jpg to distinguish them from the full-sized images.
6. Drag bechstein_thm.jpg into the thumbnail table cell of the Bechstein row. Make the alternate text **Photo of a Bechstein piano**.
7. Proportionately resize the image to 80 pixels in height (using the Shift key).
8. Resample and sharpen the image. Using the Preview option, choose the best sharpen setting for the image.
9. Link the image to bechstein-details.html.
10. Select "info »" in the Detail column of the Bechstein table row, and link the text to bechstein-details.html.
11. Continue the process. Insert the detail images into the detail pages, insert the thumbnail images (proportionately resized to 80 px high) into the piano-stock page, and provide alternate text for each image.

12. Close, saving any open detail pages, and preview piano-stock.html in your browser. Test the links you created, returning to Dreamweaver to repair any incorrect ones.

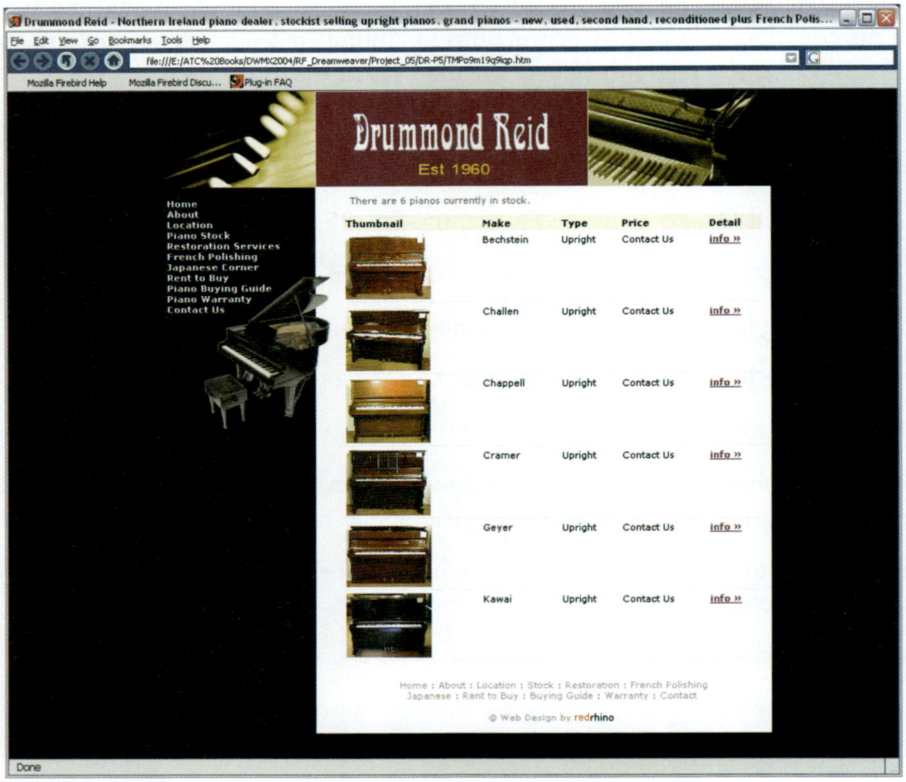


FIGURE 5.49

13. Return to Dreamweaver and close piano-stock.html.

## 2. Make the Graphics Accessible

Your task is to create appropriate descriptions of the graphics in a page. Review the discussions in this project on how to categorize images and what types of descriptions would be appropriate for images according to their category. Review the images in this page and apply the correct description to each.

1. Define a site named DF-P5 from the Project_05>DF-P5 folder using the standard site-definition settings.

2. Open visitor-stats.html.

3. Switch to the Assets panel and make note of the images for this Web page.

   You can ignore background.gif; it is a background image to the page and does not need a description. Only inline images must be described.

4. One by one, click each graphic and apply the appropriate description.

5. Close, saving visitor-stats.html.

## 3. Create a Photo Album

Your task is to create a photo album from supplied images. In the thumbs folder are duplicate copies of the photos in the photos folder. You must add (resizing, resampling, and sharpening, as necessary) photos from the thumbs folder to the filmstrip pages. You must also add photos to the detail pages; when you click a thumbnail, the larger photo of the image appears in the middle frame. You are not expected to create the frame layout, just the thumbnails, the details pages, and the links between them.

1. Define a site named Album from the Project_05>Album folder using the standard site-definition settings.
2. Open index.html and preview the page in your browser. Click the thumbnail image of the boat in the bottom frame and observe that a larger copy of the boat photograph appears in the middle frame.
3. Return to Dreamweaver and close index.html.
4. Open boats.html. Insert boat2.jpg from the thumbs folder to the right of the first thumbnail image.
5. Proportionately resize the photo to a height of 80 pixels, and resample the image. You can also sharpen and adjust the brightness and/or contrast, if you feel it is necessary.
6. Repeat the process with the remaining three boat images. Space each image from the others using an hspace setting of 5. Close, saving the changes to boats.html.
7. Open boat1.htm from the Album>details folder. Save the file as boat2.htm.
8. Replace the photo with boat2.jpg from the Album>photos folder. Proportionately resize the photo to a height of 350 pixels, and resample the image. You can also sharpen and adjust the brightness and/or contrast, if you feel it is necessary. Close, saving the changes.
9. Repeat Steps 7-8 until you have created boat3.htm, boat4.htm, and boat5.htm.
10. Reopen boats.html from the root folder. One by one, link the thumbnail images to the newly created detail pages. Close, saving the changes to boats.html.
11. Open index.html and preview the page in your browser.

## 4. Resize Images to Fit in Pop-Up Windows

You have been asked to create a photo album of the planets of our solar system, in which, when a visitor clicks a planet, a larger photo appears in a pop-up window. The image map and JavaScript have been prepared for you; your task is to insert the images into their individual pages. The images of the planets are different sizes so they need cropping and resizing.

1. Define a site named Planets from the Project_05>Planets folder using the standard site-definition settings.
2. Open index.html and then preview it in your browser. Click Mercury (first planet from the Sun) and notice that it opens in a pop-up window but the planet is too large for the window.
3. Do not close your browser but return to Dreamweaver and open mercury.html.

4. Crop the image of Mercury to remove any extra black from around the planet. Proportionately resize the remaining image so the height is 300 pixels. Resample the image and apply any of the other image-editing tools, as necessary. Close, saving the changes.

5. One by one, open the remaining planet pages, insert the appropriate photo from the images folder, and apply the procedures outlined in Step 4. Close, saving each after completing it.

6. Switch to your open browser with index.html open. Test the links from all of the planets to verify that each planet is fully visible in the pop-up windows.

7. Close your browser, return to Dreamweaver, and close any open pages.

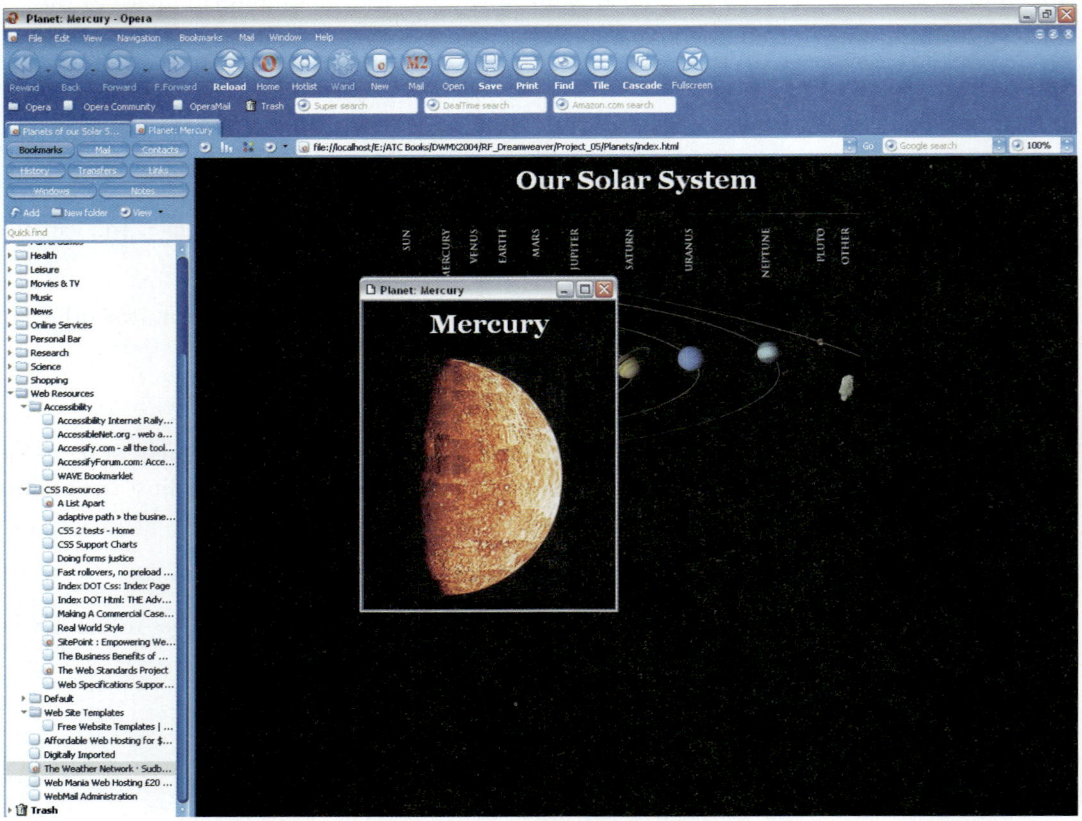


FIGURE 5.50

PORTFOLIO BUILDER

## Create an Online Image Gallery

Gallery sites provide access to photographs, illustrations, maps, and other visual objects that are either for sale or available "royalty free," which means that they're in the public domain and can be used without cost. In this assignment, you're going to create a small gallery site containing both thumbnails (small images) and links to larger, high-resolution versions of each image.

1. To see an example of this type of site, visit a commercial image library; a perfect one to look at is gettyimages.com (one of the largest commercial sites of its kind on the Web).
2. Spend some time looking through the company's offerings, making sure to note how images are organized into related categories.
3. Using a search engine such as Google.com, search the Web for "royalty free images".
4. Select five to ten images to use in your gallery site and save them to your hard drive.
5. Build a small site that provides a home page displaying small (thumbnail) images, with links to individual pages containing large versions.
6. Construct the links so the larger version of each image is displayed in a separate window when selected by the viewer.

# PROJECT 6

# Backgrounds and Colors

## OBJECTIVES

***In this project, you learn how to***

- Insert tiled, margin, and watermark backgrounds
- Identify suitable background images
- Avoid transparent background graphics
- Use Web-safe colors and correct notation
- Set text and link colors
- Choose background colors for background images
- Use CSS properties to modify background images
- Selectively apply text and background color

## WHY WOULD I DO THIS?

Once you have established the content you want to appear in your Web pages — either through structured text or images (with appropriate alternate text) — you can next turn to the task of developing a theme for your Web site. You develop this theme through the use of color and background images. You may think that you can only use color for text or the background, and that once you choose a background image for your page, you've done all that you can do. In fact, your options are not that limited any longer. By using CSS, you have many more options for applying color and background images. With CSS, you can apply color to text and backgrounds to any portion of a Web page, such as paragraphs, links, and headings. In fact, using CSS, you could even apply a different background color and text color to every paragraph, if you wanted. (You still have to provide the good taste and design sense, however.) The same might be said for background images. There are several CSS background options and, unlike HTML backgrounds, CSS enables you to apply backgrounds to almost every HTML tag in a Web page.

In this project, you explore the basic principles of using color and background images, as well as the specific methods for applying them. In all cases, you learn to apply colors and background images using CSS. Although you can apply color and background images using HTML, your options are much more limited and less powerful than using CSS. If you are going to be a designer of note, you must learn as much as you can about CSS. Although it is much more than just colors and background, by definition, CSS provides the means for creating the style of a Web site.

### Using Background Images

As noted, using CSS, you can apply backgrounds to any element in a page. Background images are similar to colored, textured, or watermarked paper — they appear behind the body of content. Unlike inline or foreground images, which only appear once where they are set to appear, background images, by default, repeat to fill the background, a process known as "tiling." Although backgrounds on Web pages are the most common use of backgrounds, the principles of background images apply to other elements, as well, such as tables, paragraphs, and headings, all of which can have a background image. CSS offers additional options for background images that are not available through HTML.

There are some important caveats and considerations for using background images:

- Text must be visible and readable against the background. It's essential that you test text colors against the background to ensure readability. You should check the color of link text as well, because text is often set to a different color than running text.
- Background graphics with transparent regions can cause problems. If you have not specified a background color, the visitor's browser may apply its own background color that shows through the transparent regions. The color showing through may not match your color patterns, so the visitor sees a very different Web page than what you intended. You should edit the graphic and disable the transparency option.

- Be careful about using complex images as backgrounds. In the past, it was recommended not to use complex graphics as backgrounds because they require more processing power to display than simpler graphics. Web pages with background graphics can hesitate during scrolling because of the processing power needed to draw the background as it moves — complex graphics exaggerate this condition. However, given the processing power of current computers, this recommendation is less relevant. On the other hand, if you need to ensure universal access to your site, even for those using older computers, you need to avoid using complex background images. There are still plenty of people in this country, not to mention around the world, using slower connections and equipment.
- Do not use animated GIFs as background graphics.
- You can use GIF, JPEG, or PNG graphic formats in the background of your Web page. The same principles used in determining the graphic format of a foreground image also apply to background graphics.
- Test your page at different monitor resolutions, especially if you are using either a margin or watermark style of background.

There are three styles of backgrounds that you can use: wallpaper patterns, margin (or strip) tiles, and watermarks. It does not matter which style of background image you choose to use — the method for inserting the background image is the same. The difference between the three styles lies in the development of the graphic.

Prior to CSS, HTML allowed background images but their use was severely limited. Only the **<body>**, **<table>**, **<tr>**, and **<td>** tags supported background images, whereas CSS enables the designer to place background images behind any or all elements of the page. Using HTML, all you could do was place an image in the background. However, using CSS, you may specify the position of the background graphic, how it is to repeat (or tile), and whether it scrolls with the page or remains fixed in the browser window. Given the versatility and flexibility of CSS, it is extremely important for you, as a designer, to know and understand the background properties of CSS and how they can empower you to create amazing Web-page designs.

## Working with the Colors of the Web

You also need to know and understand not only basic color principles but also the capabilities of computer monitors. With print design, you need to understand the capabilities of the printing process because the printer and printing process determine the colors of your printed product. Once you have that information and submit your files, your printed product remains essentially identical — fonts, images, and color selection do not arbitrarily change. With Web design, the final product displays on the computer monitors of all of your site's visitors, and you have no control over the size, color depth, or quality of their computer monitors. You may be able to make some basic assumptions, such as assuming high-technology markets have quality equipment and, equally, assuming that the K-12 educational market may not have high-quality equipment. Based on such assumptions, you can be better prepared to decide how to use colors in your Web designs.

The earliest color monitors from the early 1990s supported just 256 colors. Current monitors commonly support 16.7 million colors and even 4.3 billion colors. The color depth of monitors is described in bits, such as 8-bit, 16-bit, and 24-bit color monitors. Each bit can contain one of two numbers — a zero or a one. One-bit color has only two options, zero or one, or in color terms, black or white. Two-bit color has four options: 00, 01, 10, and 11, which can also be represented as $2^2$ or $2 \times 2$, which equals 4. For every additional bit, the number of possible colors doubles. Eight-bit color, or $2^8$ is $2 \times 2 \times 2 \times 2 \times 2 \times 2 \times 2 \times 2$ or 256 colors; 16-bit color is $2^{16}$ or 65,356 colors; 24-bit color is $2^{24}$ or 16.7 million colors; and 32-bit color is $2^{32}$ or 4.3 billion colors. Twenty-four-bit color is also known as "true color." According to recent browser statistics, 94% of Internet users use 16-bit color monitors (65,356 colors) or greater, and 44% use 24-bit color or greater.

Most developers use a system with 24-bit or 32-bit color monitors. If you are one of them, you must remember that you can't always depend on all of your visitors having similarly capable monitors. If a visitor views your graphics with a monitor displaying fewer colors, the graphic will be visible but won't seem as attractive as what you created. In many cases, the less-capable monitor uses dithering to simulate colors that it can't display. ***Dithering*** is a process of creating the illusion of new colors and shades by varying the pattern of pixels. Newspapers, which have only black and white dots, produce various shades of grays by dithering the black and white areas.

Although dithering does enable even low-color monitors to display the graphics, they do not look very attractive. In response to this problem, many authors recommend limiting the ***palette***, the set of available colors, to 256 colors or less. However, the 256 colors on Windows systems, Macintosh systems, and Unix systems are not all the same; some colors from one system dither on another. This issue further reduces the 8-bit palette of 256 colors to 216 nondithering colors, known as "the Web-safe palette."

Dreamweaver displays the Web-safe color palette in two different layouts — color cubes and continuous tones. When the mouse pointer is in the colors of the color palette, it changes to an eyedropper shape to enable you to choose a color. A pop-out menu to the right of the color palette enables you to choose the color layout, available colors, and whether or not to display only Web-safe colors.

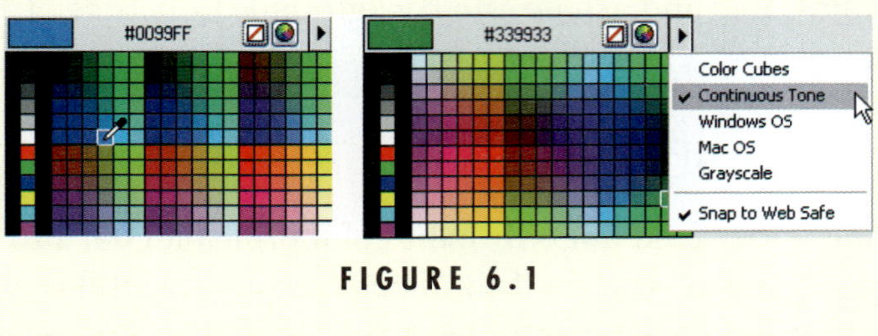


**FIGURE 6.1**

There are a variety of ways (models) to describe a color; the RGB model is used for Web graphics. The ***RGB model*** defines all colors in a palette by mixing different intensities of red, green, and blue light, such as black (0% each of red, green, and blue) and white (100% each of red, green, and blue). There are two common systems for describing colors — by name and by hexadecimal color code. Of course, the simpler method is by name, but there are only 16 color names common to all browsers. Internet Explorer has color names for all 216 Web-safe colors, but other browsers do not recognize all of those names. All browsers, however, recognize the hexadecimal color codes for all 216 Web-safe colors.

***Hexadecimal*** means 16 (***hexa*** is 6 and ***deci*** is 10). In our decimal or 10-digit system, there are 10 unique single-digit numerals, 0–9. Numbers beyond 9 in our decimal system are represented using two digits. To represent the next six single-digit numerals beyond 9 in a hexadecimal system, we use the characters A–F.

| Decimal Notation | 0 | 1 | 2 | 3 | 4 | 5 | 6 | 7 | 8 | 9 | 10 | 11 | 12 | 13 | 14 | 15 |
|---|---|---|---|---|---|---|---|---|---|---|---|---|---|---|---|---|
| Hexadecimal Notation | 0 | 1 | 2 | 3 | 4 | 5 | 6 | 7 | 8 | 9 | A | B | C | D | E | F |

**FIGURE 6.2**

The hexadecimal color system uses a group of six hexadecimal numbers to describe a color — the first pair is for red, the second for green, and the last for blue. Each primary color has six possible values equating to 0%, 20%, 40%, 60%, 80%, and 100%. If you convert percentages to hexadecimal notations from 0 to F, they would be 0, 3, 6, 9, C, and F. In the hexadecimal system, those numbers are paired to result in 00, 33, 66, 99, CC, and FF. To describe the color of pure red (which has no green or blue component), for example, you would use FF0000. Pure green would be 00FF00, pure blue would be 0000FF, white would be all colors, FFFFFF, and black would be no color, 000000. Yellow is the opposite of blue so would be FFFF00. With 6 intensities of red, 6 intensities of green, and 6 intensities of blue, you have 216 colors: multiplying 6 × 6 × 6 = 216, the number of colors in a Web-safe palette. When coding hexadecimal color codes, you must always remember to precede the color code with the hash # character.

Visibone.com's Color Laboratory (http://www.visibone.com/colorlab) provides a free, Web-based, color-picking tool that enables you to experiment with color options before applying them to your Web page. Each of the color options displays with its hexadecimal color code, and text of each color is shown in each block of color to demonstrate text color against the chosen backgrounds.

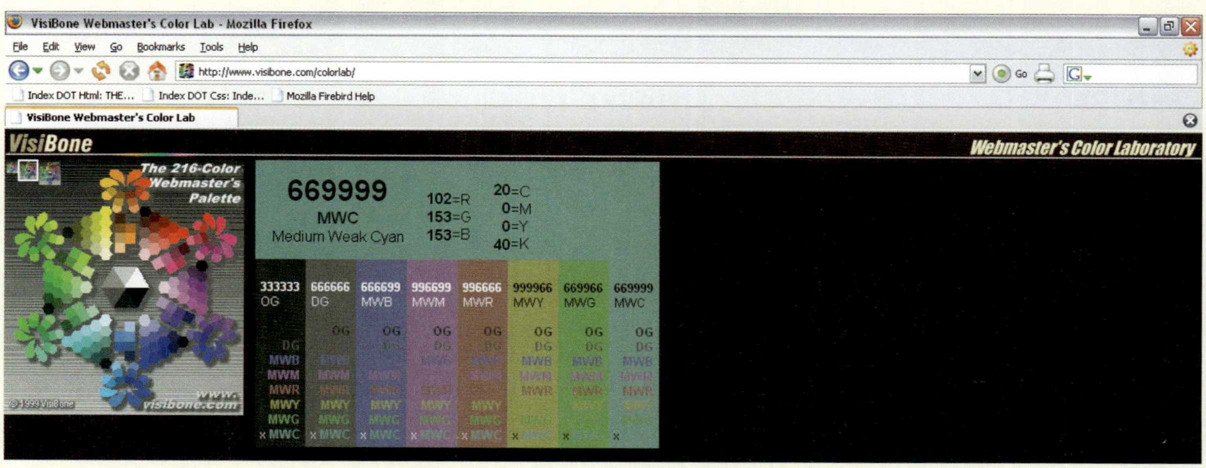


**FIGURE 6.3**

# VISUAL SUMMARY

The Page Properties dialog box has many options for setting a background color and/or a background image. You can open the Page Properties dialog box by clicking the Page Properties button in the Property inspector, choosing Modify>Page Properties from the menu, or by pressing Control-J. The Page Properties dialog box groups related properties into categories.

The Appearance category allows you to set the default text color, background color, and background image (we discuss the other options in other projects.) The Links category allows you to set the color of unvisited-, visited-, active-, and rollover-link states. The Headings category allows you to set the color of headings, such as Heading 1 and Heading 2.

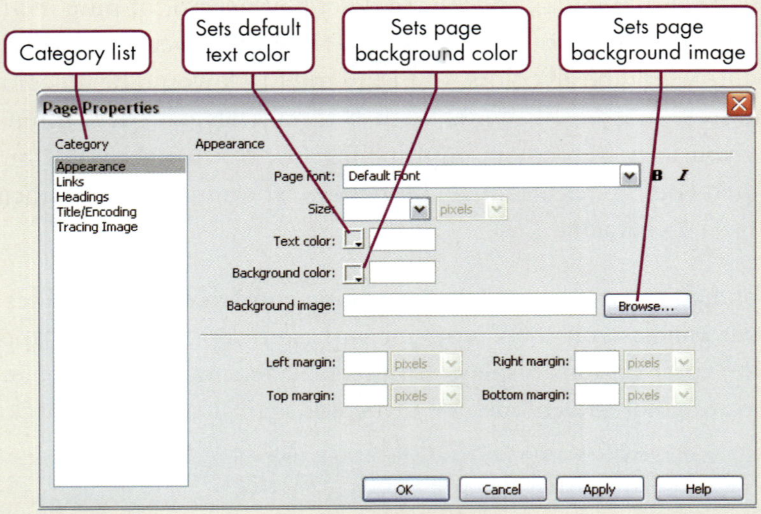


FIGURE 6.4

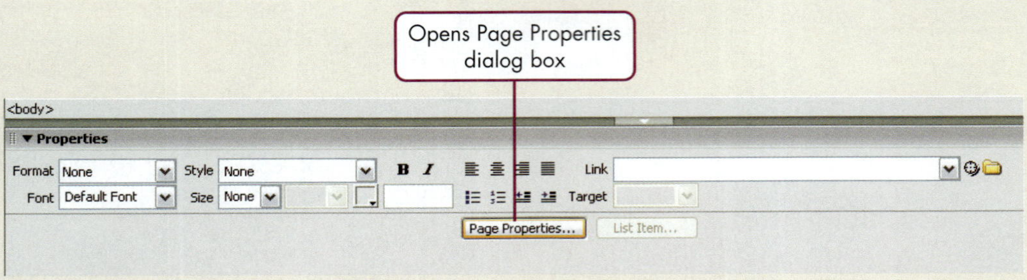


FIGURE 6.5

To specify a color, whether a text or background color, you either type the hexadecimal code of the color into the color field or click the color button. When you click the color button, a color palette appears. You can use the mouse pointer, which changes to an eyedropper, to choose a color from this palette. As the eyedropper moves across the color palette, the color swatch displays the color at the tip of the eyedropper and the hexadecimal color code displays to the right of the color swatch. The pop-out menu to the right allows you to enable/disable the use of Web-safe colors and to change the color palette to another palette.

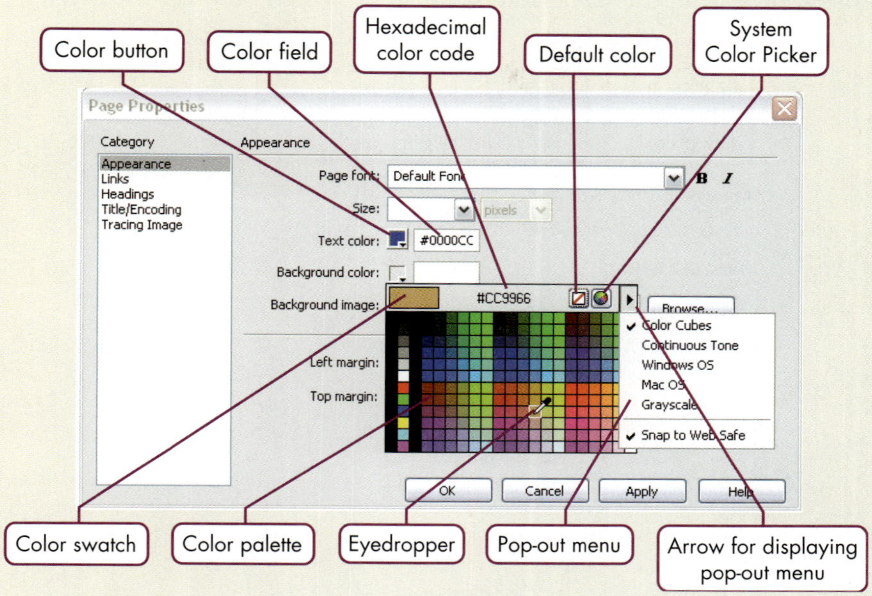


**FIGURE 6.6**

You modify CSS Styles often in this project. To view and work with existing CSS Styles, you must expand the Design panel group and click the CSS Styles tab to display the CSS Styles panel. If you Right/Control-click a style rule, a drop-down menu appears, allowing you to edit the style (among other options).

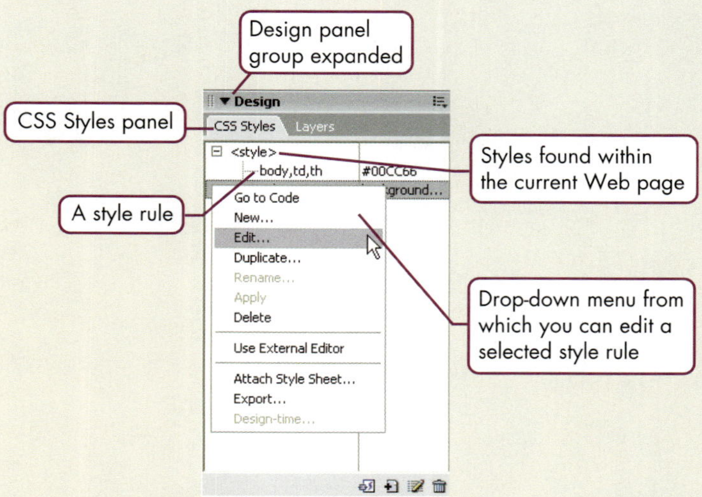


**FIGURE 6.7**

The CSS Styles Definition dialog box offers the same options as the Page Properties dialog box, plus many more. As you use more and more CSS in your designs, you will probably use the Page Properties dialog box less often and the CSS Styles definition dialog box more frequently. This dialog box also has several categories, including the Background category, which you will use often.

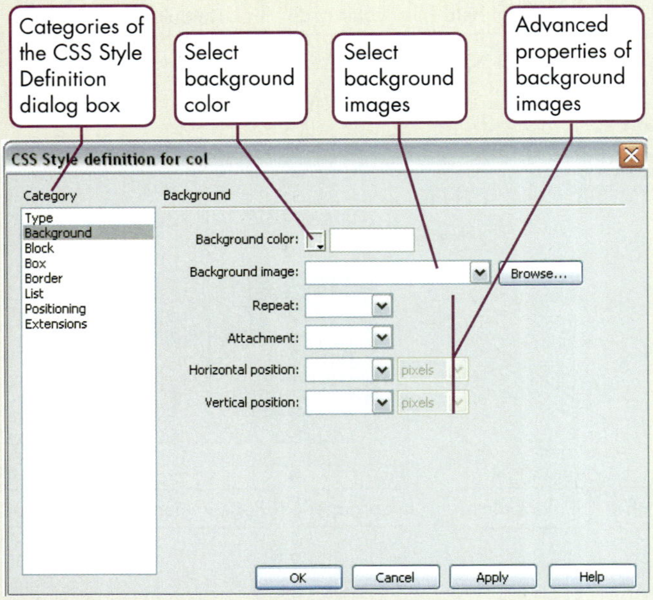


FIGURE 6.8

# LESSON 1 Using Wallpaper-Pattern Backgrounds

***Wallpaper patterns*** are tiled images that repeat across and down a page. Properly designed, wallpaper patterns are seamless — there are no clear distinctions between one tile and the adjacent tiles. Unlike the other two background styles (margin and watermark), it doesn't matter how large or small the Web page is — the tiled background image repeats horizontally and vertically until it fills the background of the page. The graphics used in wallpaper patterns are rectangular or square, commonly no larger than 300 × 300 pixels. Although wallpaper patterns were often used in Web designs in the past, they have gone out of style unless the pattern is very subtle.

It is always best to experiment with a variety of colors to test the readability and appearance of the text color against the background graphic. The BackgroundCity.com Web site (http://www.backgroundcity.com) offers free background images and displays text using different colors against your chosen background graphic.

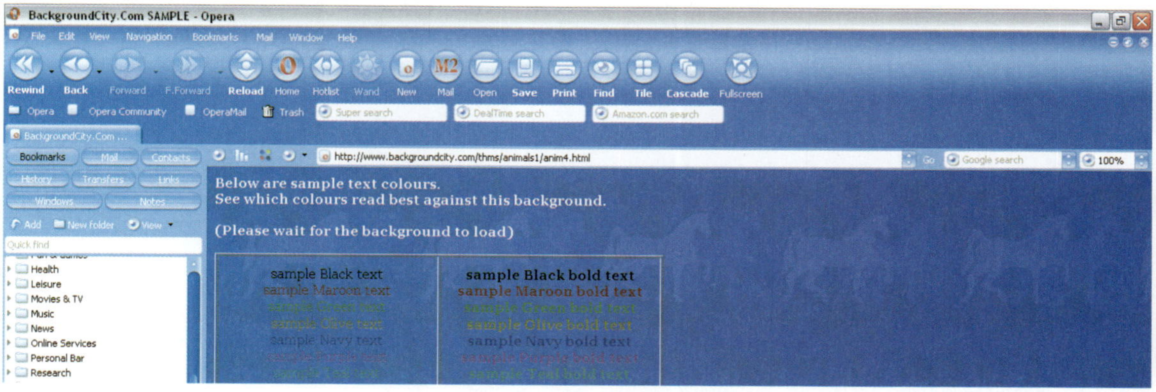


FIGURE 6.9

## Insert a Wallpaper-Pattern Background Image

In this exercise, you insert a wallpaper-pattern background image into the body of the page using the Page Properties dialog box. To do so, you simply choose the image from the bg-images folder.

1. **Define the Project_06>Backgrounds folder as a site called Backgrounds using the methods outlined in previous projects. (You may, at this time, also want to remove the site definitions from the previous project, since you won't need them again. Use the method from Project 5, Lesson 1, Step 2.)**

2. **Open index.html.**

3. **Click the Page Properties button in the Property inspector.**

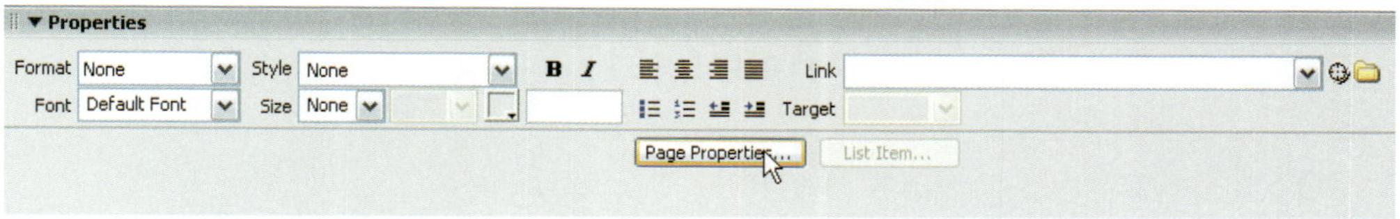


FIGURE 6.10

**4** **In the Appearance category of the Page Properties dialog box, click the Browse button (to the right of the Background Image field).**

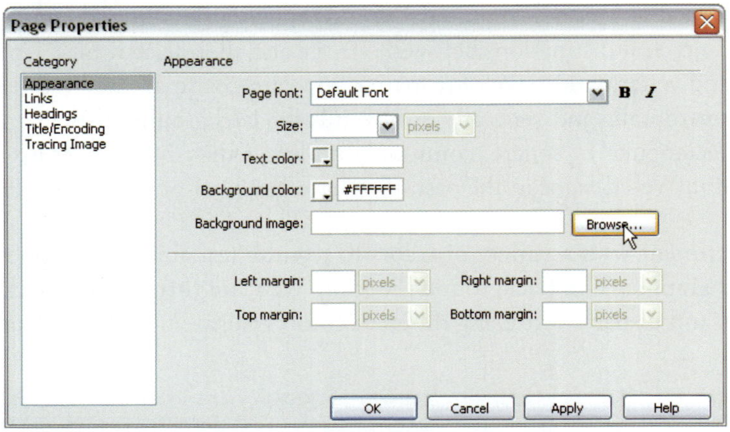

FIGURE 6.11

**5** **Open the bg-images folder, click tile-opaque.gif, and then click OK/Choose.**

The Image Preview window displays the image and, below it, various properties of the image. This image is just 160 pixels wide by 160 pixels in height, so it tiles both vertically and horizontally to fill the Web page.

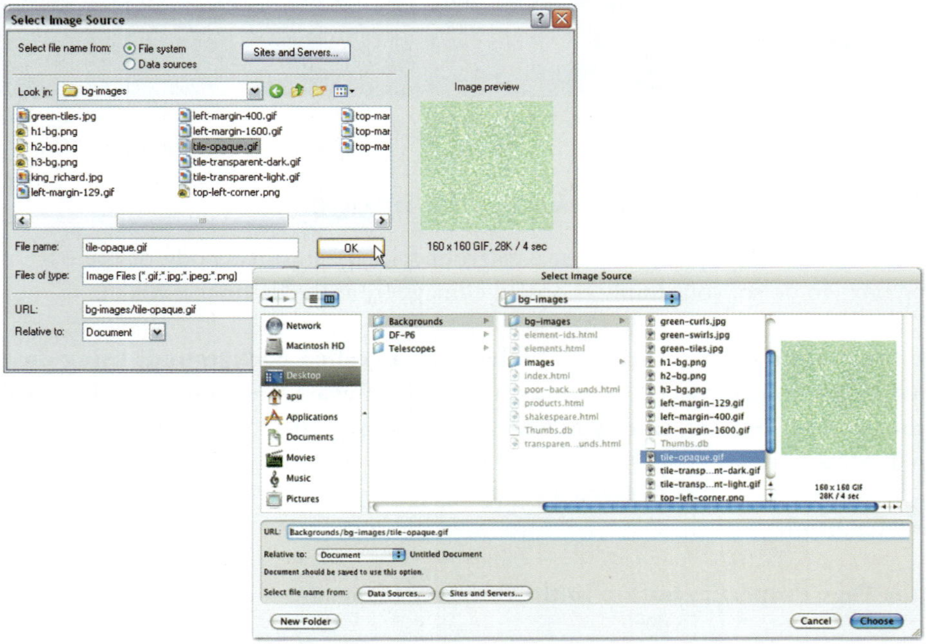

FIGURE 6.12

**6** **In the Page Properties dialog box, click OK.**

The background of the page is tiled with the background image.

**FIGURE 6.13**

**7** **Close the document, saving the changes.**

## LESSON 2 Avoiding Unsuitable Background Images

It is best to choose background graphics that are relatively ***flat in color depth*** (do not contain too many colors). If you don't, you may find it difficult to choose a color for a foreground item that can stand out sufficiently against all of those background colors. You should also choose graphics with ***low contrast***, where the difference in brightness between the brightest color and darkest color is not great. Background graphics with high contrast can make it difficult for you to choose a contrasting text color that is readable — a light text color may be hard to read against the light portion of the background and a dark text color may be difficult to read against the dark portion of the background graphic. Whether you create or simply choose an image for the background, ensure that the tiling matches properly. This is not unlike hanging patterned wallpaper — the pattern must start at the same place it ended on the adjacent strip.

In this exercise, you examine various background graphics against text on a page to see just how difficult it is to read text against a poorly chosen background. You also use the Apply button in the Page Properties dialog box to apply the changes you make to the page without having to close the dialog box and reopen it each time. With this button, it is faster and easier to experiment with different options.

## Explore Unsuitable Background Images

**1** **Open poor-backgrounds.html.**

**2** **Examine the background and overlaying text in the left cell.**

The background of the left table cell is a moderately dark and busy background pattern; only the white text can be read, and only if the text is large.

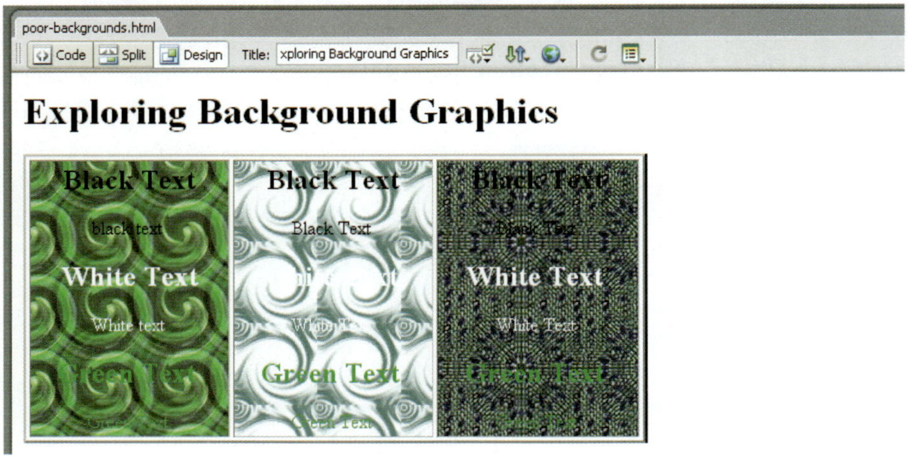


FIGURE 6.14

**3** **Examine the background and overlaying text in the center cell.**

The background of the center table cell is a lighter but still busy background pattern; because of the high contrast between the white and the darker areas, even the black text is difficult to read.

**4** **Examine the background and overlaying text in the right cell.**

Although the right cell contains a somewhat busy pattern and there is high contrast between the light areas and the dark areas, the individual areas of colors are quite small, making the white text more visible than against the other two background patterns. The pattern would be quite distracting, however, if used throughout the entire page.

**5** **Close poor-backgrounds.html.**

# LESSON 3 Exploring Problems with Transparent Background Graphics

You should avoid choosing or creating background graphics with transparent areas; because the background color shows through the transparent area. This is not an issue if the background color is the same as the transparent color (before it was chosen as the transparent color), but if the background color is different than the designer intended, a halo appears around the graphic.

Most browsers display Web pages against a default white background if no other background color or image is specified. Some browsers, however, use a gray background. You should be aware that users can specify their own background image or color. In some cases, those who do simply prefer their own background color. In other cases, they may be visually impaired (for example, having color blindness), and therefore may specify particular text and background color combinations that they can read more easily than the original design. For all of these reasons, you should avoid using background images with transparent areas. Either choose images without such regions, or remove the transparency option using an image-editing application.

In this lesson, you explore the effects of choosing a background image with transparent regions for use against an unsuitable background color. You also learn that you can specify both a background color and background image.

## Explore Problems with Transparent Background Graphics

**1** **Open transparent-backgrounds.html.**

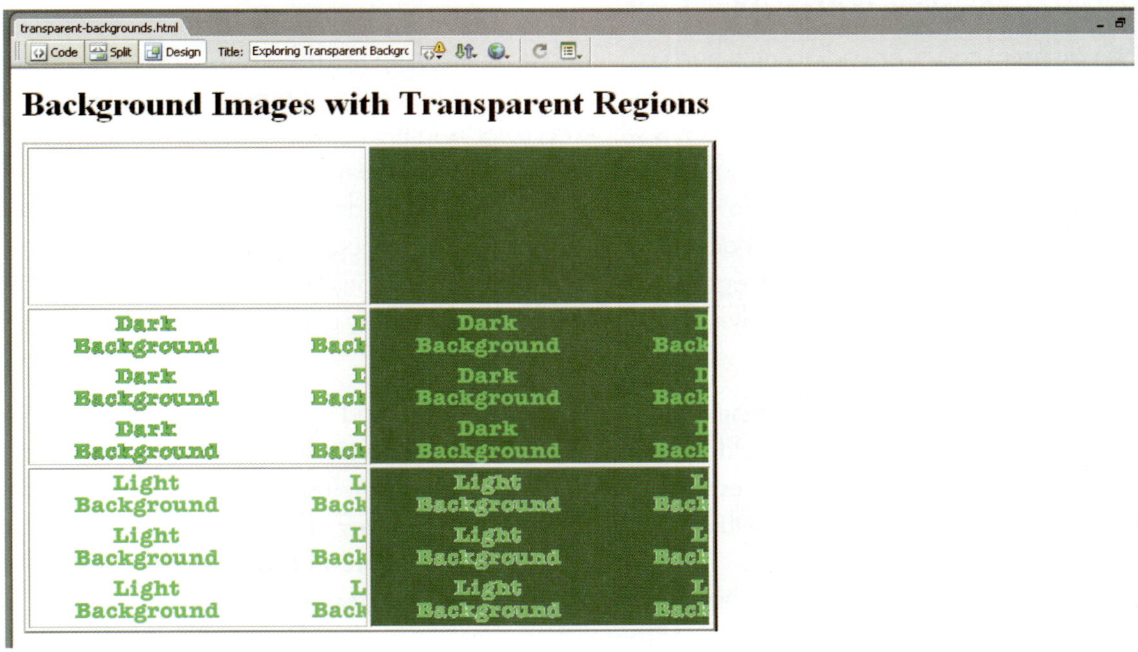


FIGURE 6.15

**2** **Examine the top two cells.**

These cells display the background color used in their respective columns.

**3** **Examine the middle row in both columns. Look closely at the background graphic and the color of the background.**

The middle row in both the left and right columns uses the same background graphic. This background graphic was created against a dark green background, like what you see in the right cell. The letters in the left cell, however, have a dark halo where the medium green of the text gradually blends with the dark green used as the original background. The gradient is apparent as a halo when the graphic is placed against a white background.

**4** **Examine the bottom row. Look at the two background colors and the background graphic.**

The bottom row displays a background graphic that was originally created against a white background and was later made transparent. The gradient or halo shows against the dark background of the right cell.

**5** **Close transparent-backgrounds.html.**

## To Extend Your Knowledge

### THE HALO AROUND TRANSPARENT GIFS

When different colors are adjacent to each other in a graphic, graphics programs create a gradient of colors in the transitional area. When the background color is made the transparent color, the gradient still exists, but the transparent region allows whatever color is in the background to show through. The halo is the remaining gradient of colors in the transition zone. For example, consider a graphic consisting of green text placed on a yellow background with the yellow identified as the transparent color. If the graphic is placed on a blue background, the blue shows through where the yellow color was. However, consider the regions in the graphic where the color is in transition from green to yellow. This gradient still exists, creating a gradient from green to almost yellow, and then blue where the background shows through. The graphic seems to have a yellow halo.

You may recognize that we're discussing index transparency. If we had used alpha transparency (PNG graphics) instead, this problem would not exist. The transition of colors between the graphic and the background would not need to be created as a transition of colors but, instead, as a transition in transparency. The closer the pixels are to the graphic, the more opaque they are, showing the graphic color more intensely; the closer the pixels are to the background, the more transparent they are, showing more and more of the background through the graphic. Therefore, it does not matter what the background color is because the gradient of transparency creates the gradient by blending the graphic and that background colors.

# LESSON 4 Using Margin Graphics

The tiled images in Lesson 2 demonstrate that when an image is smaller than the background area of a Web page, the image tiles or repeats across and down the page until it fills the background. Tiling occurs by default, no matter which type of background you choose — tile, margin, or watermark. The difference between the three is both in the design of the graphic and in the CSS background options that you set. For example, an image designed for tiling tends to be small and is also designed to hide the visible seam between images. Its small size and invisible seams make it suitable to repeat both horizontally and vertically. A margin graphic tends to be larger, generally the full width of a browser window, and therefore repeats only down the browser window. A watermark graphic tends to be an image that does not lend itself to tiling or repeating at all — a photograph, for instance, would be appropriate for this type of background.

## Margin or Strip-Tile Backgrounds

The margin or strip-tile background is generally used to create a border down the left side of the page, where a navigation bar is typically positioned. It is currently the most common style of background. Margin-style graphics are generally much wider than they are high. As long as the width of the graphic is wider than the width of the browser window, it won't repeat across the browser window, just down. The height of the repeating pattern determines the height of the graphic — it can be as little as a few pixels high, and as large as 50 pixels high. If the left border is a small buttercup flower, the graphic is short, but if the repeating graphic is an ivy vine or tall pine tree, the graphic is tall.

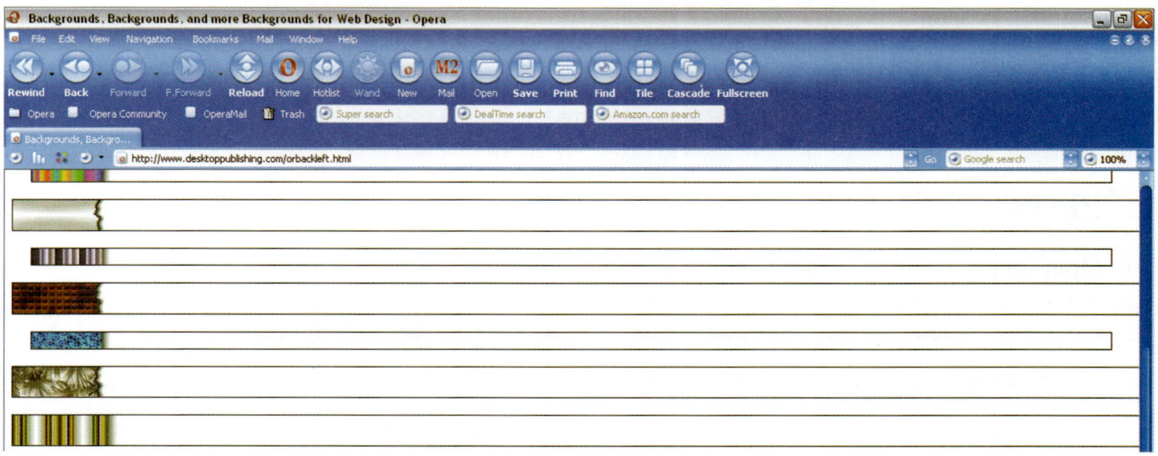


**FIGURE 6.16**

The width of the graphic is very important. If the graphic is 640-px wide, then the left border appears once on a 640 × 480 monitor, twice on a 800 × 600 monitor, and three times on a 1600 × 1200 monitor, as it repeats across the Web page. Given the nature of the compression routine in GIFs and PNGs, increasing the width of the body area of a margin-style graphic doesn't add much to its file size. For instance, using the graphic in the following figure, the 640-pixel-wide version took 2394 bytes of storage space whereas increasing the white area of the graphic to create a 1600-pixel-wide version increased the file size by only 279 bytes.

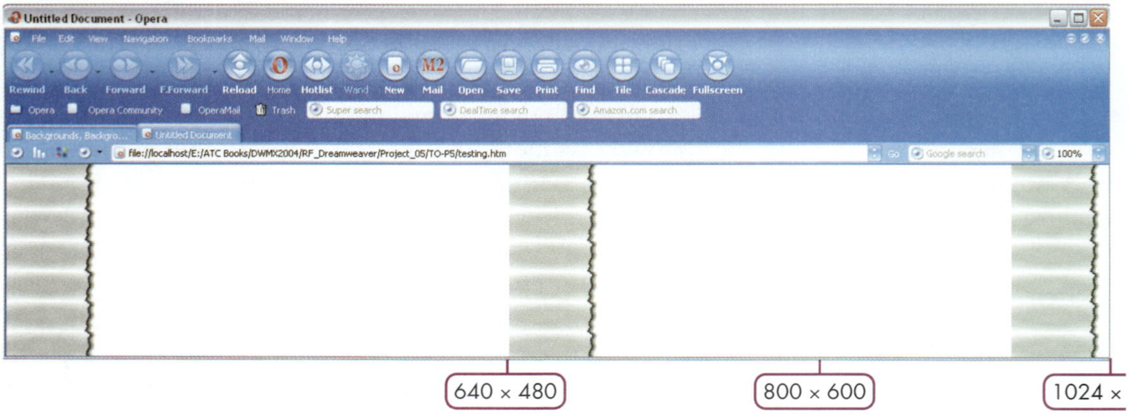


FIGURE 6.17

Although the most common form of this style of background creates a border down the left side of the Web page, it is possible to create a border along the top. The challenge with top borders is to make the graphic tall enough for all Web pages — you don't want the top border repeating partway down the page. A better solution is to use CSS to specify that the background graphic repeat across the width of the browser only, not down the height.

In this exercise, you explore different widths and heights of margin graphics. You learn firsthand that too narrow a graphic repeats across a Web page, and too short a graphic repeats down a Web page. You also learn to use the CSS **background-repeat** property to specify in which direction the repeating occurs — across or down.

## Use Appropriately Sized Margin Graphics

**1** **Open index.html, then open the Page Properties dialog box.**

**2** **Click the Browse button, choose left-margin-400.gif, click OK/Choose, and then click Apply.**

This background graphic is too narrow for the width of the Web page and repeats horizontally, giving the page a very unprofessional appearance.

FIGURE 6.18

**3** **Click the Browse button, choose left-margin-1600.gif, click OK/Choose, and then click Apply.**

This image, which is virtually identical to the one used in the previous step, differs in that it was created 1600 px wide, which is too wide to repeat.

FIGURE 6.19

**4** **Click the Browse button, choose top-margin-300.gif, click OK/Choose, and then click Apply.**

This margin graphic was designed to work as a top border, but it is too short and repeats both vertically and horizontally.

FIGURE 6.20

**5** **Click the Browse button, choose top-margin-2000.gif, click OK/Choose, and then click OK again.**

This graphic is 2000 px high. For the relatively short pages in Tropiflora Online, this height would be sufficient. In other circumstances, it might not be sufficiently tall.

**6** **Save the changes to index.html, leaving it open for the next lesson.**

## To Extend Your Knowledge

### CREATING BACKGROUND IMAGES

So far, you have explored different types of background images — some that work and some that do not. Dreamweaver's image-editing tools cannot help to create a background image; to do so, you need to use a graphics program, such as Photoshop, Fireworks, or CorelDRAW. Even modifying a background image is beyond the tools found in Dreamweaver.

When you create an image for tiling, ensure that the color depth and contrast are fairly flat. Many graphics programs come with patterns that you can use as backgrounds. There are also many Web sites, such as BackgroundCity.com, which are collections of free patterns and other graphics. In addition, there are many tutorials posted on the Internet on how to create patterns with graphics software. At http://classic.gimp.org/tut-patt1.html, for example, you'll find a tutorial on how to create patterns using the Linux graphics application called "GIMP" (which also is available for Windows). The tutorial can be adapted to other Windows or Macintosh graphics applications. (The tutorial on creating easy patterns was made for version 1.2 of GIMP, but GIMP 2.0 has now been released. With some modification, you can adapt this tutorial to GIMP 2.0.)

Left-margin patterns should not be so narrow that they repeat across a page. It is very, very rare to find a computer monitor that has a higher resolution than 1600 pixels wide. However, some designers create images that are 1610 pixels wide, just to give them an extra degree of insurance that the image is larger than the monitor width. Top-margin patterns should not repeat down a page, but that is a much greater challenge when pages are very long. Other methods are much easier to use, such as putting the top pattern in the top cell of a table or using CSS to specify that the pattern only repeat across the page, not down it.

# LESSON 5 Using Watermark Background Graphics

The difference between the first two styles of backgrounds — tiled and margin — and the third type — watermark backgrounds — is not so much how you insert the background or how you construct it, but how it is applied. Tiled background graphics are designed to create a consistent pattern in the background of the page. Margin graphics are designed to create a margin pattern that appear along just one side of the body of the page, and generally they repeat in just one direction. Watermark images are intended to appear just once on a page with no repetition in either direction. Generally, watermark background images are not generic patterns but are specific to the site, such as a photograph of the designer or a faint image of the company logo.

## Watermark Backgrounds

A watermark-style background graphic is typically made large. Generally, this style of background is restricted from repeating. You can make this restriction either by creating a large graphic or by setting the CSS **`background-repeat`** property to **`no-repeat`**. The problem with creating a large graphic is that it can appear too large in a small monitor or too small in a large monitor. Done properly, however, this background style can create some stunning Web-page effects.

In the background of the home page of Czech Web designer Petr Stanicek (aka Pixy), a flattened graphic (flattened both in contrast and color depth) of his photo shows in the background. This page uses multiple CSS techniques to push the graphic to the bottom-right corner of the page as well as to keep it from moving when the scrollbar is moved. He has added a humorous notation to the background graphic: in pale gray to the right of the top of his head, he has added <head> and just below his chin, he has added <body> — only people with HTML experience are likely to understand his joke.

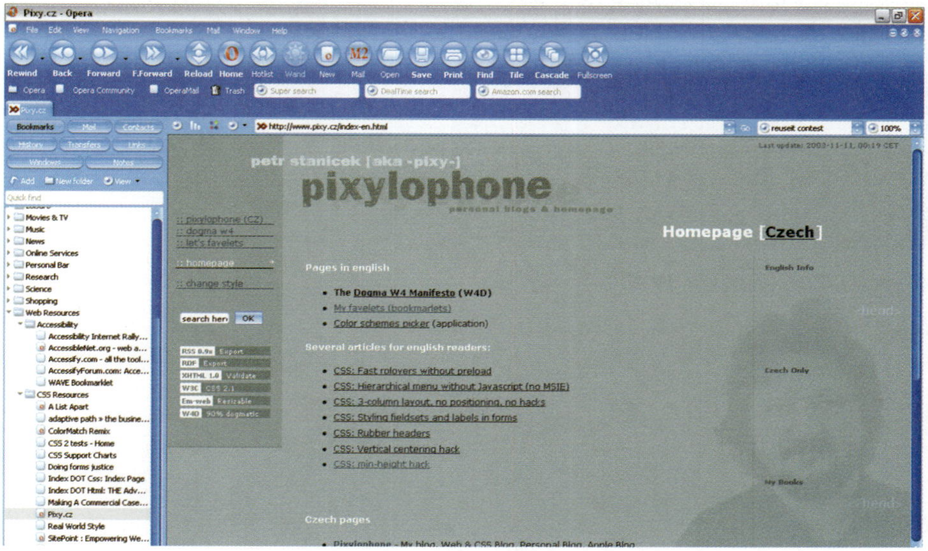


FIGURE 6.21

In the following redesign of Jakob Nielsen's Useit.com Web site, the photograph in the background is neither low in contrast nor low in color depth. However, to prevent readability issues with text over the complex background, the width of the content is restricted so it does not reach to the right side and overlap the background graphic.

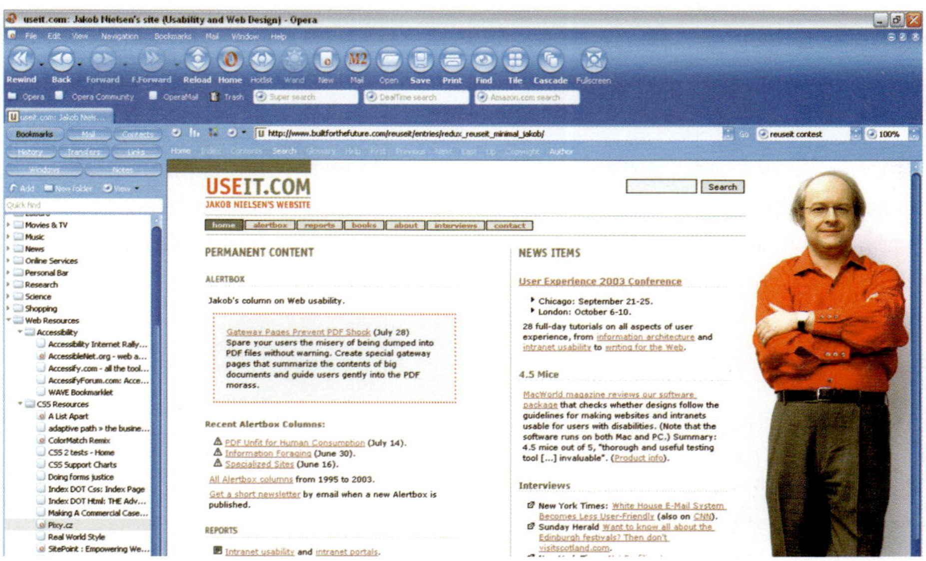


FIGURE 6.22

## Insert a Watermark Graphic

**1** **In the open document index.html, open the Page Properties dialog box.**

**2** **Click the Browse button, choose bromeliad-watermark.jpg, click OK/Choose, and then click Apply.**

This image of a bromeliad is lightened to reduce contrast and color depth. It is large but not quite large enough, as you can see where it starts to repeat on the bottom-right side.

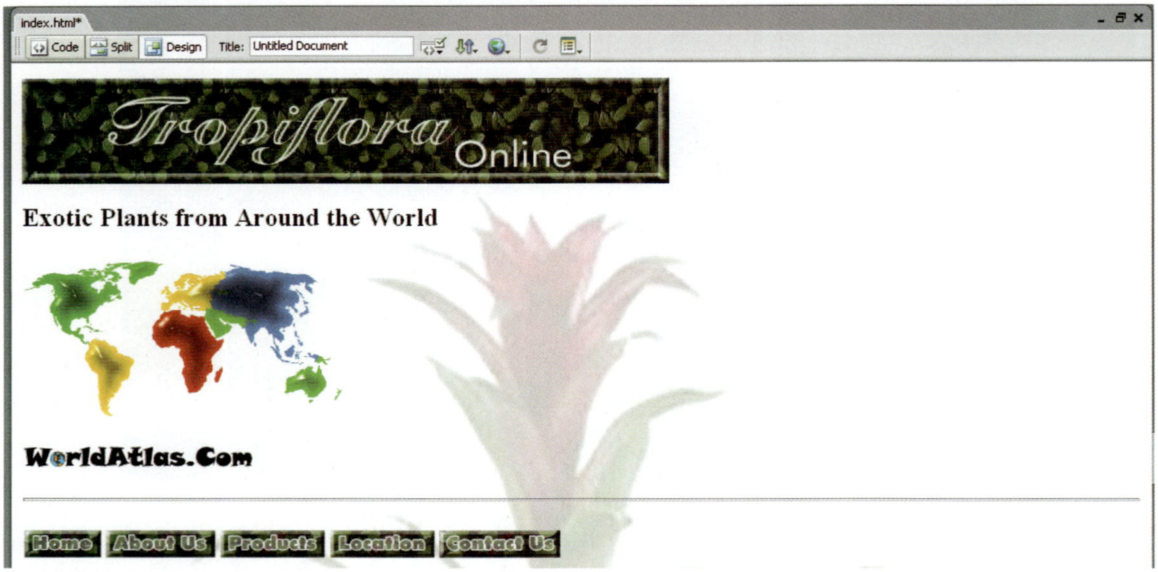


FIGURE 6.23

**3** **Close index.html, saving the changes.**

## *To Extend Your Knowledge*

### NO ALTERNATE TEXT FOR BACKGROUND IMAGES

Background images do not need and cannot have alternate text. There is no alt attribute available for background images. This fact may be useful to you when you create a Web site. If you can set a decorative graphic as a background graphic, you do not need to specify even an empty alt.

# LESSON 6 Applying Both Background Image and Color

Current browsers, by default, display Web pages against a white background. Older browsers tended to display Web pages against a light-gray background. For the most part, text colors displayed against either of these backgrounds are quite readable. However, some Web-page designers add very dark background images against their pages. This is fine except for visitors who have disabled graphics in their browser. If you use a dark background image behind your page, you use light text colors to make your text readable. However, if a visitor disables the display of graphics, the background does not display and the light text is placed against a white or light gray background so is not readable. You should, therefore, add a background color in addition to a background image if your background image is significantly different from white or light gray. Adding this color ensures that your text is visible and legible against the background.

In this exercise, you learn to apply a background color in addition to a background graphic. You also see why it is beneficial to specify both.

## Apply Both Background Color and Graphic

**1** **Define a site named Telescopes from the Project_06>Telescopes folder.**

**2** **Open index.html.**

The document appears empty because the text is colored white. You must apply a dark background.

**3** **Open the Page Properties dialog box.**

**4** **Click the Background Color button to open the color palettes.**

The square button to the right of Background Color opens the color palettes. This button appears many places in Dreamweaver and opens the same color palette dialog box each time.

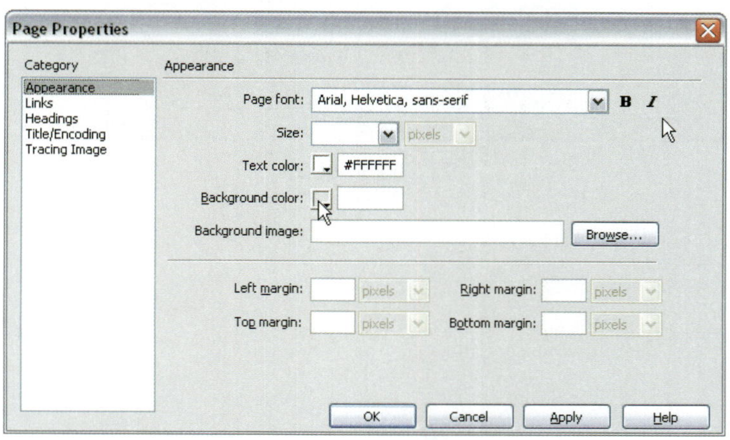


FIGURE 6.24

**5** **Move the mouse pointer around the color palette.**

Notice that the color-swatch window (top-left corner of the palette window) displays the color closest to the mouse pointer, and the top of the palette window displays the hexadecimal code of the highlighted color. Notice, also, that the mouse pointer takes the shape of an eyedropper; a tool found in many graphics programs and commonly used for choosing a color.

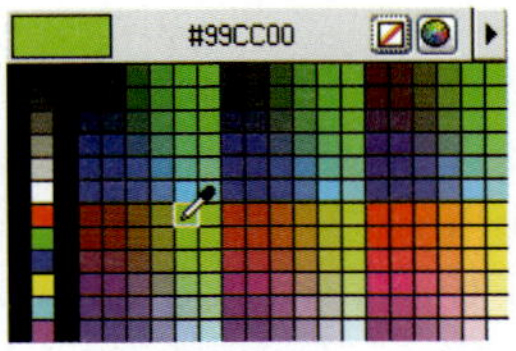


FIGURE 6.25

**6** **Click the black square at the top left of the palette.**

Black has a hexadecimal code of #000000 — you can use this code to ensure that you have found a black square.

**7** **Click Apply.**

Notice that the Background Color button has a black center and the hexadecimal code for black is in the text field to its right.

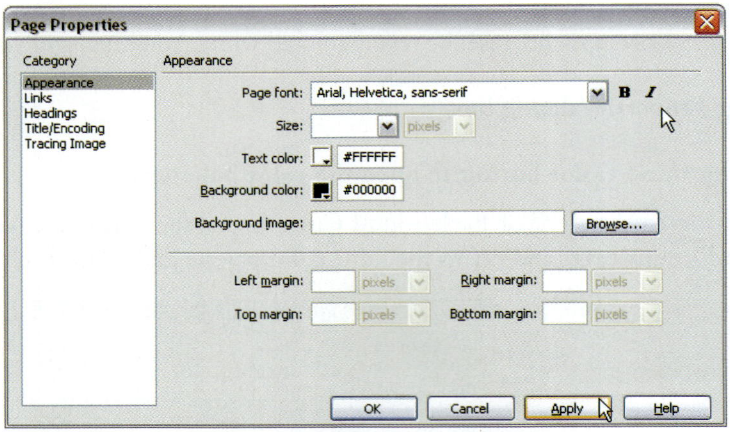


FIGURE 6.26

**8** **Click OK to close the Page Properties dialog box.**

Notice that the text is now visible against the black background color.

FIGURE 6.27

Although the background color works, it is rather boring. Next, you add a background image.

**9** **Open the Page Properties dialog box, click the Browse button, and navigate to the Telescopes>images folder. Choose stars.jpg, click OK/Choose, and then click OK/Choose again.**

FIGURE 6.28

**10** **Save the changes to index.html, leaving it open for the next lesson.**

## To Extend Your Knowledge

### BACKGROUNDS CAN REPLACE GRAPHIC BUTTONS

Many navigation bars use graphic buttons as links to provide interesting style to the navigation bar. In most cases, the buttons are identical but the text is different because they represent links to different sections of the Web site. Graphic buttons are an annoyance to create: spelling mistakes, design changes, and additional links all require the designer to modify or create new, custom graphic buttons. Because the only thing that changes from button to button is the text, many CSS-aware designers instead create a background image to place behind each link, thereby creating the appearance of a button. This has the added benefit of employing just one background graphic that is used multiple times. A change in the design requires a change to only one graphic. Spelling mistake? No problem — just fix the error in the text. A new link to add? Just type the text, create the link, and apply the same background image. Whenever there is a common background to a series of elements, whether they be links, paragraphs, or headings, consider creating a background graphic and placing it behind each of the elements rather than creating graphic buttons or graphic text.

# LESSON 7 Setting Default Text Colors

You have learned to apply a background graphic and also a background color. In this lesson, you learn to set text colors. You can set one color that applies to all text, whether it is a paragraph or a heading. However, you can set a different color for each text format, such as different colors for paragraphs and for each heading level. All of these options are available through the Page Properties dialog box. You can also apply colors to link text — link text is traditionally blue, but you can change that.

In this lesson, you learn to work with the System Color Picker. The name of this dialog box is somewhat confusing — it is titled the Color/Colors dialog box, but in the help documentation, it is also referred to as the "System Color Picker." To open the System Color Picker, you click the Color Wheel button at the top of the color palette. In the Color dialog box, the rainbow of colors is called the "Color Matrix" (Windows) and "Color Wheel" (Macintosh). There are some differences between the Windows Color dialog box and the Macintosh Colors dialog box, but these differences are cosmetic, not functional.

You drag your mouse pointer in the Color Matrix/Wheel to select a color: the cross hair/point control identifies the position of the color. In Windows, if you slide the cross hair horizontally, the Hue value below the Color Matrix changes. On a Macintosh, positions around the Color Wheel circle represent the hue; if you move the point control around the outside of the Color Wheel, you change the hue. In Windows, if you slide the cross hair vertically, the saturation value changes. On a Macintosh, the saturation value changes when you move the point control to the center of the circle. On both systems, the slider on the right changes the luminosity. In Windows, the HSL and RGB values for the current color display below the Color Matrix. In Macintosh, to obtain the RGB or HSB values, you click the Color Slider button and select either RGB or HSB (among others) from the pop-up list.

The Color/Colors dialog boxes allow you to select colors outside of the Web-safe color palette, but only if the Snap to Web-safe option in the Color Picker is disabled. The Color/Colors dialog box also allows you to see and record the RGB values of your selected color. This is useful if you want to use the **rgb()** method of specifying your color using CSS, such as **rgb(255, 0, 0)** for red.

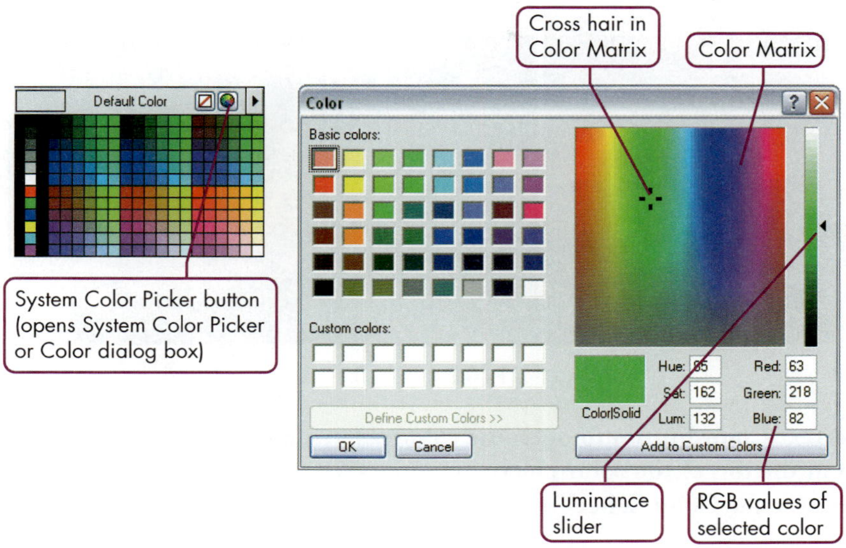


**FIGURE 6.29** Windows

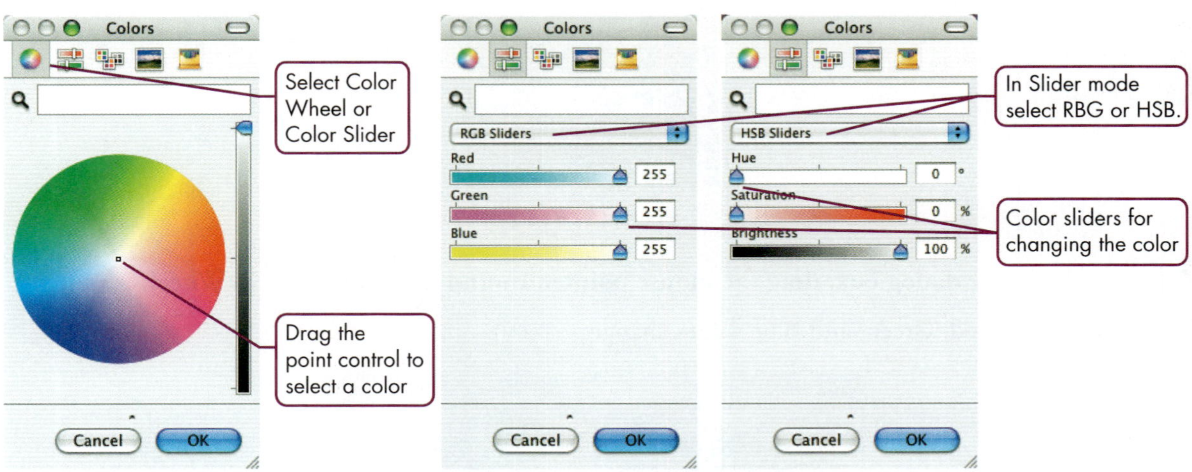


**FIGURE 6.30** Macintosh

## Set Default Text Colors

**1** **In the open document index.html, open the Page Properties dialog box.**

The white text, heading, and link colors are not the default colors for text in a Web page or Dreamweaver. Text is normally black and links are normally blue. In order to demonstrate the need to set the background color in case the background image were not downloaded in the previous exercise, the default text colors are purposely set to white.

**2** **Click the Text Color button, choose yellow with the eyedropper, and click Apply.**

Both heading and paragraph text become yellow. Link text stays white because it is controlled by a separate option.

FIGURE 6.31

**3** **Click the Text Color button to open the color palette, and then click the Color Wheel button. (The text at the top of the color palette window says "System Color Picker" when your mouse pointer is over the Color Wheel.)**

The System Color Picker is a tool that allows you to choose or specify a color from the entire range of colors available on your system.

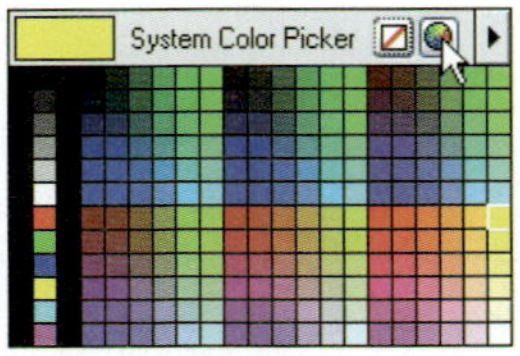


FIGURE 6.32

**4** **In the Color dialog box, drag the mouse pointer around the Color Matrix/Wheel.**

Watch the Red, Green, and Blue values change.

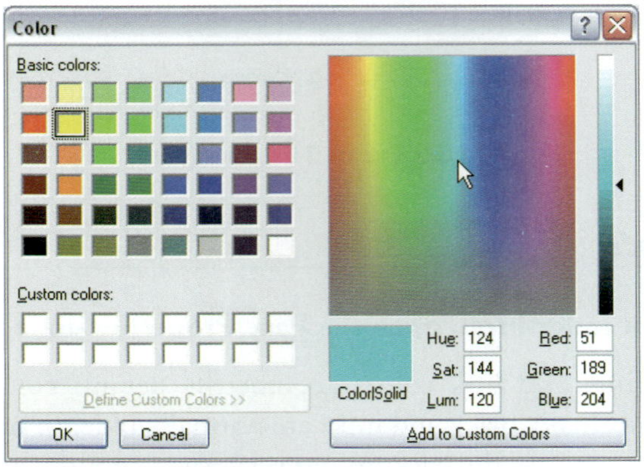


FIGURE 6.33

**5** **Drag the cross hair/point control to the most intense blue. In Windows, move the cross hair to the top of the Color Matrix. On a Macintosh, move the point control to the edge of the Color Wheel.**

The cross hair/point control indicates the position of the color in the palette.

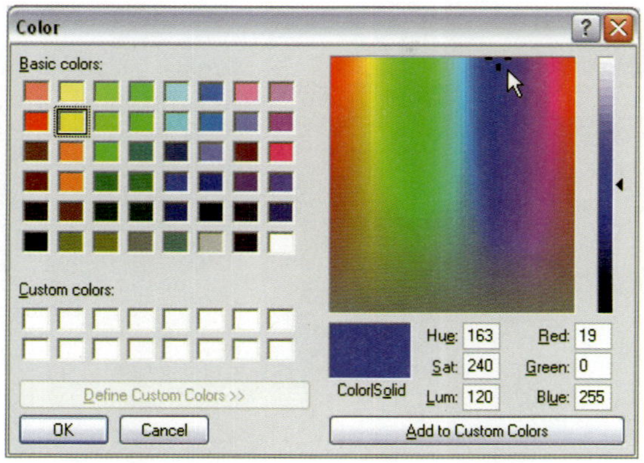


FIGURE 6.34

**6** **In Windows, drag the cross hair left and right to explore different hues, and up and down to explore different saturation levels. On a Macintosh, drag the point control around the Color Wheel to explore different hues, and to the center and back to the edge to explore different saturation levels.**

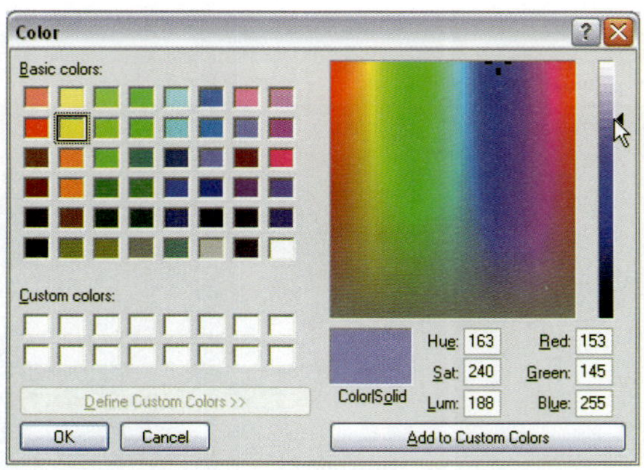


FIGURE 6.35

**7** **Drag the slider up and down to explore different luminosities (both Windows and Macintosh), then stop at a luminosity that produces a light-blue color, and click OK.**

Notice that although there were no hexadecimal color codes in the System Color Picker dialog box, Dreamweaver converts the RGB values to hexadecimal codes for you and places the code in the Text Color field.

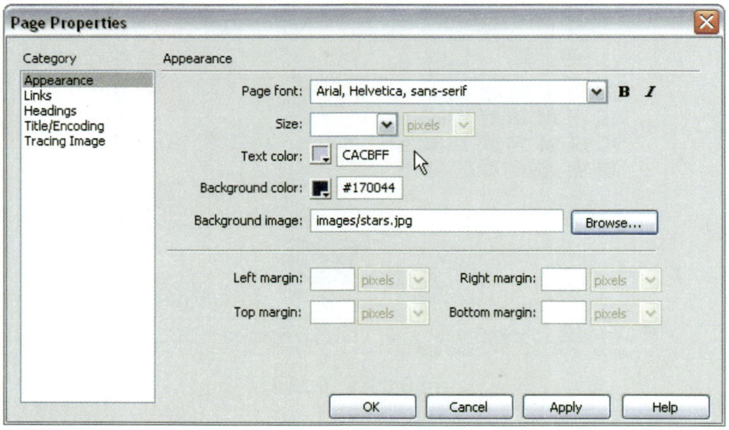


FIGURE 6.36

**8** **Click OK to apply the default text color to the document.**

The System Color Picker is another method for choosing a color.

FIGURE 6.37

**9** **Save the changes to index.html, leaving it open for the next lesson.**

## To Extend Your Knowledge

### HEXADECIMAL AND RGB

There are different palettes and methods of identifying a particular color. So far, we have identified two methods — using color names such as blue and yellow, and specifying hexadecimal color codes.

CSS allows an alternate form of hexadecimal color codes for colors that use the triplet pair of color codes. Web-safe colors use the triplet pairs of color codes, such as 003366. CSS allows a short form, in which 036 is equivalent to 003366. You can use 147 in place of 114477, despite the fact that it is not a Web-safe color — the triplet-pair pattern holds.

In the previous exercise, you saw that Dreamweaver converted the colors from the System Color Picker, which uses numerical codes for RGB, to hexadecimal color codes. Without Dreamweaver, conversion from numerical values to hexadecimal values is very difficult without using a calculator or program. CSS allows a numerical format for RGB values — for example, **`rgb(134, 87, 179)`**. This form is very simple to use because it allows you to simply type the three numbers from the System Color Picker into the format without having to convert it to hexadecimal.

# LESSON 8 Setting Link Colors

As you know, you can establish links from either text or graphics. Links were traditionally three colors, but with CSS and Dreamweaver, a fourth color option is available. Unvisited links (or just links) can use one color (traditionally blue), visited links can use a second color (traditionally purple), and active links can use a third (traditionally red). Active link colors are not often used — this color appears only briefly when you click the link. The fourth and newest link property is the CSS **`hover`** property, which allows you to apply a color that appears when the mouse pointer rolls over a link.

Dreamweaver refers to the **`hover`** property as the "rollover property", which can be confusing. This property, by whichever name, changes the color of a link when the mouse pointer rolls over the link. You set up this **`hover`** (rollover) property through the Page Properties dialog box.

As you know, Dreamweaver is not a browser. It does not respond to user-triggered events, such as the **`hover`** or **`active`** properties of CSS. Therefore, you must test the active, visited, and rollover link colors in a browser. (The unvisited link color does not respond to any user actions so appears the same in Dreamweaver as it does in a browser.)

## Set Link Colors

**1** **In the open document index.html, open the Page Properties dialog box.**

**2** **Switch to the Links category in the dialog box.**

The Link color was previously set to white so the text would show up against the dark background of the stars. Normally, link text is blue and the Link Color field would be blank.

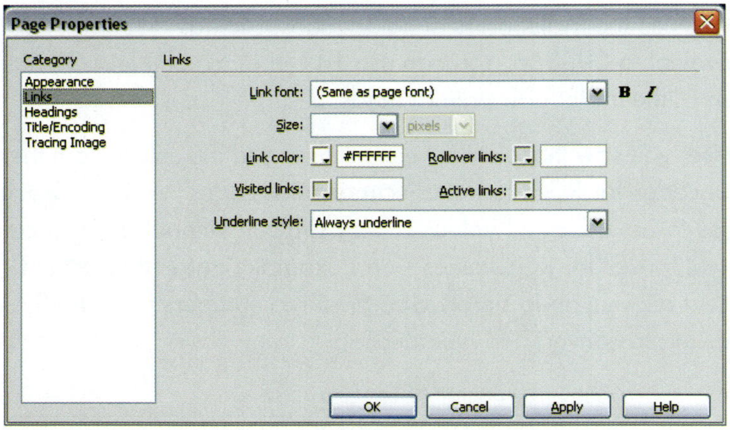


FIGURE 6.38

**3** **Change the Link Color to a light blue. Set the color of Visited Links to white, Rollover Links to yellow, and Active Links to red. Set the Underline Style to Hide Underline on Rollover.**

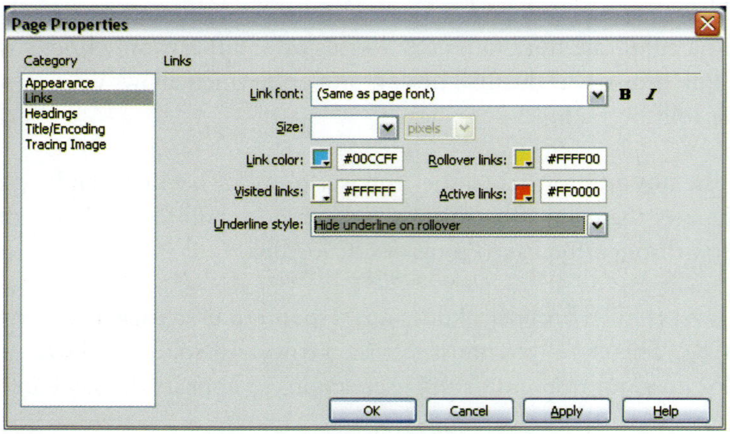


FIGURE 6.39

**4** **Click OK when finished.**

**5** **Preview the page in your browser.**

**6** **Move your mouse pointer over a link and watch as the rollover color changes to yellow and the underline disappears.**

**7** **Click a link and observe the flash of red when you click a link.**

**8** **Click the back button in your browser to return to this page, and note that the visited link has changed to white.**

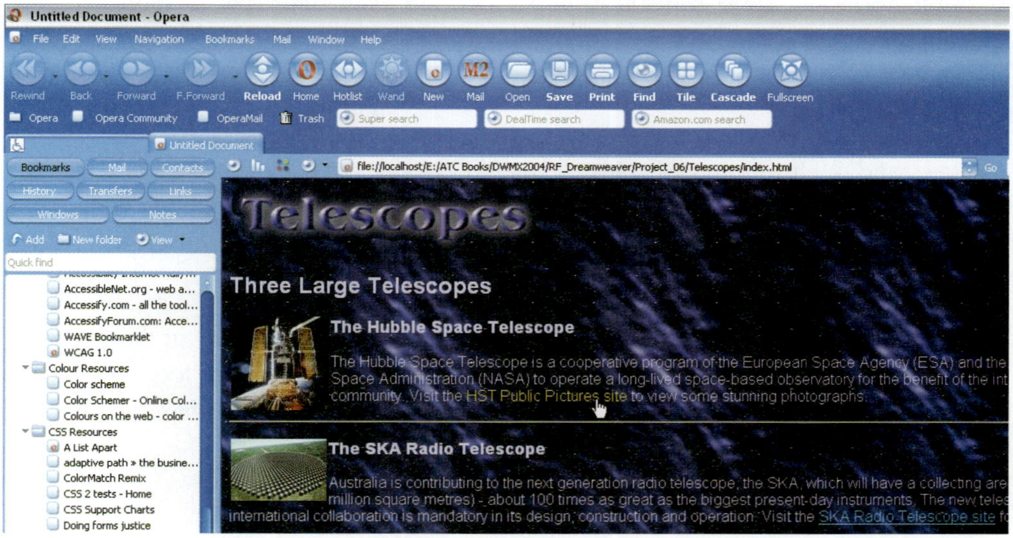


FIGURE 6.40

**9** **Return to Dreamweaver.**

**10** **Close index.html.**

## *To Extend Your Knowledge*

### CSS PSEUDO-CLASSES

The Page Properties dialog box allows you to change the text color of four link states: link (unvisited), visited, active, and hover (rollover). These states are properly known as "CSS pseudo-classes" and their forms are: **`:link`**, **`:visited`**, **`:active`**, and **`:hover`**. When you set a link color, Dreamweaver creates **`a:link`**, which means the anchor tag (**a**) has been defined with properties of a link state.

There are a few more pseudo-classes than the four discussed so far, but these are the most popular and have the widest support. Support for these pseudo-classes goes back as far as Internet Explorer 3. Other pseudo-classes include **`:focus`**, which is useful in a form — you can use it to change the background color of the text box when the user is entering text.

You can only use the link and visited pseudo-classes with the anchor tag — these pseudo-classes only make sense to a link. You can use the active and hover pseudo-class with other tags. The CSS documentation allows you to use the active pseudo-class with other tags, but browser support is virtually nonexistent. The hover pseudo-class can be used with any element, as well, and is supported by most current browsers (except Internet Explorer).

## CAREERS IN DESIGN

### USING BACKGROUNDS EFFECTIVELY

Nothing in the world can ruin a perfectly good Web site faster or more effectively than an annoying and distracting background image. Tiled, sliced, diced, or repeated, many textures and images used for backgrounds on amateur sites are so horrid that visiting them proves to be agonizing.

Professional sites stand out from amateur sites — both in layouts, the use of background images, and even (in some cases) color combinations. The amateur site designer is often a technophile with little or no sense of fashion. We're not only talking about wearing white socks with sandals, mind you — fashion sense makes itself known in many ways. Some are subtle, others not so subtle.

Use Google or Yahoo to search for bad Web designs. You will be astounded at the number of hits you receive, as much as you'll be amazed by how bad sites can look. A good place to start your search for the shocking (in a bad but not-so bad-way) is http://www.ratz.com/featuresbad.html — which provides an outline of what not to do when designing a site.

## SUMMARY

In this project, you learned different methods of using background images — as tiled backgrounds, as strip or margin backgrounds, and as watermark backgrounds. You saw that highly contrasting and highly colored background images may make it difficult to choose a foreground text color that can be read against them. You discovered that transparent images show an unwanted halo if the background color of the page is incorrect. You learned that you should add a background color similar to that of the background image in case a visitor views your pages with graphics disabled. You learned about RGB and hexadecimal color notations, and about the Web-safe color palette. You learned how to apply colors to text, headings, and the four link states. You also learned how to choose a color from the Web-safe color palette and from the System Color Picker.

## KEY TERMS

Color matrix
Color wheel
Deci
Dithering
Flat in color depth
Hexa
Hexadecimal
Low contrast
Palette
RGB model
System Color Picker
Tiling
Wallpaper patterns

# CHECKING CONCEPTS AND TERMS

## SCREEN ID

**Identify the indicated areas from the list below:**

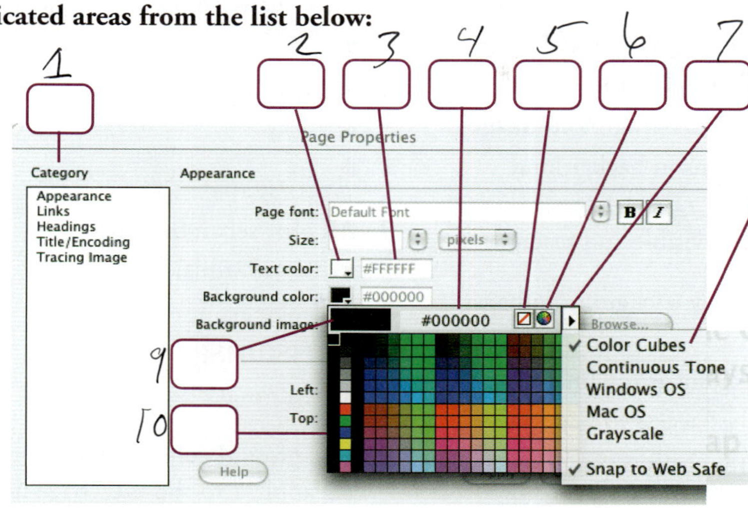


FIGURE 6.41

- **a.** Category list
- **b.** Color button
- **c.** Color field
- **d.** Color swatch
- **e.** Default color
- **f.** Hexadecimal color code
- **g.** System Color Picker
- **h.** Pop-out menu
- **i.** Color palette
- **j.** Arrow to display pop-out menu

## MULTIPLE CHOICE

**Circle the letter of the correct answer for each of the following:**

1. Which of the following is recommended when choosing a background image for a Web page?
   a. Use animated GIFs as backgrounds.
   b. Use many colors in the background image.
   c. Use transparent regions in background graphics.
   d. Make overlaying text visible and readable.

2. A reason to avoid complex background images is that they __________.
   a. can slow down scrolling as the image moves
   b. can prevent universal access to your page
   c. require more computer processing power
   d. All the above

3. Which is not one of the three styles of background images?
   a. wallpaper
   b. watermark
   c. textured
   d. margin tile

4. Color depth of monitors is described ________.
   a. as true color
   b. as 2 × 2 × 2 × 2 × 2 × 2 × 2 × 2 or 256 colors
   c. in bits, such as 8-bit, 16-bit, and 24-bit color
   d. as dithering

5. Hexadecimal __________.
   a. means 16
   b. is used for the Web color system
   c. includes numerals 0-9 and characters A-F
   d. All of the above

6. How many colors are considered Web-safe?
   a. 256
   b. 16.7 million
   c. 216
   d. 64

7. All browsers recognize __________.
   a. hexadecimal
   b. color names
   c. HSB/HSL
   d. Pantone

8. Background color and background images are applied to the Web page using the __________.
   a. Property inspector
   b. Assets panel
   c. Preferences dialog box
   d. Page Properties dialog box

9. In the Page Properties dialog box, you cannot set __________.
   a. text color
   b. syntax coloring
   c. background image
   d. All of the above

10. If you apply a background image to a Web page, you should set the background color to __________.
   a. black or #000000
   b. white or #FFFFFF
   c. a color that contrasts with the text color
   d. it doesn't matter — the color will never show

## DISCUSSION QUESTIONS

1. You can find many images and graphics on the Web — from private Web sites (belonging to individuals, companies, or organizations), from free image/graphic/photo sites, and from sites that charge a fee for their graphics. You may also have images belonging to your employer or client, and you may have access to a digital camera. Imagine that you are creating and implementing a theme and color scheme for a Web site you are designing. What would you consider the pros and cons of each of these sources of images? List at least one pro and one con for each source.

2. What different choices for colors and background images might you make if you were designing Web sites for a sports retail store, a business school, and a personal wedding? Justify your answers.

3. How can you establish the tone or mood of a Web site through the selection of background and foreground images? Give an example, stating the tone you want to create, the business or organization you are imagining designing a Web site for, and the types of choices you would make to sustain that mood with background and foreground images.

# SKILL DRILL

Skill Drill exercises reinforce project skills. Each skill reinforced is the same, or nearly the same, as a skill presented in the project. Detailed instructions are provided in a step-by-step format. You should work through the exercises in order.

## 1. Choose a Color from an Image

The reach of the eyedropper color picker extends beyond the Color Picker window. You can use it to choose a color from any component in the Dreamweaver application window. If you have a graphic with a color you would like to match, as long as you can see the graphic in the Document window, you can use the color picker to pick up a color from the graphic.

In this exercise you learn to use the eyedropper to obtain a color from a graphic, and then make the chosen color the background color.

1. Open index.html from the Telescopes site and open the Page Properties dialog box.
2. Drag to select the contents of the Background Image field (images/stars.jpg) and press Delete to remove it.
3. Click Apply to confirm that the starry background is removed.
4. Click the Background Color button.
5. Click the pop-out arrow at the top right of the Color Picker window.

6. If there is a check mark next to Snap to Web Safe, skip to Step 8. If there is no check mark next to Snap to Web Safe, click Snap to Web Safe.

   In the previous exercises, we did not need to worry about whether Snap to Web Safe was enabled or not because the colors in the color palette are all Web-safe. Colors outside of the color palette, however, may not be Web-safe.

7. Move the mouse pointer (eyedropper) over the Telescopes graphic near the top of the Document window. Watch the swatch window and hexadecimal codes change as the mouse pointer moves across the graphic.

   You can see that the hexadecimal codes are always paired triplets, such as 330066 or 003300. The Snap to Web Safe option converts the color at the tip of the eyedropper to the closest Web-safe color.

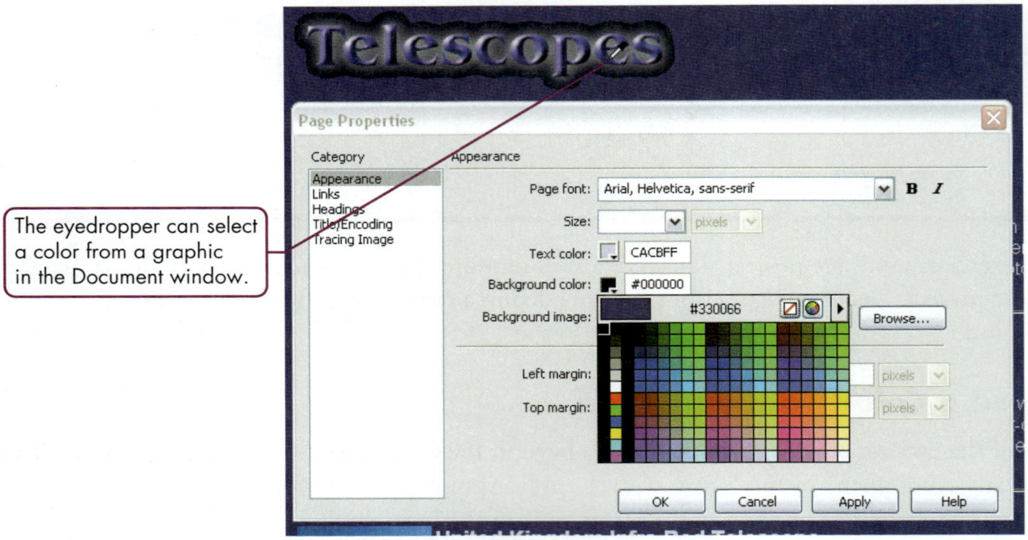


FIGURE 6.42

8. Return the mouse pointer to the color palette and disable the Snap to Web Safe option.

9. Hover the eyedropper over the same graphic.

   Notice that the hexadecimal codes are no longer paired triplets. With the Snap to Web Safe option disabled, the hexadecimal codes display the true colors at the point of the eyedropper.

10. Click a color from the Telescopes graphic. Click OK in the Page Properties dialog box to accept and apply the color.

11. Save the changes to index.html, leaving it open for the next exercise.

## 2. Set Heading Colors

So far, you have learned to apply a color to text, which sets the same color for all text in the page. However, different text elements on a page can have their own text colors, such as the different heading levels. You can apply these text colors through the Page Properties dialog box. In addition to font size, you can use colors to distinguish between heading levels.

1. In the open document index.html (from the Telescope site), open the Page Properties dialog box.
2. Choose Headings from the Category list.
3. On the right side of the Heading-1 row, click the color button and choose red from the color palette.
4. Choose yellow as the color for Heading 2 and light green for Heading 3.
5. Click OK to see the effects of the color selections.

   The Heading-1 red color is not visible in Dreamweaver because the graphic of the Telescopes text is the Heading-1 content. If the graphic did not download, the alt text Telescopes would appear in red (as shown in the Figure 6.43 of the Opera browser, in which the graphics are turned off). The white and light-blue text is link text. The alt text of the photos is also white and light blue because it represents links. The link to the Hubble Space Telescope Web site is white because the photo is a link to the home page; it has been visited, so it takes on the visited-link color (white) you defined in Lesson 8.

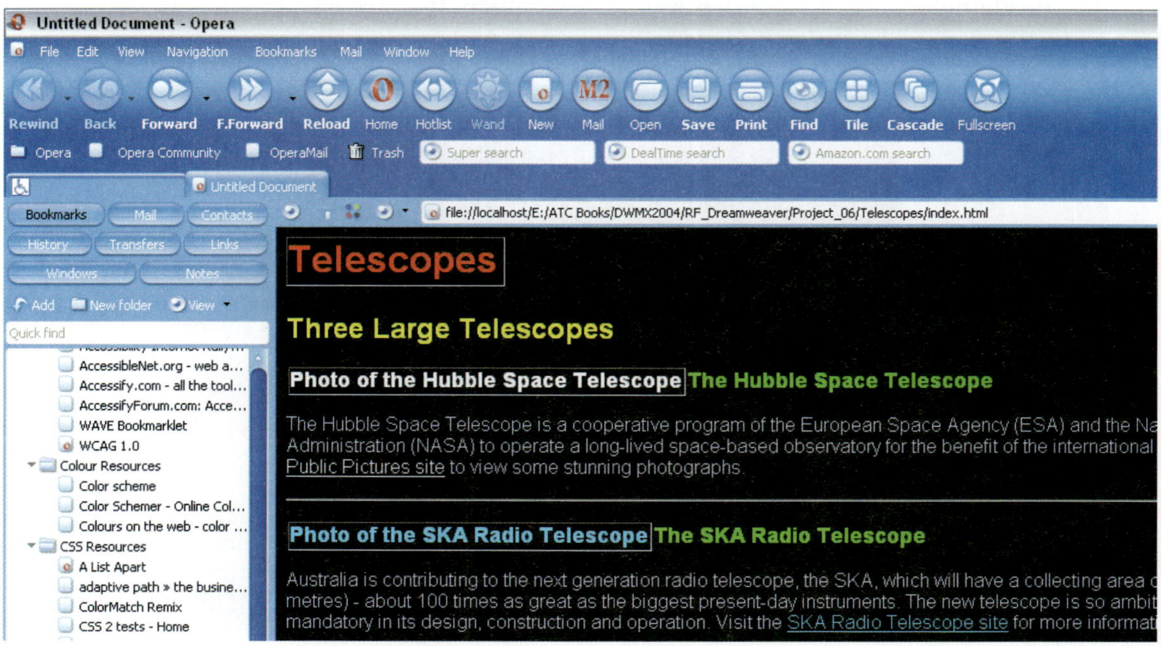


**FIGURE 6.43**

6. Close, saving the changes to index.html.

## 3. Set the Background Repeat Options

CSS has a number of useful background properties. With CSS, you can specify the direction you want your background image to repeat. You can also specify that it not repeat at all. Another background property allows you to position a background image on the page.

You can set your background images to repeat vertically or horizontally, or to not repeat at all. The vertical and horizontal repeat options allow you to use a small image and specify that it only repeat in one direction, creating a left margin (vertical repeat) or a top margin (horizontal repeat). CSS uses the values **repeat-x** and **repeat-y** to achieve these effects: x refers to the x-axis, which runs horizontally across the bottom of a chart, and y refers to the y-axis, which runs vertically up the side of the chart.

The background position options allow you to specify where in the background of the page you want your background image to appear. The pairing of background position and background repeat (set not to repeat) is a very useful combination of CSS properties, especially with a watermark style of background image.

1. Open index.html from the Backgrounds site.
2. Expand the Design panel group. If the CSS Styles tab is not selected, click it.
3. Right/Control-click body and choose Edit from the pop-up menu. Choose the Background category. Browse to choose left-margin-129.gif from the bg-images folder, click OK/Choose, and then click OK to insert the background image into the page.

   The background image is 129 pixels wide and 153 pixels high. By default, it repeats both vertically and horizontally. This image is suited to a vertical (y-axis) repeat.

FIGURE 6.44

4. Right/Control-click body in the CSS Styles panel and choose Edit.
5. In the Background category, choose **repeat-y** from the Repeat field and click OK.

   Although the image is only 129 pixels wide, it does not repeat across the background, just down the page.

6. Right/Control-click body in the CSS Styles panel and choose Edit.
7. In the Background category, browse to choose top-margin-143.gif as the Background Image, set the Repeat option to **repeat-x**, and click OK.

   This image is 143 pixels high, but because of the **repeat-x** setting in CSS, it only repeats across the page, not down it.

8. Right/Control-click body in the CSS Styles panel and choose Edit.
9. In the Background category, browse to choose bromeliad-watermark-small.jpg as the Background Image, set Repeat to **`no-repeat`**, and click OK.

   Although partly obscured by other content on this page, this image appears just once in the background of the page. You can use CSS to position a background such as this in the center of the page.
10. Right/Control-click body in the CSS Styles panel and choose Edit.
11. In the Background category, choose **`center`** from both the Horizontal Position and Vertical Position drop-down lists, and click OK.

    The single background image is positioned in the center of the page, both vertically and horizontally.

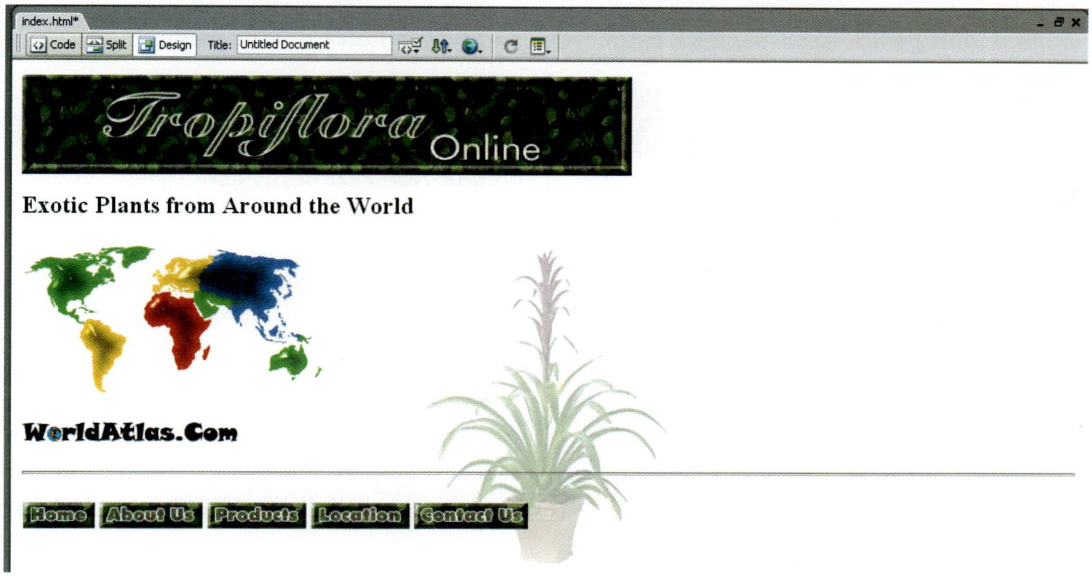


**FIGURE 6.45**

12. Close index.html, saving the changes.

## To Extend Your Knowledge

### PAGE PROPERTIES = CSS

Dreamweaver MX 2004 implements CSS very well, and uses CSS for most functions that change a style. The options you apply using the Page Properties dialog box are written into the code using CSS, which is why you can easily switch between the Page Properties dialog box and the CSS Styles panel — many of the options and features are similar. However, the Page Properties dialog box is more limiting than the CSS Styles panel. As you gain experience, you will find it easier to use the CSS Styles panel to apply a background image and modify some of its properties rather than doing some work in the Page Properties dialog box and the rest in the CSS Styles panel.

## 4. Apply Background Colors to Other Elements

Prior to CSS, you could only apply background images and colors to the Web page itself, using the body element and a few other tags. With the advent of CSS, any element can have a background — a color, an image, or both.

One significant advantage of CSS over HTML methods of styling is that when you apply a property to a particular tag, such as the Heading 2 (**<h2>**) tag, all such **<h2>** tags on the page take on that property. This ability of CSS allows you to easily create a consistent look and feel for the same element throughout the entire page. (We discuss many other advantages of CSS over HTML styles in *Essentials for Design: Dreamweaver MX 2004 Level 2*.)

1. Open elements.html from the Backgrounds site.
2. If the CSS Styles panel is not expanded, open it from the Design panel group.
3. Right/Control-click h1 in the CSS Styles panel, and choose Edit from the menu.
4. Choose the Background category, type **#005D8C** in the Background Color field, and click OK.

   Notice that a dark-blue background appears behind the Heading 1 block. You would normally have to lighten the color of the Heading 1 text so it could be read against the dark background. In this case, however, you will modify the background (in the next Skill Drill), restoring the contrast.
5. Right/Control-click h2 in the CSS Styles panel and choose Edit.
6. Choose the Background category, type **#00A4F1** in the Background Color field, and click OK.

   The medium-blue background appears behind both Heading 2 blocks on the page.
7. Right/Control-click **a:hover** in the CSS Styles panel and choose Edit.

   The **a:hover** code refers to a rollover property. It had been preset to change the text color to white when the mouse pointer rolls over the link. You added a change in background color to the **hover** pseudo-class.
8. From the Background category, set the Background Color to **#005D8C**, and click OK.
9. Preview the page in your browser and move your mouse pointer over the link text.

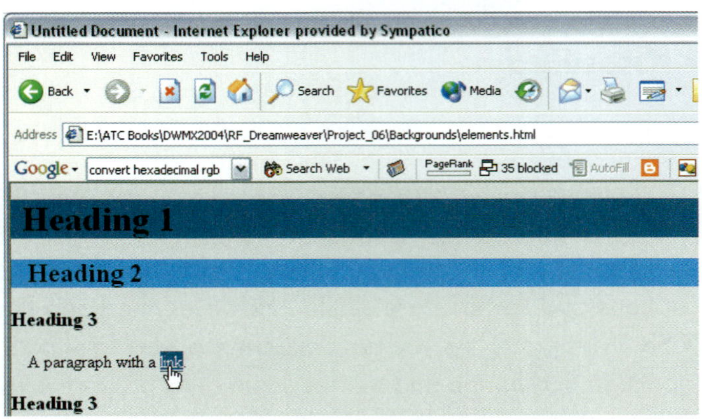


**FIGURE 6.46**

10. Return to Dreamweaver, leaving elements.html open for the next exercise.

## To Extend Your Knowledge

### TAGS AND ELEMENTS

In Project 2, you learned that HTML consists of tags, such as the paragraph tag <p>. A tag is an element surrounded by angle brackets. Therefore, **p** is the paragraph element and **a** is the anchor element. In CSS, when you want to apply a background to the body, only the element portion of the tag is used, which is why the CSS Styles panel does not display any angle brackets, just the element.

## 5. Explore Design Options with Background Images

You can apply all of the background properties you have learned equally well to any element on the page or to the page itself. You can specify **`background-repeat`**, **`background-position`**, **`background-image`**, and **`background-color`** just as you did for the background of the full page.

1. In the open document elements.html, Right/Control-click h1 in the CSS Styles panel and choose Edit.
2. From the Background category, click the Browse button beside the Background Image field, choose h1-bg.png from the bg-images folder, click OK/Choose, and then click OK.

   The background graphic for the h1 element, as you see at the bottom of the page, is too small for the space and repeats both vertically and horizontally.
3. Edit the h1 style again, set Background Repeat to **`repeat-y`**, and click OK.
4. Edit the h2 style, choose h2-bg.png from the bg-images folder as the Background Image, click OK/Choose, and click OK.

   The graphic contains a gradient from the middle white out to the top and bottom blue regions. The white part (middle) of the gradient is at the top of the h2 element, not across the middle of it.
5. Edit the h2 style again, set the Vertical Position of the Background Image to **`center`**, and click OK.

   Now the middle of the graphic is across the middle of the h2 element. The background color for the h2 element is covered by the background image and could have been removed.
6. Edit the h3 style and set the Background Image to h3-bg.png.

   Like the h1 background graphic, the h3 background graphic repeats across the width of the h3 element.
7. Edit the h3 style and set the Repeat option of the background image to **`no-repeat`**.

   The background image appears behind the Heading 3 text. However, this type of graphic can also be used as a form of underlining.
8. Edit the h3 style again and choose the Box category.

9. In the Bottom field in the Padding group, type **23** and set the units to Pixels.

   Increasing the padding around an element creates a larger area for background colors or images. Increasing the bottom padding allows you to push the background image down below the Heading 3 text, but you must still set two more options.

10. Switch to the Background category, set the Horizontal Position to **`left`**, set the Vertical Position to **`bottom`**, and then click OK.

    The background image now appears as a fancy underline below the Heading 3 text.

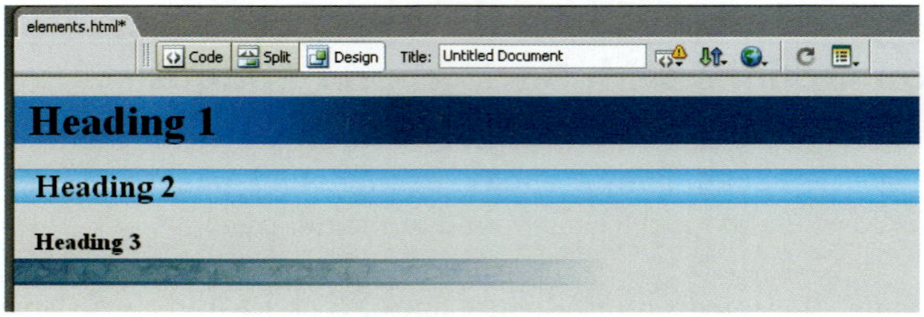


**FIGURE 6.47**

11. Close, saving elements.html.

## To Extend Your Knowledge

### PADDING VS. MARGIN

In the Box category of the CSS Styles dialog box, both padding and margin options are available (although we only discussed padding). Margin also expands the space taken by the element, but unlike padding, backgrounds (colors or images) cannot extend into the margin area.

## 6. Prevent a Background Image from Scrolling

In the Useit.com Web page, shown in the second image of the Lesson 5 introduction, the photo of Jakob Nielsen does not scroll up or down, even though the content to its left does. They achieved this by preventing the background from scrolling and specifying the position of the background image. If you use these techniques, you can then choose to use a low-contrast image, such as shown in the home page of Czech Web designer Petr Stanicek, the first image in that same lesson introduction, and allow your text to flow over it, or you can choose to use a high-contrast image, such as the photo of Jacob Nielsen, and prevent the text from flowing over it.

1. Open products.html from the Backgrounds site.
2. Using the Page Properties dialog box, insert bromeliad-solid-small.jpg from the bg-images folder as a background image.

   The background image repeats both horizontally and vertically. It is also high-contrast, so the text on top of it is difficult to read.
3. Right/Control-click body in the CSS Styles panel and choose Edit. From the Background category, set the Repeat option to **`no-repeat`**, the Horizontal Position to **`right`**, and the Vertical Position to **`top`**. Click OK.
4. Preview the page in your browser and scroll the page up and down.

   Observe that the background image scrolls up and down, just as the content does.

### ? If you have problems

If your browser window is too large, all of the page content is already visible so scrolling is neither necessary nor possible. Resize the browser window to be narrower and shorter so you can scroll.

5. Reduce the width of the browser window so it is as wide as the Tropiflora Online logo graphic.

   The top of the plant is hidden behind the logo graphic. It should be pushed down below the logo.
6. Return to Dreamweaver.
7. Edit the style of the body element again. In the Background category, set Attachment to Fixed. Change the Horizontal Position to 100% (choose % from the drop-down list) and the Vertical Position to 115 pixels, and click OK.
8. Preview the page in your browser, scrolling up and down.

   Observe that the background is now fixed and does not scroll. Dreamweaver cannot display the attachment-fixed behavior — you must preview the page in a browser to see this effect. Also notice that the position of the graphic has shifted down below the logo graphic.
9. Return to Dreamweaver.

   To create an effect similar to that of the redesign of the Useit.com Web page, in which the content does not flow over the background image, you must set the padding on the right side of the body to the width of the background graphic.

10. Edit the body styles again and switch to the Box category. In the Padding group of options, uncheck the option Same for All, type **250** in the Right field, set the units to pixels, and click OK.

    The width of the background graphic is 250 pixels. Setting the right padding of the body to 250 pixels keeps the content away from the right side.

11. Preview the page in your browser and scroll again.

    The content does not overlap the background image and the text is always readable.

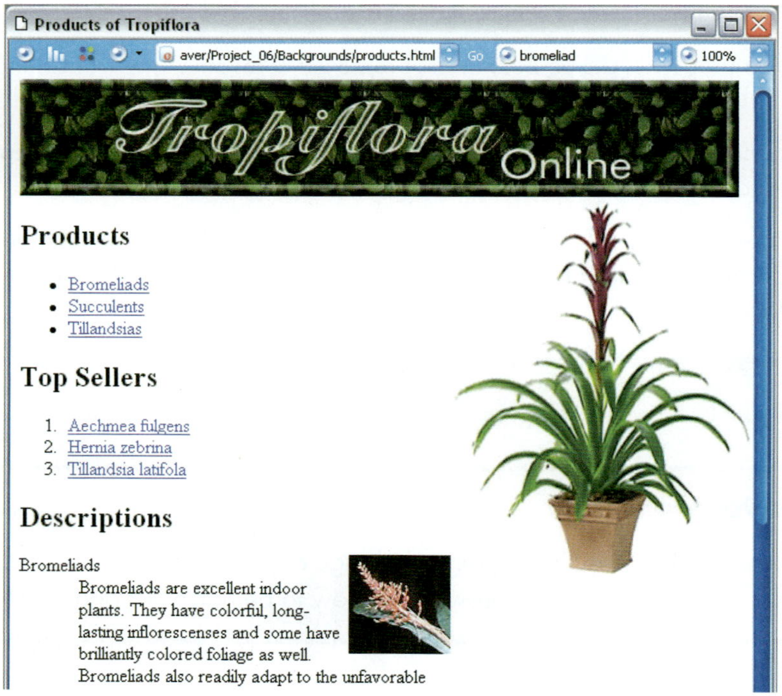


**FIGURE 6.48**

12. Return to Dreamweaver and close products.html.

## CHALLENGE

Challenge exercises expand on, or are somewhat related to, skills presented in the lessons. Each exercise provides a brief introduction, followed by instructions in a numbered-step format that are not as detailed as those in the Skill Drill exercises. You should work through them in order.

### 1. Add Decorative Corners around a Block of Content

You have learned that with proper application of CSS, you can place backgrounds, whether a color or a graphic, behind any element. However, you can use just one background image per tag — there is only one body tag, so you can only place one background image in the body tag. You can create a new background for each paragraph, but to do so you must identify each paragraph with a unique id; you then use the id to identify which background image to apply to the paragraph. Many designers use the **`<div>`** tag (the div element refers to division, such as a division or section of a document). The **`<div>`** tag by itself does nothing — it was devised as a container and, as such, you can use it to deliver styles.

In this Challenge, you surround a block of text with two **`<div>`** tags. You uniquely identify the two **`<div>`** tags with different ids and apply different backgrounds to each. This process could be extended to create four corners by creating four divs. Brian Williams wrote an article, entitled "Onion Skinned Drop Shadows," on a similar technique (http://alistapart.com/articles/onionskin/).

1. Open shakespeare.html from the Backgrounds site.
2. Select all content in the page.
3. Switch the Insert bar to the Layout mode by clicking the Menu button at the right side of the Insert bar.
4. Click the second button, Insert Div Tag. Type **`top-left`** in the ID field, ensure that Insert is set to Wrap Around Selection, and click OK.
5. With the block still selected (if not, select it), insert another div. Type **`bottom-right`** as the ID for the second div, ensure that Insert is set to Wrap Around Selection, and click OK.
6. Open the CSS Styles panel and edit the style rule div#top-left.

   When you add an **`id`** to a tag, you must use the **`#`** symbol when referring to it in styles. In this case, the div#top-left style rule, although empty, was created for you.
7. Insert top-left-corner.png from the bg-images folder as the Background Image, set Repeat to **`no-repeat`**, and click Apply.

   The background image appears directly behind the content, making the text difficult to read.
8. Switch to the Box category, uncheck Same for All in the Padding Group, apply 40 pixels to both top and left, and click OK.

   The content is now pushed down and to the right, away from the background image.

9. Edit the div#bottom-right style. Insert bottom-right-corner.png from the bg-images folder as the Background Image, set Repeat to **`no-repeat`**, set Horizontal Position to **`right`**, set Vertical Position to **`bottom`**, and click Apply.

   By default, divs extend the full width of the available space. This means the divs spread out to the right edge of the browser window. To fix this, we need to specify a width for the div.

10. Click the Box category, set the width to 325 pixels, and click OK.

    Just as we saw with the top-left corner graphic, this graphic also interferes with reading the text that overlays it.

11. Switch to the Box category, uncheck Same for All in the Padding Group, apply 40 pixels to both bottom and right padding, and click OK.

12. Close, saving the changes.

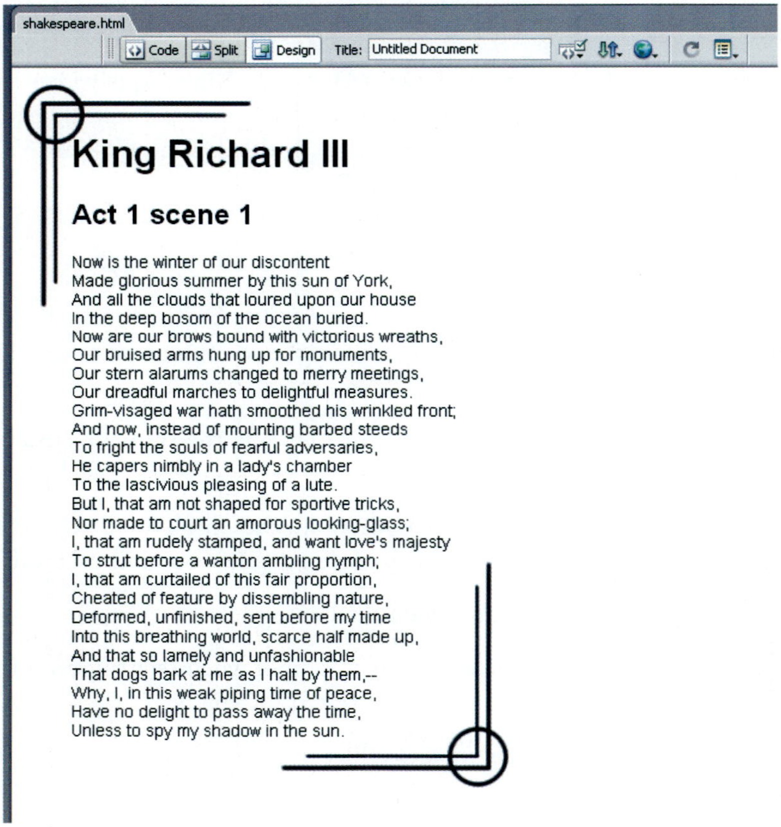


**FIGURE 6.49**

## 2. Place Decorative Graphics in the Background

As you recall, the **alt** (alternate text) attribute is mandatory for all inline (foreground) graphics on a Web page. You should assign a decorative graphic an empty alt attribute, which adds no content to the Web page. Background graphics do not need alternate text; in fact, they cannot have alternate text because they cannot be assigned the **alt** attribute. It is useful, therefore, to move foreground decorative graphics into the background. (Consider this exercise a complement to Challenge #2 in Project 5, in which you moved empty-alt graphics from the foreground and placed them in the background.)

The page you are modifying uses a table-based layout, as do many others you have worked with in this book. More and more designers take issue with table-based layout for several reasons (as we discuss in Project 8). With proper application of CSS, you can replace parts of the table with much simpler code.

1. Define a new site called DF-P6 using the Project_06>DF-P6 folder.
2. Open faqs.htm.
3. At the top of the page is a graphic of a bow tie that has been split between two cells — the top portion without text and the bottom containing the text Debonair. Click bowtie-top.gif and delete it.
4. Right/Control-click the selected **<td>** tag in the Tag selector, choose Edit Tag from the menu, and add **id="bowtie-top"** to the tag. (Don't forget to insert a space in front of **id**.)
5. In the CSS Styles panel, in the <style> group, Right/Control-click td#bowtie-top and choose Edit. In the Background category, set bowtie-top.gif from the images folder as the Background Image, set Repeat to **no-repeat**, and click OK.
6. Click in the left navigation bar and look at the Tag selector.

   Notice that there are two **<table>** tags. The navigation bar is enclosed in a small table that is enclosed in a cell in the left column.
7. Click the photo of the wrist below the navigation-bar links, and then click the front of the waistcoat, to the right of the navigations-bar links.

   The navigation bar is surrounded by two sliced graphics. You can recreate this appearance with much less code, eliminating the need for alt text.
8. Click any of the links in the navigation bar, click the <ul#menu> tag in the Tag selector, and cut the unordered list out and paste it into the clipboard.
9. Click the second **<table>** tag in the Tag selector (the one that contained the navigation bar) and press Delete/Backspace to remove the table. Paste the unordered list back into the page without the table structure around it.
10. Edit ul#menu in the CSS Styles panel from the <style> group, set menubg.gif from the images folder as the Background Image, and click Apply. Switch to the Box category, set the height to 281 pixels, and click OK.

11. Click in the main table cell containing the frequently asked questions, Right/Control-click the **<td>** tag in the Tag selector, and add **id="body"** to the tag.

12. Edit td#body in the CSS Styles panel, set background.gif as the Background Image, set Repeat to **no-repeat**, Horizontal Position to **center**, Vertical Position to **top**, and click OK.

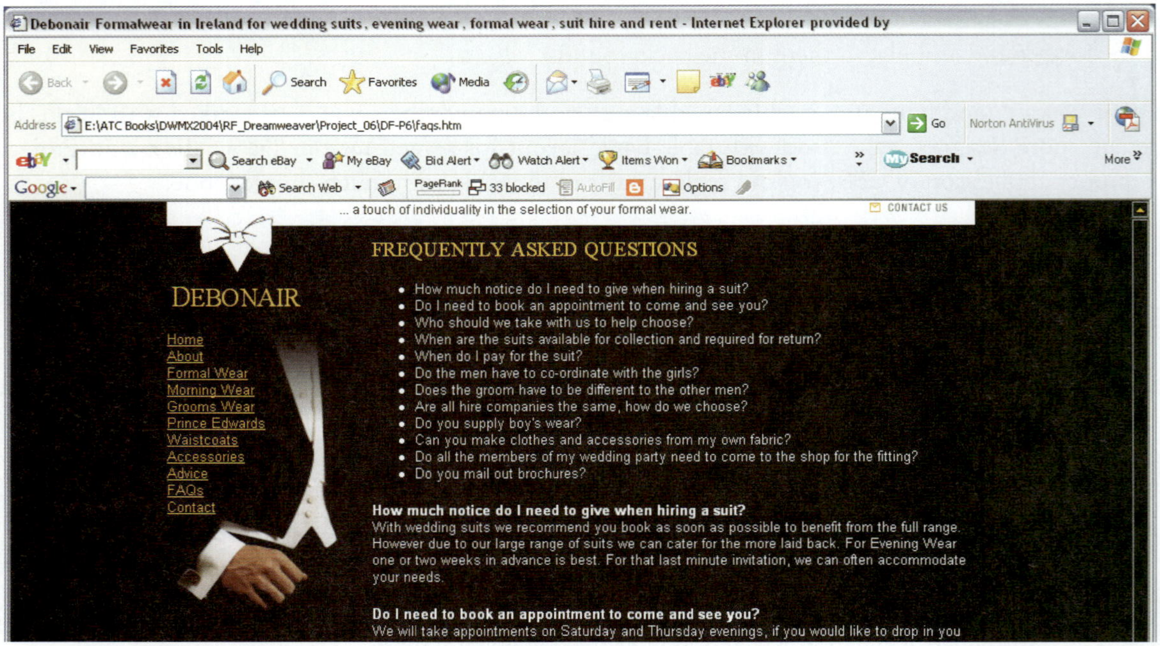


FIGURE 6.50

13. Close, saving faqs.htm.

# PORTFOLIO BUILDER

## Create Alternative Color Schemes

In this assignment, you're going to create a "comprehensive" layout to use for a client presentation. The prospective client is a furniture manufacturer, and they've indicated that their first choice for a design would be one that used a wood texture for the background of the site. You have some concerns about using such a background, because as you know, background images can easily clutter a site and distract from the content. You need to create three different page formats for the presentation.

To determine complimentary colors, try visiting the visibone.com site and looking through their color chips.

1. Search the Web for wood textures. There are a number of sites where you can download samples for use in a presentation, and then purchase the originals if you decide to use them. If you can't find one, have someone scan a wood sample for you and use that.
2. Create one design that uses the wood texture for the total background.
3. Create a second design that only uses the texture for a top or side navigation bar, leaving the balance of the site white or a light tan.
4. Create a third site that only uses the texture for buttons and navigational elements.
5. If you have access to a color printer, output the three designs so they can be presented in a physical form.

# PROJECT 7

# Tables

## OBJECTIVES

*In this project, you learn how to*

- Identify the uses and properties of tables
- Create tables
- Insert rows and columns
- Merge adjacent cells
- Add background colors and alignment to cells
- Create a layout table using the Table dialog box
- Create a layout table in Layout mode
- Create an accessible data table

# WHY WOULD I DO THIS?

Tables are important components of Web-page design. They are commonly used to lay out a Web page and to present tabular data. If you have used word-processing software, you may have worked with tables. However, there are many more options for constructing tables in HTML than in word-processing software. In this project, you learn about these options and when and how to apply them.

Basic tables consist of rows and columns, and where they intersect, cells. The names of some of these components are different in HTML than in other software. There are no columns — at least, not in the code — and cells are called "table data." The outermost HTML tags of tables are the opening and closing **<table>** tags that define the beginning and end of a table. Tables are divided into rows, which use the opening and closing **<tr>** tags. Within each row are cells or table data that are defined by opening and closing **<td>** (table-data) tags. Therefore, a basic 2 × 2 table would use the following code:

```
<table>
<tr><td>Row 1, Cell 1</td><td>Row 1, Cell 2</td></tr>
<tr><td>Row 2, Cell 1</td><td>Row 2, Cell 2</td></tr>
</table>
```

As you can see, it takes a lot of code to create a simple four-cell table. As you explore more options for tables, the code expands tremendously. One of the benefits of using WYSIWYG software like Dreamweaver is the ease with which you can create tables. You choose or specify the number of rows and columns, and Dreamweaver creates the code (and the table); you only have to add content to the cells.

HTML tables have many features, some of which are displayed in Figure 8.1. Tables can have captions, table-header cells, and ***spanned*** (merged) ***cells***. Above the table (Figure 8.1) is a caption created using the **<caption>** tag. The **<caption>** tag only exists in tables and is generally put immediately after the opening **<table>** tag. The caption can appear at the top, left, bottom, or right of the table, but the default is top. You can style caption text with a different font, bold weight, text color, or any other CSS properties.

The top row of the table, immediately below the caption, consists of table-header cells that use the **<th>** tag. These cells display bold, centered text. This special tag identifies cells that describe the cell data in their row or column. In Figure 8.1, the table-header cells are at the top of the columns; in other situations, they might run down the left row or both. By default, table-header cells are bold and aligned to the center of the cell, but you can modify their appearance using CSS.

The Florida, California, 2,500,000 and 5,500,000 cells are spanned cells. In other software they might be called "joined" or "merged" cells, but the HTML attributes responsible for these cells are the **`colspan`** and **`rowspan`** attributes — hence the origina of the term "spanned cells." (Be aware that Dreamweaver refers to the process of combining cells as "merging cells.") The **`colspan`** attribute added to the **`<td>`** tag merges cells belonging to different columns, such as the 2,500,000 cell. In this case the cell spans two columns, so the tag is **`<td colspan="2">`**. The Florida and California cells use the **`rowspan`** attribute in the form **`<td rowspan="2">`**. The 5,500,000 cell uses both **`colspan`** and **`rowspan`**: **`<td rowspan="2" colspan="2">`**.

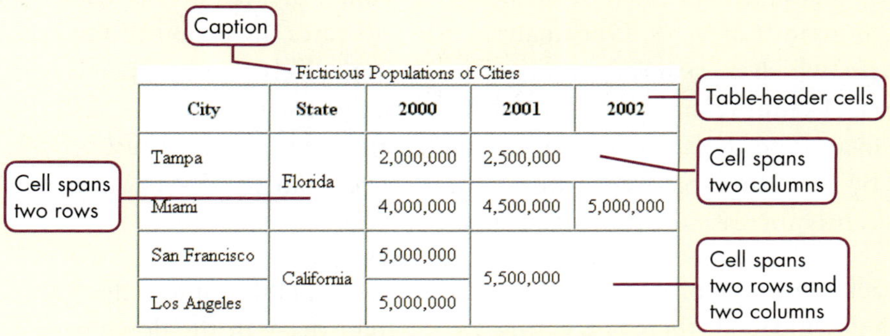


**FIGURE 7.1**

Dreamweaver provides two methods for working with tables. The Table dialog box allows you to specify the dimensions and some properties of a table. The other technique is the layout method, in which you draw cells and Dreamweaver generates the properties of the cells as you create and modify them. This is a more free-form approach and, as the term suggests, is very helpful for designing the layout of a page.

## The Pros and Cons of Table Use

The original purpose for the **`<table>`** tag and its related tags was to provide a means for presenting tabular data. Knowing this, the origin of the table-data (**`<td>`**) tag (instead of a <tc> tag for table cell) becomes clear. The **`<th>`** tag has logical significance — it specifies the relationships between table data and table headings. Table-header cells at the tops of columns indicate that the data below belong to that category. The contrasting default styles of the **`<th>`** and **`<td>`** cell contents — bold and centered versus normal and left aligned — help sighted visitors to clearly differentiate one from the other and suggest their relationship.

The other, more popular, use of tables is for laying out the components of a Web page: putting the page header in a top cell, the navigation menu in a left cell, the page footer in the bottom cell, and the content sandwiched between them, for example. Without the use of tables or frames, layout might be quite basic, relying on not much more than left, center, and right alignment. When Web designers realized how they could use tables for layout, they were able to create sophisticated designs. By using spanned cells, they merged some rows and/or columns while keeping other cells separate and individual. Furthermore, many graphic-design programs such as Adobe Photoshop and Macromedia Fireworks, enabled the designer to create a design, slice it into a complex arrangement of table cells, and then have the software create a table from the results. This process allowed graphic designers to concentrate on design while the software created the complex table layout for them.

Although using tables made possible the creation of complex designs, unanticipated problems arose. As you saw earlier, creating even simple tables requires a large amount of code. Depending on the amount of slicing a designer specified in the design software, the quantity of code could balloon into thousands and thousands of bytes. One analysis that illustrates the extent of the problem is the ***content-to-code ratio***, which measures the amount of text on a Web page compared with the amount of code. A number of commercial Web sites that use tables for layout were tested for this ratio at http://www.holovaty.com/tools/getcontentsize/ and commonly contained just 5–10% content versus 90–95% code. By contrast, table-free layouts commonly contained 45–50% content. Complex table code can significantly increase the download time of a Web page.

Another drawback to using tables for layout is that, by design, table content does not display until the whole table has downloaded, thereby creating an apparent delay in the download. This delay is not the fault of the browser manufacturers, but part of the specifications by the W3C.

The final drawback of using tables for layout pertains to screen-reader software. Whenever such software encounters a table, it reads aloud the dimensions of the table, such as: "A table consisting of 5 columns and 12 rows." When the table displays tabular data, this reading of the table is beneficial because it tells the user how much information the table contains. However, when the table is just used for layout, this information may seem merely annoying.

Table-based layouts are becoming less popular for all of these reasons. However, the table-free methods, which use advanced properties of CSS to position content, are not always well supported. Tables have been well supported by browsers for a long time, but advanced CSS properties have only gained significant ground over the last 1–2 years and still have a way to go. Therefore, despite the promise of table-free layouts, some forms of complex layouts must still use tables.

You need to understand the properties of tables for laying out tabular data, whether or not you adopt CSS-based layout. Many table features, tags, and attributes also make tabular data accessible and usable by users of screen-reading software. As more and more governments, businesses, and individuals require Web accessibility, knowing how to use these features will better prepare you for designing accessible Web sites.

# VISUAL SUMMARY

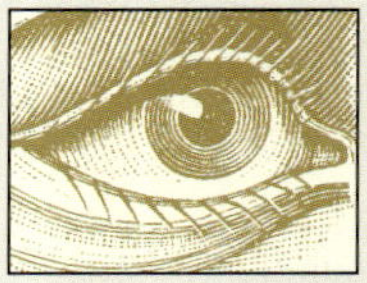

When you create tables, you commonly use the Table dialog box. You can activate this dialog box from the Common or Layout Insert bar, or by choosing Insert>Table. Using this dialog box, you can set the number of rows and columns, the width of the table, the width of the table border, and the cell-padding and cell-spacing properties. If you use a table for your page layout, you do not need the headers and accessibility features. However, if you create a table to present tabular data, you should choose a Header option and fill in the Caption and Summary fields.

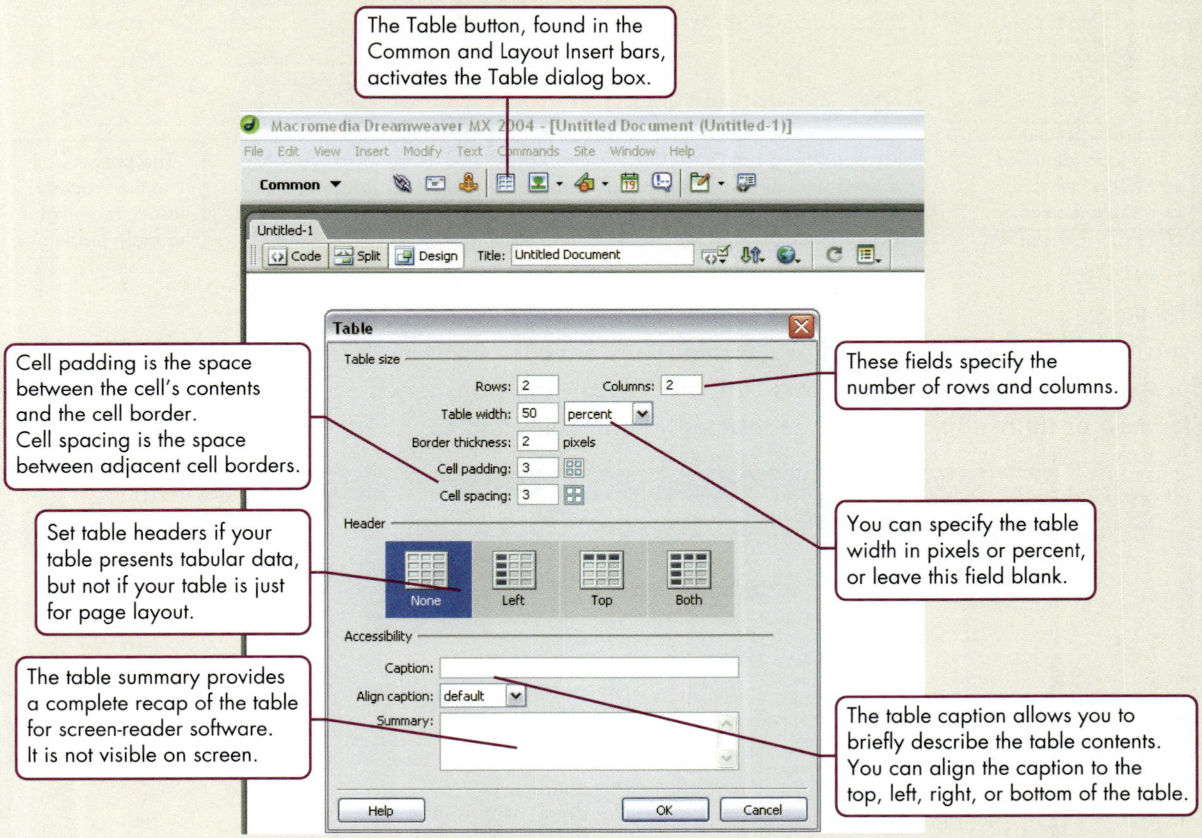


**FIGURE 7.2**

You can apply numerous properties of table cells through the Property inspector. The top half of the Property inspector displays standard text properties that you can apply to text within a cell. The bottom half of the Property inspector displays properties of table cells, table rows, or the table as a whole, depending on what is selected.

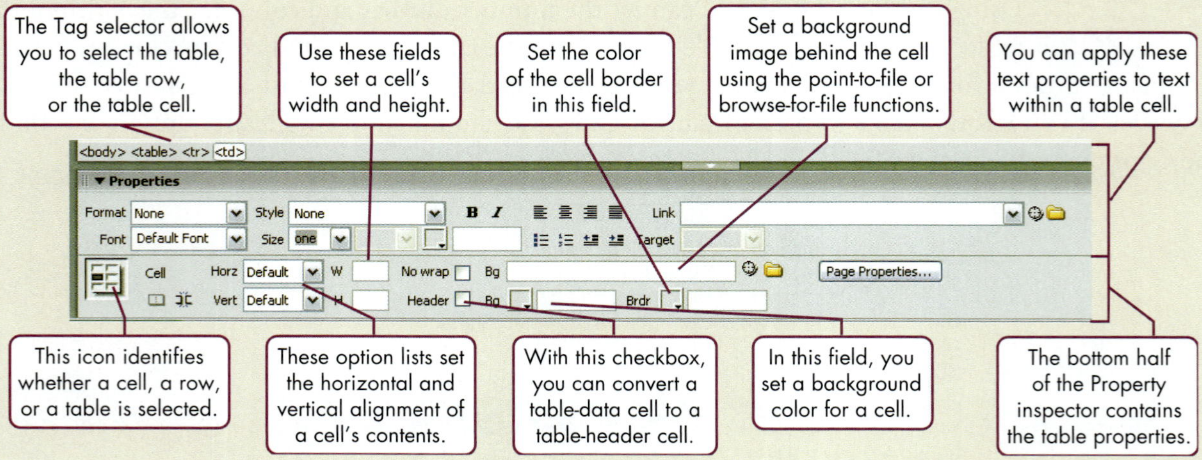


**FIGURE 7.3**

If you Right/Control-click a cell or selected block of cells as you work on a table, a contextual menu appears. This menu provides access to many useful functions, such as Merge Cells (only available when two or more adjacent cells are selected), Split Cells, and Insert Rows or Columns.

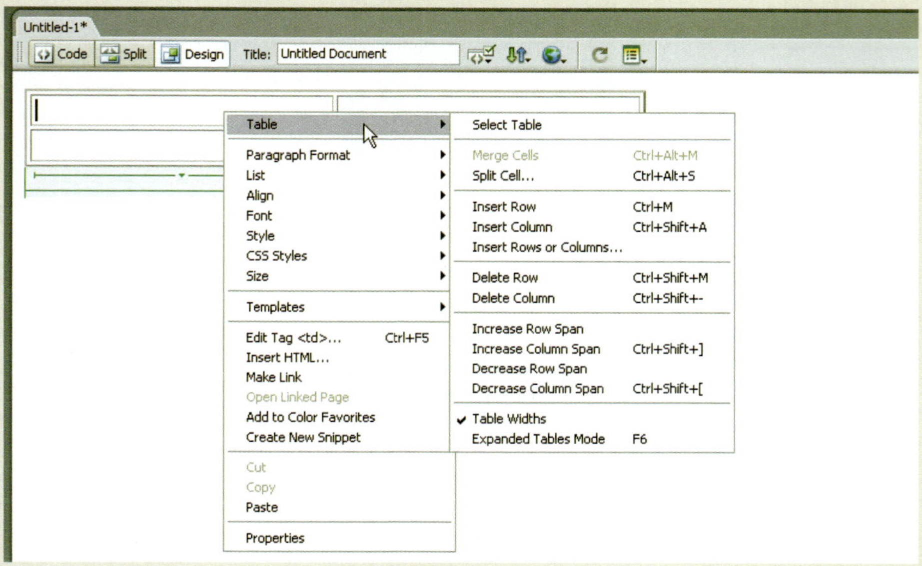

**FIGURE 7.4**

As an alternative to the Table dialog box, you can use the free-form method — the Layout mode — to create tables. To use the Layout mode, you switch to the Layout Insert bar and click the Layout mode button. Using the Layout Table button, you drag to create a table, and then using the Layout Table Cell button, you drag to create table cells. The dimensional rulers at the bottom of each column allow you to modify the column or table width.

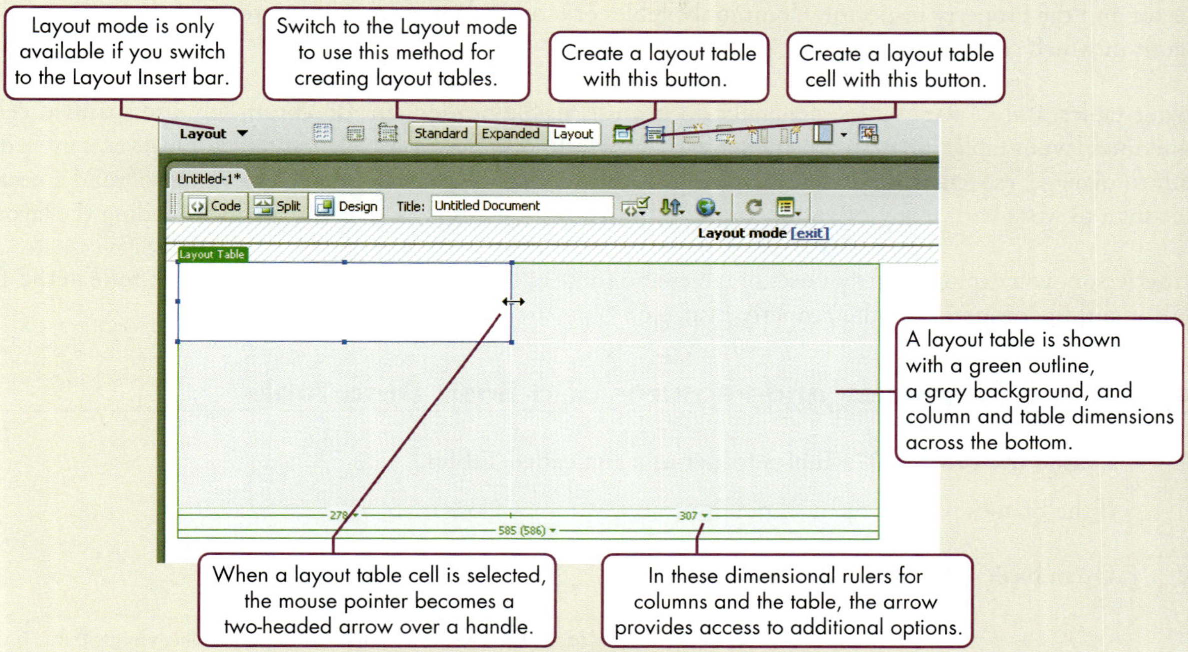


**FIGURE 7.5**

# LESSON 1 Exploring the Applications and Properties of Tables

As you learned earlier, you can use tables to present tabular data. When you do, you should use header cells to identify the information in the column or row. Header cells use the `<th>` tag, which is identified in the Tag selector and the Property inspector. Commonly, tables of tabular data have visible borders to make clear which data fit in which column.

Layout tables, unlike data tables, generally do not use visible borders but do commonly use spanned cells. Sometimes layout tables are nested — tables within the cells of other tables. Nested tables, however, can be difficult to manage, especially if you work directly with the code. Even so, it is sometimes easier to build a nested table than to work with many **`colspan`** and **`rowspan`** attributes, especially, if you are hand-coding the layout.

In this lesson, you explore different uses of tables and some of their properties. You examine the code in the Tag selector and the properties in the Property inspector.

## Explore the Properties and Features of a Basic Data Table

**1** **Define the Project_07>Tables folder as a site called Tables.**

If the Frames panel is open from last project, you may close it.

**2** **Open basic-data.html.**

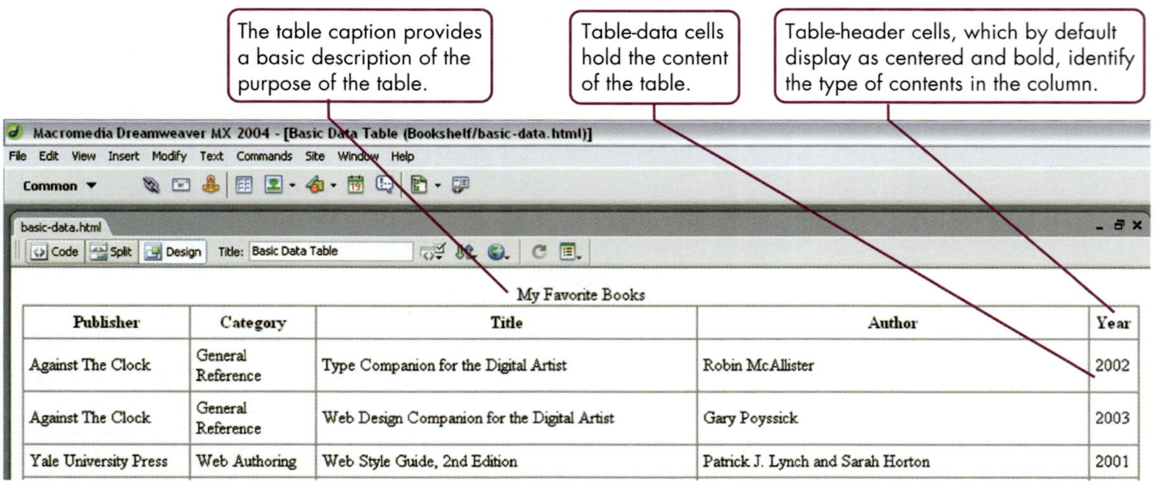


**FIGURE 7.6**

**3** **Click the Publisher text in the top-left cell, and look at both the Tag selector and the Property inspector.**

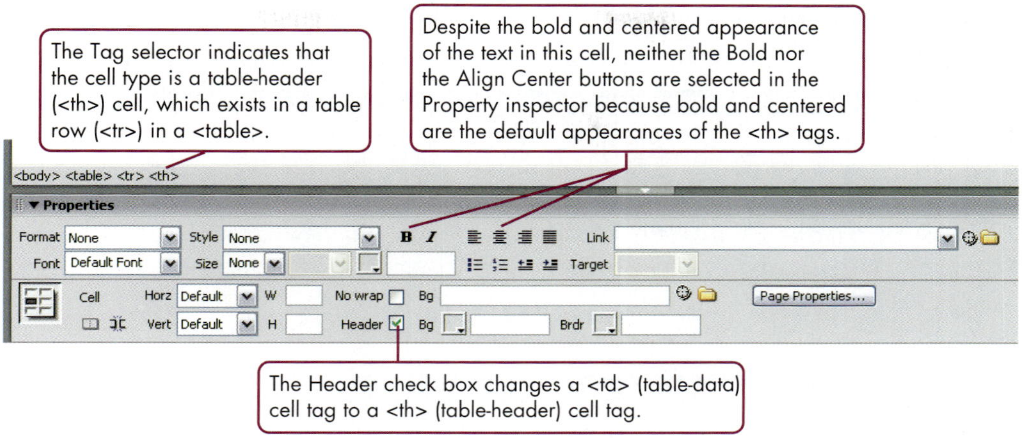


FIGURE 7.7

**4** **With the insertion point still in the Publisher text, click the Align Left button in the Property inspector and examine the Tag selector.**

Notice that a `<div>` tag appears after the `<th>` tag in the Tag selector.

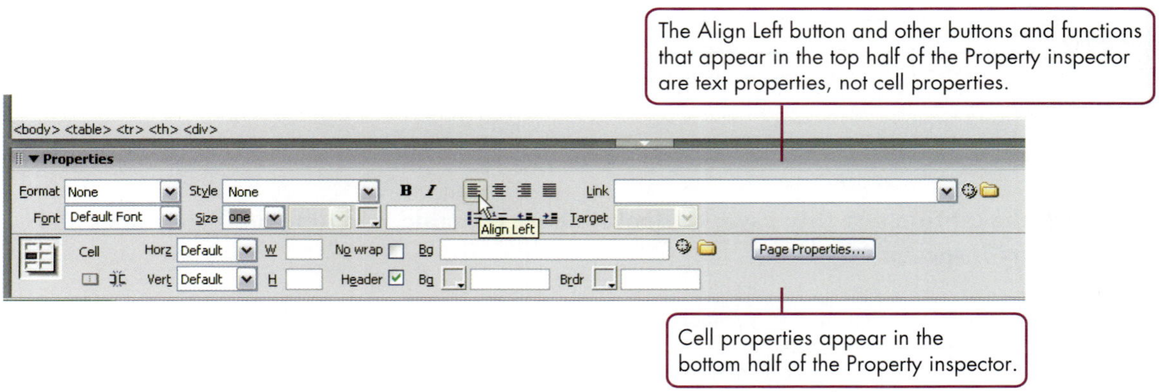


FIGURE 7.8

## If you have problems

If you do not see the bottom half of the Property inspector, click the down-pointing arrow in the bottom-right corner of the Property inspector to expand it.

FIGURE 7.9

**5** **Undo the left alignment, then choose Left from the Horz list.**

The contents of the cell are aligned to the left, and the Tag selector shows that no additional tags were created to apply the alignment property. This method applies alignment to the `<th>` tag directly as an `align="left"` attribute.

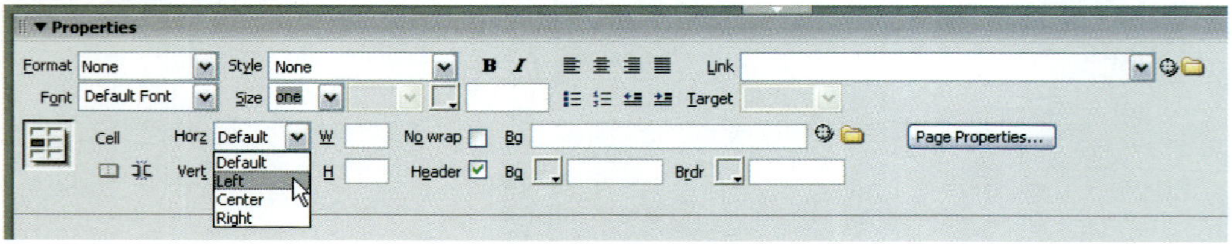

FIGURE 7.10

**6** **Control/Command-click the Category, Title, Author, and Year header cells, and then choose Left from the Horz list.**

Control/Command-clicking allows you to select cells as a group. You selected cells in the same row, but you could select multiple cells in a column or random cells throughout a table. Once you have selected the cells, you can apply any of the cell properties from the Property inspector.

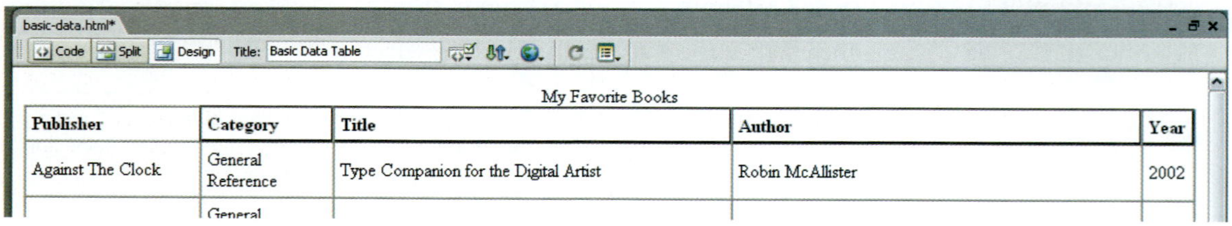

FIGURE 7.11

**7** **Click the caption text (My Favorite Books) above the table, and note the Tag selector and Property inspector.**

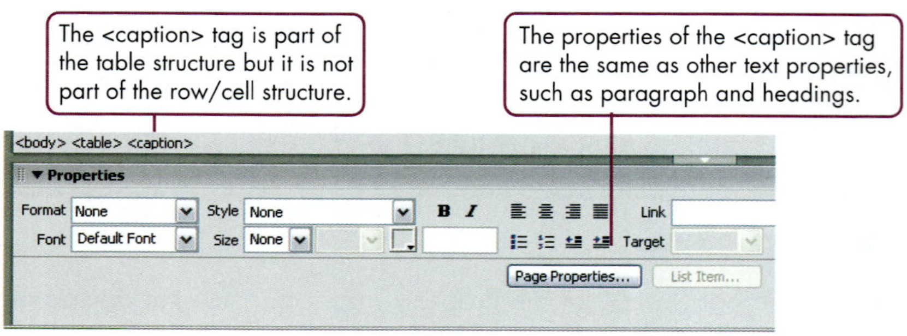


FIGURE 7.12

**8** **Close basic-data.html, saving the changes.**

## *To Extend Your Knowledge*

### ALIGNING CAPTION TEXT

You can align the **<caption>** tag for tables to the left, right, top, or bottom of the table. Unfortunately, these alignment options are not available through the Design view, only through the Code view. To apply any of these alignment options, click the caption text and click either the Code or Split button at the top of the Document window. Move the insertion point into the **<caption>** tag to the left of the closing angle bracket, and press the Spacebar once. Press "a" to choose align, press Enter/Return, press the first letter of your alignment option, and press Enter/Return. Click the Design button at the top of the Document window to close the Code window.

In Dreamweaver and most browsers, **top**, **left**, and **right** alignment appear to be equivalent of top-center, top-left, and top-right alignment respectively. Although Dreamweaver offers a center option, it is not a valid HTML option and would probably be equivalent to top. The **bottom** alignment option for captions centers the text along the bottom of the table.

Technically, Dreamweaver does not display the right and left caption alignments properly, but it has a lot of company in this respect. Captions aligned to the left should appear to the left of the table, not above it. Right alignment should place the caption text to the right of the table, not above it. Only the Mozilla-based browsers (such as Mozilla, Firefox, and Camino) properly display right and left alignment of captions. However, the alignment option has been deprecated from HTML 4 and XHTML 1.0 and has been removed from the standard in XHTML 1.1. It has been replaced by the **caption-side** property in CSS with the same values: **left**, **right**, **top**, and **bottom**. Again, however, only the Mozilla-based browsers currently display the **caption-side** property properly.

## Explore a Layout Table

In this exercise, you explore a Web page that uses tables for layout purposes. When using tables for layout, you do not use the **<th>** tag because the cells do not contain data. Layout tables routinely do not have borders because, as with frames, you typically want the layout to be seamless. Often, pages laid out with tables involve nested tables. Sometimes this occurs because the graphics application the designer used sliced the design into tables; when the designer assembles it, the coding uses nested tables.

In this exercise, you explore a page layout created using a series of nested tables. You explore the tables to see how different options were used to create the layout effects.

**1** **Open tropiflora.html from the Tables site.**

Notice that the page content appears centered in the Document window.

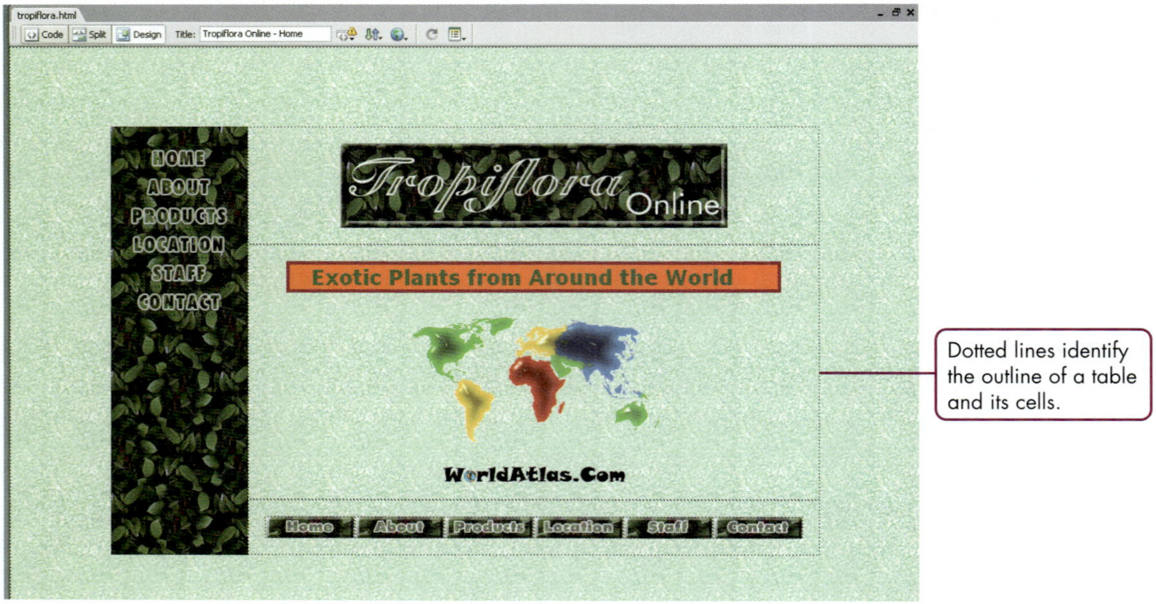


FIGURE 7.13

**2** **Click the Exotic Plants from Around the World text, and then click the `<td>` tag (to the immediate left of the `<h2>` tag) in the Tag selector.**

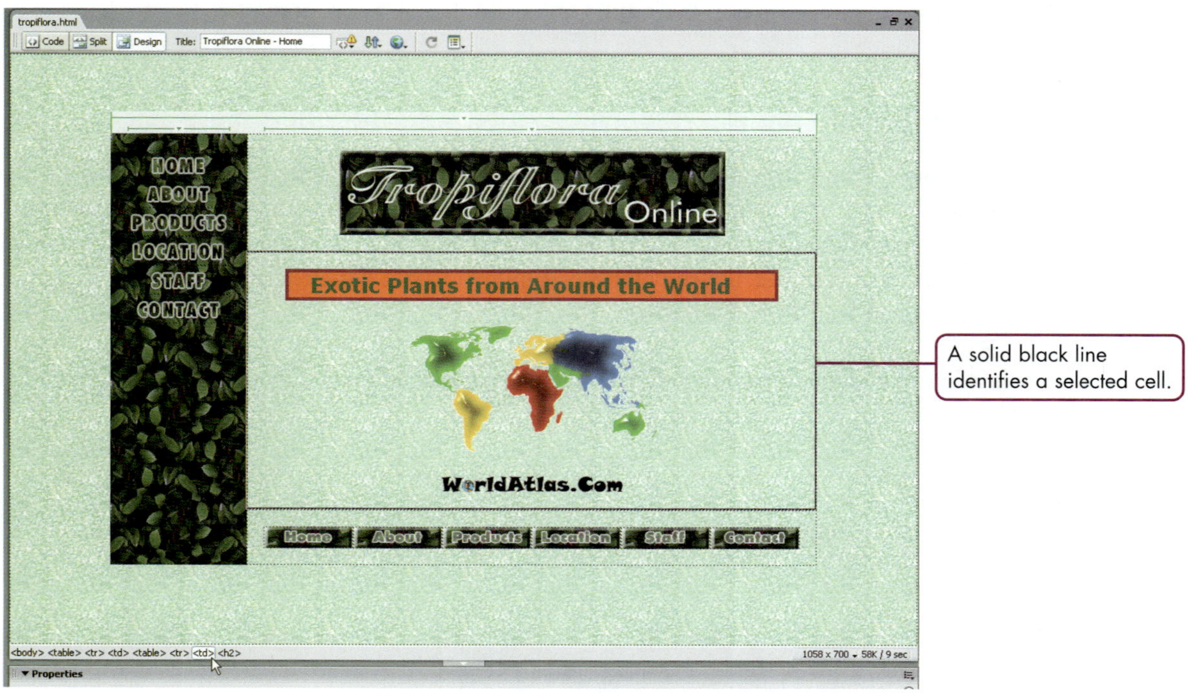


FIGURE 7.14

**3** Click the `<table>` tag (two tags to the left of the selected `<td>` tag).

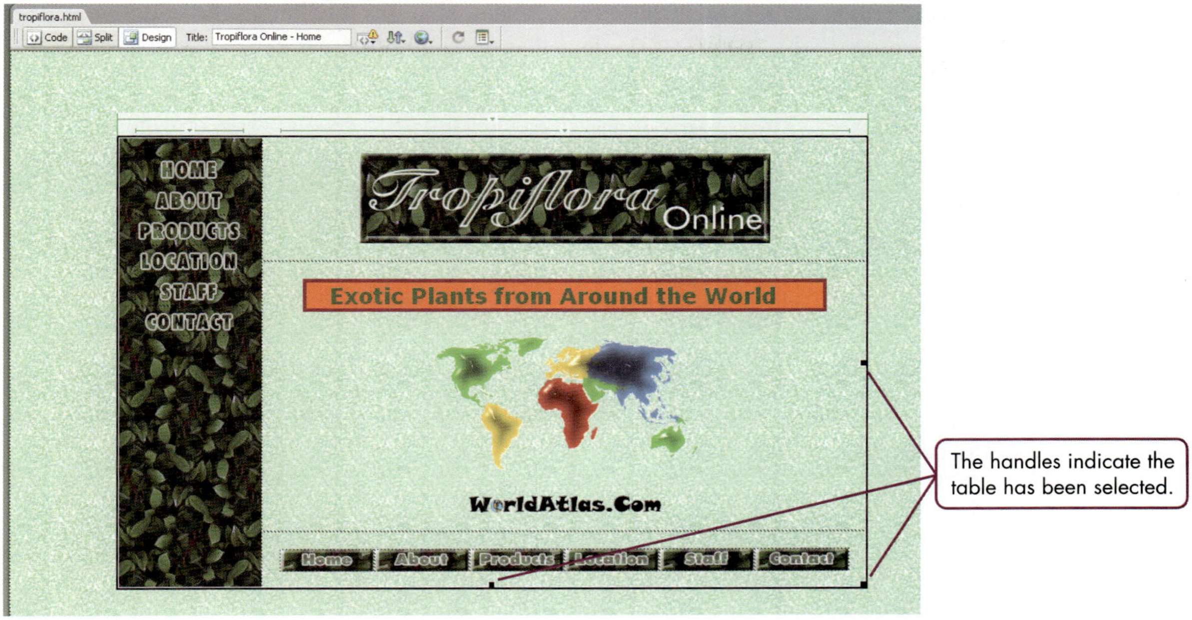


FIGURE 7.15

**4** In the Tag selector, click the `<table>` tag to the immediate right of the `<body>` tag.

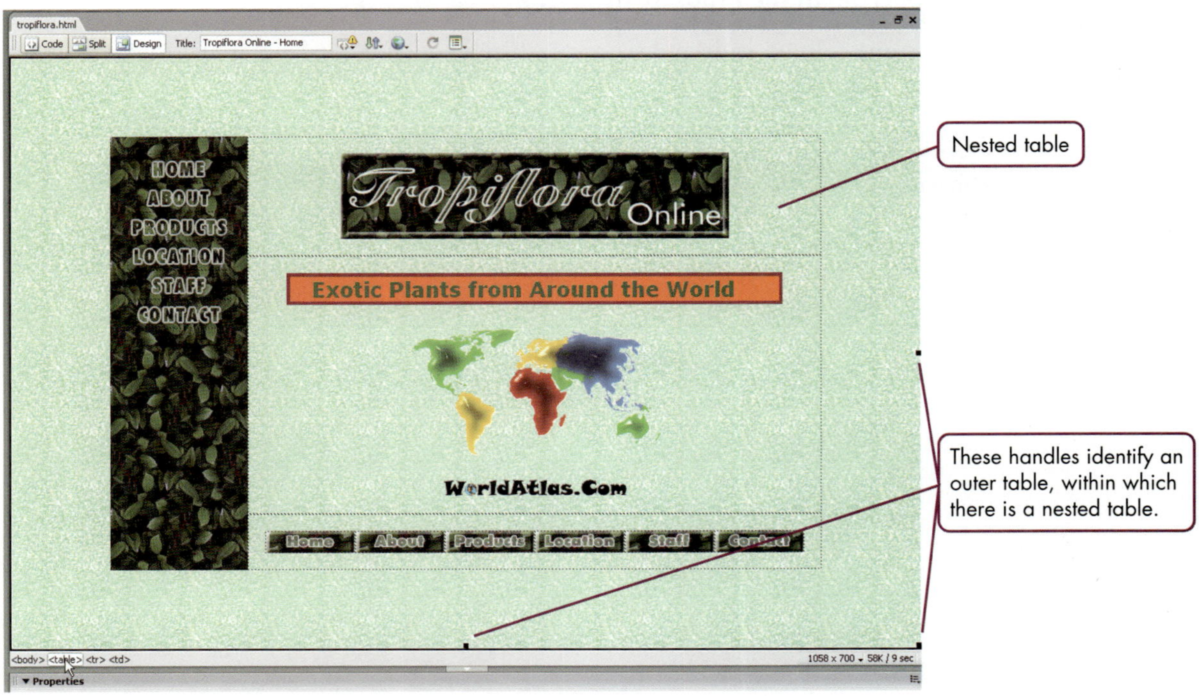


FIGURE 7.16

**5** **In the Property inspector, look at the W (width), H (height), Rows, and Cols (columns) fields.**

Both the width and height are set to 100% so the selected table fills the Document window. With just one row and one column, this table is a single-celled table whose purpose is to center the content. Within this single-celled table is a nested table.

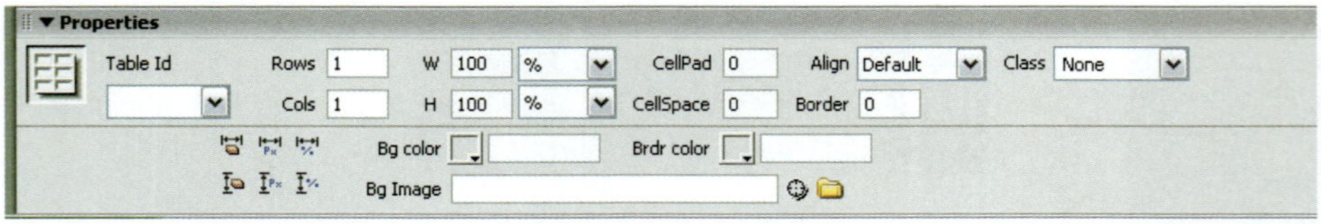


FIGURE 7.17

**6** **Click the Home graphic at the top of the left navigation bar and look at the Tag selector.**

The Tag selector indicates that this graphic is contained by the third nested table, as you can see from the three **<table>** tags.

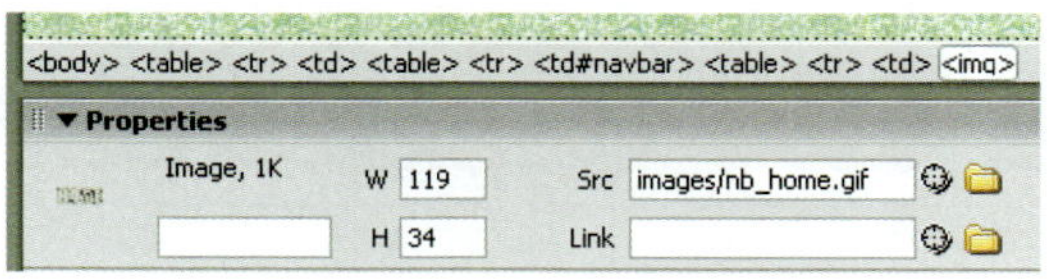


FIGURE 7.18

**7** **In the Tag selector, click the <table> tag to the immediate right of the <td#navbar> tag, and note the table properties in the Property inspector.**

This nested table is one column wide and six rows tall and contains the six graphics that will be set as links to other pages in this site.

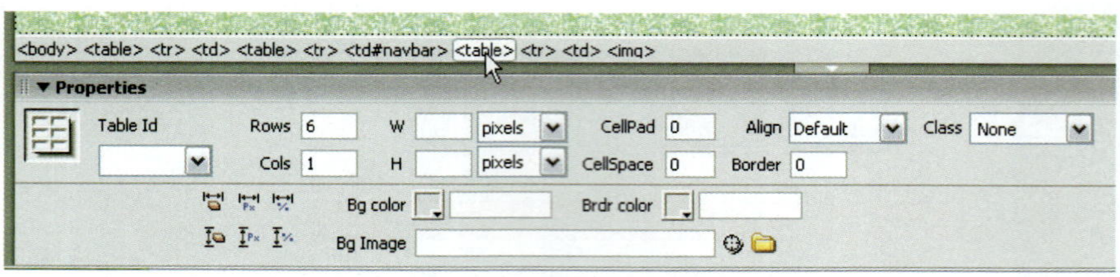


FIGURE 7.19

**8** **In the Tag selector, click the `<td#navbar>` tag, and look at the properties of this cell in the Property inspector.**

The vertical alignment is set to Top. By default, vertical alignment is middle, but that alignment would float the navigation-bar table halfway down this cell. Setting the vertical alignment to Top forces the nested navigation-bar table to the top of the td#navbar cell.

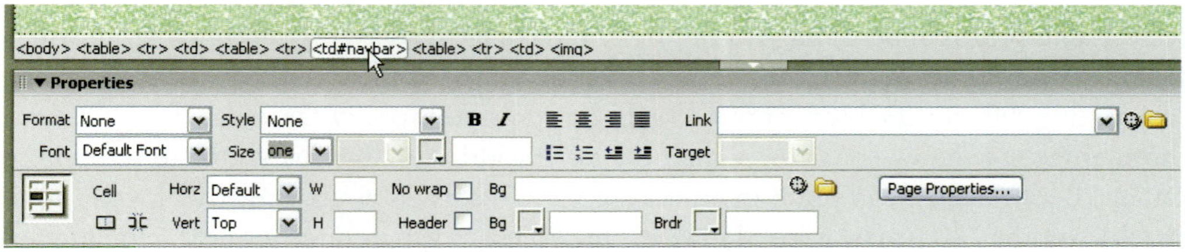


FIGURE 7.20

**9** **Click the Home graphic in the footer cell of the central table, and note the Tag selector.**

Note that the six graphics, which would normally be set as links to the pages of this site, are arranged in a six-column, one-row table.

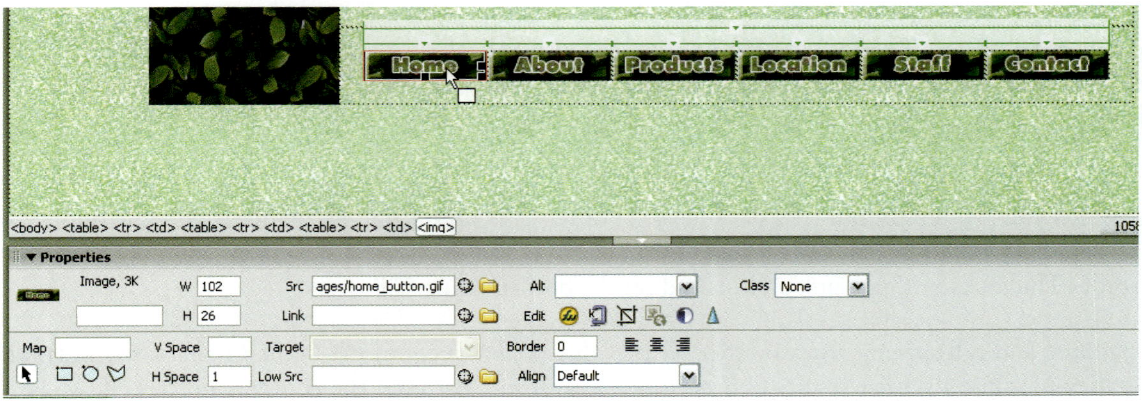


FIGURE 7.21

**10** **Click the `<td>` tag closest to the `<body>` tag, and look at its properties in the Property inspector.**

The horizontal alignment of this cell is Center and its vertical alignment is Middle, so the contents of this single-celled table are centered both horizontally and vertically.

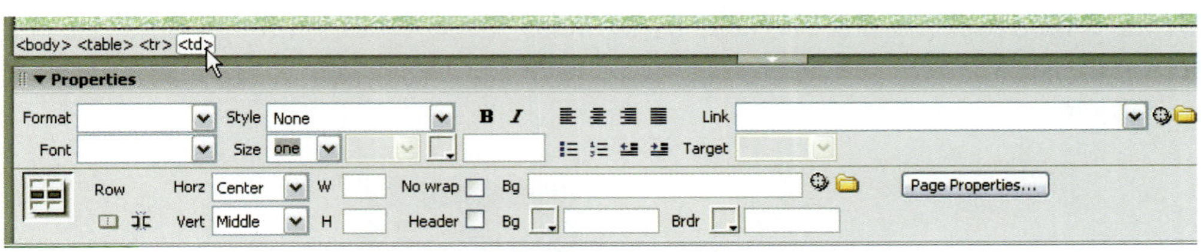


FIGURE 7.22

**11** **Close tropiflora.html.**

# LESSON 2 Creating Tables

As you know, you can create tables in two ways with Dreamweaver: using the Table dialog box or the layout method. In this lesson, you use the Table dialog box. You encounter a few properties of tables and make decisions about how to set them.

You can specify Table Width in percentage or in pixels. Percentage is based on the container in which you place the table. If, for example, you are creating a table nested in another table cell, the percentage is measured relative to the containing cell, not the browser window. If, however, you specify the width in pixels, you could have a visitor whose browser window is narrower than the table width, forcing this visitor to scroll horizontally to read the content. Because most computer monitors are set to display 800 pixels or wider, you should generally be safe with table widths 780 pixels or less. However, regardless of which units of measurement you use, if you have a 2000-pixel-wide graphic in the table, it won't matter whether the table is set to 100% or 780 pixels — the size of the graphic will force the table width to expand to whatever size is necessary to contain the graphic. The other option is to set no table width at all, and allow the content to determine the width of the table. If a table has no specified dimensions, it expands enough to accommodate the width of the content up to 100% of the available space, and, where possible, text wraps to additional lines.

Another option in the Table dialog box is Border Thickness. Any value greater than 0 displays a border that you can color as you prefer. If you set the border to 0, no border displays. You can also leave the Border Thickness field blank, which allows browsers to default to their own settings, or you can use CSS to create borders instead. By default, if no border thickness is set, browsers do not display borders.

The Border Width setting is somewhat confusing because the width applies only to the border around the table. When you give a table border any value, cell borders also appear but, no matter what table Border Width setting you use, cell borders are always just 1 pixel thick. Given this lack of flexibility, you may prefer to leave the Border Thickness setting blank and instead set the borders using CSS.

Cell padding and cell spacing are two other settings that are often confused — their names are similar and, at times, they produce a similar result. ***Cell padding*** creates space around the contents in the cell, whereas ***cell spacing*** creates space between the cells. The difference is clear when borders are present. If you set Cell Padding to 15 pixels (both measurements are in pixels) and Cell Spacing to 0 pixels, the borders around each cell press against each other but these cell borders are 15 pixels from the contents of the cell (see the left table in Figure 7.23). If you set Cell Padding to 0 pixels and Cell Spacing to 15 pixels, there is no space between the content of the cells and the cell borders but the cell borders are 15 pixels apart from each other and from the edge of the table (see the right table in the Figure 7.23). In both tables in Figure 7.23, the cells have a yellow background and the table has a blue background. The table background, if set, appears through the space created by cell spacing. You cannot set the table and cell backgrounds from the Table dialog box, but you can set them later using the Property inspector or CSS.

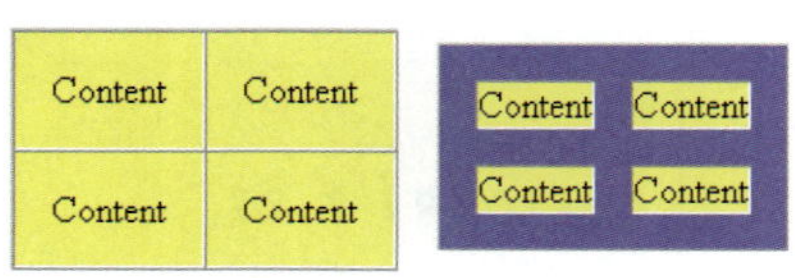


**FIGURE 7.23**

You can use the Table dialog box to create a caption and set its alignment. The Caption and Summary fields are grouped in the Accessibility section of this dialog box. (It is debatable whether or not the caption should be considered an accessibility feature because it benefits all users, not just those for whom accessibility initiatives were developed.) Unlike the **summary** attribute, the caption is visible and readable by everyone. You can use this option as a heading or as a simple description of the purpose of the table.

The final option is the Summary, which is an accessibility feature. Unlike the caption, summary text is not visible but screen readers can read it. The caption text is reserved for short descriptions; the **summary** attribute is for description that might be longer. The purpose of the **summary** attribute is to review the contents of the table, thereby reducing the need for the user of screen-reader software to listen to all of the data. Sighted users can quickly scan the table and determine trends and relationships. Screen-reader users benefit from the summary description for the same information. Consider, for example, the following browser-statistics table:

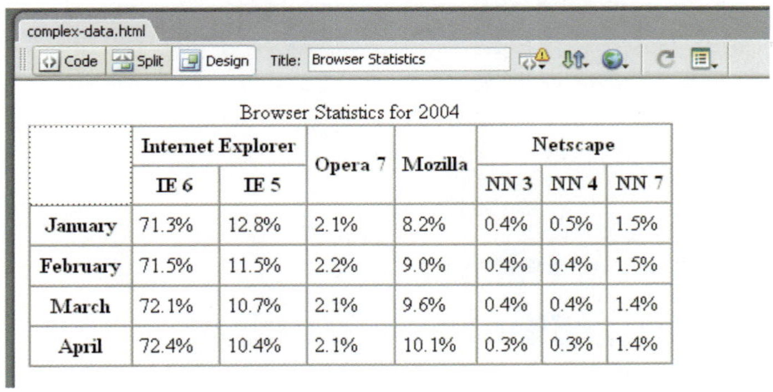


Browser Statistics for 2004

| | Internet Explorer | | Opera 7 | Mozilla | Netscape | | |
|---|---|---|---|---|---|---|---|
| | IE 6 | IE 5 | | | NN 3 | NN 4 | NN 7 |
| January | 71.3% | 12.8% | 2.1% | 8.2% | 0.4% | 0.5% | 1.5% |
| February | 71.5% | 11.5% | 2.2% | 9.0% | 0.4% | 0.4% | 1.5% |
| March | 72.1% | 10.7% | 2.1% | 9.6% | 0.4% | 0.4% | 1.4% |
| April | 72.4% | 10.4% | 2.1% | 10.1% | 0.3% | 0.3% | 1.4% |

**FIGURE 7.24**

The summary attribute for this table might be written as:

```
summary="Internet Explorer 6 accounted for approximately 72% of the visits
increasing by 1% from January to April. Internet Explorer 5 accounted for
approximately 11% and decreased by 1% during the same period. Opera 7
remained steady at approximately 2% whereas Mozilla increased from 8 to
10%. Netscape 3 and 4 remained steady at about 0.4% each and Netscape 7
changed little from its 1.5%."
```

## Create a Table

In this exercise, you create a table that will form the basis of a television schedule. Although this schedule could be considered a data table, for the purposes of this lesson, you use the table solely for layout.

**1** **Create a new HTML page with the document Title of Television Schedule. Save it (but do not close it) as tv-schedule.html.**

**2** **Type `Television Schedule` at the top of the page, format it as Heading 1, and press Enter/Return at the end of the line.**

**3** **In the Common Insert bar, click the Table button (between the Anchor and Images buttons).**

If the Insert bar is set to another mode, switch it to Common and click the Table button.

FIGURE 7.25

**4** **In the Table dialog box, set Rows to 4, Columns to 7, Table Width to 100%, Border Thickness to 1, Cell Padding to 0, Cell Spacing to 2, and Header to None. Click OK.**

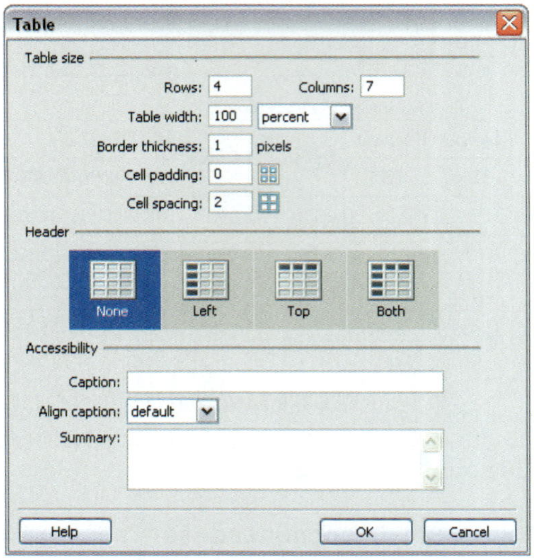


FIGURE 7.26

**5** **In the top-left cell, type `Station`; in the next cell to the right of it, type `1:00PM`. Then type `1:30PM` and so on to `3:30PM` in the last cell of the top row.**

**6** **In the cells below the Station cell, type `CTV`, `CBC`, and `TVO`.**

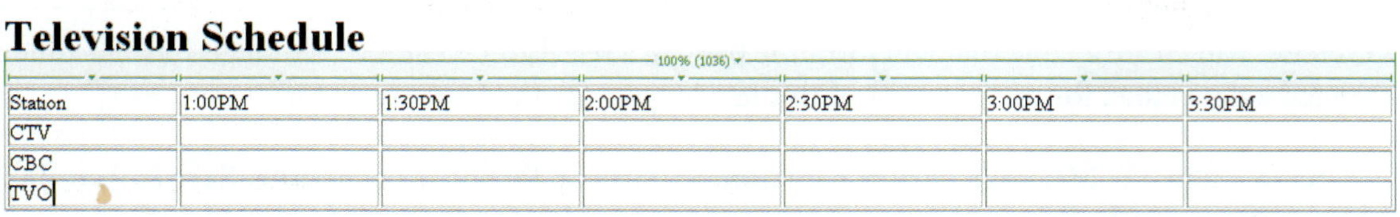


| Station | 1:00PM | 1:30PM | 2:00PM | 2:30PM | 3:00PM | 3:30PM |
|---|---|---|---|---|---|---|
| CTV | | | | | | |
| CBC | | | | | | |
| TVO | | | | | | |

FIGURE 7.27

**7** **In the CTV row, type `Vicki Gabereau` at 1:00PM, `Rosie O'Donnell` at 2:00PM, and `General Hospital` at 3:00PM.**

**In the CBC row, type `Road to Avonlea` at 1:00PM, `Canadian Gardener` at 2:00PM, `Pit Pony` at 2:30PM, and `Nothing Too Good for a Cowboy` at 3:00PM.**

**In the TVO row, type `More to Life` at 1:00PM, `Studio 2` at 2:00PM, `Your Health` at 3:00PM, and `Arthur` at 3:30PM.**

**Television Schedule**

| Station | 1:00PM | 1:30PM | 2:00PM | 2:30PM | 3:00PM | 3:30PM |
|---|---|---|---|---|---|---|
| CTV | Vicki Gabereau | | Rosie O'Donnell | | General Hospital | |
| CBC | Road to Avonlea | | Canadian Gardener | Pit Pony | Nothing Too Good for a Cowboy | |
| TVO | More to Life | | Studio 2 | | Your Health | Arthur |

FIGURE 7.28

**8** **Save the changes, leaving this file open for the next lesson.**

## To Extend Your Knowledge

### CSS BORDERS

CSS borders have three different groups of properties: **`border-width`**, **`border-style`**, and **`border-color`**. In addition to that, you can set borders the same for all, or set the top, right, left, and bottom borders differently.

# LESSON 3 Inserting New Rows and Columns

Inserting a new row at the bottom of a table is very simple — you move the insertion point to the last cell in the table and press the Tab key, and a new row appears. However, if you want to add a new row in the middle of a table, the Tab key won't work. You must use either a contextual menu or the Menu bar. To insert a new column, you can use either the Menu-bar option or the Column Width menu that appears above or below the table.

## Insert New Rows and Columns

In this exercise, you insert new rows at the bottom of the table, a new row in the middle of the table, and a column to the left of the table.

**1** **From the bottom-right cell of the table, press the Tab key.**

Notice that a new row appears.

**2** **Type `WN` in the cell under the Station cell and type `The Weather Network` at 1:00PM. Press Tab until a new row appears. Complete the rest of the table as shown in Figure 7.29.**

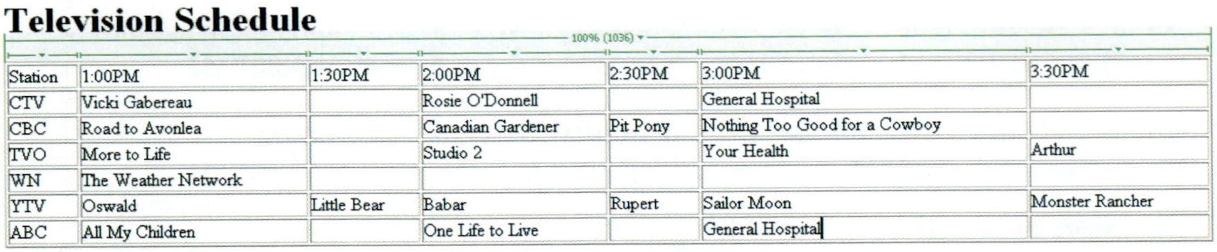


FIGURE 7.29

**3** **Right/Control-click the TVO cell and choose Table>Insert Rows or Columns. In the Insert Rows or Columns dialog box, choose Rows, set the Number of Rows to 1, set Where to Above the Selection, and click OK.**

You may notice that Insert Row and Insert Column appeared in the contextual menu. Those options are less flexible — they only allow you to insert one at a time, and rows are always above and columns are always to the left (before).

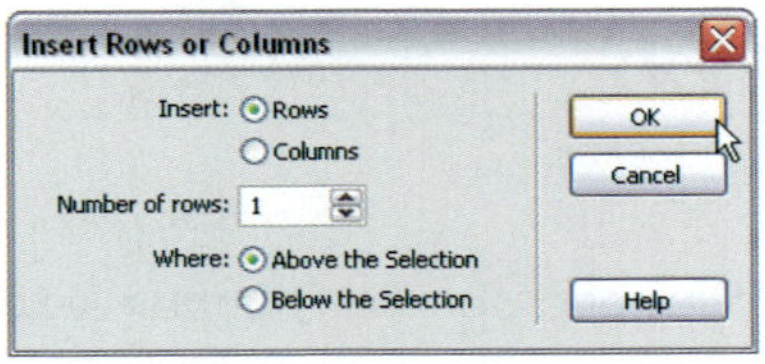


FIGURE 7.30

**4** **In the new empty row, type `TLC` under the Station cell, `While You Were Out` under 1:00PM, `Date Patrol` under 2:00PM, and `Spymaster` under 3:00PM.**

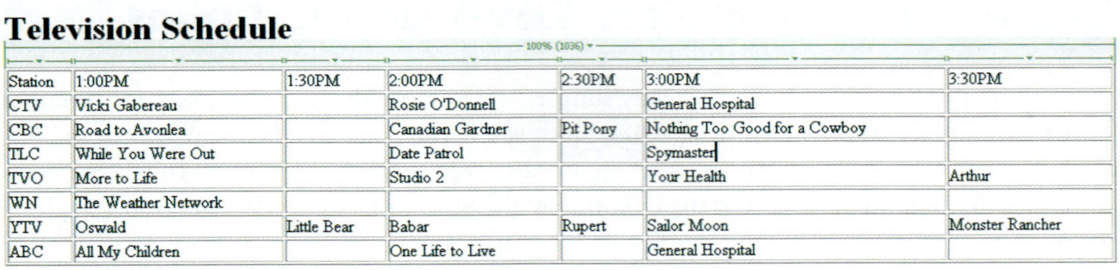


FIGURE 7.31

**5** **Above the Station cell, click the Column Width menu triangle, and choose Insert Column Left.**

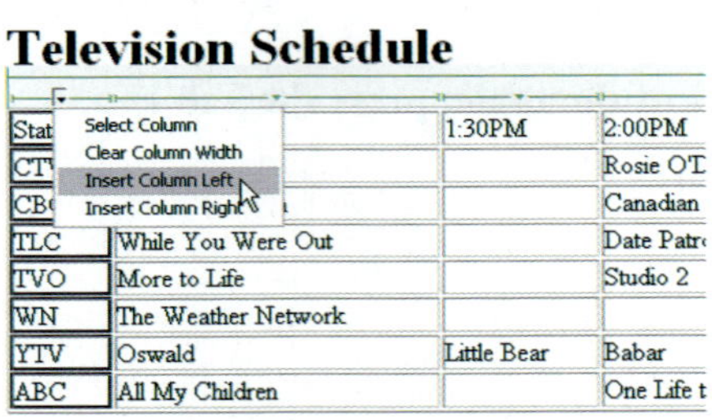


FIGURE 7.32

**6** **In the top cell of the new column, type `Source`. In the cell below, type `Cable`; in the cell to the left of WN, type `Satellite`.**

**Television Schedule**

| Source | Station | 1:00PM | 1:30PM | 2:00PM |
|---|---|---|---|---|
| Cable | CTV | Vicki Gabereau | | Rosie O'Do |
| | CBC | Road to Avonlea | | Canadian G |
| | TLC | While You Were Out | | Date Patrol |
| | TVO | More to Life | | Studio 2 |
| Satellite | WN | The Weather Network | | |
| | YTV | Oswald | Little Bear | Babar |
| | ABC | All My Children | | One Life to |

FIGURE 7.33

**7** **Save the changes, leaving the page open for the next lesson.**

## LESSON 4 Merging Cells

Merging cells is as simple as choosing a group of adjacent cells and activating the merge function. Dreamweaver automatically adds the **`colspan`** or **`rowspan`** attributes as needed. Many diehard hand-coders agree that table assembly, especially merging cells, is one feature of visual Web-design software that they could benefit by using.

In this exercise, many of the television programs are one hour long, so there is an empty cell to the right of the cell containing the name of the program. You must merge the empty cell with the cell to its left. To do so, you select the two cells (in either order) and choose Table>Merge Cells from the contextual menu or Modify>Table>Merge Cells from the Dreamweaver menu. Similarly, you must merge the Cable and Satellite cells with the empty cells below them.

### Merge Cells

**1** **In the first column, drag to select the Cable cell and the three empty cells below it.**

**2** **Right/Control-click in the selected cells and choose Table>Merge Cells.**

**3** **Select the Satellite cell and the two empty cells below it, and merge them by choosing Modify>Table>Merge Cells.**

**4** **Select the Vicki Gabereau cell (CTV, 1:00PM) and the empty cell to the right and press Control-Alt-M/Command-Option-M to merge the two cells.**

**5** **Continue to merge cells where empty cells exist to the right of filled cells. Merge all six cells in the row for The Weather Network.**

**Television Schedule**

| Source | Station | 1:00PM | 1:30PM | 2:00PM | 2:30PM | 3:00PM | 3:30PM |
|---|---|---|---|---|---|---|---|
| Cable | CTV | Vicki Gabereau | | Rosie O'Donnell | | General Hospital | |
| | CBC | Road to Avonlea | | Canadian Gardner | Pit Pony | Nothing Too Good for a Cowboy | |
| | TLC | While You Were Out | | Date Patrol | | Spymaster | |
| | TVO | More to Life | | Studio 2 | | Your Health | Arthur |
| Satellite | WN | The Weather Network | | | | | |
| | YTV | Oswald | Little Bear | Babar | Rupert | Sailor Moon | Monster Rancher |
| | ABC | All My Children | | One Life to Live | | General Hospital | |

FIGURE 7.34

**6** **Save the changes, leaving the file open for the next lesson.**

# LESSON 5 Dressing Up Tables

In this lesson, you learn to apply background colors, horizontal alignment, column widths, and border colors to a table. You can use HTML presentation tags and attributes or CSS to apply style or presentation to a table. ***HTML presentation tags*** are tags whose sole purpose is to add appearance without affecting structure. The best-known presentation tag is the `<font>` tag, which allows you to change the color, typeface, and size of text. As you learned earlier, all of these options are also available through CSS. ***HTML presentation attributes*** are attributes that apply appearances, such as colors and borders. Unlike CSS, HTML presentation attributes are coded in the tags themselves; CSS appears in the `<head>` section of the HTML document. In this lesson, you learn to specify appearances using both HTML and CSS methods, and compare the results.

You can change either or both of the background and border colors in the Property inspector. Dreamweaver provides a Format Table function that allows you to apply predefined color schemes, and to apply (and customize) any of the schemes. You apply these appearances with HTML tags and attributes through the Format Table function or the Property inspector.

There are several methods you can use to select cells to apply an appearance to the table, to a row, or to an individual cell. You can click the `<table>`, `<tr>`, or `<td>` tags in the Tag selector. You can use Control/Command-click with or without the Shift key to select multiple cells. You can move the mouse pointer to the top of a column until it becomes a down-pointing arrow, at which point clicking selects the column or, if you drag to either the left or right, you select adjacent columns. To select ***discontiguous*** (nonadjacent) columns, you Control/Command-click one column, which selects it; you then move the mouse pointer to the top of another column and, when it changes to the down-pointing arrow cursor, Control/Command-click to select that column as well.

In this lesson, you also learn to adjust the column widths using the green dimensional rulers that appear either below or above the table. You can use these rulers to adjust the width of the entire table or of individual columns. When you change the width of columns, the changes are applied to the cells in the selected columns. As you learned earlier, you build tables using the `<table>`, `<tr>` (table row), and `<td>` and `<th>` (table-cell) tags. The `<col>` and `<colgroup>` tags are rarely used because they have weak browser support, are not available through Dreamweaver's Design interface, and do not define the structure of the table. They just provide a means for applying some common attributes to columns of cells, such as column widths.

## Select, Customize, and Apply a Predefined Color Scheme

In this exercise, you change the appearance of the table of television programs using HTML styles. You use the Format Table function to create the basic style and then modify cells with different appearances.

**1** **Save the open tv-schedule.html file as tv-schedule-1.html.**

The file tv-schedule-1.html is the same as tv-schedule.html. You apply HTML presentation styles to tv-schedule.html. In a following exercise, you apply the same appearances to tv-schedule.html using CSS, and then compare the results.

**2** **Click the table and choose Commands>Format Table.**

This function offers a number of predefined table styles that you can apply to your selected table. Explore these predefined styles in the top-left list. Notice also that you can set two row colors to alternate. You can also style the top row with colors, alignment, and text styles, and the left column with alignment and text styles.

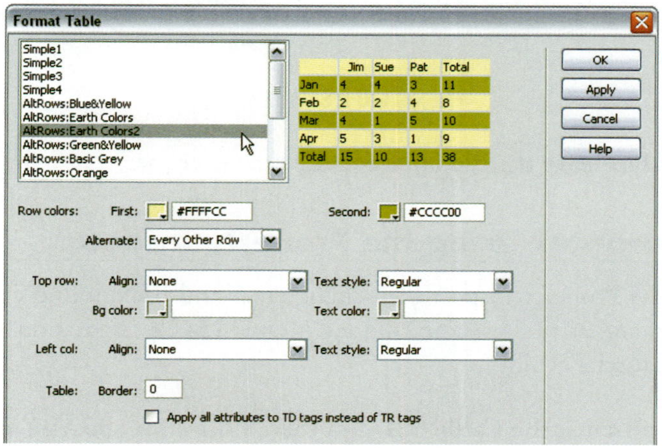


FIGURE 7.35

**3** **Choose AltRows:Earth Colors2 from the list and click the Apply button.**

When you click Apply, the table in the Document window behind the dialog box takes on the selected color scheme.

**4** **In the Format Table dialog box, set the Top Row Text Style to Bold. Set the Bg Color to #802A00 (zeros, not the letter "O") by typing this hexadecimal color code into the text field to the right of the color box. Set the Text Color to #CCCCCC. Click OK.**

Remember to type the # character for both colors.

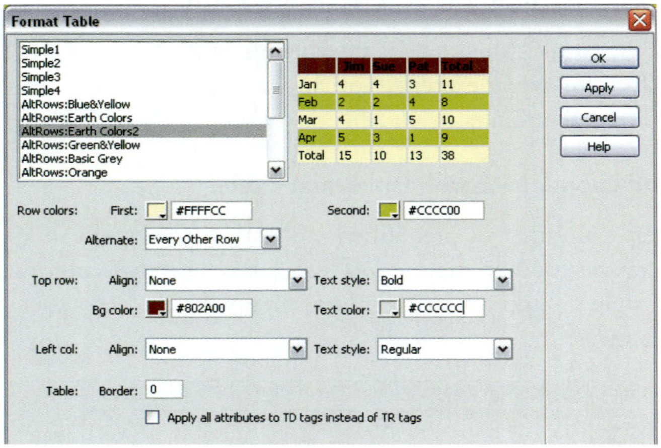


FIGURE 7.36

**5** **Save the changes but leave the file open for the next exercise.**

## Modify Cell Appearances Using the Property Inspector

In this exercise, you use the Property inspector to change text and background colors of selected cells with HTML presentational tags and attributes. The bold tag is an HTML presentational tag. The cell background color is an HTML presentational attribute.

**1** **Control/Command-click the Cable cell, and then Shift-click the ABC cell.**

There are no table borders because the table borders were set by default to 0 in the Format Table dialog box.

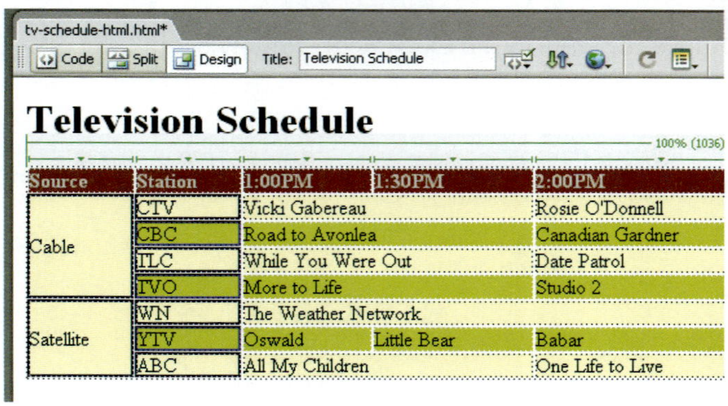


FIGURE 7.37

**2** **In the Property inspector, type #808000 in the background-color field, type #CCCCCC in the text color field, and click the B (bold) button.**

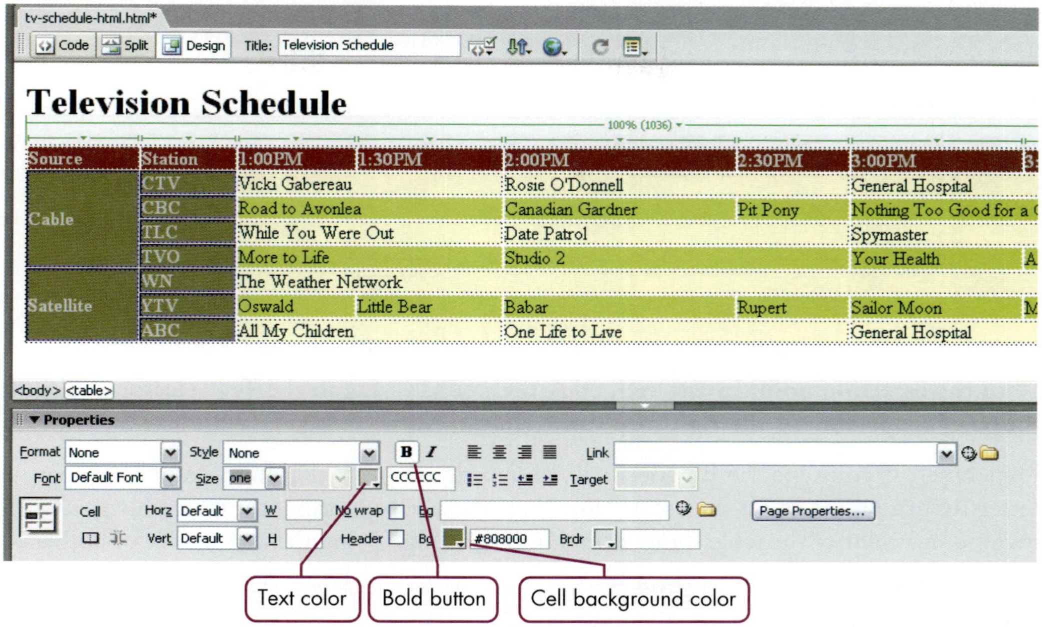


FIGURE 7.38

**3** **Control/Command-click to select the Road to Avonlea cell, then change the background color to #CC4400 and the text color to #FFFFFF (or choose white using the color box). Set the text to bold. Apply the same color scheme to the Oswald and Rupert cells.**

Although you already created the color scheme, you cannot, without going into the code, copy and paste the style properties from one cell to another because you applied the styles with HTML presentation tags and attributes.

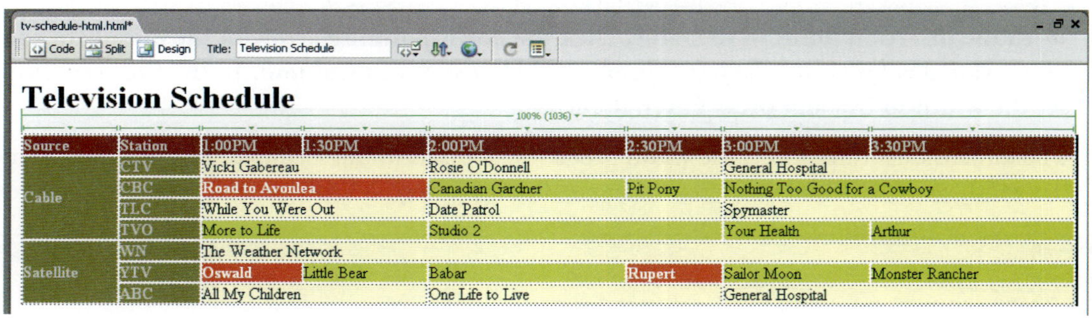

FIGURE 7.39

**4** **Control/Command-click to select all three cells highlighted with the favorite color scheme, and reverse the colors so that the text color is #CC4400 and the background color is #FFFFFF.**

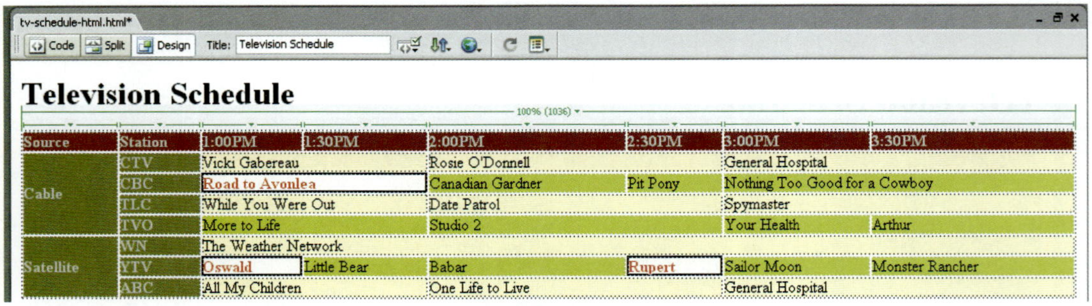


FIGURE 7.40

**5** **With the insertion point in any cell, click the `<table>` tag in the Tag selector and, in the Property inspector, set the Bg Color (background color) to black (#000000).**

Remember: if you type the hexadecimal color code in the background-color field, you must press Enter/Return or Tab to set the color. Note that when cell spacing is set to a value greater than 0, the background color of the table shows through the spacing, giving the appearance of borders.

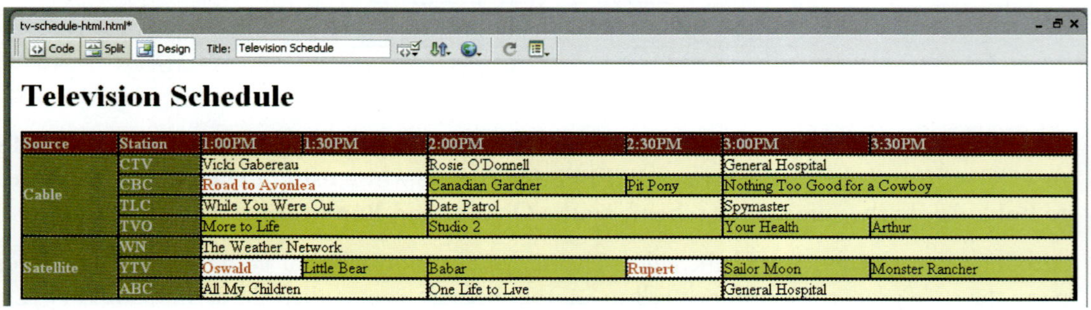


FIGURE 7.41

**6** **With the insertion point in the table, click the down-pointing arrow in the middle of the dimensional ruler above the left column, and choose Select Column. In the Property inspector, set the width to 8% and press Enter/Return.**

The dimensional ruler shows the width is 8% — 79 pixels in this example. The pixel value changes if the width of the Document window changes, but it is always 8% of the table width.

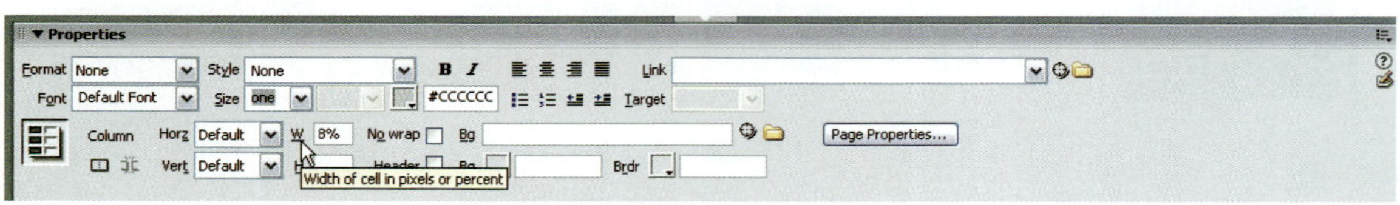


FIGURE 7.42

**7** **Using the same technique as in Step 6, set the width of the second column to 8% and the remaining columns to 14% each.**

**8** **Move the mouse pointer to the top of the first column until the pointer changes to a down-pointing arrow, and drag to the right by one column.**

The down-pointing arrow is a tool for selecting a column. You can drag to the left or right while the mouse pointer is still a down-pointing arrow to select additional adjacent columns.

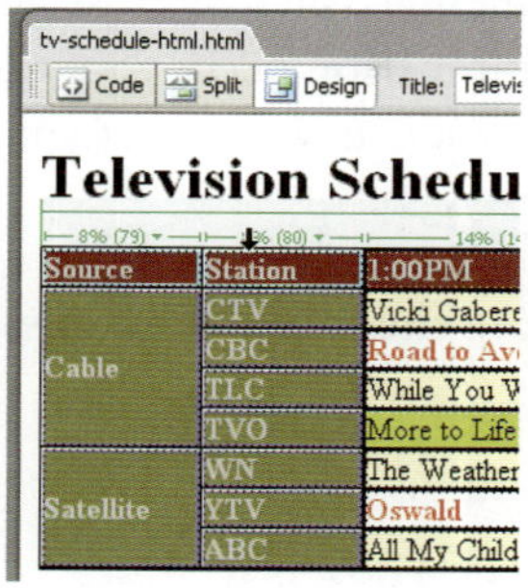

FIGURE 7.43

**9** **Choose Center from the Horz (horizontal alignment) list to center the contents of the selected cells.**

If you want to apply a common alignment to all contents of a cell, use the horizontal-alignment attribute of table cells rather than text alignment — it creates less code. However, when you are using a table for layout, you may prefer to center some paragraphs or other blocks and align others differently. In that situation, you apply the text-alignment properties, either with HTML presentation methods or the preferable CSS methods.

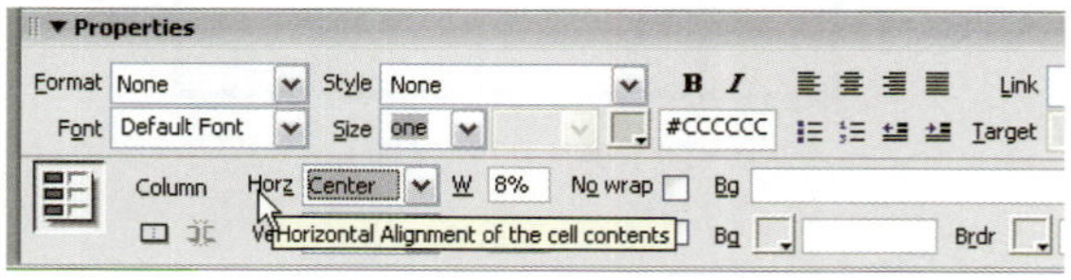

FIGURE 7.44

**10** **Close, saving the changes to tv-schedule-1.html.**

# LESSON 6 Using the Table Dialog Box to Create a Layout Table

Most Web sites use tables for layout and, for the most part, the table structures are quite basic. Commonly, there is a header, a footer, a navigation bar on the left, and a main content area.

Table-based layouts tend not to use borders, which would destroy the seamless appearance of the layout. Instead, these layouts tend to use larger cells, because they hold more content, and, therefore, also use vertical or horizontal alignment. Table-based layouts commonly use spanned (merged) cells to extend the footer or header cells across the width of the table.

## Create a Table-Based Layout Using the Table Dialog Box

In this exercise, you create a table-based layout. As in all design, it is useful to begin with a clear picture of what you want to create. At least at the beginning, you should create this image on paper. (When you become more familiar with design and layout options, you may be able to think it out by visualizing without drawing.) Before you begin any layout, you should draw it concretely, assigning the components to their own boxes or cells. To determine how many rows and columns you need, you extend all lines to the edges of the table (as we did with the dotted line in Figure 7.45). For now, imagine that you drew the layout in Figure 7.45as your plan for the layout table that you create in this exercise.

**1 Examine the provided layout. Note the number of rows and columns, and which information each contains.**

Notice that the planned layout contains two rows: the header row and the navigation/main-content row. It also contains two columns: the navigation bar and the main content. Although the header row does not have separate visible columns, it is constructed by merging the two cells in the top row. The dotted line just shows how the header row would be divided.

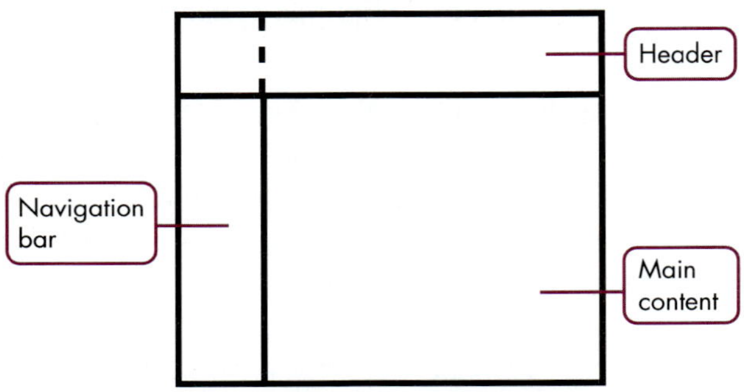


FIGURE 7.45

**2 Open f1cars.html from the Tables site.**

**3 Click the Table button and create a 2 × 2 table with a table-width setting of 100%, no borders, 3 cell padding, and 0 cell spacing. Click OK.**

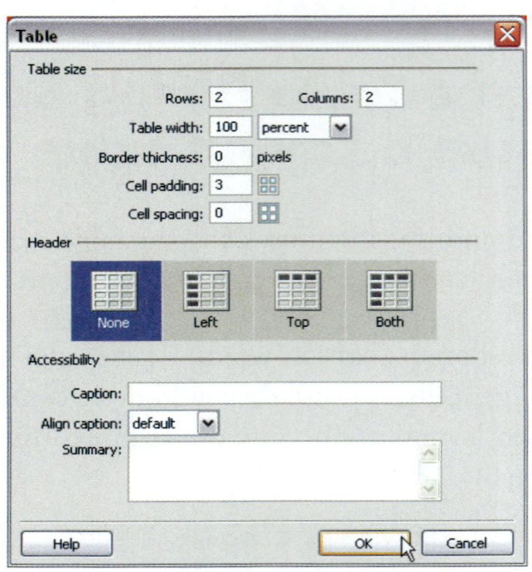


FIGURE 7.46

**4** **Drag to select the top two cells, Right/Control-click, and choose Table>Merge Cells.**

**5** **Click the top cell and insert the f1cars-logo.gif graphic from the images folder.**

**6** **Click the right cell of the second row and insert ferrari_car.jpg.**

**7** **Click the left cell of the second row and insert ferrari.gif. Press Enter/Return and insert jaguar.gif. Repeat the process and insert mclaren.gif, toyota.gif, and williams.gif.**

Notice that the top graphic and photo of the Ferrari are both left-aligned in the cells. Notice also that the small graphics on the left are centered vertically. These alignments are the defaults for horizontal and vertical alignment.

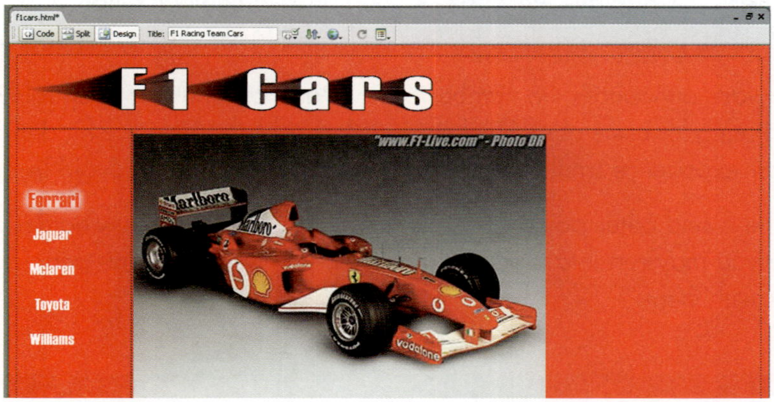


FIGURE 7.47

**8** **Save the changes, leaving the file open for the next exercise.**

## Change Cell Alignments

In this layout, the graphic buttons on the left look fine with the current content. If, however, the right cell had more content than just the photo of the car — perhaps the statistics on the car, the team, the drivers' names, and more — the left graphics would still center vertically in the cell. In a long page, these centered graphics could appear below the bottom of the browser window. In this exercise, you change the default layouts of the cells to prevent this.

**1** **Click the top cell to the right of the F1 Cars graphic.**

**2** **In the Property inspector, change the horizontal alignment to Center.**

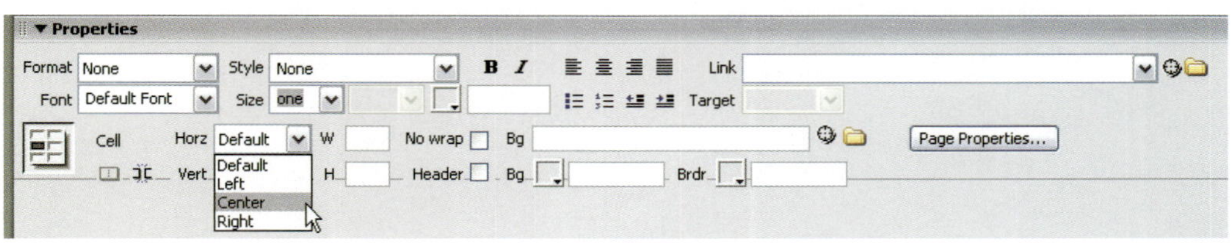


FIGURE 7.48

**3** **Click the left cell and change the vertical alignment to Top.**

**4** **Close, saving the changes.**

## To Extend Your Knowledge

### AVOID LAYOUT TABLES

As you know, tables were not designed for layout. Their complex and flexible structure and options made it possible for designers to create exciting designs. Layout tables, however, come at a high cost.

Pages do not display until the browser receives all of the table's code and contents. Nested tables add more code to download and display. When a browser displays nested tables, it also evaluates the layout once per table, so if the outer table contains five nested tables, the browser must run six passes through the code before it displays the page. If you can reduce your reliance on nested tables and work with just one table, you can produce far less code and faster-displaying pages.

Screen-reader software announces the number of rows and columns for each table, so nested tables are particularly irritating for users of such software. When table borders are hidden, sighted people do not see the tables or experience similar frustrations. Again, at least try to avoid using nested tables.

You can explore these and other points about layout tables at http://www.hotdesign.com/seybold/. However, because you may run into layout tables when you work on other people's sites, you should know how to work with them.

## LESSON 7 Creating Tables in Layout Mode

Simple tables, whether data tables or layout tables, are relatively easy to construct, so determining how many columns and rows to use is also fairly easy. For data tables, you know the number of columns and rows just from the amount of data you have. However, some layouts place graphics of different height and width beside each other. Without measuring each graphic and working your calculator to compute column and row spans, you can't easily create a table for these types of complex layouts. For this reason, Dreamweaver provides the Layout view, in which you can create cells just by dragging the borders wider or narrower. This method of creating a layout is very flexible and supports free-form design.

There are two ways you can use the Layout view to create tables. You can create a layout table and then add layout cells to it, or you can create the layout cells and allow Dreamweaver to create the table around it. Both methods have their advantages and disadvantages, so the choice is really a matter of your preference. In this exercise, you create the layout table first, and then draw the layout cells within it.

## Prepare to Use Layout Mode

**1** **Open bromeliads.html from the Tables site.**

**2** **Switch the Insert bar to the Layout Insert bar, and click the Layout mode button.**

The Layout mode is the mode in which you create the layout table. When you complete the table, you switch back to Standard mode for routine editing and design work.

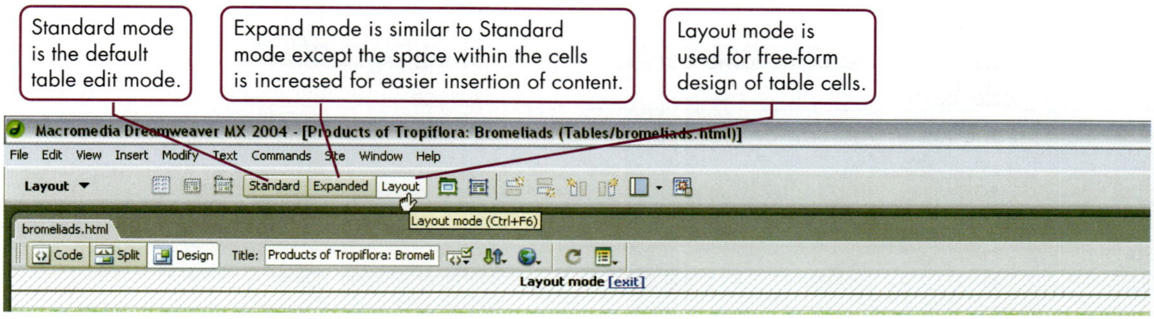


FIGURE 7.49

**3** **Read the information in the dialog box, then click OK (do not click the Don't Show Me This Message Again option).**

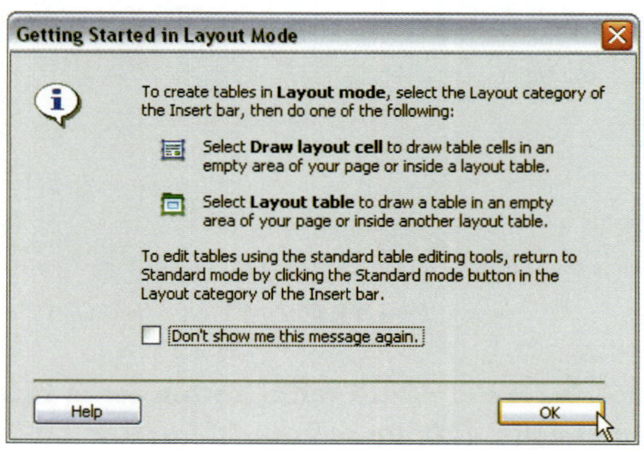


FIGURE 7.50

### ? If you have problems

(Windows only) Whether or not you have checked the Don't Show Me This Message Again option, this dialog box only appears the first time you switch to the Layout mode. If you want to access this dialog box, choose Edit>Preferences, choose the General category, click the Change Workspace button, choose Coder, click OK, and click OK again. Before you exit the Preferences dialog box, again click Change Workspace, choose Designer, and click OK twice. Click OK to close the Preferences dialog box, and then exit and relaunch Dreamweaver. When you switch to Layout mode, this Getting Started in Layout Mode dialog box appears.

## Create and Fill a Layout Table and Its Cells

You have now prepared a page and switched into Layout mode. In this exercise, you create the layout table and layout cells, and then insert different graphics into each new cell.

**1** **Click the Layout Table button (to the immediate right of the Layout button) and draw a rectangle in the Document window.**

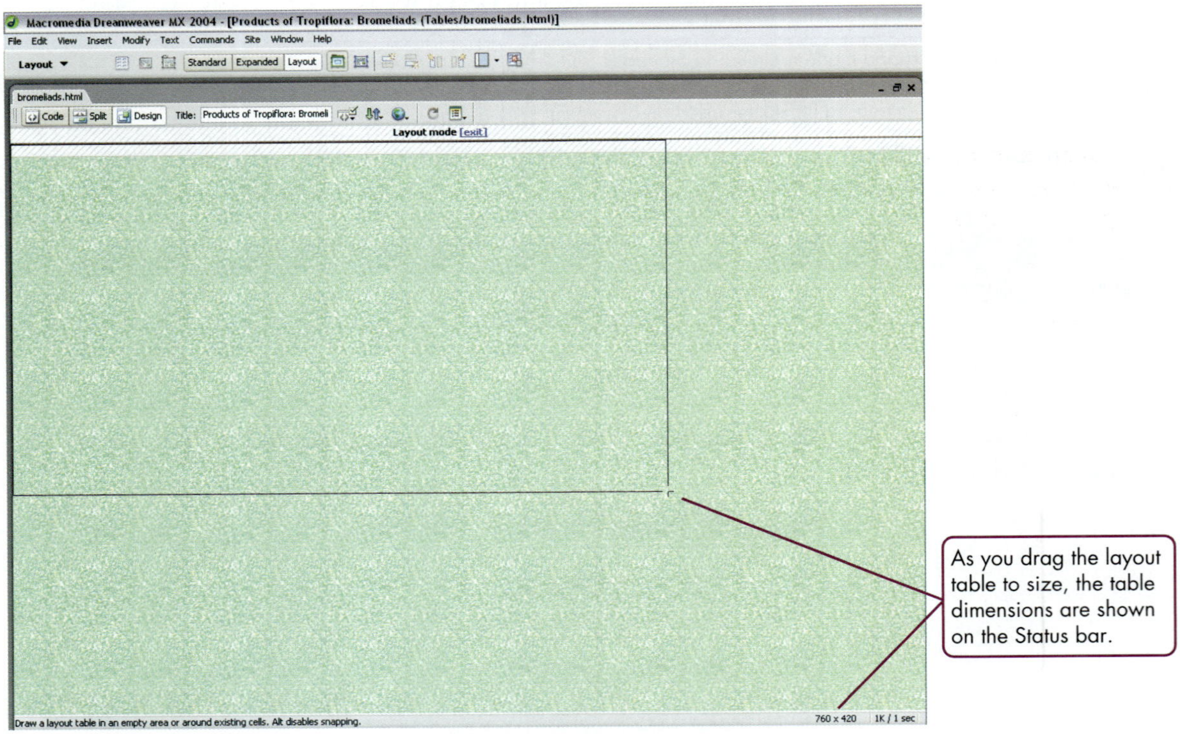


FIGURE 7.51

**2** **In the Property inspector, leave the Width radio button set to Fixed, but change the dimensions to Width: 760 and Height: 420. Press Enter/Return or Tab to register the change.**

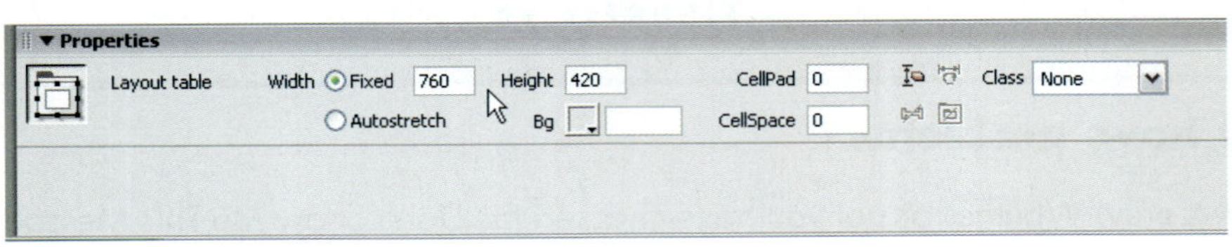

FIGURE 7.52

**3** Click the Draw Layout Cell button (to the right of the Layout Table button) and drag to create a short cell across the full width of the table.

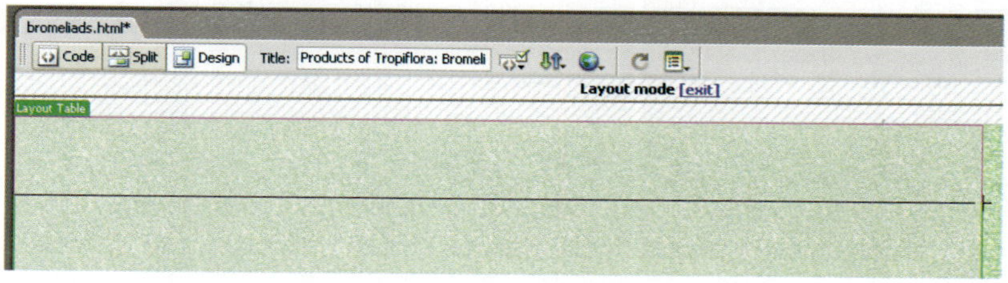


FIGURE 7.53

**4** Create another cell across the bottom of the table by clicking the Draw Layout Cell button, and dragging across the width of the table. Create three vertical cells in the center area — make the left and right cells relatively narrow and the middle cell wide.

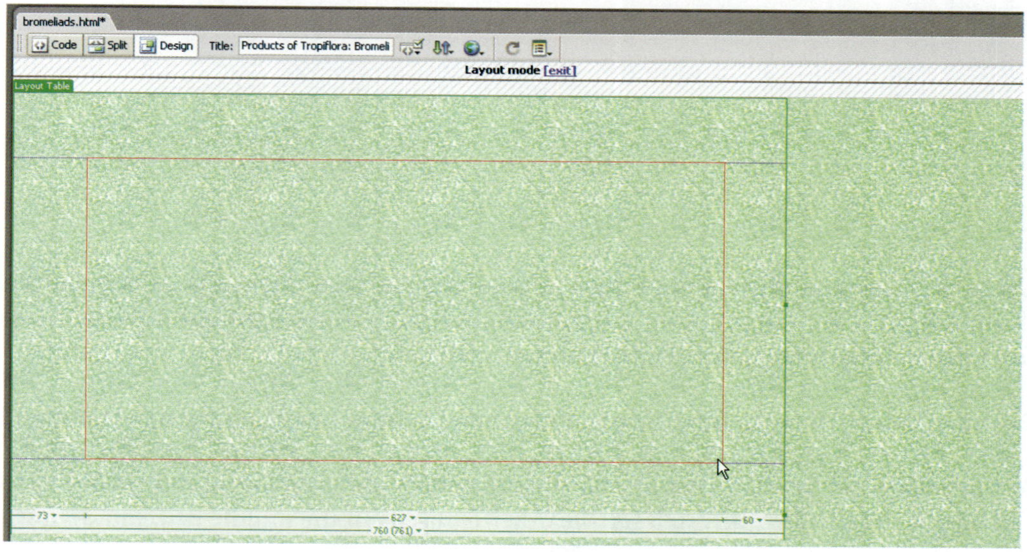


FIGURE 7.54

**5** Click the top cell. From the Property inspector, set the format to Heading 1, and drag Tropiflora_online.jpg from the images folder into the cell.

**6** Double-click to open bromeliads-navbar.html. Select all of the content, copy it, and then close bromeliads-navbar.html. Click the left cell and paste the copied content.

**7** **With the insertion point still in the left cell, Right/Control-click the `<td>` tag in the Tag selector and set the `id` to navbar.**

FIGURE 7.55

**8** **Using the same procedures as in Step 6, copy the content from bromeliads-content.html into the middle cell, the content from bromeliads-special.html into the right cell, and the content from bromeliads-footer.html into the bottom cell.**

**9** **Switch to Standard mode by clicking the Standard button (Standard Layout in the tool tip).**

**10** **At the bottom of the left (navbar) cell, click the down-pointing arrow and choose Clear Column Width. Repeat this step for the other two cells in the middle row, but do not touch the one for the entire table that reads 760.**

When you draw a table and cells in Layout mode, the process of drawing defines the width (and height) of cells in pixels. When you select Clear Column Width, the width attributes of the cells in the column are removed from the `<td>` tags. You should realize, however, that this option does not change the table width, just the selected column(s). Without specified column widths, the three columns adjust their width to their content. The graphics in the left and right cells determine those cells' minimum widths. In the middle cell, the text wraps if it cannot fit on one line.

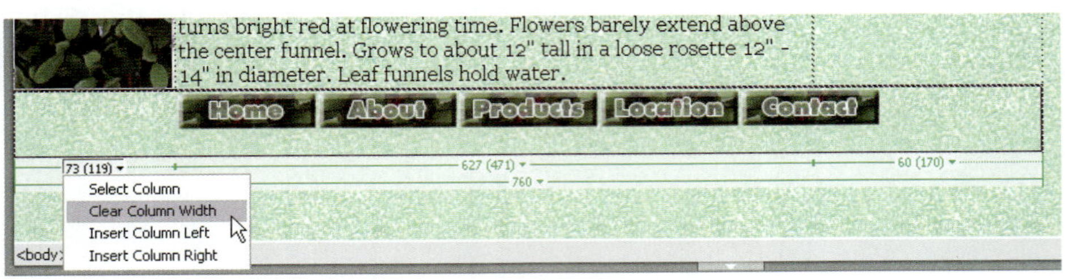


FIGURE 7.56

**11** Click the down-pointing arrow below the table dimension (760), and choose Clear All Heights.

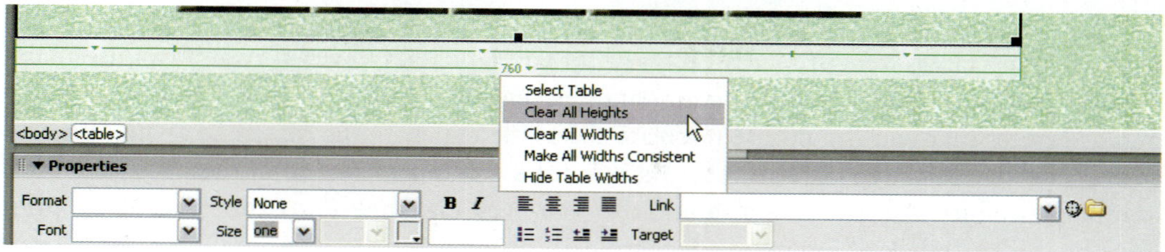


FIGURE 7.57

**12** Preview the page in your browser, then return to Dreamweaver and close bromeliads.html.

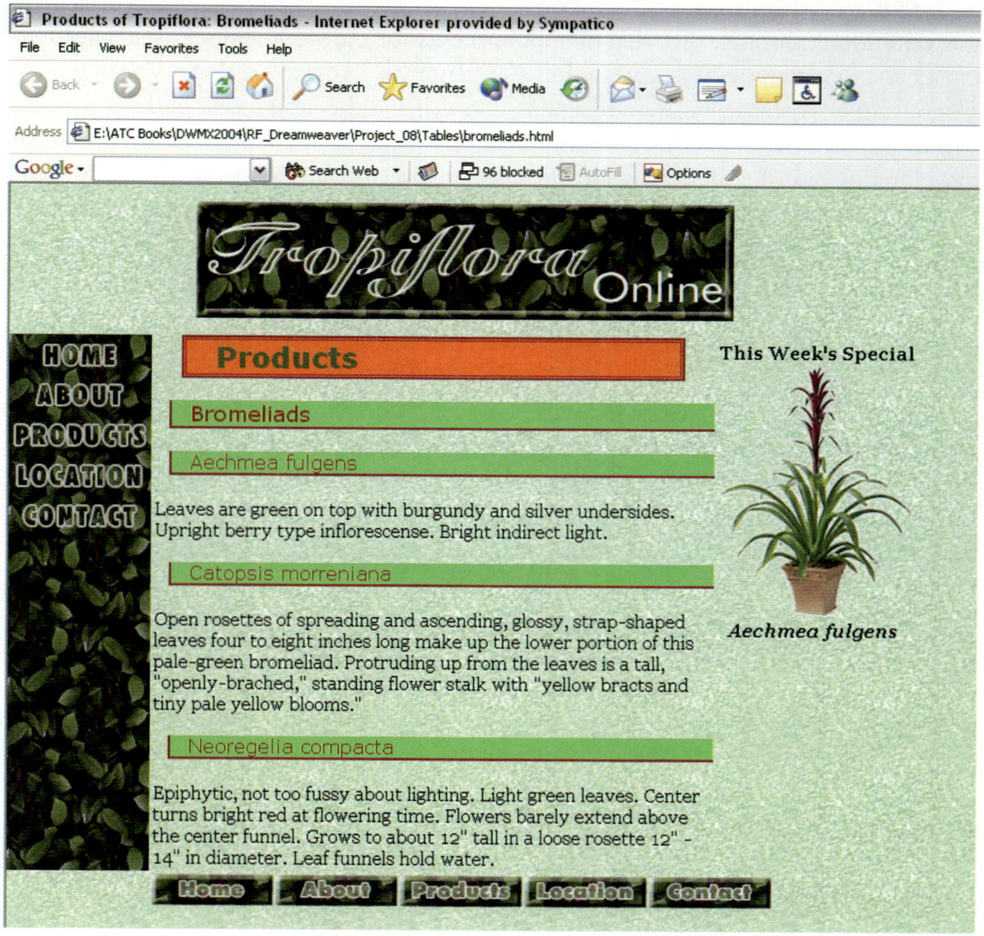


FIGURE 7.58

# LESSON 8 Creating Basic Accessible Data Tables

You learned earlier that tables were primarily designed for tabular data. However, even if you use a table to present tabular data, you have not ensured that your data is accessible to those who use screen readers. There are a few tags and attributes that you should use to create accessible tables — the **<caption>** tag, the table-header cell tag (**<th>**), and the **summary**, **scope**, **id**, and **headers** attributes. Not all of these tags and attributes are required for all data tables. All data tables should use **<th>** cell tag, the **<caption>** tag, and, optionally, the **summary** attribute. Data tables of intermediate complexity also need the **scope** attribute. Complex data tables require the **id** and **header** attributes instead of the **scope** attribute.

The issue with tables and accessibility is not whether or not screen-reader software can read your data, but whether the user of that screen-reader can work with your data. For example, if a coworker asked you when the next staff meeting is, you would look through the table of appointments for the week and see "staff meeting"; you would then look up to see that it was in the Tuesday column and then look across to see that it was in the 10:00 a.m. row. You see the relationship between the position of a table-data cell and the header cells at the top of the column and at the beginning of the row. Understanding and using this relationship is the difference between reading the table contents and interpreting or using the table contents. Users of screen-reader software can pause their software in a particular cell and direct it to read aloud the header cells that apply to it. Without proper coding, however, this relationship does not exist and they cannot use the table as well as sighted individuals.

You should use the **<th>** tags when you create a data table. You apply these tags to the header cells for the columns and/or the rows. If the table has just one ***logical header level*** (a simple data table), which means that only rows or columns require headers, all you need to do to satisfy accessibility criteria is format the header cells as table-header cells. If the table has two logical header levels (a data table of intermediate complexity), which means that both rows and columns have header cells, then in addition to table-header tags, you need to add the **scope** attribute to each header cell. The **scope** attribute identifies the direction in which the header cells apply — column or row. If the table has three or more logical header levels, then either rows or columns (or both) have multiple levels of headers. The **scope** attribute no longer suffices and you must use the **id** and **headers** attributes.

You may be concerned about how to insert the table-header tags and apply the **scope** attributes for simple and moderately difficult accessible tables, but Dreamweaver makes it easy. You must consider accessibility, however, before you start creating your data table or you lose the benefits of Dreamweaver's accessibility features, and then must either recreate the table or hand-code the modifications.

## Create an Accessible Data Table

**1** **Create a new HTML page and in the document Title field type: `Growth Charts of Boys and Girls`.**

**2** **Click the Table button in the Insert bar.**

Whether the Insert bar is set to Layout mode or Common mode, this button is available — the first button on the Layout Insert bar or the fourth button on the Common Insert bar.

**3** **Click the Table button and create a table that is 3 rows by 3 columns, and has no width setting. Set the border to 1, the cell padding to 3, and the cell spacing to 0.**

**4** **Choose the Top header option.**

**In the Caption field, type: `Growth Charts of Boys and Girls`.**

**In the Summary field, type: `Although girls are slightly shorter than boys at age 5, at ages 8 and 11 they are taller than boys. By age 14, girls have attained their adult height. Boys tend to be shorter than girls at ages 8 and 11. Between 11 and 14 they experience a growth spurt, which increases their height over girls. At age 17 their growth rate tapers off.`**

**Click OK when finished.**

As you can see, the summary is used to digest the data so screen-reader users do not have to remember the data, cell by cell, to draw their own conclusions.

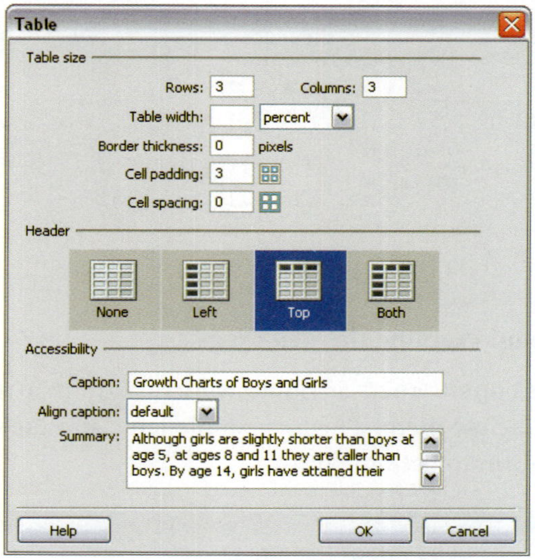


FIGURE 7.59

**5** **Type `Age`, `Boys' Height`, and `Girls' Height` in the top three cells. Complete the table with the following data, pressing Tab to move from cell to cell.**

| Age | Boys' Height | Girls' Height |
|---|---|---|
| 5 | 42.5 | 42.0 |
| 8 | 50.0 | 50.5 |
| 11 | 56.5 | 57.0 |
| 14 | 65.5 | 64.0 |
| 17 | 69.0 | 64.5 |
| 20 | 69.5 | 64.5 |

**6** **Examine the appearance and formatting of the table.**

Notice that text in the top row is bold and centered whereas the text in the data cells is normal weight and left aligned. The **<th>** tag, by default, displays text as bold and centered.

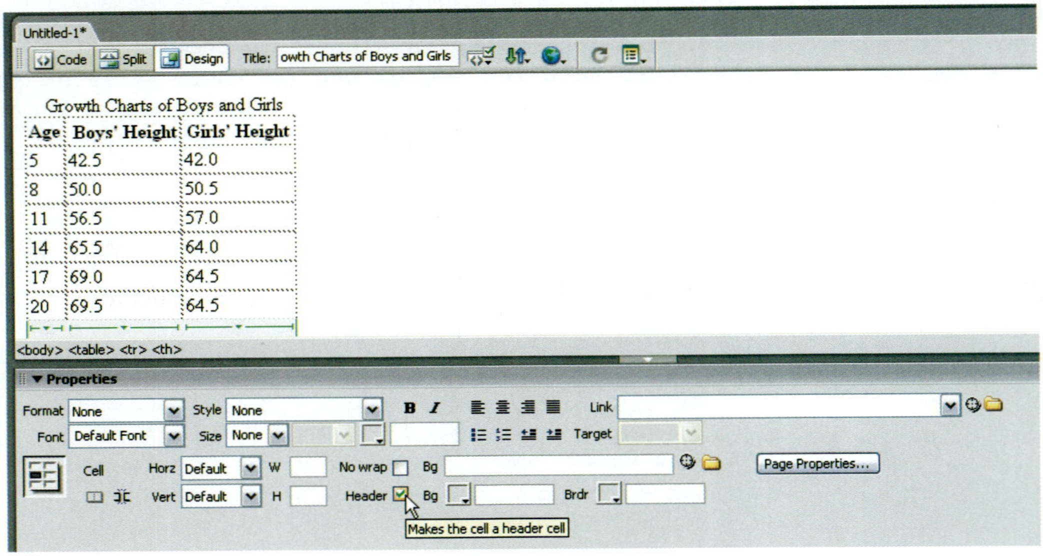


FIGURE 7.60

**7** **Click the Split button and examine the <th> tags.**

The **<th>** tags use the **scope="col"** attribute, which states that the header cells are related to the data cells in the column below them. This is a simple table and does not necessarily need the **scope** attribute, but it is good form to use it anyway.

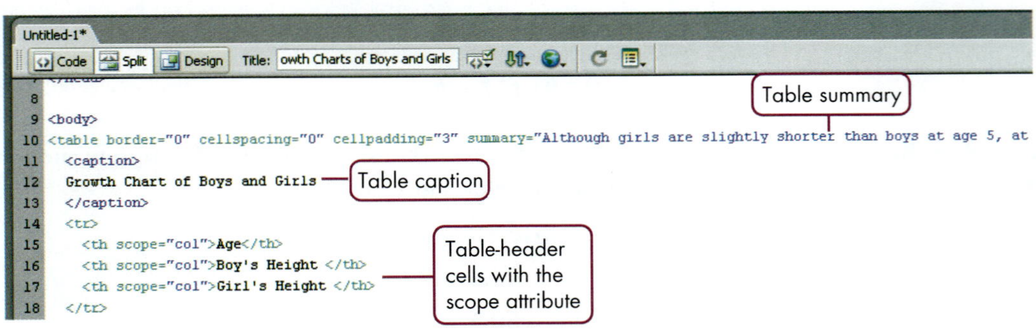


FIGURE 7.61

**8** **Click the Design button to close the Code view.**

**9** **Close this page, saving it as accessible1.html in the Tables site.**

## SUMMARY

In this project, you learned to create and modify tables. You learned that you can use tables to present data and to lay out pages. You discovered how to create data tables that make the information they contain accessible and usable by everyone. You learned to create layout tables using both the Standard mode and the Layout mode, and explored the flexibility of the Layout mode. You also learned how to modify the structure of a table by adding rows and columns, merging cells, and changing alignment and background colors.

## KEY TERMS

Cell padding
Cell spacing
Content-to-code ratio
Discontiguous
HTML presentation attributes
HTML presentation tags
Logical header level
Spanned cells

# CHECKING CONCEPTS AND TERMS

## SCREEN ID

**Identify the indicated areas from the list below:**

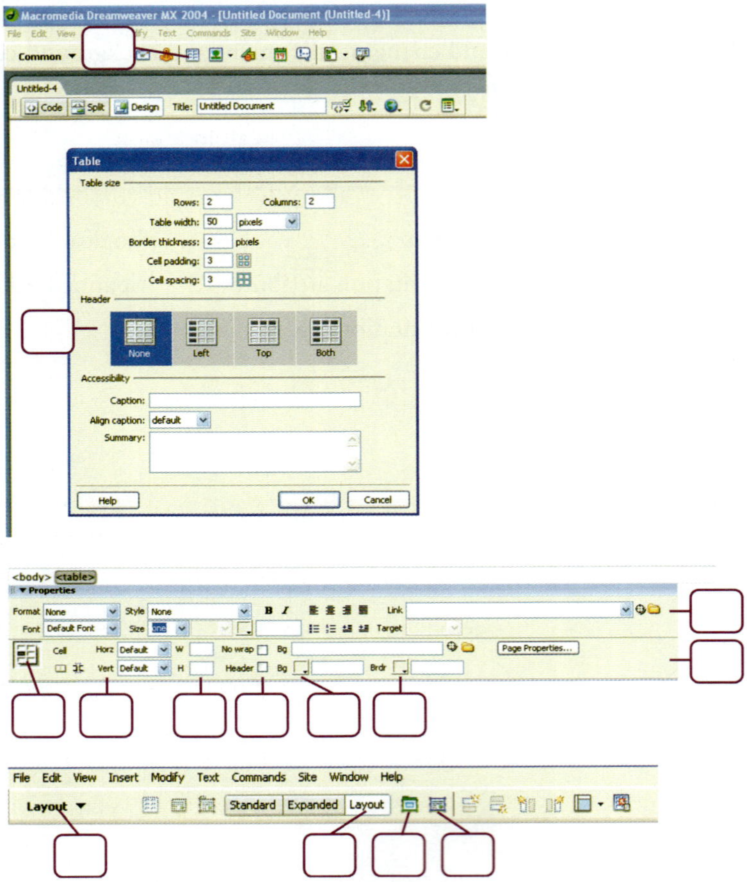


FIGURE 7.62

**a.** Table button
**b.** Text properties
**c.** Layout button
**d.** Layout Table button
**e.** Table dialog box
**f.** Cell icon
**g.** <table> tag
**h.** Draw Layout Cell button
**i.** Table properties
**j.** Horizontal/Vertical alignment
**k.** Border Color
**l.** Layout Insert bar indicator
**m.** Cell width/height
**n.** Cell background color box
**o.** Header cell check box

## MULTIPLE CHOICE

**Circle the letter of the correct answer for each of the following:**

**1.** Two tools you can use to create tables are the __________.

- **a.** Property inspector and Table dialog box
- **b.** Table dialog box and Tables panel
- **c.** Layout mode and Table dialog box
- **d.** All of the above

**2.** To use the free-form method of creating a table, you would use the __________.

- **a.** Table dialog box
- **b.** Layout mode
- **c.** Design mode
- **d.** Code view

**3.** Tables consist of __________.

- **a.** cells and borders
- **b.** columns and rows
- **c.** table data
- **d.** All of the above

**4.** The most popular use of a table in a Web page is __________.

- **a.** to generate frames
- **b.** to present tabular data
- **c.** to lay out components of a Web page
- **d.** to delimit text blocks

**5.** One problem with using tables is __________.

- **a.** they are not compatible with frames
- **b.** they require a large amount of HTML code
- **c.** tables must remain flush left in the Document window
- **d.** they must have a fixed size

**6.** Cell padding __________.

- **a.** is the same as cell spacing
- **b.** creates margin space in a cell
- **c.** creates a border around cells
- **d.** can be applied differently to each cell in a table

**7.** Which would you find in the Tag selector? __________.

- **a.** <table><body><tr><td>
- **b.** <table><row><th>
- **c.** <table><tr><td>
- **d.** <table><caption><tr><td>

**8.** Merging cells __________.

- **a.** uses the colspan and rowspan attributes
- **b.** combines adjacent cells
- **c.** allows tables to conform to design layout
- **d.** All of the above

**9.** Just like a Web page, cells of a table __________.

- **a.** can have a background color or image
- **b.** can display framesets
- **c.** must have a fixed size
- **d.** None of the above

**10.** The Format Table function __________.

- **a.** can merge and split table cells
- **b.** offers predefined table styles
- **c.** is used to create new tables
- **d.** is identical to the Table dialog box

## DISCUSSION QUESTIONS

1. Tables are the primary layout method for Web design. Both tables and frames offer methods for managing and displaying content in Web pages. What are the advantages of using tables over frames? What are the disadvantages? Provide an example of each and explain how it supports your argument.

2. You should consider accessibility before building a table. Explain why this statement is true and what types of considerations you must weigh before creating a table.

## SKILL DRILL

Skill Drill exercises reinforce project skills. Each skill reinforced is the same, or nearly the same, as a skill presented in the lessons. Detailed instructions are provided in a step-by-step format. You can work through one or more exercises in any order.

### 1. Import Tabular Data into a Table

In this Skill Drill, you import data from a Microsoft Excel file into Dreamweaver. (You don't need Excel to complete this Skill Drill — the text has already been exported.) Dreamweaver can import text files saved from Excel or Access in the Comma Separated Value (*.csv) format and convert them to data tables. This process is not automated — you can't just update the text file and expect Dreamweaver to import the data automatically. However, it is useful for inserting tabular information without having to retype it.

1. Create a new HTML file.
2. In the document Title field, type `Weather Forecast`.
3. In the Document window, type `Weather Forecast`, format it as Heading 1, and press Enter/Return.
4. Choose File>Import>Tabular Data.
5. From the Import Tabular Data dialog box, click the browse button and choose weather.csv from the Project_07>Tables folder.
6. Set the Delimiter to Comma, Width to Fit to Data, set the Cell Padding to 3, Cell Spacing to 0, Format Top Row to No Formatting, and Border to 0. Click OK.
7. Close the file, saving it as weather.html.

## 2. Make a Moderately Complex Table Accessible

In this Skill Drill, you modify an existing data table to make it accessible. It is much easier to make data accessible if you consider accessibility as you create the table and, conversely, more difficult and time-consuming to do so after creating the table. If accessibility is a requirement in your workplace, be sure to make it part of your original design specifications. In this exercise, you have information in an inaccessible table that requires the table-header cell tags with the **scope** attribute and a caption.

1. Open weather.html from the Tables site.
2. Add the **<caption>** tag and its contents by clicking the top-left cell of the table, clicking the Split button, moving the insertion point to the end of the opening **<table>** tag (to the right of the closing angle bracket), and pressing Enter/Return.
3. Type **<c** and press Enter/Return to accept **<caption>**. Type the closing angle bracket and then type **High Temperatures for the Week of May 16 to 20, 2004**.
4. In the Design window, choose the cells from 16 to 20 in the top row, and check the Header check box in the Property inspector. Select the cells from New York to Anchorage and make them header cells as well.
5. Click the 16 cell. In the Code window, click between **<th** and **>** in the opening **<th>** tag, press the Spacebar once, type **s**, press Enter/Return to accept **scope**, and type **col**.
6. Select the code you inserted (including the first space), copy the code, move the insertion point after **<th** in the opening **<th>** tag for the 17 cell, and paste. Paste the copied code into the opening **<th>** tags for the 18, 19, and 20 cells as well.
7. In the Design window, click the New York cell. In the Code window, insert **scope="row"** into the **<th>** tag for New York (don't forget the space before the **scope** attribute).
8. Copy the code you inserted in Step 7, click Los Angeles in the Design window, and paste the scope code into the **<th>** tag for the Los Angeles cell. Repeat the process for the Chicago, Houston, and Anchorage cells.
9. Close and save weather.html.

### 3. Create a Three-Column Layout Using Layout Tables

In this exercise, you create a multicolumn, table-based layout. Figure 8.63 illustrates the basic layout that you build in this exercise. In this Skill Drill, you use supplied styles. These styles assume that each cell in the layout table has specific ids, which you create.

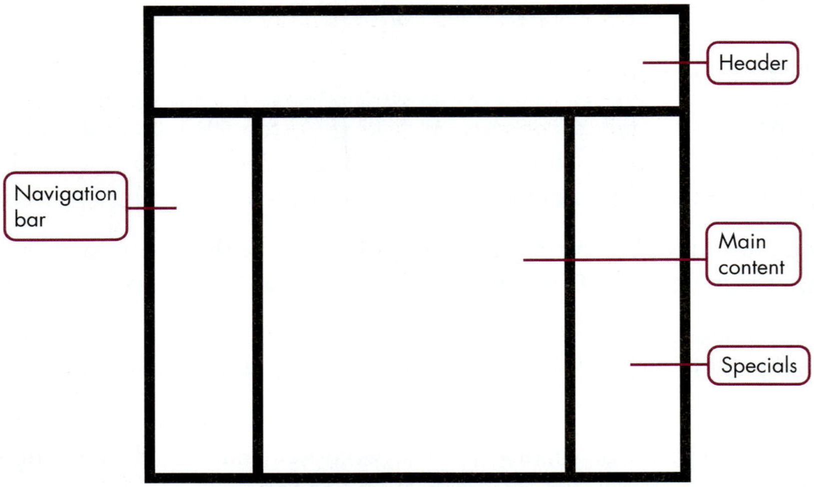


**FIGURE 7.63**

1. Create a new site definition called Carvers from the Project_07>Carver folder. Open index.html from the new Carvers site.
2. Click the Table button on the Common Insert bar and create a 2-row, 3-column table with a 100% width setting, 0-pixel border, 3-pixel cell padding, 0-pixel cell spacing, and no headers.
3. Drag to select the three cells in the top row, Right/Control-click the selected cells, and choose Table>Merge Cells.
4. From the images folder, insert carvers-logo.gif into the top row, and assign it Carver's Online as the alt text.
5. In the middle cell of the bottom row, type: **`Quality Products for Discriminating Customers`**, format the block as Heading 2, and press Enter/Return. From the images folder, insert the family.jpg photo into the new paragraph, and assign it an empty alt. Press Enter/Return again and type: **`Shop at Carver's Online`**.
6. Open leftnav.html, select all of the content (a table with graphics in each cell), copy the table, and close leftnav.html. In index.html, click the left cell of the bottom row and paste the copied table.
7. Using the same procedures as in Step 6, copy the table from specials.html into the right cell of this layout table.
8. Click the **`<table>`** tag to the immediate right of the **`<body>`** tag in the Tag selector. In the Property inspector, delete 100 from the Table Width field and press Enter/Return.

   This removes the table's width setting and allows the table to expand or contract based on its content.

9. Click the top cell and, from the Property inspector, set the cell's horizontal alignment to Center. Set the middle cell of the bottom row to centered-horizontal alignment and top-vertical alignment. Set both the left and right cells in the second row to top-vertical alignment.

10. To create the **id** for the first cell, click the top cell, Right/Control-click the **<td>** tag in the Tag selector, choose Set ID, and choose header from the list. Repeat this process to apply the correct ids to the other cells.

    Be careful with the specials cell. Apply the specials **id** to the **<td>** tag closest to the **<body>** tag — otherwise a cell in the nested table will be assigned that **id**, not the cell from the outer layout table.

11. Preview the page in your browser.

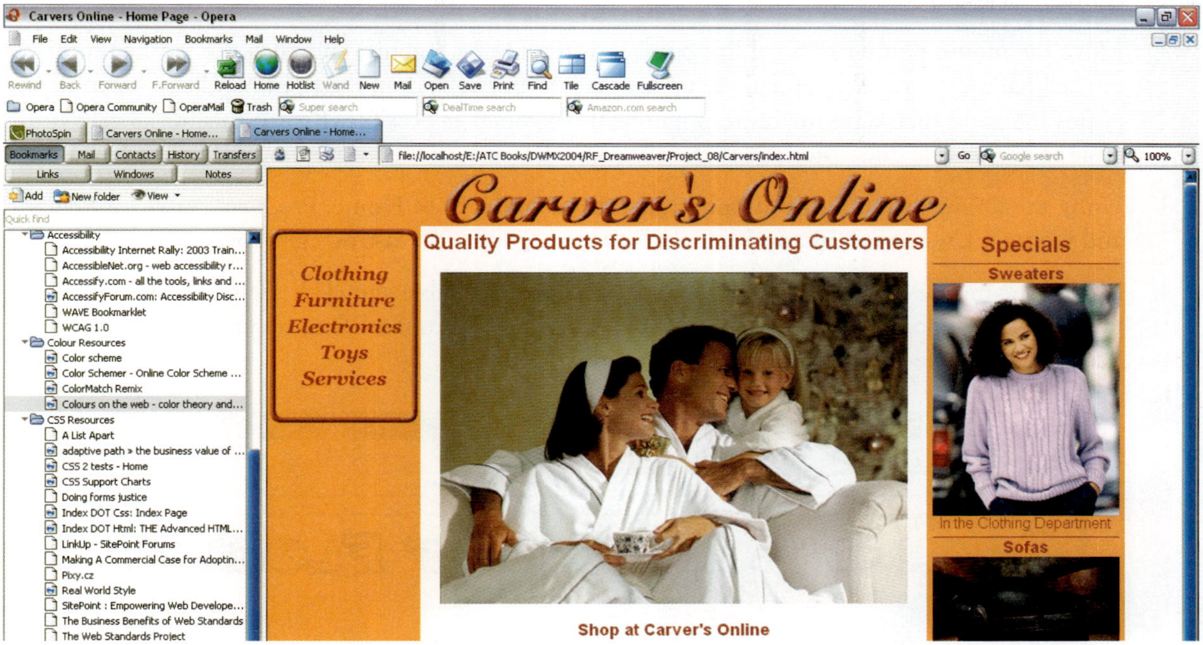


**FIGURE 7.64**

12. Close your browser, return to Dreamweaver, and close index.html.

## 4. Reassemble a Sliced Graphic in a Layout-Mode Table

In this Skill Drill exercise, you place slices of a design into a layout table using the Layout mode. This type of table would be very difficult to create using the Standard mode because the spanning would be difficult to calculate. This is an ideal situation in which to use the Layout mode to create the layout table.

1. Define a new site called Oranges from the Project_07>Oranges folder.

2. Create a new HTML page, type **Orange Growers of Florida** in the document Title field, and save the file as index.html.

3. Switch the Insert bar to the Layout Insert bar, click the Layout button, and draw a layout table about half the width and half the height of the Document window. Click the Draw Layout Cell

button, and in the top-left corner of this layout table, draw a cell that is about half the width and about one-third the height of the table.

4. From the Files panel, drag orange-gro.gif from the images folder into the empty cell.

5. Click the Draw Layout Cell button again, and draw a cell to the right of the inserted graphic but make it only about one-half the height of the other graphic. Insert wers-of-florida.gif into the new cell. Draw a cell below the last one, insert home.gif, and then click it.

6. Draw eight more layout cells — four in the left column and four in the right column. In the right cells, from top to bottom, insert products.gif, services.gif, regions.gif, and contact_us.gif. In the left cells, from top to bottom, insert left-products.gif, left-services.gif, left-regions.gif, and left-contact_us.gif.

7. Move the mouse pointer so a red line surrounds the Home graphic, and click the red line to display the cell handles. Drag the top handle up as much as possible, drag the right handle as far to the left as possible, and then drag the bottom handle up as much as possible. Repeat this for all cells in the table to reduce the dimensions of each cell to the dimensions of the graphics they contain.

8. Using the Draw Layout Cell button, create cells to the right of Home, Products, Services, Regions, and Contact Us, but not in any space that may exist below the last two graphics.

9. Move your mouse pointer to the bottom-right edge of the table and click the green line to make the table handles appear. Drag the bottom-right handle up and to the left to reduce the width and height of the table to the minimum.

**FIGURE 7.65**

10. Click the Standard button to switch to Standard mode. Close, saving the changes to index.html.

## 5. Nest a Table in a Table Cell

Tables expand in width if their content is wider than the table. If you create a 2-column table that is 400 pixels wide and insert a 300-pixel-wide graphic in each of the two columns, the table does not remain 400 pixels wide but expands to fit both graphics. It becomes a 600-pixel-wide table — wider if the settings for border thickness, cell padding, or cell spacing are greater than 0. However, text wraps, so a large amount of text in a 200-pixel-wide cell does not force the cell to be wider, just taller.

If you place a series of graphics side by side in a paragraph and if their total width is greater than the cell, one or more of the graphics is forced to a new line. However, if you place the graphics in their own cells in a table that is nested in the cell of another table, the outer table cell may be forced wider. Graphics can't be split and wrapped, nor can a table row. For this reason, many Web designers nest tables inside one another — the inner-table structure is rigid and forces the outer container to be wider if necessary.

In this exercise, you create a table nested in a cell of another table. You see why Web-site designers nest tables, despite the extra code that it creates.

1. Open index.html from the Carvers site and, if necessary, switch to Standard mode.
2. Click any of the cells in the bottom row, Right/Control-click, choose Tables>Insert Rows or Columns, and insert one row below the selection.
3. Click the middle cell of the new bottom row, Right/Control-click the **`<td>`** tag in the Tag selector, and set the **`id`** to **`footer`**.
4. Open bottomnav-paragraph.html from the Files panel.

   There are seven graphics in a row with no spaces between them — the five graphics with text and the two end graphics.
5. Select all of the content, copy it, and close bottomnav-paragraph.html. With the insertion point in the footer cell, paste the copied content.

   Some of the graphics split from the others because the cell is too narrow for them all to fit on one line.
6. Undo the insertion of the graphics.
7. With the insertion point in the footer cell, create a new table with 1 row, 7 columns, 100% table width, 0 border thickness, 0 cell padding, 0 cell spacing, and no headers, caption, or summary.
8. Insert bottomnav_r1_c1.gif into the first cell. Insert bottomnav_r1_c2.gif into the second cell. Continue to insert the graphics into the cells in order of the "c" number.

   As you near the end of the step, notice that the middle row becomes wider. Table rows cannot wrap or they would wrap to another row. Therefore, if a table row is wider than its container, the table forces the container to widen. In this case, the middle column is forced wider.
9. Close, saving the changes.

## 6. Align Tables for Layout

Aligning tables has two significant effects. The obvious effect is to place the table to the left, right, or center of its container. Of course, alignment only applies if the table is less than 100% of the width of the container.

The other effect is that you can place two or more tables beside each other, thereby creating another way to use tables for layout. The drawback to this method is that if the browser window is too narrow, the two tables do not stay beside each other — the right one shifts below the left one rather than remaining beside it. The advantage to this application of table alignment is that it can reduce the number of nested tables, thus the amount of code. Secondly, if each table is a separate entity, the browser can more quickly display the separate tables, rather than waiting for one large one with multiple nested tables. In this exercise, you create a layout using separate tables rather than an outer layout table containing nested tables.

1. Create a new site called GMMS-07 from the Project_07>GMMS-07 folder
2. Open index.html.
3. Create a 1 × 1 table that is 780 pixels wide, with 0 border width, 0 cell padding, and 0 cell spacing. From the images folder, insert gmms.png into the empty cell.
4. Click to the right of the table. Open navbar.html, select all, copy, and close the file. Paste to insert the table.

   Depending on its width, your browser window may be able to fit both the 780-pixel-wide logo table and the 140-pixel-wide navigation-bar table side by side. However, by default, the navigation-bar table always repositions below the logo-graphic table.

5. Open main.html. Click the small nested table with the university logos and map. Click the **`<table#map>`** tag to the right of the **`<body>`** tag in the Tag selector. In the Property inspector, set the table alignment to Right.

   The smaller nested table floats to the right; the text below it shifts up and flows to the left of the table.

6. Select and copy all of the content of the page. Close, saving the changes to this page.
7. In index.html, click to the right of the navigation-bar table and paste to insert the table from main.html.
8. Click the navigation-bar table, click the **`<table#navbar>`** tag in the Tag selector, and set the alignment to left.

   With the navigation-bar table aligned to the left, the main table can float up to its right.

9. Close, saving the changes.

## CHALLENGE

Challenge exercises expand on, or are somewhat related to, skills presented in the lessons. Each exercise provides a brief introduction, followed by instructions presented in a numbered-step format, that are not as detailed as those in the Skill Drill exercises. You should work through these exercises in order.

### 1. Create a Complex Accessible Table

Complex accessible tables have three or more logical levels of headers. The **`scope`** attribute does not suffice to relate a data cell to its header cells. You must use another pair of attributes: **`id`** and **`headers`**. You used the **`id`** attribute earlier with CSS. The ids do not have to be words but can be just brief or code-like; for instance, in a chart of months, you could put ja in place of january. However, the headers must match the ids.

When a screen reader speaks the headers of the selected data cell, it does not read the contents of the headers attributes. It matches the headers in the headers attributes with the ids of the header cells and speaks the contents of the table-header cells. In this Challenge exercise, you create an accessible browser-statistics chart. You explore some of the challenges of creating complex tables, which may cause you to redesign any that are supplied for sites on which you work. Dreamweaver does not provide any means of creating and matching ids and headers in the Design window. You must create it all in the Code window.

1. Open complex-data.html from the Tables site.

| | Internet Explorer | | Opera 7 | Mozilla | Netscape | | |
|---|---|---|---|---|---|---|---|
| | IE 6 | IE 5 | | | NN 3 | NN 4 | NN 7 |
| January | 71.3% | 12.8% | 2.1% | 8.2% | 0.4% | 0.5% | 1.5% |
| February | 71.5% | 11.5% | 2.2% | 9.0% | 0.4% | 0.4% | 1.5% |
| March | 72.1% | 10.7% | 2.1% | 9.6% | 0.4% | 0.4% | 1.4% |
| April | 72.4% | 10.4% | 2.1% | 10.1% | 0.3% | 0.3% | 1.4% |

**FIGURE 7.66**

2. Select the top two rows and make them header cells by clicking the Header check box in the Property inspector. Select the left column and make the cells header cells.
3. Click the Split button, then click the Internet Explorer cell in the Design window.
4. In the Code window, place the insertion point between the **`rowspan="2"`** and the **>**, press the Spacebar, and type **`id="ie"`**. Using the same basic technique, assign o7, moz, nn, ie6, ie5, nn3, nn4, and nn7 as the ids for the respective cells across the top. Assign j, f, m, and a as the ids of the month cells down the left.
5. Click the 71.3% cell in the Design window; in the Code window, place the insertion point between the **d** and **>**, press the Spacebar, and type **`headers="ie ie6 j"`** to relate the cell to Internet Explorer, IE6, and January. One by one, assign the **`headers`** attribute to all of the table-data cells, relating the data cell to the ids in the header cells above and to the left.
6. Close, saving the changes.

## 2. Minimize Reliance on Tables for Layout

There are current techniques that replace tables for layout, but not all browsers support these features. In Project 2, you learned the importance of planning your Web sites. If your plans target people who are likely to use current browsers, then you may employ the latest techniques and features in your designs. Other sites, however, attract users with a wider range of browser versions. Contrary to the chart of browser statistics in the previous exercise (which represents a current, high-technology Web site), the Ontario government Web sites, for example, find that 11–12% of their visitors use Netscape 4 browsers. You may have to modify some of your techniques so that your client does not lose customers or visitors who use older browsers.

In this Challenge exercise, you learn to apply a mixture of tables and CSS, including some commonly supported CSS properties. This mixture enables you to reduce the code and speed up delivery of your Web pages. (You also better prepare the site for later removal of all tables.) To do this, you eliminate all nested tables and replace them with structures that are lighter in code. You then recreate the appearance. In this exercise, you replace one nested table, but by further applying the same technique, you could eliminate all nested tables. The result here is similar to the look of the original nested table, but with a savings of 4,904 bytes.

1. Open index.html from the Carvers site.
2. Click the Clothing graphic in the left cell, click the **`<table>`** tag to the right of **`<td#navbar>`** in the Tag selector, and press Delete.
3. Click the Unordered List button in the Property inspector, and create a five-item list consisting of Clothing, Furniture, Electronics, Toys, and Services.
4. Right/Control-click in the CSS Styles panel and choose New. Choose the Selector Type of Advanced, type **`td#navbar ul`** in the Selector field, and click OK.
5. Choose the List category, set Type to None, and click Apply.
6. In the Box category in the Margin group, leave the Same for All option checked, type **`0`** (zero) in the Top field, and choose pixels. Click Apply.
7. In the Type category, choose Times New Roman, Times, serif from the Font list; x-large from the Size list; Bold from the Weight list; and Italic from the Style list. Set the Color to #993300. Click Apply.
8. In the Block category, set Text Align to Center and click Apply.
9. In the Background category, choose ul-bg.gif from the images folder and click Apply.
10. Return to the Box category. Set Width to 158 pixels and Height to 214 pixels. Remove the check from Same for All in the Padding Group, and set Top to 35 pixels. Click Apply.
11. Return to the Background category, set the Repeat option to no-repeat and click OK.
12. Close, saving the changes.

## 3. Use CSS for Table Styles

In Lesson 5, you learned to apply presentational HTML tags and attributes to create a style or look for the television-program table. In this Challenge exercise, you create the same appearance using CSS instead. Just as you saw in the previous Challenge exercise, using CSS results in a reduction in code, and thus in a faster downloading time. It also allows you to more effectively apply and control the look of the table and cells. Compared with the results of Lesson 5, this exercise results in an HTML page that is 54% smaller — 2,577 bytes vs. 5,616 bytes. Even with the CSS file of 598 bytes, the total (3,175 bytes) is still 43% less than the HTML page created in Lesson 5.

Another comparison between presentational HTML and CSS is the ease with which you can apply CSS. In Lesson 5, you learned that to change the text and background colors of all favorite cells, you must select them and then make the changes. If you missed one, it would not take on the color change. With CSS, the process is much easier: just assign a class to a cell and the CSS styles apply to them. Want to change the style? Just change it in the CSS Styles dialog box and the change applies to any instance in which the CSS class was applied.

1. Open tv-schedule.html from the Tables site.
2. Right/Control-click the CSS Styles panel and choose Attach Style Sheet. Click the Browser button, choose tv.css, click OK/Choose, and then click OK again.
3. Move the mouse pointer to the left of the top row until it changes to a right-pointing cursor and the cells in the row are outlined in red — click to select the row. In the Tag selector, Right/Control-click the **<tr>** tag and set the Class to top-row.
4. Click in the CTV cell, Right/Control-click the **<tr>** tag in the Tag selector, and set Class to row1. Repeat this for the TLC, WN, and ABC rows. Using the same procedure, apply the class **row2** to the CBC, TVO, and YTV **<tr>** tags.
5. Control/Command-click the Cable cell, Shift-click the ABC cell, Right/Control-click td.stations in the CSS Styles panel, and choose Apply from the contextual menu.
6. Control/Command-click the Vicki Gabereau cell, Shift-click the General Hospital cell (bottom-right corner), Right/Control-click td.programs in the CSS Styles panel, and choose Apply.
7. Control/Command-click the Road to Avonlea, Oswald, and Rupert cells; Right/Control-click td.favorites in the CSS Styles panel; and choose Apply.
8. Create a new CSS Style to change the background of the table to black by Right/Control-clicking in the CSS Styles panel, choosing New, setting the Selector Type to Tag, typing or choosing table in the Tag list, and clicking OK. In the Background category, set the background-color to black and click OK.
9. Right/Control-click td.favorite in the CSS Styles panel and choose Edit. In the Background category, set the background color to #CC4400. In the Type category, set the color to #FFFFFF. Click OK.
10. Close, saving the changes.

PORTFOLIO BUILDER

## Create a Gallery of Zoo Animals

A local zoo has hired your company to create a photo gallery of animal attractions. Your assignment is to create a table-based site that offers small thumbnail images of each animal with a link to a larger image. The larger, high-resolution images should open in their own windows, leaving the primary table-based page in tact.

1. Do some research on zoo sites to see how other designers approached the problem. Pick one that you like and use it as the basis for your design.
2. Create a page with a table, reserving cells for navigation elements and cells to hold the thumbnail images.
3. Split the page into three categories: one for primates, one for reptiles, and one for birds. Add or remove cells as necessary, and use nested tables where required.
4. Find images to use for populating the site. Since this is only an exercise and the site isn't destined for commercial use, you might consider right-clicking images you see on other sites and saving them into the folder containing the assignment pages.
5. Once it's completed, check to make sure everything works as intended.
6. Compare your design to the others you found during your research. Note what's good and bad about your site compared to the others.

PROJECT 8

# Collecting Information with Forms

## OBJECTIVES

*In this project, you learn how to*

- Insert a form
- Create different types of text fields
- Insert submit, reset, and other buttons
- Present choices via radio buttons and checkboxes
- Label form controls for usability and accessibility
- Create menus and lists
- Create groups of different but related controls
- Insert hidden fields

# WHY WOULD I DO THIS?

Forms are a very important part of the World Wide Web. They are used on many Web sites to gather information from Web-site visitors. For example, you could use a simple form to gather login information, such as username and password. Web-based email, such as Hotmail and Yahoo!, is an example of a more complex use of a form. Forms can serve a wide variety of uses, such as asking questions for online surveys and polls, sending messages through ***form mail*** forms (email composed and sent via a form on a Web site), querying search engines, setting preferences, posting comments on other people's Web sites, adding/deleting/editing content to database-driven Web sites, and writing content for blogs. (***Blogs*** are public online journals that are commonly used by the authors to discuss issues of interest to them. The term is a shortening of the phrase Web logs.)

Forms gather data that must be processed by a computer program (also known as a "Web application" or just "application"). These programs can be used to email the message to the recipient, display the results of the search query, process your purchase order, or post your article to your blog. In the past, these types of computer applications were called "CGI applications." (A ***CGI application***, or Common Gateway Interface program, is a program that processes information passed to it, typically through a Web form.) CGI commonly refers to applications written in Perl, C++, and other formal programming languages. (***Perl***, an acronym for Practical Extraction and Reporting Language, is a powerful, free, open-source programming language especially designed for processing text. Perl files commonly use the extension .pl or .cgi. ***C++*** is a high-level programming language commonly used to develop Windows, Macintosh, and Linux/Unix applications.) However, more recently, form data processing is performed using ASP, PHP, and other more current Web programming languages.

Forms collect information using a variety of ***form controls*** (functions or features of forms that enable the forms developer to control the type of data, amount of data, and format of data collected by the form). The most common form control is a text field in which users can type text, such as a text field for their first name. Other form controls include checkboxes from which they can make multiple choices (like the toppings they would like on a hamburger), radio buttons that restrict them to selecting just one of the options presented (like the size of drink they want), and text areas that allow for large amounts of text (like the entire content of an email message).

It is important to know how to create and use forms and form controls. Whether or not you create the application that processes the collected data, you should understand how to create a form, know the differences between the form controls, and understand the options available in forms and form controls. In some cases, you may need to consult with the Web developer to determine how the data is to be handled, and you may need to consult with a specialist in surveys or data gathering to ensure the right questions are asked and asked properly.

# VISUAL SUMMARY

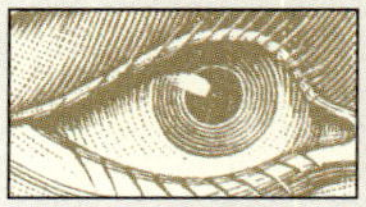

You use the buttons on the Forms Insert bar to create forms and insert the appropriate labels and form controls. If the Forms Insert bar is not visible, you click the menu button at the left of the Insert bar and select Forms to switch to the Forms Insert bar.

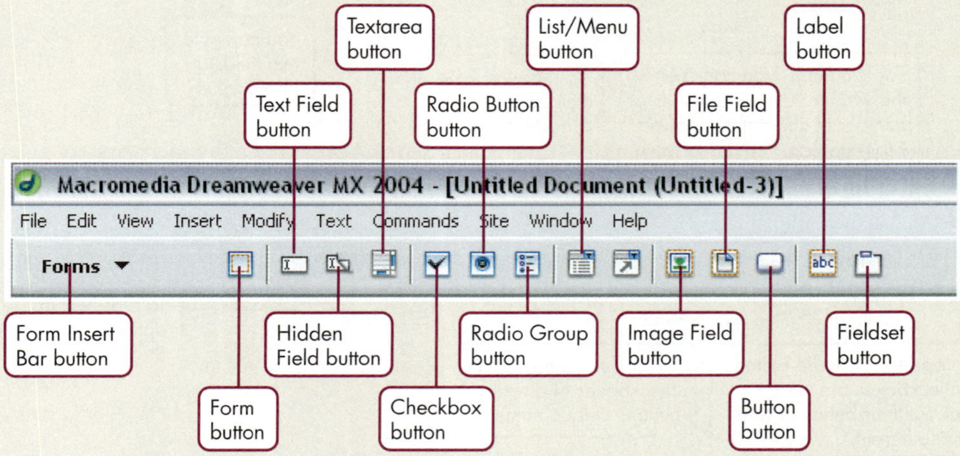


FIGURE 8.1

As with many other functions in Dreamweaver, you modify the properties of the HTML tag using the Property inspector. Forms elements are no different. After inserting a form element, you assign it a name and any other properties that are appropriate for the form or the form control.

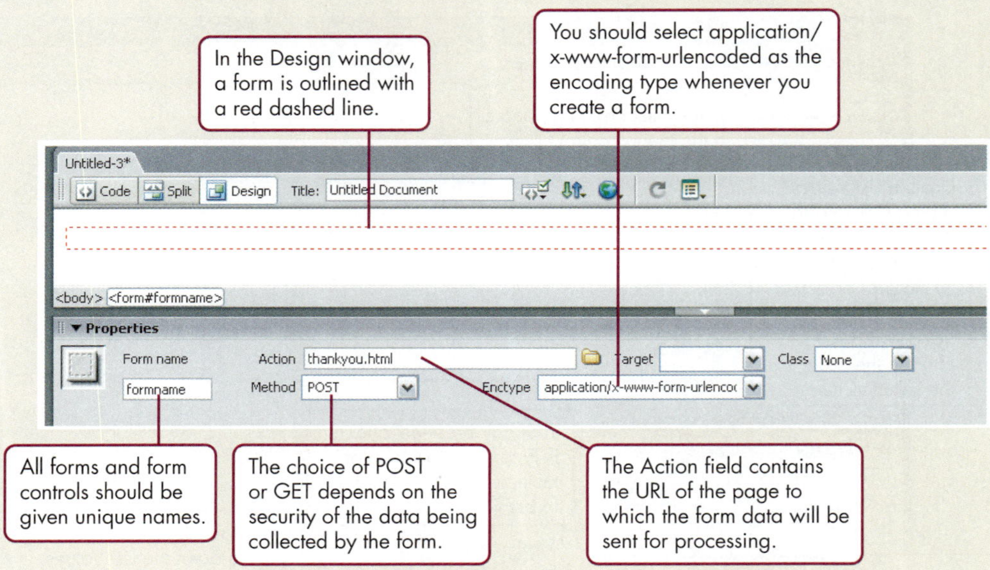


FIGURE 8.2

Text fields may be single-line or multiline text fields. Multiline text fields are called "textareas." Although you can activate text fields and textareas using different buttons on the Forms Insert bar, you can also use the Property inspector for this purpose and can use it additionally to switch between the two types of text fields. Password fields are similar to single-line text fields except that the text in the field is hidden.

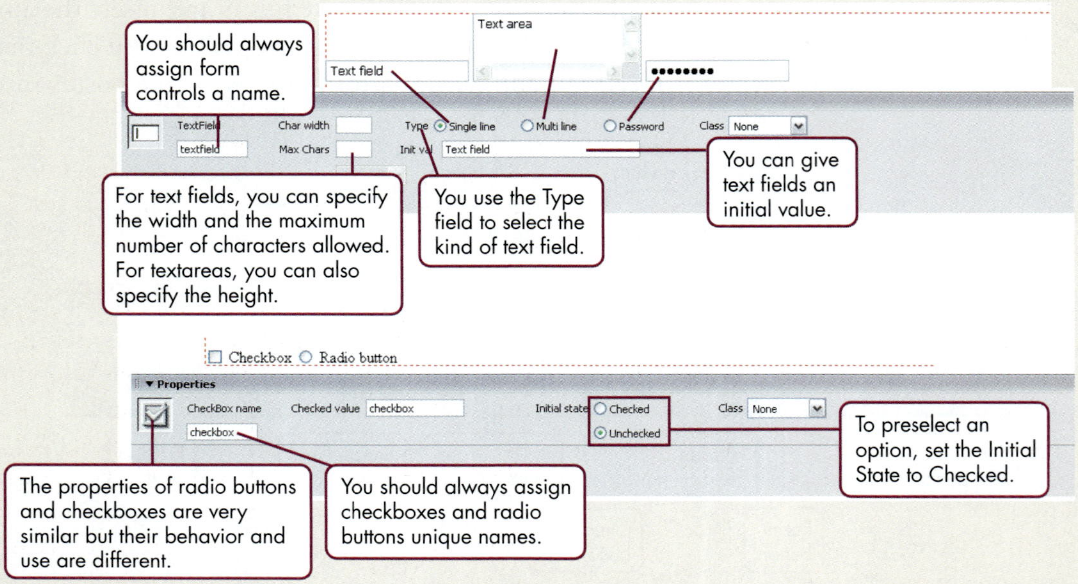


FIGURE 8.3

Menus are also form controls and are commonly used to enable a user to select a single option. Lists, which are similar to menus, allow users to make multiple selections. In addition to applying the list/menu properties in the Property inspector, you populate the list/menu with its values using a dialog box.

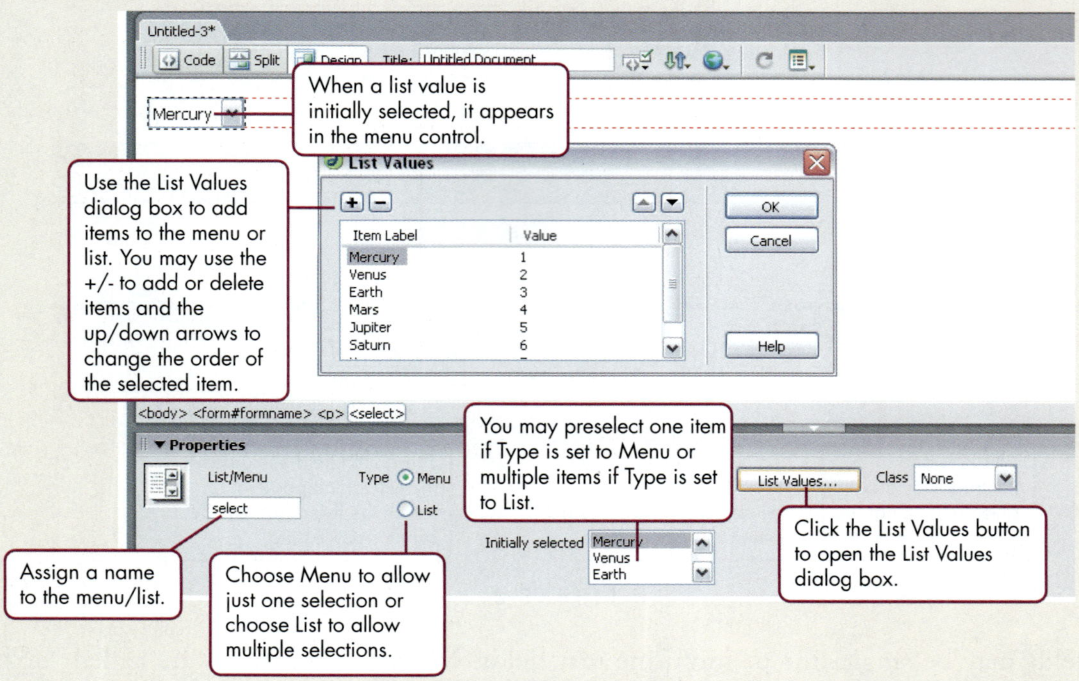


FIGURE 8.4

# LESSON 1 Creating Properties of Forms

Web forms are contained by opening and closing **<form>** tags. There are three primary options required for forms: the name of the form, the method of transmitting the data, and the encoding method for the data.

The name of the form is required for the processing application. If there is only one form on a page, the name of the form is not critical. If, however, there are multiple forms on a page or if the form is part of a series of forms for either a survey or an ***e-commerce*** (electronic commerce) site, it is important that the individual forms in the series have unique ids. (Electronic commerce can be between two businesses transmitting funds, goods, services, and/or data, or between a business and a customer.)

The **action** attribute specifies the URL of the form-processing application, such as **action="contact_me.php"**. You can use either a relative or an absolute path to the processing application. Some basic form-processing software can be ***remotely hosted*** (existing on another Web server), in which case, you would need to add **http://www.remote-host.com/** to the absolute path of the action URL. On some Web sites, you see the action URL with a cgi-bin folder, such as **action="/cgi-bin/formmail.pl"**. The cgi-bin folder is commonly below the root folder of the Web site for security reasons to prevent unauthorized access or use of any applications that may exist in the folder. The mailto: URL, such as **action="mailto:customer@domain.com"**, is a valid action URL but is rarely used and poorly supported by browsers. Its use occasionally opens a visitor's email software, which can be confusing.

The **method** attribute has two options, **post** and **get**. Search engines commonly use the get method — the data from the form are displayed in the URL sent to the search engine. For example, when searching Google.com for php editor, the get URL is http://www.google.com/search?q=php+editor&sourceid=firefox&start=0&start=0&ie=utf-8&oe=utf-8. The processing application then takes the ***query string*** (the portion of the action URL after the ?), processes it, and displays the results. It is just as easy to copy this URL from the browser's address bar as it is to bookmark the URL should you wish to return to a specific search later. The get option limits the number of characters that may be sent: a blog or news entry sent via the get method may exceed the character limit (which varies with operating system, Web-server software, and the processing application). The get option also may pose a security risk if sensitive information is revealed, such as credit card information. Furthermore, an unscrupulous user may create problems for the processing application by modifying a get URL, replacing part of it with other information. On the other hand, when you develop a form-processing application, you may want to use the get option to watch how the information is being sent so that you can adjust your programming code accordingly.

The post method does not display the query string but the data is formatted identically. The post method does not limit the amount of data sent and is more suitable for larger amounts of data. Furthermore, because the form data is not exposed in the URL, it is more secure and may also be ***encrypted*** (translated into a secret code) using the ***HTTPS protocol*** (also written as S-HTTP, a protocol for securely transmitting data between a browser and a server) that is used by e-commerce applications.

The **enctype** attribute specifies the type of data being transmitted. The **application/x-www-form-urlencoded** option transmits text. Using this option, spaces between words are replaced with **+** and certain reserved characters are replaced with hexadecimal codes for the characters. Line breaks are replaced with **%0D%0A**. The other option, **multipart/form-data**, is reserved for use when files are being ***transmitted*** (uploaded) via the form: the **method** attribute must be set to **post** when a file is being uploaded.

## Create and Set the Form Properties

In this exercise, you prepare a basic form — the login form for returning customers. You learn to set up the form options using the Forms Insert bar and the Property inspector.

**1** **Define the Project_08>Forms folder as a site called `Forms`.**

**2** **Open login.html and click in the empty cell between the header and footer cells.**

**3** **Type `Login to Place Your Order` and format it as Heading 2.**

**4** **Switch the Insert bar to Forms.**

FIGURE 8.5

**5** **Click the first button on the left of the Forms Insert bar.**

**6** **In the Property inspector, type `login` in the Form Name field, type `confirm-login.html` in the Action field, set the Method to `Get`, and set Enctype to `application/x-www-form-urlencoded`.**

FIGURE 8.6

**7** **Save the changes but leave the file open for the next exercise.**

## To Extend Your Knowledge

### FREE FORM-PROCESSING APPLICATIONS

Many of the common form-processing applications are available for free. HotScripts.com is an example of an archive that offers many programs for processing form mail. If you need to perform client-side form validation, you would search in the client-side languages, such as JavaScript or VBScript (supported only by Internet Explorer). If you need to perform server-side processing of form data and your needs are common (such as form mail), search in the languages you know your server supports, such as PHP, ASP, ASP.Net, or Perl. Generally, these programs are well documented: they come with instructions on how to install and configure them for your specific needs. Why go to the trouble of trying to learn a programming language when you can just download one and use it for free?

Not all scripts on HotScripts.com and other scripts archives are free: some are feature-limited trial versions; others are commercial; some are free for personal but not commercial use; and some are free, but to remove the script-author's Web-site link or logo, you must pay for the script. You must purchase complex or unique scripts either by downloading and paying for the script or by hiring a developer to create a script for your Web site.

# LESSON 2 Creating Short-Text, Long-Text, and Password Form Controls

One of the most commonly used form controls is the text field. Most form controls use the **<input>** tag, which employs the **type** attribute to specify the type of input. For text fields, for example, you set **type** to text, such as **type="text"**. The **size** attribute specifies the width of the text field in characters; in Dreamweaver, this field is named the Char Width field. In Dreamweaver, the default width is approximately 24 characters, but if you don't specify a width, browsers use their own default widths for the text field. The **maxlength** attribute (the Max Chars field in Dreamweaver) specifies the number of characters allowed in the text field. If you don't specify a default number, the number of characters allowed is virtually unlimited, but the width of the field makes it difficult to use. If the size of the field is smaller than the maxlength, the field contents scroll to allow the user to enter as much text as the maxlength allows. However, if the size is larger than maxlength, white space appears to the right of the contents of the field.

All form controls require a name. Although generally the **name** attribute is deprecated in XHTML 1.0 and replaced by the **id** attribute, in the case of form controls, the **name** attribute is not deprecated. The form-processing application matches the submitted data to the applicable field using the **name** attribute. Regardless of whether the get or post method is selected for the **<form>** tag, the form-control name and its value are paired in the submitted data as name=value, such as **firstname=Thomas&lastname=Denon**. The **id** attribute can also be applied to the form controls for either CSS or JavaScript. Dreamweaver, however, does not provide an id option in the Property inspector for text fields, just a class option that may also be used by CSS and JavaScript.

The Property inspector also provides an Init Value field, which is equivalent to the **value** attribute in HTML. Any text you type into the Init Value field displays in the field. You may use this option to suggest to users what they may enter into the field or in what format. For example, you could set the initial value of a comments field to **Type your comments here**, or in a telephone field, you could set the initial value to **(555) 555-5555** to suggest the expected format. There is a useful JavaScript function that you can employ when using an initial value — as soon as the user types in the field, the initial value is erased, leaving only what the user types.

## Create a Single-Line Text Field

In this exercise, you use two Dreamweaver options for the Text field: the Single Line option and the Password option. The Single Line option sets the **type** attribute of the **<input>** tag as **type="text"** and the Password option sets the **type** attribute as **type="password"**. The Multi Line option creates a different type of form control using a different HTML tag, the **<textarea>** tag, which you use in a later exercise.

1. **In the open login.html page, click inside the form area, type `Customer Number:`, and press the Spacebar.**

2. **From the Forms Insert bar, click the Text Field button.**

3. **In the Property inspector, select Single Line from the Type options, type `customerNo` in the TextField Name field, type `15` in the Char Width field, type `8` in the Max Chars field, type `123-4567` in the Init Value field, and press Enter/Return.**

FIGURE 8.7

4. **Click to the right of the text field in the Document window, and press Enter/Return.**

5. **Type `Password:` then press the Spacebar.**

6. **Click the Text Field button in the Forms Insert bar.**

7. **Set the TextField name to `password`, the Char Width to `10`, Max Chars to `6`, and Type to Password; type `abcdef` in the Init Val field; and press Enter/Return.**

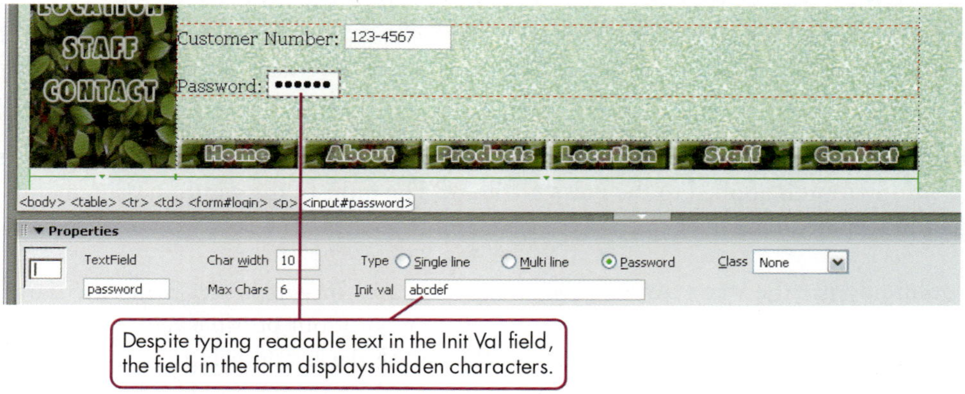


FIGURE 8.8

8. **Delete the text in the Init Val field and press Enter/Return to apply the change.**

9. **Close login.html, saving your changes.**

## To Extend Your Knowledge

### SETTING DIMENSIONS USING CSS

You may wonder why the text, password, and other form controls use characters as the measurement for width. This measurement is a throwback to early Web browsers that used a monospaced font like Courier as the common font. With the width set to a specific number of characters, users could see exactly how much space they were allowed for that particular field. Most current browsers use proportionally spaced fonts, in which iii is narrower than MMM although both are three characters. However, you may use CSS to specify the width of form controls, such as in pixels, ***ems*** (the width of the letter M), or percentage of the container width. If you want to specify different widths for different form controls, you must apply unique ids to each control so that you may specify the width for just that control. If you want several controls to be the same width, you can apply the same CSS class to each and then they may all use the same width.

# LESSON 3 Working with Multiline Text Areas

Unlike many of the form controls, the multiline text area does not use the **<input>** tag but, instead, uses the **<textarea>** tag. Dreamweaver puts both single-line and multiline form controls in the same Property inspector panel, despite the difference in tags. However, the **<textarea>** tag is a container tag requiring the closing **</textarea>** tag. Just like the single-line text control, **<textarea>** can be set with an initial value which is recorded in the Init Val (initial value) field in the Property inspector. The initial value, however, is written between the opening and closing **<textarea>** tags, such as, **<textarea>I would like to hear from you.</textarea>**, unlike any of the **<input>** form controls, which use the value attribute (which does not exist for this tag).

You set the width of the text area with the Char Width field in the Property inspector; this information is applied to the **cols** attribute. You set the height of the text area with the Num Lines field of the Property inspector; this information is applied to the **rows** attribute. The units of the width measurement are characters and the units of height are lines.

Developers commonly use the **<textarea>** tag to create an area in which users can enter large amounts of text. Dreamweaver's Property inspector offers the Wrap option with four possible values: Default, Off, Virtual, and Physical. However, the wrap attribute of the **<textarea>** tag is confusing for many reasons — it was never part of any HTML standard; some sources use Soft in place of Virtual and Hard in place of Physical; and current browsers treat Soft, Hard, Virtual, and Physical identically. Given the potential confusion and lack of validity, we recommend that you leave the setting at Default.

## Create a Multiline Text Area

In this exercise, you create a basic form to which you add a text area.

1. **Open comments.html from the Forms site.**

2. **Click to the right of Comments (smaller black text) and press Enter/Return.**

3. **Click the Text Field button on the Forms Insert bar.**

4. **In the Property inspector, select Multi Line from the Type group of options.**

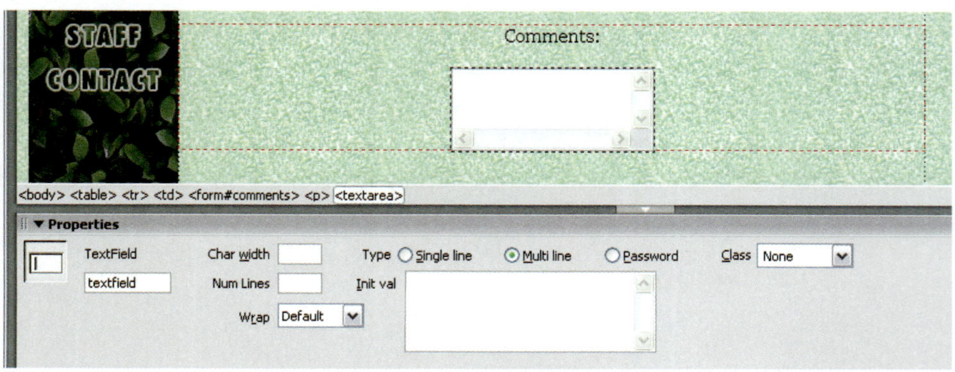


FIGURE 8.9

**5** **Press Control/Command-Z (Undo) twice, and then click the Textarea button on the Forms Insert bar.**

Notice that the result is the same: the Textarea button simply preselects the Multi Line option.

**6** **Type `comments` in the Textarea Name field, set Char Width to `35`, set Num Lines to `8`, in the Init Val field, type `Type your comment here.`, and press Tab.**

**Don't press Enter/Return while the insertion point is in the Init Val field or you create a new line in the field.**

FIGURE 8.10

**7** **Close comments.html, saving your changes.**

## To Extend Your Knowledge

### FORM CONTROLS OUTSIDE THE WWW

Form controls were not first brought into being when HTML was created but existed long before. Examine any computer application on your computer and you will recognize many of these controls in Web pages. Menus, radio buttons, checkboxes, labels, single-line and multiline text fields, and password fields — all existed in computer applications before Sir Tim Berners-Lee wrote one character of HTML. If you are having trouble figuring out which controls to place in a Web form, try to think of an example in a computer application and use that as your inspiration.

# LESSON 4 Using Submit, Reset, Image, and Other Buttons

The purpose of the submit button is to send data from the completed form to the processing application. The reset button resets the values of fields to their initial values. As with text and password form controls, you create buttons using the **<input>** tag with different types: for a submit button, **type="submit"**, and for a reset button, **type="reset"**. These types have special meaning to the browser, which submits or resets the data depending on which button the user clicks.

Two other attributes to use with these two buttons are the **name** and **value** attributes. When you select submit or reset from the Property inspector in Dreamweaver, the **name** attribute, by default, is set to that option. However, if the purpose of your form is to enable users to edit or delete items in their shopping carts, you might make the names of the buttons edit and delete and then you must program the form-processing application to pick up the name of the button selected and process the data appropriately.

You can use the **value** attribute to replace the text on the button. In Dreamweaver, you use the Label field in the Property inspector to enter the value-attribute content. For example, rather than Submit on a contact form, you might want to use Send Me Your Comments, and in place of Reset, you might want to use Clear the Form. The **value** attribute does not change the submit and reset buttons' functions — the **type** attribute specifies these buttons' functions to the browser.

If you want to provide edit and delete buttons on the form so users can edit their addresses when they move or delete items from their shopping carts, in both cases you must set the **type** attribute to **submit**, because these actions must be provided by the form-processing application. The names could be edit and delete and the values could be Edit This Address and Remove This Item. Therefore, if you want to provide a function that requires the form-processing application to act, you set the **type** to **submit** despite the name or value you assign to that button.

Dreamweaver also provides a None option which creates a generic button. You may assign it a name and value, but unlike the submit type, clicking it does not submit the form data to the action URL, nor does the browser perform a client-side action to the data as it does with the reset type. The purpose of the None type (in HTML, it is coded as **type="button"**) is to allow a Web developer to assign a JavaScript function to the button, which when clicked, triggers that JavaScript function.

The button labeled Image Field on the Forms Insert bar inserts an image form control. This form control also uses the **<input>** tag with the **type** attribute set to **image**. An image field behaves like a submit button and, commonly, an image field is simply graphic text, such as Place Your Order. Like all images, you should assign alternative text. Given that most image field buttons replace a plain submit button, the alternative text should be the same as the text that appears in the graphic. However, it is possible to use the image of a product as an image field that submits the customer's intention to purchase that product. A Web page with many product images could therefore enable customers to submit order requests using any of the product-image image fields.

In this exercise, you add both submit and reset buttons to your form. You preview the form in your browser, test the functionality of the buttons, and examine the query string sent to the action URL.

## Add Submit and Reset Buttons

**1** **Open login.html, click to the right of the password field, and press Enter/Return.**

**2** **Click the Button button (third from the right end of the Forms Insert bar).**

By default, Dreamweaver creates a submit button.

**3** **Click to the right of the Submit button and insert another button.**

**4** **In the Property inspector, change the Label field to `Clear this form` and press Enter/Return. Change the Action to Reset form**

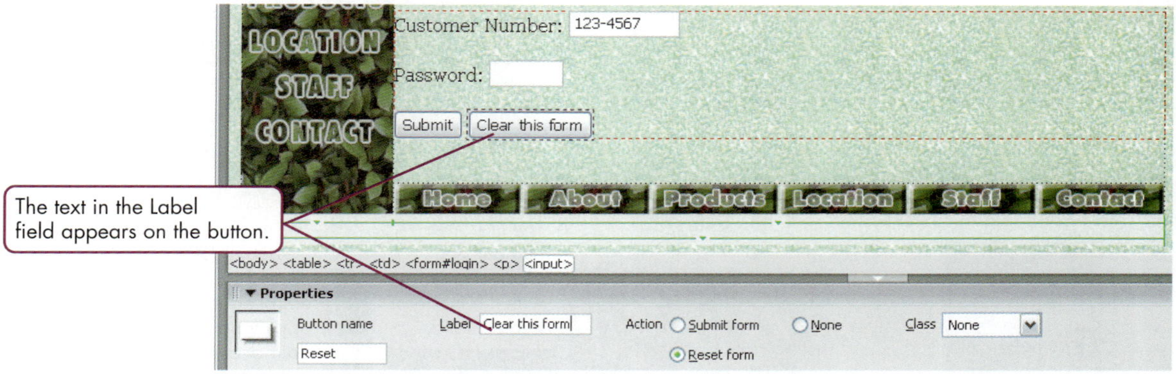


**FIGURE 8.11**

**5** **Save the changes and preview this page in your browser.**

**6** **Delete the Customer Number initial value, and type as much text as you can.**

The Max Chars property (maxlength attribute) prevents you from entering more than eight characters.

**7** **Enter some text in the Password field.**

**FIGURE 8.12**

**8** **Click the Clear This Form button.**

Both (all) fields are reset to their initial values.

**9** **Again insert a fictitious customer number and password in the form and click the Submit button.**

This time, the confirm-login.html page opens in your browser because your browser has directed you to the action URL.

**10** **Click in the address bar of your browser, and press the End key to view the end of the URL.**

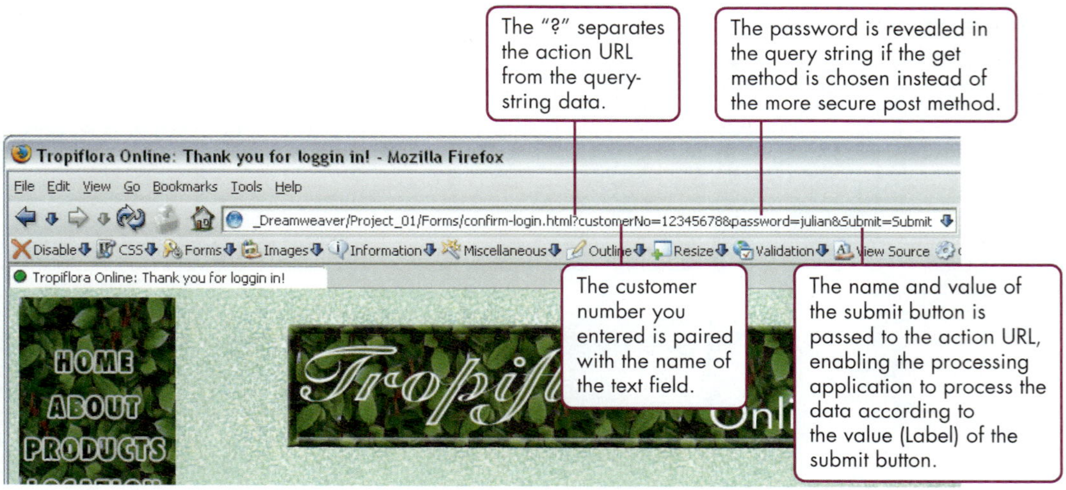


FIGURE 8.13

**11** **Close your browser, return to Dreamweaver, and close login-html.**

## To Extend Your Knowledge

### THE VALUE OF THE RESET BUTTON

Jakob Nielsen of Useit.com, a Web-site usability specialist, questions the value of the reset button (useit.com/alertbox/20000416.html). He is not saying that the reset button does not do what it is supposed to do, but rather that users who don't want to complete the form, rather than resetting it, usually click a link or type a URL and move to another page. While a generalization, this does raise the question of the value of the reset button in some forms. For example, basic contact forms found on many Web sites may not need a reset button. Visitors who change their mind about submitting a message are likely to just move on. Armed with this knowledge, you may want to rethink whether or not you need a reset button on every form.

Remember also that you may want to provide a button that clears data from a database, such as Clear This Order. While it may seem similar in function to a reset button, the Clear This Order button may actually provide an action that should be processed by the form-processing application. For that reason, you should avoid button labels that could be confused with the functionality of the reset button.

# LESSON 5 Creating Radio Button Form Controls

The radio-button form control is designed to provide users with mutually exclusive options, such as male or female. It is possible, however, to improperly create radio buttons so that they are not exclusive, for example, select three of your favorite sports. Because historically radio buttons have always been used to allow users to select just one option from a group, breaking this pattern risks alienating your visitors. A similar option, the checkbox, is meant to provide multiple options, any or all of which may be selected. Just as with the text, password, and button form controls, you create radio buttons using the **<input>** tag using the **type** attribute to identify the form control — **type="radio"**.

Radio buttons are commonly designed to work in a group, presenting options or answers to a common question. The individual radio buttons are related to each other through a common **name** attribute. For example, **name="gender"** would be common to both male and female radio buttons, and **value="male"** and **value="female"** would distinguish the two. By having a common **name** attribute, only one option from a group of radio buttons may be selected. However, if the **name** attribute for the female option were set to gender and the **name** attribute for the male option were set to sex, the two options would not be related, making it possible to select both male and female which, of course, is not possible.

Submit and reset buttons are unique in that whatever you apply to the **value** attribute appears in the button. (For buttons, this option is called the "Label field" in the Property inspector.) However, to identify the contents or purpose of the text, password, and radio button controls, the values of these **<input>** tags are not displayed in the Document window or in your browser: you must add additional text beside these controls to label them.

The **value** attribute of the text and password controls (applied using the Init Val field in the Property inspector) inserts initial or default text in the field. The radio button also has an Initial State option in the Property inspector, offering Checked and Unchecked options. Selecting the Checked option inserts the **checked** attribute in the **<input>** tag. The **checked** attribute is an unusual attribute in that there are no attribute values. If Checked is selected for the example of gender above, the **<input>** tag is written as **<input type="radio" name="gender" value="female" checked>**. Although HTML 4.01 and earlier versions allowed empty attribute values such as **checked**, in XHTML, all attributes must have attribute values: checked must be entered as **checked="checked"**. If a radio button is not to be checked, then the checked attribute is not included in the **<input>** tag at all.

Dreamweaver provides two methods of creating radio buttons: individually or in a group. In this lesson you learn both methods. Although using the radio group method is easier, there will be times when you may need to add more buttons after you have created a group. You also learn why you must use a common **name** attribute for all radio-button options.

## Create Individual Radio Buttons

1. **Open registration.html.**

2. **Click to the right of the Full Name text field and press Enter/Return. Type `Gender:` and press the Spacebar.**

**3** **From the Forms Insert bar, select the Radio Button button.**

FIGURE 8.14

**4** **In the Property inspector, type `gender` in the Radio Button name field, type `male` in the Checked Value field and leave the rest of the options at their defaults.**

FIGURE 8.15

**5** **Click to the right of the radio button, type `Male`, and press the Spacebar.**

**6** **Insert another radio button but type `sex` in the Radio Button name field and `female` in the Checked Value field. Click to the right of the radio button in the Document window and type `Female`.**

**7** **Preview the page in your browser and select both Male and Female.**

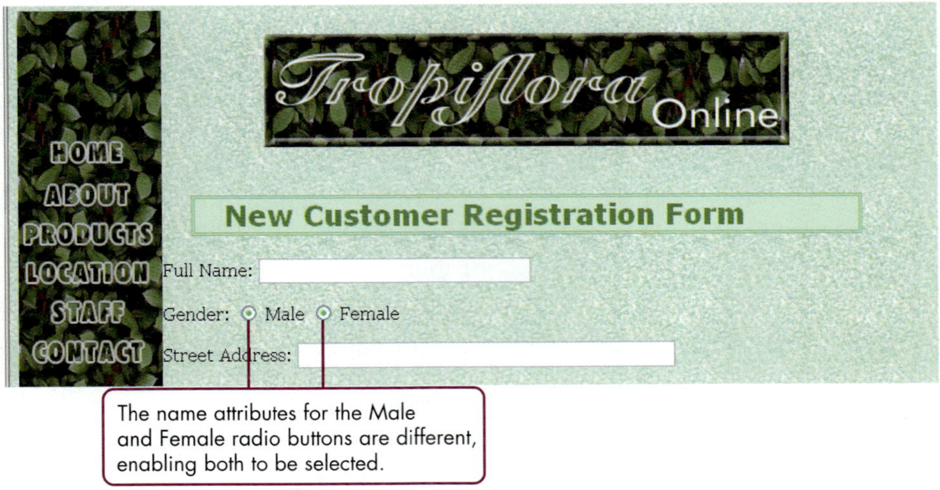


FIGURE 8.16

**8** **Return to Dreamweaver without closing your browser, change the name attribute of the Female radio button to `gender`, and preview and test the page in your browser again.**

Now that both male and female radio buttons share the same name attribute, only one of the two may be selected.

**9** **Return to Dreamweaver, leaving the file open for the next exercise.**

## Create Multiple Radio Buttons

In this exercise, you learn to create a group of radio buttons using the Radio Group button from the Forms Insert bar. This function has a few beneficial features: it creates proper labels for the radio buttons, it applies the same name attribute for all radio buttons in the group, and it gives you the option of formatting the radio buttons with line breaks or table cells.

1. **Click to the right of the Street Address text field and press Enter/Return.**

2. **Type `Dwelling Type:` and press the Spacebar.**

3. **Click the Radio Group button in the Forms Insert bar.**

4. **In the Radio Group dialog box, type `dwelling` in the Name field. Under Label, click Radio and type `Apartment`. Press Tab and type `apt` in the Value column and press Tab. Type `Row House` and press Tab. Type `rhouse`.**

5. **Click the plus symbol (+) above Label to create a new row. Type `Individual House` and press Tab. Type `ihouse`.**

6. **Leave the Lay Out Using option set to Line Breaks and click OK.**

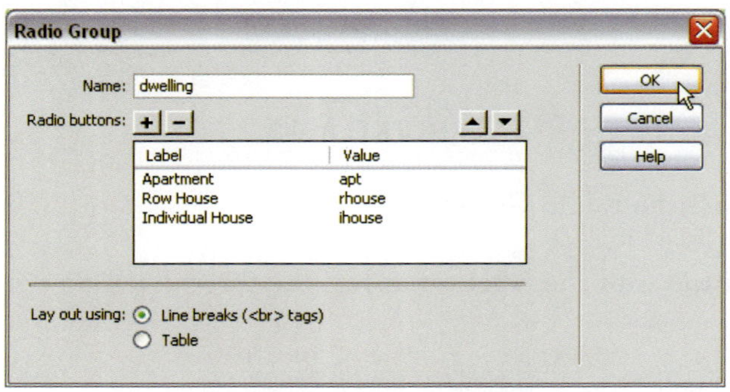


**FIGURE 8.17**

7. **To remove the line breaks, move the insertion point to the Apartment line, press the End key and then press Delete. Press End and then Delete twice more to bring all of the radio buttons onto the same line.**

8. **Preview the page in your browser and test the radio buttons.**

   The Radio Group dialog box assigns the same name attribute to all radio buttons, ensuring that only one of the options can be selected.

9. **Return to Dreamweaver, leaving registration.html open for the next exercise.**

## Add Another Radio Button to the Group

In this exercise, the option Condominium was forgotten and must be added to the group of radio buttons of dwelling types. You learn that the Radio Group dialog box is useful for creating a group of radio buttons but does not allow you to edit or add to the group. Instead, you must use the previously learned technique to add more radio buttons to a group.

**1** **In registration.html, click anywhere in the group of radio buttons of dwelling types.**

**2** **Click the Radio Group button from the Forms Insert bar.**

Notice that the settings are the same as the original default settings. This function does not pick up on the settings of the radio buttons in which the insertion point is positioned. This dialog box is only useful for creating a new group of radio buttons.

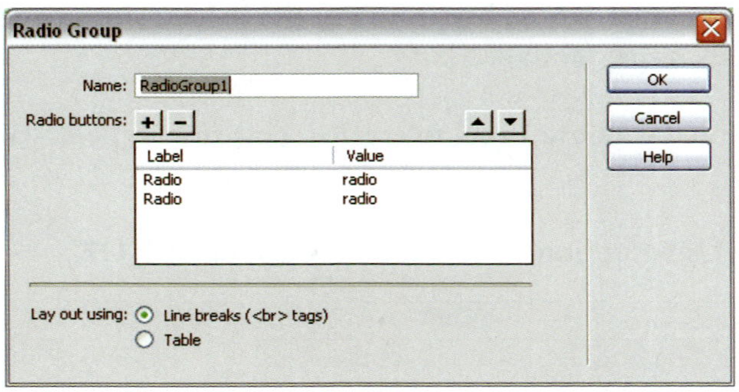


FIGURE 8.18

**3** **Click Cancel to close the Radio Group dialog box.**

**4** **Click the radio button (not the label) of any of the three dwelling options and note the Radio Button name.**

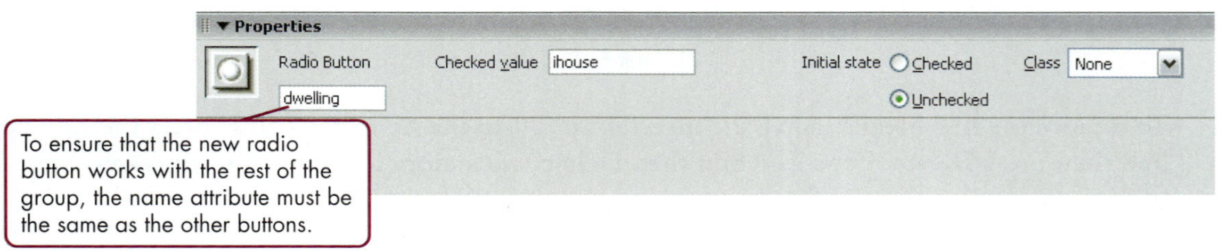


FIGURE 8.19

**5** **Click to the right of Individual House.**

**6** **Insert a new radio button (not a group, just an individual button). In the Property inspector, assign it the Radio Button name `dwelling` and the Checked Value `condo`.**

FIGURE 8.20

**7** **Click to the right of the newly created radio button in the Document window and type `Condominium`.**

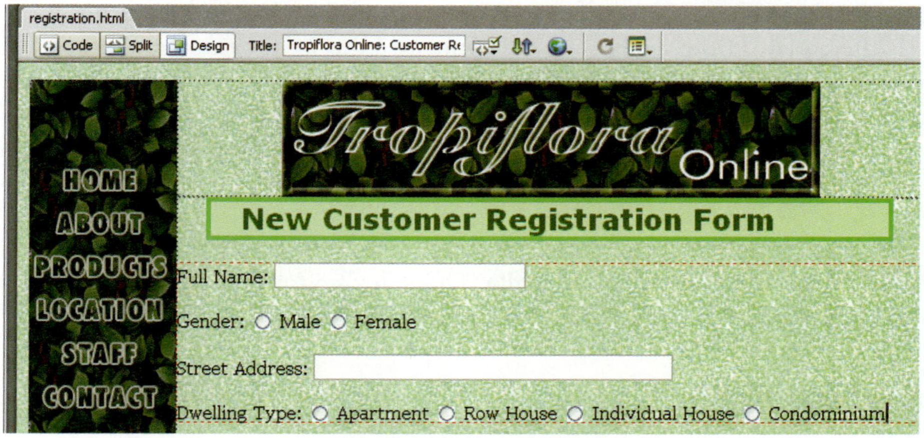


FIGURE 8.21

**8** **Preview the page in your browser to ensure that the new radio button works with the rest of the group.**

**9** **Close your browser and return to Dreamweaver, leaving registration.html open for the next exercise.**

## *To Extend Your Knowledge*

### THE OTHER OPTION

It is fairly common to see forms with several options for a particular question and the last option is Other with a text field to its right, expecting you to complete the Other text field if Other applies to you. This creates a difficult situation for the developer of the form-processing application — one that you should avoid whenever possible. For example, the radio button group might ask the visitor's profession and list options of Firefighter, Police, Retail, Management, and Other. If the listed professions were not applicable to most users of the form, more users would select Other than the identified professions. Among those who select Other, one person might type Actor in the Other text field where another might type Actress, listing essentially the same profession in two different ways (and spelling mistakes could create the same situation). Further, some might feel that they are in management in their government job and select Management, adding Government to the Other text field as well.

In all of these examples, it is virtually impossible to create a form-processing application that will handle this type of data easily. These types of situations require someone to review all entries to make sense of the data. On the other hand, it may be that Other is the best means to categorize data that does not fit within any of the listed options. Evaluate the form and try to anticipate the type of data you expect to collect before publishing the form on the Web site for visitors to complete.

# LESSON 6 Working with Multiple-Choice Checkboxes

The checkbox form control shares the **<input>** tag with all of the other form controls discussed previously and, similarly, is differentiated from them using the **type** attribute, as in **type="checkbox"**. Checkboxes are similar to radio buttons in that a group of checkboxes pertaining to the same question should all have the same name attribute; the different options presented by the checkboxes are specified in their value attributes. Checkboxes also have the Checked/Unchecked options just as radio buttons do. However, unlike radio buttons, checkboxes are designed to allow multiple selections from a group.

Dreamweaver allows you to add radio buttons individually or as a group, but the group option is not available for checkboxes: you must create them individually. Therefore, you must remember to use the same name attribute so that the options relate to the same question or topic.

## Create Checkboxes

1. **In registration.html, click to the right of Condominium and press Enter/Return.**

2. **Type `What type of plants are you looking to purchase?` and press the Spacebar.**

3. **Click the Checkbox button from the Forms Insert bar.**

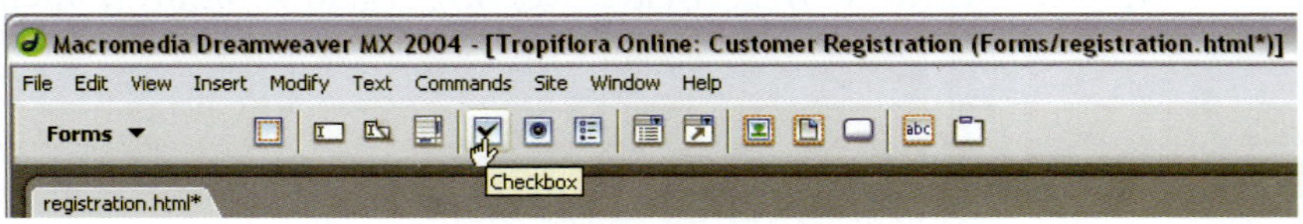


FIGURE 8.22

4. **Type `plantType` in the Checkbox Name field, type `indoor` in the Value field, and select Checked from the Initial State options.**

5. **Click to the right of the checkbox in the Document window and type `Indoor` followed by a space.**

6. **Create another checkbox with the Checkbox Name field set to `plantType` and the Value field set to `outdoor`. Leave Initial State set to Unchecked.**

7. **Click to the right of the new checkbox in the Document window, type `Outdoor`, and press Enter/Return.**

8. **Insert a submit button.**

**9** **Save the page, leaving it open for the next exercise.**

FIGURE 8.23

## Compare Radio-Button and Checkbox Query-String Data

In this exercise, you learn how the radio-button and checkbox data is sent to the form-processing application. Only one option from a radio button group may be selected, therefore there will be only one name=value pair in the query string for the radio button. However, checkboxes allow multiple selections, so for each selected item from a checkbox group, there is a corresponding name=value pair.

**1** **Preview the open registration.html page in your browser.**

**2** **Select your gender, leave Indoor selected, and click the Submit button.**

**3** **Click in the address bar of your browser, press the End key, and examine the query string.**

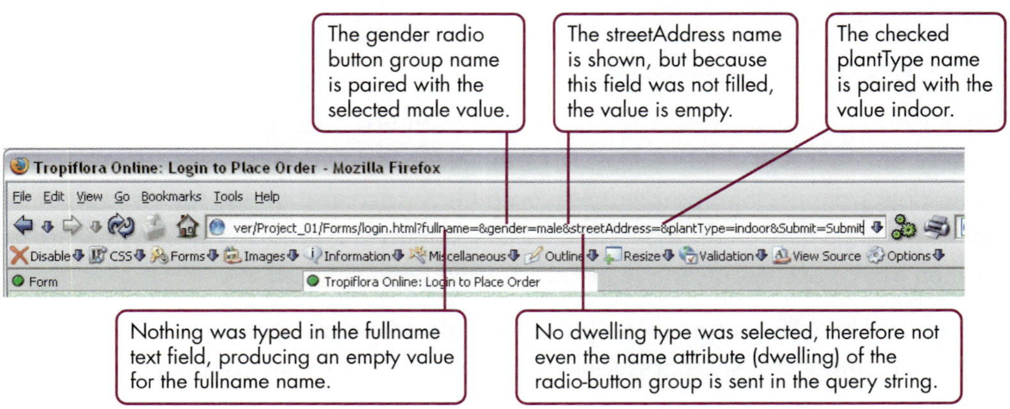


FIGURE 8.24

**4** **Click the back button in your browser.**

**5** **Select a different gender, select a dwelling type, select both Indoor and Outdoor plant types, and click Submit. Examine the query string again.**

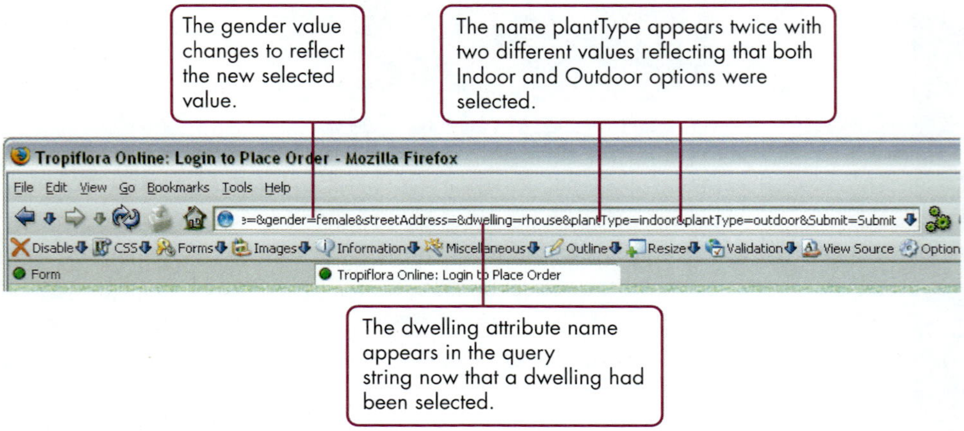


FIGURE 8.25

**6** **Close your browser and return to Dreamweaver, leaving registration.html open for the next exercise.**

## To Extend Your Knowledge

### PROCESSING RADIO-BUTTON AND CHECKBOX OPTIONS

Processing radio-buttons options is not very difficult: only one option is selected for each group. Processing checkbox options is more difficult in that you must check for multiple instances of the same name, such as plantType=indoor and plantType=outdoor.

The usefulness of the checked option for radio buttons and checkboxes may not be clear. As you saw in the previous exercise, if none of the buttons for a radio-button group are selected, the name of the group is not passed in the query string. The same principle applies to checkboxes, too. On a purchase-order form, if there are shipping options for a product, one of them must be selected or the order cannot be shipped. The Web-site designer may choose to preselect the least expensive option, leaving it to the user to accept or change the option.

Another use for preselecting an option is when information has already been entered and the user is asked to modify or confirm the information. For example, an e-commerce application remembers (by requesting the data from its database) that Bob used his MasterCard to pay for his last purchase. The e-commerce application may create the Payment Method form and preselect the MasterCard option for him: Bob is then free to accept or change the preselected payment option.

While you might not be willing to preselect (assume) Male or Female as the gender of a new customer, there are other circumstances when preselecting an option improves the usability of the form for your visitors.

# LESSON 7 Labeling Form Controls

There are two aspects to labeling forms: one obvious, the other not. In the previous exercises, you typed text beside a form control, such as a text field or radio button. It might seem logical to assume that the user would deduce the purpose of the control from the proximity of the text to the control that the text identifies. However, this relationship is not as clear to people who use screen readers. In the case of the Full Name field, the label is read before the text field is encountered, but in the case of the radio buttons and checkboxes, the labels commonly appear after the control. Using the **<label>** tag clarifies this situation for users of screen readers.

Using the **<label>** tag not only benefits people who use screen-reader software but also improves the usability of radio buttons and checkboxes for everyone. Without a **<label>** tag, to select either a radio button or checkbox option, you must click the radio button or checkbox. If you use the **<label>** tag, however, the width of the selectable area extends to include the label text. The user may click the label text to select the option, not just the control itself. If you click a label associated with a text field, the insertion point appears within the field.

There are two methods for applying the **<label>** tag: explicit and implicit. The **<label>** tag is a container tag that requires its closing **</label>** tag. The implicit method of applying the **<label>** tag is to enclose both the label text and the form control between the opening and closing **<label>** tags, as in **<label>Full Name: <input type="text" name="fullname"></label>**. The explicit method of applying the **<label>** tag separates the label text from the form control but using the **for** and **id** attributes, the relationship between the label text and the form control is explicitly stated. To apply this properly, the form control must be assigned an **id** and the **for** attribute of the **<label>** tag uses the same value as the **id** of the form control, not unlike the **usemap** attribute of the **<img>** tag and the **name** attribute of the **<map>** tag which relate the two. The following is an example of the explicit method of the **<label>** tag: **<label for="fullname">Full Name:</label> <input id="fullname" name="fullname" type="text">**.

Dreamweaver supports the implicit method with the Label button on the Forms Insert bar. You select the label text and the form control, click the Label button, and the **<label>** tag is created surrounding both the label text and the form control. Dreamweaver also automatically inserts the **<label>** tag when radio buttons are created using the Radio Button dialog box (activated by the Radio Control button of the Forms Insert bar), but the Radio and Checkbox buttons of the Forms Insert bar do not insert the **<label>** tag — you must apply these manually.

You can use tables to lay out forms, commonly with the labels in one column and the form controls in another column. You may have noticed that the Radio Button dialog box did provide a table layout option. We chose Line Breaks instead. When you use tables to lay out forms, by placing the label text in one cell and the form control in another cell, you cannot use the implicit label method as the **<label>** tag cannot cross the cell boundary. For this reason, you would need to use the explicit label method. However, Dreamweaver does not support the explicit method in the Design view. You must work in the Code view to apply the **for** attribute.

## Create Implicit Labels

In this exercise, you create implicit labels to associate label text with the form controls. You learn that the Radio Button dialog box inserts the **<label>** tag when you create a radio-button group using that dialog box. You also see how the **<label>** tag improves the usability of radio-button and checkbox controls.

**1** **In the open registration.html page, click in the text label Row House, and notice that the <label> tag appears in the Tag selector.**

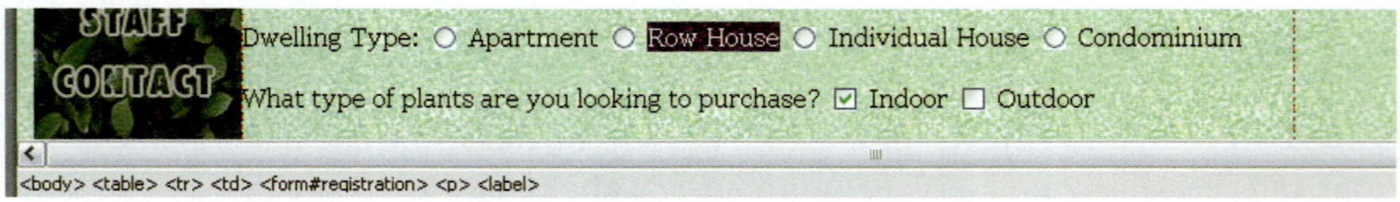


FIGURE 8.26

**2** **Click Condominium and notice that there is no <label> tag in the Tag selector.**

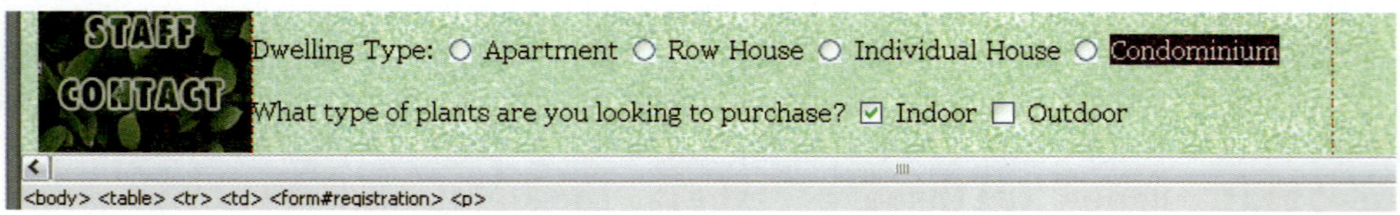


FIGURE 8.27

**3** **Preview the page in your browser and click the text Row House.**

**4** **Click Condominium and then click the radio button for Condominium.**

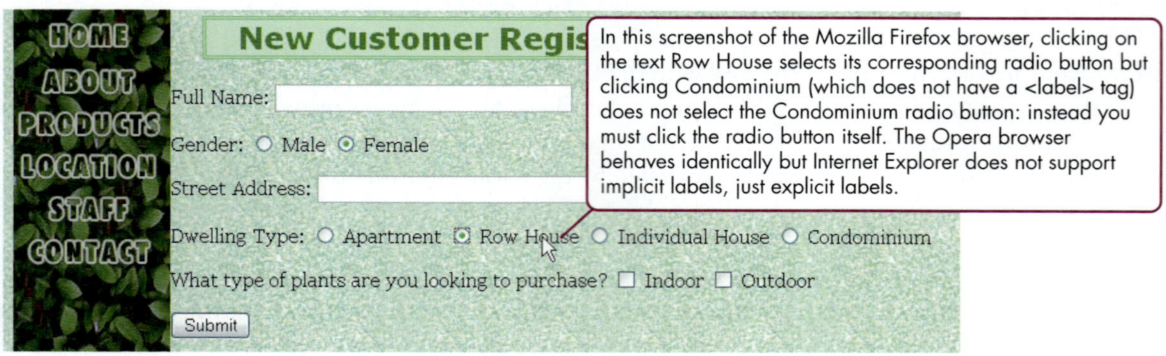


FIGURE 8.28

**5** **Close your browser and return to Dreamweaver.**

**6** **Drag to select Condominium and its radio button, and click the Label button from the Forms Insert bar.**

The Document window switches to the Split view.

**7** **In the Design window at the bottom of the Document window, select Indoor and its checkbox, and click the Label button. Select Outdoor and its checkbox, and click the Label button. Select the text label Full Name and its text field, and apply the `<label>` tag. Apply the `<label>` tag to the Street Address and its text field.**

**8** **Click the Design button to close the Code window.**

**9** **Preview the page in your browser.**

## If you have problems

Internet Explorer for Windows does not support the implicit method of applying the **<label>** tag, therefore, if you do not have access to any browser other than Internet Explorer, you won't experience the usability benefit of applying the **<label>** tag to the label text for radio buttons and checkboxes. If you have the opportunity to test this page with any of the Opera, Firefox, IE (Macintosh), or Safari (Macintosh) browsers, you will experience the benefit of implicit **<label>** tags to radio buttons and checkboxes.

**10** **Return to Dreamweaver but leave registration.html open for the next exercise.**

## Create Explicit Labels

In this exercise, you learn to apply explicit **<label>** tags to the male and female radio buttons. To do so, you must assign **id** attributes to the male and female radio buttons, apply the **<label>** tag to the Male and Female text labels, and add the **for** attribute to the **<label>** tags to explicitly relate the labels to their radio buttons.

**1** **In the open file, registration.html, Right/Control-click the radio button for Male, and select Edit Tag <input> from the contextual menu.**

FIGURE 8.29

**2** In the Tag Editor – Input dialog box, select the Style Sheet/Accessibility category, type `male` in the ID field, and click OK.

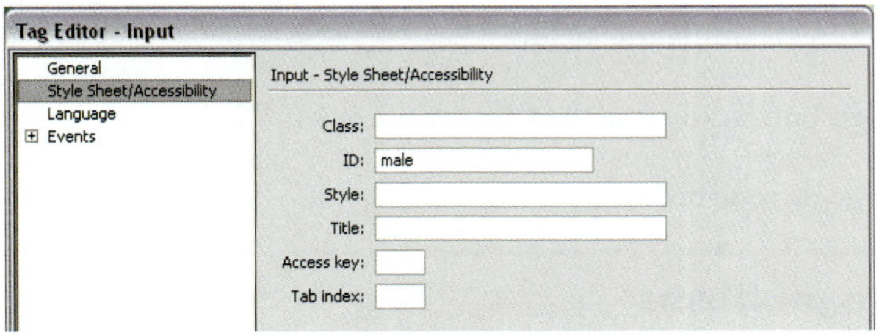


FIGURE 8.30

**3** Select the text label Male and Right/Control-click the selected text.

**4** Choose Wrap Tag from the contextual menu.

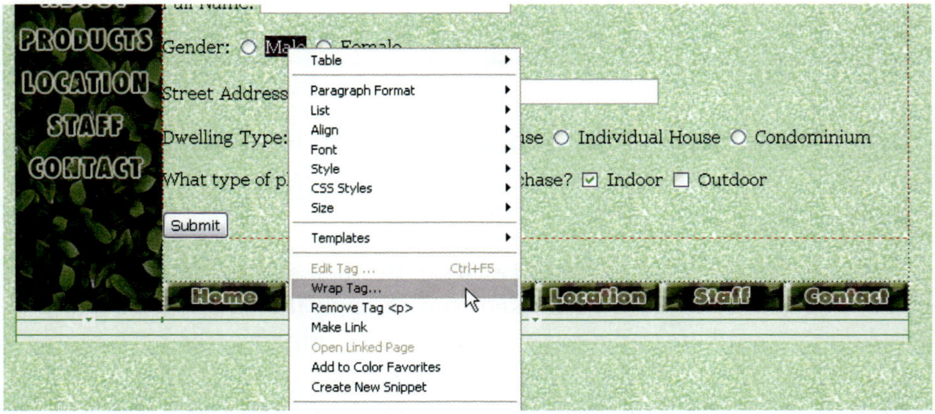


FIGURE 8.31

**5** In the little editor window, press `l` (lowercase L) and press Enter/Return to accept `label`. Press the Spacebar, press `f`, and press Enter/Return to accept the `for` attribute. Type `male` and press Enter/Return.

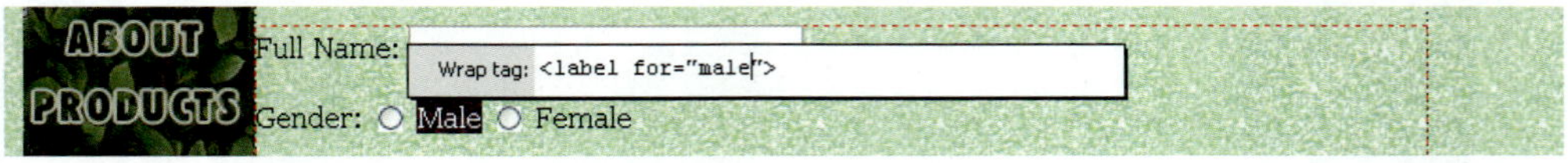


FIGURE 8.32

**6** Repeat Steps 1 to 5 for the female radio button, and then wrap the text Female with the `<label>` tag using the `for` attribute set to `female`.

**7** **Preview the page in your browser, and click either the Male or Female text label.**

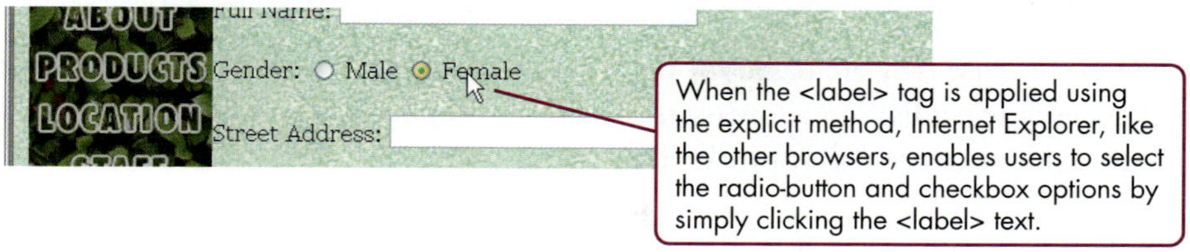


FIGURE 8.33

**8** **Close your browser and return to Dreamweaver.**

## *To Extend Your Knowledge*

### INNOVATIVE USES FOR JAVASCRIPT IN FORMS

Forms often contain JavaScript functions, and there are many scripts that increase the usability of forms.

Text fields, as you know, can have initial text. Although initial text is useful, in some circumstances, to explain what users should enter into that field, it requires that users delete the initial text before they add their own. JavaScript can be written to delete the initial-value text when the user clicks or tabs into the field.

When shipping and billing addresses are the same, clicking a checkbox with the label Same as Billing Address can be used to trigger a JavaScript function that completes the shipping-address fields with the same data as the billing-address fields.

JavaScript can be written to provide options based on previous selections. For example, if USA is selected as the country, a list of the states appears, whereas if Canada is selected as the country, a list of the provinces and territories appears. Peter-Paul Koch, an eminent JavaScript developer, has taken this principle to the extreme. His contact form changes quite significantly, depending on the purpose of sending him a message (www.quirksmode.org/contact.html). For example, if you select the subject Business from the list of possible subjects, a radio button appears with the options Nederland and Other.

Some forms contain both required and optional fields. Andy Clarke has created a form (with an accompanying tutorial) in which a JavaScript link hides the optional fields (stuffandnonsense.co.uk/archives/trimming_form_fields_3.html).

Finally, the granddaddy of all, validation: JavaScript is commonly used to validate the contents of a form to ensure that the email address is formatted correctly, the date is valid, and all of the required fields have been completed. These are just a few of the options available for JavaScript validation.

Despite the apparent benefits for usability that these JavaScript functions provide, keep in mind that if accessibility is a concern, many of these JavaScript functions may not be accessible to everyone. Some forms are so dependent on JavaScript that if people were to try to use the form with an older browser or a JavaScript-incapable or disabled browser, they would be presented with an empty page. Despite the benefits that JavaScript may provide sighted users with current browsers, be aware of your site's audience and what limitations may result if you use JavaScript.

# LESSON 8 Selecting from Lists

Select lists, named that because they are based on the **<select>** tag, can provide alternatives to both the radio buttons and checkboxes: a select list can allow users to select just one item or multiple items. This is one of the few form controls that does not use the **<input>** tag.

There are two tags used to create select lists: the **<select>** tag, which, like the unordered list **<ul>** tag, surrounds the list of options, and the **<option>** tag which, like the list item **<li>** tag, appears as often as there are items in the list. The **<select>** tag has three attributes of importance: the **size** attribute, the **name** attribute, and the **multiple** attribute.

The **name** attribute acts identically to the **name** attribute for other form controls: it identifies, to the form-processing application, the type of data being collected, such as shippingMethod or favoriteAnimal. The **size** attribute does not set the width of the control but, instead, the height in single units, such as 1, 2, or 3. When the **size** is 1 or unspecified (which defaults to 1), the select list acts as a pop-up list. However, if the **size** is 2 or more, the select list displays as a scrolling list. There is no attribute that may be used to specify the width of the **<select>** tag — by default, it stretches to fit the width of the widest item in the option list. However, the width may be specified using CSS. The **multiple** attribute, like the checked attribute of radio buttons and checkboxes, has no attribute value. If **multiple** is inserted in the **<select>** tag, the user can select multiple items from the select list, whereas without it, the user can only select one item. In Dreamweaver, a menu allows you to select just one option whereas a list allows you to select multiple options.

The **<option>** tag has only two attributes: the **value** attribute and the **selected** attribute. The **<option>** tag is unique in that the closing tag **</option>** is not required in HTML (however, it is required in XHTML). Nevertheless, Dreamweaver does insert the closing tag **</option>**, which is good form.

The **<option>** tag is also unique in that the **value** attribute is optional, too. For example, **<option>Carrot** is valid and equivalent to **<option value="Carrot">Carrot </option>**. In this example, the value is the same as the text that is visible in the list. At other times, especially if the list is populated from a database system, you may need to display a product description but code the option with the product number, such as **<option value="PN2318L">Black & Decker: Left-handed Robertson Screwdriver </option>**. In this example, although the users would see Black & Decker: Left-handed Robertson Screwdriver, the value sent to the form-processing application would be PN2318L, the product number, and the form-processing application would act on this product number rather than the displayed text.

The **selected** attribute is similar to the **multiple** attribute of the **<select>** tag: it does not have an attribute value. The **<option>** tag with the **selected** attribute displays in the list, whether it is the first, middle, or last option in the list. If the **<select>** tag has the **multiple** attribute, multiple **<option>** tags may have the **selected** attribute.

## Create a Menu

In this exercise, you create a select list from which only one option may be selected. You set one item to be initially selected and learn that you may go back and edit an existing select list.

**1** **In the open file, registration.html, click to the right of Outdoor and press Enter/Return.**

**2** **Type `How did you hear about Tropiflora Online?` and press Enter/Return.**

**3** **Click the List/Menu button on the Forms Insert bar.**

FIGURE 8.34

**4** **Type `hear` in the List/Menu name field, and then click the List Values button.**

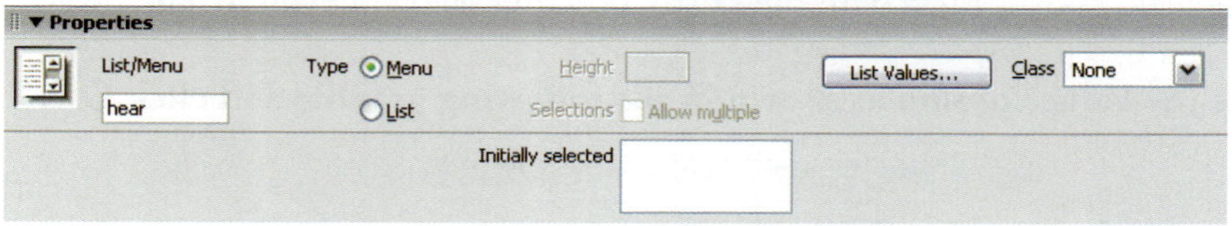


FIGURE 8.35

**5** **Under Item Label, type `Magazine`, press Tab twice, type `Search Engine`, press Tab twice, and continue to create the following list (the last item is `Got lost on Tallevast Road`). Click OK when finished.**

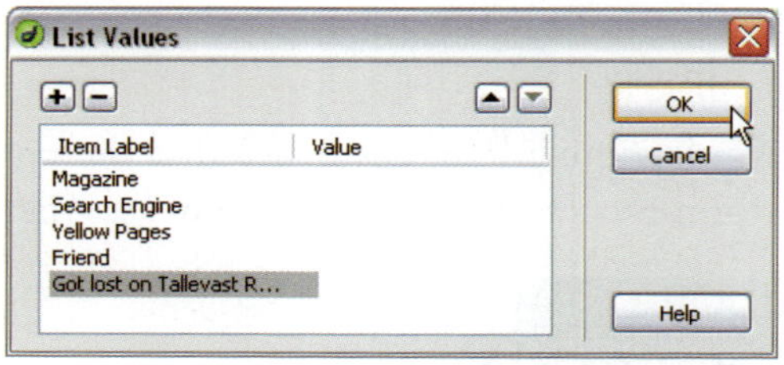


FIGURE 8.36

**6** **Click `Magazine` in the Initially Selected field, and notice that Magazine displays in the list in the Document window.**

**7** **Control/Command-click Magazine to deselect it, and then click Yellow Pages.**

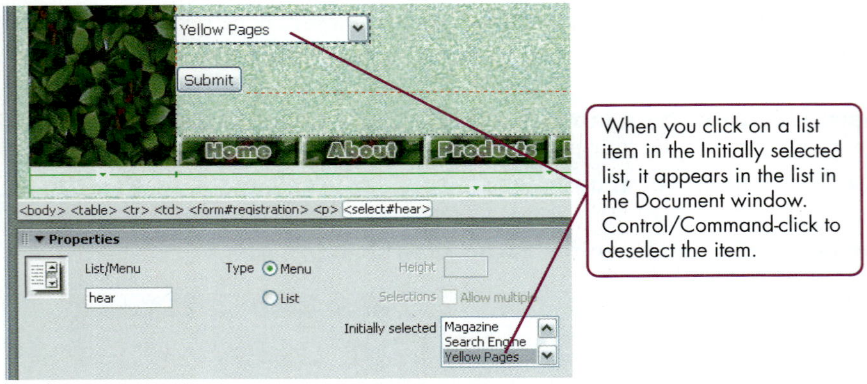


FIGURE 8.37

**8** **Click the List Values button.**

Notice that unlike the Radio Button dialog box, in which you cannot edit a group of radio buttons, the List Values dialog box is filled with the existing options, allowing you to edit, delete, or add to the list.

**9** **Complete the Value column as shown in the following graphic and click OK.**

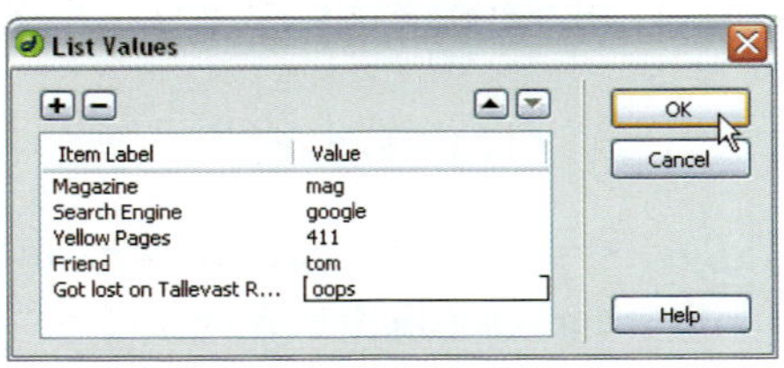


FIGURE 8.38

**10** **Preview the page in your browser.**

Notice that the browser window provides no evidence that the option values are different from the option labels. However, a form-processing application only uses the option values.

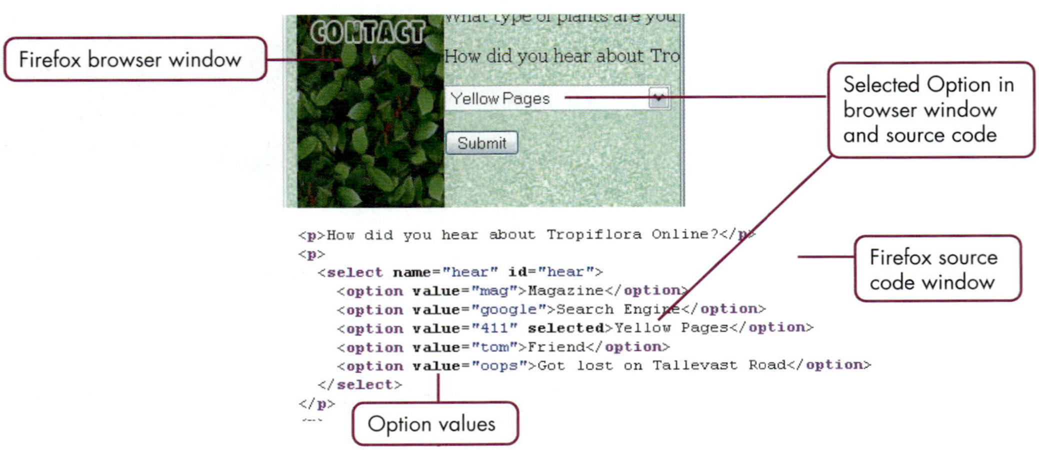


FIGURE 8.39

**11** **Uncheck the plantType Indoor checkbox, click the Submit button, and examine the query string in your browser's address bar.**

FIGURE 8.40

**12** **Close your browser and return to Dreamweaver, leaving registration.html open for the next exercise.**

## To Extend Your Knowledge

### ADDING INSTRUCTIONS TO SELECT LISTS

Many Web designers add an another option to the top of a select list. This option contains information or instructions on how to use the list, such as Select your year of birth, Choose a shipping method, or just Country. We recommend that, in collaboration with the developer of the form-processing application, you create a dummy value for the option, enabling the developer to watch for it in the program. If this is a required option, the program must send the form back to the user to complete this option. For example, in a list of countries, the first option with the Select Your Country label may be coded as follows: **`<option value="noCountry" selected>Select Your Country</option>`** and the Web developer would make the program watch for a value of noCountry.

## Create a List

Dreamweaver calls the multiple select option list a "list". In fact, the only difference between Dreamweaver's list and menu in code is that the **`<select>`** tag of the list contains the **`multiple`** attribute whereas the menu does not. Furthermore, the ability to apply the **`size`** attribute to the menu is not available from the Property inspector. What would you do to create a single select menu that is two or more lines in height? You would apply **`size="2"`** (or more) directly to the code either using the Code window or Right/Control-clicking the List/Menu control in the Design window and selecting Edit Tag <select>.

In this exercise, you create a list from which multiple items may be selected. You also preselect multiple items using Control/Command-click.

**1** **In the open file, registration.html, click to the right of the select list and press Enter/Return.**

**2** **Type** `Select the type of equipment you are interested in` **and press Enter/Return.**

**3** **Click the List/Menu button on the Forms Insert bar.**

**4** **Type `equipment` in the List/Menu name field, and select List from the Type options.**

**5** **Set the Height to `5` and enable the Allow Multiple option.**

**6** **Click the List Values button; enter `Gloves`, `Tools`, `Chemicals`, `Clothing`, and `Books` in the Item Label column; and click OK.**

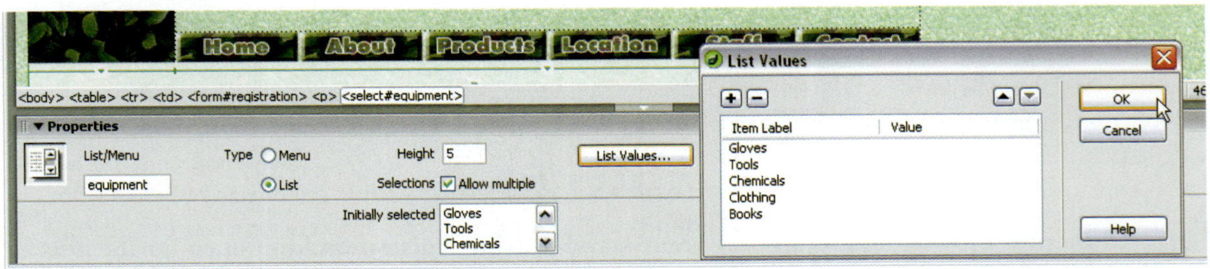


FIGURE 8.41

**7** **Using the Initially Selected list, click Gloves and then Control/Command-click Chemicals.**

**8** **Preview the page in your browser.**

Notice that both Gloves and Chemicals are selected.

**9** **Click Tools, Control/Command-click Books, click the Submit button, and examine the query string.**

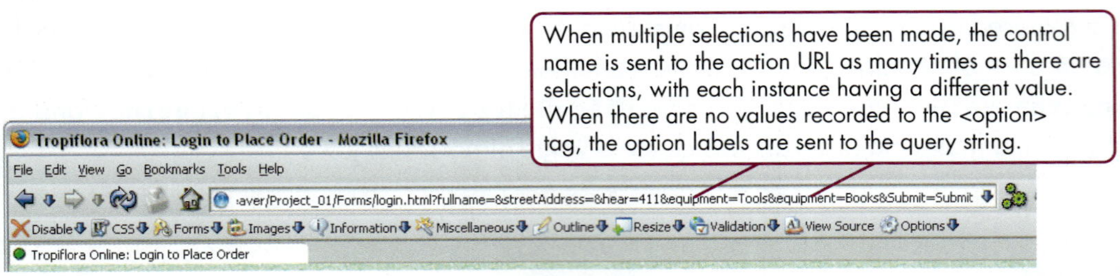


FIGURE 8.42

**10** **Close your browser, return to Dreamweaver, and close registration.html.**

## To Extend Your Knowledge

### MULTIPLE SELECT LISTS ARE UNCOMMON

It is uncommon to encounter multiple select lists. Often, when they are used, the Web-page designer adds instructional text, such as "Control-click (Windows) or Command-click (Macintosh) to select multiple items." The other option is to avoid confusion altogether. Because multiple select lists are similar to checkboxes, which are more common and understood by a greater portion of the population, unless there is a compelling reason to use multiple select lists, you might consider using checkboxes, instead.

# LESSON 9 Grouping Form Controls and Options

You have learned that the **<label>** tag benefits all users by extending the selectable area for checkboxes and radio buttons to include the area taken by the text labels. You learned that the **<label>** tag benefits screen-reader users by relating the label text to the form control. There are two other form options that provide similar benefits — the **<fieldset>**/**<legend>** pair of tags and the **<optgroup>** tag.

The **<fieldset>** tag is used to collect a group of controls. For example, a series of text fields, radio buttons, and checkboxes may be used to allow users to fill out the billing address for their orders. A virtually identical series of controls may be used to allow users to fill out the shipping address for their orders. To reduce the possibility of confusion, the billing-address controls may be enclosed in one **<fieldset>** tag and the shipping address controls may be enclosed in another **<fieldset>** tag, thereby creating, in code anyway, two groups of controls that are distinctly separated. The **<legend>** tag also plays a role: any text between the opening and closing **<legend>** tags appears above the group, thereby labeling the group. The **<fieldset>** tag also has a default presentation of creating a border around the group of controls enclosed within it.

The **<optgroup>** tag is used to group select-list options and assign names to groups. For example, UPS and FedEx both provide Regular and Express shipping services. Rather than list the four items as UPS-Regular, UPS-Express, FedEx-Regular and FedEx-Express, you may group the UPS shipping methods in one **<optgroup>** and the FedEx shipping methods in another **<optgroup>**. The **label** attribute of the **<optgroup>** tag identifies UPS or FedEx but these group names are not selectable.

## Use the <fieldset> Tag to Group Controls

In this exercise, you surround a group of controls with the **<fieldset>** tag and label the group with the **<legend>** tag. You create three fieldset groups: the shipping address, the billing address, and the preferred shipper and method. You preview the page in your browser to view the default presentation of the **<fieldset>** and **<legend>** tags. Dreamweaver does not display the border that surrounds contents enclosed in the **<fieldset>** tag.

**1** **Open addresses.html from the Forms site.**

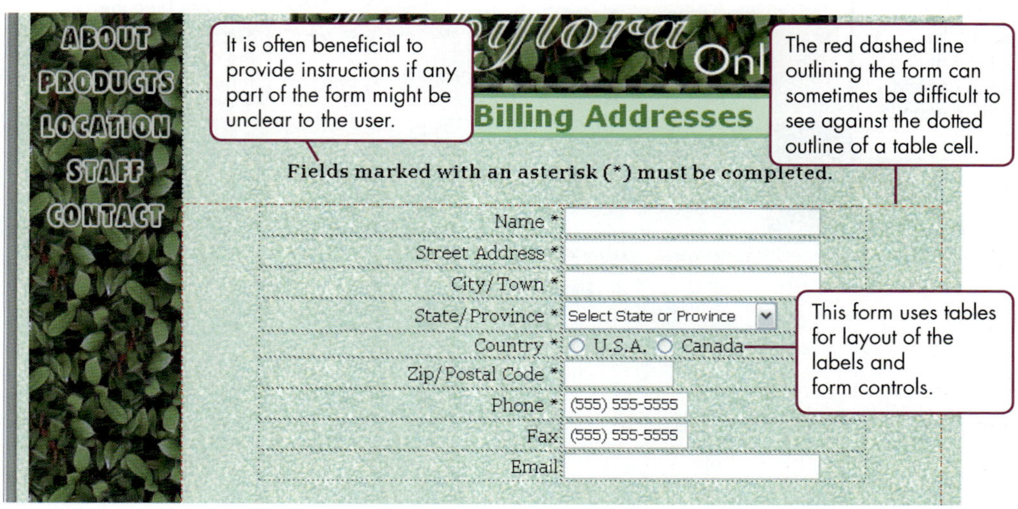


FIGURE 8.43

**2** **Click in the first table of the form, and then click the `<table>` tag to the right of the `<form>` tag in the Tag selector to select the table.**

**3** **Click the Fieldset button (last button) on the Forms Insert bar.**

When you click the Fieldset button, the Document window splits into the Split view.

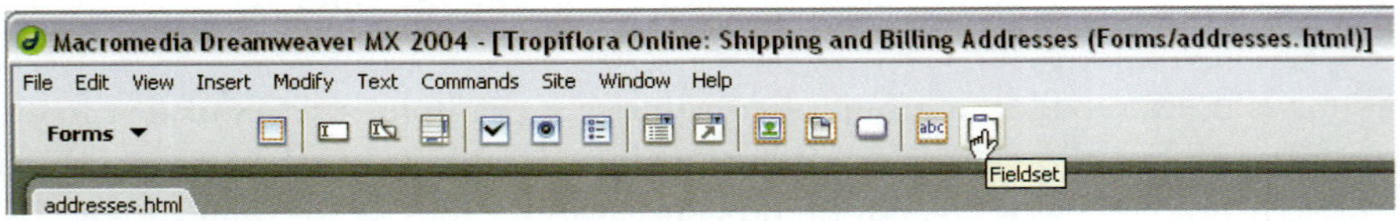


FIGURE 8.44

**4** **Type `Shipping Address` in the Label field of the Fieldset dialog box and click OK.**

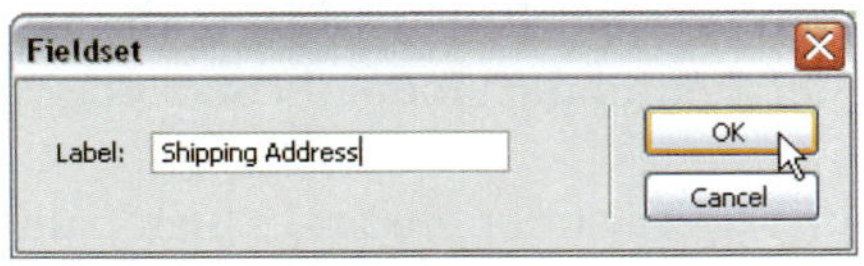


FIGURE 8.45

**5** **Do not close the Code window. Click to the right of the selected table to deselect it.**

**6** **Scroll down in the Design window. Using the same procedures as in Steps 2–4, select the second table, click the Fieldset button, and assign `Billing Address` as its label.**

**7** **Deselect the second table. Select the third table (consisting of just two cells), click the Fieldset button, and assign `Shipping Preferences` as its label.**

**8** **Scroll both the Code and Design windows so you can see the last fieldset in both.**

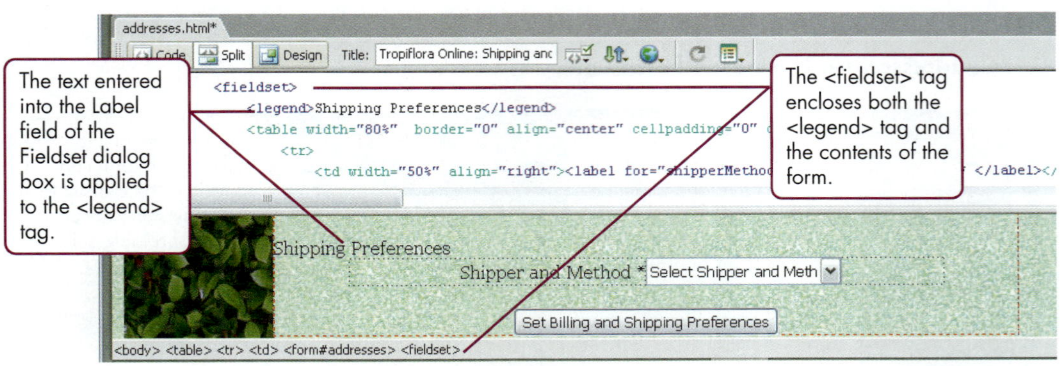


FIGURE 8.46

**9** **Close the Code window, then preview the page in your browser.**

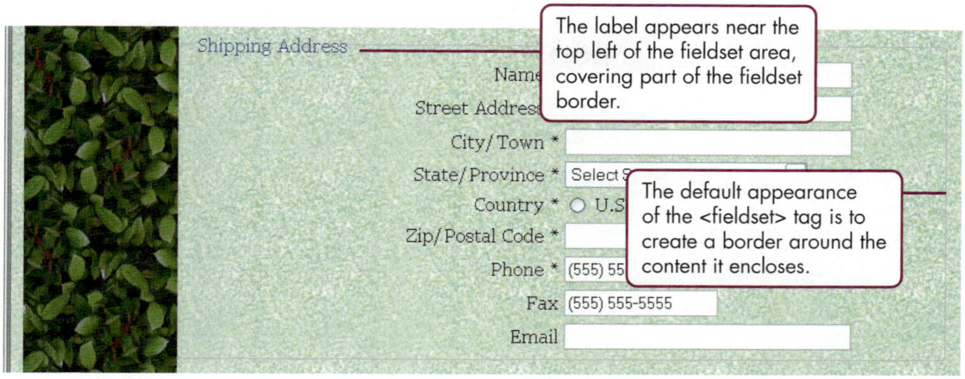


FIGURE 8.47

**10** **Return to Dreamweaver, leaving addresses.html open for the next exercise.**

## Create Option Groups in a Select List

In this exercise, we use the **<optgroup>** tag to create groups of options. This increases the usability of select lists, especially if they are long lists. The **<optgroup>** tag adds an additional item to a list, or so it appears. When you assign the **<optgroup>** tag to a group of select-list options, you are prompted to name the group. The name is then applied to the **label** attribute of the **<optgroup>** tag. This name appears in the select list but it is not selectable: it is like a heading for a block of options.

You cannot apply the **<optgroup>** tag in the Design window. You must work in the Code window.

**1** **In the open file, addresses.html, select the first select list of States and Provinces and switch to the Code view.**

**2** **Click to the left of <option>Alabama, scroll down to Wyoming, and Shift-click to the right of Wyoming to select all states of the US.**

**3** **Right/Control-click in the selected region, and select Insert Tag from the contextual menu.**

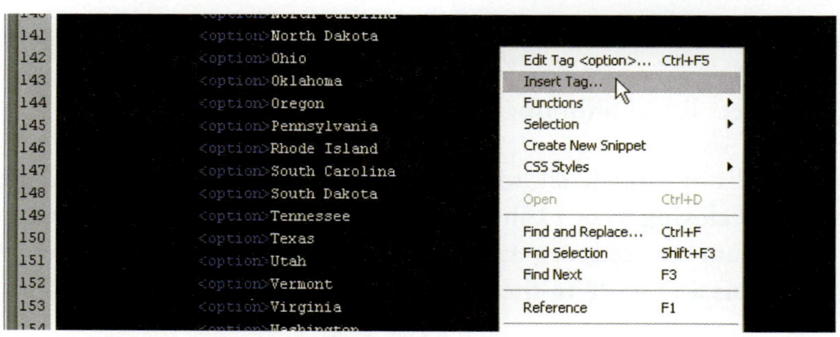


FIGURE 8.48

**4** Select HTML tags>Forms>optgroup, and click Insert.

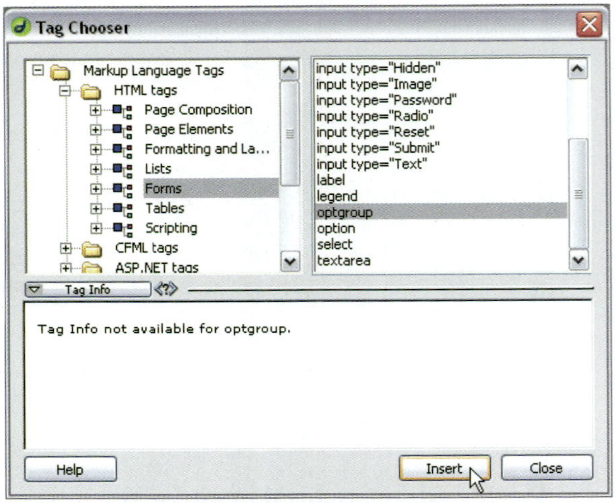


FIGURE 8.49

**5** Type `US States` in the Label field, click OK, and then click Close to close the Tag Chooser dialog box.

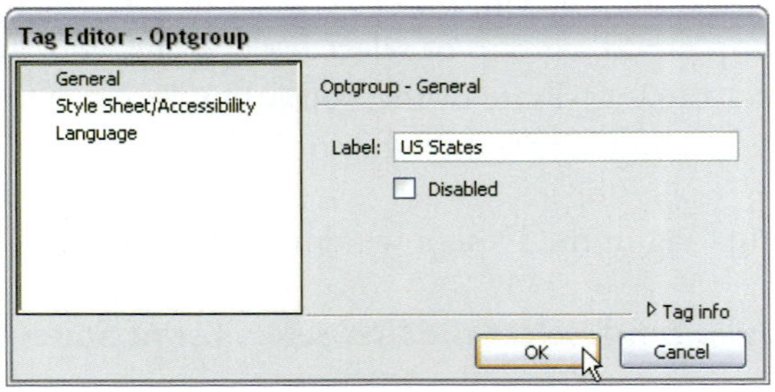


FIGURE 8.50

**6** In the Code window, click to the left of `<option>`Alberta, Shift-click to the right of Yukon Territories, and insert the `<optgroup>` tag using `Canadian Provinces` as the Label. Close the Tag Chooser dialog box and the Code window when finished.

**7** Apply Steps 1 to 6 to the second list of states and provinces.

**8** Select the third select list of Shipping Preferences.

**9** Select the two FedEx options (click to the left of the first `<option>` tag and Shift-click to the right of the second closing `</option>` tag), and insert the `<optgroup>` tag with the Label `FedEx`. Using the same procedures, assign `UPS` to the `label` attribute of the `<optgroup>` tag of the two UPS options and `USPS` to the two USPS options.

**10** **Given that the `label` attribute of the new `<optgroup>` tags identifies the FedEx, UPS, and USPS groups, delete `FedEx`, `UPS`, and `USPS` from the `<option>` label text (not the `<optgroup>` labels). For example, FedEx-Regular becomes just Regular.**

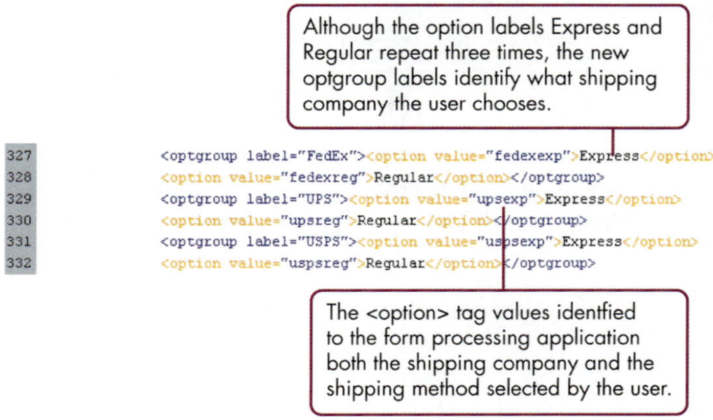


FIGURE 8.51

**11** **Switch to the Design view, preview the page in your browser, and test the modified select lists.**

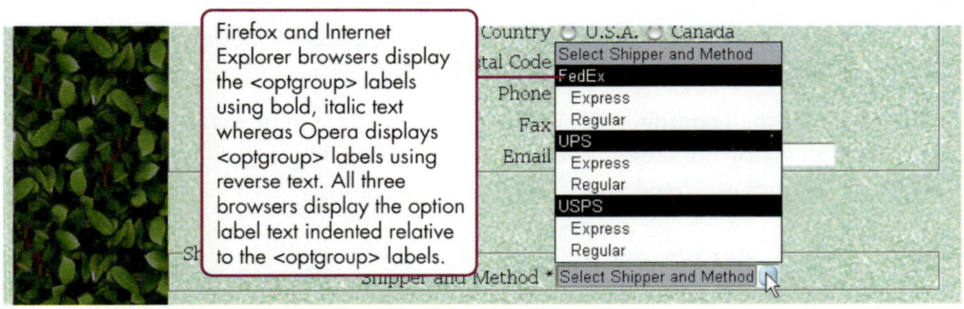


FIGURE 8.52

**12** **Return to Dreamweaver, leaving addresses.html open for the next exercise.**

## Modify the Style of <fieldset> and <legend> Tags

In this exercise, you modify the default style of the **`<fieldset>`** and **`<legend>`** tags. Legend text is blue in Internet Explorer and black in Firefox and Opera, and is the size of paragraph text. To make the purpose of the group clearer to users, you change the color and size of the legend text. The **`<fieldset>`** tag, by default, creates a border around enclosed content: in Opera and Firefox, the border is a grooved style whereas in Internet Explorer, it is a thin, flat, solid, gray borderline. You modify the borderline style of the fieldset and, to match the fieldset line, you add a borderline to the legend.

**1** **In the open file, addresses.html, Right/Control-click in the CSS Styles panel and select New. (If the CSS Styles panel is not open, click the Design panel-group title, click the CSS Styles tab, and create a new CSS Style).**

**2** **In the CSS Styles dialog box, set Tag as the Selector Type, type or select `legend` from the Tag list, ensure that Define in is set to This Document Only, and click OK.**

**3** **In the Type category, set the Font to Verdana, Arial, Helvetica, sans-serif; Size to `1.2` ems; Weight to bold; and Color to `#336600`. Click OK.**

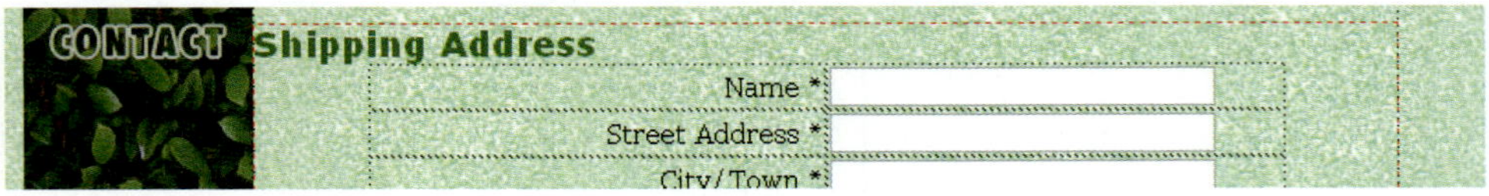


FIGURE 8.53

**4** **Using the same procedure as in Step 2, create a new CSS style for the `fieldset` tag. From the Border category, leave Same for All checked; set Style to solid, Width to thick, and Color to `#336600`, and click OK.**

As you noticed in Step 11 of the previous exercise, Dreamweaver does not display the fieldset border in the Design window.

**5** **To apply a similar border style to the legend text, Right/Control-click legend in the CSS styles panel and select Edit. In the Border category, leave Same for All checked, and set Style to solid, Width to thick, and Color to `#336600`.**

**6** **In the Box category, uncheck Same for All in the Padding group, and set Top to `3` pixels, Right to `10` pixels, Bottom to `3` pixels, and Left to `10` pixels. Leaving Same for All checked for the Margin group, set Top to `0` pixels and click OK.**

Did you notice that the Padding, Margin, Style, Width, and Color groups in the Box and Border categories of the CSS dialog box, respectively, were surrounded by the software equivalent to fieldsets and legends? Many features of Web design come from application design.

**7** **Preview the page in your browser.**

**8** **Return to Dreamweaver leaving addresses.html open for the next exercise.**

## *To Extend Your Knowledge*

### DO NOT REFER TO COLOR

One of the important practices of Web accessibility is to accommodate both the blind and the color blind. Many Web designers, when thinking about Web accessibility, forget that although the color blind can see, their eyes cannot distinguish some colors correctly. Some colors, such as red and green, can appear almost black. When designing forms, required fields are often colored to suggest to the user that those fields are required along with a statement, such as: "You must complete the fields shown in red." The color blind will have some degree of difficulty identifying the required fields and, of course, the blind will not be able to see the color at all. You must use some other method of identifying required fields, such as using an asterisk (a statement at the top of the form indicating the purpose of the asterisk is also useful). You may color the label text (and the instructions to match) as long as the color combination and contrast are usable by the color blind; just do not use the color as a criterion.

# LESSON 10 Creating Hidden Fields

Hidden fields, as the name suggests, are not visible in the browser window but these fields do exist in code. They are commonly used to pass information from the form to the form-processing application. For example, when a customer orders from an e-commerce site, his or her customer number may be stored in a hidden field and passed to the e-commerce application via the query string.

A hidden field uses the **<input>** tag with the **type** attribute set to **hidden**. The **name** attribute may be used to identify the type of data carried by the **value** attribute, such as **name="customerID" value="123456"**. You may use as many hidden fields as necessary for your application, but understand that any sophisticated user can view the information in the hidden fields by simply looking at the code. Do not store a password or any other critical information in a hidden field. There are other more secure methods available, such as ***cookies*** (text that is passed between your browser and the Web server) and session variables. (***Session variables*** are text that identifies you and may be passed as a cookie, stored in links, or in hidden fields. The session-variable text is just an identification code that is validated by the Web-server application and does not carry any recognizable information.)

## Create a Hidden Field

In this exercise, you create a hidden field that contains an encrypted session variable to identify who you are and what database record you are updating through the use of the form.

1. **In the open file, addresses.html, click in the empty paragraph between the Shipping and Billing fieldsets.**

2. **Click the Hidden Field button on the Forms Insert bar (third from the left).**

3. **In the Property inspector, type sid in the HiddenField Name field (sid is a common short name for session id), type c8b068f108ccbb25e6b43efd2dd13c66 in the Value field, and press Enter/Return.**

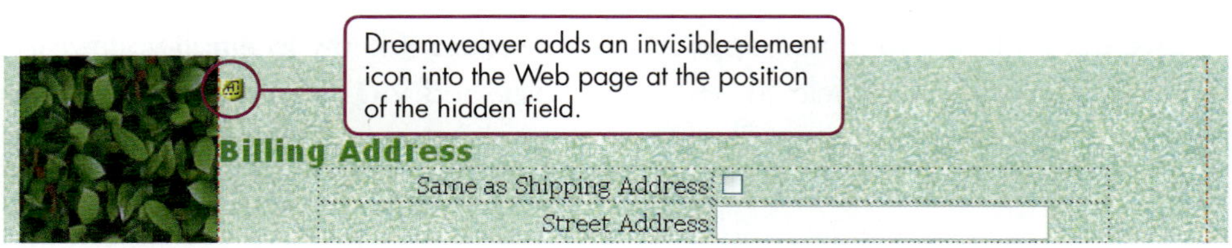


FIGURE 8.54

**4** **Preview the page in your browser, and search the query string for the sid variable. (It is a long query string, so you will have to scroll to find it.)**

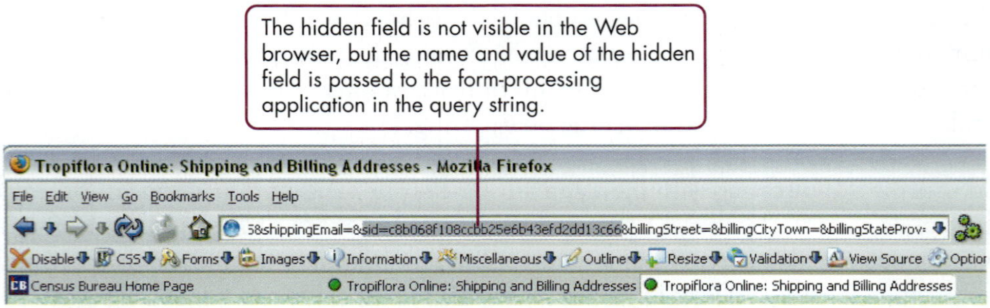


FIGURE 8.55

**5** **Close your browser, return to Dreamweaver, and close addresses.html.**

## To Extend Your Knowledge

### SPAM, FORMMAIL APPLICATIONS, AND HIDDEN FIELDS

With the exception of the mailto: action URL, form-processing applications must be installed and run on a Web server, which is not something a free Web-hosting service (whether through your ISP or a third-party service, such as Tripod.com) will allow. However, many free Web-hosting services do recognize that their clients may wish to create some basic forms, such as a contact form with the data collected from their visitors emailed to them. Rather than providing you direct access to the application, these hosting services often provide you the action URL and some instructions on how to configure the form to send your visitors' data to you via email. This is not the same as a mailto: URL: the ***formmail application*** (an application that emails collected form data to the intended recipient) uses its own programming to email the data to you.

If you don't have access to the formmail application, how does it know to email your visitors' data to you? This is done using a hidden field in which the **`name`** and **`value`** are set using **`name="email-address" value="you@domain.com"`**. The formmail application then takes the data collected by the form and emails it to the email address in the **`value`** attribute.

You learned that forms are a good way to hide your email address from spammers, but not if you use hidden fields. These hidden fields are no more secure than an email link on a Web page. If you must hide your email address, you must have access to the formmail application and store your email address right in the application. Only someone with rights to access the files on your Web server (or your space in one) can extract your email address from the programming code. However, this is hacking and beyond the ability of spammers and their email-harvesting software, so you may be assured that storing your email address in the programming code will protect it. If you cannot afford anything but free Web space, recognize that your email address in a hidden form field may be harvested at some point. You may try another free hosting service; there are many.

## CAREERS IN DESIGN

### FORMS DESIGN AND USABILITY TESTING

You have learned to create static pages that, with the exception of links, have no features with which visitors may interact. Forms add a degree of interaction between the visitor and the Web page by allowing the visitor to enter information or make selections. Even without dynamic JavaScript effects, visitors know that by clicking the submit button, some effect will occur, such as sending an email, posting a question to a discussion forum, or purchasing a book. To ensure that your visitors can use the form as you would like them to use it, however, before you create the form, you must carefully evaluate the type of data that you want it to collect and the type of form controls that you might use.

Sometimes the best input method is not obvious. For example, credit-card numbers are often in the form of 1234 2345 3456 4567. With spaces, this credit-card number takes 19 characters. One possible issue is that people may not enter the spaces and may think, therefore, that they are expected to insert the 3-digit security number, as well; if they do so, the 19-digit number is invalid. To avoid this problem, do you divide the credit card number into 4 input fields each containing 4 digits? Doing so means that after each field, the visitor must press Tab to move to the next field but, at the same time, this format makes clearer to visitors that they only need 16 numbers. Some developers add JavaScript to this type of form so after the fourth number is pressed, JavaScript moves the insertion point to the next field. If, however, a user looks at the credit card and not at the screen and presses Tab after the fourth number, JavaScript would already have moved the insertion point to the next field so the Tab would move one the insertion point one field further, leaving a field empty.

If you need to develop either a complex or a unique form, consider doing some usability testing in which people test your form and give their feedback. Usability testing can be expensive but it doesn't have to be. You can gather a group of friends or co-workers and have them test your form and provide feedback, either as written notes or in a group discussion afterwards. A Web site that depends on information collected by its forms must ensure that its forms are not an impediment to the success of the Web site.

## SUMMARY

In this project, you learned about forms and the many roles that forms play in Web applications. You explored form controls. You learned how to send form data to a form-processing application and the methods by which it may be sent. You learned how to insert single- and multiline text fields and password fields. You added submit and reset buttons, and learned how buttons may be used to trigger other actions, such as edit and delete. You explored the differences between radio buttons and checkboxes. You created menus and lists, and learned that they may be used in place of radio buttons and checkboxes. You learned why it is beneficial to everyone to properly label form controls. You grouped form controls into fieldsets and grouped options in select lists, and learned how both improve the usability of forms. You learned about hidden fields and how they may be used in a Web application. You learned that although, as a designer, you may assemble and design a Web form, that Web form is the gateway to a Web application that requires a programmer to create it so it can capture, analyze, and use the data.

## KEY TERMS

| | | |
|---|---|---|
| application | e-commerce | Perl |
| blog | encrypted | query string |
| C++ | form controls | radio button |
| CGI | formmail | scripts |
| checkbox | HTTPS / S-HTTP | session variables |
| cookies | menu | select list |

## CHECKING CONCEPTS AND TERMS

### SCREEN ID

**Identify the indicated areas from the list below:**

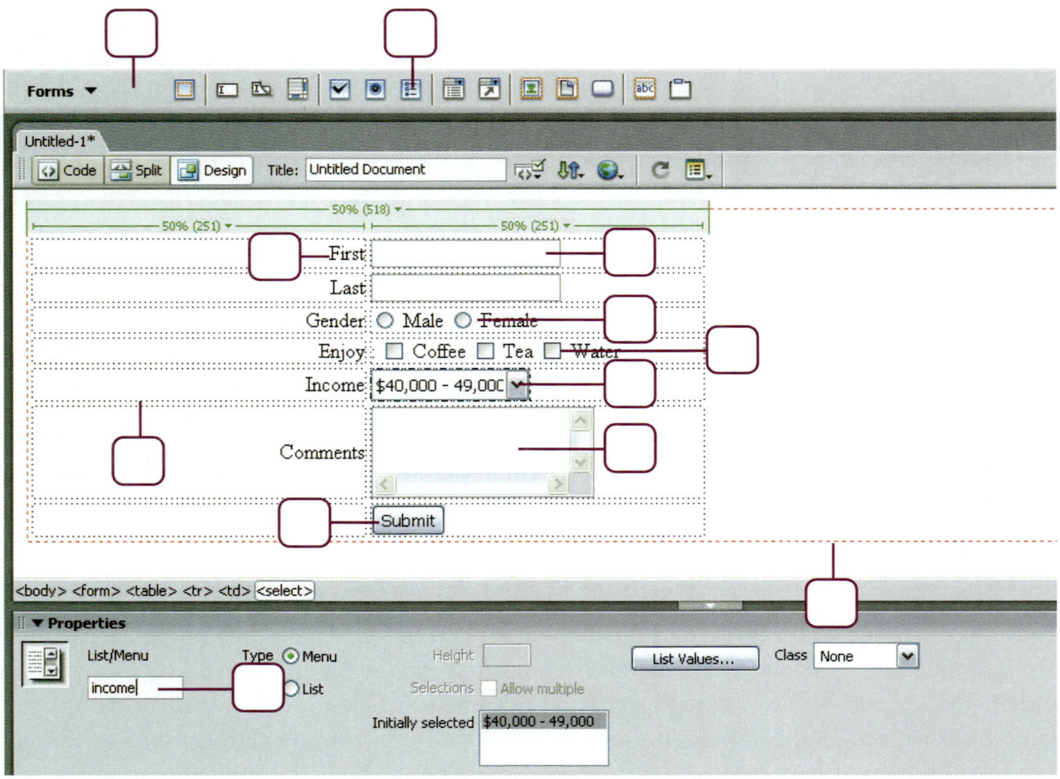


**FIGURE 8.56**

| | | |
|---|---|---|
| a. Forms Insert bar | e. Radio group button | i. Form outline |
| b. Name of select list | f. Text field | j. Layout table |
| c. Radio button | g. Checkbox | k. Menu list |
| d. Label text | h. Button | l. Textarea |

## MULTIPLE CHOICE

**Circle the letter of the correct answer for each of the following:**

1. Forms may be used to __________.
   - **a.** pay bills online
   - **b.** send an email
   - **c.** apply for a credit card
   - **d.** All of the above

2. The two controls that may be used to replace each other are __________.
   - **a.** radio buttons and checkboxes
   - **b.** checkboxes and multi select lists
   - **c.** legends and labels
   - **d.** optgroups and fieldsets

3. If the action URL is search.php, the value is 3F9J, and the name is XV9C, the correct query string is __________.
   - **a.** `search.php?value=3F9J&name=XV9C`
   - **b.** `search.php=XV9C+3F9J`
   - **c.** `search.php?XV9C=3F9J`
   - **d.** `search.php/value=3F9J+name=XV9C`

4. What attribute would you use to display the third option in a select list?
   - **a.** `display="3"`
   - **b.** `selected`
   - **c.** `checked="checked"`
   - **d.** `multiple`

5. Which button code would be best to display Modify and trigger an edit function?
   - **a.** `<input type="edit" name="edit">Modify</input>`
   - **b.** `<input type="submit" value="Modify" name="edit">`
   - **c.** `<input type="button" label="Modify" id="edit">`
   - **d.** `<input type="reset" name="Modify" action="edit">`

6. Why does the W3C recommend labeling form controls?
   - **a.** The color blind have difficulty reading some text/background color combinations.
   - **b.** Screen-reader software skips past unlabeled form controls.
   - **c.** Labeled form controls improve the usability of the form.
   - **d.** Label text displays in bold, increasing its readability.

7. In a select list of country names, which option would a Web application reject and request the user select a valid country?
   - **a.** `<option>Select a country`
   - **b.** `<option value="none">Select a country</option>`
   - **c.** `<option value="notSelected" selected>Select a country</option>`
   - **d.** All of the above

8. Which of the following is true?
   - **a.** A group of radio buttons should allow only one item to be selected.
   - **b.** A group of checkboxes can allow multiple items to be selected.
   - **c.** The multi select list is uncommon and unfamiliar to most users.
   - **d.** All of the above.

9. The <fieldset> and <legend> tags may be used to identify __________.
   a. a group of radio buttons
   b. a collection of a variety of form controls
   c. a group of related select-list options
   d. all of the above

10. The post method __________.
   a. sends the form data to the action URL
   b. encrypts the form data so a hacker can't snoop it
   c. emails the form data to your email address
   d. all of the above

## DISCUSSION QUESTIONS

1. Online stores, from which you can purchase items, require a large amount of information to enable you to complete your purchase. What type of information would you need to collect from customers to enable them to complete their purchases? For each type of information, identify what type of form control you would use to simplify data entry for the customers.

2. HTML forms are the most important types of Web pages. Do you agree or disagree with this statement and why?

# SKILL DRILL

Skill Drills reinforce project skills. Each skill reinforced is the same, or nearly the same, as a skill presented in the lessons. Detailed instructions are provided in a step-by-step format. Work through these exercises in order.

## 1. Create a Web Form to Sign in for an Online Exam

In this Skill Drill, you create a basic form that serves as the opening page for an online examination for the Web Design 301 course. (In Challenge Exercise 1, you add to this series of examination pages.)

1. Create a new site definition called **`Casual University`** from the Project_08>CasualU folder.
2. Open signin.html.
3. Click in the empty paragraph below the last sentence and create a **`2`**-row, **`1`**-column layout table with no width setting, **`0`** border thickness, **`0`** cell padding, **`0`** cell spacing, and no headers. With the table selected, set the table (not cell) alignment to center.
4. Insert casualu-logo.jpg from the images folder into the top cell, and assign **`Casual University`** as the alternate text.
5. Select the bottom cell and set the horizontal alignment to center. In the bottom cell, type **`Web Design 301`** and format it as Heading 1. Press Enter/Return, and type **`Mid Term Exam`**, and format it as Heading 2. Press Enter/Return and type **`You are required to complete all fields in all pages of this examination.`** Select this paragraph and apply bold to it. Click to the right of this paragraph and press Enter/Return.
6. Create a form where the name is signIn, the Method is POST, the Action is **`q1.html`**, and the Enctype is set to application/x-www-form-urlencoded.

7. In the form area, insert a **3**-row, **2**-column table with the width set to **60%**, border thickness set to **0**, cell padding set to **3**, cell spacing set to **0**, and headers set to none. Select the top four cells and set the cell width to **50%**. Select the top and middle left cells, and set the cell alignment to right.

8. In the top-left cell, type **Student Name**, and in the cell below, type **Student ID**. In the top-right cell, insert a text field named **studentName** that is **35** characters wide. In the middle-right cell, insert a password field named **studentID** that is **35** characters wide.

9. Merge the bottom two cells. Set the horizontal alignment of the merged cell to center. In the merged cell, insert a submit button with the name **signIn** and a Label **Sign Me In**.

10. Right/Control-click the studentName text field, and select Edit Tag <input>; in the Style Sheet/Accessibility category, ensure that the ID is **studentName** (add it, if it isn't). Using the same procedures, ensure the studentID text field has the ID of **studentID**.

11. Select Student Name in the left cell, Right/Control-click and wrap the selected text with the **<label>** tag, with the **for** attribute set to **studentName**. Using the same procedures, wrap Student ID with the **<label>** tag, setting the **for** attribute to **studentID**.

12. Close signin.html, saving your changes.

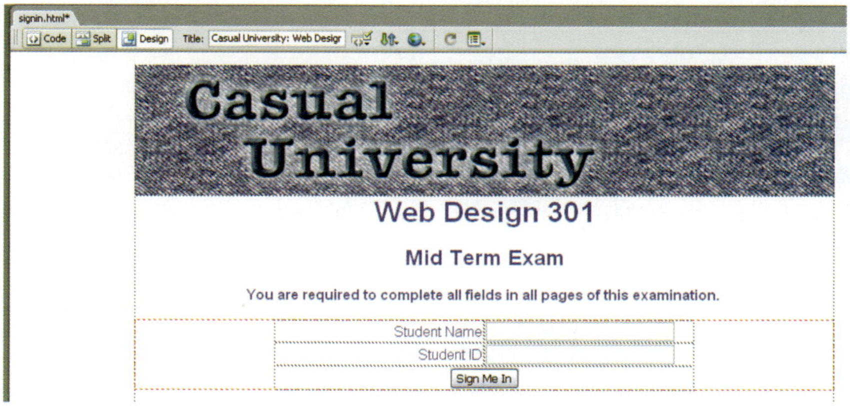


**FIGURE 8.57**

## 2. Create a Contact Form

A contact form is one of the most common means of contacting a company. It provides the employees some degree of protection against spam by hiding their email from direct access. A contact form can accommodate changing staff when a contact person changes position, department, or employers. A contact form can also help categorize the message based on the types of questions the customers/visitors have and the department they want to contact, making it easier for the company to respond.

In this exercise, you create a contact form that includes the basic Name and Email fields as well as lists of departments and types of questions the visitor might have.

1. Open contactus.html from the Forms site.

2. In the empty paragraph below the Contact Us heading, insert a form with the name **contactus**, Method set to POST, Action set to **thankyou.html**, and Enctype set to application/x-www-form-urlencoded.

3. In the form, insert a 7-row, 2-column table, with the width set to 100%, border thickness set to 0, cell padding set to 2, cell spacing set to 0, and headers set to none. Select the left column and set the horizontal alignment to right. Merge the bottom two cells and set the horizontal alignment to center.

4. In the top-left cell, type `Your Name:`, and in the right cell, insert a text field with a name of `contactName` and a width of 35. In the left cell of the second row, type `Your Email:`, and in the right cell, insert a text field with a name of `contactEmail` and a width of 35. In the left cell of the third row, insert one checkbox with a name of `ccSender`, a Checked Value of `yes`, and Initial State set to Checked. In the right cell, type `Send a copy of the message to you`.

5. In the left cell of the fourth row, type `Department:`. In the right cell, create a menu list named `department` with the following five items: `Select a department` (assign a value of `noDept`), `Sales`, `Service`, `Human Resources`, and `Web master` (no values for the last four items). Set Select a department as the Initially selected item.

6. In the left cell of the fifth row, type `Reason for Contacting Us:`. In the right cell, create a menu named `reason`. Using the chart below, create a list of items. When finished, set Choose a reason as the Initially Selected item.

| *Item Label* | *Value* |
|---|---|
| `Choose a reason` | `noReason` |
| `Order not arrived` | `notArrived` |
| `Order received broken` | `broken` |
| `Other` | `otherSales` |
| `Warranty enquiry` | `warranty` |
| `Schedule a repair` | `schedRepair` |
| `Order a part` | `partOrder` |
| `Other` | `otherService` |
| `Privacy and other Policies` | `policies` |
| `I would like a job` | `employment` |
| `Other` | `hrOther` |
| `Broken Web link` | `brokenLink` |
| `Other` | `webOther` |

The fact that there are multiple instances of an option labeled Other requires that they be distinguished using different values.

7. Switch to the Code view. Select from Order not arrived to otherSales.
Right/Control-click in the selected region, select Insert tag, and insert the **<optgroup>** tag with a label of `Sales Department`. Select from Warranty enquiry to otherService, and insert the **<optgroup>** tag with the label `Service Department`. Select from Privacy to hrOther, and insert the **<optgroup>** tag with the label `Human Resources`. Select the last two options, and insert the **<optgroup>** tag with the label `Web Site`. Switch to the Design view when finished.

8. In the sixth left cell, type **Comments:**. In the right cell, insert a multiline text field with a name of **comments**, a Char Width of **35**, and a Num Lines of **10**.

9. Apply the **<label>** tag to all of the labels, assigning the **for** attribute the same value as the **id** attribute of the related form control. Right/Control-click a form control, select Edit tag, and check for an ID in the Style Sheet/Accessibility category of the Tag Editor dialog box. If an ID does not exist, create one that is identical to the control name (found in the General category of the Tag Editor dialog box). Select the form control's label text, and wrap it with the **<label>** tag, assigning it the **for** attribute identical to the ID attribute of the form control. Repeat these procedures for all six form controls.

10. In the bottom merged cell, insert an image field using the Forms>images>contactusform.gif graphic. Type **submit** in the ImageField field and **Send Your Message** in the Alt field.

11. Preview the page in your browser and click the image-field button.

    A thank you message is very respectful of your customers. It may contain a static message, like this one or, through the magic of the form-processing application, may contain a copy of the message they sent via the form.

12. Close your browser, return to Dreamweaver, and close contactus.html.

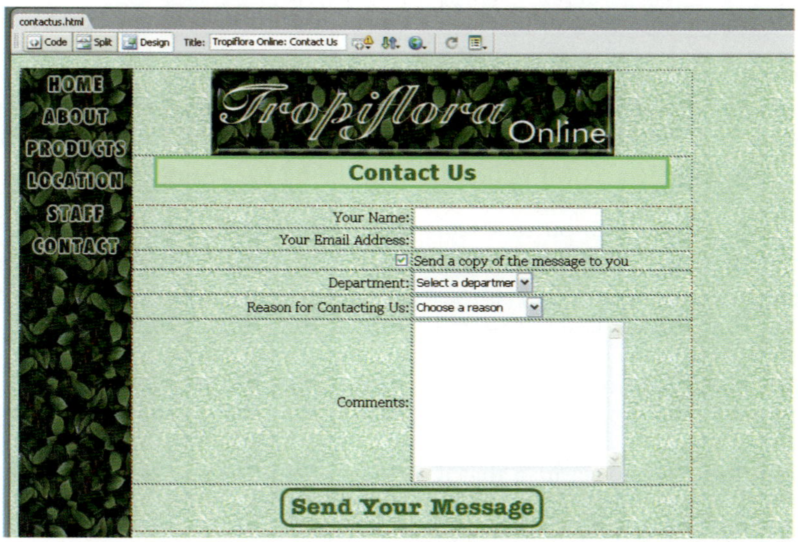


FIGURE 8.58

## To Extend Your Knowledge

### ONE LIST AFFECTS ANOTHER

This form uses optgroups to help the user select a reason that matches the department selected from the other list. However, this is a perfect example of a form in which JavaScript could be used so instead of optgroups, the selection of a department from the first list would hide all reasons except those that apply to the selected department.

## 3. Create a Marketing-Survey Form

In this exercise, you create a market-survey form using radio-button groups to provide the options while restricting the user to selecting just one from each group.

1. Create a new HTML page, title it `Market Survey`, and save it (but do not close it) as `survey.html` in the Forms site.
2. Type `Market Survey`, format it as Heading 1, and press Enter/Return.
3. Insert a form with the name `survey`, the Method set to POST, Action set to `market-survey.html`, and Enctype set to application/x-www-form-urlencoded.
4. Type `1. Select your age group` and press Enter/Return. Create a Radio Group called `age`. Create four radio buttons labeled `Under 25`, `25 to 34`, `35 to 44`, and `45 and older`. Make up your own values for the four radio buttons, keeping them short and without spaces. If necessary, use the plus button to add new rows, and the up and down arrows to sort the entries from youngest at the top to oldest at the bottom. Lay out the buttons using a table.
5. Click to the right of the radio-buttons table and press Enter/Return. Type `2. Select your family income.` and press Enter/Return. Create a radio-button group called `income` using `Less than $30,000`, `$30,000 to $45,000`, `$45,000 to $60,000`, and `Over $60,000`, and create your own values to match the labels. Lay out the buttons using a table.
6. Click to the right of the radio-buttons table and press Enter/Return. Type `3. Select your dwelling type.` and press Enter/Return. Create a radio-button group called `dwelling` using `Apartment`, `Row House – Rented`, `Row House – Owned`, `Condominium`, `Duplex`, and `House` as the labels, and create your own values. Lay out the buttons using a table.
7. Click to the right of the radio-buttons table and press Enter/Return. Type `4. Select your current profession.` and press Enter/Return. Create a radio-button group called `profession` using `Retail`, `Government`, `Health Services`, `Business Owner`, and `Other`, and create your own values. Lay out the buttons using a table.
8. In the last cell to the right of Other, click and press Enter/Return. Type `If you selected Other, please specify.` Insert a text field called `specifyOther` with a width of `25`.
9. Insert a submit button, and set it so that it displays `Thank You!` on the button.
10. Close survey.html, saving your changes.

## 4. Create a Book Wish-List Form

For the purpose of this exercise, pretend you have created an application in which you, your family, and your friends may add entries to a Book Wish-List database. If anyone is trying to think of a perfect birthday gift, all they need do is consult the database. In this exercise, you create the front-end form that will submit the book details to the database. As part of the form, you add the URL to the Web site of the book (if there is one), and insert a little JavaScript function with which you may test the book Web-site URL.

1. Create a new HTML page, title it **Book Wish List**, and save it as **wishlist.html** in the Forms site.
2. Type **Book Wish List** and format it as Heading 1. Press Enter/Return, type **Add a new entry**, and format it as Heading 2. Press Enter/Return and type **All fields marked with an asterisk must be filled.** Select this paragraph and apply bold. Press Enter/Return.
3. Create a form with the name **wishlist**, Action set to **wishlist.html**, Method set to POST, and Enctype set to application/x-www-form-urlencoded.
4. Create a **7**-row, **2**-column table with the width set to **60%**, the border thickness set to **0**, cell padding set to **2**, cell spacing set to **0**, and no headers. Select the left column of cells and set the horizontal alignment to right. Merge the two cells in the bottom row, and set the horizontal alignment to center.
5. In the left column type **Title***, **Author(s)***, **ISBN**, **Publisher***, **Publication Date***, and **Book Web Site**. In the right columns, insert text fields for the **title**, **author**, **ISBN**, and, **publisher** with appropriate names and widths. Create a text field for the book Web site and name it **bookURL**. (The name is important as it is used in a JavaScript function added in Step 8.)
6. To enable the user to insert the publication date, create two menus. The first menu is a list of the months of the year, so name it appropriately. Above **January**, insert **Month**, assign it an appropriate value, and then add the rest of the month names (with or without values, your choice). The second menu is a list of years starting with **Year**, then listing **2004** backwards to **2000**. Assign an appropriate name for this list and also an appropriate value for Year, the top item in the list.
7. In the merged cell, insert a submit button that displays **Add To Wish List**.
8. Open testurl.html, press Control/Command-A to select all of the content, copy it to the clipboard, and close testurl.html. Click to the right of the book Web-site text field, and paste the copied code.
9. Preview the page in your browser.
10. Complete the form as follows: **Speed Up Your Site** is the title, **Andrew B. King** is the author, **0-7357-1324-3** is the ISBN, **New Riders** is the publisher, **January 2003** is the publication date, and **http://www.websiteoptimization.com** is the book's Web site. Click the Test URL link and observe that the book's Web site opens in a pop-up window.
11. Close the pop-up window, close your browser, return to Dreamweaver, and close wishlist.html.

## CHALLENGE

Challenge exercises expand on, or are somewhat related to, skills presented in the lessons. Each exercise provides a brief narrative introduction, followed by instructions in a numbered-step format that are not as detailed as those in the Skill Drill section. You can work through one or more exercises in any order.

### 1. Create a Multiple-Choice Exam

In this challenge, you create three forms containing questions from a multiple-choice exam. The action URLs send the student to the next question. Hidden fields contain the answers to previous questions. Although using hidden fields this way may not be very secure, it is possible to ***obfuscate*** (make obscure or unclear) the answer using a ***hash*** (a process of encrypting text whereby the result cannot be reversed to reveal the original text, but two encryptions of the same text produce the same result, enabling comparison) of the answer so that the student cannot simply change the answer in the hidden field from A to B. This exam process, and the generation of the hash (which is an available function in PHP and other programming languages) would normally be done with a form-processing application. However, this exercise will provide you with an understanding as to the type of process one might apply to a form-processing application.

1. Open q1.html from the Casual University site, and click in the empty paragraph below the instructions.
2. Create a new form called `q1` with the Action set to `q2.html`, the Method set to POST, and the Enctype set to application/x-www-form-urlencoded.
3. In the form, type `1. Which text format displays using the largest text size?` and press Enter/Return. Create a radio-button group with the name `q1`. Type `Heading 6`, `Heading 2`, `Paragraph`, and `Heading 1` as the labels, and `a`, `b`, `c`, and `d` as the values. Lay out the radio-button group using line breaks.
4. Press Enter/Return after the last answer and insert a hidden field with `studentID` as the name and `25D55AD283AA400AF464C76D713C07AD` as the value.

   This 32-character string is a hash of 12345678.
5. Create a submit button with `next` as the name and `Next Question` as the value.
6. Close, saving the changes.
7. Open q2.html. Use the same procedures as you did in Steps 2 to 6 with the following changes: set the form name as `q2` and the form's action to `q3.html`. The question is `2. Absolute links are necessary when linking:` and the answers are `a page to a named anchor`, `to a target window`, `to a page in another Web site`, and `alternate text`. Insert the same `studentID` hidden field plus another hidden field called `answer1` with a value of `8277E0910D750195B448797616E091AD`. When finished, close q2.html, saving your changes.
8. Open q3.html. Use the same procedures as in Step 7 with the following changes: set the form name as `q3` and the form's action to `results.html`. The question is `3. GIF and JPEG image formats:` and the answers are `are bitmapped graphics`, `are limited to 256 colors`, `can be animated`, and `are the storage formats of digital cameras`. Insert the same `studentID` and `answer1` hidden fields plus another hidden field called `answer2` with a value of `4A8A08F09D37B73795649038408B5F33`. When finished, close q3.html, saving your changes.

9. Open results.html. Below Results, insert a Definition List from the Text Insert bar. Type **`1. Which text format displays using the largest text size?`**, press Enter/Return, type **`Heading 1`**, and press Enter/Return. Type **`2. Absolute links are necessary when linking:`**, press Enter/Return, type **`to a page in another Web site`**, and press Enter/Return. Type **`3. GIF and JPEG image formats:`**, press Enter/Return, type **`are bitmapped graphics`**, and press Enter/Return twice.
10. Type **`Congratulations! Perfect!`**.
11. Insert the same three hidden fields as you did previously: **`studentID`**, **`answer1`**, and **`answer2`**. Create a fourth hidden field called **`answer3`** with a value of **`0CC175B9C0F1B6A831C399E269772661`**. Close, saving the changes.
12 Open signin.html and preview it in your browser. Sign in and answer the questions in the forms. When finished, close your browser, return to Dreamweaver, and close signin.html.

## *To Extend Your Knowledge*

### A HASH CALCULATOR

If you search for hash calculator using your favorite search engine, you will find a number of downloadable, free calculators that enable you to calculate different forms of hashes. You may also go to bfl.rctek.com/tools/?tool=hasher for an online version. When you compare the MD5 hash for a, d, and c (individually), you see that these values are equal to the values of the answer1, answer2, and answer3 hidden fields.

## 2. Create a Two-Form Page

When working with forms, one common programming technique is that when two or three forms are related to each other, all two or three forms are created within the same HTML page. The form data sent by the first form is used by the programming code to determine that the second form is to be displayed. For example, the first form could ask for your name. When the form is sent back to itself, the programming code sees that your name has been completed and sends you the second form (with the name stored in a hidden field). The second form asks you for your gender. When the form is sent back to itself, the programming code takes your name from the hidden field, your gender from the most recent form data and creates a suitable message for you.

In this exercise, you create both forms on the same page and insert some ***pseudo-code*** (programming-like code written in understandable English instructions to describe the process that will be used) that, on a Web server, might be used to populate the employee-details form with the information about the employees.

1. Open edit-student.html from the Casual University site, and click in the empty cell below the top graphic.
2. Type **`Select a Student`** and format it as Heading 1. Press Enter/Return.
3. Insert a form with a name of **`selectStudent`**, the Action set to **`edit-students.html`**, the Method to GET (for the time being so we can analyze the query string), and Enctype to application/x-www-form-urlencoded.

4. In the form, type **Select a student** and press Shift-Enter/Return. Insert a menu named **studentID** with the following five student names and values (student IDs): **Carole Brown** (**1234**), **Bruce Carter** (**2345**), **Jane Higgins** (**3456**), **Tommy Kettle** (**4567**), and finally, your own name and a four-digit number. Select both the label text (**Select a student**) and the menu control, and click the Label button to insert an implicit label.

5. Click to the right of the menu control and press Enter/Return. Insert a submit button with the name **submit** and a label of **Edit Student Record**.

6. In the empty paragraph below this form, type **Edit Student Record** and format it as Heading 1. Press Enter/Return and create another form named **editStudent**, set Action to **edit-student.html**, the Method to GET, and Enctype to application/x-www-form-urlencoded.

7. In the form, create a **9**-row, **2**-column layout table. In the left column, create the following labels: **Student ID**, **First Name**, **Last Name**, **Street Address**, **City/Town**, **State**, **Home Phone**, and **Birth Date**. In the right column, insert text fields for the first seven labels, and create three for Birth Date with the labels **Day**, **Month**, and **Year**. Merge the bottom row and insert a select button with the name **submit** and the label **Save Changes**.

8. Insert your name and particulars as the initial values for all of the fields.

9. In the empty paragraph below the second form, type **Student Record Updated** and format it as Heading 1.

10. Switch to the Code view and scroll to approximately line 17 where **<h1>Select a Student</h1>** appears. Open edit-student.php.txt, select lines 2 to 6, copy the text, switch to edit-student.html, and paste the text between the **<form>** and **<h1>** tags around line 17. Switch to edit-student.php.txt and select lines 10 to 17, copy them, switch back to edit-student.html, and paste them between the **<form>** and **<h1>** tags near line 34. Switch to edit-student.php.txt, copy lines 21 to 26, switch back to edit-student.html, and paste them between the last **<form>** and **<h1>** tags near line 86.

    Read the three inserted blocks of pseudo-code. The first block says that if there is no query string, the first form is displayed. The second block says that if the query string identifies that the Edit Student Record button is clicked and contains the studentID, the database will be queried using that studentID, and the second form is populated with the student's details and displayed. The third block says that if the Save Changes button was clicked, the database is updated with the new data and the third part of the page is displayed.

11. Preview the page in your browser. Select your name from the top form, click the Edit Student Record button, and examine the query string for submit=Edit+Student+Record and your studentID. Click the second submit button and examine the query string for submit=Save+Changes.

    In this situation, it is fine to have three Heading-1 blocks because only one displays at a time.

12. Close your browser, return to Dreamweaver, and close edit-student.html and edit-student.php.txt.

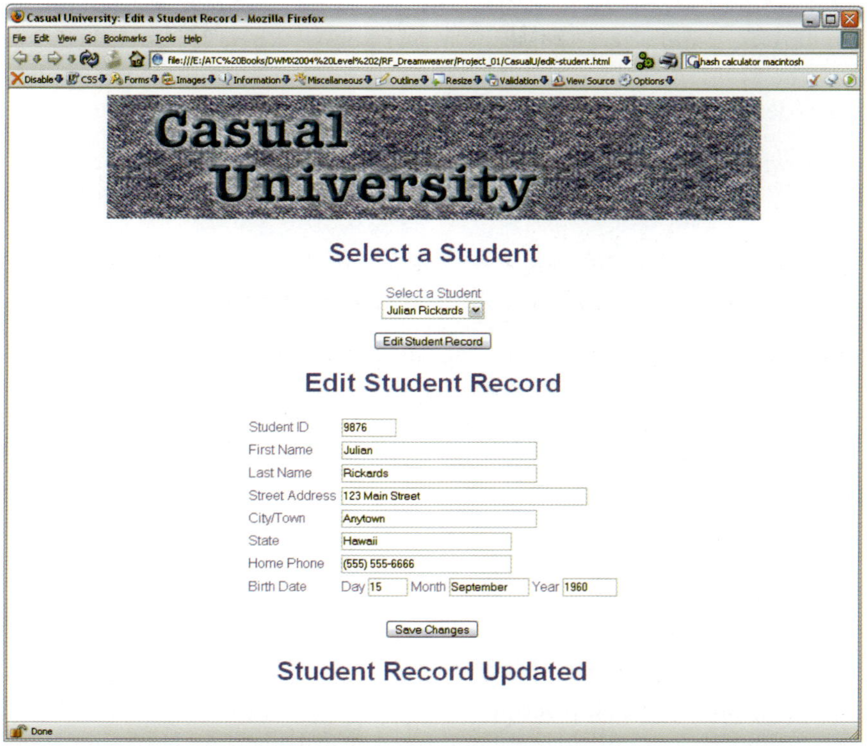


**FIGURE 8.59**

## 3. Using Image Buttons to Submit Orders

The image button is useful, not only for decorating the text of a submit button but also, on a shopping site, for submitting an item to the ***shopping cart*** (a term used to describe the shopping process used on an online store) for purchase. In this exercise, you complete the form that students may use to purchase books for their courses. In place of plain buttons, you use image buttons that are images of the book covers.

1. Open order-books.html from the Casual University site.
2. Click in the cell to the left of the description of the Dreamweaver book. Click the Image Field button from the Forms Insert bar, and insert ATC_DW_MX_Cover.JPG from the images folder. Type **`Order this Dreamweaver book`** in the alternate-text field. Copy the ISBN number from the right cell, and paste it into the name field of the Image Field button.
3. Repeat Step 2 and insert Image Field buttons for each of the books. Change the alternate text to reflect the book, and change the name of the field to reflect the ISBN number.

   The ISBN number is a unique identifier of each book and is used by the database system to manage the shopping cart as well as other business functions of the online store.
4. In the empty cell at the bottom of the table, insert a submit button with the name **`submit`** and the label **`Checkout`**.

5. Preview the page in your browser, click any of the book covers, and examine the query string.

   Image field buttons appear twice in a query string because they indicate not only which image was clicked, but also the x and y position of the mouse pointer where it was clicked. In some other applications, the position of the mouse pointer is useful, but for this type of application, all that is needed is the identity (ISBN) of the selected book.

6. Close your browser, return to Dreamweaver, and close order-book.html.

**FIGURE 8.60**

## 4. Hide Optional Fields Using JavaScript

You have read often in this project that JavaScript is commonly used to enhance the usability of forms. In this exercise, you create a form that has both required and optional fields. The JavaScript function in this page, when clicked, hides the optional fields and, when clicked again, reveals the optional fields. You don't need to insert or type any of the JavaScript: it is configured to act on certain classes and ids. When you create the optional fields in this form to enable JavaScript to work on them, you must assign them the class name optional. The JavaScript code looks for all instances of the class optional and hides or reveals them depending on how many times the link is clicked. The link to also is dynamically created using JavaScript. In Dreamweaver, the link is not visible because Dreamweaver does not run the JavaScript.

1. Open contactus.html from the Casual University site.
2. Click to the right of Contact Us and press Enter/Return.
3. Press Control/Command-B to apply bold, type `Labels with the asterisk (*) are required.`, press Control/Command-B to disable bold, and press Enter/Return.
4. Right/Control-click the empty paragraph, and select Edit Tag <p> from the contextual menu. From the Style Sheet/Accessibility category of the Tag Editor dialog box, type `hidedisplaylink` in the ID field (the spelling and letter case is important or the JavaScript won't be able to act on it).

### If you have problems

If you have problems Right/Control-clicking the empty paragraph, type some text, and then Right/Control-click and complete the rest of Step 4. Delete the text but not the paragraph tag when you are finished with Step 4.

5. Create a form with the name **contactus**, the action set to **thankyou.html**, the method set to POST, and Enctype set to application/x-www-form-urlencoded.

6. In the form, create a **6**-row, **2**-column layout table. In the left cells, insert the following field labels: **Full Name**, **Student ID**, **Email address**, **Subject ***, and **Comments ***. In the right columns, create appropriate text fields for each of these fields, except the Comments field. The Comments field should be a text area field, **35** characters wide and **10** lines high.

7. Merge the bottom two cells and insert a **submit** button with the label **Send us your comments**.

8. Click in Full Name and, using the Tag selector, click the **<tr>** tag. Right/Control-click the **<tr>** tag, select Edit tag, add **class="optional"** to the tag, and press Enter/Return. Repeat the process for the **<tr>** tag of the Student ID and Email address rows.

9. Preview this page in your browser.

   Notice the link that wasn't visible in Dreamweaver: the JavaScript function has been programmed to create this link and text dynamically.

10. Type information in all of the fields.

11. Click the link and notice that the optional fields are hidden (by hiding the table rows in which they exist), and the link-text changes, enabling you to reveal the optional fields.

    Notice that the contents of the fields are not erased when the fields are hidden and revealed again. The hiding processing does not erase the table rows and its contents; it hides them.

12. Close your browser, return to Dreamweaver, and close contactus.html.

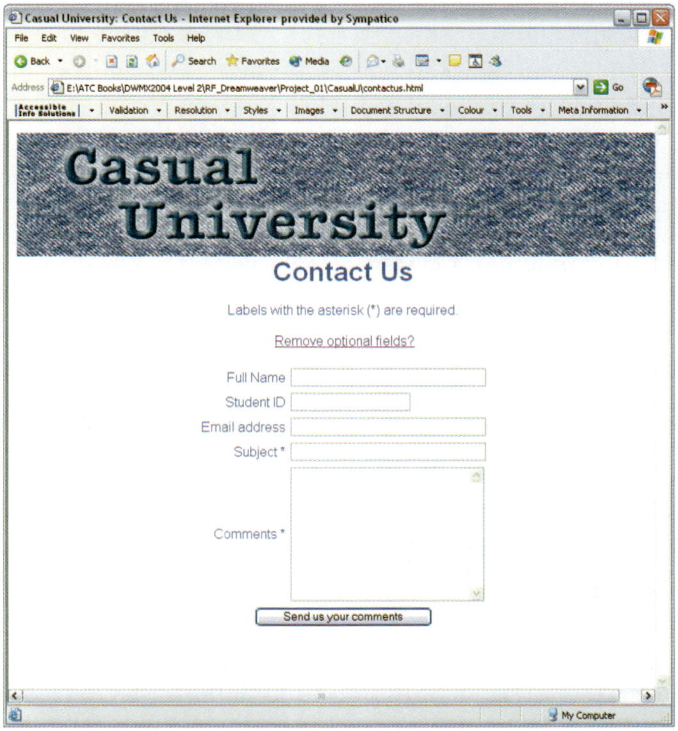


**FIGURE 8.61**

# PORTFOLIO BUILDER

## Create Forms to Process a Purchase

Online stores require a large amount of information to enable customers to complete their purchases. In this assignment, you're going to create a series of forms that collect and process customer and purchase information for an online bookstore.

Before you begin, write down the author and title of three books you own, and use these as the selected products from your online bookstore. Assume that the books you have chosen are stored in a shopping-cart database. Consider the following options when you create the forms:

1. The customer may be a new or returning customer. Given that you need information about the customer but don't want to ask returning customers to enter their personal information each time they visit your site, create the form or forms necessary to gather information from a new customer. Provide an option to allow returning customers to identify themselves without having to reenter this information.
2. A purchase-confirmation page allows customers to view their purchase selections and, if necessary, reconsider their selections. Create a form that displays their shopping-cart items and allows them to make some changes. Consider the type of changes you would allow customers to make to their orders and provide the appropriate options in the form.
3. Create a form that displays the customer's shipping information and provides shipping options.
4. Create a payment form allowing users to select how they will pay for their products. Do you only accept credit cards or would you also allow other payment methods? What type of information do you need from the customers and what information might customers need from the store for their selected payment option?
5. Create a page that displays their final invoice. This page is not a form but gathers information from the previous forms. Do not display sensitive information, such as credit-card information.

# PROJECT 9

# Working with Cascading Style Sheets

## OBJECTIVES

*In this project, you learn how to*

- Use element selectors singly or grouped
- Apply styles using classes and ids
- Create style rules using contextual selectors
- Use pseudo-class selectors
- Create custom styles using the <span> tag
- Create and apply external style sheets
- Use design-time style sheets
- Create print and alternate style sheets

## WHY WOULD I DO THIS?

***Cascading style sheets*** (***CSS***) is a coding language that is part of the W3C Web technologies. Its purpose is to handle the presentation while leaving the document structure to (X)HTML. CSS version 1 was released in late 1996, just months before HTML 4.0. The current version is CSS2.1; CSS3 is in draft form. Despite the many years that CSS has been around and the intent that CSS be responsible for the presentation of Web pages, many designers use design software that does not make it easy to apply CSS. Dreamweaver MX 2004 is better than other Web-design software in its support for CSS, but even in Dreamweaver there are many options for applying CSS that cannot easily be chosen from a dialog box. In some ways, CSS may be considered a weak programming language because parts of it rely on relationships between HTML elements and these types of relationships cannot be easily offered through dialog boxes. In this project, you learn how CSS works and how you can make it work effectively for you.

The term Cascading Style Sheets requires some explanation. Style is obvious; CSS is used to add style, such as color, backgrounds, and borders, to Web pages. The word sheet indicates the most common methods of creating CSS — collecting all of the styles into a block or sheet. Style sheets can be embedded or external. Embedded style sheets appear in the **<head>** section of an HTML document between opening and closing **<style>** tags. External style sheets are separate files attached to all pages in a Web site. The word cascading refers to the fact that if you apply a style to the paragraph **p** element, the style applies or cascades to every paragraph on the page or in the Web site.

Two questions may occur to you when you think about CSS: what does CSS do and how may it be applied? Using CSS, you can add or change text styling, colors, backgrounds, bullet characters, and many other properties. How to apply CSS is a more difficult question to answer because applying CSS is more complex than the old HTML presentation methods which use presentation tags, such as the **<font>** tag, and presentation attributes, such as the **bgcolor** (background color) attribute. Applying CSS is the primary focus of this project.

You may wonder why you should learn CSS. Perhaps the most obvious reason is its power. Through one simple modification, you can change the paragraph typeface from Arial to Times, not just for the current paragraph, or even all paragraphs in the current page, but all pages in your site, whether 10, 100, or 100,000 pages. Another reason why CSS is so important is its versatility. For example, HTML allowed backgrounds (background colors or images) behind only a few elements: the body, tables, table rows, and table cells. Using CSS, you can apply backgrounds to any element on the page. Variety is another reason why CSS is important to learn. HTML does not allow you to create a custom bullet for lists, change line spacing, remove bold from headings, or remove underline from links. These are examples of commonly supported features of CSS that HTML cannot match. CSS can be written to apply certain combinations of styles just on the basis of relationships between HTML elements. For example **h2+p** tells CSS to apply a combination of styles to the first paragraph after a heading 2 whereas all other paragraphs after that one have a different style. CSS can help reduce ***page weight*** (the amount of bytes required to render a Web page) in two ways. It takes fewer bytes of CSS to define the style of a page than HTML presentation. For example, to change 10 paragraphs to Arial font,

HTML would use **<font face="Arial"></font>** ten times (26 × 10 = 260 characters) whereas **p {font-family: Arial}** uses only 22 characters and, unlike the **<font>** tag, additional paragraphs in the page do not need any additional characters. Redesign is another good reason to learn to use CSS. Property structured HTML determines the document structure and that does not change when there is a redesign of a Web site. However, the look and layout of the Web site may well change with a redesign and they are controlled with CSS. Of course, the design graphics may also require changing, such as background graphics.

Whenever you embark on a CSS-based design, you should start with a page with properly formatted content but with no style whatsoever — no text alignment, no colors, no background, nothing. This becomes your blank canvas on which you build your creative design. As a result, you build a Web page or Web site in which the structure is completely separate from the presentation: structure and presentation are the separate domains of HTML and CSS.

Web designers limit their creativity by not knowing and using CSS. However, just knowing the properties, such as background images or text color, is not sufficient. When you learn how CSS may be applied, what options are available to you, and how you may combine them, then you have learned to design using CSS.

## VISUAL SUMMARY

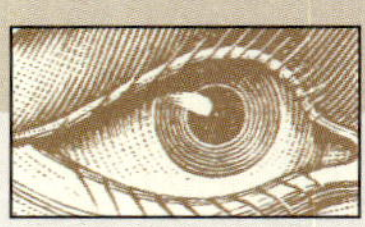

This project focuses more on helping you understand how to apply CSS and less on the properties and values of CSS. However, you should be familiar with the CSS Styles dialog box with which you create the styles.

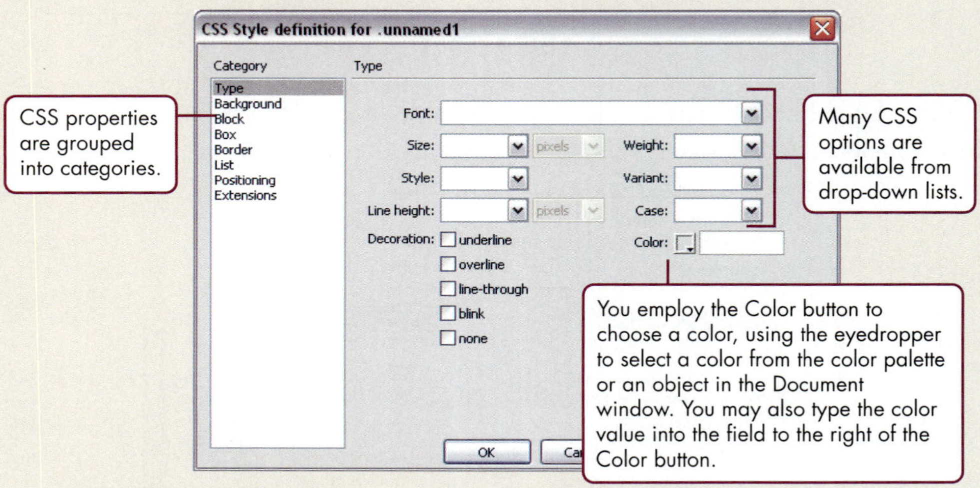


FIGURE 9.1

However, before you assign a CSS property, you must identify the tag, class or other selector to which you are applying the style. You also must identify where the styles are to be stored: in the current document or in a style-sheet file.

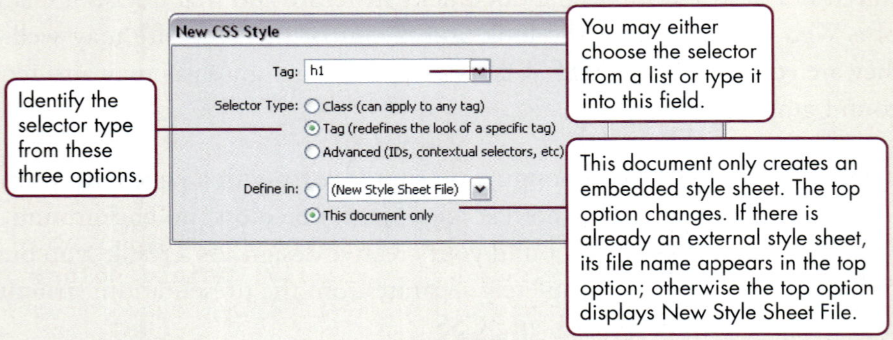


FIGURE 9.2

If you have an external style sheet, you must attach it to the Web pages so that the styles within it can be applied to the pages. The Link method is the most common method for attaching an external style sheet but the Import method is also useful.

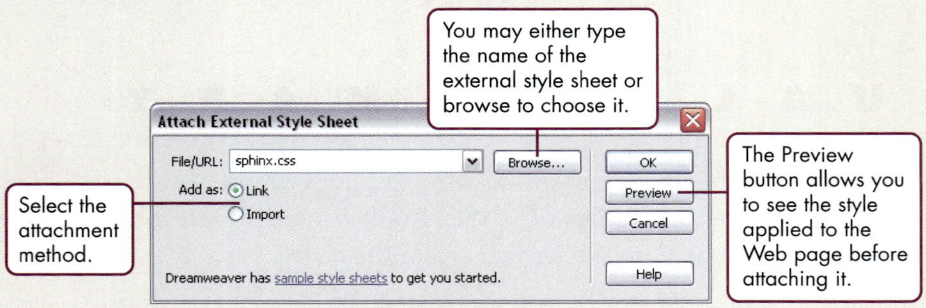


FIGURE 9.3

The Design Time Style Sheet function allows you to hide or display selected style sheets during the design process. This is very beneficial when developing an alternate or print style sheet.

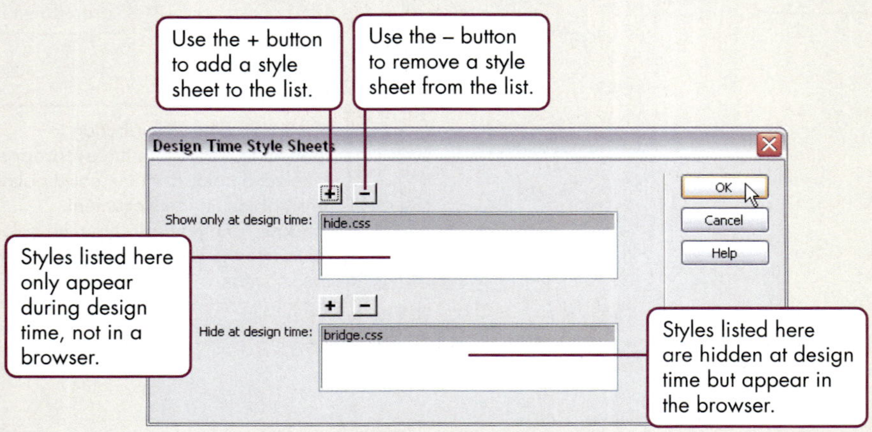


FIGURE 9.4

# LESSON 1 Using Element Selectors and Grouping

CSS, like any technology, has its own terminology. CSS uses ***properties*** (types of appearances) and ***values*** (options for the properties), such as the property **`color`** (used to change the color of text) and the value **`red`** (one of many possible values of the **`color`** property). In code, a property and its value are separated from each other using a colon (:), such as **`color: red`**. Some properties accept multiple values, such as font-family in which you can list multiple fonts in case the first font is not installed on a visitor's computer. For example, **`font-family: Georgia, Times, "Times New Roman", serif`**. Quotation marks are inserted around Times New Roman because the phrase as a whole identifies the font and the spaces would cause a problem.

A CSS property: value pair is called a "style declaration." You can group declarations; when you do so, you must separate declarations with semicolons (;), such as: **`font-family: Arial; color: red`**. Many CSS hand-coders add a semicolon after the last declaration — it is not necessary and it doesn't cause any problems, they just like to use it in case they should want to add another declaration and might forget to begin the next declaration with the semicolon. When you choose multiple properties in the CSS Style dialog box in Dreamweaver, it creates a grouped declaration. A ***style declaration block*** is a complete set of style declarations surrounded by curly braces, such as **`{font-family: Arial; color: red}`**. A declaration block can contain one or more declarations; it does not require multiple declarations to be considered a declaration block, but curly braces must surround it.

Despite the fact that a declaration block has been created, you don't know which text is red Arial because it is not identified in the declaration block. A ***selector*** is the HTML code to which the declaration block will be applied. The simplest form of selector is an ***element selector***: a single HTML tag, such as **`p`** or **`h1`**. Element selectors in CSS are the HTML tags without the angle brackets (**`<p>`** is the paragraph tag whereas **`p`** is the paragraph element). A ***style rule*** is the complete package of selector and declaration block, such as **`p {font-family: Arial; color: red}`** which styles all paragraph text as red Arial.

Just as declarations can be grouped, selectors can also be grouped, but the format is slightly different. Multiple selectors must be separated with commas, such as **`h1, h2, h3`**, which would apply the same style to text in any of these heading levels. Dreamweaver does not provide a click-and-point method of grouping selectors using its dialog boxes, but you can group them quite easily using the advanced selector option and typing the selector group in the Tag field.

## Add Styles to Element Selectors

In this exercise, you add some basic styles to a Web page to learn the difference between single and grouped element selectors and single and grouped declarations.

1. **Define the Project_09>My Travels folder as a site called `My Travels`. Do not click Done — leave the Site Definition dialog box open for the next step.**

2. **Click the first site in the list from a previous project, and click the Remove button. When asked to confirm the removal, click Yes. Repeat until you have removed all sites from the list (except the My Travels site you defined in Step 1). Click Done when finished.**

3. **Open index.html.**

**4** **Right/Control-click in the CSS Styles panel (if it is not open, click the Design panel group title to expand it, then click the CSS Styles tab if it is not visible) and choose New. In the New CSS Style dialog box, set Selector Type to Tag, choose (or type) `body` in the Tag field, set Define in to This Document Only, and click OK.**

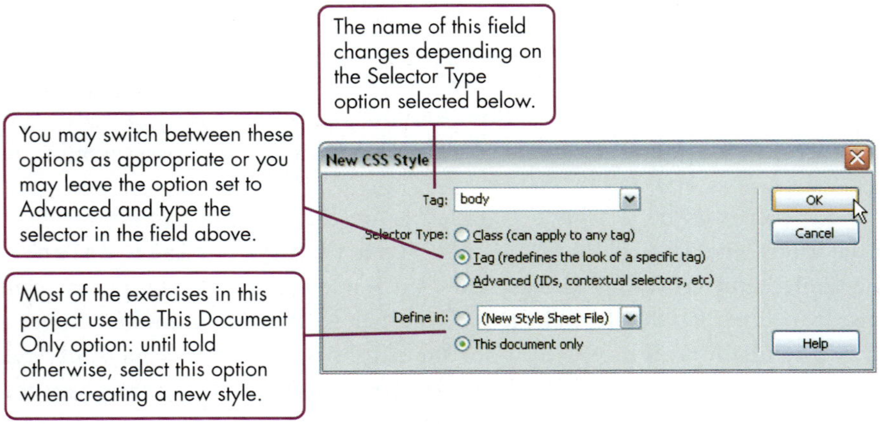


FIGURE 9.5

**5** **In the Background category, set Background color to `#969696` and click OK.**

**6** **Right/Control-click in the CSS Styles panel and choose Go to Code.**

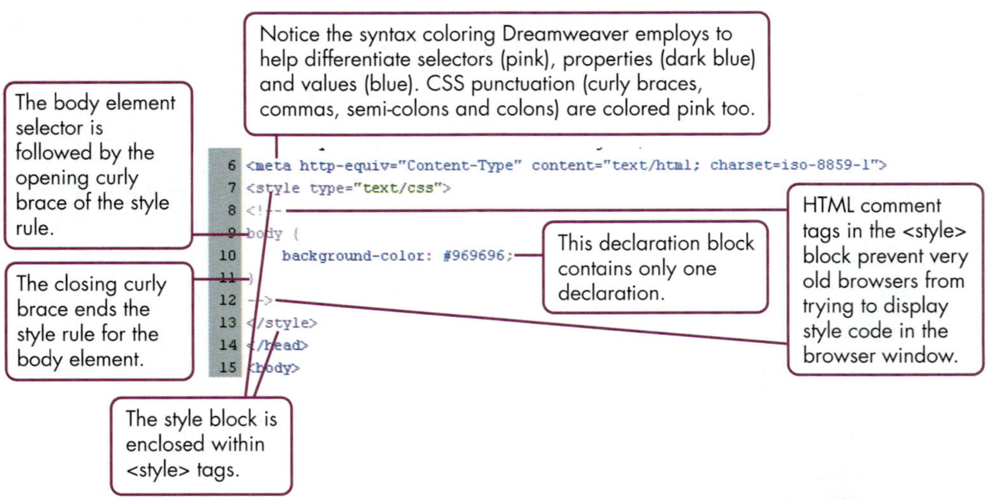


FIGURE 9.6

**7** **Right/Control-click body in the CSS Styles panel and choose Edit.**

**8** In the Box category, keep Same for All selected for both Padding and Margin, set both Padding and Margin to `0` pixels, and click OK.

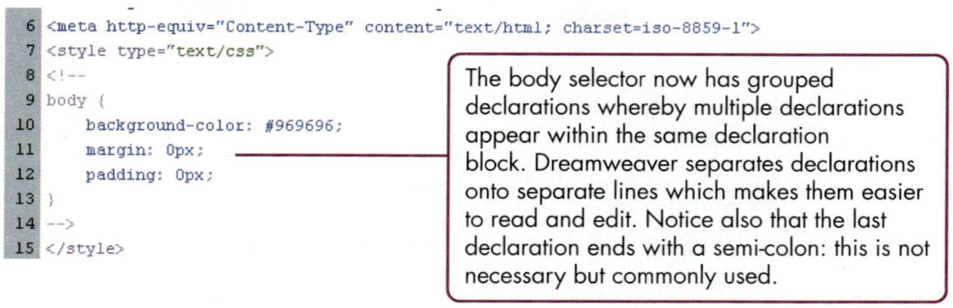


FIGURE 9.7

**9** Close the Code window.

**10** Create a new style for the blockquote tag by Right/Control-clicking in the CSS Style panel, selecting New, selecting or typing `blockquote` in the Tag field, setting Selector Type to Tag, setting Define in to This Document Only, and clicking OK.

**11** From the Type category, set Style to italic. From the Block category, set Text Align to center. Click OK.

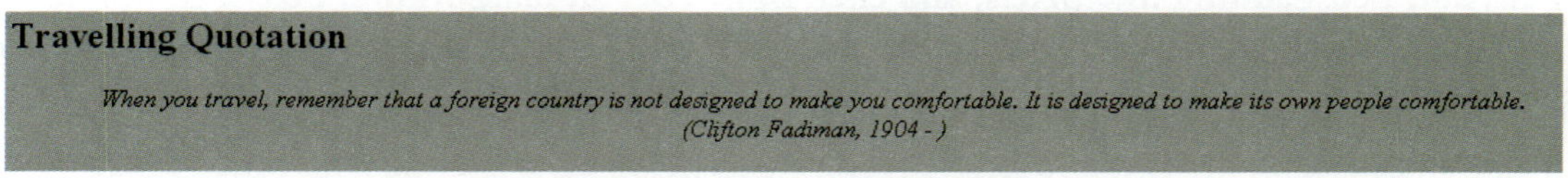


FIGURE 9.8

**12** Save the changes but leave index.html open for the next exercise.

## Assign Common Styles to Multiple Selectors

In this exercise, you learn to group selectors. Dreamweaver does not provide any point-and-click tools to simplify this process, but it is not difficult. You simply choose the Advanced option from the Selector Type group of radio buttons and type the comma-separated list of selectors in the Selector field. When you are considering using grouped selectors, you must plan ahead, because although it is easy to create a group, if you decide that one member of the group should be removed, you must go into the code to remove it from the comma-separated list. You could consider creating the styles separately rather than grouping them, but that would increase the size of the CSS file and therefore the page weight.

**1** **Create a new CSS Style; choose Advanced from the Selector Type group; in the Selector field, type `h1, h2, h3`; and click OK.**

Throughout the rest of this project, you will create styles for the Tag selector type, the Class selector type, and the Advanced selector type. Rather than switching between the types, use the Advanced selector type for all of them: the Advanced selector type allows all types of selectors. Also, until Lesson 6, set Define in to This Document Only.

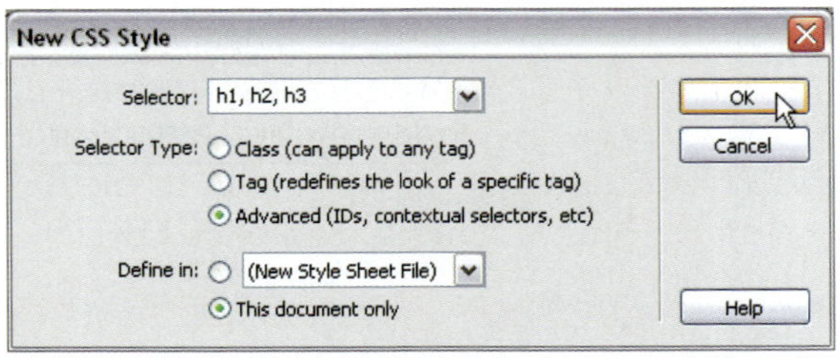


FIGURE 9.9

**2** **In the Type category of the CSS Style dialog box, set Color to `#C4C4C4` and click Apply. In the Background category, set the Background Color to `#969696` and click Apply. In the Block category, set Letter Spacing to `2` pixels and click Apply. In the Box category, uncheck Same for All for Padding; set Top Padding to `15` pixels, Right Padding to `0` pixels, Bottom Padding to `0` pixels, and Left Padding to `5` pixels; and click Apply. Set all margins to `0` pixels. In the Border category, uncheck all Same for All; set the Top Border to solid, `1` pixel, `#000` (three zeros); and click OK.**

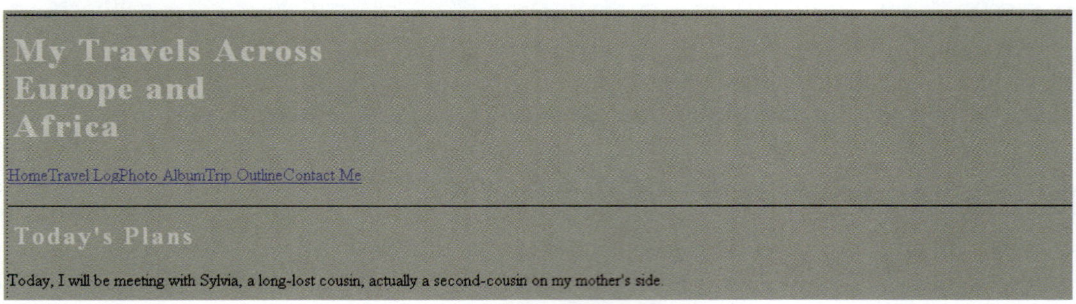


FIGURE 9.10

**3** **To remove the h1 selector from this group, Right/Control-click `h1, h2, h3` in the CSS Styles panel and choose Go to Code.**

**4** **In the Code window, delete `h1`, from the selector group and close the Code window.**

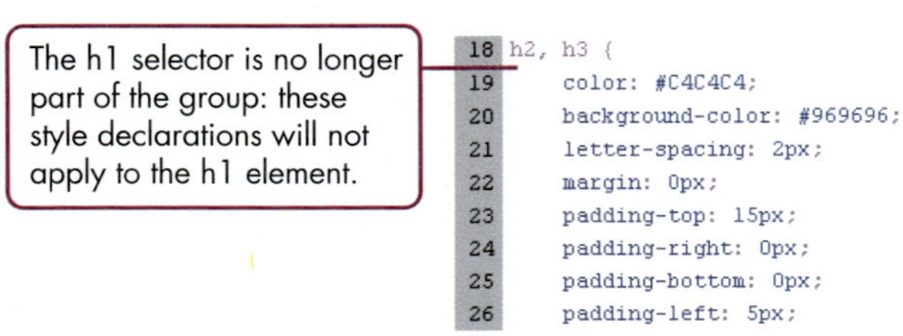


FIGURE 9.11

## If you have problems

If the style of the Heading-1 block at the top of the page does not revert to its previous style, click the Refresh button in the Property inspector.

**5** Create a new CSS Style for the `h1` tag. In the Type category, set Color to `#C4C4C4`. In the Block category, set Text Align to right. In the Background category, set Background Color to `#965156`, Background Image to images>london-bridge.jpg, Background Repeat to no-repeat, Horizontal Position to left, and Vertical position to top. In the Box category, set Height to `200` pixels, set all paddings and margins to `0` pixels, and click OK.

FIGURE 9.12

**6** Create a new CSS Style for the selector group `p, li`. In the Type category, set Line Height to `1.4` ems and click OK.

**7** Scroll to the contact-form table at the bottom of the page, and click to the right of Name. Create a new CSS style for `input, textarea`. In the Box category, set Width to `200` pixels and click OK.

**8** Create a new CSS Style for the `textarea` tag. In the Box category, set Height to `120` pixels and click OK.

FIGURE 9.13

**9** Save the changes to index.html, leaving it open for the next exercise.

## To Extend Your Knowledge

### CSS SHORTHAND FORMATS

There are a number of CSS shorthand formats that Dreamweaver knows about and can apply. There are six font properties: **`font-style`** (normal or italic), **`font-variant`** (normal or small-cap), **`font-weight`** (normal or bold), **`font-size`** (various measurements), **`line-height`** (also referred to as "leading" in print publishing), and **`font-family`** (typeface). To specify all of them individually would take quite a bit of space. However, the **`font`** property, a shorthand CSS property, can be used to apply all of the individual font properties together. When this shorthand format is used, the values are separated by spaces, except **`font-size`** and **`line-height`**, which are separated with a forward slash (/). Comma-separated typeface names are also allowed. For example, to set a font property for the **`p`** element, you could use **`p {font: italic small-cap bold 12pt/16pt Arial, Helvetica, sans-serif}`**. To enable the shorthand formats, choose Edit>Preferences, choose the CSS Style category, and enable any or all shorthands you want Dreamweaver to use.

Another shorthand can be used to shorten hexadecimal color values. If all three colors (RGB) use pairs of hexadecimal numbers, they can be shortened to singles. For example, black is **`#000000`** which can be shortened to **`#000`** and white can be shortened to **`#FFF`**. The three pairs do not need to be identical: **`#F07`** is a valid shorthand of **`#FF0077`**, but you cannot shorten **`#929292`**.

# LESSON 2 Using Class and ID Selectors

Element selectors are beneficial when you want to apply the same style to all instances of those selectors. At times, however, you may want to either single out one instance of an element or specify that some instances of an element be treated differently than others. In these situations, you would use classes or ids, so you need to understand the differences between them to be able to use them correctly. Classes are selectors that may be applied multiple times whereas ids may only be used once per page.

There are two types of classes and ids — regular and generic. ***Regular classes*** and ***regular ids*** are assigned to an element, such as **`p.warning`** or **`tr#odd`**, which mean the warning class of the paragraph element and the odd id of the table-row element. When you define the style for a regular class, such as **`p.warning`**, and try to assign the warning class to the **`h2`** element, the style does not transfer because it is assigned to the paragraph element. If you want to apply a class (for example, the warning class, which you may have designed as bold red text against a yellow background with an orange border) to multiple elements, you would use a generic class. A ***generic class*** style rule is defined without an element, for example, **`.warning`**. Therefore, the regular warning class of the paragraph element would appear in the style block as **`p.warning {color: red; font-weight: bold; background-color; yellow; border: solid 2px #FFA500;}`** whereas the generic warning class would differ only in that the selector would not have an element, such as **`.warning`**.

When creating a style rule for a class, whether generic or regular, you must precede the class name with a period and, if the class is a regular class, with the element selector. When creating a style rule for an id, the id name is preceded by the pound (#) symbol, such as **`#odd`**, and if it is a regular id, the element must precede the **`#`**, such as **`tr#odd`**. When assigning a class or an id in HTML, you use the class attribute, such as **`class="warning"`** or **`id="odd"`**. In Dreamweaver, you can use the Tag editor or Tag selector to assign a class or id to an element. However, if you create a **`p.warning`** regular class, the Tag selector does not allow you to assign the warning class to an h2 block because the class was defined as a regular class.

Because classes can be used multiple times, you may encounter a situation in which you want to apply two classes to the same element. For example, **`.bgcolor1`** may be a style rule for a background color and **`.fgcolor1`** may be a style rule for a foreground (text) color: you may apply both to the same paragraph by adding **`class="bgcolor1 fgcolor1"`** to the paragraph tag using the Tag editor or entering the code directly in the Code window. You may also use this principle to assign **`class="bgcolor1 fgcolor2"`** to one h2, **`class="bgcolor2 fgcolor1"`** to another h2, **`class="bgcolor1 fgcolor2"`** to a paragraph, and **`class="bgcolor2 fgcolor2"`** to another paragraph.

In contrast to classes, an id may only be used once per page, even if it is a generic id. For example, if you define a generic id called **`#unique`**, you may assign p with **`id="unique"`** or h1 with **`id="unique"`**, but once you have assigned it once in a page, you cannot use it again. Some older browsers display the styles from multiple uses of ids on a page, but current, standards-compliant browsers do not, just the first time. You also cannot assign two or more ids to the same element — that would be similar to saying that you have two different names or two different student IDs. However, you can assign both an id and a class (or multiple classes) to the same element, such as **`id="footer" class="bgcolor1 fgcolor2"`**.

Dreamweaver's New CSS Style dialog box offers a Class option for the Selector Type, but it accepts only generic classes, not regular classes. However, if you choose the Advanced Selector Type, you are free to create whatever type of class, id, or combination of selectors that may or may not be understood or supported by Dreamweaver.

## Create and Apply CSS Style Classes

In this exercise, you create both regular and generic classes, and assign them to the Web page. You learn that a regular class is restricted to its element but a generic class may be applied to any element.

**1** **In the open file, index.html, create a new CSS Style, choose Class as the Selector Type, type `.right` in the Name field and click OK. From the Block category, set Text Align to right and click OK.**

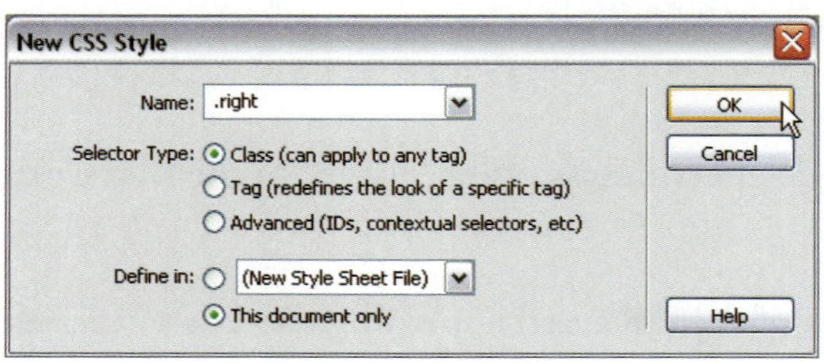


FIGURE 9.14

**2** **Scroll to the table below the heading Summary of Photographs. Click in the # Photos cell. Right/Control-click the `<th>` tag in the Tag selector, and choose Set Class>right from the pop-up menu. Right/Control-click in the `<td>` cell below, and apply the right class to the cell.**

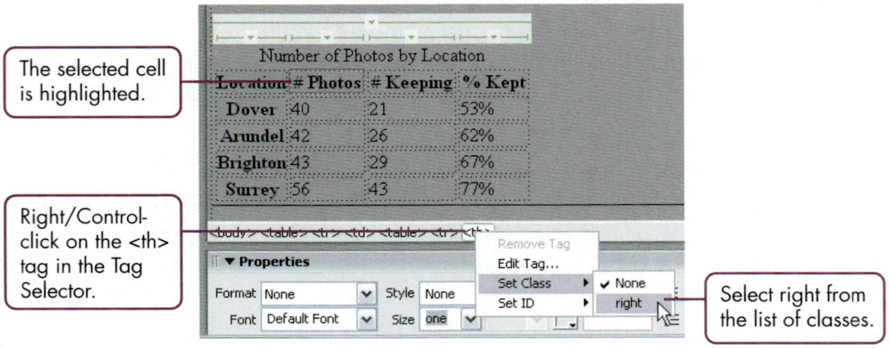


FIGURE 9.15

**3** **Click again in the # Photos cell and then Shift-click in the 77% cell. Right/Control-click in the selected block of cells, and then choose CSS Styles>right from the contextual menu.**

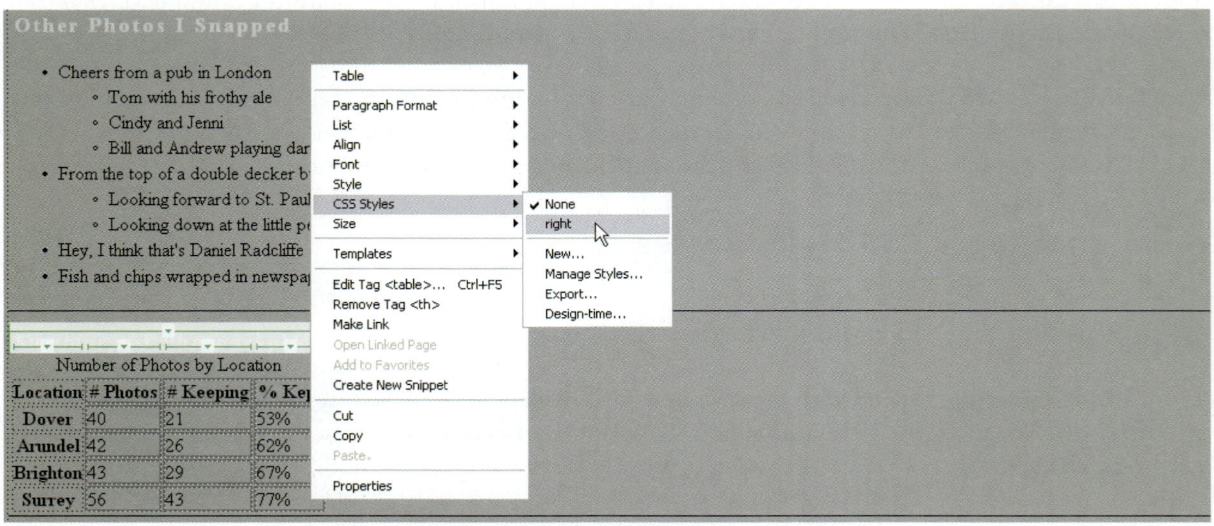


FIGURE 9.16

**4** **Create a new CSS Style generic class called `.left`. In the Block category, set Text Align to left and click OK.**

**5** **Select the left column of the table and apply the left class to the selected cells.**

**6** **Click in the caption above the table, and then click the `<caption>` tag in the Tag selector. In the Property inspector, choose left from the Style list to the right of the Format menu.**

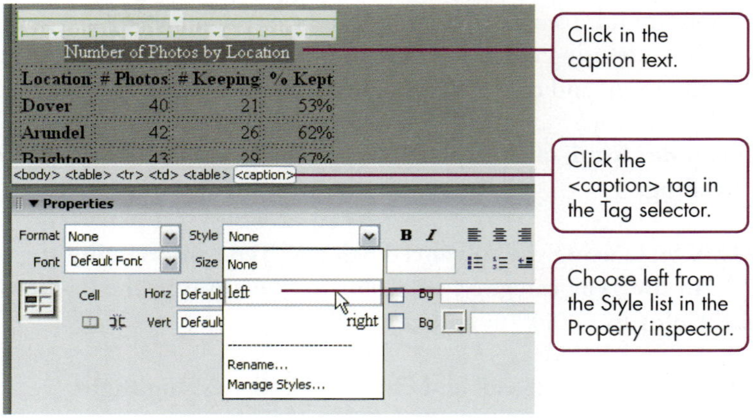


FIGURE 9.17

**7** **Create a new CSS Style, choose Advanced from Selector Type, and type `p.first` in the Selector field. In the Box category, uncheck Same for All from both Padding and Margin, and then set Top to `0` pixels for both Padding and Margin. Click OK.**

**8** **Click in the first paragraph below the Today's Plans heading and choose the style named first from the Style list in the Property inspector. Using the same methods, apply the first class to the first paragraph below the Recent Photos heading, and to the first paragraph below the Friends heading.**

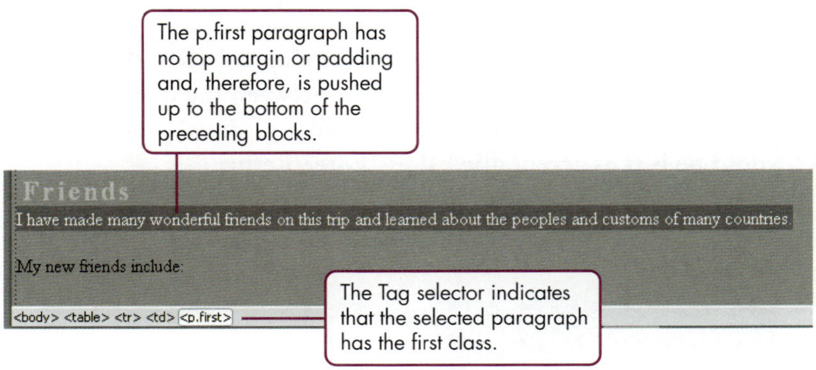


FIGURE 9.18

## If you have problems

At times, the paragraphs tend to overlap each other. Press F5 to refresh the Design-view display.

**9** **Save your changes, but leave the file open for the next exercise.**

## Combine Multiple Classes

In this exercise, you create a CSS class and learn how to apply it to an element that already has a class. Dreamweaver does not support multiple classes from its interface. You must add any additional classes (you can apply more than two) to the code using either the Tag editor or the Code window. Dreamweaver does understand the multiple classes, however, and displays them correctly.

**1** **In the open file, index.html, click in the 53% cell in the table below the Summary of Photographs heading.**

**2** **Create a new CSS Style using the Advanced Selector Type and naming the selector `td.highlight`. In the Type category, set Color to `#965156`; in the Background category, set Background Color to `#F0F0F0`; and click OK.**

**3** **Right/Control-click in the 53% cell and choose CSS Styles>highlight.**

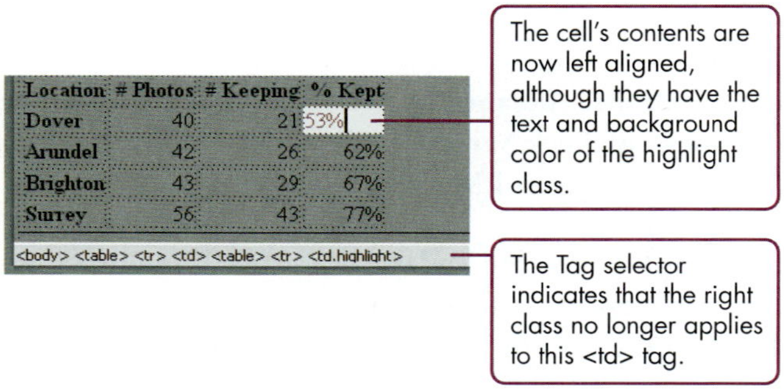


FIGURE 9.19

**4** **With the insertion point in the changed cell, Right/Control-click the `<td.highlight>` tag in the Tag selector, and choose Edit Tag. Type `right` between the quotation marks so that you end up with `class="highlight right"`. (The order of the classes doesn't matter; `right highlight` would be just as acceptable.) Press Enter/Return.**

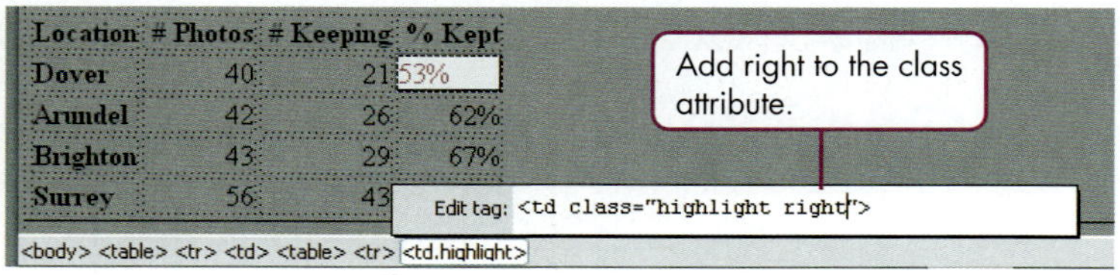


FIGURE 9.20

**5** **Repeat Step 4 for the rest of the table-data cells in the right column so all of the cells have both the right and highlight classes.**

**6** **Save your changes, leaving the file open for the next exercise.**

## Create and Apply Styles Using Ids

In this exercise, you create style rules that are based on id selectors. As you learned earlier, you cannot use a specific id more than once on a page, so before you create an id, you should think about whether or not you will need it again on the same page. If so, use a class instead. As you saw with classes, there are no limitations as to what style properties may be applied to a class; all style properties may be applied to ids, as well.

**1** **In the open file, index.html, create a new CSS Style for the Advanced Selector `p#navbar`. In the Type category, set Size to `1.2` ems, and Line Height to `2` ems. In the Background category, set Background Color to `#000`. In the Block category, set Text Align to center. In the Box category, set both Padding and Margin to `0` pixels (Same For All in both cases). Click OK.**

**2** **Click in the paragraph below the photo of the London Bridge. Right/Control-click the <p> tag in the Tag selector, and set the ID to navbar.**

FIGURE 9.21

**3** **Create a new CSS Style for the Advanced Selector `ul#places`. In the List category, set the Bullet image to images>redball.gif. Click OK.**

**4** **Create two similar styles as you did in Step 3. Make the first with the selector of `ul#photos` and the Bullet image as images>redsqare.gif; make the second with the selector of `ul#friends` and the Bullet image as images>reddiamd.gif.**

**5** **Click in the list below the heading Places I Saw, Right/Control-click the <ul> tag in the Tag selector, and set the ID to places. Click in the list below the heading Friends, Right/Control-click the <ul> tag in the Tag selector, and set the ID to friends.**

**6** **Click the first list item (Cheers from a pub in London) and set the ID of the <ul> tag to photos.**

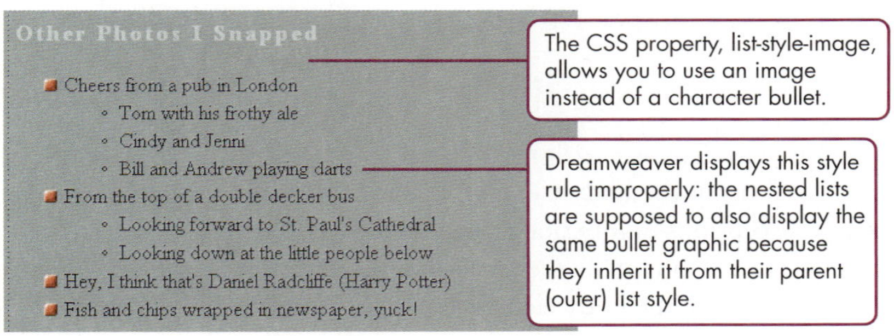


FIGURE 9.22

**7** **Save the changes to index.html and leave it open for the next lesson.**

## To Extend Your Knowledge

### MANAGING CLASSES AND IDS

Classes and ids allow you to customize elements within a page. While this is desirable, it means that you must continuously modify the code of every new page to apply the custom classes and ids. It is not uncommon to see a page created by a beginner that is littered with classes. A style sheet with many classes and ids is quite difficult to manage. In later lessons in this project, you learn about inheritance that, with proper use, can greatly reduce the number of classes and ids on a page.

Another common mistake of beginning CSS designers is naming classes and ids based on the style that they create, such as boldred or italicyellow. What do you do when you redesign the site and decide that the elements with the boldred class no longer should be bold or red? It is best to use class and names that either describe their purpose or the contents within them, such as navbar, footer, header, datatable, and warning. In doing so, you do not limit yourself to the style described by the name of the class or id, or force yourself to rename all instances of boldred to italicyellow.

# LESSON 3 Working with Selectors Based on Context

Although you hear more about the ***DOM*** (the Document Object Model, a hierarchical organization of HTML elements in a page, often shown as branching diagram) in JavaScript, it also applies to CSS. The following figure displays a Web page and its DOM. The second row of elements are children of the body element and adjacent to each other. The third row of elements are children of row-2 elements, descendents of the body element, and adjacent to each other, and so on with subsequent rows.

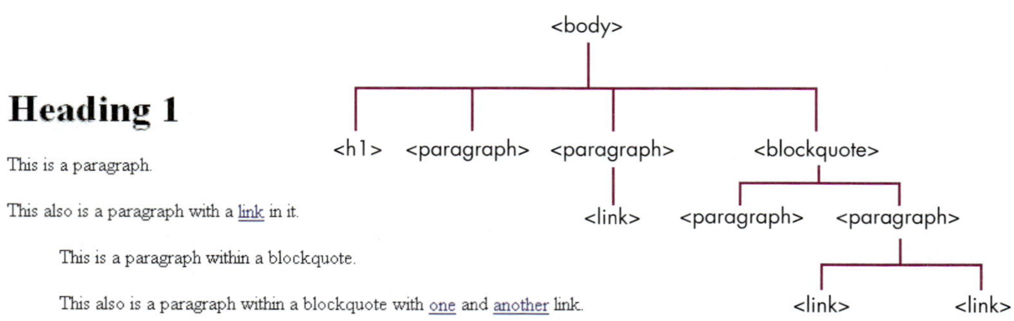


**FIGURE 9.23**

In most cases, styles you apply to elements are inherited by the descendents of that element. For example, if you set the font property to Arial using the body element selector, then the heading, paragraph, blockquote, and link text use that font. The exceptions to inheritance occur when the default appearance of an element conflicts with the new style setting: the default style takes precedence. For example, if you apply the **`font-weight: normal`** (which disables bold) using the body element selector, headings still appear bold. Also, if you use the body element selector to change the text color to red, link text still is blue. To override default appearances, you must apply the changed properties directly to the elements, such as **`h1 {font-weight: normal;}`** or **`a {color: red;}`**.

There are different methods of describing the relationships between elements on a page, and there are CSS selector methods that you can use to specify these relationships. There are descendent selectors, child selectors, and adjacent selectors. Descendent selectors are commonly supported, but child and adjacent selectors, despite being part of CSS2 (released in 1998), have less support.

The simplest selector based on inheritance, and the one with the most support, even in ***version 4 browsers*** (a term generally used to describe Netscape 4.x and Internet Explorer 4.x — Mozilla and Safari are still in their version 1 generations but are much more advanced than NN4 and IE4 ever were), is the descendent selector. You are a descendent of your parents as well as your great-great-great-great-grandparents. It does not matter how many generations there are, as long as there is a straight line of inheritance. All elements are descendents of the body element, but if you want to apply one color to links in paragraphs and another color to links in blockquotes, then you must create descendent selectors that account for these two situations. Descendent selectors are written with spaces between them, such as **`blockquote p`** and **`p a`**. To change the color of link text in blockquotes to red and the color of link text in paragraphs outside of blockquotes to green, the style rules would be written as: **`p a {color: green;}`** and **`blockquote a {color: red;}`**. In the second example, it is not necessary to specify the complete ancestry, such as **`blockquote p a`**, because **`a`** is a descendent of **`blockquote`**, however many layers may exist between them.

Children are the immediate descendents of their parents. To create a style rule for child selectors, you insert the **>** between selectors, such as **`body>p`** (or with spaces, such as **`body > p`**). The selector **`body>p {text-style: italic;}`** would make all paragraph text italic except paragraphs within the blockquote because those paragraphs are not children of the body element, just descendents.

Adjacent selectors are those that describe two elements that share the same parent and are immediately adjacent to each other. To define an adjacent selector, the plus (+) symbol is inserted between the elements. For example, **`h1+p {text-decoration: underline;}`** adds an underline to the first paragraph after the h1 element but not to any other paragraphs.

All of the previous discussions in this project about the application of CSS apply to selectors based on context. You may group descendent selectors, such as **`blockquote a, p a`**. You may specify adjacent classes, such as **`p.warning+p.navbar`**; descendent selectors to ids, such as **`p#navbar a`**; or any other combination of selectors.

There are some things you cannot do with style rules. You cannot create exceptions. If you want all paragraph text to be in the Times font except paragraphs within blockquotes, you can't exclude blockquotes. Instead, you must create a rule for all paragraphs, such as **`p {font-family: Times;}`** and then reverse blockquote paragraphs with **`blockquote p {font-family: Arial;}`**. You cannot create rules that apply to ancestors — for example, if you want paragraph text to be blue if the paragraph has a link in it, but to be red if the paragraph does not have a link in it (compare the first and second paragraphs following the h1 block in the preceding figure). The only way to achieve this is to use classes, and apply one class or another based on whether or not there is a link in the paragraph.

## Observe Inheritance of the Font Property

In this exercise, you observe the effect of inheritance by creating a style rule for the body and seeing it applied to descendents of the body element. You observe that the default font property for the `<textarea>` tag is monospaced and does not take the font style applied to the body element. You must create a textarea element selector style to override its font.

**1** In the open file, index.html, Right/Control-click the body style in the CSS Styles panel and choose Edit.

**2** In the Type category, set Font to Arial, Helvetica, sans-serif and click OK.

**3** Preview the page in your browser. Scroll down to the form and type in the large text area.

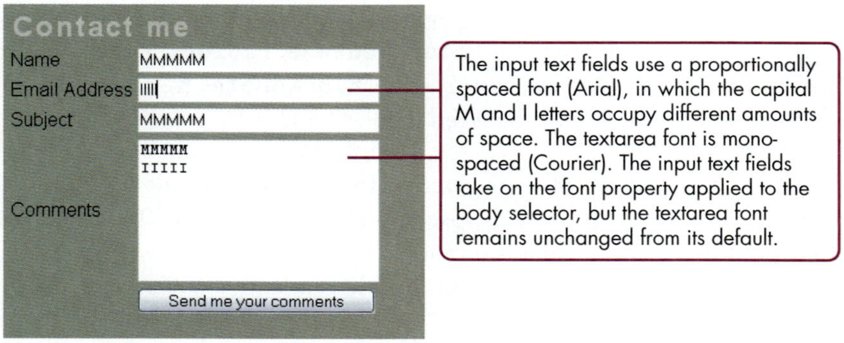


FIGURE 9.24

**4** Return to Dreamweaver.

**5** Edit the textarea style rule in the CSS Styles panel; set the font to Arial, Helvetica, sans-serif; and click OK.

**6** Preview the page in your browser and type in the textarea.

**7** Return to Dreamweaver, saving your changes to index.html and leaving it open for the next exercise.

## Create Descendent Selectors

In this exercise, you create descendent selectors. You learn how powerful descendent selectors are and how they can reduce the number of classes used in a page. You apply a style to the links in the navbar paragraph, but the styles do not affect any other links because of the descendent selector. You create a style for a nested list. Using descendent selectors cleans up the styles and clears the problem of unwanted styles.

**1** **In the open file, index.html, create a new style for the selector `p#navbar a`. Set the Text color to `#C4C4C4`. In the Box category, uncheck Same for All for Padding, and set both left and right padding to `15` pixels. Click OK.**

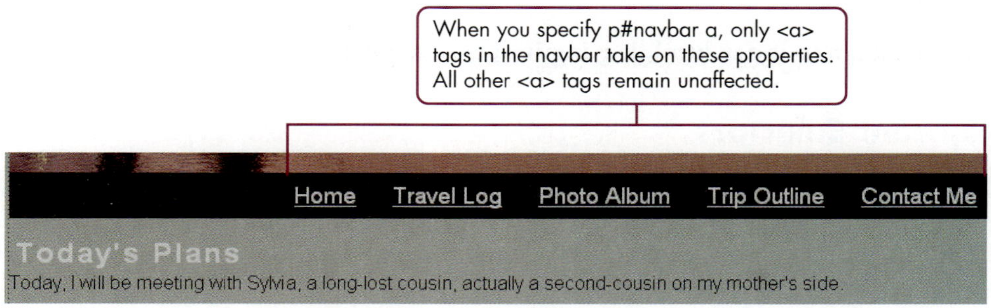


FIGURE 9.25

**2** **Create a new style for the selector `ul#photos ul`. In the List category, set the Bullet image to images>redarrow.gif and click OK.**

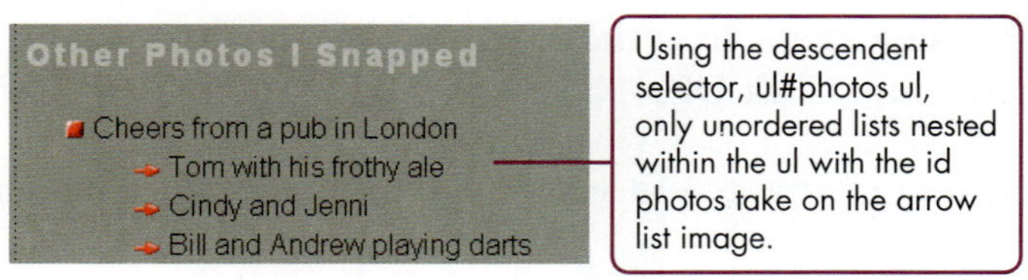


FIGURE 9.26

**3** **Create a new style for the `table` tag. In the Box category, set the width to `750` pixels, uncheck Same for All for Margins, and set both Left and Right margins to auto (choose from list) and both Top and Bottom to `10` pixels. Click OK.**

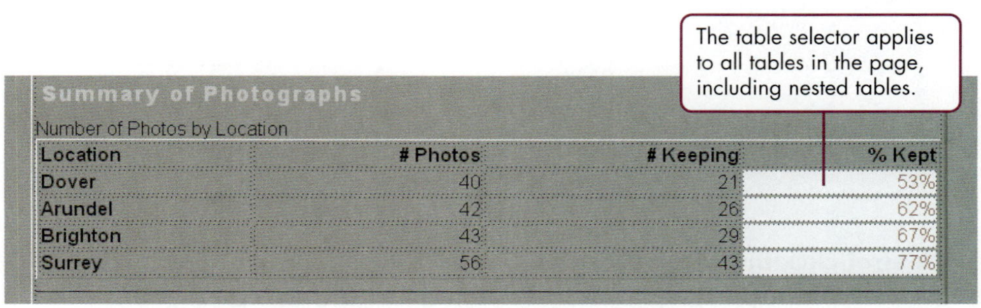


FIGURE 9.27

**4** **Create a new style for the selector `table table`. Set the Background color to `#E1E1E1`. In the Box category, set the width to `400` pixels and click OK.**

FIGURE 9.28

**5** **Save the changes to index.html, leaving it open for the next exercise.**

## Create Adjacent Selectors

In this exercise, you observe the usefulness of adjacent selectors. Unlike descendent selectors, adjacent selectors are less well supported by browsers: the Opera, Mozilla, and Safari browsers support this property, as does Dreamweaver, but Internet Explorer does not. You see that although you can replace classes created earlier with adjacent selectors, if the style for your Web-page design depends on the adjacent selectors working in current browsers, you may need to revert to using classes or ids to achieve the style you desire.

**1** **In the open file, index.html, scroll down to the form at the bottom of the page and click to the left of Name.**

**2** **Create a new style using `form td` as the selector. In the Block category, set Text Align to right and Vertical Align to top. Click OK.**

**3** **Create a new style using `form td+td` as the selector. In the Block category, set Text Align to left and click OK.**

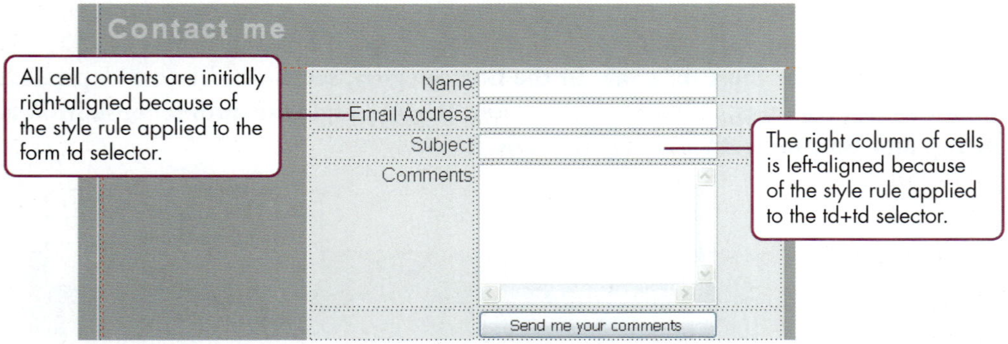


FIGURE 9.29

**4** **Right/Control-click the `p.first` selector in the CSS Styles panel and choose Delete. One by one, click each of the paragraphs immediately below the headings, Right/Control-click the `<p.first>` tag in the Tag selector, and set its class to none.**

The paragraphs are no longer assigned the class of first and the p.first style rule no longer exists.

**5** **Create a new style using `h2+p, h3+p` as the selector. In the Box category, set all paddings and margins to `0` pixels and click OK.**

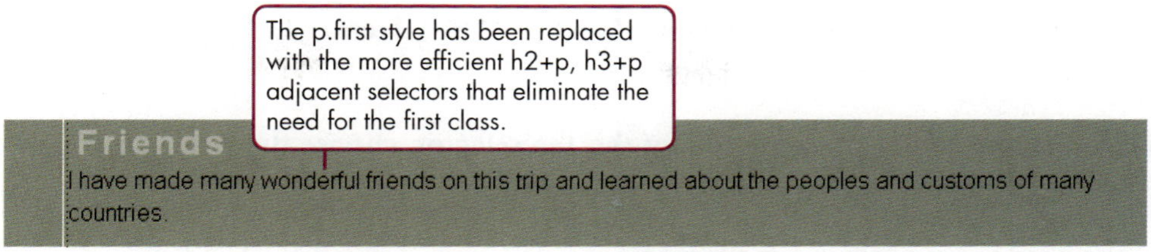


FIGURE 9.30

**6** **Preview the page in your browser.**

## If you have problems

The adjacent selector (element+element) is not supported by Internet Explorer but is supported by the Mozilla, Safari, and Opera browsers. If you have a style rule that uses adjacent selectors and want to retain that appearance in IE, you must create a class or an id and apply that class or id to the appropriate blocks in the document.

**7** **Return to Dreamweaver, leaving index.html open for the next exercise.**

## Use a Child Selector

A child element is also a descendent element but not all descendent elements are child elements. Because the child selector is not as well supported as the descendent element, you may have to resort to using either descendent or class/id selectors instead.

**1** **In the open file, index.html, create a new style using the selector `body>table`. In the Background category, set the background color to `#DADADA`. In the Border category, leaving Same for All checked, set Style to groove, Width to thick, and Color to `#969696`. Click OK.**

**2** **Right/Control-click the table table selector and choose Edit. Apply a solid, `1` pixel, black border around all sides and click OK.**

**3** **Preview the page in your browser. Scroll down to examine the other two tables.**

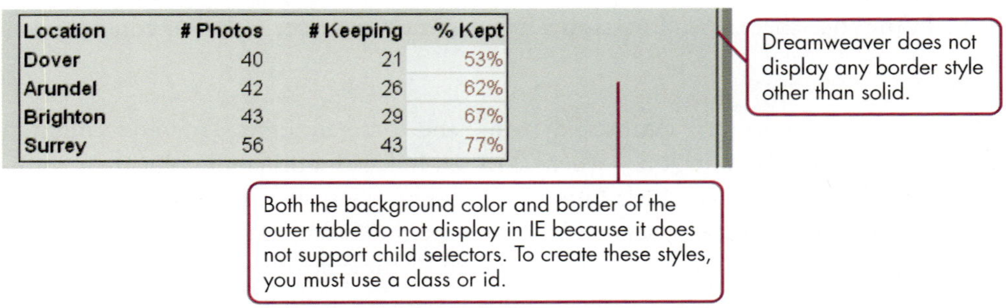


FIGURE 9.31

**4** **Return to Dreamweaver.**

**5** **Right/Control-click the body>table selector and choose Go to Code. Delete the selector `body>table` (not the style declaration block, just the selector) and type `table#body`. Close the Code window.**

**6** **Click in the content of the page. Using the Tag selector, choose the left-most `<table>` tag, Right/Control-click the tag, and set its ID to body.**

**7** **Save the changes but leave index.html open.**

## *To Extend Your Knowledge*

### IE5, IE6, AND IE7

Internet Explorer is the most commonly used browser in the world — most browser statistics place its use at about 94%. The most recent version for Windows is IE6 whereas for the Macintosh, the latest version is IE5.2. Despite the difference in version numbers, these two browsers are similar in capabilities. However, both versions suffer from a number of weaknesses in support for some Web technologies, such as the abbreviation and acronym tags, `<abbr>` and `<acronym>`, respectively. IE also has weaker support for some CSS selectors (adjacent and child) and properties (width is sometimes miscalculated) than the Opera, Mozilla, and Safari browsers.

Although it is not known what the next version of Internet Explorer will bring (it will only be available for the next version of Windows, not for the Macintosh), Dean Edwards has been developing an advanced script in JavaScript, that he calls IE7, in which many of the deficiencies in IE5 and 6 for Windows are being resolved. At his Web site at dean.edwards.name/IE7/compatibility/ you can see which deficiencies he has been able to eliminate. The IE7 script is free to download and simple to install. With it in place, you are able to use more CSS selectors and properties without having to wonder if IE5/6 can support them. There are two caveats to using IE7: this code does not work if a user has disabled JavaScript, and the IE7 script is reported to slow the display of a Web page at times.

# LESSON 4 Creating Pseudo-Class Selectors

You can deduce all of the preceding selectors from the document tree. You can examine HTML code of an unstyled page and identify which styles will apply and where based on the hierarchy of the elements of the page and the selectors in the style sheet. Pseudo-classes allow designers to create styles for conditions outside of the document tree.

There are seven pseudo-class selectors; some are dynamic and some are rigid. The most commonly used and understood pseudo-classes are used for links, where a visited link has a different color than an unvisited link, and an active link flashes red when clicked. These pseudo-classes are the `:link`, `:visited`, and `:active` pseudo-classes respectively. These three pseudo-classes replace the `link`, `alink`, and `vlink` attributes of the `<body>` tag. HTML only supported color changes for each of these attributes but CSS is not limited to just color — any CSS property can be used in these pseudo-classes. These three pseudo-classes are unique in that they only play a role for anchor tags.

The **:hover** pseudo-class does not have an HTML equivalent. You can use this pseudo-class to change the appearance of a link when the mouse moves over it, such as removing the underline or changing the text or background color. Although the **:hover** property can be applied to elements other than the anchor tag, Internet Explorer and version 4 browsers only support the **:hover** pseudo-classes when applied to anchor tags.

When you create a style rule for the a element selector, the rule applies consistently whether the link is visited, unvisited, or active, or the mouse pointer rolls over it. Occasionally, you may see a style sheet in which someone has specified **a:link, a:visited, a:hover, a:active {color: white;}**. It is simpler to simply use **a {color: white;}**. You can create a common style for all four states using the a element selector, such as **a {color: white; font-family: Arial; font-size: 1.2em}** and then use the pseudo-classes to create modifications of the default, such as **a:active {color: red;}**. If you are creating separate style rules for these pseudo-classes, they must be created in the following order whether you use some or all of these pseudo-classes: **:link**, **:visited**, **:hover**, and **:active**. Use LoVe HAte as a mnemonic to remember this order.

The **:focus** pseudo-class is commonly used in form fields to highlight the field in which the visitor is entering information. Many Web designers use the **:focus** pseudo-class to change the background (and sometimes, text) color of an input form control. Unfortunately, Internet Explorer does not support the **:focus** pseudo-class. There are no CSS workarounds for this deficiency — only JavaScript may be used to create a similar effect, one of the successes that Dean Edwards has had with his IE7 script.

The two static pseudo-classes are exceptions to the general rule of pseudo-classes in that you can infer them from the document tree; regardless, the W3C calls them "pseudo-classes." The **:first-child** pseudo-class is somewhat similar to the **>** child selector in that it applies to a child of the identified element, but it is different in that the first child may not always be the same. For example, if one table cell (td) contains an h2 block and then a p block, and another table cell contains two p blocks, **td:first-child** would apply the style rule to the h2 element in the first cell and to the first p element in the second cell. The **:lang** pseudo-class can be used to change the style based on the language specified. For example **:lang(fr) {text-style: italic;}** applies italic to any text in which the **lang="fr"** attribute (fr=French) is applied, such as **<p lang="fr">Bonjour!</p>**.

## To Extend Your Knowledge

### COMBINING PSEUDO-CLASSES

It is possible, although uncommon, to combine some pseudo-classes. Often you see different link properties for links in the body than for links in a navigation bar. Some designers take this a step further by combining pseudo-classes. For example, **a:hover {color: red;}** changes the link color to red when the mouse pointer rolls over it, and **a:visited {color: purple;}** sets the color of visited links to purple. However, you may want to have a different **:hover** color (or other property) for links that have been already visited. Therefore, you must combine **:visited** with **:hover**, such as **a:visited:hover {color: green;}**, which causes visited links to change to green when the mouse pointer rolls over them whereas unvisited links change to red when the mouse rolls over them.

As you may have guessed, Internet Explorer does not support this combination of pseudo-classes, but it is something to keep in mind.

## Create Pseudo-Classes for Links

In this exercise, you create pseudo-classes for links in the page. You can combine pseudo-classes with any of the other selectors types, such as classes, ids, and any of the relational selectors.

1. **In the open file, index.html, create a new style using the selector `a:visited`. In the Type category, set the Text color to `black` and click OK.**

2. **Create a new style using the selector `a:active`. In the Text category, set the Type color to `red` and click OK.**

3. **Create a new style using the selector `a:hover`. In the Type category, choose none from the Decoration group of radio buttons and click OK.**

4. **Create a new style using the selector `a:link`. In the Text category, set the Type color to `#965156` and click OK.**

5. **Preview the page in your browser. Move your mouse pointer over the links in the content section of the page (not the navigation bar). Click a link, then use the back button to return to this page. Return to Dreamweaver when finished.**

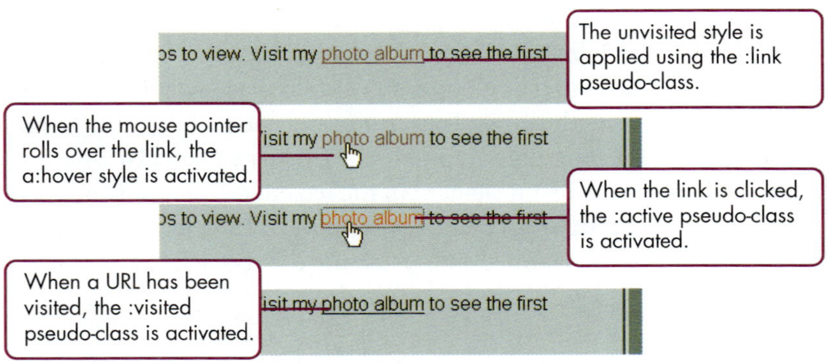


FIGURE 9.32

6. **Create a new style using the `p#navbar a:hover` selector. In the Type category, set the Text color to `black`. In the Background category, set the Background color to `#C4C4C4` and click OK.**

7. **Preview the page in your browser and roll your mouse pointer over the navigation-bar links. Return to Dreamweaver.**

FIGURE 9.33

8. **Keep index.html open for the next exercise.**

## To Extend Your Knowledge

### PADDING VS. MARGIN

The links in the navbar paragraph were separated from each other using left and right padding set at 15 pixels each, which means that the space between the e in Home and the T in Travel Log is 30 pixels. This space could have been created using either padding or margin. However, padding extends the content area of the element whereas margins are outside of the content area. If you apply a background to the element, the background extends into padding but does not extend into the margin. Therefore, the wide band of gray around the links in the navbar paragraph when the :hover pseudo-class is active is created because the padding extends around the links. If margin were used, only the background of the text would change to gray.

## Add the :focus Pseudo-Class for the Form Text Fields

In this exercise, you use the :focus pseudo-class selector to change the text and background color of the input fields when the visitor is entering information into these fields. Just as JavaScript can improve the usability of forms, this pseudo-class can improve the usability of the input fields by clearly identifying to users which field they are working in.

1 **In the open file, index.html, create a new style using the selector `input:focus, textarea:focus`. In the Type category, set the Text color to `#FFF`. In the Background category, set the Background color to `#969696`. Click OK.**

2 **Preview the page in your browser. Type in one of the input fields, and then tab through the rest of them.**

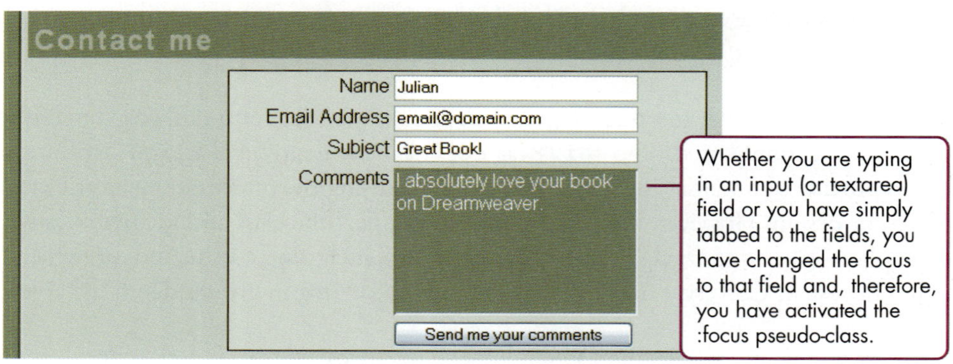


FIGURE 9.34

3 **Return to Dreamweaver but leave index.html open for the next exercise.**

## *To Extend Your Knowledge*

### SEPARATING PRESENTATION FROM BEHAVIOR

Much has been said about the separation of presentation from structure where structure is defined using HTML and presentation is created using CSS. Peter-Paul Koch and other advanced JavaScript developers are displeased with some of the CSS pseudo-classes, specifically, **`:visited`**, **`:active`**, **`:hover`**, and **`:focus`**. These CSS pseudo-classes border on creating behavioral effects that they feel should be in the domain of JavaScript. In his article, "Separating Behavior and Presentation" (digital-web.com/articles/separating_behavior_and_presentation/), Koch explains how CSS has moved into the arena of behavior and how one might evaluate which technology, CSS or JavaScript, should be used to create these types of behaviors. Peter-Paul Koch recognizes that **`:hover`** and other quasi-behavioral pseudo-classes can be used very simply and effectively to create very beneficial results. However, these pseudo-classes can and have been used to create more complex effects, such as Eric Meyer's Pure CSS Menus (meyerweb.com/eric/css/edge/menus/demo.html). Koch believes that effects at this level of complexity and sophistication should be the domain of JavaScript and not CSS. His articles, his Web site, and those of Simon Willison (simon.incutio.com) are very interesting reading.

# LESSON 5 Working with the <span> and <div> Tags

The **`<span>`** and **`<div>`** tags have a special role, and unlike most other HTML tags, they serve no purpose in document structure. Their role is simply to be containers that deliver CSS styles. There are differences in their intended purposes, however. The **`<span>`** tag is meant to serve as an inline container whereas the **`<div>`** tag is intended to serve as a block container. A ***block*** fills the width of the browser window and separates itself from other blocks with white space. Paragraphs and headings are both block containers, but unlike div blocks, paragraphs and headings have a role in the structure of the document. An element is considered ***inline*** if it exists within a block, just as links or italicized words are contained within paragraphs.

Divs (a colloquial term used to refer to **`<div>`** tags and their contents) are commonly used to create CSS layouts whereas spans are less commonly used. The **`<div>`** tag does have the deprecated **`align`** attribute, but given that its current use is to provide a container for layout through CSS, using the presentational attribute **`align`** is contrary to using CSS for design. However, the **`<div>`** tag does support the class and id attributes with which CSS selectors can be applied. The **`<span>`** tag has very few attributes, including **`class`** and **`id`**, which, again, can be used for selection purpose in CSS style rules. We discuss the **`<div>`** tag in greater depth in Project 3.

Whenever you create a custom style in the Design view, Dreamweaver creates a class and a style rule for you using the **`span`** selector. The style is added to your style sheet. You can use it at any other time.

## Create a Span Style

1. **In the open file, index.html, select Sylvia (in the first paragraph). Using the Property inspector, click the bold and italic buttons, and, using the Text Color color box, choose a dark red color, #990000.**

**2** Click away from Sylvia, and then click in Sylvia again. Click the Split button to open the Code window.

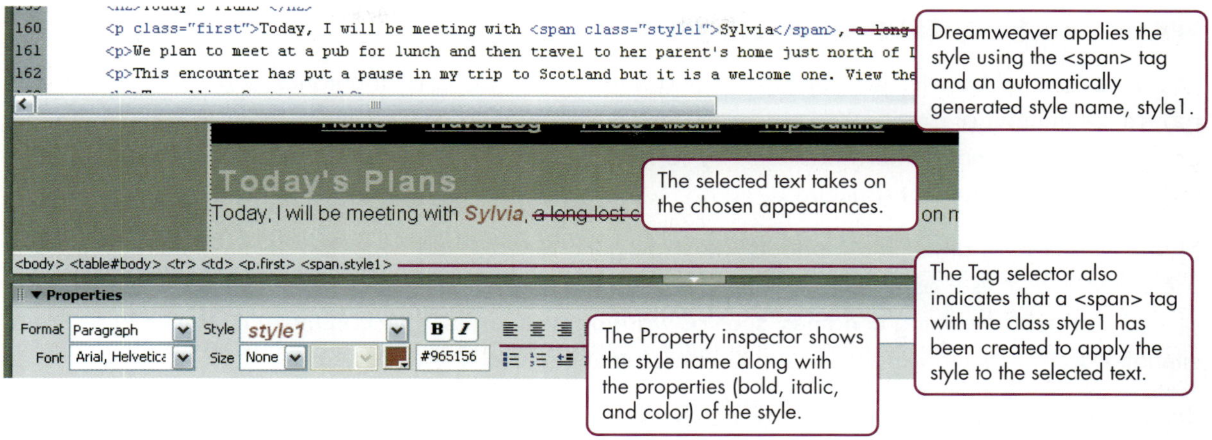


FIGURE 9.35

**3** Close the Code window. Select the word cousin from the same paragraph as Sylvia. Using the Style list in the Property inspector, choose style1 from the list.

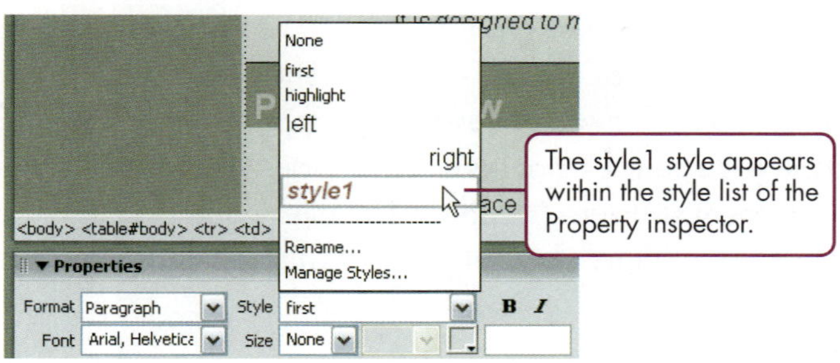


FIGURE 9.36

**4** In the CSS Styles panel, scroll down to the bottom of the list. Select another word from the same paragraph, Right/Control-click .style1 from the CSS Styles panel, and choose Apply.

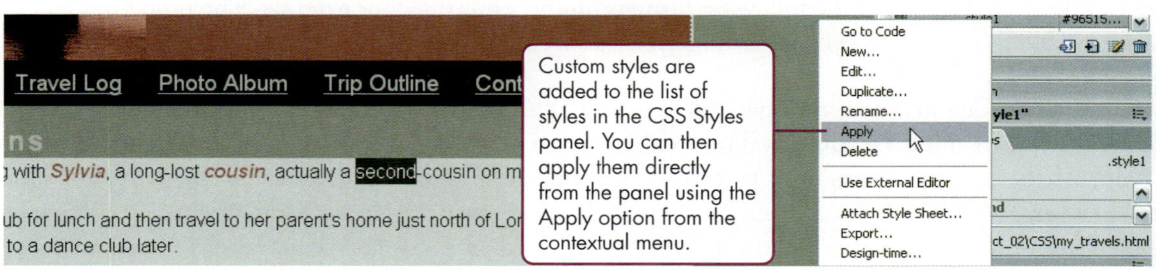


FIGURE 9.37

**5** Save the changes to index.html, but leave it open.

## To Extend Your Knowledge

### SPANS CAN BE OVERUSED

You have learned how to use CSS classes and how styles based on inheritance and relationships can reduce the number of classes. You can apply the same thought process to styles that use the **<span>** tag as the delivery agent. Where possible, try to reduce your use of **<span>** styles and, instead, create styles based on document structure.

Span styles can be difficult to manage. They are generally applied when the document structure does not support their use, as if you randomly decided to change the style of some text. Even if you have given span styles meaningful names, such as warning or address, they can make it difficult to restyle a site later on. Try to keep span styles to the absolute minimum.

Be aware of conflicts with accessibility: if you are applying a span style to emphasize a word or phrase, remember that using span only adds visual style; the emphasis does not originate in the document structure. If you want to emphasize something, use **<strong>**, **<em>**, or both, and if you wish, add additional style.

The **<span>** tag can be used to add additional style to an element. For example, elements may have only one background image but your design may require two background images. Therefore, some designers add a **<span>** tag to deliver the second background image. For example, **<h1><span>Text</span></h1>** allows the designer to apply one background to the **h1** selector and another background to the **h1 span** selector. While this is an effective use of the **<span>** tag that does not damage the basic document structure (Heading 1 is still Heading 1), this technique does require a designer to add another tag to each **h1** element just so that the design remains intact.

# LESSON 6 Using Inline, Embedded, and External Style Sheets

Styles can be created in any of the following formats: inline, embedded, or external. The properties and values are available to all forms of styles, but each method has its advantages and disadvantages.

An ***inline style*** is one in which the style rule is added as an attribute and attribute values to a tag. The style attribute is required and the attribute values are the CSS properties used anywhere else. For example, to change the color of the text in a paragraph to green, an inline style would be written as **<p style="color: green;">Text</p>**. Style declarations are formatted just as they are always formatted: the style property is separated from the style property value with a colon and style property:value pairs (declarations) are separated from each other with semicolons. However, curly braces are not allowed. Instead, a pair of quotation marks surrounds the style declaration block. One disadvantage of inline styles is that if you need to edit the style, you must edit right in the code of the tag. Secondly, if the style is required again, you either have to recreate it in the other location(s) or rebuild it as either an embedded or external style.

An ***embedded style sheet*** appears in the **<head>** section of an HTML document. Opening and closing **<style>** tags surround the style rules. The **<style>** tag requires one attribute, the **type** attribute, that is set to **text/css**, as in **<style type="text/css">**. Commonly, inside the **<style>** tags are comment tags **<!--** and **-->**. The purpose of the comment tags is to hide the style rules from old browsers (NN3, IE3, and earlier browsers), which would not understand the **<style>** tags and would, therefore, attempt to display the style rules in the browser window. Between the opening and closing comment tags are the style rules. Embedded styles have the advantage that you can apply them to any of the elements in the current page, but if you open another page on the site, the styles do not transfer.

An ***external style sheet*** exists in a separate file and is called into use by the Web page. The format of the style rules is identical to those in embedded style sheets with one minor exception: there is no need for the **<style>** or comment tags. However, in order to bring the style rules into use by the Web page, the **<link>** tag is commonly used. The **<link>** tag is an empty tag which has no closing </link> tag. There are three required attributes and attribute values: **type="text/css"**, **rel="stylesheet"**, and **src="style_sheet_filename.css"**. The **type** attribute tells the browser the format of the information, the **rel** attribute identifies the relationship of the external file, and the **src** attribute identifies the URL of the external style sheet. The URL can be absolute or relative: absolute is recommended because the pages that depend on the style sheet can be found in different folders at different folder depths. An alternate method of calling an external style sheet uses the **@import** method. The **@import** method uses the **<style>** tag in the format of **<style type="text/css"> @import(style_sheet_filename.css); </style>**.

You can use any or all of these methods, as needed. Although it is rare to use inline styles, it is not uncommon to combine embedded and external style sheets, where the external style sheets have the styles for the whole Web site and an embedded style sheet provides either additions or modifications for the current page. You can use multiple external style sheets. Some designers divide their styles into logical blocks and save each block to a different file. For example, the navigation-bar styles may appear in one style sheet, the main-content styles may appear in another, and the styles that control layout may appear in yet another. You must be aware of the order of the style sheets in the code. If two styles conflict, such as one color for h1 text in the embedded style sheet and another color for h1 text in the external style sheet, the last one to appear in code is the one that displays. Commonly, external style sheets are listed first followed by the embedded style sheet, so the embedded style sheet's rules take precedence if there is a conflict.

Using external style sheets is the primary method for reducing page weight. Exporting the style rules to an external style-sheet file reduces the number of bytes in the HTML page. Many professional CSS-based designers redesign a Web page by removing presentational HTML, rebuilding the appearance using CSS, and then exporting the styles to an external CSS file, thus losing as much as 80% of the HTML page weight. Of course, the CSS file takes space, but never as much as the lost HTML tags and attributes. There is another benefit to external style sheets — browsers cache external style-sheet files if they are used more than once. To ***cache*** is to store the file in the browser's temporary files from which the file may be recalled when needed again. This means that if a person visited a site, their browser would download the HTML document and the CSS file. If the person links to another page on the same site that uses the same CSS file, the browser does not download the CSS file again but recalls it from the cache. This further reduces the page weight to just the HTML document.

Dreamweaver does not create inline styles with the exception of layers, which we discuss in the next project. Even span styles are not inline styles. Span styles can be created on the fly but are stored in the style sheet, either embedded or external. When you create a style, you have the option of defining it in the current document or in a style-sheet file. Choosing current document creates an embedded style whereas choosing a style-sheet file creates an external style sheet.

## Create an External Linked Style Sheet

In this exercise, we create a style that is stored in an external style sheet.

**1** **In the open file, index.html, create a new style using the `h1` selector. In the New CSS Style dialog box, set Define in to New Style Sheet and click OK.**

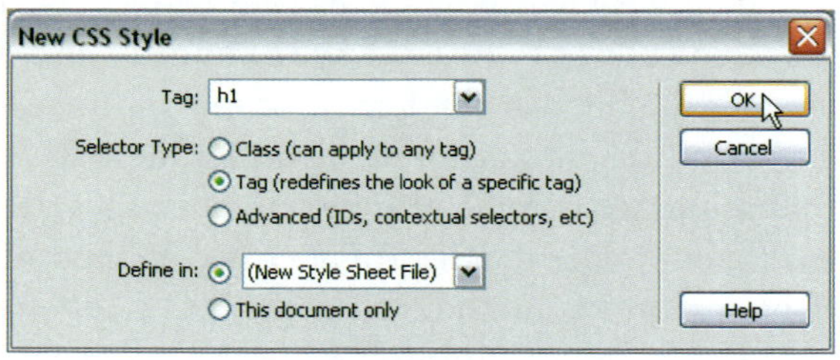


FIGURE 9.38

**2** **In the Save Style Sheet File As dialog box, type `test.css` in the File Name field. Ensure that the My Travels folder is the current folder and click Save/Choose.**

**3** **In the Type category, set the Text color to `#FFF` and click OK.**

**4** **In the CSS Styles panel, scroll to the top of the list of styles, and click the –/down-arrow (Macintosh) beside <style> to collapse the list of style rules in the <style> block.**

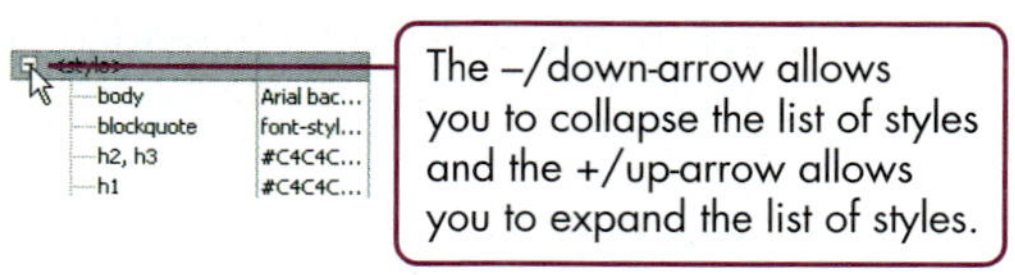


FIGURE 9.39

**5** **Click the test.css tab (Windows)/Document title bar (Macintosh), and then close the external style-sheet file, saving your changes.**

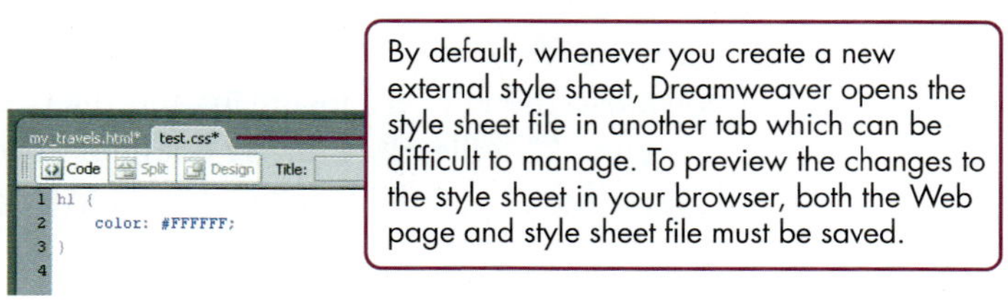


FIGURE 9.40

**6** **Choose Edit>Preferences/Dreamweaver>Preferences (Macintosh), choose the CSS Styles category, remove the check from Open CSS Files When Modified, and click OK.**

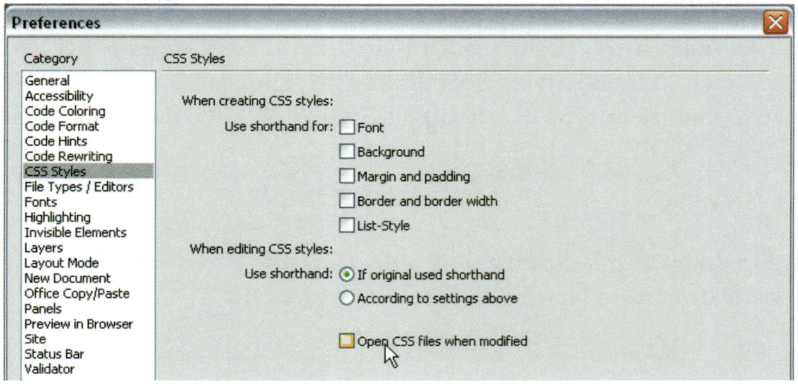


FIGURE 9.41

**7** **Save the changes to index.html, leaving it open for the next exercise.**

## Export an Embedded Style Sheet

In this exercise, you export all of the style rules you have created to an external style sheet. In the process of exporting, Dreamweaver also creates a link to the external style sheet so you don't have to attach the style sheet as an additional step.

**1** **In the open file, index.html, Right/Control-click <style> in the CSS Styles panel and choose Export.**

**2** **Type `bridge.css` in the File Name field and click Save.**

**3** **Again Right/Control-click <style> in the CSS Styles panel and choose Delete.**

**4** **Right/Control-click test.css in the CSS Styles panel and choose Delete.**

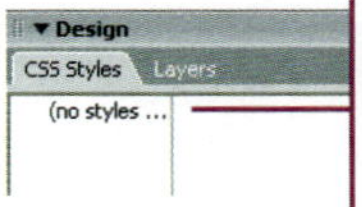


There are no longer any styles associated with the current Web page. By deleting the <style> block, the embedded styles within the <head> of thedocument are gone. However, they do exist in the external style sheet called bridge.css.

FIGURE 9.42

**5** **Save the changes to index.html, leaving it open for the next exercise.**

## Attach an External Style Sheet

In this exercise, you attach a style sheet with the link method and examine the **<link>** tag.

**1** **In the open file, index.html, Right/Control-click in the CSS Styles panel and select Attach Style Sheet. In the Attach External Style Sheet dialog box, choose Link from the Add as options, either Browse to choose or type `bridge.css` in the File/URL field, and click OK/Choose.**

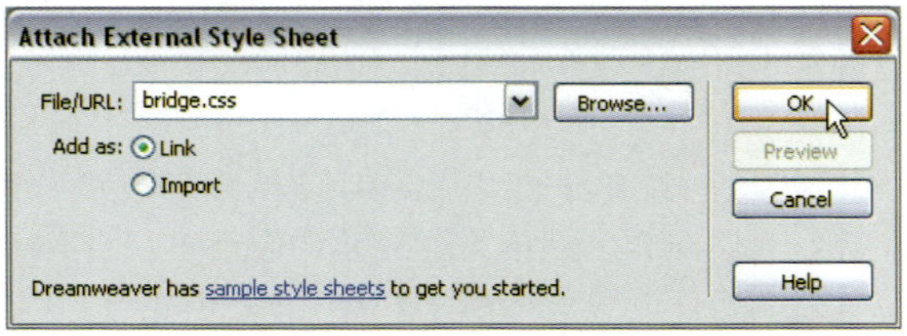


FIGURE 9.43

**2** **Again, Right/Control-click in the CSS Styles panel and choose Attach Style Sheet. In the Attach External Style Sheet dialog box, choose Add as Import, type or Browse to choose `test.css`, and click OK/Choose.**

**3** **In the CSS Styles panel, click the +/up arrow to the left of <style>. Also, open the Code window.**

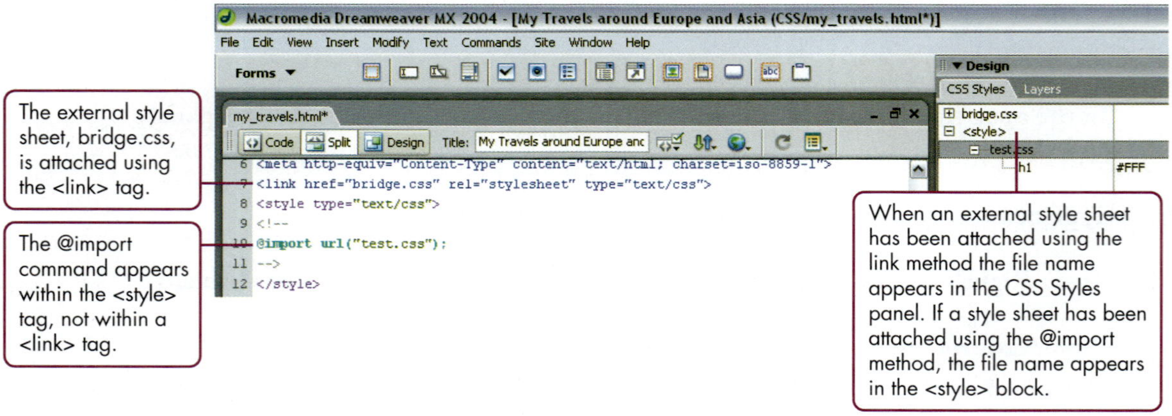


FIGURE 9.44

**4** **Right/Control-click <style> in the CSS Styles panel and choose Delete.**

When an external style sheet has been deleted from the CSS Styles panel, the file still exists but is no longer attached to the current Web page. However, if the styles are embedded in the current page, deleting <style> deletes all of the style definitions. Although you can use Undo to recover the deleted style rules from the **<style>** block, be careful when considering that option.

**5** **Close the Code window and close index.html.**

## To Extend Your Knowledge

### @IMPORT HIDES STYLES FROM NN4

Netscape Navigator 4.x is notorious for its poor support for CSS. You may wonder why this particular browser is picked on so much — why not IE3, Mosaic (the precursor to both Netscape and Internet Explorer), or Opera 2? The problem is twofold. For a long time, NN4 was the browser of choice for many individuals and corporations, so many, many visitors used this browser. Even today, 4% of all visitors use this browser. Secondly, NN4 has inconsistent support for CSS: some properties are supported, some are not, some display improperly, and some crash the browser. For these reasons, efforts are made to prevent NN4 browsers from seeing the styles. If successful, visitors using this browser do not see the styles but at least they can read the content and see inline images (another reason for creating proper document structure with HTML).

NN4 does not understand the `@import` method of attaching a style sheet and, therefore, those styles are hidden from it. Some designers use multiple style sheets, putting the styles that don't work in NN4 into an imported style sheet and the rest in linked style sheets. All other current browsers support the `@import` method of attaching an external style sheet, so they can use all of the styles — those attached using the `@import` method and those attached using the link method.

## Create a Consistent Design

In this exercise, you attach the bridge.css style sheet to all other pages on your site. Where necessary, you apply classes to elements so that the style rules that need classes apply.

1. **Open contact_me.html.**

2. **Right/Control-click in the CSS Styles panel and choose Attach Style Sheet. Using Link as the Add as option, choose bridge.css, and click OK/Choose.**

3. **Click in the navigation-bar paragraph. From the Tag selector, select the <p> tag, then Right/Control-click on the <p> tag and set the ID to navbar.**

4. **Close, saving your changes.**

5. **Repeat Steps 2 to 4 for photo_album.html, travel_log.html, switcher.html, and trip_outline.html.**

6. **Open index.html.**

**7** **Scroll down to the Contact Me heading and the form below it. Select both the heading and the form, and delete them.**

The form was beneficial to have in this page to help develop the style rules for forms. However, now that the bridge.css style-sheet file has been attached to contact_me.html, the form in index.html is no longer needed. The link in the navigation bar provides access to the contact form.

**8** **Preview this page in your browser. Click any of the links in the navigation-bar paragraph, and note the consistent look of the Web pages in this site.**

**9** **Close your browser and return to Dreamweaver, leaving index.html open for the next lesson.**

## LESSON 7 Using Design-Time Style Sheets

Dreamweaver has an innovative feature called "design-time style sheets" that allows you to enable or disable style sheets when you are creating or designing Web pages. The style sheets are no different than any other style sheet — this option is purely a Dreamweaver feature. Design-time style sheets can have several beneficial roles as you develop a Web site. Some CSS properties and values are not well supported by Dreamweaver. You have seen some of these although none of them are very critical. Dreamweaver has great difficulty with some CSS properties, making it difficult to create new pages with the style sheet enabled. The design-time feature allows you to disable those properties and develop the pages without hindrance. You can use design-time style sheets when developing alternate style sheets. By hiding the primary style sheet, you prevent it from interfering with the alternate. At times, part of a Web page, such as the navigation bar, is created using a server-side language that, of course, doesn't run in Dreamweaver. Therefore, this may create a hole in the page where this dynamic content would appear. You can create a design-time style sheet to hide this empty area.

The design-time style-sheet feature works by allowing you to choose which style sheets you want to have active when designing or working with a page and which style sheets you want to disable. Unlike the earlier suggestion, you cannot enable or disable individual style rules, but if you make a copy of the primary style sheet, you can delete the rules that cause a problem, and then, using the design-time feature, disable the primary style sheet and enable the less-problematic duplicate.

Design-time is not a Web technology but purely a Dreamweaver feature. There is nothing in the HTML code that indicates how Dreamweaver manages this feature: it is managed from within the site-definition settings. Therefore, Dreamweaver is not creating any custom or special code that will cause any problems with your browser. Furthermore, because there is no HTML code controlling the design-time style sheets, the browser sees the intended production style sheets, not any that are used during design-time.

The Design Time dialog box enables you to choose which style sheets you want to show when designing and which style sheets you want to hide when designing. Notice the reference to multiple style sheets. When you plan to use design-time style sheets, you create a style sheet that has the properties you want to see when this style sheet is active or one that has properties that reverse other properties that are causing problems.

## Create and Apply a Design-Time Style Sheet

In this exercise, you want to hide the navigation bar and the contact form during Web-page development. You create a design-time style sheet that hides those parts of the Web page and see that the properties in the design-time style sheet are active only in Dreamweaver.

**1** **In the open file, index.html, create a new style for the selector form, `p#navbar`, but choose New Style Sheet File from the Define in option, and click OK. Type `hide.css` in the File name field and click Save.**

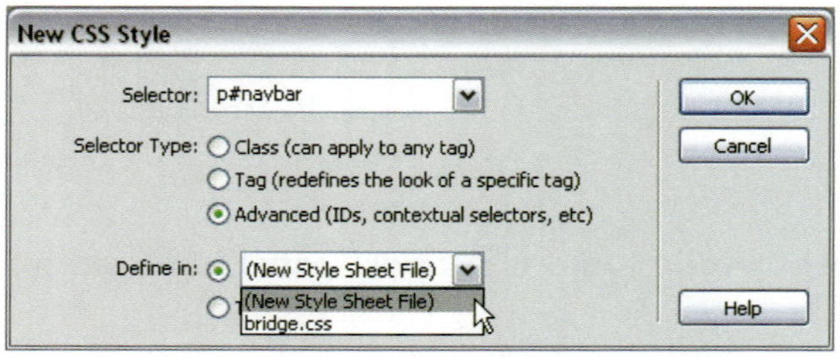


FIGURE 9.45

**2** **From the Block category, choose none from the Display list and click OK.**

**3** **Preview the page in your browser.**

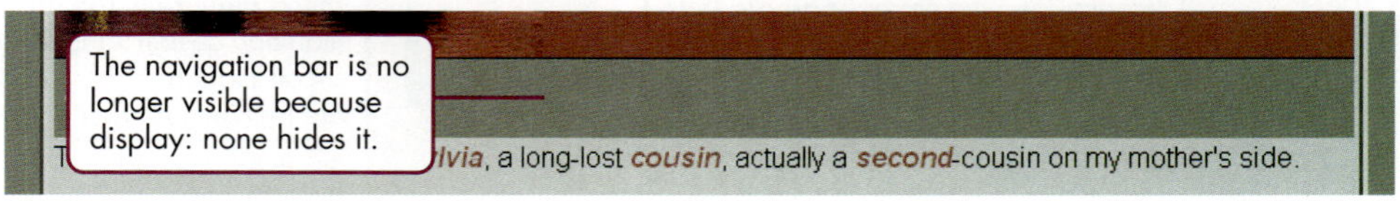


FIGURE 9.46

**4** **Return to Dreamweaver.**

**5** **Right/Control-click hide.css in the CSS Styles panel and choose Delete.**

**6** **Right/Control-click in the CSS Styles panel and choose Design-time. Click the + button above Show Only at Design Time, choose hide.css, and click OK/Choose. Click the + above Hide at Design Time, choose bridge.css, and click OK/Choose. Click OK to close the Design Time Style Sheets dialog box.**

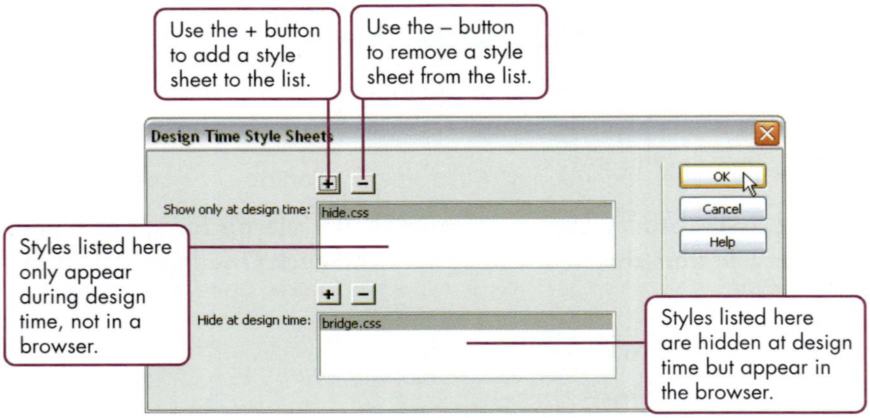


FIGURE 9.47

**7** **Examine the Document window and CSS Styles panel in Dreamweaver.**

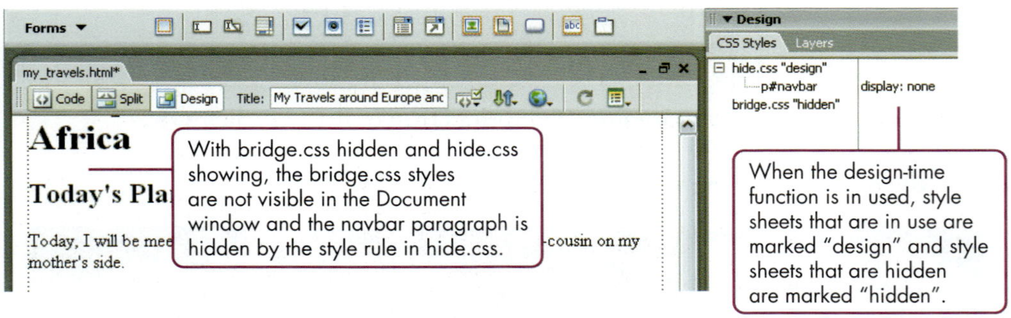


FIGURE 9.48

**8** **Preview the page in your browser.**

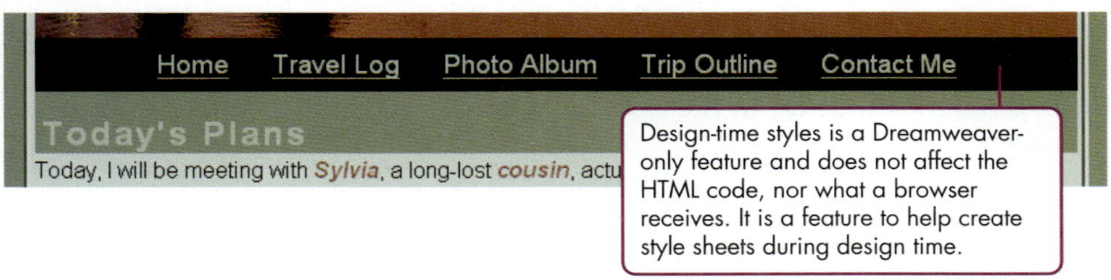


FIGURE 9.49

**9** **Return to Dreamweaver.**

**10** **Right/Control-click in the CSS Styles panel, choose Design-time, and click both – buttons to remove both hide.css and bridge.css from their fields in the dialog box. Click OK when finished. Leave index.html open for the next lesson.**

## To Extend Your Knowledge

**PROS AND CONS OF DESIGN-TIME STYLE SHEETS**

The design-time style-sheet function is a useful feature of Dreamweaver. You can hide CSS properties that cause problems for Dreamweaver, you can hide dynamic content, and you can hide the current style sheet while you are developing a new look or design for the Web site.

Although this feature is beneficial, it is not perfect. If you want to use this feature for all pages in a site, you must enable it for all pages individually. Macromedia Contribute is software designed for Web-content contributors. Design-time style sheets would be beneficial for users of Contribute in that areas of a Web page that contributors are not authorized to modify could be hidden. However, Contribute 2 does not support design-time style sheets. As long as you understand the limitations, you may find design-time style sheets quite useful at times.

# LESSON 8 Working with Print Style Sheets

Many news-related Web sites provide a link to a printable version of the current Web page, sometimes using an icon of a printer. The printable version commonly does not have colors or background images and sometimes, navigation bars are not present. Creating printable versions of your Web pages using this method involves creating a duplicate of every Web page either through server-side programming or manually. Style sheets have more uses than just styling content on a computer screen; they can also be developed for printers, televisions, and handheld devices, such as cell phones and ***PDAs*** (portable digital assistants, such as the Palm® devices). If a visitor decides to print a page that has a print style sheet attached, the browser displays the Web page on the printer using the print style sheet. This process is automatic and eliminates the need to create printable versions of the page. As long as the Web page is attached to the print style sheet, the browser uses the style rules in the print style sheet to style the printout.

There are no differences in the format of print and screen style sheets, although some screen options don't make sense for printing, such as the **`:hover`** pseudo-class. There also is one change that you should apply to the **`<link>`** tag to tell the browser not to display a print style sheet on screen, but only use it when printing. The default format of the tag is **`<link rel="stylesheet" href="filename.css" type="text/css">`**. The **`media`** attribute, not normally added by Dreamweaver, specifies for what type of device the style sheet is intended: **`media="screen"`** is for computer screens, **`media="print"`** is for printers, and **`media="all"`** is for all devices. Without a **`media`** attribute, the browser assumes that the style sheet can be used in all media.

There are some print-specific CSS properties that enable the designer to specify what size of paper is to be used for printing, such as letter, legal, or A4, and where to place page breaks, but these properties are poorly supported. Also, text size more commonly uses points as the unit of measurement. Points are more appropriate for printers than computers, televisions, or cell phones.

## Create a Print Style Sheet

In this exercise, you create a print style sheet. You use the design-time feature during the design of the print style sheet to hide the styles in bridge.css. You create the print style sheet, and modify the `<link>` tag to specify that the print style sheet is intended for the printer and bridge.css is intended for the screen.

**1** **In the open file, index.html, create a new style sheet using the selector `body`, and choose New Style Sheet File from the Design in options. Type `print.css` in the File name field and click Save.**

**2** **In the Type category, choose Times New Roman, Times, serif. Set the color to `#000` and click OK.**

**3** **Right/Control-click in the CSS Style panel and choose Design-time. Click the + button to add bridge.css to Hide at Design Time and click OK/Choose.**

**4** **Create a new style for the `h1` selector in the print.css file. In the Border category, create a solid, thin, black border around all sides. Click OK.**

**5** **Create a new style for the form, `p#navbar` selector in the print.css file. In the Block category, set Display to none and click OK.**

**6** **Create a new style for the `a` selector in the print.css file. In the Type category, choose none from the Decoration group of radio buttons, and set the Text color to `#000`.**

The navigation bar has no value on paper, so it was hidden. On a similar note, links in the document also have no value on paper, which is why the underlines were removed and the text color was changed to the same as normal paragraph text.

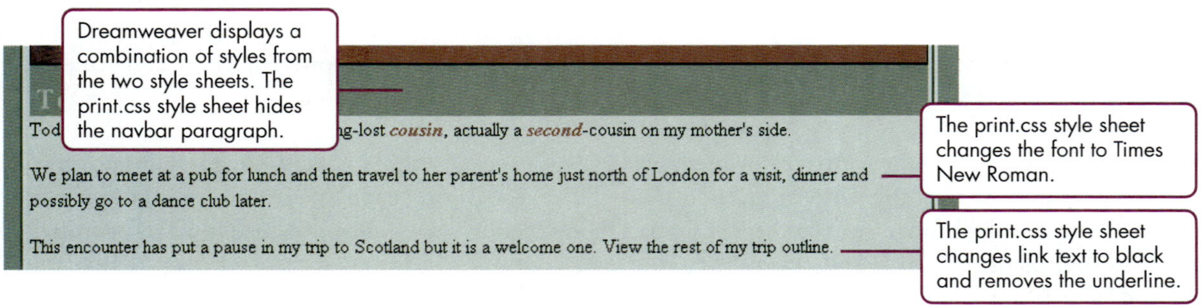


FIGURE 9.50

**7** **Right/Control-click in the CSS Styles panel and choose Design-time. Click the – button to enable the display of bridge.css.**

**8** **Open the Code window and locate the line beginning with `<link href="print.css"` (approximately line 8). Move the insertion point to the left of > and press the Spacebar. Type `m`, choose media, and press Enter/Return. Type `p`, choose print, and press Enter/Return.**

**9** **Locate the line beginning with <link href="bridge.css". Using the same methods as in Step 8, set the media attribute to screen. Close the Code window when finished.**

```
<title>My Travels around Europe and Asia</title>
<meta http-equiv="Content-Type" content="text/html; charset=iso-8859-1">
<link href="bridge.css" rel="stylesheet" type="text/css" media="screen">
<link href="print.css" rel="stylesheet" type="text/css" media="print">
</head>
```

When media has been set, the browser knows when to use the style sheet: screen for onscreen display and print when printing the page.

FIGURE 9.51

**10** **Preview the page in your browser, and either print the page or choose File>Print Preview in your browser.**

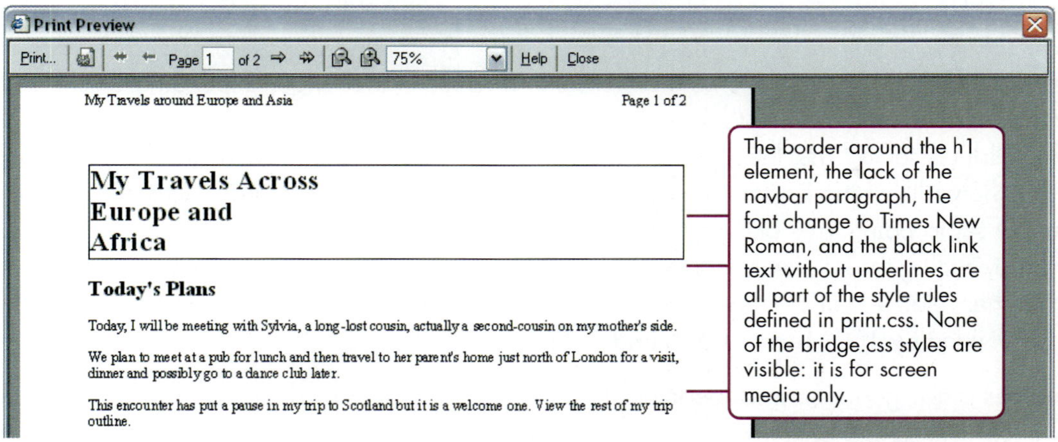


FIGURE 9.52

**11** **Close your browser and return to Dreamweaver, leaving index.html open for the next exercise.**

## LESSON 9 Using Alternate Style Sheets

An alternate style sheet is a feature of CSS that cannot be duplicated in HTML without completely redesigning the Web site. An alternate style sheet is essentially a second (or third or more) style sheet that has been created for the Web page or Web site. In developing the alternate style sheet, you may completely rethink your design and layout of the Web page or you may just apply very limited changes, such as colors. The differences between primary and alternate style sheets are not in the creation or methodology used, but in how they are attached to the Web pages. Another difference between primary and alternate style sheets is that when you have at least one alternate, you are able to provide your visitors with the option of switching between style sheets. Finally, if you want to use alternate style sheets, all of your style sheets, including the primary, should be external style sheets. It is possible but more difficult to switch between primary and alternate style sheets if the primary is an embedded style sheet.

## To Extend Your Knowledge

### POINTS VS. PIXELS VS. EMS VS. ...

There are many units of measurements available to CSS: some have good browser support and others do not. The units of measurements can be classified as absolute units and relative units.

***Absolute units of measurement*** are fixed and unchanged. The most understood absolute unit is the point: there are 72 points per inch so a 12-point font is one-sixth of an inch in height. Another absolute unit is the pixel: you have used this often to set the dimensions of images, thickness of borders, and dimensions of some elements, such as the height of the h1 element. Pixels are absolute because the only way you can change the number of pixels on your computer monitor is to change the resolution. CSS also supports inches and centimeters, but those are more appropriate for setting dimensions on the printed page than on-screen.

***Relative units of measurement*** create dimensions or sizes that change, depending on the situation. Percentage is measured relative to the dimensions of the container or default font size. For example, if the table width is set to 50%, the outer table is 50% of the width of the browser window, a nested table is 50% of the width of the containing cell, and so on. All browsers have a default setting for font size (commonly set to point sizes between 12 and 14 points). This is the base font size for paragraph or normal text. Setting the h1 size to 200% displays the text at 24 to 28 points, depending on the browser. Em is another relative unit of measurement. For all intents and purposes, you can think of ems as percentages divided by 100: 1em = 100% and 0.8em = 80%.

Percentages make good sense to people, but unfortunately, some browsers do not interpret percentages well for text size: 0.8em text size should be the same as 80%, but in IE, it is not. Furthermore, font sizes less than 70% on IE5.2 for the Macintosh are very difficult to read, whereas 70% on IE6 for Windows is readable, albeit small.

For reasons of accessibility, the W3C recommends that you use a relative font size. This recommendation targets people who have poor vision and would like to enlarge the font on their computer screen to make it easier to read. Font sizes specified in absolute units cannot be resized, whereas relative units can be resized. Although the menu option varies from browser to browser, under the View menu is a font- or text-size option enabling you to change the size. If other elements use em as the unit of measurement, such as a table with of 30em, its width also change when you change the text size from the menu. Go to webstandards.org and resize the text size. Go to cnn.com and try the same process. CNN.com uses (at the time of writing) points for font size that cannot be resized in a browser. The Opera browser is the exception, in which the zoom feature resizes everything, including images, no matter what units were used.

You have learned how to create an external style sheet. You have used design-time to create a new style sheet, the print style sheet. Using design-time allowed you to see the changes to the style of the page as you created them without interference from the screen style sheet. A print style sheet is not considered an alternate style sheet because it is intended for a different medium. An alternate style sheet is one that has been designed for the screen and displays the same Web page with a different look. There are two changes that you need to make to the `<link>` tag to set an additional style sheet as an alternate style sheet: you must modify the `rel` attribute from `rel="stylesheet"` to `rel="alternate stylesheet"`, and you must apply a name to the alternate style sheet using the `title` attribute, so that the user can choose the alternate style sheet.

There are two methods for allowing visitors to switch between alternate style sheets. The easiest method is available to the Mozilla and Opera browsers. In these browsers, you choose View>Use Style or View>Style and choose the style sheet — the browser automatically unloads the current style sheet, loads the selected style sheet, and redisplays the page using the current style sheet. Unfortunately, Internet Explorer does not support alternate style sheets within the application. The second method is called "style-sheet switching." It depends on either a JavaScript or server-side script with a link on a Web page to choose the style sheet. These methods are supported by all browsers.

CSSZenGarden.com is a Web site designed specifically to highlight CSS-based redesigns of a single page. In order to achieve this, every contributor creates the equivalent of an alternate style sheet, submits it to the site and, using a server-side application, visitors to the site can choose style sheets from the links provided. Besides the promotion of CSS, there are a number of applications where alternate style sheets are beneficial. Some Web designers use them to provide more accessible versions of their Web pages with higher-contrast color schemes, and/or larger fonts. Other Web designers use it to show off their design talents by demonstrating different design options for their Web sites. On a similar note, Web designers could use it to demonstrate to their clients some of the different design options they have come up with for their Web sites.

## Attach an Alternate Style Sheet

In this exercise, you are given an alternate style sheet that you must attach to the Web page, configure properly, and test in your browser.

**1** **In the open file, index.html, Right/Control-click in the CSS Styles panel and choose Attach Style Sheet. Add the style sheet using the Link method, and browse to choose sphinx.css. Click OK/Choose, then OK again.**

FIGURE 9.53

**2** **Switch to the Code view and scroll up to approximately line 7 where you find the `<link>` tag to the bridge.css style sheet.**

**3** Click to the left of the > at the end of the tag and press the Spacebar. Type `t`, choose `title` from the Code Hint, and press Enter/Return. Type `London Bridge`.

**4** Find the `<link>` tag for the sphinx.css file. Insert `alternate` before stylesheet in the rel attibute to produce `rel="alternate stylesheet"`.

**5** Click to the left of the > at the end of the tag, and press the Spacebar. Type `m`, press Enter/Return to choose `media`, type `s`, and press Enter/Return to choose `screen`. Insert a `title` attribute, as in Step 3, and title the style sheet `The Sphinx`.

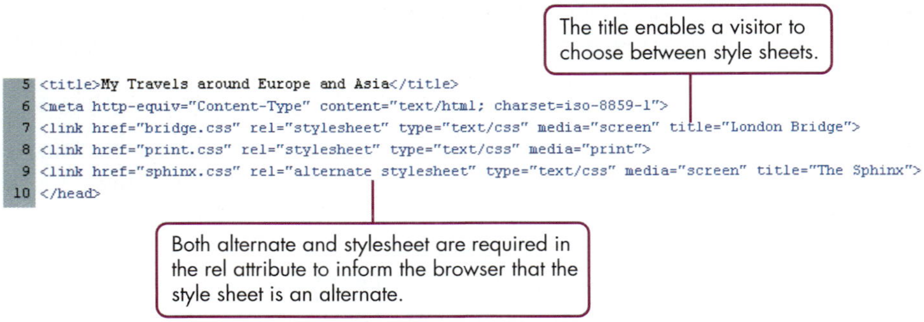


**FIGURE 9.54**

**6** Switch back to the Design view and preview the page in your browser.

**7** Switch style sheets using the appropriate method for the browser: in Opera, choose View>Style; in Mozilla, choose View>Use Style; in Firefox, click the icon in the Status bar and choose The Sphinx.

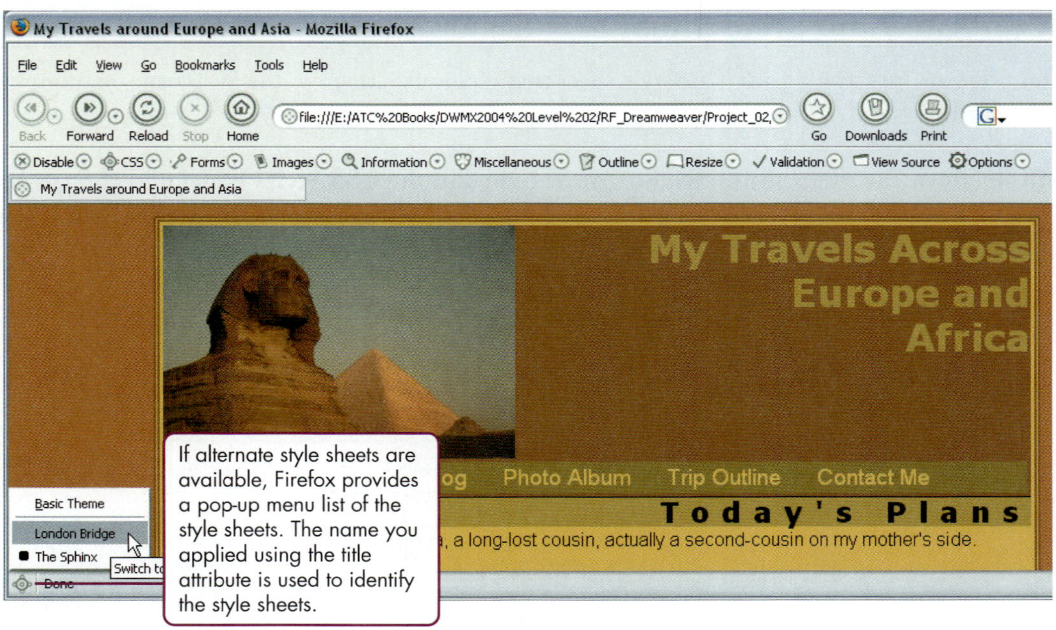


**FIGURE 9.55**

**8** Close your browser, return to Dreamweaver, and close index.html.

## To Extend Your Knowledge

### BROWSER SUPPORT FOR CSS

There are many CSS properties and values for the properties. Even the best browsers, which currently are the Mozilla-based browsers (Mozilla, Firefox, and Camino), suffer from bugs, weaknesses, misinterpretations, or lack of support for some CSS properties or values. Current browsers support most of the CSS1 properties, with the exception of some units of measurement, such as the ex. However, CSS2 is not fully supported, and it would be nice to know which browsers support what properties. There are two sources of this type of information: browser-support charts and Dreamweaver's results panel.

Westciv.com has an excellent series of CSS browser-support charts at westciv.com/style_master/academy/browser_support/; you can also purchase a printed copy of these charts (with more information) from that Web site. At blooberry.com/indexdot/css/, you can find a wealth of CSS information, and for each property, browser support is indicated. Other CSS browser-support charts are available if you search for css support chart using your favorite search engine.

Dreamweaver also provides support information through the Browser Check function. You click the Browser Check button to the right of the Document Title field at the top of the Document window, and choose Show All Errors. In the Results panel that opens up below the Property inspector, any code that is poorly supported or unsupported is flagged with red (serious problem for the identified browsers), yellow (warning, may not appear as intended), or white (informational, unsupported code but has no visible effect) markers. To check your CSS file for browser-support issues, open the CSS file in Dreamweaver, run the browser check, and review the messages in the Results panel.

## SUMMARY

In this project, you learned how CSS works and how to make it work for you. You learned what an element selector is and how to group element selectors so that the same style declaration can apply to multiple elements. You learned the difference between class and id selectors, how they should be used, and how to apply them to your Web pages. You learned about inheritance of CSS properties, about relationships between elements, and how to use these principles to reduce dependency on classes and to create sophisticated style rules. You learned about pseudo-classes and how they can be applied to links. You learned how the **<span>** tag is used to create custom styles. You created an embedded style sheet, discovered how to export it to an external style sheet, and learned how an external style sheet you can attach to every page in a Web site to create a consistent look and feel. You learned how the design-time feature of Dreamweaver is beneficial for the development of other style sheets without interference from the primary style sheet. You created a print style sheet and learned how it can be used to create a style for printing and to hide elements that have no usefulness on paper. You learned how to attach alternate style sheets so that your visitors or clients can be presented with different styles of the same page.

## KEY TERMS

absolute units
block
cache
class
DOM
element selector
embedded style sheet
external style sheet
generic class/id
id
inline
inline style
page weight
PDA
properties
regular class/id
relative units
selector
style declaration
style-declaration block
style rule
values
version 4 browsers

## CHECKING CONCEPTS AND TERMS

### SCREEN ID

**Identify the indicated areas from the list below:**

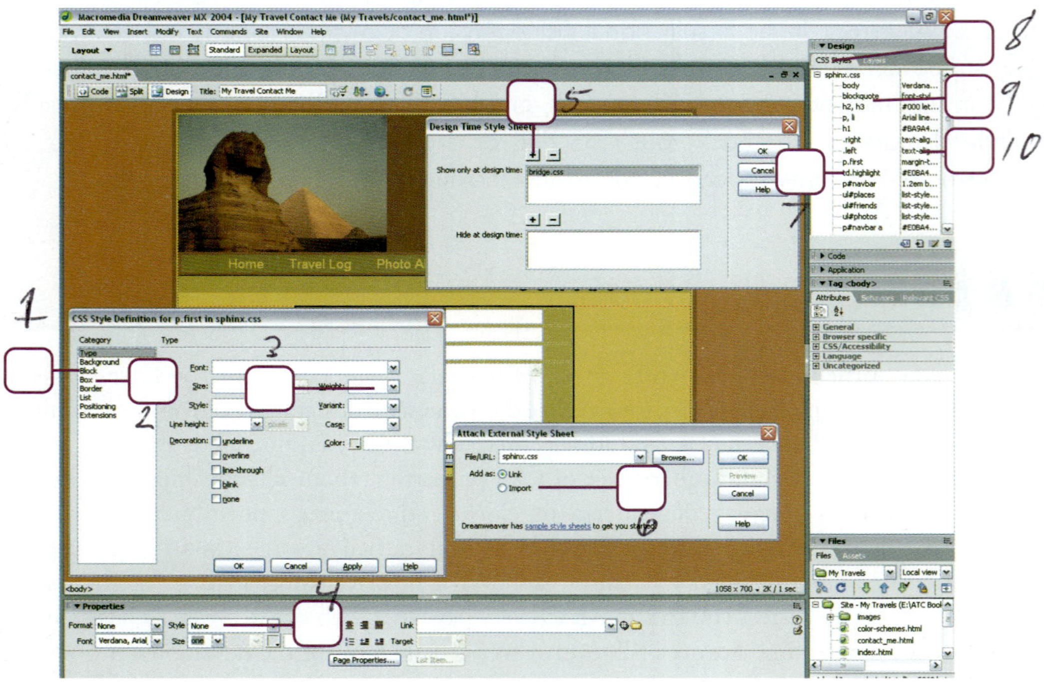


FIGURE 9.56

a. Enable or disable bold

b. @import

c. Style declaration

d. Show more style sheets at design time

e. Category containing width, height, margins, and padding

f. Element selector

g. CSS Styles panel

h. List of available styles

i. Regular class selector

j. Category containing text alignment

## MULTIPLE CHOICE

**Circle the letter of the correct answer for each of the following:**

1. Identify the correct application of the selector **.alert**.
   - **a.** <p class="alert">, <a class="alert">
   - **b.** <blockquote id="alert">, <h1 class="alert">
   - **c.** <h2 id="alert">, <h2 id="alert">
   - **d.** All of the above

2. **a {color: red;}** is an example of _______.
   - **a.** an element selector
   - **b.** a style rule
   - **c.** a style declaration block
   - **d.** a regular class

3. The correct format of a child selector is _______.
   - **a.** a:child
   - **b.** p+p
   - **c.** h1, h2
   - **d.** ul>li

4. A style sheet between the **<head>** and **</head>** tags is called _______.
   - **a.** applied
   - **b.** enclosed
   - **c.** embedded
   - **d.** exported

5. An external style sheet is attached to a Web page using _______.
   - **a.** <link href="hicontrast.css" rel="alternate stylesheet" type="text/css" media="screen" title="High Contrast">
   - **b.** <link href="styles.css" rel="stylesheet" type="text/css">
   - **c.** <link href="print.css" rel="stylesheet" type= "text/css" media="print">
   - **d.** All of the above

6. The Design Time Style Sheets dialog box allows you to _______.
   - **a.** create element selectors
   - **b.** hide and display style sheets
   - **c.** create and delete style sheets
   - **d.** attach or detach style sheets

7. To change the appearance of a link when the mouse pointer rolls over it, you use _______.
   - **a.** p.navbar:active {color: red;}
   - **b.** a:visited {background-color: blue;}
   - **c.** a.body:hover {text-decoration: none;}
   - **d.** p#navbar a {padding: 0px; padding-left: 15px; padding-right; 15px;}

8. Which is an example of a group of id selectors?
   - **a.** p#navbar {color: red;}, p#footer {color: blue;}
   - **b.** .style1, .style2 {font-weight: bold;}
   - **c.** p#navbar, .style1 {text-align: center;}
   - **d.** #navbar, #footer {text-decoration: underline;}

9. Which color code produces the color black?
   - **a.** #00000
   - **b.** #black
   - **c.** #000
   - **d.** All of the above

10. In a Web page in which you have **<h2>Job Experience</h2><p>I made hamburgers at <a href="http://www.bk.com"> Burger King</a>.</p>**, which selector would change the color of Burger King to blue?
    - **a.** h2+p>a
    - **b.** p a, blockquote a
    - **c.** body a
    - **d.** All of the above

## DISCUSSION QUESTIONS

1. You have experienced the power, flexibility, and versatility of CSS, and, as a designer, you can make great use of these features. What reasons might non-CSS designers have for not learning and applying CSS in their Web-site designs? What means can you think of to encourage designers to learn more about and use CSS?

2. The **media** attribute of the **<style>** tag has several options; **screen**, **print**, and **all** are the most commonly used. You have been asked to create a **handheld** media (cell/mobile phones and PDAs) style sheet for the My Travels Web site (the one used for much of this project). Assume that the devices can display color and images (as most current ones can) and assume that these devices support all current CSS selectors and properties. What changes would you make to the style sheet and/or Web page(s) to allow users to comfortably browse this Web site using these small screen devices?

## SKILL DRILLS

Skill Drills reinforce project skills. Each skill reinforced is the same, or nearly the same, as a skill presented in the lessons. Detailed instructions are provided in a step-by-step format. Work through these exercises in order.

### 1. Lay the Foundation Styles

In the following exercise, you're going to build the basic styles for the Philosophy Department's Web site. You create the body styles and the basic layout styles. Although the instructions state to click OK at the end of creating a style rule, you can click Apply after each new property has been assigned to see the changes taking place gradually.

1. Create a new site definition called **Philosophy** from the Project_09>Philosophy folder.

2. One by one, open and examine the three Web pages in the folder.

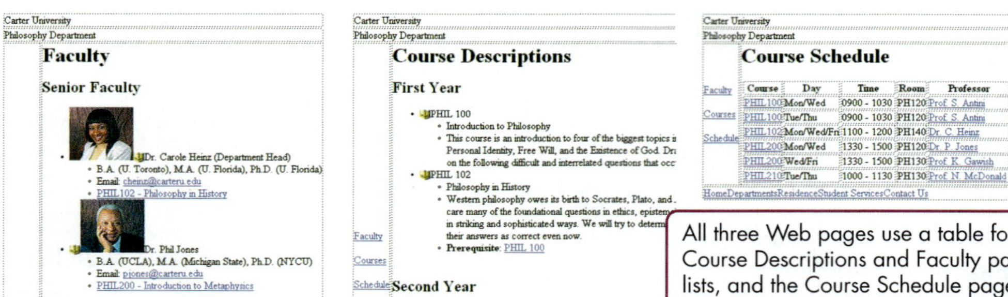


All three Web pages use a table for layout. The Course Descriptions and Faculty pages have nested lists, and the Course Schedule page has a nested table. All three have a left cell with the navigation-bar links and a bottom cell with more links.

FIGURE 9.57

3. Open faculty.html. Create a new style for the **body** selector, set Define in to New Style Sheet File, and click OK. Type **styles.css** in the File name field and click Save.

4. In the Type category, set the Font to Verdana, Arial, Helvetica, sans-serif. In the Background category, set the Background Image to images>body-bg.png, Attachment to fixed, Horizontal Position to center, and Vertical Position to top. Click OK.

5. Create a new CSS style for the **table#body** selector. In the Background category, set the Background Color to **#000000**, the Background Image to images>table-bg.jpg, Repeat to no-repeat, Horizontal Position to left, and Vertical Position to top. In the Box category, set Width to **750** pixels, uncheck Same for All for Margins, and set both Left and Right margins to auto. Click OK.

6. Click in the table in the Document window. Right/Control-click the **<table>** tag in the Tag selector and set the ID to body.

7. Create a new CSS style for the selector **td#header**. In the Type category, set the Font to Georgia, Times New Roman, Times, serif; the Size to **4** ems; the Weight to bold; and the Color to **#1C438C**. In the Box category, set the Height to **178** px. Click OK.

8. Click inside the top cell containing the text Carter University. Right/Control-click the **<td>** tag in the Tag selector and set the ID to header.

9. Create a new CSS style for the selector **td#dept**. In the Type category, set the Weight to bold, the Line Height to **30** pixels, and the Color to **#FFFFFF**. In the Block category, set Text Align to right. In the Box category, uncheck Same for All for Padding, and set the Right padding to **15** pixels. In the Border category, uncheck Same for All for all border properties, and create a bottom border that is solid in style, medium in thickness, with a color of **#5C7FA7**. Click OK.

10. Click inside the second cell containing the text Philosophy Department. Right/Control-click the **<td>** tag in the Tag selector and set the ID to dept.

**FIGURE 9.58**

11. Keep faculty.html open for the next exercise.

## 2. Create the Navigation-Bar Styles

In this Skill Drill, you create the styles for the left navigation bar. You create a navbar id for the **<td>** tag. You then create styles based on descendent selectors using the **td#navbar** as the ancestor, so that these styles are not confused with any other styles. By using the id selector, you do not need to create or assign multiple classes to the content within the navbar cell.

1. Create a new CSS style for the **td** selector. In the Block category, set Vertical Align to top and click OK.

   By default, table-data cells are aligned left (horizontally) middle (vertically); this change forces the content of all table-data cells to the top.

2. Create a new CSS style for the **td#navbar** selector. In the Block category, set Text Align to center. In the Box category, set the width to **120** pixels. In the Border category, uncheck Same for All, and create a Right border with a solid style, a medium thickness, and a color of **#5C7FA7**. Click OK.

3. Click inside the left cell containing the three text links. Right/Control-click **<td>** tag in the Tag selector and set the ID to navbar.

   It is possible to select the **<td>** tag of the left cell and add the code, **id="navbar"**, using the Tag editor before creating the style for the id. However, creating the style first adds the id name to the ID list. It's easier to choose an id from the list to apply than to use the Tag editor. At times, however, you may have to add the id using the Tag editor before creating the style or for the purposes of JavaScript.

4. Create a new CSS style for the **td#navbar p** selector. In the Box category, set all paddings and margins to **0** pixels. Click OK.

5. Create a new CSS style for the **td#navbar a** selector. In the Type category, set Color to **#FFFFFF**, Decoration to none, and Weight to bold. In the Block category, set Display to block. In the Box category, set the width to **120** pixels, and set all Paddings and Margins to **0** pixels. In the Border category, create a bottom border that is solid, **1** pixel thick, with a color of **#5C7FA7**. Click OK.

FIGURE 9.59

6. Keep faculty.html open for the next exercise.

## 3. Create the Content-Area Styles

The content cell contains the greatest variety of HTML tags, such as headings, paragraphs, links, lists, and nested tables. For this reason, it takes more effort to create the styles for the content area. Additionally, some HTML elements may not exist in the current page (such as a nested table), so you may have to add to the style sheet after examining other pages.

1. Create a new CSS style for the **td#content** selector. In the Type category, set Color to **#DDDDDD**. Click OK.

   The content cell, with the exception of the top portion, has a black background, which is the table background color. The text color could have been set to white, but white can be too bright against a black background. **#DDDDDD** is a light gray that provides decent contrast without appearing too bright.

2. Click inside the main content cell. Right/Control-click **<td>** tag in the Tag selector and set the ID to content.

3. Create a new CSS style for the **td#content h1, td#content h2** selector. In the Type category, set Weight to normal. In the Box category, set all margins to **5** pixels and all paddings to **0** pixels. Click OK.

   Headings, by default, are bold. They are also larger in size (headings 1 to 3 are larger than normal paragraph text, which is equivalent in size to heading 4). Therefore, these headings stand out on the basis of their size. Remember, styles using CSS do not affect the HTML structures of the document. Removing bold from the appearance of these headings does not change their heading level, just their appearance, and removing bold is only one of multitudes of different style changes that you could apply to these elements.

4. Create a new CSS style for the selector **td#content ul**. In the Type category, set Weight to bold, and set Line Height to **1.3** ems. In the List category, set Type to none. Click OK.

   Both the outer and nested list take on the same style. The next style rule uses a selector that targets the nested list.

5. Create a new CSS style for the selector **td#content ul ul**. In the Type category, set Weight to normal. In the Box category, set the bottom margin (only) to **20** pixels. In the List category, set the Type to square. Click OK.

   This rule reverses the bold and bullet settings applied in the previous rule. The bottom-margin setting creates a space below each nested list.

6. Create a new CSS style for the **td#content img** selector. In the Box category, set Float to right, all paddings to **0** pixels, and the right margin to **5** pixels. In the Border category, set all borders to solid style, **2**-pixel thickness, and a color of **#666666**. Click OK.

   This style rule is very generic. On other pages, there may be images that you might not want to float to the right. Therefore, you may have to modify the selector for this page to **td#content ul img** or, if that is not specific enough, you may have to create a class, such as **img.faculty**. For the purposes of this Skill Drill, this selector is sufficiently specific.

7. Create a new CSS style for the **td#content a** selector. In the Type category, set Color to **#97B5EB**. Click OK.

**FIGURE 9.60**

8. Leave faculty.html open for the next exercise.

## 4. Create the Footer Styles

The footer is just another navigation bar, but, compared with the left navigation bar, its layout is different (horizontal) and allows for a different styling.

1. Create a new CSS style for the **td#footer** selector. In the Type category, set Line Height to **2** ems. In the Background category, set Background Color to **#2E3B6B**. In the Block category, set Text Align to center. In the Border category, create a top border with a solid style, medium thickness, and a color of **#5C7FA7**. Click OK.

2. Click inside the bottom cell. Right/Control-click **<td>** tag in the Tag selector and set the ID to footer.

3. Create a new CSS Style for the **td#footer a** selector. In the Type category, set Color to **#DDDDDD**, Weight to bold, and Decoration to none. In the Box category, set all margins to **0** pixels, and set the paddings as: Top to **0** pixel, Right to **15** pixels, Bottom to **0** pixel, and Left to **15** pixels. Click OK.

4. Create a new CSS Style for the **td#footer a+a** selector. In the Border category, create a left (only) border with a solid style, **3**-pixel thickness, and a color of **#FFFFFF**.

   Internet Explorer does not support the adjacent selector, a+a, in Step 4, although Dreamweaver and the Mozilla, Opera, and Safari browsers support it. To create this style for IE, you must create a class or an id to style the first link in the footer differently from the other links.

5. Right/Control-click the **td#footer a+a** selector in the CSS Styles panel and choose Go to Code. Delete **a+a** and replace it with **a.notfirst** to create **td#footer a.notfirst** as the selector. Close styles.css and save the changes.

6. Click the second link (Departments) in the Design window, Right/Control-click the selected **<a>** tag in the Tag selector, and apply the class notfirst. One by one, select the remaining links to the right and apply the notfirst class to them.

**FIGURE 9.61**

7. Keep faculty.html open for the next exercise.

## 5. Create the Pseudo-Class Styles

Unlike all of the styles created so far, the pseudo-class styles cannot be tested in Dreamweaver. Therefore, after creating these styles, you preview and test them in your browser.

1. Create a new CSS style for the **td#content a:hover** selector. In the Type category, set Decoration to none and click OK.
2. Create a new CSS style for the **td#content a:active** selector. In the Type category, set Decoration to none, Color to **#FFFFFF**, and click OK.
3. Create a new CSS style for the **td#content a:visited** selector. In the Type category, set Color to **#DDDDDD**, and click OK.
4. Create a new CSS style for the **td#navbar a:hover** selector. In the Type category, set the color to **#5C7FA7**. In the Border category, create a bottom (only) border with a solid style, **1**-pixel thickness, and a color of **#FFFFFF**. Click OK.

   It is common practice not to create a **:visited** pseudo-class for navigation-bar links. (An **:active** pseudo-class style could be created but won't be.)
5. Create a new CSS style for the **td#footer a:hover** selector. In the Type category, set Color to **#46537D**. In the Background category, set Background Color to **#BBBBBB**. Click OK.
6. Preview the page in your browser. Roll your mouse pointer over the links in the content, navbar, and footer cells. Click any of the links in the content cell and watch the link color flash white (the **:active** pseudo-class). Click the back button in your browser and note the color of the visited link.
7. Close your browser, return to Dreamweaver, and close faculty.html.

## 6. Apply the Style Sheet to the Other Web Pages

When you linked to the other pages, you noticed that they were not styled. The next step is to attach the style sheet you created to the other Web pages in this site. Most of the style rules depend on ids, such as **table#body** and **td#navbar**. These ids do not yet exist in these pages. Even when the style sheet is attached, the id hooks won't be present and most of the styles will not appear. If there are classes, they, too, must be applied to the elements that require them. The only class is the **notfirst** class that must be applied to all but the first link in the footer cell.

1. Open courses.html.
2. Right/Control-click in the CSS Styles panel and choose Attach Style Sheet. Using the Add as Link option, choose styles.css.
3. Click in the table. Right/Control-click the **<table>** tag in the Tag selector and set its ID to body.
4. Click in the top cell. Right/Control-click the **<td>** tag in the Tag selector and set its ID to header.
5. Click in the second cell. Right/Control-click the **<td>** tag in the Tag selector and set its ID to dept.
6. Click in the left cell. Right/Control-click the **<td>** tag in the Tag selector and set its ID to navbar.
7. Click in the main cell. Right/Control-click the **<td>** tag in the Tag selector and set its ID to content.
8. Click in the bottom cell. Right/Control-click the **<td>** tag in the Tag selector and set its ID to footer.

9. One by one, click the links in the footer cell (excluding Home), Right/Control-click the **<a>** tag in the Tag selector, and set the class to notfirst.
10. Close courses.html, saving your changes.
11. Open schedule.html. Repeat Steps 2 to 9.
12. Save the changes to schedule.html and leave it open for the next exercise.

## 7. Create New Styles

The document structures in the content cells of the Faculty and Course Descriptions pages are very similar. However, there is a nested table in the Course Schedules page for which no style has been developed. In this exercise, you create a style for the nested table.

1. Create a new CSS style for the `td#content table` selector. In the Background category, set the Background color to `#21355A`. In the Box category, set all margins to `20` pixels. In the Border category, create a border around all sides that is solid, thin, and has a color of `#CCCCCC`. Click OK.
2. Create a new CSS style for the `td#content th, td#content td` selector. In the Block category, set Text Align to center. In the Box category, set all paddings to `5` pixels. Click OK.

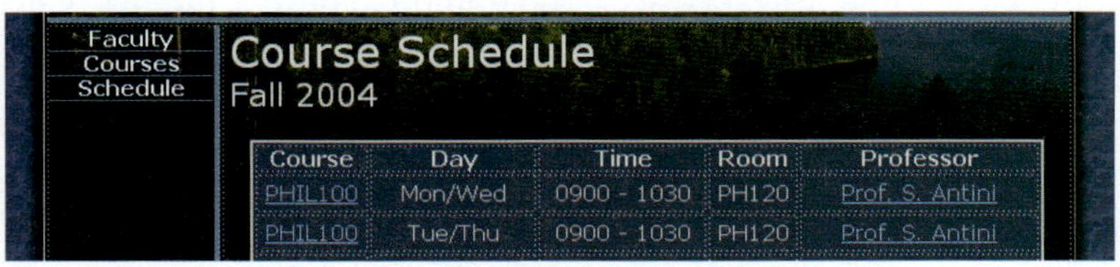


FIGURE 9.62

3. Close schedule.html, saving your changes.

# CHALLENGE

Challenge exercises expand on, or are somewhat related to, skills presented in the lessons. Each exercise provides a brief narrative introduction, followed by instructions in a numbered-step format that are not as detailed as those in the Skill Drill section. Work through the exercises in the order presented.

## 1. Create a Print Style Sheet

In this Challenge exercise, you create a print style sheet for the Philosophy Department Web site.

1. Open schedule.html from the Philosophy site.
2. From the CSS Style panel, open the Design Time dialog box and set styles.css to be hidden.
3. Create a new CSS style using `body` as the selector. Set Define in to New Style Sheet File, and name it `print.css`. Set the Font to Arial, Helvetica, sans-serif; the text color to `#000000`; and all margins and paddings to `0` pixels.

4. Create a new CSS style for the **a** selector. Set the text color to **#000000** and Decoration to none.
5. Create a new CSS style for the **table#body** selector. Set the box width to **100**%. Create a bottom border that uses the solid style, is **5** points in thickness, and has a color of **#000000**.
6. Create a new CSS style for the **td#header** selector. Set the font size to **18** points, the weight to bold, and the font to Times New Roman, Times, serif. Create a bottom border that uses the double style, is **3** points in thickness, and has a color **#000000**.

   The solid, dotted, and dashed border styles can be as thick or thin as you wish, but the other styles require at least a medium, 3-pixel, or 3-point thickness. Experiment with different thicknesses — you can use the relative measurements (thin, medium, or thick) or pixels for on-screen presentation and points for printing.

7. Create a new CSS style for the **td#dept** selector. Set the font size to **13** points and the text alignment to right.
8. Create a new CSS style for the **td#footer p, td#navbar p** selector. Set Display to none.
9. Create a new CSS style for the **td#content table** selector. Set the width to **100**%, the bottom margin to **20** points, and a border around all sides that is solid in style, **1** point in thickness, with a color of **#000000**.
10. Right/Control-click the **td#content table** selector in the CSS Styles panel and choose Go to Code. Add the following new style declaration to the **td#content table** style rule: **border-collapse: collapse;**. Close print.css, saving your changes.

    When adjacent cells have a border around each cell, the cell-border thicknesses are doubled. The **border-collapse: collapse** declaration removes the duplicate border when cells share a border. Dreamweaver does not display collapsed borders, but all current browsers support this CSS property.

11. Create a new CSS style for the **td#content td, td#content th** selector. Set the text alignment to left, all paddings to **5** points, and borders around all sides that are solid in style, **1** point in thickness, with a color of **#000000**.
12. Unhide styles.css using the Design Time dialog box. Switch to the Code view and add **media="screen"** to the styles.css **<link>** tag and **media="print"** to the print.css **<link>** tag. Return to the Design view and close schedule.html, saving your changes.

## 2. Add Additional Styles to the Print Style Sheet

In this Challenge exercise, you attach the print style sheet to the other two pages and determine whether or not additional style rules need to be created to accommodate document structures that are not found in the Course Schedules page.

1. Open faculty.html.
2. Attach print.css to faculty.html and set the media attributes for the two style sheets as you did in Step 12 of the previous exercise.
3. Using the Design Time Style Sheets dialog box, hide styles.css.

4. Examine the appearance of the Web page, and note the differences in document structures that exist in this page — notably the images, lists, and nested lists.

5. Using any of the style properties learned in this project, create new style rules to accommodate the new document structures in this page. Do not create any new classes or ids — use the elements, ids, and classes that currently exist (the only class is the notfirst class in the footer) and their relationships to apply the styles.

6. When finished, redisplay styles.css using the Design Time Style Sheets dialog box, and then close faculty.html, saving your changes.

7. Open schedule.html and apply the same procedures as outlined in Steps 2 and 3. Examine schedule.html and determine whether or not additional style rules are needed. If so, create them, but keep in mind that the structure of schedule.html is very similar to that of faculty.html, and changes you make to the style sheet may affect the Faculty page.

8. When finished with schedule.html, preview the page in your browser, and either print or print preview the page. Link to the other pages, also, and print or print preview those pages, as well.

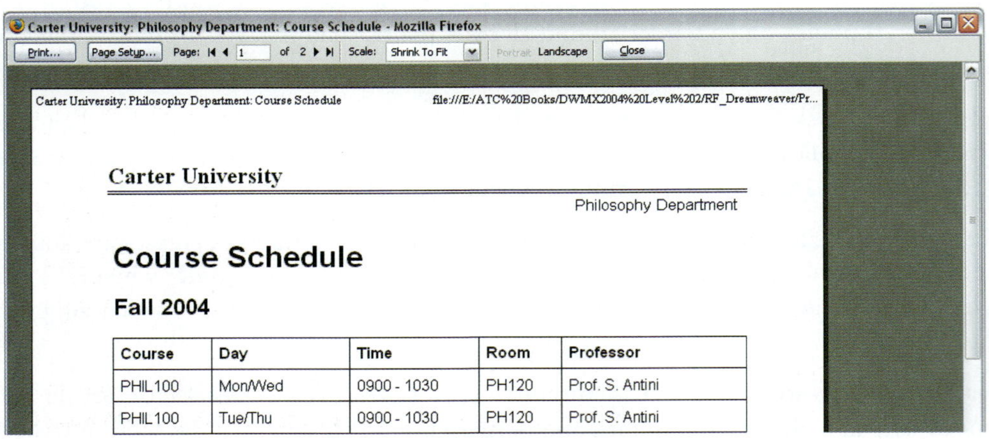


**FIGURE 9.63**

9. Close your browser, return to Dreamweaver, and close schedule.html.

## 3. Create an Alternate Style Sheet

In this Challenge exercise, you will be given some freedom to create your own alternate style sheet.

1. Open index.html from the My Travels site and open color-schemes.html from the My Travels site.

2. In the color-schemes.html page are images and color schemes to match the images. Choose an image to replace the image of the London Bridge. Click in the cells containing the background colors and make note of the hexadecimal color codes. You can close color-schemes.html or keep it open to refer to as you are working.

3. If you are not happy with the colors for your chosen image, you may create your own color scheme using the same technique employed for these images. Set your chosen image as the background image for the h1 element, replacing the image of the London Bridge. Click the color button and, using the eyedropper, pick a color from the image. Note the hexadecimal color code for the color. Open your browser and go to either color.twysted.net or colorschemer.com/online.html. Type the hexadecimal color code into the hexadecimal color field, and click the Use It or Set Hex button (depending on which site you have chosen to use). Make note of the colors in the scheme (whether or not they are provided, you can also use white, black, and grays) and return to Dreamweaver.
4. Using the Files panel, make a copy of the bridge.css file and name it with your personal name (no spaces in the filename — use a hyphen or underscore to create a fake space). The filename will be beneficial in the next Challenge exercise.
5. Attach your new style sheet to index.html.
6. Using the Design Time Style Sheets dialog box, hide all other style sheets.
7. Apply as many or as few of the colors from the color scheme as you want to the text and background colors by modifying the existing selectors. You can also change alignment, and add or delete borders.
8. When you have finished modifying the styles, open the Code window and apply the screen media attribute and the title attribute to the new style sheet `<link>` tag, and modify the rel attribute to alternate stylesheet. Return to the Design view and unhide the style sheets from the Design Time Style Sheet dialog box.
9. If you have access to the Opera, Mozilla (or Firefox or Camino) or Safari browser, preview the page in that browser and switch to your new style sheet.
10. Return to Dreamweaver, leaving index.html open for the next exercise.

## 4. Use a JavaScript Style-Sheet Switcher

In this Challenge exercise, you set up a JavaScript style-sheet switcher. If you have used the Mozilla, Opera, or Safari browser, you have seen how you may switch between style sheets. However, as soon as you switch to another page, the style sheet reverts to the primary style sheet. Style-sheet switchers remember which style sheet you chose and remember the style-sheet selection for all pages in your site.

There are two steps to setting up a style-sheet switcher. Assuming you already have an alternate style sheet, the first step is to attach the alternate style sheet to all of the pages in your site. The second step is to create a mechanism with which you can choose a style sheet: in this exercise, you use a menu list. The third step is to attach the external JavaScript file to all of the pages in your Web site. Once configured, you choose a style sheet from the list and browse your Web site.

If you are working in a classroom setting, get together with some of your classmates and share the style sheets you created in the previous Challenge exercise. You can then switch between even more style sheets than those you created.

1. Open index.html. In the navbar paragraph, click to the right of Contact Me, and type **`Styles`** (you won't be able to see the black text against the black background). Double-click Styles and link the selected text to switcher.html.

## If you have problems

If the text Styles appears as soon as you typed it, it is because you added this text to the Contact Me link text. Do not delete it, but select Styles, remove the contact_me.html link from the Link field in the Property inspector, and press Enter/Return. With the Styles text still selected, link it to switcher.html.

2. If you are working in a classroom setting, share your style sheet with some classmates by copying the files to a floppy disk or a common folder on the network, or emailing them. Save the ones you have received in the My Travels site. Attach the shared style sheets as alternate style sheets (**`rel="alternate stylesheet"`**) and create a title for each.
3. Open the Code window. Select and copy all of the **`<link>`** lines to the clipboard.
4. Open switcher.html, open the Code window, if necessary, and paste the copied lines above the closing **`</head>`** tag. Also, write down on some paper the title attributes for all of the attached alternate style sheets (you can omit print.css).

   The JavaScript code has been added to this file on line 6: do not disturb it.
5. In switcher.html, switch to the Design mode, click the menu list at the bottom, and then click the List Values. Click The Sphinx in the Value column, click the + to add new list items, and add the new title attributes noted in Step 4 in both the Item Label and Value fields. Press Tab after each entry to add more. Click OK when finished.
6. Preview the page in your browser and test the link switcher. Return to Dreamweaver when finished.

   The style switcher works in this page but it will not work in the other pages because the JavaScript code needed to remember the chosen style sheet is not attached to the other pages.
7. Open the Code window. Select from line 6 to the last **`<link>`** tag, and copy it into the clipboard.
8. Close switcher.html. In the open index.html, select and delete the **`<link>`** tags in the Code window, and paste the copied lines from switcher.html. Close, saving your changes.
9. One by one, open the remaining pages in this site, delete the **`<link>`** tag lines from the **`<head>`** section, and paste the copied lines. When finished, close saving your changes.
10. Open index.html and preview it in your browser. Switch to a different style and then follow one of the links to a new page.

    There are two types of functions in the JavaScript program: one is used to switch style sheets when chosen from the list; the other function enables the other pages to remember the chosen style sheet.
11. Close your browser, return to Dreamweaver, and close index.html.

PORTFOLIO BUILDER

## Convert a Web Page to CSS

Many Web sites do not make much use of CSS other than for basic text styling and for links, with the :hover property. Search for the Web site of a business and view the HTML code. When you find one for which the code contains **<font>** tags and a tables-based layout, save the HTML code as a file on your computer.

1. Examine the code for **vlink**, **link**, **alink**, and **bgcolor** attributes in the **<body>** tag and record the colors. Delete these attributes from the **<body>** tag.
2. Create an embedded style sheet and reinstate these colors using CSS.
3. Examine the **<font>** tags and record the font names, font sizes, and font colors as well as what tag (**<p>**, **<h2>**, **<blockquote>**, or **<b>**) the **<font>** tag is modifying.
4. Record the location of the **<font>** tag, such as **<p>** tags in the left table cell have green text whereas **<p>** tags in the right table cell have blue text.
5. Delete all **<font>** tags and **bgcolor** attributes of **<body>**, **<table>**, **<tr>**, and **<td>** tags. (When deleting the **<font>** tags, don't forget to delete the closing **</font>** tags, as well.)
6. Assign ids to different table cells.
7. Create CSS selectors and rules to replace the **<font>** tags.
8. Look for **bgcolor** attributes in the **<table>**, **<tr>**, and **<td>** tags, and record the colors.
9. Delete the **bgcolor** attributes from the **<table>**, **<tr>**, and **<td>** tags, and reinstate these colors using CSS.
10. Compare the file size of the CSS page with that of the non-CSS page.

PROJECT 10

# Snippets, Library Items, and Templates

## OBJECTIVES

*In this project, you learn how to*

- Insert a snippet into a Web page
- Create and save a new snippet
- Create a library item
- Insert a library item into a Web page
- Revise a library item
- Create a template
- Create a child page from a template
- Revise a template
- Create a repeating region

# WHY WOULD I DO THIS?

A consistent look and feel is one goal of good design in a Web site and to achieve this, you must find ways to maintain this consistency. One way is to build a template, which many designers have done with or without Dreamweaver. A template would include all of the common components, such as the logo, navigation bar, and footer, but would leave the body area empty, ready to fill with new content as it arrives. A design change requires a large effort to bring all of the pages in line with the new design or layout. Dreamweaver, however, provides very powerful and sophisticated tools for accomplishing this with great ease.

Certainly, one of the tools that can help to build a consistent look to the site is CSS. In *Project 9: Working with Cascading Style Sheets,* you learned how to create a style and layout using CSS, and that, with the assistance of a JavaScript style-sheet switcher, you can change the layout and look of a site. However, CSS only affects style, not structure: if you need to add another link to the navigation bar, a jump menu, or a search form to every page, CSS cannot help you. All of these changes are structural changes that require a different approach.

You learned how to create a basic Web-site template without any content and save it as a template page. You then opened the template in Dreamweaver, saved it with a different name, and added the content specific for that page and continued the process. This is one method of templating and, until something new is needed, this process would work. It is when you need new common content on every page that this process fails because you must add the new content, such as an additional link, to every page. Dreamweaver has two tools that ease this process: library items and templates.

The Dreamweaver templating function allows you to create a ***master template page*** for a group of pages on your site. Once you have created the master template, you can lock areas you don't want modified and unlock content areas. If you discover that you have forgotten a link or any other structural change, you merely edit the master template page, make whatever changes necessary, and save the changes. When you change the master template, Dreamweaver automatically transfers the changes to the other pages that were built from the template — the ***child pages***, pages built from the master, take on the change(s) applied to it. Of course, depending on the nature of the change, you may need to tweak your CSS, as well.

The other Dreamweaver technology that assists with the development of a consistent look and feel for a site is called "library items." In many respects, they are similar to Dreamweaver templates in that all pages that use a library item take on the same changes if the master library item changes. The difference between library items and templates is that templates are whole pages whereas library items are just parts of pages. For example, a department store may have the same header, footer, and primary navigation for all pages, but the clothes-department navigation bar may be different from the furniture-department navigation bar. Therefore, you would build a template for the header, footer, and primary navigation, and would use library items for the departmental navigation bars.

In this project, you also learn to use snippets. ***Snippets*** are parcels of code that may be just a single word, a paragraph, or larger. Although snippets and library items may be the same size, there are significant differences between them that affect their use. Library items, like templates, are linked to their masters, so if a change is made to the master, the change cascades to all uses of the library item. Not so with snippets: if you make a change to the stored snippet, only it changes, not any instances of its use. Secondly, templates and library items are specific to site definitions, which is perfectly reasonable: it would not make sense to use or even have access to the Tropiflora templates and library items from the Jungle Cat World site. However, snippets are global and may be used in any site — if you create a useful snippet when working on one site, you can open the snippets folder from another site and use that same snippet.

In this project, you learn how to create, modify, and use snippets, library items, and templates. You learn how to use them to create a consistent look and feel to your site. You learn that library items and templates could be considered the structural equivalents of CSS, and discover how using both of these technologies can greatly simplify your design and development of a Web site.

## VISUAL SUMMARY

Snippets are stored in the Snippets panel that is part of the Code panel group. To open the Snippets panel, you choose Window>Snippets or click the Code panel group and then the Snippets tab. Snippets are organized into folders: when you create your own snippets, you may add them to currently existing folders or you may create your own folders. Be careful when considering the deletion of a folder: to restore a Snippet folder that was part of the Dreamweaver installation, you must reinstall Dreamweaver.

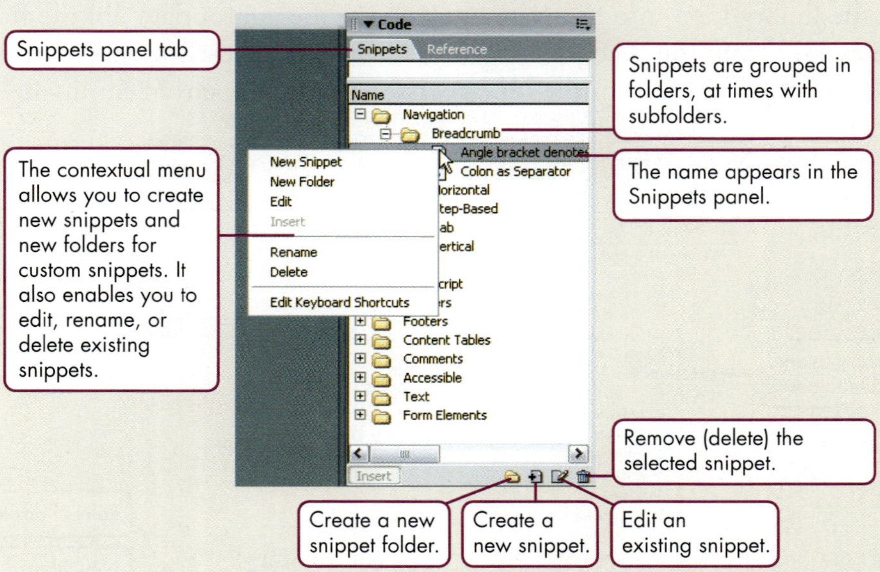


FIGURE 10.1

When you create or edit a snippet, you must assign it a name, choose the type of snippet, and insert the code; the description is optional. Wrap-selection snippets have two components, the before block and the after block, and both blocks display separately in the Snippet dialog box. Insert-block snippets have just one part, shown in the Insert Code field of the Snippet dialog box.

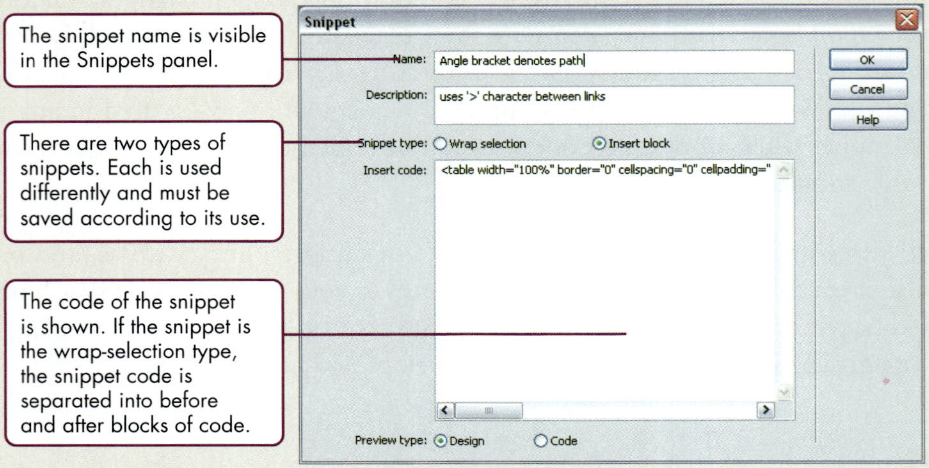


**FIGURE 10.2**

You find library items in the Library folder of the Site folder or in the Library section of the Assets panel. The Library folder does not exist in a site until you create the first library item. Library items have the filename extension .lbi. If you select a library item in the Assets panel, a preview of the library item appears at the top of the panel.

You can use any of the buttons at the bottom of the Library Assets panel to insert the selected library item into the Web page, to create a new library item, or to edit or delete the selected library item. You can also insert the library item into the page by dragging the appropriate .lbi file from the Library folder in the Files panel into the Web page. However, if you double-click a library item, either from the Library folder of the Files panel or the Library Assets panel, it opens in edit mode.

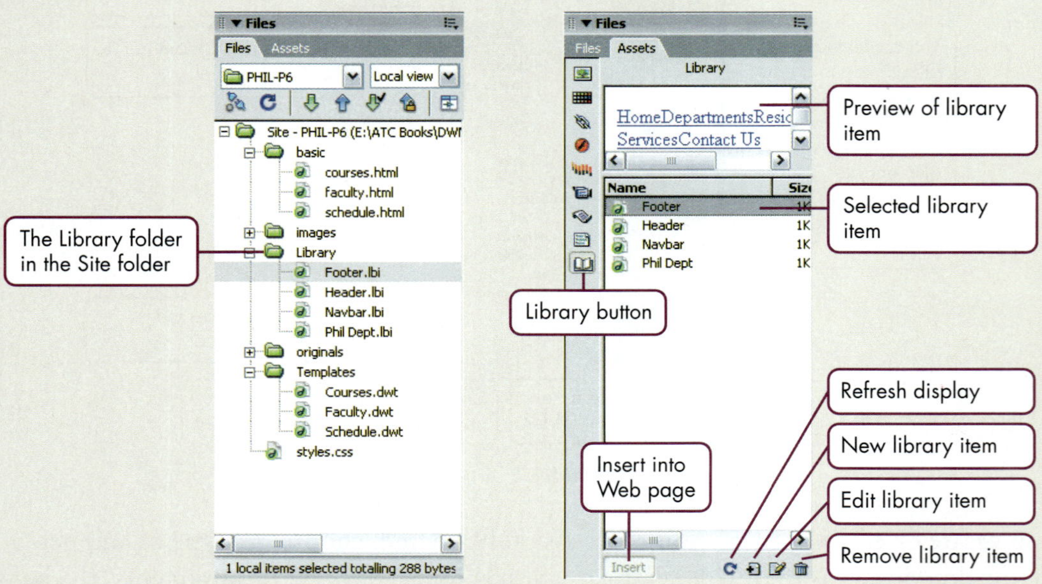


**FIGURE 10.3**

When preparing a new template file, you use the Templates drop-down menu from the Common Insert bar to specify editable and repeating regions. In this project, you create the template by working with an existing page — one with the features you need in a Web page for the site — and preparing it as a template.

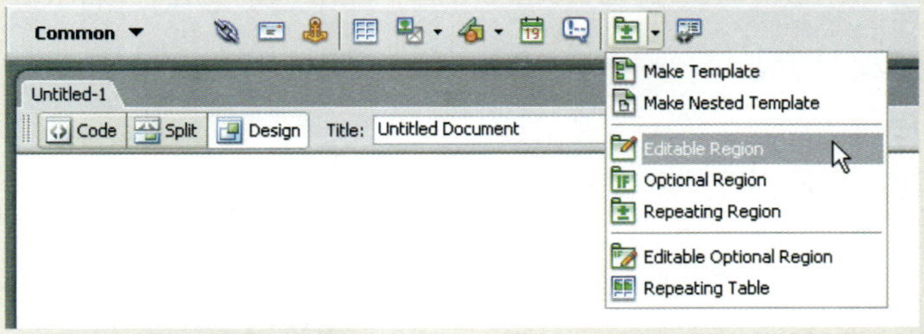


FIGURE 10.4

When you create and save a template, Dreamweaver creates a Templates folder below the Site folder and the template is stored there. Dreamweaver templates have the .dwt (Dreamweaver templates) extension. Templates are also listed in the Templates Assets panel from which you may apply the template, create a new one, and edit or delete an existing one. You can create multiple templates, each for a different purpose.

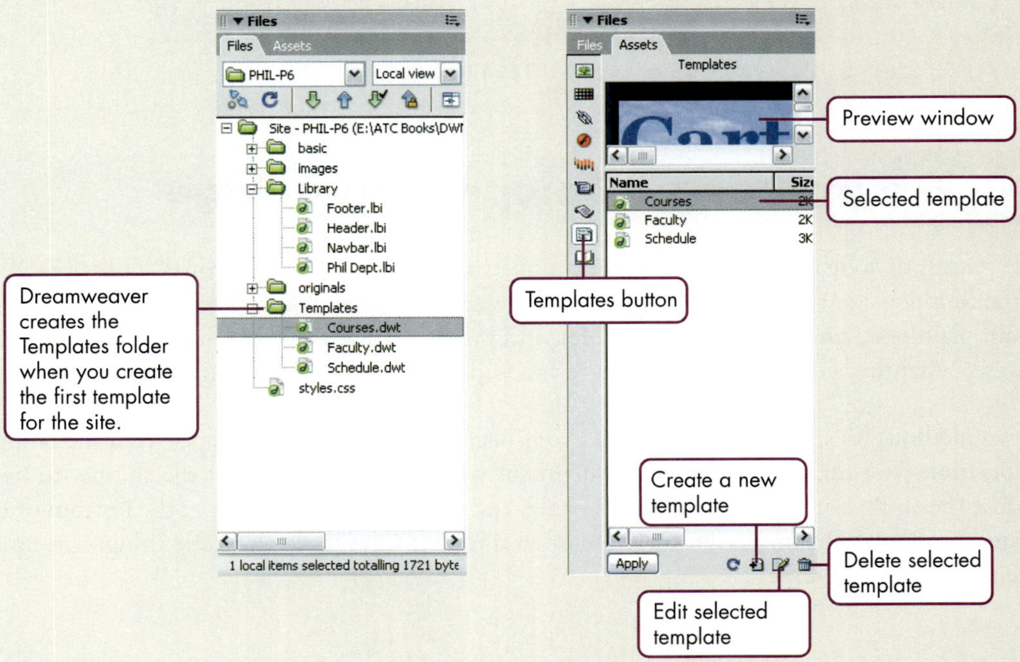


FIGURE 10.5

When you build a child page from a template, you choose File>New and click the Templates tab. You then choose the site from which the template is stored and choose the specific template, if necessary. You can see the template in the Preview window. The child page of the template allows you to edit or create content in the editable regions but not in the noneditable regions, preventing you or other users of the template from damaging the template; it thereby enforces a consistent structure from page to page.

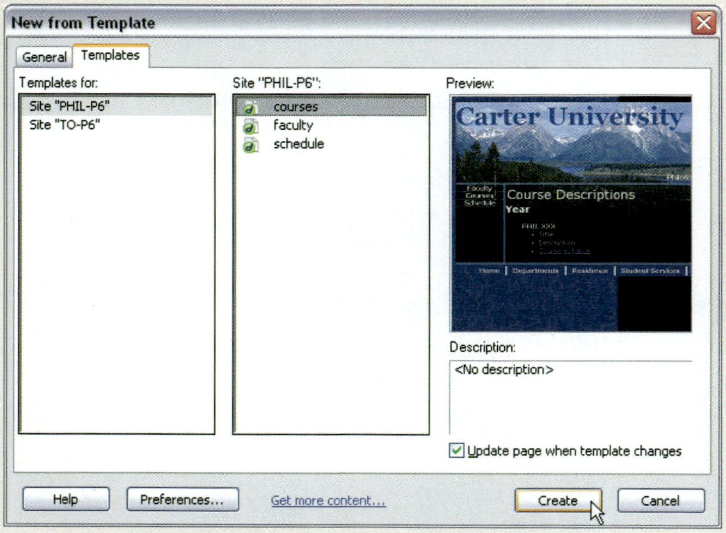


FIGURE 10.6

## LESSON 1 Inserting a Snippet into a Page

Snippets are parcels of code that are stored in the Snippets folder in the Snippets panel. They are grouped into folders in the Snippets panel, and each snippet has a description to enable you to identify what it contains. Some contain plain text, some contain small tables, and others even contain JavaScript. Experimentation will allow you to see what they contain and may inspire you with some ideas of how you might be able to use them.

There are two methods for inserting snippets into your page. You can drag the snippet from the Snippets Asset panel into position. You can also click in the Document window where you want the snippet to be inserted, click to choose the snippet in the Snippet Assets panel, and click the Insert button at the bottom of the panel. As with many features of Dreamweaver, there are often different ways to do the same thing; it is up to you to decide which method you prefer.

## Insert a Snippet

In this exercise, you add a snippet to the order form. When you ask for credit-card information in an order form, you must collect both the month and year of the expiration date. A select list of month numbers already exists in the Snippets panel. You can quickly insert and use this snippet in a Web page.

**1** **Define the Project_10>TO-P10 folder as a site called `TO-P10`. Do not click Done, but remove all previously defined sites from the Manage Sites dialog box, and then click Done.**

**2** **Open order_form.html, scroll down, and click in the empty cell to the right of Expiration Date.**

**3** **Type `Month:` and press Spacebar.**

**4** **Open the Snippets panel by selecting Window>Snippets.**

**5** **In the Snippets panel, double-click the Form Elements folder, and then double-click the Dropdown Menus folder to open it.**

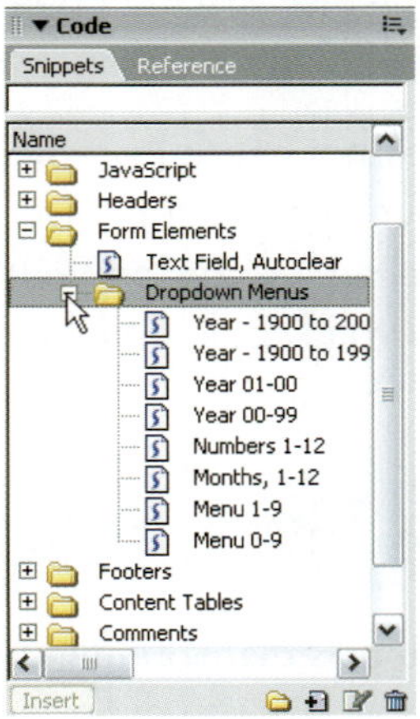


FIGURE 10.7

**6** **Drag the Months, 1-12 snippet to the right of Month: in the table cell.**

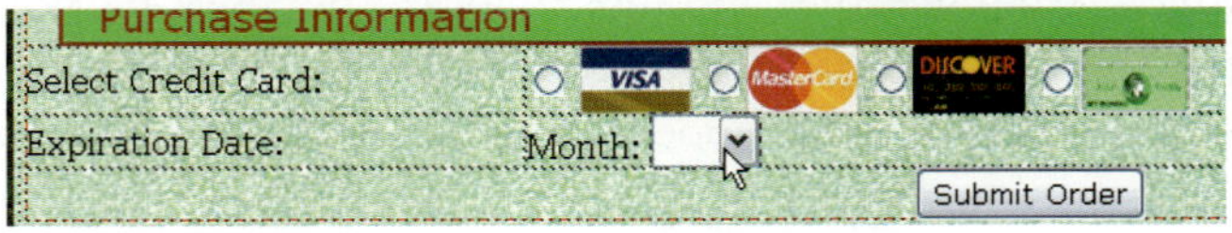


FIGURE 10.8

**7** **Click the new List control. From the Property inspector, change its name to `cc_exp_month` and press Enter/Return.**

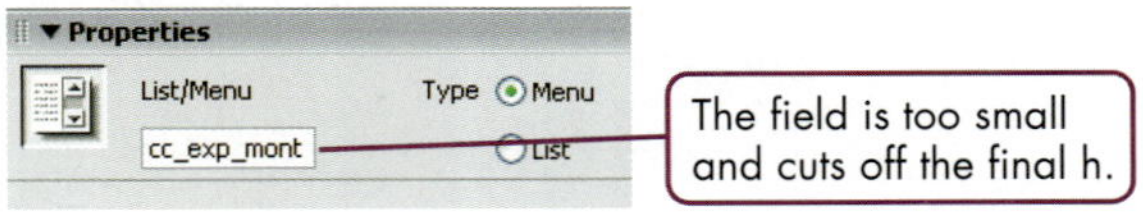


FIGURE 10.9

**8** **Save your changes to order_form.html, but leave it open for the next exercise.**

## To Extend Your Knowledge

### CONTENTS OF SNIPPETS

You can create and insert snippets to use in the **<head>** or **<body>** section of the Web page. In most cases, you will probably create snippets to use in the Document window or the **<body>** section of the Web page. However, there are HTML tags that Dreamweaver does not offer through its menus or that are missing some of the attributes, such as the **rel** attribute of the **<style>** tag, and, therefore, snippets may be the way you want to store and reuse them.

Snippets may contain virtually any tag content or text content, with some limitations. There are no limitations on what you can insert into a snippet — you could even, for instance, insert all of the code of an HTML document in a snippet, but you wouldn't be able to use the snippet because a Web page cannot have two **<body>**, **<html>**, **<head>** or **DTD** (Document Type Definition) tags. Therefore, avoid the **DTD**, **<body>**, **<head>**, and **<html>** tags in your snippets. Also do not use snippets to create parts of tags or components, such as **<tr><td>**, which are the opening tags of a table row and a table cell, because it is quite possible that you won't always remember to complete the unfinished tags.

Remember, also, that Dreamweaver does not check the validity of snippets, so if you try to create a **<bold>** tag, Dreamweaver does not check your snippet for valid tags, whereas Dreamweaver does check the Web page if you try to create such a tag on your page. It is best to create the content in Dreamweaver so that it creates good and valid code, and then you can create a snippet from that code.

# LESSON 2 Creating a New Snippet

Dreamweaver does not contain all of the snippets that you might find useful. You may create snippets of your own that might be useful in other projects. You may also discover pieces of code on other Web sites that could be useful to you, such as a list of countries of the world or the states of the US. In both cases, these parcels of code are quite long so saving them as reusable snippets could save you a lot of typing time in the future.

There are two types of snippets: wrap selection and insert block. The insert-block snippets are blocks of code that appear where you insert them. There is only one component to the snippet. The wrap-selection type of snippet consists of two pieces of code: one that appears before and one that appears after. When you create a new snippet, you must first determine which type of snippet it will be and enable the appropriate options in the Snippet dialog box.

## Create a New Snippet

In this exercise, you create a new insert-block snippet and save it for later use. The code does not yet exist so you must create it first. This snippet will be the years from 2004 to 2010, created for use as the credit-card expiration year. You save the snippet in a new folder that you create in the Snippets panel.

**1** **In the open file, order_form.html, click to the right of the cc_exp_month List control.**

**2** **Type `Year:` and from the Forms Insert bar, insert a new List. Name it years. Populate the list values with 2004, 2005, 2006, 2007, 2008, 2009, and 2010.**

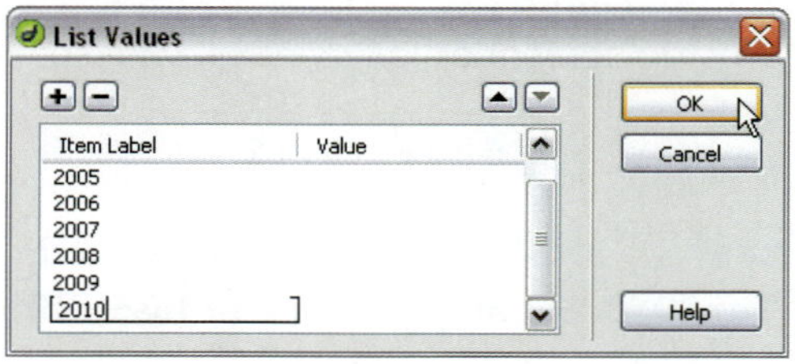


FIGURE 10.10

**3** **In the Snippets panel, close any open folders.**

**4** **Right/Control-click below the last folder in the Snippets panel and choose New Folder.**

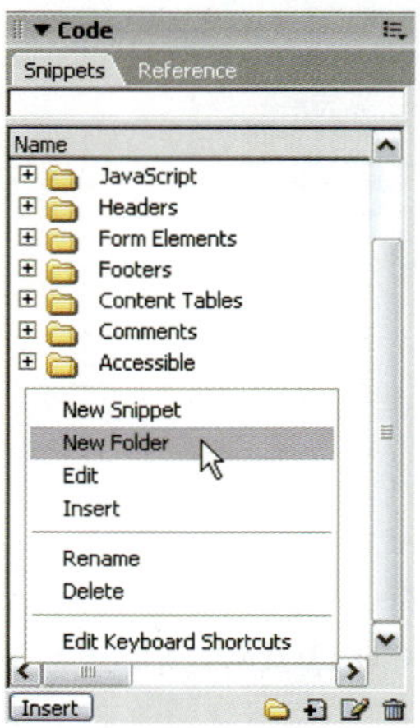


FIGURE 10.11

**5** **Type your name (such as Bob) and press Enter/Return.**

**6** Click the new list of years in the Document window. Right/Control-click the new folder in the Snippets panel and choose New Snippet.

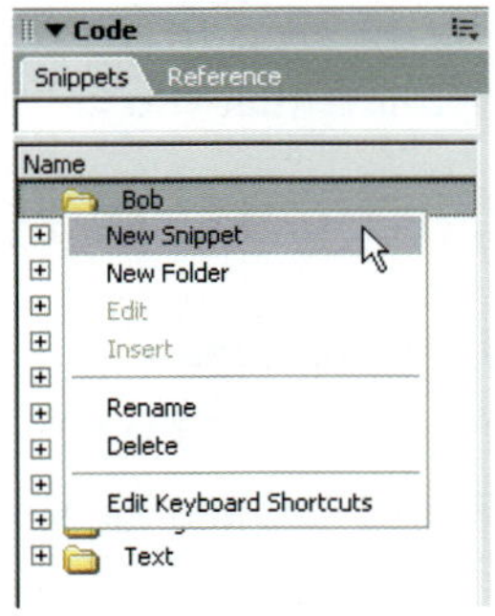


FIGURE 10.12

**7** In the Name field, type `Years, 2004 to 2010`. In the Description field, type `A select list of years from 2004 to 2010`. Set Snippet Type to Insert Block. Set Preview Type to Design and click OK.

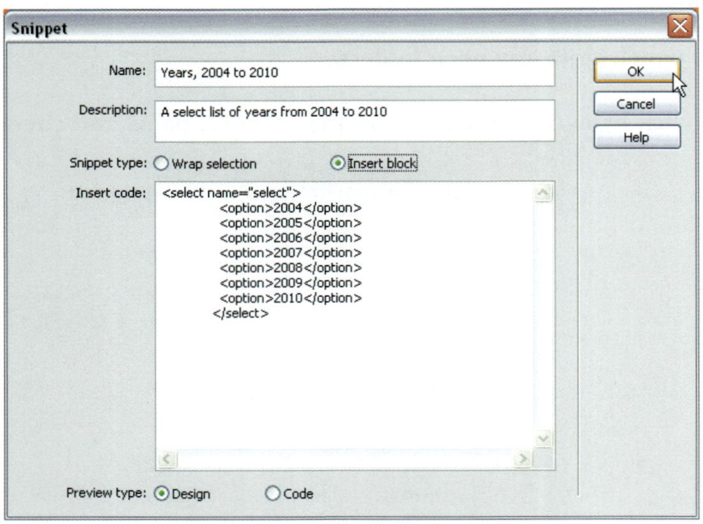


FIGURE 10.13

**8** Click the year list in the Document window and, in the Property inspector, name the list `cc_exp_year`.

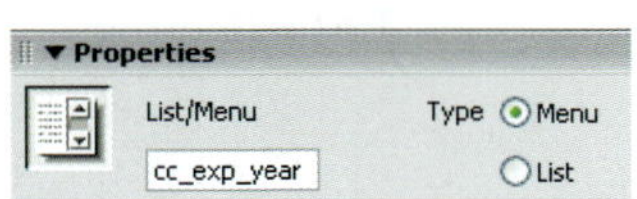


FIGURE 10.14

**9** Save the changes to order_form.html, but leave it open for the next exercise.

## To Extend Your Knowledge

### WRAP-SELECTION SNIPPET TYPE

The wrap-selection snippet allows you to surround selected content with two parts of a snippet: the insert-before and insert-after parts. This is very handy if you use an HTML tag that Dreamweaver does not present except in the Tag Chooser dialog box. You may find that opening the Tag chooser to insert a tag is cumbersome; the wrap-selection snippet may be more to your liking. For example, if you find that you use the **<q>** quote tag often, you may create a quote-tag snippet, where the insert-before code is **<q>** and the insert-after code is **</q>**. To use the quote-tag snippet, simply select the quote text, insert the quote-tag snippet, and the quote will be surrounded by the **<q>** and **</q>** tags.

# LESSON 3 Creating Library Items

Most people are familiar with the concept of a template; we explore the Dreamweaver template function later in this project. A template is a complete Web page without the information that changes from page to page. A library item is a small component, such as a menu bar or header, not a complete Web page. Although smaller and more focused, a library item is still a powerful tool and time saver. The power of a library item is not simply the consistency from page to page that uses it, but also that if you make a change to the library item, any page using it reflects the change. Need to add a new link to the navigation bar? Just create a navigation bar library item and, when you add a new link to it, all pages that use that library item reflect that change, whether there are 4 or 4,000 pages on your site.

The first step in working with a library item is to create it. The library item must first exist as a component of your pages (at least one page) and then you may add it to the library-items folder or assets. When you create your first library item, Dreamweaver creates a Library folder in the Site folder; any library items you create will be stored there. Library items are also listed as assets of the site and, as such, are found in the Library collection of the Assets panel.

## Create a Library Item

In this exercise, you create a library item from the Tropiflora logo image. As you do so, Dreamweaver creates the Library folder for you. You see that when you examine a library item in the Property inspector, it displays the library-item properties, not the properties of the content in the library item.

1 **In the open file, order_form.html, click the Tropiflora Online graphic at the top of the page.**

2 **Open the Assets panel either by clicking the Assets tab at the top of the Files panel or by selecting Window>Assets.**

**3** **Click the Library icon at the bottom of the list of icons on the left side of the Assets panel.**

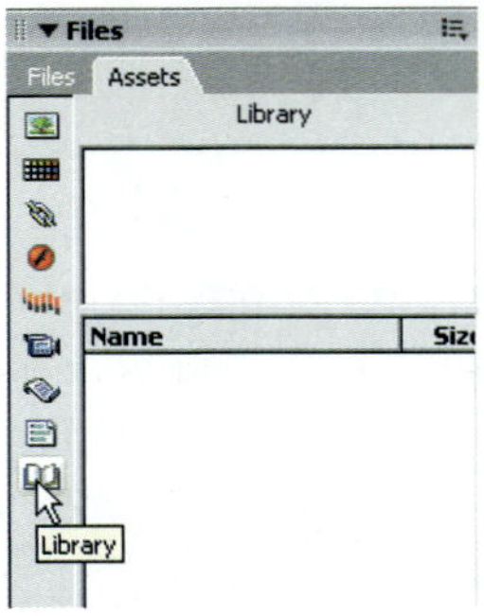


FIGURE 10.15

**4** **Drag the Tropiflora Online graphic into the Library Assets panel. Type `Tropiflora Logo` and press Enter/Return.**

FIGURE 10.16

**5** **Click the Files tab to view the Files panel and click the Refresh button (or press F5).**

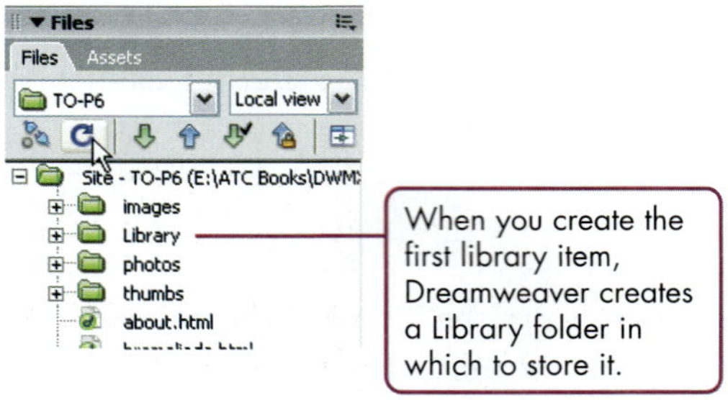


FIGURE 10.17

**6** **Click the graphic at the top of the Document window and observe the Property inspector.**

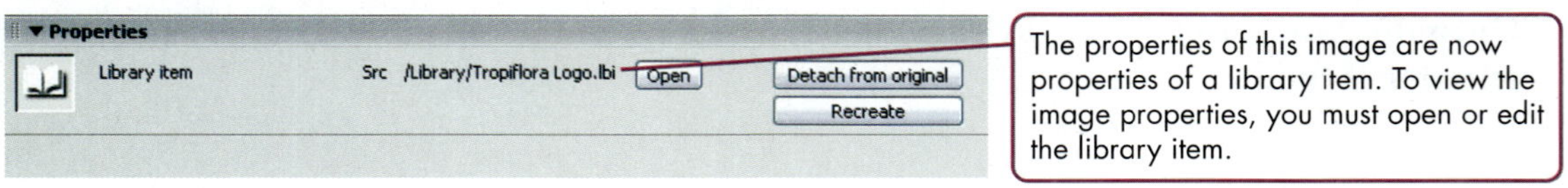


FIGURE 10.18

**7** **Close order_form.html, saving your changes.**

## To Extend Your Knowledge

### CONTENTS OF LIBRARY ITEMS

Snippets may contain code for either the **<head>** or **<body>** section of an HTML document, but a library item may only contain **<body>** section content, with one exception. This means that the content must be viewable in the Document window in the Design view. The exception to this rule applies when JavaScript is involved.

Many JavaScript scripts have two components: the event handler as an attribute of a tag in the **<body>** section of the HTML document and the function called by the event handler that is in the **<head>** part of the HTML document. For example, an image rollover has the **onMouseOver** and **onMouseOut** events and event handlers in the **<a>** tag, but the Swap Image behavior function is written in the **<head>** section of the HTML document. If you create a navigation bar with image rollovers in it and save it as a library item, you might assume that because the Swap Image JavaScript is in the **<head>** section and the navigation bar is in the **<body>** section, the Swap Image JavaScript would not be carried by the library item. If you create the behavior using Dreamweaver's own behaviors and the Behavior panel, however, Dreamweaver does transfer the JavaScript with the library item. Examine the JavaScript function for the Swap Image behavior in the **<head>** section of the HTML document and you will see that the function begins with **MM_**. All Dreamweaver behavior functions begin with **MM_**. This has special significance to Dreamweaver library items because Dreamweaver recognizes that the event handler in the navigation bar is calling a JavaScript function that begins with **MM_** and Dreamweaver automatically adds that JavaScript function into the **<head>** section of any page in which you insert the library item.

However, if you create a custom JavaScript script that has a function in the **<head>** section of the HTML document, Dreamweaver does not know to copy the function to pages that use the custom function; you must copy it yourself. On the other hand, if you create a template with the custom script, because the template is a complete Web page, the custom code in the **<head>** section will be transferred to pages built from the template.

# LESSON 4 Inserting Library Items into Other Pages

You can only apply the power of library items if the library item exists on other pages. Although the Tropiflora Online graphic appears on all other pages of this site, it does not exist as a library item on these other pages, just as a graphic. To set this graphic as a library item on the other pages, you must replace the graphic with the library item of the same graphic.

You might not generally replace common elements with library items while working on an existing site. Instead, you would be likely to use library items as you design the site for the first time using templates. When you build a new page from the template, it has the library items already in it because they were in the template. At times, however, you may be asked to rebuild a Web site and you might use library items in the rebuilding. Therefore, you would identify the common elements on the pages, store them as library items, and then replace the common elements with the library items created from them. In doing so, you have prepared the common elements so that should any further changes be required later, you could update all of the common elements with the alterations.

There are two methods for inserting a library item into a page. You can click at the position where the library item is to go and drag the library item from the Library Assets panel. Your other option is to click at the position where the library item is to go, click the library item in the Library Assets panel, and click the Insert button at the bottom of the panel. You cannot add a library item from the Library folder of the Files panel nor by double-clicking the library item: double-clicking just opens the library item in edit mode.

## Add the Library Item to the Other Pages

In this exercise, you add the Tropiflora Logo library item to the other pages in the site. You switch between the Files and Assets panels to open the page, and then insert the library item. There are no real shortcuts although you may open the page using File>Open.

**1** **Open about.html and click the Tropiflora Online graphic at the top of the page.**

**2** **Switch to the Assets panel and click the Tropiflora Logo library item. (If necessary, first click the Library icon at the bottom left of the Assets panel.)**

**3** **Click the Insert button at the bottom of the Assets panel.**

FIGURE 10.19

### If you have problems

If the Tropiflora Logo library item did not replace the Tropiflora Online graphic but, instead, appeared beside it, the graphic was not selected when you clicked the Insert button. You may either delete the Tropiflora Online graphic or you may press Control/Command-Z to undo, click the Tropiflora Online graphic, and reinsert the library item.

**4** **Close about.html, saving your changes.**

**5** **Repeat Steps 1 to 4 with the remaining HTML pages in the site.**

To open the pages you can switch to the Files panel, open the file, and then switch to the Assets panel to insert the library item. You may also choose File>Open to open the page, keeping the Assets panel open all of the time.

## *To Extend Your Knowledge*

### LIBRARY ITEMS ON THE WEB SITE

Most of the content that you create in the Site folder will be uploaded to the Web server and, generally, is publicly viewable. However, library items and template files have no role in a Web site outside of its design and development. Dreamweaver will upload the Library and Template folders if you upload the whole site to the Web server unless you are selective or you cloak these folders. Cloaking is a feature of Dreamweaver with which you may mark folders and file types: Dreamweaver does not upload cloaked files and folders.

# LESSON 5 Revising a Library Item

Simply replacing the Tropiflora Online graphic with a library item that contains the same graphic is not the value of the library-items feature. The value is that if you change an aspect of the library item, all pages that use the library item receive the updated content, as well. In this lesson, you edit the Tropiflora Logo library item and, as you do so, you see how every page containing the library item is updated with the changes.

You have two choices for editing a library item: you can open the Library folder of the Files panel and double-click the library item, or you can double-click the library item in the Assets panel. In edit mode, the library item appears alone in a new Document window. You may make changes to it as you see fit. As soon as you close the Document window, you are prompted to save the library item. If you choose to save, you are then prompted to update all pages that use the library item.

## Edit a Library Item

In this exercise, you change two aspects of the Tropiflora Logo library item: you add alt text to the image and you change the image. You make both changes at the same time. After you close the Document window containing the library item, you save the changes and update the pages that contain the library item.

**1** **Open the Assets panel and double-click the Tropiflora Logo library item.**

You don't need to have a document open to edit a library item.

**2** **Double-click the image in the Document window and replace it with images>tropiflora_online2.jpg.**

**3** Type `Tropiflora Online` in the Alt field and press Enter/Return.

FIGURE 10.20

**4** Close, saving the library item.

**5** Click Update to update the pages that contain the library item.

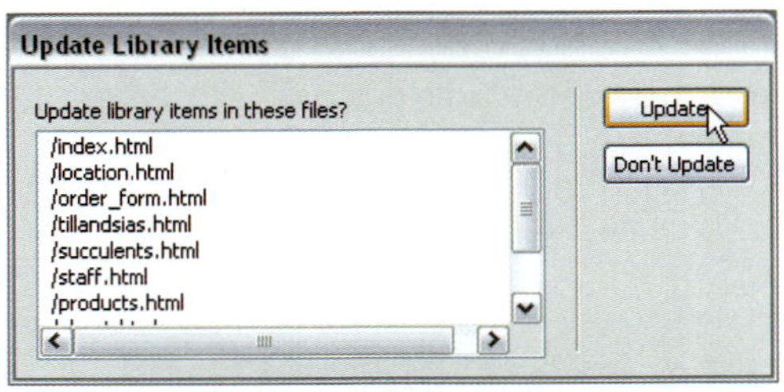


FIGURE 10.21

**6** After the update is complete, you see a report on the update process. Click Close after reviewing the report.

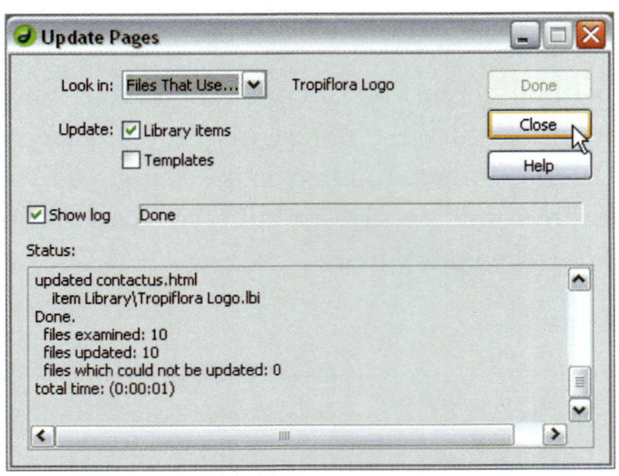


FIGURE 10.22

## To Extend Your Knowledge

### SSI IS SIMILAR TO LIBRARY ITEMS

In ***SSI*** (server-side includes) — a technology very similar in function to library items — common parcels of code are inserted into Web pages. The technology differs, however, in that the insertion occurs when the visitor requests the page, not during the design of the Web page. In most cases, SSI requires access to a Web-programming language, such as PHP or ASP, but if your Web server is running Apache Web-server software, you can use SSI without a Web-programming language.

The drawback to library items is that if you have many pages that use the same library items, whenever you change a library item, Dreamweaver must inject the changes to the library item into all of the pages. With many pages, this process can take a long time. SSI simply uses a command that states "insert file abc.inc here," but that command is not processed until a visitor requests the page. As long as the SSI command remains the same, the code in the include file can change as much as you like during the development of the site.

The primary difference between library items and SSI is that when you use library items, the complete code of the library item exists within the Web pages that use the library item, but the SSI command is just a line of code that states the filename of the include to insert. This difference has another effect on file uploading: because the code of library items are in the pages that use them, it does not matter if the Library folder is uploaded to the Web server because the pages on the Web site do not rely on the presence of the files in the Library folder. However, SSI is a command to the Web server to insert the include file into the page before delivering it to the visitor. You must, therefore, remember to upload the include files to the Web server; otherwise, the SSI command tries to include a nonexistent file.

Dreamweaver supports SSI in the Design view: you can create the code for SSI and Dreamweaver displays the contents of the included file in the Design view. However, you cannot see the effect of SSI if you preview a local page in your browser unless your computer is running either Apache Web-server software or a Web-programming language.

# LESSON 6 Creating Templates

There are two methods for creating a template: start from scratch and prepare a Web page as a template or take an existing page and save it as a template. The method you choose may simply be based on your preferences; there are no compelling reasons to choose one method over another. However, be certain that the template is in good shape when you start to use it. Although you may make changes to the template later, you shouldn't make too many changes, because the more child pages you create from the template, the longer the update process takes. When you have laid out the common elements of a template, you save the file as a template by choosing File>Save as Template, where you can also add a description of the template in case you create several for the same site.

Templates are commonly thought of as Web pages with the common elements of the Web pages for the site. However, Dreamweaver templates are more sophisticated than that — the common elements are protected from change unless you edit the template file. This is beneficial because if you are working on a page based on a template, you cannot make changes to the common elements on that page, thus rendering parts of that page different from other pages. Instead, if you discover a mistake with the template while working on a child page, you edit the template, fix the mistake, and update all of the pages that use the template with the fix.

After you have laid out the common elements of the template, you must identify what areas of the template are editable. By default, none of the parts of the template are editable, which means that when you create a child page from the template, you can't add any content. If you forget to specify an editable region (or regions) when you save the template, you will be warned that the template has no editable regions; you can then go back and assign editable regions. Only in child pages are some regions noneditable. In the template all regions may be edited, but to make the template useful for creating child pages, you must set at least one editable region.

Templates, like library items, are stored in their own Templates folder. Templates also are collected in the Assets panel in their own group, which is accessible by clicking the Templates icon, the second from the bottom. Templates may contain library items, a feature that can greatly simplify the development of a Web site. This saves the work of re-creating the components of the library item in each template if a library item is quite complex and used throughout the site, or if you have multiple templates for the Web site, all containing the same library item. Of course, if you change the library item, both templates and child pages update with the change.

## Create a Template from an Existing Page

In this exercise, you create a template from an existing page. In a situation where you need to add more pages to a site and want to use the Dreamweaver template technology, it makes sense to take an existing page and develop it into a template. You must remember to set the editable area or you won't be able to use it to create child pages.

1. **Open about.html from the TO-P10 site.**

2. **Choose File>Save as Template.**

3. **Type `Basic` in the Save as field and click Save.**

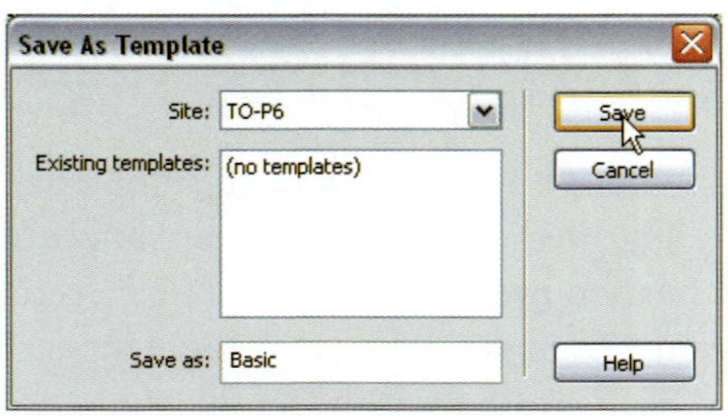


FIGURE 10.23

**4** **Click Yes to update the links in the template.**

The links in the about.html page are relative to the location of about.html, the root folder of the site. However, templates are stored in a Templates folder, so the links must be adjusted to compensate for the location of the recently created template.

FIGURE 10.24

**5** **Examine the filename tab.**

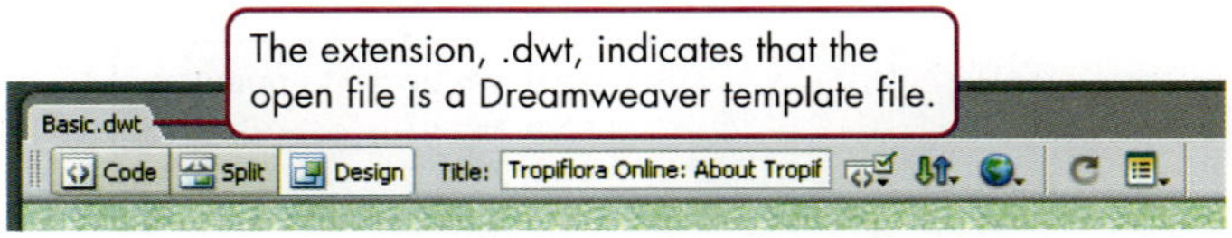


FIGURE 10.25

**6** **Choose File>Close. Do not check the Don't Warn Me Again checkbox, but instead click Cancel.**

Unless another user before you has checked the Don't Warn Me Again checkbox, this warning appears, indicating that there are no editable regions in the template.

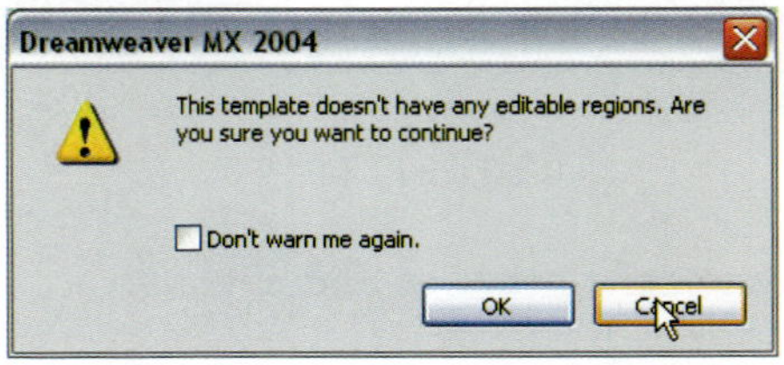


FIGURE 10.26

## If you have problems

If someone before you has checked the Don't Warn Me Again checkbox, you won't see the warnings in Steps 4 or 6 and the template file closes. You must reopen Template.dwt from the Templates folder. You may have to refresh the Files panel by clicking the Refresh button at the top of the Files panel. If you have had to reopen Template.dwt, continue with Step 7.

**7** Click OK to acknowledge the information.

FIGURE 10.27

**8** Click in the main content cell of the page, click the `<td>` tag in the Tag selector, and press Delete.

**9** With the `<td>` tag in the Tag selector still selected, switch to the Common Insert bar, and choose Editable Region from the Template drop-down menu.

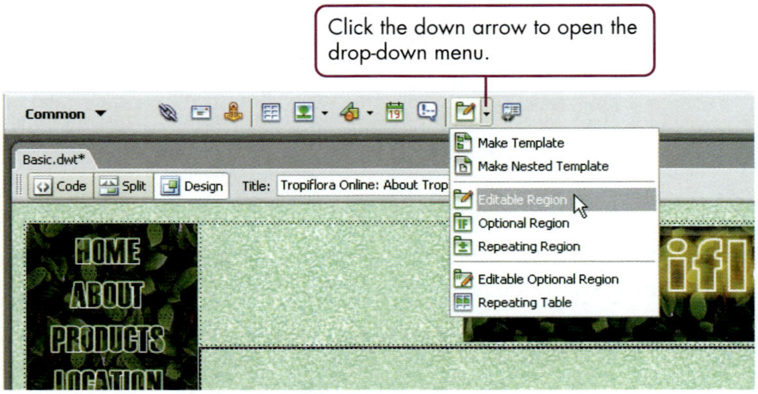


FIGURE 10.28

**10** Name the editable region `Content Region` and click OK.

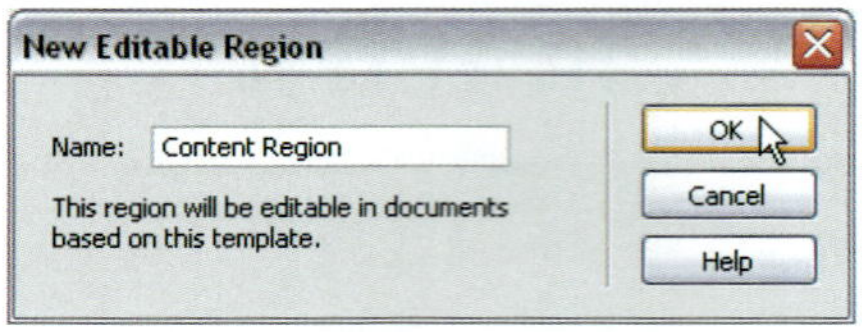


FIGURE 10.29

**11** Examine the Document window and notice the blue label identifying the editable region.

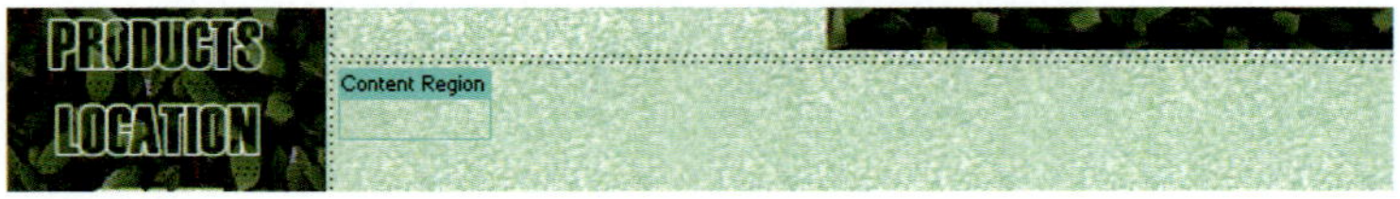


FIGURE 10.30

**12** **In the document Title field at the top of the Document window, remove About Tropiflora and replace it with `Template`.**

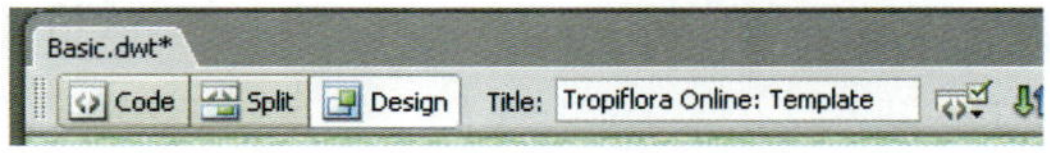


FIGURE 10.31

**13** **Close Basic.dwt, saving your changes.**

## To Extend Your Knowledge

### TEMPLATES AND LIBRARY ITEMS

Templates may contain library items as well as regular HTML components. There may be times when you need to create different templates for a Web site, such as a template for a product-category page as well as a template for a product-detail page. Both may use the same footer content (links to the contact, copyright, privacy, and other pages) and primary navigation (links to primary product-category pages). There is no need to go to the trouble of re-creating these components of the templates each time you create a new template and risk creating them differently. If you create a library item for each of these components, you just need to insert them into the two templates and any other templates that you create later. Then, if you need to make a change to any of these library items, the update process not only updates the child pages created from the templates but also updates the templates themselves.

# LESSON 7 Creating a Child Page from the Template

Once you have created a template, you can use it to build other pages, child pages. To create a child page from a template, you choose File>New to create a new page. Click the Templates tab at the top of the New dialog box, choose the site from which the template is to be drawn, choose the template page from the list, and click Create (or double-click the template page name).

When creating a child page, you learn that there are only two sections of a page that are editable: the editable regions, of which there may be more than one, and the document Title. Only these sections can be edited in a child page. Even in the Code view, you cannot edit any section outside of the editable regions.

To enable this functionality, Dreamweaver creates special tags based on the standard HTML comment tags: <!-- and -->, for which special Dreamweaver-specific attributes are added. For example, the code inserted into the page to indicate the editable region named Content Region is **`<!-- TemplateBeginEditable name="Content Region" -->`**Content Region**`<!-- TemplateEndEditable -->`**. In any other HTML editor, these tags could be edited and deleted, but in a child page of a template while using Dreamweaver, these tags cannot be edited. Dreamweaver respects the purpose of these tags — to identify editable and noneditable regions. It is not HTML but Dreamweaver that prevents the designer from editing noneditable regions.

## Create a Child Page from the Template

In this exercise, you create a new page from the Basic template. When creating a new page from a template, you change the mode of the New dialog box to New from Template by clicking the Templates tab. In that mode, the dialog box displays all sites current in Dreamweaver on the left, and, after you click a site, any templates that have been created for the selected site display in the middle.

**1** **Choose File>New and click the Templates tab.**

**2** **Click the TO-P10 site, choose the basic template, and click Create.**

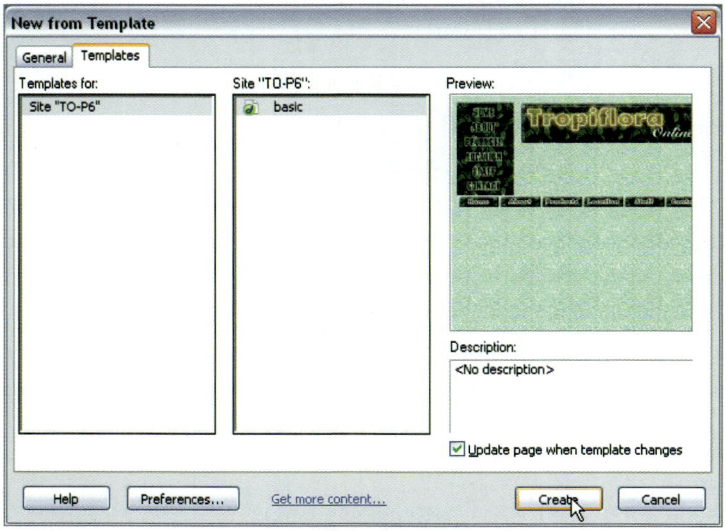


FIGURE 10.32

## To Extend Your Knowledge

### MACROMEDIA CONTRIBUTE

Not only Dreamweaver but also another of Macromedia's products, Contribute, respects the template-specific coding. Contribute, in version 3 at the time of this writing, is an application specifically developed for contributors to a Web site. Not all people adding content to a Web site are Web designers or Web developers. Some contributors simply add content to new pages. Furthermore, the cost of the Contribute application is significantly less than the cost of Dreamweaver, making it quite affordable for an organization to purchase a few copies of Dreamweaver and many more copies of Contribute for the content writers. Contribute can use templates, but, unlike Dreamweaver, Contribute can neither create nor edit templates, thus reassuring the Dreamweaver designer that the templates will not be damaged by Contribute users.

**3** **Move your mouse pointer around the template, including over the Content Region.**

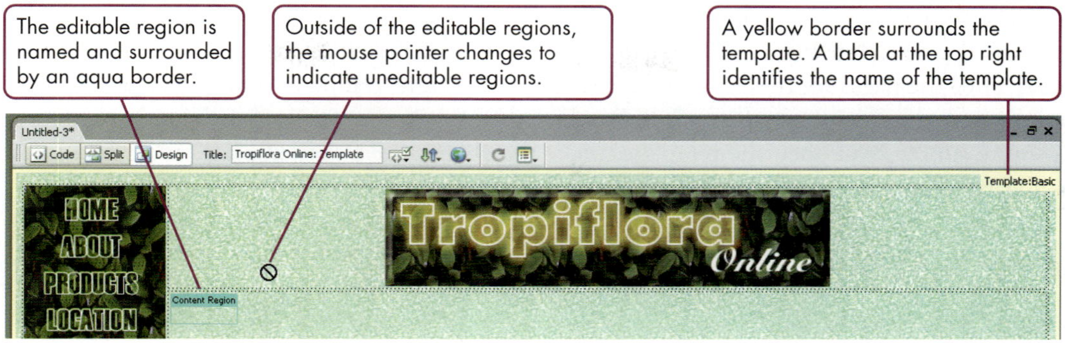


FIGURE 10.33

**4** **Without closing the Untitled page, open basic_events.html. Select all of the text in the page, copy it to the clipboard, and close the page.**

**5** **Click in the Content Region of the Untitled page and paste the copied content.**

**6** **Delete Template from the document Title field and replace it with `Upcoming Events`.**

FIGURE 10.34

**7** **Close, saving the new child page as `events.html`.**

## *To Extend Your Knowledge*

### DRAWBACKS TO TEMPLATE TECHNOLOGY

As you have learned, both library items and template technologies are very beneficial for the development of a Web site, and its consistent look and feel. As mentioned earlier, CSS can help with this, too. However, whenever you need to make a change to either a template or a library item, the update process runs and updates all pages affected by the changes. If there are only 10 pages in a site, at most, only 10 pages need to be uploaded to the Web server. However, if there are 10,000 pages on a site, this is more problematic. Although all 10,000 pages can be uploaded, the upload can take a very long time and the update process may also take a very long time. Many Dreamweaver professionals recommend limiting the use of Dreamweaver template technologies to sites with 50 or fewer pages. Larger sites should consider the use of SSI or other technologies.

# LESSON 8 Revising a Template

You have created a new page from the template but no pages are linked to the new page. In this exercise, you assume that all of the pages on the site were created from this same template. Therefore, when you add a link in the template to the new page, all pages built using the template are revised to include the new link. The process is quite simple: you open the template, make the change, save the template, and when Dreamweaver asks if you want to update all pages built from the template, you click Update.

## Revise the Template

In this exercise, you open the Basic template and make two changes. In both cases, you create links to the new events.html page. Just like library items, when you save the changes to a template, you are prompted to update all pages that use the template.

**1** **From the Templates folder, open Basic.dwt.**

You can also open a template by opening the Assets panel, clicking the Template icon, and double-clicking the name of the template.

**2** **In the left navigation-bar table, click the Products graphic link, and choose Modify>Table>Insert Rows or Columns. Set the Insert Rows or Columns dialog box to insert one row Below the Selection and click OK.**

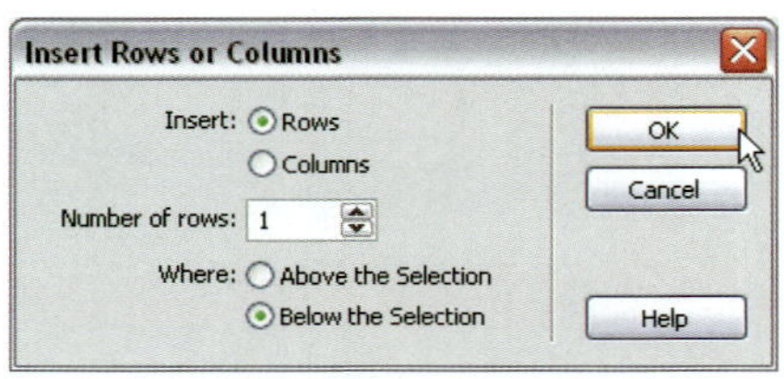


FIGURE 10.35

**3** **Into the empty cell, insert the images>nb_events.gif graphic and link it to events.html. Add `Events` as the alternate text.**

FIGURE 10.36

**4** **Click the Products graphic link in the bottom navigation bar and choose Modify>Table>Insert Rows or Columns. Set the Insert Rows or Columns dialog box to insert one column After the Selection and click OK.**

FIGURE 10.37

**5** **Insert the images>events_button.gif graphic into the empty cell, and link it to events.html. Add `Events` as the alternate text.**

**6** **Close Basic.dwt, saving your changes.**

**7** **When prompted, click Update. When finished, click Close.**

**8** **Reopen events.html and observe that both navigation-bar graphics appear in the page.**

## LESSON 9 Creating Repeating Regions in a Template

Repeating regions of a template enable you, the designer, to create a consistent look and feel within small parts of a page. There are times when a type of information may be repeated multiple times in a page. For example, you may create a What's New page where each story has a title, date, author, and ***précis***, (a summary of the main points of a story). You may want to design a format or layout for this collection of components and allow the collection to be repeated as many times as necessary. You would, therefore, create a template with repeating regions. In the repeating regions, you can have a mixture of both editable and noneditable regions. For example, the date area might be editable but the word Date, the heading, might not be editable.

Repeating regions are more work to set up but quite simple to use. When you are working on a child page developed from a template with a repeating region, you can add and delete repeating regions and change their order. For example, when a story has been added out of date order, you may move it up or down into the correct order. Also, if a story is old and no longer appropriate on the What's New page, you can remove it by deleting its repeating region.

When you create a template with a repeating region, you should lay out one of the regions with actual content so that you can arrange it properly and determine which content needs repetition and which does not. Then you select the content that is to be editable and set it as editable regions (with names). You select the content that is to be repeated and set it as a repeatable region (also with a name). Finally, you save the template and build a child page from the template.

## Create a Template with a Repeating Region

In this exercise, you create a template with a repeating region. You set some of the content area to be editable and specify which region in the template may be repeated. Finally, you save the template.

**1** **Open about.html from the TO-P10 site, choose File>Save as Template, and name it `Books`. When asked to update links, choose Yes.**

**2** **Click in the main content cell, click the <td> tag in the Tag selector, and press Delete.**

**3** **Click in the empty cell, type `From the Bookshelf`, format the block as Heading 2, and press Enter/Return.**

**4** **Create a `2`-row, `2`-column table that is `50`% in width (and leave all other settings blank).**

**5** **With the table still selected, set the alignment to center in the Property inspector.**

**6** **Select the two cells in the top row and check the Header option in the Property inspector.**

**7** **In the top-left cell, type `Title`, and in the top-right cell, type `Price`.**

FIGURE 10.38

**8** **Click in the bottom-left cell, click the last <td> tag in the Tag selector, and choose Editable Region from the Templates drop-down menu of the Common Insert bar. Name the Editable Region `Title` and click OK.**

**9** **Click in the bottom-right cell, click the last <td> tag in the Tag selector, and choose Editable Region from the Templates drop-down menu of the Common Insert bar. Name the Editable Region `Price` and click OK.**

**10** **With the insertion point in the bottom row, click the last <tr> tag in the Tag selector, and choose Repeating Region from the Templates drop-down menu of the Common Insert bar. Name the Repeating Region `Book Details` and click OK.**

FIGURE 10.39

**11** **Remove About Tropiflora from the document Title field and replace it with `Template`.**

**12** **Close Books.dwt, saving your changes.**

## Create a Child Page Using the Repeating Region

Creating a child page from a template with repeating regions uses the same procedures as you used in the previous template until you need to repeat the regions. As you notice, there are four icons above the repeating region: a plus symbol (+) to add a copy of the repeating region, a hyphen (-) to remove the current repeating region, an up arrow to move the current repeating region up in order, and a down arrow to move the current repeating region down in order.

**1** **Choose File>New, choose the Templates tab, and choose books from the TO-P10 site.**

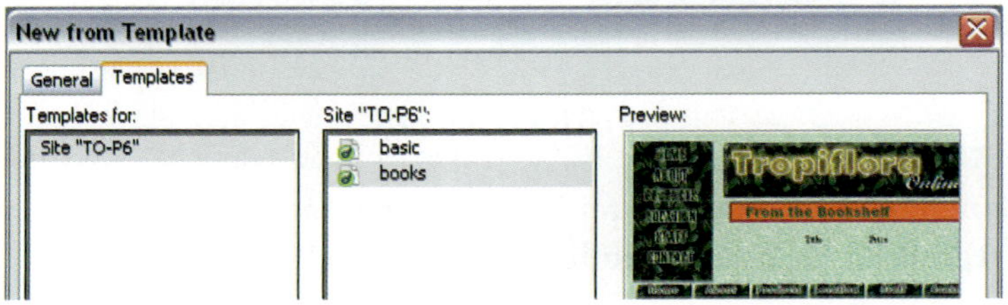


FIGURE 10.40

**2** **Change the document title to `Products: Books`.**

**3** **Choose File>Save and save the child page as `books.html`.**

**4** **Click in the Title editable area and type `Bromeliads: A Cultural Manual`. Click in the Price editable area and type `$39.95`.**

**5** **Click the plus symbol (+) to add a new repeating region.**

FIGURE 10.41

**6** **Type `The Tillandsia Handbook` in the Title editable region and `$27.00` in the Price editable region.**

**7** **Add a new repeating region, type `Bananas You Can Grow` as the title, and type `$19.95` as the price.**

**8** **Add a new repeating region, type `Succulents: The Illustrated Dictionary` as the title, and type `$24.95` as the price.**

**9** **Using the up and down areas at the top of the repeating region, sort the books so that, from top to bottom, the books are Bananas You Can Grow, Bromeliads: A Cultural Manual, Succulents: The Illustrated Dictionary, and The Tillandsia Handbook.**

FIGURE 10.42

**10** **Click in the Bananas You Can Grow repeating region and click the hyphen button (-) to delete the repeating region. (This book is no longer available.)**

**11** **Close books.html, saving your changes.**

## *To Extend Your Knowledge*

### PROGRAMMING THE TEMPLATE TECHNOLOGY

Dreamweaver's template technology is much more sophisticated than what you have seen, including capabilities such as conditional and optional regions in a template. Dreamweaver's templates have a programming language and the code described to you earlier for a template's editable and noneditable regions is just the tip of the iceberg. Unfortunately, most of these features and functions are based on programming concepts that are outside of the scope of these books. The template programming language is based on JavaScript, but unlike the Behaviors panel, many of the features of this language are not available through dialog boxes and require hand-coding.

For additional information about the programming technology of Dreamweaver templates, review the information available in the Help resources of Dreamweaver or at macromedia.com/devnet/mx/dreamweaver/templates.html.

## CAREERS IN DESIGN

### WORKING WITH DOCUMENTS DESTINED FOR PRINTING AND THE WEB SITE

Web designers may be assigned different roles and responsibilities in an organization, depending on a variety of factors, including their knowledge, skills, and experience, as well as the size of the department. Among the possible roles and responsibilities they may take on are print-based graphic and publication design.

Communications departments often continuously produce print-based publications from smaller single-page documents such as press releases to larger documents of 100 pages or more. Many such documents are destined for multiple paths — printed to paper, saved as PDFs, and made into Web pages. However, the ways in which readers use these types of documents differ from each other depending on the final formats, and Web designers should be aware of the differences. Although it is possible to export a publication from a graphic-design or desktop-publishing application to Web-page format, the result may not be satisfactory for either the end user or the Web-site designer.

A printed publication is commonly read from beginning to end, but information on Web sites is typically scanned by users searching for specific information, a much more focused approach. A one- or two-page press release may be posted to a Web site with little or no modification, but longer documents require restructuring and reorganization. As a result, a large document must be split into multiple pages so that the users may more easily find the information they are seeking. It may also be necessary to include a link to a search engine or even build a search engine into the Web site. You may download code from Google.com, or one of several other search engines, that creates a form on your site linked to the search engine and provides search-engine functionality to enable searching for content from pages within your site. This functionality goes a long way to helping the users of your site search for the information they are seeking.

In other words, File>Save As is not an appropriate method for transferring content from a print publication to a Web site. Web designers and their managers should be aware that the two different media require different treatments. Effective use of templates and CSS can greatly ease the creation of Web pages from multipage publications and should be considered from the outset when the project is initiated.

## SUMMARY

In this project, you learned several means of efficiently updating and planning for updating your Web sites. You learned to insert a snippet into your document. You created a new snippet and a folder in the Snippets panel, and stored the snippet for later use. You learned about library items and how they can help you create a common look and feel to your Web site. You learned how they are beneficial to the development of a Web site and enable you to make changes that are reflected throughout your Web site. You created, inserted, and updated a library item. You also learned about templates and how they, too, help with the development and rebuilding of a Web site. You discovered how to create a template from a combination of a library item and nonlibrary-item code. You created a template from an existing page, but also learned that you could create the template from scratch. You created a child page from the template, modified the template, and saw the child page update with the changes. You created a template with a repeating region. You built a child page from the template with the repeating region, added more repeating regions, and sorted them.

## KEY TERMS

child page
editable region
insert after
insert before
insert block
Library folder
library item
master template
repeating region
snippet
template
Templates folder
update
wrap selection

## CHECKING CONCEPTS AND TERMS

### SCREEN ID

**Identify the indicated areas from the list below:**

**FIGURE 10.43**

a. Snippets panel
b. Noneditable region
c. Template name
d. Add repeating region
e. Snippet name
f. Create new page from template
g. Library folder
h. Name of an editable region
i. Assets panel

## MULTIPLE CHOICE

**Circle the letter of the correct answer for each of the following:**

1. Which of the following is true?
   - **a.** Snippets can be opened from either the Snippets panel or the Snippets folder of the current site.
   - **b.** A snippet of an <img> tag contains both the HTML code and the image.
   - **c.** Snippets can contain a JavaScript event handler.
   - **d.** None of the above.
2. By default, all areas in a template are __________.
   - **a.** not editable
   - **b.** unstyled
   - **c.** table cells
   - **d.** All of the above
3. Templates can be created using __________.
   - **a.** library items
   - **b.** snippets
   - **c.** HTML
   - **d.** All of the above
4. To insert a library item into a document, you can __________.
   - **a.** drag it from the Templates folder
   - **b.** select the content in the page and click the New Library Item button
   - **c.** choose the item in the Library Assets panel and click the Insert button
   - **d.** All of the above
5. Which of the following can contain the `<body>` tag?
   - **a.** an editable region
   - **b.** a snippet
   - **c.** a library item
   - **d.** a template
6. To wrap a selected block of text with <span class="sidebar"> before it and </span> after it, you would create __________.
   - **a.** a library item
   - **b.** a snippet
   - **c.** a template
   - **d.** None of the above
7. Which layout method is not supported by templates?
   - **a.** layers
   - **b.** CSS
   - **c.** frames
   - **d.** tables
8. Which feature does not apply to templates?
   - **a.** consistent HTML structure
   - **b.** site-wide updating
   - **c.** less effort for contributors to a Web site
   - **d.** consistent appearance and styles
9. Which component of a Web page is always editable in a template?
   - **a.** `<body>` content
   - **b.** `<title>` content
   - **c.** `<!-- -->` comments
   - **d.** None of the above
10. Which feature is not site-specific?
    - **a.** snippets
    - **b.** templates
    - **c.** library items
    - **d.** All of the above

## DISCUSSION QUESTIONS

1. You have been asked to design a Web site for a client. You plan to use Dreamweaver templates to provide consistency to the structure. Your client would like you to show them a few sample pages before giving final approval. Would you or would you not use templates and/or library items in the sample pages? Explain your reasoning.

2. The snippet function can save a significant amount of time in the development of a Web page by reducing some of the tedious development time. Review the procedures and methods you have used in the past to create components of a Web page, list those that could be saved as a snippet for later use, and explain why. If you think of others uses for snippets that you haven't tried yet, add those to your list as well.

# SKILL DRILL

Skill Drills reinforce project skills. Each skill reinforced is the same, or nearly the same, as a skill presented in the lessons. Detailed instructions are provided in a step-by-step format. Work through these exercises in order.

## 1. Create Snippets from Code

It is very easy to add a snippet, such as a list of the states of the US, from a Web page in Dreamweaver: you just open the page in Dreamweaver, click the list in the Design view, and add it to the Snippets panel. It is more difficult to copy code. The purpose of this Skill Drill is not to make it difficult for you to copy some useful code and save it as a snippet. The purpose is to create a more realistic scenario whereby you might find a piece of code on someone else's Web site and want to save it for use on yours. You would, therefore, have to view the source code from your browser, search through the code for the code you want to copy and save as a snippet, and then copy/paste it into the Snippets panel. Recognize that you should not save copyrighted code unless you ask permission of the owner of the Web site. In this Skill Drill, the information is publicly available and not copyrighted.

1. Open survey.txt from the TO-P10 site.
2. Scroll to line 245. Select lines 245 to 297, inclusive, and copy the code into the clipboard.
3. Right/Control-click your named folder in the Snippets panel and choose New Snippet.
4. Name the snippet **`States of the US`**. In the Description, type **`A select list of the states of the US`**.
5. Set Snippet Type to Insert Block and set Preview Type to Design.

   If the selected code does not automatically appear in the Insert Code area, paste the selected code into it.
6. Click Close/OK.
7. In the open file, survey.txt, select lines 19 to 237, inclusive, and copy the code to the clipboard.
8. Create a new snippet in your named folder called **`Countries`** with a description of **`A select list of the countries of the world.`**

9. Set Snippet type to Insert Block and set Preview Type to Design.

   If the selected code does not automatically appear in the Insert code area, paste the selected code into it.

10. Click Close/OK.

11. Close survey.txt.

## 2. Insert Snippets into a Web Page

In this Skill Drill, you insert the snippet containing the list of states that you saved in the previous exercise. You use it to replace a text field in which the visitors are expected to type their billing and shipping states. To meet the needs of the form-processing application, you must rename the form field names from the default names stored with the snippet.

1. Open order_form.html from the TO-P10 site.

2. Click the State text field in the Billing Information area of the form and delete it.

3. From your named folder in the Snippets panel, insert the States of the US snippet.

4. Click the new list field and change the name of the form control in the Property inspector to **`billing_state`**.

5. Repeat Steps 2 to 4 with the state text field in the Shipping Information area of the form. Name the new form control **`shipping_state`**.

6. Close order_form.html, saving your changes.

## 3. Create and Add Library Items to the Template

In this Skill Drill, you enhance the Basic.dwt template by making more of the common components — the left and bottom navigation bars — into library items so, if you need to, you can use them in other templates.

1. Open Basic.dwt from the Templates folder of the TO-P10 site.

2. Click any of the graphic links in the left navigation bar.

3. In the Tag selector, click the **`<table>`** tag to the right of the **`<td#navbar>`** tag.

4. Open the Assets panel and click the Library icon at the bottom of the column of icons on the left.

5. At the bottom of the Assets panel, click the New Library Item button, read the message, and click OK. Name the new library item **`Left Navbar`**.

6. In the Document window, click any of the graphic links in the bottom navigation bar.

7. In the Tag selector, click the nested **`<table>`** tag.

8. At the bottom of the Assets panel, click the New Library Item button, read the message, and click OK. Name the new library item **`Bottom Navbar`**.

9. Close Basic.dwt, saving your changes.

10. When prompted, click Update and then Close.

## 4. Build a Site with Revised Templates

In this Skill Drill, you use the revised template to rebuild most of the pages from the TO-P10 site folder, ensuring that the entire site uses the same template and library items. After completing this exercise, you are prepared to make any changes to the site that you or the owner of the site requires — your changes will cascade through all of the pages.

1. Choose File>New, if necessary click the Templates tab, choose the basic template from the TO-P10 site, and click Create.
2. Open about.html from the TO-P10 folder.
3. Drag to select all of the content in the main content cell and copy it to the clipboard. Close about.html.
4. Paste the copied content into the editable region. Set the document Title field to `Tropiflora Online: About Tropiflora`.
5. Close, saving your changes to about.html and overwriting the existing file.

   The links will be broken until you save the file and Dreamweaver updates the links.
6. Repeat Steps 1 to 5 as follows:

| *Source of Content* | *Document Title Field* | *Save as Filename* |
|---|---|---|
| bromeliads.html | `Tropiflora Online: Products: Bromeliads` | bromeliads.html |
| contactus.html | `Tropiflora Online: Contact Us` | contactus.html |
| index.html | `Tropiflora Online: Home` | index.html |
| location.html | `Tropiflora Online: Location` | location.html |
| order_form.html | `Tropiflora Online: Products: Order Form` | order_form.html |
| products.html | `Tropiflora Online: Products` | products.html |
| staff.html | `Tropiflora Online: Staff` | staff.html |
| succulents.html | `Tropiflora Online: Products: Succulents` | succulents.html |
| tillandsias.html | `Tropiflora Online: Products: Tillandsias` | tillandsias.html |

## 5. Create a Template with Repeating Regions

In this Skill Drill exercise, you create a staff directory with a repeating region. Each repeating region consists of a table with a left cell containing an editable image placeholder and cells on the right containing the name, phone number, and email address of each staff member. The heading cells between the two columns are not editable.

1. Open about.html from the TO-P10 site, choose File>Save as Template, and name it **`Staff Directory`**. When asked to update links, choose Yes.
2. Remove About Tropiflora from the document Title field and replace it with **`Staff Directory`**.
3. Delete the content in the main content cell. Type **`Staff Directory`** and format it as Heading 2. Click to the right of the text and press Enter/Return.
4. Create a **`4`**-row, **`3`**-column table that is **`500`** pixels wide. Leave all other fields empty and click OK.
5. With the table selected, set the alignment of the table to center from the Property inspector.
6. Select the three cells of the bottom row and merge them. From the HTML Insert bar, insert a horizontal rule into the merged cell.
7. Merge the three remaining cells in the left column. Set the merged cell's horizontal alignment to center and vertical alignment to middle.
8. From the Common Insert bar, Images drop-down menu, insert an image placeholder named **`photo`**, with dimensions of **`100`** by **`100`**, into the merged cell.
9. In the middle column, type **`Name:`**, **`Phone Number:`**, and **`Email Address:`**. Select the three cells and apply bold.
10. In the right column, type **`name`**, **`phone`**, and **`email`** in the three cells.
11. Click in the right cell containing the word name, click the **`<td>`** tag in the Tag selector, and, from the Common Insert bar, set it as an editable region named **`Name`**. Repeat the same procedure for the two other cells on the right, naming the editable regions **`Phone`** and **`Email`**, respectively.
12. Click in the left cell with the image placeholder and click the **`<td>`** tag in the Tag selector. Set this cell to be an editable region named **`Photo`**.
13. Click the nested **`<table>`** tag to select the inner table. From the Common Insert bar, set this table to be a repeating region named **`Staff Details`**.

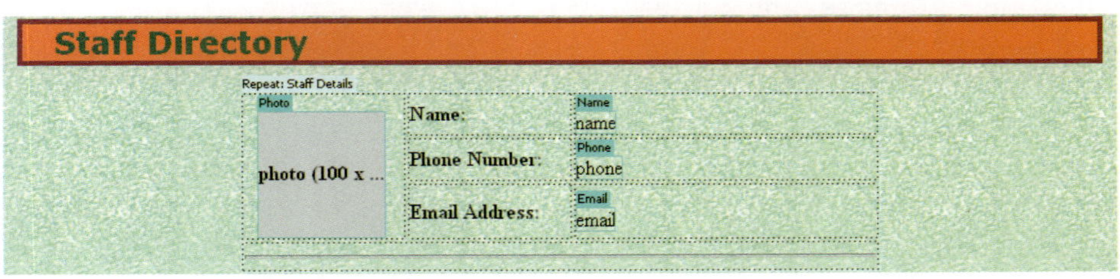


**FIGURE 10.44**

14. Close Staff Directory.dwt, saving your changes.

## 6. Fill a Template with Repeating Regions

In this Skill Drill exercise, you use the Staff Directory template and build a staff directory using repeating regions. The advantages of repeating regions become very clear when you develop a layout using them. You never have to think about the process of creating a nested table; you just click the Add button and a new region appears, identical in structure to the previous one. This is a real time saver.

1. Choose File>New, click the Templates tab if necessary, choose staff directory, and click Create.
2. Save the new file as **staff-directory.html**.
3. Double-click the image placeholder and replace the placeholder with alan.jpg from the thumbs folder. In the Name editable region, type **Alan**. In the Phone editable region, type **351-2267 ext. 122**. In the Email editable region, insert an email link using the Email button on the Common Insert bar and the address **alan@tropiflora.com** in both the Text and E-mail fields of the Email Link dialog box.

FIGURE 10.45

4. Add a new repeating region by clicking the plus symbol (+). Replace the image placeholder with alex.jpg from the thumbs folder. In the Name editable region, type **Alex**. In the Phone editable region, type **351-2267 ext. 134**. In the Email editable region, insert an email link using the Email button on the Common Insert bar and the address **alex@tropiflora.com** in both the Text and E-mail fields of the Email Link dialog box.
5. Repeat Step 4 with the following information:

| *Photo* | *Name* | *Phone* | *Email* |
|---|---|---|---|
| david.jpg | **David** | **351-2267 ext. 133** | **david@tropiflora.com** |
| debbie.jpg | **Debbie** | **351-2267 ext. 214** | **debbie@tropiflora.com** |
| dennis-linda.jpg | **Dennis and Linda** | **351-2267 ext. 115** | **cathcarts@tropiflora.com** |
| gregoria.jpg | **Gregoria** | **351-2267 ext. 212** | **gregoria@tropiflora.com** |
| jeff.jpg | **Jeff** | **351-2267 ext. 144** | **jeff@tropiflora.com** |
| pilar.jpg | **Pilar** | **351-2267 ext. 114** | **pilar@tropiflora.com** |
| ray.jpg | **Ray** | **351-2267 ext. 224** | **ray@tropiflora.com** |
| veronica.jpg | **Veronica** | **351-2267 ext. 234** | **veronica@tropiflora.com** |

6. Close staff-directory.html, saving your changes.

## CHALLENGE

Challenge exercises expand on, or are somewhat related to, skills presented in the lessons. Each exercise provides a brief introduction, followed by instructions in a numbered-step format that are not as detailed as those in the Skill Drill exercises. Work through the exercises in order.

### 1. Create Library Items from a CSS Layout Page

In the preceding exercises, you learned that that you can create library items where the pages use tables for layout. However, the containers of the contents of tables-based layouts are the **<td>** table-data cells and they cannot be separated from the rest of the table structure. When you create a library item from a table cell, you create a library item of the contents of the table cell, not the table cell and its contents. When using CSS-based layouts where the **<div>** tags are the containers, the situation is different in that the **<div>** tag and its contents can be captured in the library item.

In this exercise, you create library items from a CSS-based layout. Because the layout uses **<div>** tags as containers and CSS to position the containers, Dreamweaver warns you each time you create a library item from a **<div>** that the styles will not be saved with the library item. This is fine because the styles are stored in an external style sheet. However, there is a problem that may not be clearly evident. If you create a library item of a **<div>** with the id of header and then edit the library item and change or remove the id, the styles do not apply to that **<div>** and its contents because the id, which is used as a selector, does not exist in the form that CSS needs. Be aware of the need to maintain ids and classes for CSS styling when you modify a library item.

1. Define a new site called **PHIL-P10** from the Project_10>PHIL-P10 folder.
2. Open faculty.html from the basic folder.
3. Open the Assets panel to the Library Items panel.
4. Click in Carter University at the top of the page, click **<div#header>** tag in the Tag selector, and drag the selected block to the Library Items Assets panel. Click OK to acknowledge the message about styles. In the Library Items Assets panel, name the new library item **Header**.

   It may seem odd to store the name of the college in a library item because it is unlikely that the name would change. However, you may need to change the contents of the header div, and to effect the change across the whole Web site, you must store the change in a library item.

5. Click in Philosophy Department, click the **<div#dept>** tag in the Tag selector, and drag the selected block to the Library Items Assets panel. Click OK to acknowledge the message about styles. In the Library Items Assets panel, name the new library item **Phil Dept**.

   Again, to accommodate the possibility that the department div might change in the future, you create a library item. This library item would only be used on pages for the Philosophy Department. The university's Web pages would need other library items for the other departments, as well.

6. Click in the left navigation bar and click the **<div#navbar>** tag in the Tag selector. Click the New Library Item button at the bottom of the Library Items Assets panel. Click OK to acknowledge the message about styles. In the Library Items Assets panel, name the new library item **Phil Navbar**.

   Each department can have its own navigation-bar links so the Philosophy Department navigation bar is saved as its own library item.

7. Scroll down if necessary, click in the footer, and click the **<div#footer>** tag in the Tag selector. Click the New Library Item button at the bottom of the Library Items Assets panel. Click OK to acknowledge the message about styles. In the Library Items Assets panel, name the new library item **Footer**.

   Like the Header library item, the Footer library item would be consistent across all of the university's Web pages and is saved as a library item to allow for the possibility of additional links.

8. Keep faculty.html open for the next exercise.

## 2. Create a Template with Nested Library Items

In this exercise, you prepare the template for the Faculty page. You use the library items you created and specify editable regions.

1. In the open file, faculty.html, choose Save as Template and save the template as **Faculty**. When prompted to update links, click Yes.
2. Select the text Faculty Group Name. From the Common Insert bar, choose Editable Region from the Templates drop-down menu, name the New Editable Region **Faculty Group Name**, and click OK.
3. Click in Professor Name and click the **<li#prof_name>** tag in the Tag selector. Choose Editable Region from the Templates drop-down menu, name the New Editable Region **Faculty Details**, and click OK.
4. Save the changes to Faculty.dwt but leave it open.

## 3. Create the Remaining Templates for the Web Site

In this exercise, you create the Courses and Schedule templates, using Faculty as the base.

1. In the open file, Faculty.dwt, choose File>Save as Template. Read and then click OK to acknowledge the warning. Name the new template **Courses**. At the end of the document Title field, change Faculty to **Courses**.
2. Without closing Courses.dwt, open courses.html from the basic folder, select all of the content, copy it to the clipboard, and close courses.html.
3. Click in the content div of Courses.dwt, click the **<div#content>** tag in the Tag selector, and paste the copied content.
4. Select the text Year. From the Common Insert bar, choose Editable Region from the Templates drop-down menu, name the New Editable Region **Year Group Name**, and click OK.
5. Click in the text PHIL XXX and click the **<li#phxxx>** tag in the Tag selector. From the Common Insert bar, choose Editable Region from the Templates drop-down menu, name the New Editable Region **Course Details**, and click OK.
6. Save the changes to Courses.dwt but leave it open.
7. Choose File>Save as Template. Read and then click OK to acknowledge the warning. Name the new template **Schedule**. At the end of the document Title, change Faculty to **Schedule**.

8. Without closing Schedule.dwt, open schedule.html from the basic folder, select all of the content, copy it to the clipboard, and close schedule.html.

9. Click in the content div of Schedule.dwt, click **<div#content>** tag in the Tag selector, and paste the copied content.

10. Select the text Term. From the Common Insert bar, choose Editable Region from the Templates drop-down menu, name the New Editable Region **Term Group Name**, and click OK.

11. Select PHILxxx in the second row and set it as an Editable Region called **Course**. Select Mon/Wed and set it as an Editable Region called **Days**. Select 0900-1030 and set it as an Editable Region called **Time**. Select PH120 and set it as an Editable Region called **Room**. Select Prof and set it as an Editable Region called **Professor**.

12. Close Schedule.dwt, saving your changes.

## 4. Create Nested Repeating Regions

Each of the pages created so far in the Challenge exercise may be set up with repeating regions — there is more than one professor, more than one course description, and more than one course listed in the schedule.. However, professors are grouped according to whether they are full or assistant professors, courses are grouped according to their year, and schedules are grouped into different terms. This provides the opportunity for you to learn how to create nested repeating regions.

1. Open Schedule.dwt from either the Template Assets panel or the Templates folder in the Files panel.

2. Click in any cell of the second row of the table and then click the **<tr>** tag in the Tag selector.

3. From the Common Insert bar, choose Repeating Region from the Templates drop-down menu and name the repeating region **Course Region**.

4. Click in the text Term, and then click the **<h2>** tag in the Tag selector. Shift-click to the bottom right of the table to select from the **<h2>** tag to the end of the table.

5. From the Common Insert bar, choose Repeating Region from the Templates drop-down menu and name the repeating region **Term Region**.

6. Close Schedule.dwt, saving your changes.

## 5. Create Nested Repeating Regions in the Template Pages

In this exercise, you create nested repeating regions in the Courses and Faculty pages. To prepare repeating regions, especially nested repeating regions, takes a bit of practice. The Schedule.dwt template page is slightly easier than the Courses and Faculty template pages, but with careful attention to the instructions, you can set up these nested repeating regions.

1. Open Courses.dwt from the Templates folder or the Templates Assets panel.

2. Click in the text PHIL XXX, and then click the **<ul>** tag in the Tag selector.

3. From the Common Insert bar, choose Repeating Region from the Templates drop-down menu and name the repeating region **Course Region**.

4. Click in the text Year, and then click the `<h2>` tag in the Tag selector. Shift-click to the bottom right of Course Syllabus.
5. From the Common Insert bar, choose Repeating Region from the Templates drop-down menu and name the repeating region `Year Region`.
6. Close Courses.dwt, saving your changes.
7. Open Faculty.dwt from the Templates folder or the Templates Assets panel.
8. Click in the text Professor Name, and then click the `<ul>` tag in the Tag selector.
9. From the Common Insert bar, choose Repeating Region from the Templates drop-down menu and name the repeating region `Faculty Region`.
10. Click in the text Faculty Group Name, and then click the `<h2>` tag in the Tag selector. Shift-click to the bottom right of Course Title.
11. From the Common Insert bar, choose Repeating Region from the Templates drop-down menu and name the repeating region `Faculty Group Region`.
12. Close Faculty.dwt, saving changes.

## 6. Create and Test Child Pages

In this exercise, you create child pages from the templates and test the nested repeating regions. You learn that each repeating region has its own controls to add, remove, and sort the regions. You can add Fall, Winter, and Spring terms to the Schedule page and, within each term, can display multiple courses in the schedule tables. Nested repeating regions could also be created for the Courses and Faculty pages.

1. Create a new page from the schedule template in the PHIL-P10 site.
2. Click the plus symbol to the right of the Repeat: Course Region label.
3. Click the plus symbol to the right of the Repeat: Term Region label. In the second Term Region, click the plus symbol to the right of the Repeat: Course Region label.
4. Close without saving the changes.
5. Create a new page from the courses template in the PHIL-P10 site. Use the plus symbols to add new Course and Year regions. When finished, close without saving the changes.
6. Create a new page from the faculty template in the PHIL-P10 site. Use the plus symbols to add new Faculty Group and Faculty regions. When finished, close without saving the changes.

## PORTFOLIO BUILDER

### Assess the Need for Templates and Library Items

You have learned that templates and library items are very beneficial to the development, maintenance, and consistent appearance of a Web site. Some Web sites, such as the Canadian federal governments' Web sites, have a "common look and feel (CLF)" policy. Templates and library items could help realize similar policies. In this assignment, you build a Dreamweaver template for a Web site using a free page from freesitetemplates.com.

1. Go to freesitetemplates.com. On the left, under the Free Templates heading, are categories of templates. Browse through these templates and find one that appeals to you.
2. Register and confirm the registration when the email arrives.
3. Download the file and save it in a new folder called **PB**, under the Project_10 folder.
4. Create a new site for the **PB** folder called **PB10**.
5. Open the downloaded page and create library items from selected components of the page.
6. Create a template from the page and set an editable area.

# INTEGRATING PROJECT

This integrating project reflects a real-world Web-site job, drawing on the skills you learned throughout this book. The files you need to complete this project are in the RF_Dreamweaver>IP folder.

## Independence Hummer Web Site

The management of Independence Hummer, a car dealership, has hired you to recreate their existing Web site. While this site actually exists (IndependenceHummer.com, graphics and photos used by permission), for the purposes of this project, imagine you are on the Web team creating the site. The client has supplied the information and the images, and has approved the design concepts. The team has planned the basic strategy for creating the site and assembled the components. The final site will feature a frames-based layout that includes tables within the individual pages, as well as text and graphic links.

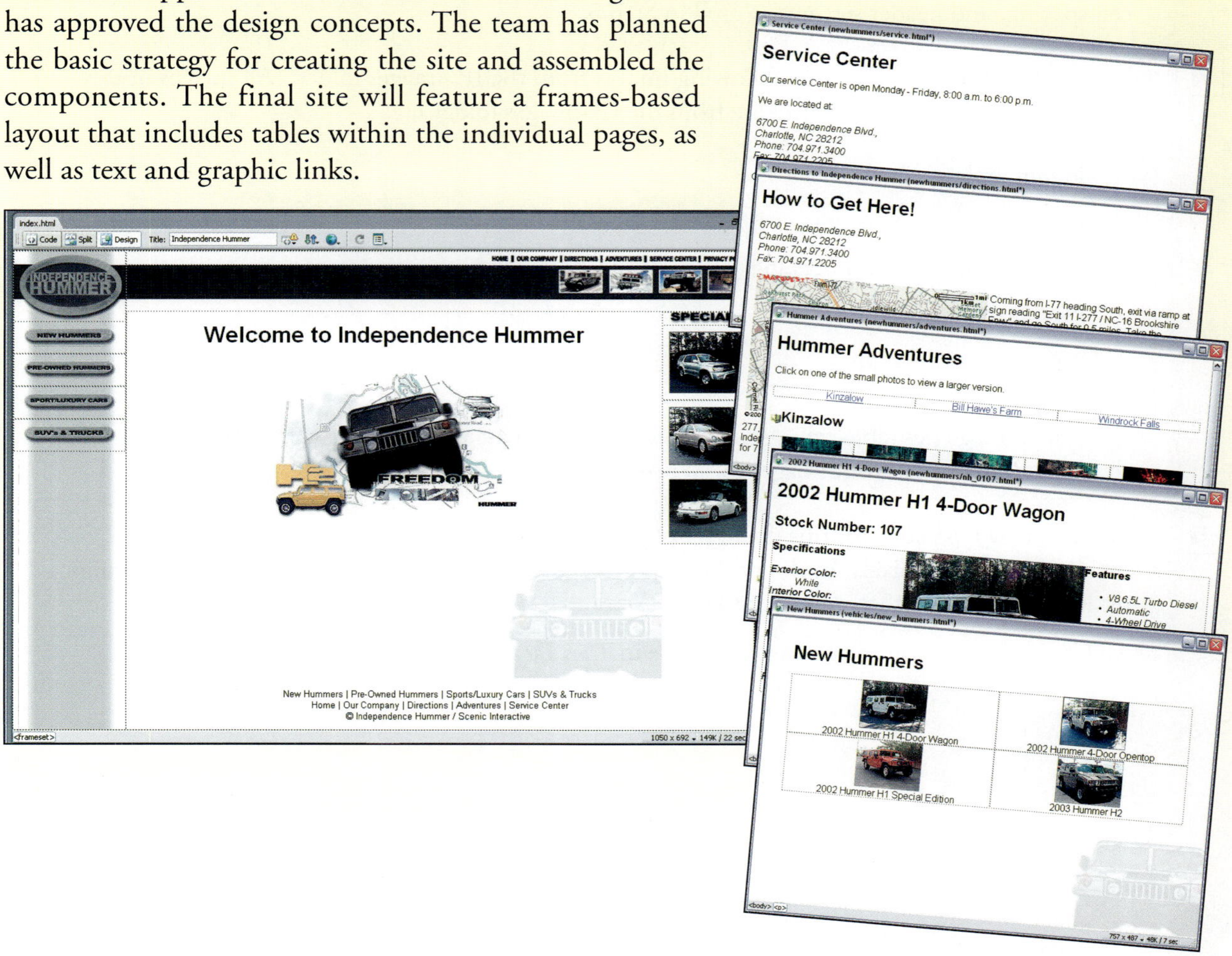

# PART 1 Creating the Basic Frames and the Home Page

In this section, you create the pages that appear in the frames that surround the main-content area of the frameset. You create the home page, which later becomes a nested frameset, and then create the main frameset that binds together all of the frames.

## Create the Left Page

1. Create a site definition called "Independence Hummer" in the WIP>IP folder.

2. Create a new basic HTML page, title it "Left Navigation", and save it as "left.html" (but do not close the file).

3. Create a 5-row, 1-column table. Set the width to 159 pixels, border to 0, Cell Padding to 0, Cell Spacing to 0, and Header to None. Click OK.

   Whenever you use a layout table in this integrating project, apply the same border, cell padding, cell spacing, and header settings as used in Step 3.

4. From top to bottom, insert the following images from the IP>images folder. (All images in this section of the integrating project are from the IP>images folder.)

   logomain.jpg

   menu_newhummers.jpg

   menu_preownedhummers.jpg

   menu_sportsluxury.jpg

   menu_suvstrucks.jpg

   Insert one image per table cell. Assign appropriate alternate text for each image. Set the vertical spacing of the bottom four images to 10 pixels.

5. Create a new CSS style for this document for the **body** Tag selector. In the Box category, set all margins to 0 pixels. In the Background category, set the Background Image to bgmenu.jpg, set Repeat to **repeat-y**, and click OK.

   All CSS styles in this project use the Define in This Document Only option.

**6** Close left.html, saving the changes.

FIGURE IP.1

## Create the Top Page

**1** Create a new HTML page, title it "Top Navigation", and save it as "top.html" (but don't close the file).

**2** Create a 2-row, 1-column layout table with a width of 100%.

**3** Insert the following graphics into the top cell in this order, and assign appropriate alternate text for each graphic:

top_home.jpg

top_ourcompany.jpg

top_directions.jpg

top_adventures.jpg

top_service.jpg

top_privacy.jpg

**4** In the bottom cell, insert top_pics.jpg. Assign it an empty alt.

**5** Create a new CSS style for the **body** Tag selector. In the Box category, set all margins to 0 pixels. In the Background category, set the Background Image to bgtop.jpg and set the Repeat option to **repeat-x**. Click OK.

**6** Create another new CSS style for the **td** Tag selector. In the Block category, set the Text Align to **right**. Click OK.

**7** Close the file, saving your changes.

FIGURE IP.2

## Create the Bottom Page

**1** Create a new HTML page, title it "Bottom Navigation", and save it as "bottom.html" (but do not close the file).

**2** Type: `New Hummers | Pre-Owned Hummers | Sports/Luxury Cars | SUVs & Trucks`, and press Enter/Return.

You create the " | " (pipe) character by pressing the Shift key and typing the " \ " character.

**3** Type: `Home | Our Company | Directions | Adventures | Service Center`, and press Enter/Return. Insert the Copyright character from the Text Insert bar Character list, and then type: `Independence Hummer / Scenic Interactive`.

Scenic Interactive is the name of the Web-design agency that originally built this Web site. You may substitute your name in place of Scenic Interactive.

**4** Create a new CSS style for this document for the **p** Tag selector. In the Type category, choose Arial, Helvetica, sans-serif from the Font list and set the Size to **small**. In the Block category, set Text Align to **center**. In the Box category, set all margins to 0 pixels, and then click OK.

**5** Close the file, saving your changes.

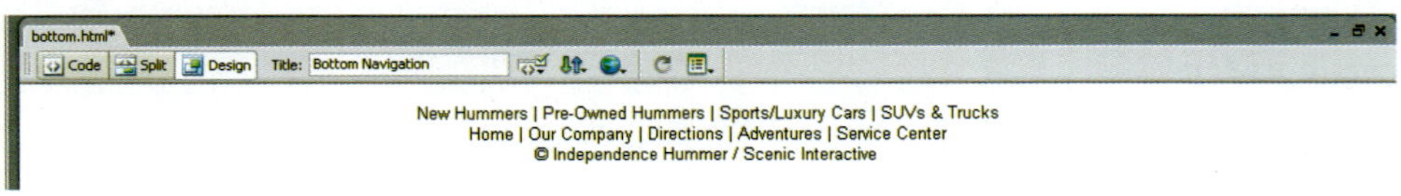


**FIGURE IP.3**

## Create the Main Page

The home page will be a nested frameset containing the main page and a specials page. You create the main page first, then develop the specials page, and then create the frameset page.

1. Create a new HTML page, title it "Main Page", and save it as "main.html".

2. Type: `Welcome to Independence Hummer` and set the Format to Heading 1.

3. Press Enter/Return, insert main_body.jpg, and assign the image an empty alt.

4. Create a new CSS style for this document for the **`body`** Tag selector. In the Type category, choose Arial, Helvetica, sans-serif from the Font list. In the Background category, choose bgbody.jpg as the Background Image, set Repeat to **`no-repeat`**, Horizontal Position to **`right`**, Vertical Position to **`bottom`**, and Attachment to **`fixed`**, and then click OK.

5. Create a new CSS style for this document for the **`h1`** Tag selector. In the Block category, set Text Align to **`center`** and click OK.

6. Create a new CSS style for this document for the **`p`** Tag selector. In the Block category, set Text Align to **`center`** and click OK.

7. Close the file, saving your changes.

**FIGURE IP.4**

## Create the Specials Page

1. Create a new HTML page, title it "Current Specials", and save it as "specials.html".

2. Create a 1-column, 4-row layout table. Set the width to 130 pixels.

3. In the top cell, insert specials.jpg and add the appropriate alt text.

4. In the remaining cells, insert the following images from the IP>vehicles>images folder:

    suv_0201sm.jpg
    sl_0229sm.jpg
    sl_0227a.jpg

Assign the graphics the following alt text, in order:

    2000 Toyota 4Runner
    1998 Mercedes CLK 320
    1990 Porsche 911 Carrera

5. Apply 10 pixels of horizontal spacing and 10 pixels of vertical spacing to each of the three car photos.

6. Create a new CSS Style for this document for the **body** Tag selector. In the Box category, set all margins to 0 pixels and click OK.

7. Close the file, saving your changes.

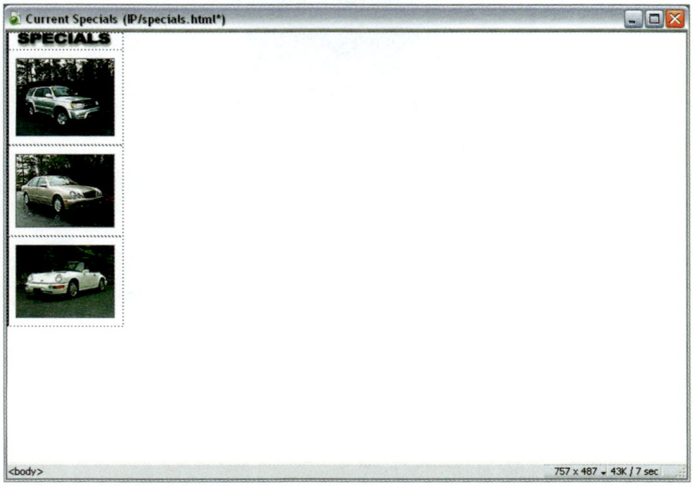


**FIGURE IP.5**

## Create the Home-Page Frameset

**1** Create a new Frameset from the Fixed Right predefined layout, title it "Home Frameset", and save the frameset page as "home.html".

**2** Using the RowCol Selection area in the Property inspector, click the right frame and set the column width to 130 pixels.

**3** Press Shift-F2 to open the Frames panel.

**4** Click the right frame in the Frames panel, and in the Property inspector, name the frame "specials". Set specials.html as the source of the frame.

**5** Click the left frame in the Frames panel, and in the Property inspector, name the frame "main". Set main.html as the source of the frame.

FIGURE IP.6

**6** Close home.html, saving your changes.

## Create the Primary Frameset

1. Create a new frameset page using Fixed Left as the template, title it "Independence Hummer", and save the frameset as "index.html".

2. Rename the left frame "leftnav", resize it to 159 pixels wide, and set its source to left.html.

3. Select the larger frame. From the Frames button on the Layout Insert bar, choose Top and Bottom Frames.

4. Rename the top frame "top", resize it to 88 pixels high, and set the source to top.html.

5. Rename the bottom frame "bottom", resize it to 75 pixels high, and set the source to bottom.html.

6. Rename the middle frame "main" and set the source to home.html.

7. Save the changes to index.html and leave it open for the next exercise.

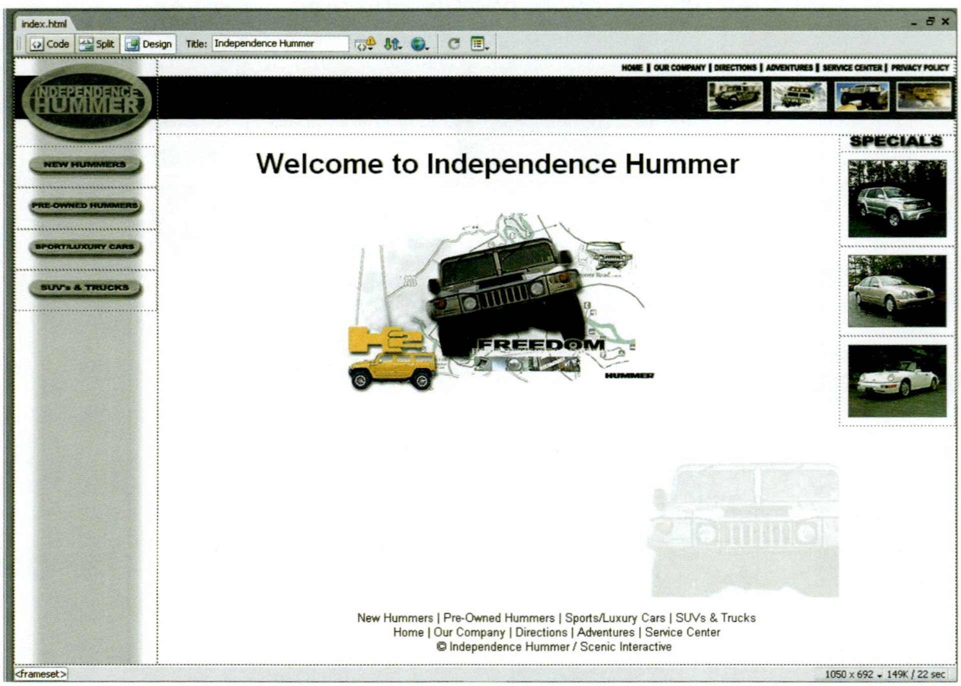


FIGURE IP.7

## Evaluate the Frameset Scroll Options

**1** Preview index.html in your browser.

**2** Resize your browser both in width and height. Observe the scroll bars and determine whether or not they are necessary.

When you create custom frame layouts in Dreamweaver, the scroll bars may not be set correctly. If the scroll bar setting is Auto, the scroll bars can appear when not needed; if they are set to No, scroll bars are prevented from appearing when they are needed.

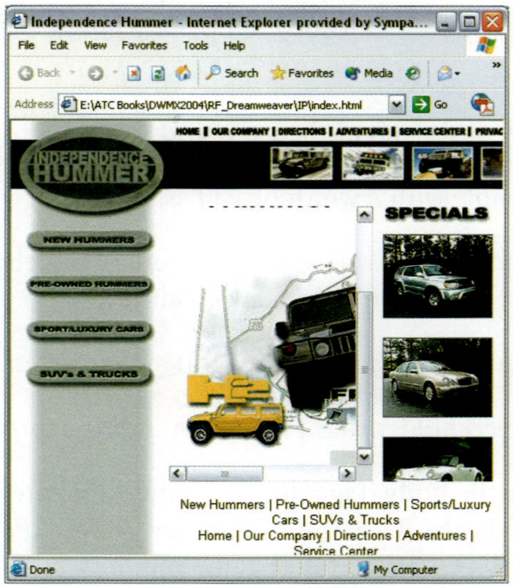


**FIGURE IP.8**

**3** Return to Dreamweaver.

**4** If you need to modify the Scroll option for any of the frames, click the frame in the Frames panel and change the Scroll option in the Property inspector.

**5** If you made changes to the Scroll option for any of the frames, preview index.html in your browser and review your changes.

**6** Return to Dreamweaver and close index.html.

# PART 2 Creating Vehicle-Category Pages

In this section, you create one page for each of the four categories of vehicles: New Hummers, Pre-Owned Hummers, Sport/Luxury Cars, and SUVs/Trucks. You create a template page, and then use that template to build pages with information for each vehicle. You do not work with the frameset in the next few exercises, so you can close the Frames panel if you wish.

## Create the Category Template

1. Create a new HTML page, title it "Category Template", and save it as "category-template.html" in the IP>vehicles folder.
2. Type **Vehicle Category** at the top of the page, and set the Format as Heading 1.
3. Create a 2 × 2-cell layout table with a width of 100%.
4. Click the top-right cell, and create a 110 × 110-pixel image placeholder with the name "vehicle_photo", assign any color, and do not assign alt text.
5. Click to the right of the image placeholder, press Enter/Return, and type **Vehicle Description**.
6. Copy the text and image placeholder, and paste them into the three empty cells.
7. Create a new CSS style for the **body** Tag selector. In the Type category, set the Font to Arial, Helvetica, sans-serif. In the Background category, choose IP>images>bgbody.jpg as the Background Image, set Repeat to **no-repeat**, Horizontal Position to right, Vertical Position to **bottom**, and Attachment to **fixed**. In the Box category, set all margins to 40 pixels and click OK.
8. Create a new CSS style for the **p** Tag selector. In the Block category, set the Text Align to **center**. In the Box category, uncheck Same for All for the margins, and set both Top and Bottom margins to 0 pixels. Click OK.
9. Close the file, saving your changes.

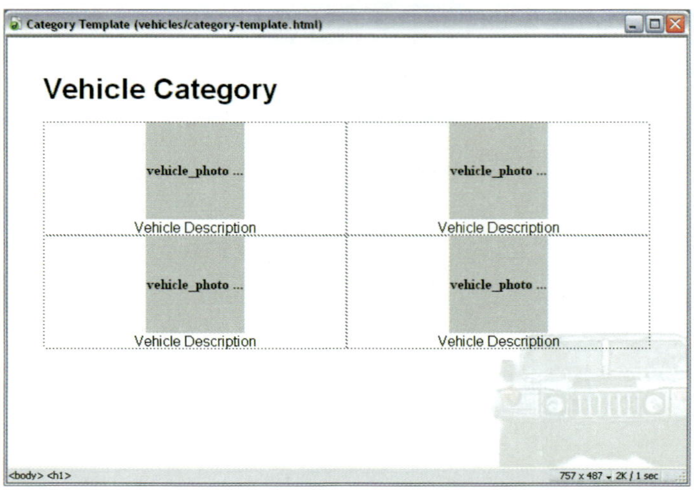


FIGURE IP.9

## Build Category Pages from the Template

**1** Open category-template.html and save it as "new-hummers.html" in the IP>vehicles folder.

**2** Change both the document title and Heading 1 text to "New Hummers".

**3** Replace the four image placeholders with the images identified below. In all cases, the image filenames end with sm.jpg (thumbnail images), and the images are in the IP>vehicles>images folder. Also, set an empty alt for these images. Replace the Vehicle Description text with the text provided below.

| Placeholder | Image | Description |
|---|---|---|
| 1 | nh_0107sm.jpg | 2002 Hummer H1 4-Door Wagon |
| 2 | nh_0203sm.jpg | 2002 Hummer 4-Door Opentop |
| 3 | nh_0271sm.jpg | 2002 Hummer H1 Special Edition |
| 4 | nh_h2h2sm.jpg | 2003 Hummer H2 |

**4** Close new-hummers.html, saving your changes.

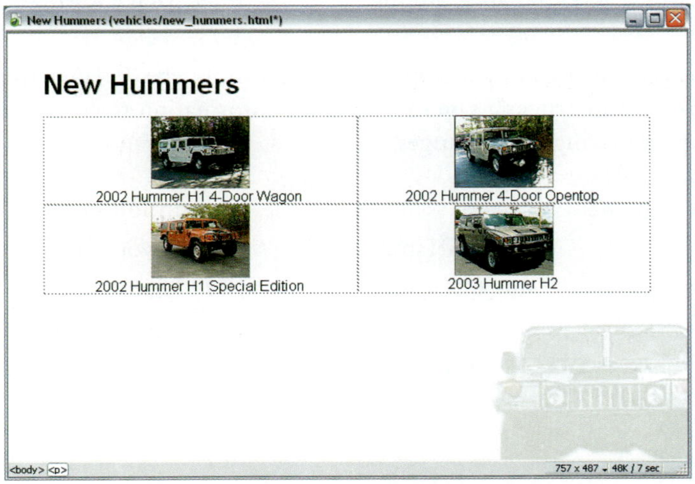


**FIGURE IP.10**

**5** Open category-template.html and save it as "preowned-hummers.html".

**6** Change both the document title and Heading 1 text to "Pre-Owned Hummers".

**7** Applying the same procedures as you used in Step 3, use the following information to complete the page. When you finish, close the page, saving your changes.

| Placeholder | Image | Description |
|---|---|---|
| 1 | poh_0104sm.jpg | 1993 Hummer H1 4-Door Opentop |
| 2 | poh_0145sm.jpg | 2001 Hummer H1 4-Door Opentop |
| 3 | poh_0206sm.jpg | 2000 Hummer H1 4-Door Wagon |
| 4 | poh_0218sm.jpg | 1995 Hummer H1 4-Door Opentop |

**8** Create "sports-luxury.html" from the category-template.html page. Change the document title and Heading 1 to "Sports and Luxury Vehicles". Use the following information to complete the page. When you finish, close the page, saving your changes.

| Placeholder | Image | Description |
|---|---|---|
| 1 | sl_0140sm.jpg | 1994 Red Lotus Esprit G4 |
| 2 | sl_0227asm.jpg | 1990 Porsche 911 Carrera 2 |
| 3 | sl_0229sm.jpg | 1998 Mercedes CLK 320 |
| 4 | sl_0247sm.jpg | 1997 Mercedes-Benz E320 |

**9** Create "suvs-trucks.html" from the category-template.html page. Change the document title and Heading 1 to "SUVs and Trucks". Use the following information to complete the page. When you finish, close the page, saving your changes.

| Placeholder | Image | Description |
|---|---|---|
| 1 | suv_0201sm.jpg | 2000 Toyota 4Runner Limited |
| 2 | suv_0219sm.jpg | 1999 Lexus LX470 |
| 3 | suv_0246sm.jpg | 1993 Land Rover Defender 90 |
| 4 | suv_0313sm.jpg | 1999 Land Rover 4.6 HSE |

# PART 3 Building Vehicle-Detail Pages

In this section, you apply the same methodology you used to create the category pages. You create a template for an individual vehicle page, and then use that template to create the specific pages. Given that there are 16 vehicles in the site (4 per category), 12 of the vehicle-detail pages were created for you. Your task is to create the detail pages for the New Hummers category.

## Create the Vehicle-Detail Template Page

1. Create a new HTML page, title it "Detail Vehicle Template", and save the page as "detail-template.html" in the IP>vehicles folder.

2. Type `Vehicle Name` and set the Format as Heading 1. Press Enter/Return, and type: `Stock Number: 1234`, set the Format as Heading 2, and press Enter/Return.

3. Create a 1-row, 3-column layout table with a width of 100%. Select all three cells, set the vertical alignment to **`top`**, and set the width to 33%. Click the middle cell and set the horizontal alignment to **`center`**.

4. In the left cell, type `Specifications`, set the Format as Heading 3, and press Enter/Return. Create a definition list (click "dl" in the Text Insert bar) and type `Exterior Color`. Press Enter/Return and type `xxx`.

5. Continue to create the definition list, making the following blocks of text the definition terms — "Interior Color:", "Make:", "Model:", "Year:", and "Price:" — and using "xxx" as the definition description.

6. In the right cell, type `Features`, set the Format as Heading 3, and press Enter/Return. Create an unordered list and type `engine`.

7. In the middle cell, insert a 250 × 250 image placeholder with the name "vehicle_photo" and no alt text.

8. Create a new CSS style for the **`body`** Tag selector. From the Type category, set the Font to Arial, Helvetica, sans-serif. In the Background category, choose IP>images>bgbody.jpg as the Background Image, set Repeat to **`no-repeat`**, Horizontal Position to **`right`**, Vertical Position to **`bottom`**, and Attachment to **`fixed`**. In the Box category, set all margins to 40 pixels and click OK.

9. Create a new CSS style for the **`dt`** Tag selector. In the Type category, set the Weight to Bold and click OK.

10. Create a new CSS style for the **`dd`** Tag selector. In the Type category, set the Style to Italic and click OK.

11. Create a new CSS style for the **`ul`** Tag selector. In the Type category, set the Style to Italic and click OK.

12 Close the file, saving your changes.

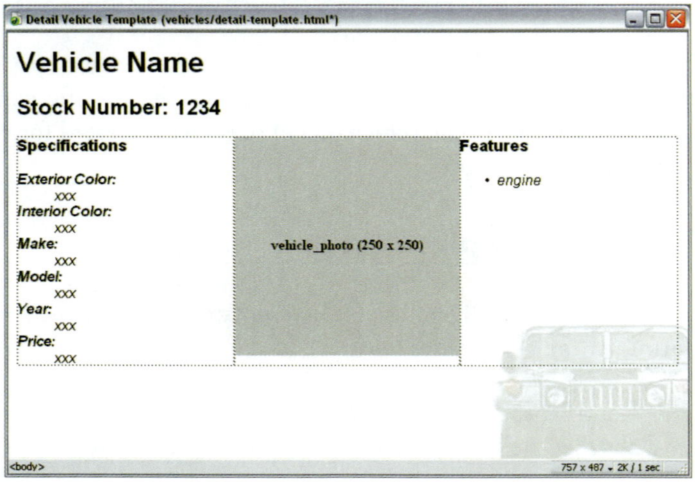


FIGURE IP.11

## Build Details Pages from the Template

1 Create a new folder called "newhummers" below the IP>vehicles folder.

It should appear with the other category folders.

2 Open detail-template.html and save it as "nh_0107.html" in the IP>vehicles>newhummers folder.

3 Change both the document title and Heading 1 text to "2002 Hummer H1 4-Door Wagon", and change the stock number to "107".

4 Replace the image placeholder with nh_0107lg.jpg from the IP>vehicles>images folder, and assign it an empty alt.

5 Replacing the "xxx" in each case, change the Exterior Color to "White", Interior Color to "Tan", Make to "Hummer", Model to "H1 4-Door Wagon", Year to "2002", and Price to "$111,302".

6 Under Features, create an unordered list with the following list items: "V8 6.5L Turbo Diesel", "Automatic", "4-Wheel Drive", "Luxury Package", "All Power Options".

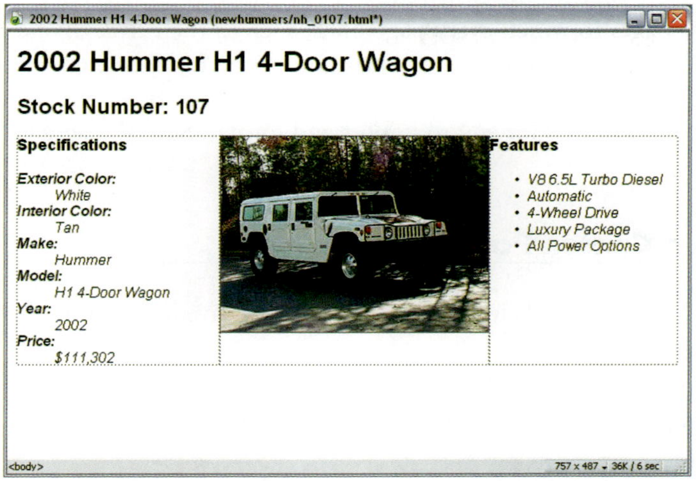


**FIGURE IP.12**

7 Close the file, saving your changes.

8 Repeat Steps 2–7 using the following information to create the three remaining vehicle-detail pages.

| **Filename** | nh_0203.html | nh_0271.html | nh_h2h2.html |
|---|---|---|---|
| **Document Title** | 2002 Hummer 4-Door Opentop | 2002 Hummer H1 Special Edition | 2003 Hummer H2 |
| **Stock #** | 203 | 271 | H2h2 |
| **Image** | nh_0203lg.jpg | nh_0271lg.jpg | nh_h2h2lg.jpg |
| **Specifications** | Pewter, Tan, Hummer, H1 4-Door Opentop, 2002, $104,049 | Bronze Metallic, Tan, H1 10th Anniversary Edition, 2002, $116,560 | Pewter, Gray, Hummer, H2, 2003, $56,500 |
| **Features** | V8 6.5L Turbo Diesel, Automatic, ABS, Air Conditioning, Full-Time 4WD, Brush Guard, Towing Package, Heated Mirrors, Heated Windshield, Keyless Entry, Monsoon Stereo with CD, Aluminum Wheels | 10th Anniversary Special Edition (#4 of 65), First One Released to the Public for Sale after Arnold Schwarzenegger, First H1 to Offer Factory Leather, Heated Seats, Wood-Grain Panels | V8 5.0 liter, Automatic, 4Wheel Drive, Adventure Package, Towing Package, Alloy Wheels, Roof Rack |

# PART 4 Creating Common Pages

Common pages are those pages to which every page links, such as the Privacy Policy, Directions, and Service Center pages. Your task is to create and format these pages for the Independence Hummer Web site. For this section, the text is in the IP>common folder and the images are in the IP>common>images folder. The text is in MS Word document format, ready for you to import and format. Save all pages you create in this section in the IP>common folder.

## Create the Service-Center Page

1. Create a new HTML page, title it "Service Center", and save it as "service.html".

2. Windows users: Import service.doc into this empty page.

   Macintosh users: Open service.txt, select and copy all of the text, close service.txt, and paste into the empty page.

3. Select the top line and format it as Heading 1.

4. Format the address line using the **<address>** tag (Common Insert bar, Tag Chooser button).

5. In the address block, insert line breaks in front of Charlotte, Phone, and Fax.

6. Create a new CSS style for the **body** Tag selector. Set the font to Arial, Helvetica, sans-serif. Set the Background Image to IP>images>bgbody.jpg, set Repeat to **no-repeat**, Horizontal Position to **right**, Vertical Position to **bottom**, and Attachment to **fixed**.

7. Close the file, saving your changes.

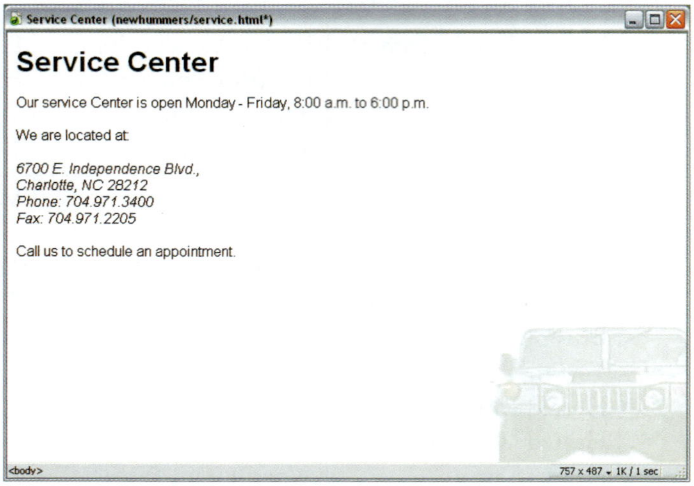


FIGURE IP.13

## Create the Directions Page

**1** Create a new HTML page, title it "Directions to Independence Hummer", and save it as "directions.html" (but do not close the page).

**2** Windows users: Import directions.doc into this empty page.

Macintosh users: Open directions.txt, select and copy all of the text, close directions.txt, and paste into the empty page.

**3** Format the top line as Heading 1.

**4** Format the address with the **`<address>`** tag, as you did in Step 3 of the previous exercise. Insert a line break in front of Charlotte, Phone, and Fax.

**5** Insert ih_map.gif at the beginning of the first paragraph of directions, align the image to the left, and assign it an empty alt.

**6** Create a new CSS style for the **`body`** Tag selector. Set the font to Arial, Helvetica, sans-serif. Set the Background Image to IP>images>bgbody.jpg, Repeat to **`no-repeat`**, Horizontal Position to **`right`**, Vertical Position to **`bottom`**, and Attachment to **`fixed`**.

**7** Close the file, saving your changes.

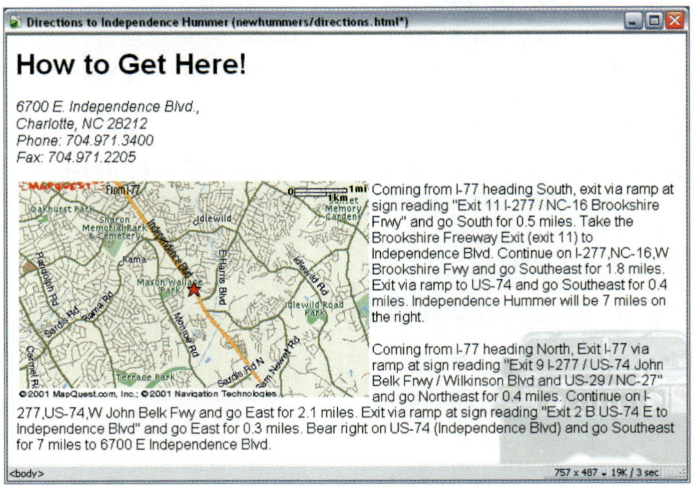


FIGURE IP.14

## Create the Adventures Page

**1** Create a new HTML page, title it "Hummer Adventures", and save it as "adventures.html".

**2** Type **Hummer Adventures** and format it as Heading 1. Press Enter/Return. Type: **Click on one of the small photos to view a larger version.** and press Enter/Return.

**3** Create a 1-row, 3-column layout table with a width of 100%. Select all three cells and set the horizontal alignment to **center**. In the left cell, type **Kinzalow**; in the center cell, type **Bill Hawe's Farm**; and in the right cell, type **Windrock Falls**.

**4** Below the table, type **Kinzalow** and format it as Heading 2. Insert an anchor named "kinzalow" in front of the text you just typed.

**5** Create a 1-row, 5-column layout table with a width of 100%. Select all five cells, and set the horizontal alignment to **center** and width to 20%. Insert into the table cells the small Kinzalow photos from the images folder (they all begin with kinzalow and end in sm.jpg). Proportionately resize and resample the images so they are 100 pixels wide.

**6** Repeat Steps 4 and 5 twice, using "Bill Hawe's Farm" and "Windrock Falls" as the Heading 2 text and "billhawes" and "windrock" as the anchor names. After each of the two headings, create a 1-row, 5-column table and insert the appropriate sm.jpg photos, resizing and resampling all images.

**7** Create links from each small photo to the larger version of the photo (same filename except it ends with lg.jpg).

You won't be creating Web pages for each photo, just links to the photos.

**8** Create a new CSS style for the **body** Tag selector. Set the font to Arial, Helvetica, sans-serif. Set the Background Image to IP>images>bgbody.jpg, set Repeat to **no-repeat**, Horizontal Position to **right**, Vertical Position to **bottom**, and Attachment to **fixed**.

**9** Close the file, saving your changes.

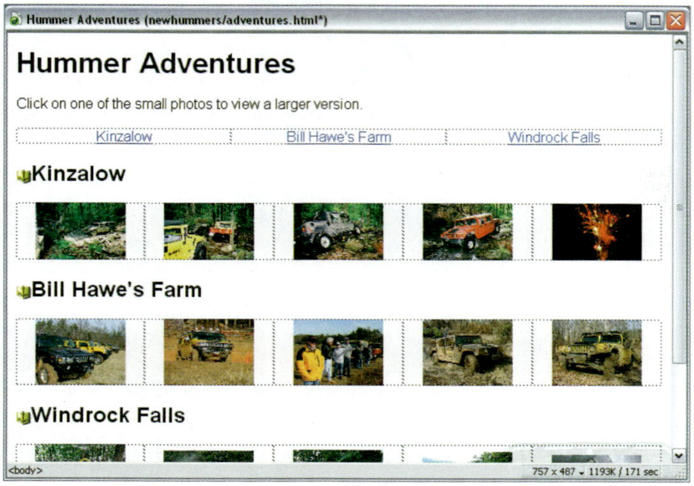


FIGURE IP.15

## Create the Privacy Page

1. Create a new HTML page, title it "Privacy Policy of Independence Hummer", and save it as "privacy.html". Import privacy.doc into this empty page.

2. Format the top line as Heading 1.

3. You may use either of two methods to format the rest of the page. Either format each short block of text as Heading 2 or create a definition list in which the short blocks of text are the definition terms and the paragraphs below are definition descriptions.

   Either is appropriate document structure for this text.

4. Create a new CSS style for the **`body`** Tag selector. Set the font to Arial, Helvetica, sans-serif. Set the Background Image to IP>images>bgbody.jpg, set Repeat to **`no-repeat`**, Horizontal Position to **`right`**, Vertical Position to **`bottom`**, and Attachment to **`fixed`**.

5. If you chose to use a definition list, create the following two styles (otherwise skip to Step 6). Create a new CSS style for the **`dt`** Tag selector. In the Type category, set the Weight to Bold and click OK. Create a new CSS style for the **`dd`** Tag selector. In the Type category, set the Style to Italic and click OK.

6. Close the file, saving your changes.

## Create the Company Page

In this exercise, the staff names, title, photos, and descriptions are provided. You may lay out the staff directory page as you see fit. You might use a table, paragraphs, or a list, if you feel that is appropriate. You could use a nested frameset, as you did in Project 7. You could create JavaScript pop-up pages using the JavaScript code you learned in Challenge 4 of Project 5. You might align the photos to the left, right, or alternating, and could even resize and/or crop them, if you find them too large.

1. Create a new HTML page, title it "Independence Hummer Staff Directory", and save it as "company.html" (but do not close the page).

2. Type `Company Profile & Expert Staff` and format it as Heading 1.

3. Create a new CSS style for the **`body`** Tag selector. Set the font to Arial, Helvetica, sans-serif. Set the Background Image to IP>images>bgbody.jpg, set Repeat to **`no-repeat`**, Horizontal Position to **`right`**, Vertical Position to **`bottom`**, and Attachment to **`fixed`**.

4. Create a new HTML page and import company.doc into the empty page. Examine the information, consider various layout options, choose one you would like to use, and create it.

   Remember, if you use one method for creating multiple pages, give each page a document title and a Heading 1 block that identifies the purpose of the page. You may want to repeat Step 3 above for each page to keep the styles the same for all pages. You may also want to create a template page first and then build the specific pages from the template.

5. When you are finished, close, saving the page (or pages).

# PART 5 Linking the Pages

In this final exercise, you create the links that enable your visitors to navigate the pages on your Independence Hummer Web site. You first create the links from the initial frameset pages and then create the links from the vehicle-category pages. As often as you feel is necessary, preview in your browser and test the links to ensure that they open the correct pages in the correct frames.

## Create Links from the Initial Frameset Pages

1. Open index.html.
2. Create links from the bottom four graphics in the left frame to open the appropriate category pages in the main frame.

   (Remember to use the **<base>** tag to assign a target when most or all links in a page use the same target.)
3. Create links from the text graphics in the top frame to the appropriate pages (in the IP>common folder), so they open in the main frame.
4. Create links from the text in the bottom frame to the appropriate pages, so they open in the main frame.
5. Link the three special vehicle images to their specific pages. Choose a target that opens the destination pages in the main frame and replaces the home.html frameset page.
6. Close, saving your changes to all pages.

## Create Links from the Category Pages

1. Open new-hummers.html from the IP>vehicles folder, and link the photos to the appropriate vehicle-detail pages. Evaluate whether or not you need to specify a target; if so, determine which target, and whether or not you need to use the **<base>** tag. Close the file, saving your changes.
2. Open index.html and preview it in your browser. Click a link to open the New Hummers category page. Test the links from the category page to ensure these links are targeted correctly.
3. Repeat Steps 1 and 2 with the three remaining category pages.
4. Test any links you created in the staff directory page. When you are finished, close the file, saving your changes.

# TASK GUIDE

| Task | Windows | Macintosh |
|---|---|---|

## Managing Files

| Task | Windows | Macintosh |
|---|---|---|
| New document | Control-N | Command-N |
| Open an HTML file | Control-O | Command-O |
| Open in frame | Control-Shift-O | Command-Shift-O |
| Close | Control-W | Command-W |
| Save | Control-S | Command-S |
| Save as | Control-Shift-S | Command-Shift-S |
| Exit/Quit | Alt-F4 or Control-Q | Option-F4 or Command-Q |

## Opening and Closing Panels

| Task | Windows | Macintosh |
|---|---|---|
| Insert bar | Control-F2 | Command-F2 |
| Properties | Control-F3 | Command-F3 |
| CSS Styles | Shift-F11 | Shift-F11 |
| Tag Inspector | F9 | F9 |
| Reference | Shift-F1 | Shift-F1 |
| Site | F8 | F8 |
| Assets | F11 | F11 |
| Show/Hide panels | F4 | F4 |

## Viewing Page Elements

| Task | Windows | Macintosh |
|---|---|---|
| Page Properties | Control-J | Command-J |
| Selection Properties | Control-Shift-J | Command-Shift-J |

## Previewing and Debugging in Browsers

| Task | Windows | Macintosh |
|---|---|---|
| Preview in primary browser | F12 | F12 |
| Preview in secondary browser | Shift-F12 | Shift-F12 |

| Task | Windows | Macintosh |
|---|---|---|

## Inserting Objects

| Task | Windows | Macintosh |
|---|---|---|
| Any object (image, Shockwave movie, etc.) | Drag file from the Explorer or Site panel to the Document window | Drag file from the Finder or Site panel to the Document window |
| Image | Control-Option-I | Command-Option-I |
| Table | Control-Option-T | Command-Option-T |
| Named Anchor | Control-Option-A | Command-Option-A |

## General Editing

| Task | Windows | Macintosh |
|---|---|---|
| Undo | Control-Z | Command-Z |
| Redo | Control-Y or Control-Shift-Z | Command-Y or Command-Shift-Z |
| Cut | Cut Control-X or Shift-Delete | Cut Command-X or Shift-Delete |
| Copy | Control-C | Command-C |
| Paste | Control-V or Shift-Insert | Command-V or Shift-Insert |
| Clear | Delete | Delete |
| Bold | Control-B | Command-B |
| Italic | Control-I | Command-I |
| Select All | Control-A | Command-A |
| Move to page up | Page Up | Page Up |
| Move to page down | Page Down | Page Down |
| Select to page up | Shift-Page Up | Shift-Page Up |
| Select to page down | Shift-Page Down | Shift-Page Down |
| Select line up/down | Shift-Up/Down | Shift-Up/Down |
| Move to start of line | Home | Home |
| Move to end of line | End | End |
| Select to start of line | Shift-Home | Shift-Home |
| Select to end of line | Shift-End | Shift-End |
| Go to previous/next paragraph | Control-Up/Down | Command-Up/Down |
| Go to next/previous word | Control-Right/Left | Command-Right/Left |
| Delete word left | Control-Backspace | Command-Backspace |
| Delete word right | Control-Delete | Command-Delete |
| Select character left/right | Shift-Left/Right | Shift-Left/Right |
| Find and Replace | Control-F | Command-F |

| Task | Windows | Macintosh |
|---|---|---|
| Find next/find again | F3 | Command-G |
| Replace | Control-H | Command-H |
| Preferences | Control-U | Command-U |

## Code Editing

| Task | Windows | Macintosh |
|---|---|---|
| Print code | Control-P | Command-P |
| Open Quick Tag Editor | Control-T | Command-T |
| Insert tag | Control-E | Command-E |
| Edit tag (in Design view) | Control-F5 | Command-F5 |
| Go to line | Control-G | Control-, |
| Move to top of code | Control-Home | Command-Home |
| Move to end of code | Control-End | Command-End |
| Select to top of code | Control-Shift-Home | Command-Shift-Home |
| Select to end of code | Control-Shift-End | Command-Shift-End |

## Text Editing

| Task | Windows | Macintosh |
|---|---|---|
| Create a new paragraph | Enter | Return |
| Insert a line break <BR> | Shift-Enter | Shift-Return |
| Insert a nonbreaking space | Control-Shift-Spacebar | Command-Shift-Spacebar |
| Move text or object to another place in the page | Drag selected item | Drag selected item |
| Copy text or object to another place in the page | Control-drag selected item | Option-drag selected item |
| Open and close the Property inspector | Control-Shift-J | Command-Shift-J |
| Check spelling | Shift-F7 | Shift-F7 |

## Working in Tables

| Task | Windows | Macintosh |
|---|---|---|
| Move to the next cell | Tab | Tab |
| Move to the previous cell | Shift-Tab | Shift-Tab |
| Insert a row (before current) | Control-M | Command-M |
| Add a row at end of table | Tab in the last cell | Tab in the last cell |

| Task | Windows | Macintosh |
|---|---|---|

## Working with Images

| Task | Windows | Macintosh |
|---|---|---|
| Change image source attribute | Double-click image | Double-click image |
| Edit image in external editor | Control-double-click image | Command-Double-click image |

## Working with Frames

| Task | Windows | Macintosh |
|---|---|---|
| Select a frame | Alt-click in frame | Shift-Option-click in frame |
| Select next frame or frameset | Alt-Right Arrow | Command-Right Arrow |
| Select previous frame or frameset | Alt-Left Arrow | Command-Left Arrow |
| Select parent frameset | Alt-Up Arrow | Command-Up Arrow |
| Select first child frame or frameset | Alt-Down Arrow | Command-Down Arrow |
| Add a new frame to frameset | Alt-drag border of selected frame | Option-drag border of selected frame |
| Add a new frame to frameset (push method) | Alt-Control-drag border of selected frame | Command-Option-drag border of selected frame |

## Managing Hyperlinks

| Task | Windows | Macintosh |
|---|---|---|
| Drag and drop to create a hyperlink from a document | Select the object, then Shift-drag the selection to a file in the Site panel | Select the object, then Shift-drag the selection to a file in the Site panel |
| Drag and drop to create a hyperlink using the Property inspector | Select the object, then drag the Point-to-File icon in Property inspector to a file in the Site panel | Select the object, then drag the Point-to-File icon in Property inspector to a file in the Site panel |
| Open the linked-to document in Dreamweaver | Control-double-click link | Command-double-click link |

## Previewing and Debugging in Browsers

| Task | Windows | Macintosh |
|---|---|---|
| Preview in primary browser | F12 | F12 |
| Preview in secondary browser | Shift-F12 | Shift-F12 |

## Getting Help

| Task | Windows | Macintosh |
|---|---|---|
| Using Dreamweaver Help Topics | F1 | F1 |
| Using ColdFusion Help Topics | Control-F1 | Command-F1 |
| Reference | Shift-F1 | Shift-F1 |

| Task | Windows | Macintosh |
|---|---|---|

## Site Map

| Task | Windows | Macintosh |
|---|---|---|
| View site files | F8 | F8 |
| Refresh Local pane | Shift-F5 | Shift-F5 |
| View as root | Control-Shift-R | |
| Show page titles | Control-Shift-T | Command-Shift-T |
| Zoom in site map | Control-Plus (+) | Command-Plus (+) |
| Zoom out site map | Control-Hyphen (-) | Command-Hyphen (-) |

## Site Management and FTP

| Task | Windows | Macintosh |
|---|---|---|
| Connect/Disconnect | Control-Alt-Shift-F5 | Command-Option-Shift-F5 |
| Refresh | F5 | F5 |
| Create new file | Control-Shift-N | Command-Shift-N |
| Create new folder | Control-Alt-Shift-N | Command-Option-Shift-N |
| Cut file | Control-X | Command-X |
| Delete file | Del | Command-Delete |
| Copy file | Control-C | Command-C |
| Paste file | Control-V | Command-V |
| Duplicate file | Control-D | Command-D |
| Rename file | F2 | F2 |
| Get selected files or folders from remote site | Control-Shift-D | Command-Shift-D |
| Put selected files or folders to remote site | Control-Shift-U | Command-Shift-U |
| View site map | Alt-F8 | Option-F8 |
| Refresh Local pane | Shift-F5 | Shift-F5 |
| Refresh Remote pane | Alt-F5 | Option-F5 |

# GLOSSARY

**_blank** A predefined target that opens the destination of the link in a new blank browser window.

**_parent** A predefined frame target that replaces the parent frameset of the current frame with the page identified by the link.

**_self** A predefined target that opens the destination of the link in the current window. Not commonly used because _self is the default target of a link but if the <base> tag defines a different base target, the _self target will override the base target and open the page in the same frame as the linking page.

**_top** A predefined target that opens the destination link in the current browser window, replacing all framesets.

**above the fold** The area of a Web page that a user can view without scrolling either vertically or horizontally.

**absolute path** The location of a file or Web page beginning with the root. Includes all necessary information to find the file or page. In the case of a Web page, called "absolute URL". See relative path.

**absolute positioning** Specifying the position of a div using the upper-left corner of the page as a fixed reference point. See also div and relative positioning.

**accessibility** The ability for a disabled user to use a Web site.

**action** The URL that receives data from a form.

**alert box** A pop-up box with a message for the user to acknowledge.

**alt text** Alternate Text. In Web-page design, text that can be displayed in lieu of an image.

**anchor** In a Web page, a type of hyperlink destination in which the destination is a specific location on a page.

**background** A static object or color that lies behind all other objects.

**animation** The technique of simulating movement by creating slight changes to an object or objects over time.

**animated GIF** A type of sequential file format where multiple bitmap images are displayed one after another.

**anonymous FTP** FTP protocol that allows users access to files for downloading. The user ID is anonymous, and the password is any valid email address.

**anti-aliasing** A graphics software feature that eliminates or softens the jaggedness of low-resolution curved edges.

**ASP** Active Server Pages. A specification for a dynamically created Web page that contains either Visual Basic or JavaScript code. When a browser requests an ASP page, the Web server generates a page with HTML code. Only available on Windows servers.

**asset** An image, sound, video, or other file that may be in use in a Web page.

**assistive device** Hardware enabling a disabled viewer to use a Web site.

**attribute** Attributes augment the element in which they appear. They also provide additional information about the element. Attributes appear as name-value pairs in the element's start-tag.

**bandwidth** The transmission capacity, usually measured in bits per second, of a network connection.

**behavior** A JavaScript action or reaction to an event.

**bit (binary digit)** A computer's smallest unit of information. Bits can have only two values: 0 or 1.

**bit depth** A measure of how many colors can be contained in an image. 8-bit color is 256 colors, 16-bit color is 32,768 colors, and so on.

**bitmap image** An image constructed from individual dots or pixels set to a grid-like mosaic. The file must contain information about the color and position of each pixel, so the disk space needed for bitmap images can be very large.

**browser** Software program that allows you to surf the Web. The most popular browsers are Netscape Navigator and Microsoft Internet Explorer. The very first browsers, such as Lynx, only allowed users to see text. Also called "Web browser."

**browser compatibility** A term that compares the way a Web page functions on different browsers. Incompatibilities often exist due to the way a browser interprets the HTML. The differences may be very slight or significant.

**bullet** A marker preceding text, usually a solid dot, used to add emphasis; generally indicates the text is part of a list.

**button** An element a user can click to cause an effect, such as the submission of a form.

**button state** A visual version of a button. For example, when clicked, the button is in its down state; when dormant, it is in its up state. When the mouse is hovered over the button, the button is in its over state.

**byte** A unit of measure equal to 8 bits (decimal 256) of digital information, sufficient to represent 1 text character. The standard unit measure of file size.

**Cascading Style Sheets (CSS)** Part of a Web page file listing properties that affect the appearance of content, the content to which those properties apply, and their values.

**cell** A unit of information within a table.

**cell padding** The margin around the inside of a table cell.

**cell spacing** The margin between table cells.

**CFML** Cold Fusion Markup Language. A proprietary markup language owned by Macromedia that is mixed within HTML. Cold Fusion may perform functions and interact with databases. It only runs on a Cold Fusion Server.

**CGI** Common Gateway Interface. Interface that allows scripts to run on a Web server. CGI scripts can be used to put the content of a form into an email message, to perform a database query, or to generate HTML pages on the fly.

**CGI script** A CGI program used to process a form or provide other dynamic content.

**cgi-bin** The most common name of a directory on a Web server in which CGI scripts are stored.

**checkbox** A square that can be clicked to cause the form to send a name-value pair to the action; a form element that allows a user to choose zero or other choices.

**class** A style designation that can be added to multiple elements.

**click-through rate** A measure that reflects the percentage of users who clicked through to a Web site divided by the total number of messages that were delivered, inviting them to do so.

**client** A computer system or application that requests a service of another computer system on the network. See server.

**client-side** Scripting or other actions that take place within the browser, as opposed to the server.

**clip art** Collections of predrawn and digitized graphics.

**code hint** A pop-up menu presenting code options for HTML tags, attributes, and options; CSS; and some programming languages. Code hints are only available when working with the code directly.

**comment** A line in a piece of programming code that is intended to be read, not executed.

**conditional statement** A statement that evaluates as either true or false. Conditional statements are used in if-then and while clauses that must evaluate whether or not the condition is true before proceeding or repeating.

**contextual menu** A menu containing options relative only to the object for which the menu is activated.

**cookie** Information a Web server writes to your computer hard disk via your browser, containing data such as login information and user preferences. This data can be retrieved so Web pages can be customized before they are sent to the visiting browser.

**CSS** Cascading Style Sheets. Part of a Web-page file listing properties that affect the appearance of selectors, the content to which those properties apply, and their values.

**color picker** A function within a graphics application that assists in selecting or setting a color.

**column** A series of cells arranged vertically.

**compression** A technique used to reduce file size by analyzing occurrences of similar data. Compressed files occupy less space, and their use improves digital transmission speeds. Compression can sometimes result in a loss of image quality and/or resolution.

**copyright** Ownership of a work. Permits the owner of material to prevent its use without express permission or acknowledgement of the originator. Copyright may be sold, transferred, or given up contractually.

**dead link** A link whose destination has been changed or removed. Also called broken links.

**deprecated** The status of a tag or attribute that can still be used, but will eventually be removed, and so should be avoided, if possible.

**development server** A server that houses a Web site while it is still being created and tested. (See server.)

**DHTML** Dynamic HTML. JavaScript programs that dynamically change cascading style sheet properties, allowing parts of your Web page to be hidden, shown, or animated.

**div** A block of content that can be positioned on the page. See absolute positioning and relative positioning.

**digital camera** A camera that produces images directly into an electronic file format for transfer to a computer.

**disabilities** Challenges that hinder some people from using computers in general including Web pages. Included are blindness, low vision (requiring magnification), color blindness, motility (shakiness or loss of function) and some mental challenges such as dyslexia. The goal of the WAI is to provide guidelines for Web designers to enable their sites to accommodate disabilities in their design.

**dithering** A technique in which a color is represented using dots of two different colors displayed or printed very close together. Dithering is often used to compress digital images and in special screening algorithms.

**DNS** Domain Name Server or Domain Name System. Maps IP numbers to a more easily remembered name. When you type http://www.somedomain.com into a browser, the DNS searches for a matching IP address (228.28.202.95).

**document root** The main directory for a Web site.

**domain name** A unique name that is used to identify a Web site, FTP site, and/or email server. A domain name always points to one specific server, even though the server may host many domain names.

**domain name registrar** A company who may sell domain names. Some provide hosting and other related services as well.

**download** Transfer of data from a server to your computer's hard disk.

**DTD** Document Type Definition. A separate document that contains formal definitions of all of the data elements in a particular type of HTML, SGML, or XML document. By consulting the DTD for a document, a program called a parser can work with the markup codes that document contains.

**dynamic** Content that changes according to client-side or server-side scripting.

**ECMA** The European Computer Manufacturers Association.

**ECMAScript** An official, standardized version of JavaScript maintained by the ECMA.

**e-commerce** Electronic Commerce. Conducting business online, including product display, online ordering, and inventory management. The software, which works in conjunction with online payment systems to process payments, resides on a commerce server.

**editable text** A text element that the user can modify by entering or deleting keystrokes.

**element** The portion of an HTML tag between the angle brackets. <p> is the paragraph tag whereas p is the paragraph element.

**em** A printers measurement; the height, in points, of the font size.

**email address** An electronic mail address. Email addresses are in the form of: user@domain.com (for example, chris@webguest.net).

**empty tag** A tag that has no closing element tag.

**embedded style sheet** Style information included within a Web page.

**event** An action or occurrence detected by JavaScript. Events can be user actions (such as clicking a mouse button or pressing a key), timed events, or the loading and unloading of a Web page.

**event handler** A function or method containing program statements that are executed in response to an event.

**export** To save a file generated in one application into a format that is readable in another.

**external style sheet** Style information included in a separate file referenced by a Web page.

**FAQ** Frequently Asked Questions. A document that contains the most common questions and answers on a particular subject or product.

**file compression** The process of reducing the number of bytes in a file, file compression is usually used when transferring files between computers.

**flat color** Color that lacks contrast or tonal variation. Also called flat tint.

**flowchart** A sketch that shows the relationships of each page to the other pages in the site.

**folder** The digital equivalent of a paper file folder, used to organize files in the Macintosh and Windows operating systems. Double-clicking the icon opens it to reveal the files stored inside.

**font** A font is the complete collection of all the characters (numbers, uppercase and lowercase letters, and in some cases, small caps and symbols) of a given typeface in a specific style; for example, Helvetica Bold.

**font class** In Web design, the type of font (serif, sans serif, monospace, cursive, or fantasy) that will be used if the user's computer does not have any of the font-family members. See CSS.

**font family** In Web design, a grouping of (supposedly) similar fonts, which will be used to display text in the Web page.

**form** A page that enables a user to type information and send it to a site via form elements such as text boxes and pull-down lists.

**form validation** The process of making certain a Web form contains all required data and no invalid data.

**frame rate** The number of successive images that are displayed in one second. Designated fps (frames per second).

**frame-by-frame animation** Animation using a series of keyframes with no tweening; it creates a flipbook type of animation.

**frame** A section of the browser window displaying a content document that is independent of all other areas within the browser window. This window-within-a-window can be referenced by links in other frames.

**frame trapping** Improper use of a frames-based layout in which an external Web site's page is displayed within the frame of another site and not allowed full access to the whole browser window.

**frameset** The document defining the layout on a framed page and breaking it into one or more frames.

**freeware** Software available at no cost. Freeware does not necessarily mean copyright free.

**FTP** File Transfer Protocol. Internet method to transfer files through the Internet from one computer to another. FTP is used to download files from another computer, as well as to upload files from your computer to a remote computer.

**function** A script that can be referenced by name.

**get** A method for sending form data by appending it to the action URL. See post.

**GIF** Graphics Interchange Format. A popular format for online clip art and drawn graphics. Graphics in this format are acceptable at low resolution. See JPEG.

**graceful degradation** A technique that ensures content remains usable, even if all features are not available. Graceful degradation is the goal when designing pages using standards that may not be supported in older browsers.

**grayed out** Any option (menu selection, button, etc.) that is not available.

**grayscale** An image composed in grays ranging from black to white, usually using 256 different tones.

**gradient** A gradual transition from one color to another. The shape of the gradient and the proportion of the two colors can be varied. Also known as blends, gradations, graduated fills, and vignettes.

**handles** Black squares (commonly 8) at the corners and sides of a selected image enabling the user to resize the graphic.

**header information** Information at the beginning of a Web-page file that defines the contents and characteristics of the page.

**hex values** Numbers specified in the hexadecimal system, commonly used for specifying colors on Web pages.

**home page** Main page of a Web site. A Web site containing only one page is also called a home page.

**hotspot** A region in an image map that has been marked up as a link. A hotspot may be a rectangle, circle or polygon.

**HREF** Hyperlink Reference. HTML code that specifies a URL as the linked resource.

**HSB** Color model used to define color in terms of hue, saturation, and brightness.

**HSV** A color model based on three coordinates: hue, saturation, and value (or luminance).

**HTML** HyperText Markup Language. A tagging language that allows content to be delivered over the World Wide Web and viewed by a browser.

**HTML frameset** A version of HTML that includes all tags that are part of HTML 4.01, including those involving frames.

**HTML strict** A version of HTML that does not include any presentational tags or attributes.

**HTML transitional** The most common version of HTML. Includes all tags and attributes that are part of HTML 4.01 except for those involving frames.

**HTTP** Hypertext Transfer Protocol. The method used by browsers and Web servers to communicate, such as to request and deliver content, respectively.

**hue** The wavelength of light of a color in its purest state (without adding white or black).

**hyperlink** An HTML tag that directs the computer to a different anchor or URL. A hyperlink can be a word, phrase, sentence, graphic, or icon. A hyperlink can also cause an action, such as opening or downloading a file.

**hypertext** Organization of content that enables the user to select related content.

**image compression** The process of reducing the amount of digital data that makes up an image.

**ID** An identifier for a particular tag, added as an attribute and typically used to add style information.

**if-then statement** A programming construction that executes one section of code if a conditional statement is true, and a second section if it is not.

**IIS** Internet Information Server. Microsoft's Web server that runs on Windows NT platforms. IIS comes bundled with Windows NT 4.0. IIS is tightly integrated with the operating system, so it is relatively easy to administer.

**image map** A graphic containing hotspots, or areas of an image that are defined as links. When a viewer clicks the part of the image that is a hotspot, they are actually clicking on a link.

**information architecture** The structure and organization of the data on a Web site.

**inline graphic** A graphic that is inserted within a body of text, and may be formatted using normal text commands for justification and leading; inline graphics move with the body of text in which they are placed.

**interlacing** A characteristic of GIF and PNG files, in which the file is displayed in progressively greater detail as it is downloaded.

**Internet** A global system of interconnected computers.

**input** An element, such as a text box, that receives information from the user.

**IP address** A unique, 32-bit Internet address consisting of four numbers, separated by dots and sometimes called a dotted quad (90.0.0.95).

**InterNIC** Internet Network Information Center. The entity that keeps track of the domain names. Recently the right to register domain names has been widely granted to private companies, so the cost and services associated with obtaining a new domain can vary.

**intranet** A private network dedicated to information and resources about and for the corporation or organization that maintains it, enabling a company to share resources with employees without confidential information being made available across the Internet.

**ISP** Internet Service Provider. An organization that provides access to the Internet for such things as electronic mail, bulletin boards, chat rooms, or use of the World Wide Web.

**JavaScript** A scripting language, designed by Netscape, which can be embedded into HTML documents.

**JPEG** A compression algorithm that reduces the file size of bitmapped images, named for the Joint Photographic Experts Group, which created the standard. JPEG is lossy compression; image quality is reduced in direct proportion to the amount of compression.

**JScript** Microsoft's version of JavaScript.

**JSP** Java Servlet Pages. Web pages created using the Java programming language run on a Web server.

**KB** Kilobyte. 1,024 bytes, the nearest binary equivalent to decimal 1,000 bytes. Also abbreviated and referred to as K.

**keyframe** An individual frame in a sequence of animation, from which other frames are extrapolated. For instance, a linear movement can be extrapolated from two keyframes, one at the beginning and one at the end of the movement.

**keywords** Words that identify the content of a Web page and can be used by search engines as part of their process of determining the results of searches.

**layout** The arrangement of text and graphics on a page.

**leading** Space added between lines of type. Named after the strips of lead that used to be inserted between lines of metal type. In specifying type, lines of 12-pt type separated by a 14-pt space is abbreviated 12/14, or 12 over 14. The CSS property for leading is line-height.

**letter spacing** The insertion or addition of white space between the letters of words.

**left alignment** Text having a straight left edge and a ragged (uneven) right edge.

**linking** The act of placing a reference to one file (sound, graphic, or video) into another file. When the referenced file is modified, the placed reference is automatically (or manually, depending on the application) updated.

**Linux** UNIX-based operating system for personal computers that is available for little or no cost, and offers developers free access to the uncompiled code.

**list** A series of items.

**LiveScript** The original name for JavaScript.

**log in** Enter into a computer system. Also the account name (or user ID) that you must enter before you can have access to some computer systems.

**looping** The process of continually returning to a location until another action occurs, such as the movement of the mouse pointer or the selection of a button.

**lossless** Refers to data compression techniques in which no data is lost.

**lossy** A data compression method characterized by the loss of some data.

**Lynx** A text-only browser.

**mail server** Server that handles incoming and outgoing email.

**mailto:** A protocol used to tell the browser to create a new email message.

**meta tag** An optional HTML tag that is used to specify information about a Web document. Some search engines index Web pages by reading the information contained within the meta tags.

**mouseover** The event triggered at the moment the user rolls the mouse pointer over an area or item on a Web page. Typically used to tell the browser to do something, such as execute a rollover script.

**MIME** type An indication of the kind of data being sent to the browser. Used by the browser to know what to do with the data.

**Mosaic** The first Web browser (developed by NSCA) with the ability to display graphics. The Mosaic browser caused a major breakthrough in the way people could access the resources of the World Wide Web.

**Mozilla** The organization created when Netscape Corporation decided to open source the code of their Netscape browser. Mozilla.org has released the powerful and sophisticated Mozilla, Firefox and Camino browsers. Netscape version 6+ is based on Mozilla code. All Mozilla-based browsers are free to download.

**MySQL** Fast, free, open-source database suitable for Web database functionality.

**named anchor** An <a> anchor tag which uses the name attribute. Commonly, the named anchor is empty such as <a name=header></a> where no content exists between the opening and closing <a> tags. Consider removing all named anchors and linking tags with ids instead such as <div id=header>.

**named colors** A set of colors specifically designated for reference by name, rather than by RGB or hexadecimal values.

**named target** A frame that has a designated name, allowing links to specify that content should be displayed within that frame.

**nested frameset** A frameset that is the content of the frame of another frameset.

**nested tag** A tag contained within another tag.

**Netscape Navigator** A common Web browser.

**noframes section** Content provided for browsers that do not support frames contained within a noframes element.

**obsolete** HTML tags that have been removed from a specified standard.

**ODBC connectivity** A standard database access method developed by Microsoft. The goal of ODBC is to make it possible to access any data from any application, regardless of which database management system (DBMS) is handling the data.

**opening tag** The indication of the start of an element containing the name of the element and any attributes.

**Opera** Popular, advanced browser for Windows, Macintosh, Linux/Unix and cell phones from Opera.com. The free version is supported by advertising which may be removed for a fee.

**operating system (OS)** The software that allows your computer to function. An example of an operating system is Mac OS X or Microsoft Windows.

**orphaned files** Files that exist below the root of the site but are not linked or used in any pages in the Web site.

**over state** A button state that occurs when the user passes the mouse pointer over a button.

**page properties** In Web design, the characteristics of a layout page, including default background and text colors, page width, and background image.

**page title** Text that appears in the Title bar of the user's browser when the page is viewed. Also called the document title.

**page weight** The total number of bytes required to download the HTML document and all associated assets such as images, CSS, and JavaScript files. Dreamweaver's Download indicator identifies the page weight. You should try to keep the page weight below 60 KB.

**palette** As derived from the term in the traditional art world, a collection of selectable colors.

**panel** In Macromedia's workspace, the name given to palettes of tools and options.

**parameter** In programming, the term parameter is a synonym of argument, a value that is passed to a routine or function.

**password** Secret code you must enter after your user ID (login name) in order to log on to a computer.

**password box** A text box that replaces all characters with a bullet or asterisk to hide their identity.

**Perl** Practical Extraction and Report Language. A powerful computer language, especially used for writing CGI scripts that handle input/output actions on Web pages.

**PHP** An open source server-side Web programming language capable of running on Unix, Linux, Windows and Macintosh Web servers. Not only easy to learn but capable of powerful and sophisticated functionality.

**PNG** Portable Network Graphics. PNG is a new graphics format similar to GIF. It is a relatively new file format, and is not yet widely supported by most browsers.

**pixel** Picture Element. One of the tiny rectangular areas or dots generated by a computer or output device to constitute images. A greater number of pixels per inch results in higher resolution on screen or in print.

**point** A unit of measurement used to specify type size and rule weight; equal to approximately 1/72 inch.

**post** A method for sending form data using headers. See get.

**preloading** Causing the browser to download images or other items before they are needed, so when they are needed, they are already in the browser cache; improves the speed with which they appear.

**presentational HTML** HTML tags and attributes that provide only style. The <b> (bold) tag and the align attribute are examples of presentational HTML. When designing a Web page, avoid using presentational HTML and use CSS instead.

**progressive display** A characteristic of JPEG files, in which the file will be displayed in increasingly greater detail as it is downloaded.

**protocol** A set of rules and conventions that describe the behavior computers must follow in order to understand each other.

**pt** Abbreviation for point.

**pull quote** An excerpt from the body of a story; used to emphasize an idea, draw readers' attention, or generate interest.

**PWS** Personal Web Server. A feature-limited free version of IIS, available for Windows 98, enabling new developers to experiment with ASP and SQL Server database.

**query** Request for specific information from a database.

**radio button** A single round button that can be clicked to cause the form to send a name-value pair to the action.

**radio group** A group of radio buttons with the same name. Only one radio button may be selected at a time within a radio group.

**redirect** To cause the browser to load a different page without intervention from the user.

**relative positioning** Specifying the position of a section of content, such as a div, based on the original location of the content. (See div and absolute positioning.)

**raster image** A type of picture created and organized in a rectangular array of bitmaps. Often created by paint software, scanners, or digital cameras.

**refresh** To reload.

**relative path** The location of a file or Web page that uses the location of the current file or page as a reference. In the case of a Web page, called relative URL. See absolute path.

**reload** To re-retrieve and redisplay a Web page in the browser.

**resample** Resizing an image to decrease the physical size of the file, not just change the appearance on the page.

**RGB** Red Green Blue. A means of specifying a color by indicating the amount of each of these components (channels) of the color.

**RGBa** Red Green Blue alpha. Similar to RGB plus a fourth channel to specify transparency. Used in PNG graphics to allow individual pixels to have different levels of transparency.

**root** Top-level directory from which all other directories branch out.

**royalty-free** Content that you may purchase and use in your published Web pages without having to pay a royalty to the creator of the content each time you use it. The content may be text- or image-based.

**sans-serif** Fonts that do not have serifs. See serif.

**screen reader** Software that captures the onscreen content, stores it into a buffer then passes it onto the user either through computerized speech processor or refreshable Braille displays.

**scripting** The process of adding programming capabilities to a program (e.g., AppleScript), file (e.g., ActionScript), or Web page (e.g., JavaScript).

**search engine** A Web site that allows users to search for keywords on Web pages. Every search engine has its own strategy for collecting data.

**search engine optimization** (SEO) Judicious incorporation of keywords and alt text in creating Web sites to maximize the likelihood that those sites will be found by various search engines.

**select** Place the cursor on an object and click the mouse button to make the object active.

**select list** A list of potential choices that can be displayed as a menu that appears when the user clicks on it, or as a box with its own scroll bar.

**select option** A potential choice listed in a select list.

**selector** Information used to determine the content to which style changes should apply.

**server** A computer that has a permanent connection to the Internet. A Web site is stored on a Web server.

**serif** A line or curve projecting from the end of a letterform. Typefaces designed with such projections are called serif faces.

**server-side** Pertaining to functions that are run at the computer that operates as a server before the results are sent to the client.

**SGML** Standard Generalized Markup Language. The predecessor to Hypertext Markup Language; a means for creating universally available content using tagging.

**shareware** Software you can test for a certain amount of time to determine whether or not you want to buy it.

**shopping cart** A piece of software that acts as the interface between a company's Web site and its deeper infrastructure, allowing consumers to select merchandise, review what they have selected, make necessary modifications or additions, and purchase the merchandise.

**SHTTP** Secure HyperText Transfer Protocol. An encrypted version of HTTP used to transfer private information, such as credit-card information.

**site map** A list of pages in a Web site. Commonly, the page names are links to the pages.

**site root directory** The parent folder that contains all other files and directories for a Web site.

**source** The actual text that makes up the Web page received by the browser, including HTML/XHTML, client-side scripting, and other information.

**spam** To send identical and irrelevant postings to many different newsgroups or mailing lists. The name comes from a Monty Python song and is considered to be a serious violation of netiquette.

**spamming a search engine** Providing false or repetitive information in the hope of improving search-engine rankings.

**span** A section of inline content that can be styled.

**spider** Program, also known as a bot, used by some search engines to index Web sites. Spiders search the Web to find URLs that match the given query string.

**SQL** Structured Query Language, SQL is a standardized query language for requesting information from a database. SQL also supports database updates, inserts and deletes and also user management.

**storyboard** A small sketch that represents each page in a Web site.

**structural tags** Tags that provide information about content.

**style** A defined set of formatting instructions for font and paragraph attributes, tabs, and other properties of text.

**style sheet** A defined set of formatting instructions for font and paragraph attributes, tabs, and other properties of text.

**SVG** Scalable Vector Graphics. A language for the creation of graphics using only tags.

**syntax highlighting** A method of distinguishing different components of code (such as tags, attributes, comments, and text) by coloring the code or background differently or applying bold, italic or normal styling.

**template** A document file containing layout, styles, and repeating elements (such as logos) by which a series of documents can maintain the same look and feel. A model publication you can use as the basis for creating a new publication.

**text box** A box into which users can type.

**this** Keyword that refers to the object that generated an event.

**tweening** A process by which the in-between frames of an animation are automatically generated by the developing application.

**thumbnails** Small images used to indicate the content of a computer file.

**title attribute** An attribute that may be used to expand an acronym and an abbreviation with the full term. It may also be used in the anchor tag to provide more information about the destination of the link.

**tool tip** Small text explaining the item to which the mouse is pointing.

**transparency** The quality of an image element that allows background elements to partially or entirely show through.

**UNIX** Multi-user computer operating system. The Internet and the Web matured on UNIX, and these days UNIX is still the most common operating system for servers on the Internet.

**up state** Normally a button's default state, which occurs when the user has not clicked or passed over the button with the mouse pointer.

**uploading** The process of sending a file from one computer to a remote server.

**URL** Uniform Resource Locator. Address of any resource on the Web.

**usability** The ease with which a user can access, navigate, and achieve goals on a Web site.

**user ID** Unique identifier you must enter every time you want to access a particular service on the Internet. The user ID is always accompanied by a password.

**validate** To analyze a file to ensure the structure, tag names, and attributes are correct, according to the DTD selected.

**variable** A unit of information that can be referred to by name.

**variable-width page** A characteristic of Web pages that allows the page to expand or contract horizontally, displaying as a percentage of the user's browser window. Also known as a liquid layout.

**VBScript** A Microsoft scripting language used for client-side scripting.

**vector graphics** Graphics defined using coordinate points and mathematically drawn lines and curves, which may be freely scaled and rotated without image degradation in the final output.

**W3C** An abbreviation for the World Wide Web Consortium.

**WAI** Web Accessibility Initiative. A project at the W3C to create guidelines for actions that developers should take to increase the accessibility of their sites and applications.

**watermark** An impression incorporated in paper during manufacturing showing the name of the paper and/or the company logo. A watermark can be applied digitally to printed output as a very light screened image.

**WCAG** Web Content Accessibility Guidelines: a list of guidelines for Web page designers identifying what they must do to ensure their Web sites are accessible to everyone. WCAG is the result of the work of the WAI.

**Web designer** An individual who is the aesthetic and navigational architect of a Web site, determining how the site looks, how it is designed, and what components it contains.

**Web developer** A person who builds the technical architecture of Web sites, providing the programming required for a particular Web product to work.

**Web host** A company that provides access to a server on which you can place your Web site content. This server is connected to the Internet, allowing the general public to access your Web site.

**Webmaster** The person who is responsible for the Web server (usually the system administrator).

**Web page** A single file or Web address containing HTML or XHTML information. Web pages typically include text and images, but may include links to other pages and other media.

**Web-safe color** Color palette used for images that will be displayed on the Internet; a specific set that can be displayed by most computer-operating systems and monitors.

**Web site** A collection of HTML files and other content that visitors can access by means of a URL and view with a Web browser.

**World Wide Web** Client/server hypertext system for retrieving information across the Internet.

**World Wide Web Consortium** (W3C) The group responsible for definition of HTML Standards (http://www.w3c.org).

**WYSIWYG** What You See Is What You Get.

**XForms** An emerging specification defining advanced functionality for Web forms.

**XHTML** An abbreviation for eXtensible HyperText Markup Language. The reformulization of HTML 4.01 in XML.

**XML** A markup code similar to HTML which allows the developer to define how data is structured when it's published on a web site or printed.

**z-index** Value used for determining which of a set of overlapping layers will be displayed.

# INDEX

# INDEX

## N



## O



## P



## Q



## R



## S

# INDEX